A HISTORY OF
MODERN CULTURE

BY

PRESERVED SMITH

HON.LITT.D. AMHERST
PROFESSOR OF HISTORY IN CORNELL UNIVERSITY

VOLUME I

THE GREAT RENEWAL

1543–1687

NEW YORK

HENRY HOLT AND COMPANY

Printed in the United States of America by
J. J. LITTLE AND IVES COMPANY, NEW YORK

TO

CHARLES HOMER HASKINS

IN HONOR AND IN FRIENDSHIP

PREFACE

Though the duties of the professoriate are arduous they allow considerable intervals of leisure which may be devoted to reading and writing. In addition to summer vacations I have been granted, by Cornell University, two longer periods of freedom from academic duties. An appropriation from the fund for the promotion of research given by Mr. August Heckscher, to whom I tender my thanks, allowed me during the spring term of 1926 to transfer the burden of teaching to other shoulders and thus to devote my time to study. A second and longer interval of leisure was granted me in 1928-29, in the sabbatic year which it is the wisdom of our universities to allow professors after six or seven years of academic labor.

For assistance in coping with a task which would otherwise have far exceeded my capacity, I am indebted to kind and able friends. The introductory chapter and those on Laws and on Morals and Manners, have been read and corrected in manuscript by Professor Carl Becker of Cornell University; the chapters on Astronomy, Physics, and Mathematics by Professor Frederick A. Saunders of Harvard; the chapter on Philosophy by Professor Charles H. Toll of Amherst College; the chapter on Political Theory by Professor George E. G. Catlin of Cornell University; the chapters on Religion, Free-thought, Superstition, and Tolerance by Professor George Lincoln Burr of Cornell University; the chapters on Literature and Art by my sister, Professor Winifred Smith of Vassar College. The first and second chapters have been read in proof by Professor Burr, and the fifth and sixth chapters by Dr. W. T. W. Forbes, of Cornell. While the careful criticisms of these eminent scholars have been invaluable to me, I must relieve my collaborators of all responsibility for the general point of view adopted throughout the book, as well as for the expression of certain opinions with which they might not agree. Their help has enabled me, I hope, to present the various subjects treated with that degree of accuracy and in that perspective suitable to a work on so large a scale as this. My purpose has been to survey the intellectual progress of Western culture as a whole, not to amplify and qualify every detail with the meticulous refinement rightly demanded in the history of a small subject. One rule governs the drawing of a world map, another the drafting of the plan of a city or county.

For making the index, for reading the proof, and for other help, I am indebted to my wife.

P. S.

Ithaca, New York,
April 14, 1929.

TABLE OF CONTENTS

PART III. SOCIAL CONTROL

A HISTORY OF MODERN CULTURE

CHAPTER I

INTRODUCTORY

I. PURPOSE OF THE PRESENT WORK

The best excuse for writing the history of anything is the intrinsic interest of the subject. Most men of past generations have thought, and many men still think, of politics as the warp and woof of social life. History for a long time therefore treated chiefly politics. Then came the economists to arouse the interest of scholars and of the public in the production and distribution of wealth. Economic history rightly absorbs much attention, for it illumines, with its new searchlight, many a dark corner of the past, and explains many features of present-day society.

But to many men today the most interesting thing about society is its culture; just as the most interesting thing about an individual is his thought. Indeed, it has begun to be suspected that even politics and economics, each sometimes worshipped as a First Cause, are but secondary effects of something still deeper, namely, of the progress of man's intellectual life. The present volume aims to exhibit, as a unified whole, the state and progress of modern culture. There is the more reason for doing this, as it has hardly ever been done. Histories of literature, of science, of philosophy, of learning, of religion, and of all branches of them, as well as of many other particular divisions of culture, there are; but hardly any history of that complex whole that includes knowledge, belief, morals, law, customs, opinions, religion, superstition, and art.

Like the epic poet the historian must always begin in the middle of the plot. The roaring loom of time weaves

3

but one seamless web from which for purposes of examination a fragment must be torn. Even though ragged edges betray the fragmentary character of any narrative, some attempt must be made to define the topic, the period, and the social group treated. The present work will confine itself to the North Atlantic peoples in modern times.

The cultural group is usually different from the political. The peoples of Europe west of Russia and Turkey, and their children in their colonies, have a common culture, descended in part from Greece, Rome, and Judea, modified by the Teutonic conquest of the Middle Ages, and still further altered and developed by the extraordinary achievements of modern science. This culture now dominates the world; military conquest and commercial contact have imposed it on all peoples.

It must be recognized, of course, that the culture of all members of the white races is not the same. There are infinite varieties and shades not only as between geographical divisions of the earth but as between the strata of the classes. Perhaps the differences between the culture of the several classes is now more important than that between the various nations of the white race. In a sense, a history of culture is really a history of the intellectual class. Civilization is imposed by the leading classes on the masses, often against their stubborn opposition, generally without their full knowledge of what is taking place, and always without their active co-operation.

The period selected for treatment in this work is the last four hundred years. Whether the division of history into great eras is purely arbitrary, depending on the convenience of the student, or whether it corresponds to some objective change in the underlying material (thought, or culture)—a change as real as that from ice to water or from water to steam, or as real as the change from one season to another in the year,—is a deep problem as yet unsolved. That the former alternative is the true one is made probable by the fact that the periods into which history seems naturally to fall differ for different nations and for different subjects. One chronological scheme suits England, another Japan; the dates most important in the history of mathematics are not remarkable in the history of music.

For the annals of world culture dates of universal import must naturally be selected. The common division of the ages into ancient, medieval, and modern, was first introduced into church history in the seventeenth century, and from that taken over into general history. The dividing lines at the fall of the Roman Empire and at the beginning of the Reformation (say 476 and 1517) have little to commend them to the student of culture. Among the large number of chronological schemes proposed to replace the traditional one, those which seem to have the most to recommend them are the following. (1) A division depending on the shift of commerce and the center of civilization from the Mediterranean to the Atlantic, about 1500. (2) A division depending on technical progress in the use of stone or metals, distinguishing a stone age, a bronze age, an iron age, and a steel age. (3) A division depending on the status of the laboring class, distinguishing a gentile system (Asiatic), a servile system (Greek and Roman), a feudal system (medieval), and a capitalistic system of production (modern). (4) A division depending on the perfection of man's methods of communicating his thoughts, distinguishing an ancient period from the development of language to the invention of the alphabet, a middle period to the invention of typography (in Europe, about 1440), and a modern period from that time to the present, when perhaps the radio, phonograph and cinema are introducing the contemporary and future age. It will be observed that three out of these four schemes discover an important break in the fifteenth century. But the transition was gradual and did not fully announce its import until the dawn of modern science dazzled the world in the works of Copernicus and Vesalius (1543). The decisive factors in the creation of modern culture were the invention of printing (c. 1440), the geographical discoveries of the late fifteenth and early sixteenth centuries, the rise of capitalism at the same time, and the growth of science. The century from 1440 to 1543 may be regarded as an age of transition from the first (or second) great era of world history to the second (or third) great era. For the present history of culture the year 1543 has been selected as a convenient starting point.

Certain general characteristics mark off the modern from all previous periods of history. The first of these is the growth of world unity. Before the discoveries of Columbus and Magellan there could be no such thing as universal history, because there could be no such thing as a world society. But the continued exploration of the globe and the vast improvement of means of travel and of communication have made civilization a unified whole. A second note of modern times is the enormous increase of wealth and of population. The growth of population depends on the increase of wealth, and that, in the last analysis, is due to the improvement of technical methods of production and to the exploitation of the natural resources of America. Thirdly, only in modern times have vast democracies arisen and spread over practically the whole earth. This equalization of the various classes is in the main dependent on the cheapening of knowledge through the invention of printing. As a corollary to this development must be noted the spread of popular education. Fourthly, modern society is secular to an extent unknown in any previous age. Religion has decayed among the highly educated classes, and to some extent even among the masses; superstition has been banished to dark corners; and tolerance has won a hard, but notable victory over the forces making for persecution and bigotry. This development is due directly to the growth of modern science, which may be taken as the fifth note of modernity. To the historian of culture the rise and development of the natural sciences in the last four centuries may well seem the most distinguishing characteristic of modern times, and perhaps the most important event (if, for convenience, a protracted process, still un-folding, may be called an event) in all history. In addition to material conquests, the triumphs of science have produced a new mentality, not, indeed, as yet among the masses, but among the intellectuals, who constitute a small, but important and leading, class. If we may speak of their mentality as the modern spirit, it is, as distinguished from the spirit of earlier ages, rational, free, forward-looking, and self-conscious. To trust reason rather than tradition or authority, to assert the liberty of the individual, to look to the future rather than to the past, to regard truth as relative and subjective rather than as absolute and objective, are the notes of the modern spirit.

The division of the last great age into smaller periods is necessary for purposes of narrative and analysis. I have therefore subdivided the whole epoch into four chronological sections, each to be treated in one volume. This first volume will exhibit the history of culture from Copernicus to Newton (1543-1687). As the scientific rebirth is the most distinguishing trait of the period, I have called it, after Bacon, The Age of the Great Renewal (*Instauratio Magna*).

2. THE POLITICAL BACKGROUND OF THE PERIOD 1543-1687

The vast cultural changes which took place during this century and a half worked themselves out against a political background itself ever changing under the impact of cultural forces. Of these determining factors the least important, and the most overrated, is the Renaissance. Defining that word in the proper sense of the rebirth of classical antiquity, we can attribute little to the Renaissance except some instruction to the generation emerging from medievalism in the art, literature, morals, philosophy, and science of the ancient Greeks. This was valuable to an age that had much to learn, but it was soon outgrown and thereafter acted as an oppression rather than as an emancipation. The ideal of the humanists was in the past; they looked backward not forward; they derided or opposed all the progressive or emancipating forces in their own age except those for which some analogy could be found in antiquity.

Considerably more important for the history of the sixteenth and seventeenth century is the Reformation, though that, too, was in some respects a reactionary movement, the return to an ideal of a long past age and the revival in some respects of the medieval spirit, just as it was, in other ways, being outgrown. But on the other hand the Reformation ushered in momentous forward movements, both consciously and unconsciously. In the large sphere of religion it represented the growing individualism and the philosophic monism of modern times. Though far from being very tolerant or very rational, the Protestants were driven, by the logic of their revolt, to be a little more tolerant and a little more rational than their forefathers or than their Catholic brothers. More progressive was the new Protestant ethics, emphasizing the virtues of industry, giving a good conscience to the activities and desires of the rising merchant classes, and thereby making Calvinism and capitalism allies.

But probably the positive effects of the Reformation were less decisive in the long run than were its undesigned, or negative, results. Luther and his followers, by rending the unity of the Western church, divided Europe into two armed camps, and at the same time struck a hard blow at all authority and tradition. The fierce persecutions and the devastating wars of the sixteenth and seventeenth centuries were the direct and baleful consequences of the religious hatred born of the schism; but after they had passed away a freer field than before was left to reason, tolerance, and secularism.

More important even than the Reformation was the commercial revolution which raised the merchant class into the dominant position in the state and left the hitherto privileged classes of clergy and nobility in a much reduced situation. An economic shift is always followed by a political, and then by an ethical and cultural revolution. When money, and not birth or sacred character, became the key to power in the state the political institutions and the artistic and moral ideas of society were bound to change. To a considerable extent, the cultural changes of modern times have been but the working out, in various fields, of the logical consequences of the rise of capitalism.

Politically, the first effects of the rise of the bourgeoisie took two forms—the growth of despotism and the formation of republics. In countries like France and Spain, in which the third estate was unable to match the power of the second and first estates unaided, and where a powerful army was needed for protection against foreign foes, the bourgeoisie sought and found in the monarch the ally, and then the master, who cast down their common foes at home and abroad. But in England and Holland, and still more in the North American colonies, the third estate became so strong that it was able not only to pillage the church and to curb the feudal nobility but to dispense with the burdensome aid of the king and to establish republics.

A fourth factor in the evolution of Europe was the influence of the new geographical discoveries. By them at first the imagination of the time was deeply stirred; but presently, and with surprising rapidity, the material effects of commerce with the newly accessible continents began to make themselves felt. The center of world culture and of world power was shifted from the Mediterranean to the Atlantic. A stream of wealth pouring into the laps first of Portugal and Spain and then of Holland and England upset the balance of power and laid the foundations of new experiments in civilization. Sea-power became the "abridgment of empire"; wars for trade and colonies began to take the place of wars for religion and conquest. And new settlements, west of the Atlantic, laid the foundations of states destined to become as powerful and as civilized as their mother countries.

Perhaps the rise of nationalism should be included among the formative factors of modern culture. In all ages the devotion of the individual to his group has been a strong and a constant, because a biological, factor. But in different ages the group varies. The Middle Ages felt the compulsion of two great international states, the Roman Catholic Church and the Holy Roman Empire. The medieval man, moreover, owed a strong local allegiance to the city or to the dukedom or to the county which constituted a group smaller than the kingdom or empire of which it was a part. But in modern times the national state has been the strongest group in the world, and the one within which all forms of cultural life tend to take shape. Even in religion national churches have largely taken the place of the universal church. The Holy Roman Empire, not quite killed until the time of Napoleon, received hard blows with the Peace of Augsburg (1555) and the Peace of Westphalia (1648).

In that age of poor communications the differences between the several nations were greater than they are now. The light of culture shone strong on the central nations of Western Europe—England, France, the Netherlands, Germany, Switzerland, and Italy. In the penumbra round about lay Scandinavia, Scotland, Portugal, Spain, and Poland. Ireland to the west and Turkey and Russia to the east then lay outside the circle of European civilization.

After taking the lead in the age of the Reformation, Germany sank in prosperity and in culture during the century from the outbreak of the Schmalkaldic War to the end of the Thirty Years War. From the fearful havoc caused by this last conflict the nation did not really recover for another century. Not less destructive to civilization than the vital and economic losses was the moral decline. The peasantry were reduced to serfdom; the inhabitants of the cities were ruined; the princes, though impoverished, established an absolutism in which the popular elements of government (the Estates, or local Diets) were suppressed and the army took the leading position as an instrument of government. As the authority of the emperor relaxed, the Empire became a loose confederacy of states. Among these Brandenburg, under the Great Elector (1640-88), began to take the leading position which was later to make it, under the name of Prussia, the most powerful state of the European continent.

France, though terribly wasted by the religious wars of the last half of the sixteenth century, recovered rapidly enough in the seventeenth to become the mightiest state in the Western world under her Great Monarch, Louis XIV. The military force which made the nation dreaded abroad established a heavy despotism at home. In 1614 the States General met for the last time before the Revolution. The feeble efforts of the Parlement of Paris and of the nobility to make a stand against tyranny made the Fronde (1649-53) no more than a ghastly parody of the contemporary English establishment of liberty under the Commonwealth. But the chains of despotism were gilded by the military glory and diplomatic prestige of the monarchy. Greater than the achievements of French arms and of French statesmen were the conquests, during the seventeenth century, of the French writers. A galaxy of genius added luster to the splendor of Versailles. Under the combined impression of French military success and of French philosophy and poetry, the whole of Europe fell under the spell of Gallic thought and of Gallic manners. French became the language of diplomacy, of culture, and of polite society.

While France was rising the other great Catholic monarchy, Spain, was sinking into decay. With the annexation of Portugal and her extensive colonial empire in 1580 the might of the Spanish Hapsburgs reached its apogee. But the revolt of the Netherlands, the defeat of the great Armada by the English in 1588, the defeat of a second Armada by the Dutch in 1639, the revolts and the expulsion of the Moors, the defeat of the Spanish army by the French at Rocroy in 1643, the successful revolt of Portugal in 1640, marked the visible stages of Spanish decadence. Despotism and priest-craft flourished on the decay of the population. General corruption in administration and a savage bigotry in religion kept the people miserable and enslaved. But while science and philosophy languished under the terror of the Inquisition, a wonderful art and literature consoled the nation for its loss of power and of freedom.

As the trident of sea-power fell from the grasp of Spain the commerce of the world came into the hands of the Dutch and of the English. The war of independence, waged by the Netherlands against Spain, tore the country in two. While the ten southern provinces remained under the Spanish yoke, the seven northern provinces united to form a new nation. The extraordinary power wielded by this tiny people, who first defeated Spain, then repulsed the unjust attacks of France, and finally contested with England the command of the sea, was based upon the enormous wealth of the colonial trade which, for some years, they succeeded in nearly monopolizing. After deposing Philip, the Dutch created a federal republic with a somewhat complicated constitution. The prestige and ability of the House of Nassau first threatened and finally destroyed the republican form of government in favor of one which was quasi-monarchical. But throughout the seventeenth century the wealth, the culture, the freedom, and the art of the Dutch Republic continued to be the admiration and envy of the world.

In the meantime the southern provinces were left under the nearly autonomous rule of their archdukes. The purpose of Spain in waging the war to keep the Netherlands had been chiefly to preserve them for the Catholic church. This object having been secured, the Spanish Netherlands were little vexed by their foreign king. But, their land fearfully wasted by the war, their commerce cut off by the Dutch, and their liberty of thought crushed by the church, the men of Flanders and Brabant contributed little to European culture except a remarkable luxuriant art which, perhaps, as in the case of Spain, served them as a compensation for lost freedom and lost power.

Among the smaller nations of Europe Switzerland continued to enjoy a republican form of government, though one which was narrowly oligarchical. Like Germany, Switzerland was torn into two parts by the Reformation, and the opposing leagues of cantons occasionally came to blows.

For one brief moment Sweden like a meteor dominated the European constellation. When Gustavus Adolphus intervened to save Protestantism in Germany, he carried all before him until his premature death in 1632. But the resources of neither Sweden nor Denmark were sufficient to establish a Scandinavian empire around the Baltic, and the constant efforts to do this were therefore frustrated. In Sweden, and in Denmark, as in most of the rest of Europe, the monarch became despotic or nearly so, with the support of the third estate against the two privileged orders.

The Italian states lost, in the latter sixteenth and in the seventeenth century, whatever political importance they may have previously enjoyed. The transfer of the oriental trade from the Mediterranean to Atlantic routes ruined Venice and Genoa. The papacy no longer held the supreme place in the European polity that had once belonged to it. The intellectual glory of Florence, indeed, was worthily prolonged until the church crushed, in forcing Galileo's recantation, the hope of free thought. But Italy continued to produce many great artists and a few great poets.

The history of England during the century between the Armada and the Revolution (1588-1688) shone bright with the double glory of establishing an empire over seas and liberty at home. The bourgeoisie, which in the rest of Europe had made an ally of the monarch only to fall into bondage to him later, in England was strong enough to call even him to account. By the Puritan Commonwealth the king was executed for treason to the nation and by the sons of the Republicans the son of the justly punished king was exiled. Of all periods in the history of English letters that from the first play of Shakespeare to the death of Milton was the most glorious.

While they were consolidating liberty at home the English mariners laid the foundations of a great colonial empire. The settlement of Virginia in 1607 and of Plymouth in 1620 marked the birth of a new people, destined for more than a century and a half to flourish under the protection of the mother country and then to assert its full maturity as an independent nation. Here, in the New World, was built a new type of state, freer and more popular than any that had gone before. Though, in their infancy, the colonies could contribute little directly to the culture of the world, it is remarkable that even in the seventeenth century interest in science and in literature flourished mightily beyond the Atlantic.

Through all these nations, so various in spirit and in manner of life, sometimes so hostile to one another, pulsed the strong current of a common tradition. The Republic of Letters is an international state; the City of Man a dwelling place for all peoples. The history of culture must take the international or supernational point of view. There were men three hundred years ago, as there have been in all ages before and since, who could say with Bacon, "We bestow our supreme love on the Republic of Man as on a common fatherland." [1] The story of this great republic is spread at large upon the monuments of the science, of the learning, of the literature, and of the art of every age.

[1] "Humanam Rempublicam"; *Prodromi sive Anticipationes philosophiae secundae. Works*, v, 182.

PART I. THE SCIENCES

CHAPTER II

ASTRONOMY

I. THE COPERNICAN SYSTEM

Of all the elements of modern culture, as of all the forces moulding modern life, science has been the greatest. It can be shown that all other changes in society are largely dependent upon this. Thought, philosophy, religion, art, education, laws, morals, economic institutions, are to a great extent dependent upon the progress of science. Not only does science alter technique in the production of wealth, but it alters man's view of the world in which he lives. The world-view is perhaps the decisive factor in moulding life and civilization.

To the astonished eyes of the men of the sixteenth and seventeenth centuries science revealed that they had been living in a dream sent by the shades of their ancestors through the ivory gates of the past. In the transvaluation of all values produced by studying the facts of nature instead of relying on the wisdom of the past and on the common opinion of mankind, revelation faded into mythology and tradition into poetry; the very testimony of the eyes was shown to be delusive, and the world, which had stood so fast through all ages, was loosed from its moorings and sent spinning at terrific speed through space.

Of course the implications of the new science were not felt, were still less admitted, all at once. The brain of man has an enormous *vis inertiae* resistant to all sudden change. Generations, even centuries, are required for a really novel idea to win acceptance. And the impact of science was so fresh in man's experience as to cause him first astonishment, then pain, and then anger; he found it at first ridiculous, then horrible, and then blasphemous, before he finally learned to prize it as the supreme good.

New it was to the sixteenth century even though there had been something like it in ancient Greece. Glorious as it was, however, the science of the Greeks had been a unique phenomenon, leaving no immediate posterity. Neither Rome nor medieval Europe added anything of importance to pure science, though some practical discoveries of the highest value had enriched the twelfth and subsequent centuries. And then suddenly, within two years, appeared three of the most momentous works of science that the world has ever seen, Copernicus *On the Revolutions of the Heavenly Orbs* (1543), Vesalius *On the Structure of the Human Body* (1543), and Cardan's *The Great Art* (a treatise on algebra, 1545). And from that time to the present almost every decade has seen an increasing number of discoveries in many fields.

Of the three men it is hard to say which contributed most to the particular science which he studied, but there can be no doubt that Copernicus sent the shock through Europe which, when it was later repeated with a much higher voltage by Kepler and Galileo, first convulsed and then liberated the mind of the race. Copernicus was not, indeed, the first to assert that the earth and five planets revolve around the sun, and that the earth spins on its own axis, for Aristarchus of Samos in the third century before Christ had advanced the same theory, and this theory had been accepted by some Arabian philosophers; but Copernicus first put the proof so powerfully that he convinced the leading astronomers and finally the whole world. While the heliocentric theory, like many modern discoveries, including the atomic system and evolution, had been conjecturally anticipated in ancient times, he is rightly honored as the establisher of the new truth who first made the particular idea he espoused a permanent and living part of the thought of the intellectual world.

Nicholas Copernicus (1473-1543), the son of a Polish father and of a German mother, was born at Thorn in

Poland, and studied at the national university of Cracow. After taking holy orders, as did many men who desired leisure for study, he was enabled, by an ecclesiastical appointment, to spend ten years in Italy, a large part of it at the universities of Bologna, Padua, and Ferrara. With an omnivorous appetite for knowledge he mastered medicine and mathematics and took the degree of doctor of canon law at Ferrara in 1503. In later life, besides his books on astronomy, he wrote a treatise on trigonometry and one on political economy, pointing out the effect, in raising prices, of debasing the currency. When he returned to Poland he was again indebted to his uncle, an influential bishop, for an ecclesiastical benefice, this time as a canon of the cathedral of Frauenburg. If character is built in the stream of affairs, the ideas that move the world are nursed in the stillness of an uneventful life. Thirty-one years (1512-43), except for brief intervals, he spent in the little tower on the wall of the cathedral close, observing the planets with his naked eyes and measuring their altitudes and their longitudes with the poor instruments made with his own hands.

Not so much as the result of his own observations, which were not numerous and which added little to the already assembled mass of facts, but from a high capacity for colligating details in general formulae he was led to propound the astronomical system ever since known by his name. While the apparent orbits of the sun, moon, and five planets had long been known, the explanation of their irregularities was unsatisfactory, and was becoming more and more complicated and unconvincing with every accretion of new knowledge. Early Greek philosophers had held the theory that the earth is the center of the universe and that around it move a number of transparent spheres, in one of which was carried the sun, in another the moon, in separate ones each of the planets, and in one the fixed stars; and outside of that they placed the *primum mobile,* the crystalline heaven needed to explain the precession of the equinox. But as the ancients themselves soon saw that no such simple system could account for the complicated movements of the planets, they began to modify it by adding more spheres, some of them concentric with the original spheres, but moving in different directions, some of them epicycles, which were supposed to revolve around points revolving in the main sphere. Before the time of Aristotle the number of spheres had been raised to 27; he more than doubled the number, adding epicycles that moved retrograde, and some of a second degree. As even this machine could not suffice to explain the orbits of the planets, later astronomers added still other spheres until by the sixteenth century the number had reached 77, making in all a system of such inconceivable complexity as to stagger belief.

While Copernicus was in Italy, the Venetian printer Aldo published, in 1499, a collection of ancient writings on astronomy (*Scriptores astronomici veteres*). Though this contained nothing of Aristarchus, the Polish student learned from it that there had been Greeks who believed that the sun is the center of the solar system. As he observed and computed further he saw that this hypothesis would reduce to simplicity and order the apparently wry and complex motions of the heavenly bodies. For many years, however, after he had attained conviction of the truth—which dawned on him first at some time between 1506 and 1515—he kept his conclusions to himself, fearing, as he later explained in a dedicatory letter to Pope Paul III, that the novelty of his opinions would raise clamor against him and cause him to be hissed off the stage. Then, like Pythagoras, whom he perhaps regarded as a precursor in maintaining the heliocentric theory, he began cautiously to intimate his esoteric doctrine to a few friends and disciples. About 1530 he issued a summary and prospectus of his planned book, under the name of *A Brief Commentary concerning the Celestial Movements*. After another decade, his young disciple, Georg Joachim, called Rheticus, who had left Wittenberg to sit at the master's feet, published a fuller explanation of the theory in a tract entitled *The First Account* (1539).

Not long afterwards Copernicus sent the manuscript of his great work to be printed at Nuremberg. While in press it fell into the hands of a Lutheran pastor, Andrew Osiander, who was so struck by the novelty of the apparently convincing theory, that he wrote and inserted an anonymous preface stating that the hypotheses in the book were not intended to be taken as absolutely true, or even probable, but were merely put forth to facilitate calculation. Though he thus advanced a proposition difficult for the philosopher to accept, and though he doubtless expected to have his preface pass for that of the author, Osiander probably acted in agreement with the leading Lutheran theologians, and certainly with the intention of mitigating the shock likely to be caused by the book, of facilitating its publication, and of preventing its suppression. He even, as he wrote in excuse to Rheticus, believed that any one who read the book would be convinced of its truth. But, as a matter of fact, the preface, long taken as Copernicus's own, proved a nasty stumbling-block to the readers of the book and an aid and comfort to its enemies. It is fairly amazing to see how often it was quoted against the Polish astronomer, as if offering evidence that he himself did not believe in his own propositions, but regarded them merely as unproved hypotheses. In 1597 Kepler discovered and revealed to the world that the author of the preface was Osiander, and a few years later he wrote [1]

It is a highly absurd process to explain natural phenomena by assigning them false causes, but this method must not be imputed to Copernicus, who believed and proved that his hypotheses were true. The Preface [quoted against him] is by Osiander.

But the truth is ever a laggard in overtaking the accepted falsehood. In the eighteenth century there were still men who regarded the Copernican system not as a proved truth but as a "learned hypothesis."

But to return to the astronomer of Frauenburg. When the completed volume was brought to him, as he lay on his death-bed, he must have felt that the labor of his life

[1] *Kepleri Opera*, iii, 136.

had been crowned and the work of his hands established for ever. On the title-page of the handsome quarto he read: [1]

On the Revolutions of the Celestial Orbs. Six books. By Nicholas Copernicus of Thorn. Printed at Nuremberg by John Petreius. 1543.

In this recently composed and published work you have, Studious Reader, the motions of the fixed stars and planets restored according to ancient and recent observations and set in order according to new and admirable hypotheses.

At the bottom of this same crowded title-page is a Greek motto, borrowed from the door of Plato's academy: "Let no one ignorant of geometry enter here."

The first of the six books into which the work is divided examines the previous authorities, the second propounds the new theory, the third explains the precession of the equinoxes, the fourth proves that the moon circles the earth, the fifth and weightiest book proves that the planets, including the earth, move around the sun, and gives correctly the time of the orbits of all the planets then known, from Mercury with eighty-eight days to Saturn with nearly thirty years. The last book treats the determination of latitude by the fixed stars.

The judgment often passed on Copernicus' work, that it was not convincing until further proofs were offered by Kepler and Galileo, is not a fair one. The great argument on which he relied, that his hypothesis was the only one fitting the observed facts, is absolutely convincing if tested, and did in fact convince Kepler and Galileo and other astronomers. Those who, like Tycho Brahe, and Francis Bacon, still rejected it in whole or in part, did so not for astronomical reasons, but by arguments drawn chiefly from other than astronomical authorities. It is true that the Copernican system was as yet incomplete. The discrepancies

---

[1] *Nicolai Copernici Torinensis de revolutionibus orbium coelestium Libri VI.* Norimbergae apud Joh. Petreium. MDXLIII. A copy of the first edition is at Cornell University. This title is largely Osiander's. Copernicus never spoke of his "hypotheses," and apparently called his work simply *De revolutionibus.*

he noticed between his calculations and the observed positions of the planets led him at one time to entertain the true theory that the planets move in elliptical orbits, but unfortunately he abandoned this theory for the classical hypothesis of circular orbits, and so the passage dealing with this matter, found in his manuscript, was deleted and never printed. Another limitation on the Copernican work was that it dealt with the solar system only. The astronomer of Frauenburg was content to leave the fixed stars in a globe around the earth, though, in order to account for the absence of any change in their apparent position (parallax), he removed that globe to an almost infinite distance.

In such matters the man who did more to break a path for modern thought than almost any other was still under the spell of antiquity. At every point he tried to buttress his hypothesis by showing that it could be defended by ancient authority. Bruno's verdict that he collected and polished the rusty and worthless fragments of antique learning is a just one, if one looks at the form rather than at the spirit of the work. Moreover, Copernicus, unlike most modern scientists, carefully cultivated a persuasive as well as a dialectic style. While he could write as dryly and as objectively as Euclid, he could also drive home his ideas with poetical imagery worthy of an artist. The wonderful passage (Book I, chapter X) on the harmony of creation and the grandeur of the divine workshop breaks into a hymn which has been compared, though extravagantly, with the twenty-second canto of Dante's *Paradiso*.

The first adherents of the new theory were naturally astronomers. Rheticus of Wittenberg had been convinced before 1540. Erasmus Reinhold in 1551 published a catalogue of the stars (the *Tabulae Prutenicae*)[1] calculating their positions on Copernican principles. Five years later (1556) John Field in England printed his *Almanac for the year 1557 according to the rules of Copernicus and Reinhold*.

But Tycho Brahe, the leading astronomer of the next

[1] So called because dedicated to Duke Albert of Prussia.

generation, while admitting that the other planets circled the sun, refused to believe that the earth could do so. His main contribution to science was not his system of the world, a compromise between the Ptolemaic and Copernican, but his careful cataloguing of the stars and his studies of comets.

Tycho Brahe (1546-1601) was born of a noble Danish family in Scania, the southernmost district of the Scandinavian peninsula, then belonging to Denmark. His interest in astronomy, first excited by seeing the eclipse of August 21, 1560, was fostered at the universities of Leipzig and Rostock, and was further stimulated by the extraordinary spectacle of the bright new star which suddenly appeared in the constellation Cassiopeia on November 11, 1572, and which gradually became dimmer until it disappeared eighteen months later.

From 1576 to 1597 Tycho lived on the little island of Hveen in the sound between Denmark and Sweden. Here he built a fine observatory and called it, perhaps with a pun on the name of the island, and with an allusion to the building's purpose, Uraniborg, or the Castle of Heaven. Therein he set up a large brass-plated sphere on which he marked the positions of the stars calculated afresh with painstaking accuracy. The observatory consisted of a circular stone tower with little windows around the upper part just under the roof. Through these windows any given star could be seen by an observer on the floor and its position then accurately marked on a great mural quadrant at the base of the tower's interior. The improvement of this method over the older one was in the size of the instrument used and the length of the distance between the eye of the observer and the aperture through which the star appeared. This left a much smaller error in the angle marking the star's elevation than the error likely to vitiate observations with the older quadrants and astrolabes, small instruments held up to the eye.

Tycho's quadrant, a quarter-circle of metal, with a radius of six feet and nine inches, could mark nicely the angle formed by the intersection of the line of vision with a horizontal plane, or the angle marking the apparent distance of one star from another. Other instruments he carefully described in his *Astronomiae Instauratae Mechanica,* published in 1598. One of these was an armillary sphere, a combination of iron circles in a skeleton globe, the various circles representing the meridian, the ecliptic, and the colures.

With these aids Tycho added greatly to the descriptive astronomy of his time. In his *Progymnasmata* (written in 1572, printed by Kepler, after the author's death, in 1602) he accurately marked the position of 777 fixed stars. His study of the comet of 1577 proved that its orbit lay far beyond the moon, and thus upset the then accepted idea that comets are atmospheric, and hence sublunary, exhalations. His estimate of the earth's semi-diameter as 860 German miles (3956 English miles) was not much wrong, but he went far astray in calculating the distances of the heavenly bodies. He believed the moon to be 206,000 (English) miles from the earth, whereas it is now known to be about 238,800; and he thought Saturn distant 48 million (English) miles from the earth instead of the modern figure of 887 million miles from the sun.

Trying to find a *via media* between Ptolemy and Copernicus he excogitated a solar system that had much vogue among old-fashioned philosophers and ecclesiastical writers for many years. Keeping the earth as the center of the system, he believed that the sun and moon revolve around it, and that the five planets are satellites of the sun. While his conclusions were doubtless influenced largely by tradition and biblical authority, he advanced two specious arguments against the Copernican hypothesis, first that so swift a revolution of the earth on its axis would hurl it to pieces, and secondly that, as the earth moved from one end of its orbit to the other, a change in the position of the fixed stars should be apparent, while as a matter of fact no such parallax had as yet been perceived. Both these arguments, well taken though they were, could be and later were answered by the further progress of science.

2. KEPLER'S LAWS

Leaving Uraniborg in 1597 Tycho wandered for the last four years of his life around the German Empire, matriculating at Wittenberg on February 20, 1598, and settling for some time at Prague. Here he had as an assistant a younger and abler man, Johann Kepler, whom he labored hard but vainly to persuade of the truth of his system. So isolated was the position of Brahe among scientists by this time that Kepler was able to say in 1596 that all famous astronomers were by that time Copernicans.[1]

Kepler himself was destined to become, with Galileo, the most famous of them all, and the perfecter of his master's hypothesis. The presiding principle that governed his prolific energies was the endeavor to find behind the multifarious phenomena of nature the mathematical formulæ binding them together. By this method he was able to discover some natural laws of the utmost importance and to deserve the title of "legislator of the sky." But the mind so penetrating and alert in disclosing the true and useful relation of things was also capacious of much that was fanciful, if not absurd. Hardly any scientist of equal rank has written so much pure rubbish on his own subject. Three-quarters of the work of this Wordsworth of astronomy is valueless; the remaining quarter is priceless.

Johann Kepler (1571-1630) was born at Weil in Württemberg and educated at the University of Tübingen. His early wish to be a divine was fortunately thwarted by the bigotry of the Lutheran divines who disliked his Calvinistic view of the eucharist and who, perhaps, looked askance at his already eager championship of the Copernican system. But, though he turned to astronomy at the age of twenty-four with the avowed purpose of making the stars declare the glory of God, he was subject to constant

[1] *Kepleri Opera*, i, 76.

persecution, to defend himself against which he published a *Confession of Faith,* testifying his orthodoxy, in 1623. As a convinced Protestant he suffered some persecution in Catholic lands.

Nor did his only troubles come from the intolerance of his compatriots. Poverty was then generally, as it is often still, the lot of the lonely scientist. Even after his works had brought him great fame they brought him little income. He supported himself in part by writing almanacs, in part by appeals to patrons. The matter of income was made more pressing by an early and fruitful marriage. When his first wife died, in 1610, he made a list of the ladies whom he considered as candidates for the vacancy, marking them carefully on a graded scale of qualities and ranging them in order according to the average mark obtained by each. This method of choosing a wife seems so prudent that it must have come to him as an inexplicable contrariety in the fitness of things that the lady clearly proved by his calculations to be the most eligible declined the honor, and he was obliged to go further down on the list before the equation of mathematics and matrimony was solved.

Great difficulties were placed in his path by the ravages of the Thirty Years War. Though he found in Wallenstein a patron and protector, he was driven from place to place —from Gratz to Prague, from Prague to Linz, from Linz to Sagan, and then to other cities. But, through the tempest which prostrated Germany, he continued to work. "While the raging whirlwind threatens a national shipwreck," he wrote in the last year of his life, "we have nothing better to do than to cast the anchor of our harmless studies in the rock-bottom of eternity." [1] Those studies were, indeed, more momentous for the future of the world than all the rage and uproar of the fearful war.

His first considerable work, entitled *A Preface to Cosmography, or the Mystery of the Cosmos,*[2] was published

[1] Nov. 6, 1639. *Bayerische Akademie d. Wiss., Math.-Naturwissenschaftliche Abt.* xxxi, i, 1927, p. 55.
[2] *Prodromus Dissertationum Cosmographicarum seu Mysterium Cosmographicum,* Tübingen, 1596, reprinted, *Opera,* i, 1ff.

in 1596. The most valuable part of it was the defence of
Copernicus, but the author's main purpose was to present
and maintain a characteristic and fanciful scheme of the
solar system. He believed that the planets might be conceived as moving in the surface of concentric spheres, and
that the size of each sphere was dependent on the supposed
fact that it was circumscribed about a regular solid which
in turn was circumscribed about the sphere of the planet
next in order in distance from the sun. Thus, said he, the
largest of the spheres, that of Saturn, contains a cube, which
contains the sphere of Jupiter, in which is inscribed a tetra-
hedron; then, in regular order, come the sphere of Mars,
a dodecahedron; the sphere of the earth, an icosahedron;
the sphere of Venus, an octahedron, and the sphere of Mercury. Though this method of calculating the relative sizes
of the planetary orbits is worthless, not even agreeing with
the data at Kepler's disposal, the author was so much
wedded to it that he wrote Galileo his positive conviction
that no more than six planets could exist because there are
only five regular polyhedrons to determine the distances
between them.

The accepted theory that the planets move in perfect
circles was seen by Kepler to contradict the facts of his
observations of the orbit of Mars as early as 1602. Seven
years he spent in unremitting toil verifying his theory that
the planet moves in an ellipse of which one focus is the
sun. This is known as his first law. Even after his formulation of the theory his work was rendered arduous by
his initial error of supposing that the planet moves at a
uniform velocity. In truth a planet moves more rapidly
the nearer it is to the sun, a fact illustrated by comparing,
in the case of the earth, the length of the period from the
vernal to the autumnal equinox with the period from the
autumnal to the vernal equinox. As the earth is nearer the
sun during our northern winter it travels the part of its
orbit from the September to the March equinox in about
179 days, whereas its journey through the other part of
its orbit occupies about 186 days. Not knowing the amount

of variation in the planet's velocity, Kepler performed the calculation of the orbit and velocity of Mars seventy times —a problem infinitely laborious without the aid of logarithms—before he was able to announce his second law, namely: That a planet moves more rapidly when near the sun and more slowly when farther from it, and that its speed in all parts of its orbit is such that the area of all segments swept in equal times by a radius drawn from the sun to the planet is equal. From the accompanying figure it will readily be seen that if we suppose O to be the orbit

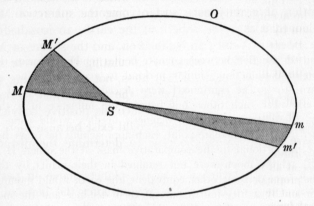

FIG. 1.—Illustrating Kepler's law.

of Mars, of which S (the sun) is one focus, and if the segment MM′S be equal to the segment mm′S the segment with the shorter radii must have the longer arc. According to Kepler's law, this means that the planet will cover the longer arc MM′ in the same time that it covers the shorter arc mm′, provided the segments swept out by the line joining the planet and the sun are equal.

These two important truths were announced to the world in a treatise with a long title, here translated with the display words in capitals: *A new cause-explaining Astronomy or celestial Physics presented in a Commentary ON THE MOTIONS OF THE PLANET MARS, from the Observations of Tycho Brahe, elaborated with long and pertinacious study by Johann Kepler, Prague, 1609.* Among the miscellaneous matter contained in this treatise was some interesting, if erroneous, speculation as to the cause of the varying velocity of the planet in different parts of its orbit. In the then imperfect state of physics Kepler believed that the planet would need a continual application of force to keep it going, just as would a wagon on land or a ship at sea. This force he thought to be derived from the sun, and he accounted for the greater speed of the satellite near the sun by saying that the emanation of energy would naturally be stronger nearer its source. From Gilbert he derived a notion of gravity as a sort of magnetic attraction, and he defined it as

a mutual affection between cognate bodies tending towards their union or conjunction, similar in kind to magnetic virtue. · . . . If two stones [he continued] were placed in some part of the universe near each other but beyond the influence of a third body, these stones, like two magnetic needles, would come together at an intermediate point, each approaching the other by a space proportional to the comparative mass of the other. If the earth and the moon were not retained in their orbits by their animal force or some other equivalent, the earth would mount to the moon by a fifty-fourth part of their distance and the moon would fall towards the earth by the other 53 parts, and they would meet, assuming that the matter in each is of the same density [and that the mass of the earth is to that of the moon as 53 to 1].

This definition of gravity is notable not only as a probable starting point for Newton's speculations, but as showing how much more successful was Kepler—and the same is true of most other scientists—in describing and calculating phenomena than in assigning them true causes.

Just ten years after the *Commentary on the Motions of Mars* Kepler published a work on *The Harmony of the World,* in which a vast mass of fanciful and useless speculation formed the background of some valuable observations and of one extremely brilliant generalization, commonly known as Kepler's third law. This was a statement of the periodic times of the planetary revolutions in relation to each other and to the size of their orbits. It had been noticed that the planets more distant from the sun move at a slower rate, thus making the time of their revolution around the sun much longer than that of the nearer planets, and proportionately longer than might be indicated by the ratio of their orbits. In a flash of genius Kepler saw the true relation of things, and announced that "the squares of the periodic times are proportional to the cubes of the mean distances of the planets from the sun." This so-called sesquiplicate ratio may be simply illustrated. If there is a planet the mean distance from the sun of which is nine (3^2) times as great as that of another planet, its year will be twenty-seven (3^3) times as long; because nine cubed equals twenty-seven squared, *i.e.* 729. This ratio comes very near that actually obtaining between the earth and Saturn; with an orbit a little more than nine times as big as that of the earth Saturn has a year a little more than twenty-seven times as long (29 years and a fraction).

About the time that he published this work Kepler prepared and printed in two parts (1618, 1621) an *Epitome of the Copernican Astronomy,* containing the first comprehensive exposition of the new system, together with his own discoveries and certain fantastic notions, of which one, emphasized by him, was the supposed relation of the distances of the planets to the notes of the musical scale. After his death his son published (1634) an entertaining *jeu d'esprit,* called *Kepler's Dream, or the Astronomy of the Moon.* In it the author showed how different the universe would look to an observer on the moon.

Besides enunciating the three great laws known by his name, Kepler gave to astronomy a host of careful observations and of stimulating suggestions, and he also wrote works on optics and on mathematics. Taken all in all his insight into the intricate mathematical relations of the cosmos was more penetrating and profound than any man's before Newton.

3. GALILEO'S DISCOVERIES

Far different, but hardly less important, were the services to astronomy of Galileo Galilei. Science walks, like a man, on two legs: one leg is the accumulation of facts, and the other leg the colligation of large classes of isolated facts in those great generalizations, economical of thought, called natural laws. Neither process can go on satisfactorily without the other. Data without binding theory soon bewilder and clog the mind; theory without supporting fact wanders off into barren illusion. Kepler was the master of theory; his great contemporary, Galileo, by a marvellous ingenuity in devising new methods of observation and experiment, added enormously to descriptive science. And he, rather than his northern rival, aroused first the interest and then the passions of the multitude, and thus brought on himself the animadversion of the Inquisition. The sight of the satellites of Jupiter and of the mountains of the moon impressed the masses more vividly than did the calculation of the sesquiplicate ratio or the elliptical orbits of the planets. While Kepler hid his jewels of thought in a heavy casket of abstruse and technical Latin, Galileo displayed many of his celestial marvels under the clear glass of a transparent Italian style. And, as he raised the first great storm that has broken over modern science, his thrilling, tragic, and yet triumphant career has become the very type and exemplar of the warfare that has since raged between new truth and old superstition.

Galileo, the son of Vincenzo Galilei, a musician, was born at Florence on February 15, 1546, about two months before Shakespeare saw the light in England. At the age of thirteen he was sent to the monastery school at Vallombrosa, where he saw the leaves of two autumns thickly strew the ground. When he matriculated at the University of Pisa (September 5, 1581) he found the instruction offered in the regular curriculum less to his liking than were the lessons in mathematics privately given by Ostilio Ricci, a practical engineer. The new life already pulsating in the arteries of the applied sciences, as practiced by their masters, had not yet flowed into the somewhat dry and senile veins of the universities. From Ricci the young Florentine learned all that the mathematicians and engineers of the age had to teach, and from him he acquired that marvellous skill in making and in using instruments which was to prove the foundation of his later work.

According to tradition it was at Pisa that he made his first two important discoveries in mechanics—that of the isochronous pendulum by watching a lamp swinging in the cathedral, and that of the equal speed of falling bodies by dropping weights from the famous leaning tower. The truth of these traditions has been doubted, but, though the circumstances are purely legendary, there is good reason to believe that the discovery of the law of the pendulum, at least, does date from his student days.

After eight years of study at Pisa he was given the chair of mathematics in the university at the salary of $1.25 a week—no munificent sum even allowing that money then had eight or ten times its present purchasing power. Three years later he was called to a better position at Padua, the university town of Venice. Here he remained eighteen years, continuing to make important discoveries in physics and to try his hand at various forms of literary composition.

In these he doubtless formed that animated style that is the best in Italian literature of the seventeenth century. An artist to the finger-tips, Galileo read and criticized the poets and even imitated them. He treated the "size, site and conformation of Dante's hell" in a way that showed he could yet accept the medieval cosmology. He was drawn deep into the quarrel then agitating Florentine literary circles as to the respective merits of Tasso and Ariosto. As Tasso had been accused of hostility to Florence, Galileo was perhaps influenced by patriotic as well as by æsthetic considerations when he branded that poet's allegory as "meager, poor, and miserable," while praising Ariosto as "rich, magnificent, and wonderful." The theater interested him so much that he wrote the scenario for a *commedia dell' arte.*

Not as a critic or as a dramatist, however, was he destined to win immortal fame, but as a scientist. It is remarkable that in his university lectures he continued to expound the old Ptolemaic system, even after he had become convinced in his own mind of the truth of the Copernican system. Indeed, his *Treatise on the Sphere,* as late as 1605, developed the older astronomy for his pupils without a word of criticism.[1]

It is not clear how he first learned of the Copernican system, though he might have done so in various ways, as it had become a matter of interest throughout Europe by this time. It is possible, but not certain, that he meant to be autobiographical the passage in his later *Dialogue* in which he makes the speaker say that he had been converted by hearing a North European lecture on Copernicus at an Italian academy. If so, Galileo in his old age confused the name of the lecturer with that of Christian Wurstisen.[2] But before 1596, at latest, his own inquiries had convinced him of the truth of the heliocentric hypothesis. By that date his fame had increased to such a point that Kepler sent him his new work, *The Precursor,* which Galileo acknowledged in an interesting letter, the first of a goodly number that passed between the two astronomers:

Many years ago [he says [3]] I adopted the opinion of Copernicus, for I discovered many causes of natural effects which are inexplicable on the common hypothesis. In support of this position, and in refutation of the arguments against it, I wrote many reasons, which I have hitherto not dared to publish, fright-

[1] *Trattato della Sfera, Opere,* ii, 211ff.

[2] Wurstisen was a well known chronicler of Basle who wrote on astronomy, (1544-88). He cannot be traced in Italy. The lists of lectures at Bologna show that Germans lectured on astronomy there in 1585-6, 1586-7, and 1598-9, (U. Dallari: *Rotuli dei lettori.......dello studio Bolognese,* ii, 1889, pp. 222, 225, 265). Unfortunately the records of other Italian universities have not been published. Galileo was offered a chair at Bologna in 1587. He tells of the lectures of Wurstisen in his *Dialogue on the Two Systems of the World,* Book ii, *Opere,* vii, 154.

[3] Padua, Aug. 4, 1597. *Opere,* x, 67.

ened by the fortune of Copernicus who, though he has obtained immortal fame among the few, is, nevertheless, ridiculed and hissed by the many, who are fools.

In reply Kepler urged Galileo to join forces with the supporters of Copernicus, saying that when the vulgar, swayed ever not by reason but by authority, see the learned go over to his opinion, they will follow.

Not only did Galileo now come out openly for the new astronomy, but he brought to its support proofs drawn from sensational discoveries which he was enabled to make by turning on the heavens the recently invented telescope. Like so many other ideas in the history of science, that of the combination of lenses to magnify and elongate vision came to several men about the same time. While antiquity had learned the power of glass blown into the shape of a bean or lentil (and hence called a lens) to refract light, the knowledge had been so little used in the Middle Ages that Roger Bacon, in the thirteenth century, had won the fame of a magician by having two glasses with one of which he could light a candle and with the other of which, it was said, he could see his friends in the distant parts of the earth. Though spectacles became common aids to vision not long after Bacon's time, no one thought of the *combination* of lenses to augment their power until the end of the sixteenth century. After the telescope had excited public attention Giovanni Baptista della Porta, a scientist known for curious experiments with the *camera obscura,* loudly claimed to be the inventor, and his claim receives some contemporary corroboration.[1] What he had really done was apparently to combine two lenses without fitting them into the ends of a

---

[1] See his letter of 1613, printed in Galileo's *Opere,* xi, 611, saying that he had invented the first telescope and that the name had been given it by the King of Naples. Some corroboration of his claim to have had an early telescope is found in a letter from Spinola to Galileo, dated Antwerp, Jan. 22, 1621, *Opere di Galileo,* xiii, 56. Spinola says that he had been shown a telescope many years before by Della Porta, though he attributes the invention to Fracastoro. In Holland Spinola had talked with the man who claimed to have invented telescopes, but whom he does not name. See Huygens' *Œuvres,* xiii, 434ff, 591.

tube; and the same ineffective combination had been made by Leonard Digges in England as early as 1579. The credit of making the invention practical must go to Dutch opticians, of whom one, Zacharias Jansen, about 1591, began to make microscopes for magnifying objects near at hand, and two others, Jan Lippershey and Jacobus Metius, manufactured a telescope or field-glass for spying out distant objects, in 1608.

Very soon after this Galileo heard of the instrument and, without ever having seen one, proceeded to make a telescope by fitting into a tube a convex lens at the far end and a concave lens as an eye-piece. This instrument, which he exhibited to the Venetian Council in 1609, had an aperture of an inch and a half diameter and magnified an object by three diameters, or, as Galileo preferred to put it in terms of the area, nine times. By the next year he had made a much more powerful glass, five and a half feet long and with a diameter of two and a quarter inches, which magnified objects by thirty diameters or 900 times the area.

Almost the first glance with which, through this artificial and piercing eye, he swept the nocturnal heavens, revealed to his amazed and feverishly excited mind more of the heavenly bodies than had hitherto been seen by man. With delight in its beauty he gazed at the moon apparently so near that he could trace the mountains and the valleys on its surface. The number of fixed stars had increased tenfold, and the Milky Way now seemed to him to be not a nebula but a "mass of innumerable stars planted together in clusters."

Three small luminous bodies near the planet Jupiter attracted his attention; his first idea that they were small fixed stars was soon refuted by their rapid motion, by which he recognized them as what they are, the moons of Jupiter. Here was a tiny model of the Copernican system, an ocular demonstration of the big machine on a small scale. Presently he noticed that Venus, like our moon, has phases of waxing and waning. When he turned his telescope on

Saturn he saw the phenomenon now known as the ring, but thought by him to be two small and oddly shaped satellites, which appeared and disappeared in a perplexing manner; so that Saturn seemed, as in the legend, to be alternately eating and disgorging his own children. (Its true form, that of a ring, was first described by Huygens in 1655.)

Fairly intoxicated with these draughts of new knowledge Galileo hastened to communicate them to the public in a little Latin book entitled *The Sidereal Messenger* (1610). The work had an enormous, a sensational success. Kepler wrote a dissertation approving it, while many others tried to refute it. The author was at once elected into the Academy of the Lynx-eyed (*Accademia dei Lincei*) at Rome. A professor who lectured on the discoveries in the Eternal City was heard by a throng of nobles and prelates and by no less than three cardinals. Orders for telescopes poured in on Galileo from Germany, England, France, and Spain, as well as from Italy. The Emperor asked for an instrument so powerful that by its aid he could read a book a mile away and see not only the mountains in the moon but the boats on its seas and the stags in its glades. One of the first to receive a telescope was Marie de Médicis, Queen of France, who used it with interest. John Wells of London wrote Galileo in 1613 that he had made a telescope that would magnify the area one thousand times and that he had heard of still more powerful glasses. Giovanni Baptista della Porta announced in 1614 that he was making a telescope one hundred times as powerful as Galileo's by which he intended to examine the fixed stars and the empyrean,—but of this nothing more was heard.

When Galileo left Padua in 1610, living most of his life thereafter at Florence, his fruitful labors did not end. In 1611 he discovered the spots on the sun, which he at first took to be planets traversing it, but which he soon saw to be dark dots on the surface of a revolving sphere. From the fact that the fixed stars were not, like the planets, magnified by the telescope, Galileo drew the correct conclusion that they appeared larger on account of radiation, and that they were immensely more distant than had been supposed even by Tycho Brahe. In 1638 he discovered the slight oscillations known as the librations of the moon.

4. THE OPPOSITION TO THE COPERNICAN ASTRONOMY, AND ITS FINAL ACCEPTANCE

The sensational success of Galileo's work now brought to a crisis the conflict waged between the champions of Copernicus and the defenders of the older system. Hitherto the new hypothesis might pass for the mere vagary of a few students, of whom the popular opinion is doubtless expressed in the German proverb, that the more learned they are the crazier they are (*je gelehrter desto verkehrter*). But, as the prophet who produces signs in the heavens always wins followers, at last the suspicion began to insinuate itself into the mind of Europe that perhaps the heliocentric theory might be true—and against this dire thought all the instinctive habits and subconscious emotions of mankind mobilized themselves. Though the conflict between the old theory and the new has generally been envisaged as a battle between science and religion, such a view of its history unduly narrows it. What men prize more than anything else, what they fight for as for their lives, are their mental habits, be they religious or rational. The young can be educated in different habits; the old are condemned, or privileged, to die in their inveterate beliefs. That religion played a prominent part in the conflict was natural, first because religion was then the largest part of the mental habit of the masses, and secondly because the church has always been an organized conservatism, one of the chief agencies by which the traditional group mentality has been imposed on rebellious individuals.

The amount of popular opposition to a given scientific discovery is proportional to the contact that it makes with, and to the impact that it makes on, the body of commonly held beliefs. New theorems in mathematics, revolutionary as they may be to that science, can be propounded without

raising a ripple on an uncomprehending public opinion. Discoveries in physics and anatomy had to overcome some opposition in the schools, but not much in the indifferent public.
But the Copernican astronomy changed the whole picture
of the world as it had been viewed by all generations.
Hitherto the universe had been a snug little place, and the
earth occupied its center both in space and in importance.
Around a globe not too big to make one feel comfortably
at home the concentric spheres of the heavens curtained off
the scene on which was enacted the drama of the universe.
Like convenient coulisses, hell, purgatory, and heaven were
at hand to receive the several actors after their exits, while
on the stage of the world men played that absorbing melodrama, conceived and put on by God, half spoiled by Satan
as impresario and villain, and viewed with rapt attention
by a large audience of supernatural beings. And as a
guarantee that this idea of the universe was correct, man
had the witness of his own senses, which could see the sun
and the planets rise and set, and he had also the testimony
of the abnormally wise generations of old and of prophets
inspired by God to write the first acts of the divine comedy
in order to give the actors entering later their proper cue.

And now, at one blow from an infatuated star-gazer, the
world, which had stood so fast on its foundations for six
thousand years, began to twirl giddily on its axis and spin
like a fretful midge around a candle. Though the implications of the new science were not worked out immediately, it
began even from the first to be suspected that, if the theories
advanced were true, man had lost his birthright as the creature for whose sake all else existed, and had been reduced to
the position of a puny and local spectator of infinite forces
unresponsive to his wishes and unmindful of his purposes.
True, this conclusion was not directly taught, but was rather
dissembled by the first Copernicans; nevertheless it insinuated itself, in a nimbus of painful emotion, as the logical
corollary of their thought. True, with the humiliation went
a great exaltation,—that the tiny parasite of a little planet
could, with godlike mind, penetrate the secrets of nature,

and sound the abysses of an endless universe. But, even with this consolation to mitigate the shock, it was terrible. With the possible exception of Darwinism, there has never been such a blow to man's pride, nor one involving such a complete subversion of all his most cherished prejudices. The war between the old and the new beliefs was long and bitter.

Among the first to take alarm were the Wittenberg theologians who had heard of the heliocentric hypothesis from their colleague, Rheticus. On June 4, 1539, Luther in his table talk spoke of the theory as a paradox produced by the vanity of its promulgator. On October 16, 1541, Melanchthon wrote to Burkhard Mithob, at Münden, calling a certain opinion as absurd "as that of the Sarmatian astronomer who makes the earth move and the sun stand still. Wise rulers," he ominously added, "ought to repress such wanton ingenuity." It is probable that he suggested to Osiander the misleading preface to the *De Revolutionibus*.[1] In the first edition of his text-book on *The Elements of Physics* (1549) he argued against the heliocentric theory on biblical and common-sense grounds. Later he struck the allusion to it out of the second edition of his book (1550). Calvin, in a *Commentary on Genesis,* condemned all asserters that the earth is not the immobile center of the universe, citing as his authority Psalm xciii, 1, "the world also is stablished that it cannot be moved."

Italian philosophers trained in the old ways were as shy of the new light as were the German and Swiss theologians. Cardan, the brilliant algebraist, rejected the Copernican hypothesis in the following words: [2]

That the earth is entirely stable, is round, and is situated in the middle of the universe, is demonstrated by mathematics. The earth is no more able to stir from its place than the sky is able to stand still.

[1] This suspicion, suggested to me by Professor Burr, can be confirmed by a careful study of Melanchthon's correspondence.
[2] *De Subtilitate Rerum,* 1550, quoted by Morley: *Cardan,* ii, 62.

One year after these words were written Archbishop Alessandro Piccolomini of Siena published a book of popular science on *The Globe* (*Della Sfera*) refuting the doctrines of the plurality of worlds and of the revolution of the earth, though without mentioning Copernicus, whom the author evidently had in mind. The interest of the people in the astronomical question was aroused by the sermons of the clergy against the heterodox view. An early proof of this is a book called *Marmi* (*Marbles*) by Anton Francesco Doni, a publicist or journalist before journals existed. In this book of gossip and timely topics he represented two Florentines discussing the heliocentric theory, which they had heard mentioned and refuted in sermons. It is possible that the writer, who did not mention Copernicus, was dependent on Piccolomini; but it is equally probable that he heard sermons from the Florentine pulpit, as he avers.

As time went on both interest in the new science and opposition to the heliocentric system waxed hot. Before the church had spoken, the poet Alessandro Tassoni in his *Random Thoughts* (*Pensieri diversi,* 1608) denounced Copernicus and his hypothesis as contradicting universal opinion, nature, religion, science, and common sense.

In France, while Jean Bodin tried to rebut the new theory, Montaigne emitted the characteristically hyperskeptical opinion that Copernicus, having overthrown his predecessors, would be in time himself overthrown by his successors. The popular French opinion in 1578 was reflected by Du Bartas, in the following words in his poem on creation, called *The Week:*

> Some clerks now think—think how absurd a jest!—
> That neither heavens nor stars do turn at all
> Nor dance around this great round earthly ball,
> But the earth itself, this massy globe of ours
> Turns round-about once every twice twelve hours.[1]

[1] Sylvester's translation, slightly revised.

Among the British foes of the Copernican theory, the famous Scotch publicist, George Buchanan, argued that if the earth turned on its axis a violent east wind would sweep everything from its surface.

With far less excuse, because he knew the *Sidereal Messenger* of Galileo, Francis Bacon, after speaking in *The Advancement of Learning* (1604) of the heliocentric theory as possible, later took a strong stand against it. Bacon could never see good in other men's work, neither in that of Aristotle among the ancients nor in that of Gilbert and Galileo among his own contemporaries. Moreover he was impressed by Tycho Brahe's compromise system, and was misled by that officious preface of Osiander to the *De Revolutionibus*. Shortly after he read Galileo's *Sidereus Nuntius*, he answered it in a work entitled *The Sphere of the Understanding*,[1] in which he urged against the Copernican system that the sun must be one of the planets because they had in common many like "passions." In one of his *Essays* (XXIII), first published in 1612, he said that the earth stands fast upon its center. On April 14, 1610, Tobie Matthew wrote Bacon from Italy that Galileo had refuted his (Bacon's) theory of the tides, and this personal note confirmed in hostility the mind of the philosopher, not too celestial to feel jealousy and anger. In the *De Augmentis* (1622-23) Bacon attacked the Copernican hypothesis vigorously by appealing to the evidence of sight, to inveterate opinion, and to the argument from gravitation that the earth must be the center of the universe because of its weight. Elsewhere [2] he said that, though the heliocentric theory agrees with astronomical appearances, it is refuted by arguments drawn from natural philosophy.

The popular opinion in England, favoring the Ptolemaic system, is reflected in the Elizabethan dramatists. Not only was Shakespeare's acceptance of it unquestioning,[3] but

---

[1] *Globus Intellectualis, Works,* vii, 303.
[2] *On the Interpretation of Nature,* no date, *Works,* vi, 44.
[3] *Hamlet,* II, ii, 127ff, and note in the modern "First Folio Edition." Cf. *Troilus,* I, iii; *John,* III, i; *Merry Wives,* III, ii.

Ben Jonson, biased by veneration for antiquity, and ever sensitive to currents of popular interest, gave, with his learned sock, a hard kick to astronomers who make discoveries with "perplexive glasses"—a pun on "perspective glasses" as telescopes were then called. In the satiric masque, *News from the New World discovered in the Moon* (1620), he ridiculed the idea that the moon "is an earth inhabited, with navigable seas and rivers, variety of nations, policies, laws," and with all else that is found on earth. This, of course, does not prove his rejection of the Copernican theory, but it indicates the trend of the author's thought.

But while the inertia of the human mind resisted the impact of the strange knowledge, and while many of the philosophers and poets refused to harbor it, a small but ever increasing band of thinkers hailed the fresh truth with enthusiasm and championed it boldly. Among the first to adopt it was the English mathematician, Robert Recorde. Whereas most of the universities were long hostile, the University of Salamanca in 1561 began to allow the students to choose which system they would learn, heliocentric or geocentric. One of the teachers of Salamanca, Didacus à Stunica, introduced the Copernican hypothesis into a *Commentary on Job* published in 1579.

A brilliant and passionate partisan of the modern astronomy was found in Giordano Bruno, of Nola, near Naples. Early sent to the Dominican friary, for which he had no vocation, he soon fled from it, and wandered all through Europe, teaching at several universities and proclaiming everywhere the religion of science. At Geneva he met the leading Calvinists; in France he came to know many distinguished men; and in England he was befriended by Sir Philip Sidney and lectured at Oxford. Thence he went to Wittenberg (where he matriculated August 20, 1586) and thence to Prague. In 1593 he was lured back to Italy, was imprisoned by the Inquisition, and after long years of suffering in a dungeon he was burnt at the stake in Rome on February 17, 1600.

More than any man of his century he drew the deductions, for religion and science, from the principles of the new cosmography. Breaking through the crystal globe which had bounded the universe even for Copernicus, Bruno came to see that

> this world is merely one of an infinite number of worlds similar to this, and all the planets and stars are infinite worlds without number composing an infinite universe, so that there is a double infinitude, that of the magnitude of the universe and that of the multitude of worlds.[1]

And his words bore fruit among contemporaries. If Shakespeare rejected his message, Edmund Spenser accepted of it at least the astronomical part, saying:[2]

> What, if within this moon's fair shining sphere,
> What, if in every other star unseen
> Of other worlds he happily should hear?

More temperate advocates than Bruno, but in the long run more effective, were found in a group of mathematicians, physicists, and philosophers. William Gilbert, the investigator of magnetism, accepted the Copernican hypothesis and praised its author,[3] Simon Stevin, the Dutch inventor of decimals, by teaching the heliocentric theory, drew on himself the animadversion of the Calvinist theologians, who again quoted Osiander's unfortunate preface against him, and accused him of giving the Holy Ghost the lie.[4]

Among the most ardent of Galileo's disciples was the philosopher and publicist, of generous sympathies and tragic fate, Campanella. Hardly had the *Sidereal Messenger* been published before he thanked the author for the pleasure he had found in reading the secrets of God, unlawful for a man to utter. Feeling the implication of the new thought, he speculated on the inhabitants of the other planets, all of

[1] *De immenso et innumerabilibus,* lib. III, cap. i.
[2] *Faery Queen,* Introduction to book ii.
[3] *De Magnete,* lib. vi, cap. 3.
[4] H. Brugmann: *Briefwechsel des Ubbo Emmius,* 1923, ii, 55. Stevin: *Wisconstige Gedaechtenissen,* 1608. *Bib. Nat.* xxiii, 919.

whom, said he, doubtless imagine themselves, as does vain man, the center and prime care of the universe.[1]

This growing popular interest, ominous of a dreaded change, led the conservatives to use the Catholic church as a willing instrument to crush by force an opinion inexpugnable by reason. Relying on the authority of the Bible and of the almost equally revered Aristotle, the leaders of the church and of the schools attacked the novel doctrines as impious and rash. Many of the answers called forth by the *Sidereal Messenger* preferred to refute it rather by citing Scripture than by scientific investigation. While the theoretical arguments could be brushed aside as if sophistical, the actual facts revealed by the telescope proved a formidable obstacle in the path of the Aristotelians and of the divines. Most interesting is the letter revealing the perplexity of Cardinal Robert Bellarmine, a famous apologist of Catholic doctrine and a potent champion of the papacy. Having verified by looking through a telescope the existence of many stars invisible to the naked eye, of the phases of Venus, and of the satellites of Jupiter and Saturn, he wrote to inquire of the mathematicians of the Roman College whether these phenomena *which he had seen with his own eyes* were real or only an illusion.[2] Their reply confirmed the reality of most of the phenomena.

There were others fatuous enough to deny the witness of the telescope by alleging that faults in the instrument created delusive appearances. One Martin Horky alleged that, having stolen a glance through a telescope one night— after a convivial dinner?—he had noticed that all the fixed stars looked double. Another gentleman, named Zugmann, testified that through one of these strange glasses he had seen the sun in triplicate!

The campaign was opened in earnest at Florence by a zealous priest, in a sermon delivered in December, 1614, on a particularly apposite text taken from Acts i, 11: "Ye

---

[1] Letter of Jan. 12, 1611, *Opere di Galileo*, xi, 21.

[2] *Opere di Galileo*, xi, 87, letter of April 9, 1611. The reply, April 24, *ibid.* p. 93.

Galileans, why stand ye gazing up into heaven?" As the attack was pressed, Galileo began to defend himself by attempting to prove that his doctrine was not contradicted by the Bible. The inspired writers, he urged, in a long letter to Cristina de Lorraine, Grand Duchess of Tuscany, often spoke figuratively in order to be easily understood, as when they attributed to God hands, feet, eyes, and human passions, and even forgetfulness of the past and ignorance of the future. In support of his own teaching he quoted passages from the Fathers of the church importing that questions of natural science should be decided by experiment and demonstration. Some of his disciples went much further than did he in this line of reasoning, Campanella rashly offering to prove that the biblical writers, the rabbins, and the Fathers, had all been of Galileo's opinion about the solar system! [1] Of course this was absurd; it would, as Campanella himself admitted, revolutionize theology. But even the more reserved form in which Galileo tried to reconcil his science with Scripture was untenable. As soon as the case was appealed to the Bible, it was lost for the Copernicans. Not only did Bellarmine and other defenders of the geocentric theory have little trouble in proving that such texts as that relating how Joshua made the sun stand still and the one stating that "the sun ariseth and goeth down and hasteth to his place where he arose," [3] should be taken literally, but they were able to show that the Council of Trent had forbidden any novel exegesis contrary to the consensus of patristic tradition,[4] and they angrily accused their opponent of saying that many propositions in the Bible were false, at least in their obvious sense.

In order to settle, once for all, the question in dispute, the ecclesiastical authorities summoned Galileo, on February 26, 1616, before the bar of the Inquisition, and there he was "warned to forsake the opinion he had hitherto held, that

[1] Galileo: *Opere*, xii, 32, 1614. See also his *Apologia pro Galileo*, written 1616, published at Frankfort 1622.
[2] Josh. x, 12.
[3] Ecclesiastes, i, 5.
[4] Bellarmine to Foscarini, April 12, 1615, Galileo: *Opere*, xii, 171.

the sun is the center of the sphere and immovable, and that the earth moves," and, according to the minutes of the Holy Office, "he agreed to do so." [1]

Some scholars hold that the record of the Inquisition's dealings with Galileo in 1616 was tampered with, shortly before his trial in 1632, in order to make the charge against him, at that time, more precise. In my judgment, however, the theory that the true record of the proceedings of 1616 was erased and a false one inserted in its stead, is untenable; whereas the theory that the true record was interpolated does not offer, for the small interpolations which would have been the only ones possible, a sufficient motive to a forger. The question, however, of the existence and extent of a forgery, is not yet conclusively decided.[2]

But to return to the acts of the Holy Office in 1616. On March 5, a week after the alleged admonition to Galileo, the Congregation of the Index, the body officially charged with licensing and prohibiting books, passed the following decree: [3]

Inasmuch as it has come to the notice of the said Congregation, that that false Pythagorean doctrine, directly contrary to the Holy Scripture, about the mobility of the earth and the immobility of the sun, taught by Nicholas Copernicus in his book *On the Revolutions of the Celestial Orbs,* and by Didacus à Stunica in his *Commentary on Job,* has now become widespread and is received by many, . . . therefore, lest such an opinion should creep further to the destruction of Catholic truth, the Congregation has decreed that the said books of Copernicus and Stunica be suspended until they are corrected, . . . and that all

[1] A. Favaro: *Galileo e l'Inquisizione. Documenti del Processo Galileiano,* 1907, p. 16.

[2] E. Wohlwill: *Galileo,* ii, 1926, 171. Pastor: *Geschichte der Päpste,* xii, 204. R Laemmel: "Untersuchung der Dokumente des Galilei'schen Inquisitionsprozesses," *Archiv f. die Geschichte der Mathematik* &c., x, 1928, 405ff.

[3] C. Mirbt: *Quellen zur Geschichte des Papsttums und des römischen Katholizismus,*[4] no. 510. The same originally printed in an appendix to the *Index Librorum Prohibitorum* of 1596, added in the edition of 1624, with a separate title page: *Librorum post Indicem Clementis VIII prohibitorum decreta,* 1624, p. 133. The list of passages to be corrected in Copernicus, *ibid.* p. 144. This rare book, bound with other Indices, is at Cornell.

other books teaching the same doctrine be prohibited; and in the present decree the Congregation prohibits, condemns, and suspends them all.

Even after this comprehensive decree, there still seemed to be one loophole by which the scientist might elude the censure of the church at least sufficiently to pursue his own studies. This method of evasion was suggested to Foscarini, one of the warmest supporters of Galileo, by no less a personage than Cardinal Bellarmine himself. There was no harm, according to this prelate,[1] in treating the Copernican system as a mere hypothesis designed to facilitate mathematical calculations, provided it were not regarded as really true; it was thus—here the cardinal echoed the misleading preface of Osiander—that Copernicus had treated his own system.

Nevertheless, Galileo prudently kept aloof from the dangerous subject for many years. His position was rendered delicate by the galling attacks of his enemies, the Peripatetics, particularly some Jesuit scholars who tried in every way to entrap him into an unqualified assertion of the truth of the Copernican theory. Wary enough to avoid the set snares, and stung by a constant fire of attack, Galileo produced a counter-attack in a work called *Il Saggiatore* (*The Balance,* or *Scales*). This masterpiece of Italian prose, though somewhat baroque in style, pilloried the ignorance and malice of his enemies. It was the crushing manifesto against Jesuit science, as the *Provinciales* of Pascal was the manifesto against Jesuit morality. The work, while consummately able, naturally did not make its author's position safer. In it he had avoided direct endorsement of the Copernican system. A few years later, however, courage to grapple with that perilous problem was given him by the accession of his reputed admirer, Barberini, as Pope Urban VIII (1623).

Not only did the new pontiff write with great affection and high praise of Galileo to the astronomer's patron, the

[1] Letter of April 12, 1615; Galileo: *Opere,* xii, 172.

Grand Duke of Tuscany,[1] but he even remarked that Holy Church had condemned the heliocentric hypothesis not as heretical but only as rash, "for there was no danger," he added, "that anyone would ever prove it necessarily true." [2]

Thus encouraged, the Florentine astronomer completed the most famous of his works, his *Dialogue on the Two Principal Systems of the Universe*. For many years, perhaps since 1597, he had been planning a comprehensive defence of the new astronomy, and had collected material for it, which he put into literary form in the years 1626-29. The next three years were spent in getting the necessary licence from the papal censors. This was given at last on the ground that the work did not champion the heliocentric theory but merely presented the arguments on both sides. A special preface by the author was demanded and inserted, praising the edict of 1616 and alleging that the Copernican idea was not treated as proved but only as possible. In 1632 the large work, famous on account of its brilliant argument, of its attractive Italian style, and of the storm it raised, appeared under the title: *Dialogue of Galileo Galilei . . . on the two Principal Systems of the Universe, the Ptolemaic and the Copernican, propounding, without deciding for Either, the natural and philosophical Reasons in favor of Each.*

The dialogue, divided into four days, is sustained by three interlocutors. The first, given the name of Salviati, a dear friend and disciple of the author, who had died in 1614, naturally advocates the Copernican system. Sagredo, another friend, though he is really also a Copernican, plays the part of an impartial seeker after truth. To the third speaker, the champion of Ptolemy and of Aristotle, is given the name of Simplicio, happily chosen as that of a real and noted medieval Peripatetic, and as at the same time suggesting, with fine malice, the mental quality of the anti-Copernicans.

On the first day Simplicio advances the familiar argument that the earth must be the center of the universe because it is heavy, while the fire of which the stars are made is light.

---

[1] Galileo: *Opere*, xiii, 183.   [2] *Ibid.*, vi, 501.

To this Salviati replies that if Aristotle had possessed a telescope he would have judged the structure of the heavens differently.

The second day's conversation canvasses the motion of the earth. Salviati argues for the simplicity of the theory of the earth's revolution on its axis as against the difficulty of supposing that so many bodies as the stars move at such an inconceivable speed as would be necessary to produce so vast a revolution. Simplicio answers with the old Aristotelian and Tychonian arguments for a stable earth.

In the course of the third day the strongest batteries of the attack open fire upon the stubborn defence. The difficulties of explaining the motions of the planets by cycle and epicycle, the moons of Jupiter, the phases of Venus, impress the reader as unanswerable arguments, though of course they fail to convince Simplicio. The final day is given to a discussion of the tides, which Galileo explained as due to the motion of the earth alone, and not to the attraction of the sun and moon, as was even then held by some investigators.[1]

However carefully the author may have guarded himself against summing up in favor of either side, when his book appeared it was at once hailed as the most powerful defence of Copernicus in existence. Campanella forthwith expressed [2] his delight, congratulating the author on having shown once for all how conclusive were the arguments for the new hypothesis, and on the skill by which each interlocutor was made to do his part, "even Simplicio, as the buffoon of your philosophic comedy, perfectly revealing the folly of his sect."

From France the noted philosopher and scientist Gassendi wrote that the author had soared higher than any man had ever done, and had made all the hypotheses and arguments of the ancients appear, compared with his *Dialogue,* mere idle dreams.[3]

[1] *E.g.* by Stevin and by Gilbert.
[2] Letter of Aug. 5, 1632, Galileo: *Opere,* xiii, 366.
[3] *Ibid.,* xiv, 422.

Grotius, too, sent the homage of the Netherlands in letters declaring that Galileo's works had surpassed all previous human effort, had rendered the ancients superfluous, and would hardly be surpassed by posterity.[1] From all quarters of Europe similar testimonies poured in.

Roused by the thunders of applause for Galileo, the napping church started up to do mortal battle with a doctrine which she now dreaded as "more scandalous, more detestable, and more pernicious to Christianity than any contained in the books of Calvin, of Luther, and of all other heretics put together."[2] Immediately the pope appointed a commission to examine the *Dialogue,* and within a month he heard their report to the effect that Galileo had treated the Copernican system not as a hypothesis but as a reality, and that he had procured the *imprimatur* of the censors by fraudulent misrepresentation.

Cited to answer the dreaded Roman Inquisition, Galileo, though so ill at the time that he had to be carried in a litter, obeyed the summons, appearing before its bar five times, on April 12, April 30, May 10, June 21, and June 22, 1633. For his decision to submit and deny his true opinions no one but a fanatical transcendentalist will blame him. Science could not benefit by his martyrdom, but it did benefit enormously by his prolonged life. Nor did the cause of progress suffer by his act. As every one understood that his recantation was forced, so no one was convinced by it. The act of the Holy Office, by intimidating other scientists, postponed popular enlightenment, but this was not Galileo's fault. The blood of the martyrs is not the seed of science; and had every astronomer in the world proved his faith at the stake, had a scientific Reformation been followed by a Thirty Years War between the Ptolemaeans and the Copernicans, it would rather have retarded than advanced the cause of truth.

When Galileo first presented himself, on April 12, before the tribunal in the Palace of the Holy Office in Rome, he

[1] *Ibid.,* xvi, 266, 488.
[2] Galileo: *Opere,* xv, 25; xvi, 458.

was informed that he was vehemently suspected of heresy for defending the heliocentric hypothesis after he had been warned, in 1616, not to do so. Denying that he had defended the theory, he pleaded that he had submitted to the licensers the book on which the charge was based. On April 30, in humble tone, he stated that he had intended in his *Dialogue* not to defend but to attack Copernicus; and if he had advanced specious arguments in his support, it was due merely, he confessed, to the natural complacence felt by everyone in his own subtlety. He offered to rewrite the book, strengthening the arguments for Ptolemy, and making it clear that he had always adhered to that opinion. Called again before the judges on May 10, he was told to prepare a written defence, and was informed that the Congregation had examined his book and had found it unequivocally teaching the Copernican system. His written defence relied on the same arguments previously advanced orally.

As his excuses failed to convince his judges, he was again summoned before them, informed that he had held and defended the heretical doctrine, and that he must recant. Though he was ready and anxious to do all demanded by the Inquisition, he was brutally threatened with the torture, if not, as there is some reason to believe, actually tortured. The next day he was again summoned to sign a formal recantation, and to hear his sentence. The recantation, sworn to and signed with his own hand, is in part as follows: [1]

Since I was instructed by this Holy Office that I ought by all means to abandon the false opinion that the sun is the center of the world and immovable, and that the earth is not the center of the world and that it moves, and that I could not hold, defend, or teach in any manner, orally or in writing, the said false doctrine, and inasmuch as after I had been warned that the said doctrine is contrary to Holy Scripture, I wrote and had printed a book in which I treat the said doctrine already condemned, and set forth powerful reasons in support of the said doctrine without any decision, I am judged vehemently suspected of

[1] Galileo: *Opere*, xix, 402ff. M. Cioni: *I Documenti Galileiani del S. Uffizio di Firenze*, 1908, no. 27.

heresy. . . . Wherefore, wishing to relieve myself, in the minds of your Eminences and of all faithful Christians, of the vehement suspicion reasonably conceived against me, with a sincere heart and unfeigned faith, I abjure, curse, and renounce the said errors and heresies . . . [Signed] I, Galileo Galilei have abjured as above with my own hand.

He was then sentenced to perpetual imprisonment and to a penance of frequent repetition of the penitential Psalms. Satisfied with its crushing victory over the leading intellect in Europe, the Holy Office interpreted the sentence with sufficient lenity to allow its illustrious penitent to live under surveillance at Florence. The ecclesiastical officials at that city did not even entirely succeed in preventing him from seeing northern visitors, though they took pains to hinder this when possible. In 1638 the States General of the Netherlands sent to the illustrious astronomer an ambassador with a gold chain in payment for his services in attempting to solve the problem of finding longitude at sea, but the church would not allow Galileo to receive either the present or the messenger. They did not, however, stop his studies, which continued to be fruitful in physics, until his eyes, strained by long study of the sun, failed him.

Though the legend that as he rose from his knees after recantation he murmured "eppur si muove"—"the earth does move, however"—lacks foundation, it squares with the truth that his opinion remained unaltered. Soon after his trial Galileo got a copy of the work by the Jesuit Antonio Rocco, published in 1633, and intended to defend Ptolemy. The marginal notes of Galileo, refuting Rocco's arguments, while branding him as "an ignoramus, an elephant, a fool, a dunce, a malignant, a big animal, an ignorant eunuch, and a rascal," have survived.

Again when in 1641 the Florentine ambassador at Venice sent Galileo, under protection of the diplomatic seal, a letter expressing pleasure that the discovery of the proper motion of the fixed stars by Giovanni Pieroni furnished an additional proof of the Copernican system, and asking his opinion of the discovery, Galileo replied that, though the heliocentric system must be rejected, as condemned by religion, yet the arguments used against it by the Peripatetics were worthless, as both Aristotle and Ptolemy could be proved wrong.

Though Galileo never published anything on the question again, there are extant notes in his own hand, most probably written after his trial, setting forth additional arguments in favor of Copernicus and saying that his system had been condemned by those who did not understand it.[1] His last years were brightened by the homage of many eminent men, some of it offered in letters, some in person, as when John Milton visited him. He died, full of years as of fame, on January 8, 1642.

The Catholic foes of Galileo followed up its victory by a vigorous campaign against his doctrines and his disciples. Not only were Copernicans regularly dealt with by the Inquisition,[2] but several works were written to defend the orthodox view and the action of the Inquisition in enforcing it. One of the first of these, the *Anticopernicus Catholicus*,[3] by Giorgio Polacco of Venice (1644), excuses the Inquisition for condemning Galileo and adds to the old arguments against the heliocentric theory a new one drawn from his recantation. A far more pretentious presentation of the orthodox astronomy was the *Almagestum Novum* published by the Jesuit Riccioli in 1651. This vast treatise on the stars adopts a modification of the Tychonian system, proving the immobility of the earth by Scripture and by the ancient philosophical arguments. By these means the church kept at least the Italian schools in the strait and narrow path throughout the seventeenth and eighteenth centuries.[4]

But the mind of educated Europe was largely convinced before the ink on Galileo's recantation was dry. The fear of the Inquisition made some hypocrites but no converts. At Amsterdam the astronomer Martin Hortensis defended the Ptolemaic system in such a way as fully to expound the con-

[1] These notes are in a copy of the *Dialogue* now in the Library of the University of Padua, and are reprinted in the *Opere*, vii, 356ff.

[2] Examples of these, in 1641, given in Cioni, *op. cit.*, no. 48.

[3] A copy of this rare book at Cornell.

[4] Casanova: *Mémoires*, i, 40, and ii, 210. (1740-50).

trary views.[1] A disingenuous effort to elude the censure of the church, while maintaining the position she condemned, was made by Descartes. Having already adhered to Galileo's opinion, he heard with astonishment and horror of its condemnation.

> I confess, [he wrote in November, 1633,[2]] that if this [the Copernican hypothesis] is false, all the foundations of my philosophy are also false, for it is plainly demonstrated by them, and is so bound up with other parts of my treatise that I cannot exscind it without mutilating all the rest.

Though he expressed the opinion that what the Inquisition decided was not made thereby an article of faith, he preferred to evade its censures, for, less amorous of his convictions than of life and quiet, he professed the motto "bene vixit, bene qui latuit." [3]

After ten years of prudent silence, he propounded what claimed to be a new theory reconciling religion and science, but what was in reality nothing but an adroit equivocation, intended to pay verbal homage to the geocentric formula while recognizing the heliocentric fact. According to this new scheme, the earth did not move of its own motion, but was carried along in a liquid vortex of ether, which circled about the sun.[4] Thus the earth might be said to remain still as truly as a sleeping man carried in a ship, or as a ship drifting in a current, might be said to stay still,—or, as a witty critic phrased it, as a dead worm in a cheese might be said to keep still even though the cheese was carried from Amsterdam to Sumatra.

Among the followers of Descartes who rejected the Copernican theory in words, while admitting that it was irrefutable by science, were the philosopher Gassendi, and the astronomer André Taquet of Mechlin. Somewhat bolder were the

---

[1] So Voss wrote Grotius on May 28, 1634, Galileo: *Opere*, xvi.
[2] Letter to Mersenne, Galileo: *Opere*, xv, 341.
[3] April, 1634, Galileo: *Opere*, xvi, 88.
[4] *Principia Philosophiae*, 1644, *Œuvres*, 1905, viii, 86; cf. v. 544, 550; iii, 258.

scientist Mersenne who explained Galileo to his countrymen in French, and the Jesuit Honoré Fabri who took part in the proceedings of the *Accademia del Cimento* at Florence and, under the protection of the Cardinal de'Medici, revived Galileo's arguments. Boldest of all, among the pious Catholics, was Pascal, who sought to reconcile the claims of science and of religion by advancing the theory that the church, while infallible in matters of faith, is not proof against error in deciding matters of fact. It is thus that, in his immortal *Provincial Letters,* he pays his respects to the Jesuits:

> It was in vain that you obtained against Galileo that decree of Rome which condemns his opinion touching the movement of the earth. This decree will never prove that the earth remains stationary; and, if constant observations prove that it turns, all the men in the world will not prevent its turning, and will not even prevent themselves from turning around with it.[1]

It is interesting to note, however, that Pascal's mind was too skeptical definitely to decide whether Ptolemy, Tycho, or Copernicus was right.[2]

But the stars in their courses fought for Galileo and against the decree of the Inquisition. By 1686 the question had been decided, in France at least, so that it was safe to praise Copernicus and to defend his system, as was done by Fontenelle in a brilliant work of popular science, entitled *Conversations on the Plurality of Worlds* (*Entretiens sur la Pluralité des Mondes*).

In other countries north of the Alps the Copernican system continued to gain ground, particularly after the translation of the *Dialogue* of Galileo into Latin by Martin Bernegger in 1635. The English poet John Donne thrilled with the discoveries of Galileo, while the Cambridge Platonist Henry More compared his persecutors to the Titans who sought in vain to scale Olympus and to subdue the gods. Even in New England the Copernican system had some

[1] *Lettres Provinciales,* no. 18.
[2] *Pensées,* no. 218.

adherents at Harvard by 1670, after which date it made rapid progress, not without some opposition by the clergy.

In old England, too, there were some men who continued, until the time of Newton, to reject the heliocentric hypothesis, or to leave the question undecided. Harvey, the discoverer of the circulation of the blood, though he had heard Galileo lecture at Padua, rejected the Copernican hypothesis flatly in 1628, and referred to it as conjectural and unsatisfactory in 1649.[1]

Another great Englishman, John Milton, though he perhaps read the *Dialogue* soon after its publication, and though he visited "the famous Galileo, grown old and a prisoner of the Inquisition," and though his epics sing of telescopes and microscopes, of the mountains in the moon and of sun spots, and though he fully describes the heliocentric system and refers to the possibility that every star may be a world, yet refrains from expressing a preference for the new or for the old theory. It is possible, indeed, that in *Paradise Lost* he felt constrained by the dramatic setting borrowed from Genesis, which betrays no knowledge of the Copernican hypothesis, to leave Adam unenlightened by the angel, and yet it is significant of the times and of his own temper that he did not anywhere tell which theory he favored.[2]

Milton is the last eminent man known to maintain even a suspended judgment on the matter in question. Just twenty years after the publication (1667) of *Paradise Lost,* Newton's *Principia* banished the last shadow of doubt in the minds of the educated classes, and even in the minds of the masses. Within 150 years after the *De Revolutionibus* appeared, the new cosmography, at first neglected as paradoxical and then damned as heretical, had at last been thoroughly assimilated, and came in its turn to be taken for granted and to be treated as a dogma.

[1] Curtis: *Harvey,* 155.
[2] *Paradise Lost,* i, 287; iii, 588; iv, 591; v, 261; vii, 210, 225; 621; viii, 17, 30, 120, 160; *Paradise Regained,* iv, 42, 57. The reference to the visit to Galileo is in the *Areopagitica.* Diodati, Milton's bosom friend, took a copy of the *Dialogue* to England in 1632, Galileo: *Opere,* xiv, 422.

Last of all, the Catholic church accepted, as she always does, the accomplished fact, and quietly changed her position without admitting that she had ever been wrong. How far the Inquisition's condemnation of the heliocentric theory has compromised the church's infallibility may be decided by those for whom such a question still has interest. In 1757 the revised *Index of Prohibited Books* omitted the phrase banning all works teaching the Copernican theory. But, as licence was refused to a book of 1820 for this reason, the Holy Office, at the direction of Pius VII, issued a decree on September 11, 1822,[1] declaring:

There is no reason why the present and future Masters of the Sacred Palace should refuse licence for printing and publishing works treating of the mobility of the earth and the immobility of the sun, according to the common opinion of modern astronomers.

The *Index of Prohibited Books* in 1835 first omitted the works of Copernicus, Kepler, and Galileo, which have since then been allowed to the faithful.

There has never been a greater revolution in the history of thought than that marked by the establishment of the Copernican astronomy. The abandonment of a geocentric universe of matter was logically followed by the relinquishment of an anthropocentric universe of thought. But the importance of the new idea lay less in the changed picture of the world, vast as that change was, than in the triumph of that great instrument for probing nature, science. To a reflecting mind—and there have been a few such in every generation—no victory could possibly have been more impressive than that of science in this battle with the senses, with common opinion, with inveterate and all but universal tradition, and with all authority, even that claiming to be divine revelation.

[1] A Favaro: *Galileo e l'Inquisizione*, 1907, p. 31.

CHAPTER III

PHYSICS

I. THE BIRTH OF A NEW SCIENCE

While Astronomy, waging a fierce battle with Church and School, attracted the gaze of the whole European amphitheatre, her triumphs in the realm of pure science are, even in this glorious period, hardly as important as are those of her kindred discipline, Physics. For, whereas astronomy, already old when the Chaldean astrologers named the days of the week after the planets and when the engineers of Cheops adjusted the entrance of his pyramid to look towards the North Star, was very ancient in the time of Galileo, physics was the new-born child of his generation. Not only had Greek and medieval thinkers failed to differentiate physics from the vague body of science called by them natural philosophy, but their unhappy ventures into this field had burdened their successors with a series of principles and maxims almost invariably wrong. Such hoary errors as that bodies fall with a velocity proportional to their weight, or that the ability of a given substance to float in water depends on its shape, had passed almost without challenge for more than two thousand years not so much because, as is often stated, of veneration for Aristotle, as because they were just such rules of thumb as the untutored layman believed that he could verify in his own daily experience. Everyone has seen the stone fall briskly and the thistledown float lazily to earth on a still summer's day; everyone knows that a lump of metal will sink in water but that a silver bowl or an iron ship will swim; and everyone can draw the obvious but incorrect deductions. Other maxims of the schools were based not only on misunderstood experiment

but upon the sandy foundations of metaphysical speculations. The maxim that "Nature abhors a vacuum," originating in a hasty generalization from the phenomenon of suction, was afterwards justified by a generation of thinkers
who identified emptiness with nothingness, a vacuum with
nonentity.

Not only were the physicists of the late sixteenth and
early seventeenth century burdened with a considerable
mass of pseudo-science, but they were crippled by a total
lack of instruments for that exact measurement necessary
to the progress of knowledge. When we remember that by
the year 1600 there was no method of measuring heat, no
method of measuring the pressure of the air, no method
even of measuring small intervals of time, we have found
a partial explanation of the fact that there had been so little
progress in physics before this date and that it came so
rapidly thereafter. The invention of the thermometer, the
barometer, and the pendulum clock had for certain branches
of physics the same significance that the invention of the
telescope had for astronomy.

A good deal of popular interest in and study of natural
phenomena during the Renaissance had proved fruitless
because it was directed rather to the collection of the marvellous than to careful investigation of the common. The
same appetite for crude sensation that made biology largely
a study of monstrosities made of physics a search for
curiosities. A good gauge of the popular interest at that
time, as well as a compendium of the state of contemporary
knowledge and an example of the science that came just to
the verge of important discovery, is furnished by the work
of that versatile Neapolitan, Giovanni Baptista della Porta
(c. 1539-1615). This precocious youth at the age of twenty,
not, as he later vaingloriously asserted, at the age of fifteen,
published a work in four books *On the Miracles of Nature*
(1558), which he expanded thirty years later into twenty
books under the name *Natural Magic* (1589). The title of
the last book, *Chaos,* might well designate the whole vast
and disorderly collection of information and misinforma-

tion on a wide range of topics, practical and speculative, scientific and superstitious. In addition to much homely instruction, partly based on ancient writers and partly on current old wives' lore, on such subjects as medicine, aphrodisiacs and anaphrodisiacs, cosmetics, animal breeding, domestic economy, fireworks, cryptographs, powders for making invisible writing, diet, tests for chastity, and parlor tricks, he imparted some information of a more nearly scientific character. Among the many constructions, some possible, some impossible, and nearly all obscure, described by him, are machines for testing the amount of steam given off by a particular quantity of water, and the amount of expansion of air by heat—which latter might have made a thermometer if only he had practically perfected it. His best work is in the field of optics, though he cannot justify his insistent claim to be the inventor of the telescope. He did, however, write intelligently on refraction, on the mechanism of the eye, on colors, on the power of concave and convex mirrors to distort reflections, and on the power of lenses to modify vision and to ignite combustibles by focusing the rays of sunlight. He described and improved, though he did not discover, the *camera obscura*. If, as he correctly explained, a room is completely darkened except for a small hole on one side, a reversed image of objects passing in the light outside will be cast on the opposite side of the room, and this image will be improved by slightly enlarging the aperture and filling it with a convex lens. But the main interest of the whole work, as shown by the title, is in expounding extraordinary phenomena, not in careful experiment and generalization. Had the age continued to confine its interest in such matters, and in the construction of perpetual motion machines—as was still done by James I [1] of England, for example—it would have contributed little or nothing to science. But a new method applied by men of patient industry and of mighty genius was destined to transform the whole subject in nearly all its branches.

[1] His machine is described in a letter of Antonin to Galileo, Feb. 4, 1612.

2. MAGNETISM

A few important discoveries in magnetism and the invention of the word "electric" were due to William Gilbert of Colchester (1540-1603). Educated at St. John's College, Cambridge, where he took the degree of B.A. in 1560, and in various Italian universities, one of which gave him the degree of M.D. in 1569, he returned to England to serve the Royal College of Physicians at first as Fellow, then as Censor, then as Treasurer, and finally as President. Most of his leisure, and a large inherited fortune, he spent in investigating the laws of magnetism. His researches were given to the public in 1600 in a Latin work, *On the Loadstone and Magnetic Bodies and on the Earth as a Great Magnet.*

A knowledge of the attractive power of magnets, and some superstition connected with it, had descended from antiquity. One of the momentous discoveries of the later Middle Ages was that of the mariner's compass. Gilbert thought that it was brought to Italy from China by Marco Polo, but earlier allusions to it in European chronicles—a certain one by Alexander Neckham about 1200, and a doubtful one in an earlier Icelandic saga—make it probable that it was an independent invention of European sailors. Those who first speculated on the weird power of the needle to point north hazarded the guess that it was attracted either by a magnetic island near the pole or by the North Star. Much confusion was caused by the fact, observed independently by Nuremberg geographers, by Columbus, by Sebastian Cabot and perhaps by earlier navigators, that the needle does not point true north but varies slightly and by amounts differing according to places and to time. In addition to this declination of the needle, as it is called, the inclination, or dip from the true horizontal position to one at an angle with the earth's surface, was noticed by Hartmann of Nuremberg in 1544, and by Robert Recorde in 1576.

Gilbert began by canvassing the work of his ancient and

recent forerunners and by giving a history of the mariner's compass. He then described the properties of loadstones, stressing their polarity, or tendency to attract each other in one position and to repel each other in the reverse position. His two great discoveries were first, that the earth itself is a magnet and second, that the loadstone is nothing but iron in a special state induced by exposure to magnetic influence. Hence, any bar of iron may be turned into a magnet, and this can be done simply by laying it in a north and south position and leaving it thus for several years, or by heating and hammering it in this position. Gilbert goes too far in assuming that the constant position of the earth's axis is due to magnetic force pervading the universe. It is tempting, but impossible, to see in his attribution of the rotary movement of the earth to magnetic properties a prophetic glimmering of modern theories of circular movement in fields of magnetic force. Nor can we accept as a truth demonstrated by him the hypothesis which commended itself to many of his contemporaries that gravitation is a form of magnetism.

In detail, his careful examination of loadstones illuminated their various properties and also swept away "the figments and falsehoods which," he says, "in earliest times no less than nowadays are commonly put forth by smatterers and copyists to be swallowed of men." But when he came to explain the cause of magnetic attraction he became mystical. He thought of magnetism as "a soul or like a soul, in many things superior to the human soul as long as it is bound to bodily organs," and he argued that this soul is that of the sun and of the stars, and that attraction is a love or an appetite. Though here again it is possible to bring his ideas into relation with the speculations of recent hylozoists like Haeckel, it is certain that in uttering them he passed out of the safe bounds of physics into the less explored region of metaphysics.

Gilbert's final service was in noticing and naming certain phenomena as "electric." The word he derived from the Greek word for amber, because amber rubbed on fur will attract straw, hair, chaff, and many other things. This attraction he measured by a freely swung iron needle which he called a versorium but which would now be called an electroscope. This attraction, which he compared with that of magnetism and of gravitation, he explained as due to subtle effluvia—but to go further he was unable. The word "electricity" is first found in Sir Thomas Browne's *Pseudodoxia,* 1646.

Gilbert's "painful and experimental work," as Bacon called it, found wide reading throughout the republic of letters. Little advance was made on it for two hundred years. The secular variation of the needle was noticed by the English mathematician Gellibrand in 1633-35; the diurnal variation by Graham in 1722; the annual variation by Cassini in 1782-91. Further experiments with electric bodies were made by the Magdeburg burgomaster Otto von Guericke about 1663. Though he has sometimes been credited with having discovered electric induction and the electric current, all that he really noticed was that feathers and other things rubbed on balls of sulphur would acquire attractive and repulsive properties which he attributed to a half mystical, half mechanical, "earth force" (*virtus mundana*). The electric spark, which had been noticed by Erasmus [1] and probably by others, was not particularly studied by Gilbert, but attracted the attention of Leibniz.

So swift is the human mind to anticipate the possibilities latent in new discoveries, that the electric telegraph was almost suggested within a few years after Gilbert wrote. The Jesuit Famianus Strada in a work called *Prolusiones Academicae,* published in 1617, suggested that two friends at a distance might communicate by utilizing the sympathy of two magnetic needles which should simultaneously point to the same letters of the alphabet. This suggestion was brought to the notice of Galileo in the vain hope that he could make it practicable. [2]

[1] *Colloquies,* "Inquisitio de Fide." 1524. See my *Key to the Colloquies of Erasmus,* 1927, p. 24.

[2] Sandys: *History of Classical Scholarship,* ii, 281; Galileo: *Dialogo sopra i due massime sisteme del mondo,* p. 88.

3. OPTICS

Naturally, the age of the telescope devoted much attention to optics. This science had been divided by the Greeks into two parts, catoptrics (from the Greek word for mirror) embracing the phenomena of reflection, and dioptrics (from the word meaning transparent) embracing the phenomena of refraction, or the bending of a ray of light when passing obliquely through the surface of two media. The principal medieval writer on the subject had been the thirteenth-century Thuringian Vitello (or Vitellio).

Johann Kepler studied optics in two works, the *Supplements to Vitellio,* 1604, and the *Dioptrics,* 1611. The first part of the former book treats of the nature of light in a number of propositions. Color he was unable to explain except on the old, false theory that it was due to different degrees of dilution or absorption of pure white light by the body on which it fell. Practically, Kepler was able to do more than he could theoretically justify. Asked the question why the light coming through the aperture of the *camera obscura* outlined the bright object from which it came and not the shape of the aperture through which it passed, he answered by holding a book at some distance from a wall, putting between it and the wall a piece of paper cut into a different shape. If strings, representing the beams of light, were passed from the single corner of the book to the wall, touching the edges of the paper, they would outline the shape of the paper, but if they were passed from all corners of the book, they would outline the shape of the book. In a valuable supplement to his first work, Kepler examined the structure of the eye which he rightly explained as a *camera obscura.* "Seeing" he defined as "a sensory activity of the retina stimulated and filled with the spirit of vision; or, one may say, seeing is feeling the stimulation of the retina. This retina is painted with colors from the visible world." He rightly maintained that the retina is modified by the beams of light falling upon it, and that the image must be carried from the eye to the brain.

He gave the answer now generally accepted to a problem that Huygens later declared insoluble, why it is, namely, that we do not see things upside down and right side left, as the image is received by the retina. This problem, rather psychological than physical, Kepler rightly saw to be purely a question of judgment and of names.

In his second book, that on *Dioptrics*, Kepler was more successful in discovering phenomena than in explaining them mathematically. He learned by experiment on transparent bodies that rays entering a thicker medium, like glass, tend by refraction within the body to approach the perpendicular erected on the surface at the point of entrance. He measured the angle of the refraction but could not discover the law governing it. At a later time he also improved the telescope by using two convex lenses instead of one convex and one concave. The prime improvement of this type of telescope over the Galilean is that for the same magnifying force the field of view is larger.

The fundamental law of refraction, sought in vain by Kepler, was discovered by Willibrord Snell and independently by the French philosopher and mathematician Descartes, who expressed it in a neater way. He began his *Dioptrics* [1] by defining light in a luminous body as "nothing but a certain motion, or visible and vivid action which, sent through the air and other transparent bodies, comes to the eyes," but he soon modified this by the further statement that "what we call the light of a luminous body is not so much its motion as its impulse or propensity to motion; hence we can easily deduce that the rays of light are nothing but the lines along which this action tends to express itself." This definition easily allows a mathematical treatment of light, which Descartes thought of fundamentally as small active particles running along straight lines from the center of emission. Reflection he compared to the action of a bounced ball; refraction he explained by imagining such a ball slightly deflected from its course by encountering the resistance of a thin tissue. If the ball strikes the tissue, as

[1] *Œuvres de Descartes*, vi, 81ff.

when the light falls upon a denser medium, the speed will be altered and, unless the light falls perpendicularly, the direction also. Descartes found that for any two given media the ratio of the sines of the angles of incidence and of refraction is constant, but that it differs with other combinations of media. This constant is now called the relative refractive index of the second medium to the first.

In explaining color Descartes maintained the old theory that it is dependent on the amount of light absorbed in the colored surface. The beam, said he, which penetrates a little way appears red, that which penetrates farther is green, that which goes still deeper is blue. This is all wrong, as is his theory that light is and must be propagated instantly. So convinced was he that he had demonstrated this last proposition that he once said that if it were proved wrong he would admit that his whole philosophy had been overthrown.[1] He was a little more successful in explaining the mechanism of the eye, and particularly how the combined action of the two eyes enables one to judge solids and distances—though he does not use the modern word "stereoscopic."

4. MECHANICS, STATICS, HYDROSTATICS

Since the day when Archimedes, while engaged in solving a problem, was cut down by a Roman soldier, little advance had been made in the sciences of mechanics or of hydrostatics for eighteen centuries. The first to break new ground in these fields during the great renewal of science was Simon Stevin. Though born at Bruges in the Southern Netherlands, in 1548, and though serving for a short time as bookkeeper at Antwerp, when the war of independence tore the country in two he settled in the North, matriculating at Leyden in 1583, and thereafter filling the positions of military and civil engineer and controller of finances for Maurice of Nassau in whose good graces he stood high until his death in 1620. Besides important works on mathematics he wrote

[1] *Œuvres*, i, 308.

three small but meaty tracts on statics and hydrostatics, all
published in 1586 in Dutch and almost immediately translated into French as *L'Art Ponderaire, ou de la statique.*[1]
He begins with the postulate that weights can be treated in
the abstract apart from matter, and with the definition of
weight as "the force that a body has in falling." He further
defines the center of gravity as the point by which, if we
imagine a body to be hung, it will remain motionless in any
given position. From very simple propositions, such as: of
two weights in equilibrium the heavier will have the same
ratio to the lighter as the longer beam of the scale has to
the shorter, he advanced to more complex problems of
finding the center of gravity, and of the properties of pulleys,
levers, and other mechanical devices. He also solved the
problem of the parallelogram of forces in an original way,
proving that for inclined planes having the same altitude
any given force along the plain will sustain a weight which
is proportional to the length of the plane.

In hydrostatics Stevin discovered that the pressure of
a liquid on the bottom of a vessel depends solely on the
height of the column of liquid and not, as hitherto believed,
partly on the shape of the vessel. He also examined the
pressure of water on the sides of a vessel and the so-called
"hydrostatic paradox" of Archimedes, that bodies heavier
than water when weighed in water lose just the weight of
the liquid they displace. He showed that the center of
gravity of a floating body is in a vertical line with the
center of gravity of the displaced water and that, if a floating body is in equilibrium, its center of gravity lies higher
than the center of gravity of the displaced water.

A vastly greater advance in several branches of physics
was made by Galileo. After the Inquisitors had wrung from
him the recantation of his great Copernican heresy they
allowed him, with unwonted, indeed unique, clemency, to
retire under surveillance to his villa of Arcetri at Florence. Here the old man, warned on pain of death to publish

[1] *De Beghinselen der Weeghconst. De Weeghdaet. De Beghinselen des
Waterwichts.* 1586. I use the French edition quoted in the bibliography.

nothing on astronomy, turned his attention to physics, in which he had made many important discoveries ever since he was a student at Pisa. Indeed, though it was his astronomy that excited the passionate interest of the public, it was in physics that his genius burned brightest and that, for the progress of science, his most revolutionary discoveries were made. He found this branch of natural philosophy little but a mass of ignorance and error; he left it a well-built and comely science.

Having written a treatise *On Motion* [1] as early as 1590, and another on *Hydrostatics* [2] in 1612, he now gathered up the principal results advanced in them and occasionally elsewhere, together with much new material, in a comprehensive work entitled *Discourses and Mathematical Demonstrations Concerning Two New Sciences*. For this work, which he sent to Venice to be printed in 1635, he could get no licence in the Catholic world. Seeking a subterfuge by which he could disavow the work if necessary, he allowed one of the great Dutch publishing house of the Elzevirs to "steal" the manuscript, thus giving to free Holland and to learned Leyden the glory and advantage of printing, in 1638, the work on which all subsequent physical researches have rested.

The two new sciences begotten though not named by Galileo were mechanics or "that science treating the resistance which solid bodies offer to fracture," and dynamics or "that science treating of motion." The literary form of the treatise is again the dialogue, with the same interlocutors as had spoken in the momentous *Dialogue on the Two Chief Systems of the World*. Here again Simplicio represents the orthodox Aristotelian dogma, Salviati propounds the new views, to which Sagredo, as the candid searcher for truth, is ultimately drawn. Can there be clearer proof than is furnished by this *mise en scène*, that here, too, the Florentine

---

[1] *De Motu, Opere,* i, 245ff.

[2] *Delle cose che stanno in su l'Aqua, Opere,* iv, 1.

[3] *Discorsi e dimostrazione matematiche intorno a due nuove scienze, Opere,* viii, I. Translated into English as *Dialogues concerning Two New Sciences,* by H. Crew and A. de Salvio, 1914.

consciously acted the rebel and revolutionary against the *beati possidentes* of the schools, the Peripatetics and their tyrant the Stagirite?

The first dialogue "demonstrates geometrically that the larger machine is not proportionately stronger than the smaller," for the strength of a beam increases as it is enlarged, only in proportion to its cross section, *i.e.* as the square of its diameter, whereas its weight increases as its solid mass, *i.e.* as the cube of the diameter. Speculating on the cause of the cohesion of metals and other solids Galileo imagined that it might be due to the presence of a number of infinitesimal vacua between the component atoms.

To Galileo the world owes the happy union of static and dynamic laws in the doctrines of "virtual velocities" or "displacements." Stevin, whom he did not know, had shown that if two weights, one of one pound and the other of two pounds, are in equilibrium on a scale, the beam supporting the one pound will be just twice as long as the beam supporting the two pounds. Galileo went further, showing why this is, and thereby explaining the principle of the lever. The reason is that if the scale be tipped the long beam will move just twice as far in the same time; in other words, the same work is done in lifting one pound two feet as in lifting two pounds one foot. The same law holds good for all mechanical contrivances, such as the pulley. What is gained in weight is lost in speed, and *vice versa*. In short: If two bodies move in equilibrium their movements in distance are in inverse proportion to their weights.

With all his insight Galileo never solved the parallelogram of forces nor did he ever attain an idea of potential energy, or "energy of position" as it is now called. He conceived only of a moving body as doing work, whereas in more modern thought rest is but one form of movement. Taking up the ancient problem as to why a light blow would drive a wedge further than a heavy steady pressure, he wrongly answered that speed being one factor in force the power of a blow is infinitely greater than that of a quiet weight, which he therefore called "dead weight."

The most famous of Galileo's experiments is that by which
he tested the ancient maxim that bodies fall with a velocity
proportional to their weight. The story told, some years
after his death, by one of his disciples, is that as a youth at
Pisa he had dropped from the top of the campanile, or
leaning tower, two iron balls, one weighing ten times, or a
hundred times, as much as the other, and had thus discovered that they fell so nearly in the same time that the
heavier ball outstripped the lighter one by only two finger-
breadths. This story has recently been branded as a legend,
on the ground that Galileo nowhere speaks of the experiment himself. Nevertheless, it has been shown that Philo-
ponos in the sixth century, and Leonardo da Vinci and
Benedetto Varchi and Girolamo Varchi in the sixteenth, had
before Galileo contradicted the Aristotelian maxim, though
none of them had devised a conclusive experiment to test
it. Galileo's words rather indicate that he was following
the lead of others than devising an absolutely new principle
when he asserted that all bodies fall at the same speed,
making allowance for the slight differences caused by the
resistance of the air. And very likely he had discovered or
learned this principle while still at Pisa.

Further experiments on falling bodies soon revealed to
Galileo many other physical laws. He showed that the
speed of a falling body, starting at zero, increases all the
time at an even rate, so that, for example, its speed at a
hundred feet from its starting point would be just twice
that at fifty feet. Hampered by the lack of accurate instruments he was not able to estimate at all closely the
speed of a falling body, for he thought that it would
cover 60 metres in five seconds, instead of the true measure
of 122 metres in this time.

As the velocity of a freely falling body was too great
for direct observation with the timepieces at his command,
Galileo constructed inclined planes of boards seven feet long
with a groove covered with smooth parchment. Down this
he would roll balls, on the correct assumption that their
behavior would be exactly that of a falling body at a much

diminished speed. Finding that a ball would roll one quarter of the way in half the time it took to roll the whole way he concluded that the space covered by a falling body is proportionate to the square of the time taken.

One of the most fruitful of all his discoveries was that the time of the oscillation of a pendulum depends not on the width of the swing but on the pendulum's length. So imperfect, at that period, were the means of measuring small intervals of time that Galileo was at first obliged to use his pulse which "did temperately keep time" in a more literal sense than was intended by Hamlet when he used that phrase. Very soon he recognized in the pendulum a special case of a falling body, and was therefore able to deduce and to verify the hypothesis that the length of the pendula varies as the squares of their times of oscillation. He discovered that the pendulum would always rise to the height from which it fell, disregarding a small decrease due to friction; and this he found true even if he changed the path of a pendulum on a flexible string, by inserting a nail at some point which would intercept the upward stroke.

As the weight at the end of a pendulum falls not along a straight line but along a curve, Galileo was soon able to show that the path of quickest descent for any body falling not in the perpendicular is not a straight line but a curve.

In ballistics Galileo also recognized special cases of the laws governing falling bodies. He showed that if there were no friction the movement of a ball along a horizontal plane would be perpetual and unchanged in speed and direction. If a moving body be subjected to the action of a new force the resultant will be a new movement. Thus he showed, as perhaps Tartaglia had done before him, that a stone thrown in a horizontal direction, acted upon by gravity, will fall to earth along a half parabola.

As early as 1590 Galileo's investigations of hydrostatics had convinced him that Aristotle was in error in assuming the existence of a principle of "levity" in addition to that of "gravity," and still more in identifying these principles with air and earth. Weight, he showed, can be measured with absolute accuracy in a vacuum; in all denser media, including air, it is diminished by the amount of the medium displaced. He demonstrated that weight is a purely relative thing by making balls just a little heavier than fresh water, which would rise when the weight of the water was increased by adding salt.

To explain the difference between solids and liquids Galileo resorted to a mathematical analogy and to metaphysical speculation. Infinity, he argued, is a number like unity, for there are as many squares as there are numbers in unity and in infinity. But the higher one goes in finite numbers the more unlike both unity and infinity do they become in this respect. For, in the first hundred numbers there are ten squares, or one-tenth as many squares as numbers; whereas in the first ten thousand numbers there are only one hundred squares, or one one-hundredth as many squares as numbers. Now, according to Galileo, a solid is like a finite number; if it is one piece it has certain characteristics as, for example, ice has transparency, but if it is broken up it begins to lose this character, for, the finer ice is ground the less transparent it is. In this it resembles the finite numbers which, the more they are multiplied, the less do they resemble unity. But when we can break it into an infinite number of parts we obtain a liquid; and thus water resembles infinity in again acquiring the characteristics of its former unity and with it transparency. Ingenious as is this speculation it is valuable rather for the light it casts on Galileo's mathematical conception of physics than as a scientifically useful clue.

Galileo, the son of a musician, also investigated sound.[1] Rightly comparing the vibrations of the strings of a lute to the oscillations of a pendulum, he recognized that sound is an undulation in the air, and that its tone is due to the different lengths of the several waves. This he demonstrated by scattering sand on a copper plate, and then stroking it with a sharp iron. As he did this the plate would emit a sound and the vibration which produced the sound would also

[1] *Opere,* viii, 141ff.

shake the sand into little ridges which admirably illustrated, though of course they did not measure, the waves in the air. For the higher tones these ridges were narrower and closer together. Galileo by this means made the correct calculation that in playing the scale up, the original note, the fourth, the fifth, and the octave, stand in the following numerical relation: 6:8:9:12. He also inferred that harmonics are notes of which the waves strike the ear with a certain regularity.

The torch that fell from the hands of the dying Galileo was seized and carried farther by his friend and disciple Evangelista Torricelli, whose work on the cycloid, on the barometer, and on various problems of mechanics rather completed the unfinished tasks of his master than started new lines of investigation. Born at Faenza in 1608, educated in the classics by the Jesuits and in science by Galileo's disciple Benedetto Castelli at Rome, in 1641 Torricelli went to Arcetri to be the secretary of Galileo. Taken into favor by the grand duke of Tuscany, Torricelli became, on the death of his master, the successor to his position and emoluments, for the five years until his early death in 1647. Apart from a valuable correspondence his principal contributions to physics were made in a work *On the Motion of Falling Bodies*,[1] published in 1644.

This work advanced a series of propositions, geometrically demonstrated, on dynamics and hydrostatics. Torricelli showed that the path of a stream of water flowing sideways out of a hole in a barrel is a parabola the arc of which reaches its maximum size when the hole is in the middle of the barrel; whereas holes at equal distances above and below the central point emit streams in parabolas with arcs equal to each other but smaller than that of the central stream.

Whereas Descartes' system of the world is a contribution rather to metaphysics than to physics, a few of his more concrete ideas may best be considered here. In this, as in all other matters, the mind of the French philosopher, keen beyond all others in seizing and in generalizing the logical

[1] *De motu gravium naturaliter descendentium, Opere di E. Torricelli,* ii.

and mathematical implications of given premises, was so closely bound by a network of syllogistic cords to a starting-point in his inner consciousness that he was not only blind to facts contrary to his system but that he continued to reject them after experimental proof in the sublime confidence that nothing could exist which he had proved to be impossible. Indeed, his chief criticism of Galileo was that he built his science without a foundation of general theory, seeking only the proximate causes of special effects, and not the nature of things as a whole.[1]

That this was really the strength and not the weakness of Galileo's method is evident from the fact that much which Descartes advanced as his own has been proved wrong by experiment. In some matters of purely mathematical reasoning, however, Descartes was able to clarify the operations of nature. Thus, he gave a clearer explanation than had yet been done of the engines by which a great pressure can be exerted by a small force—the pulley, the wedge, the lever, the wheel, and the vise.[2] He was inclined to see all the laws of nature as laws of motion to be geometrically explained. As the most general laws of motion he laid down three: 1. The law of inertia, or, as he expressed it, "that all bodies strive with all their might to stay as they are." The measure of a body's force he defined as the product of its mass and its speed. 2. His second law is really a special case of his first, that a moving body tends to keep moving at the same speed and in the same direction as that with which and in which it started. 3. His third law, that of impact, is based on his favorite notion that there is no such thing as a vacuum, and that therefore a moving body must be in a state of perpetual collision. This condition results in making the body go slower, or rebound, or stop—and all the various cases of these reactions are worked out.

True to his theory that all natural phenomena are due to movement, Descartes explained the difference between solids and liquids by saying that the former consist of particles

[1] Descartes to Mersenne, Oct. 11, 1638, *Opere di Galileo*, xvii, 387ff.
[2] Descartes, *Œuvres*, i, 435ff.

internally at rest, and the latter of particles internally in motion.

As the tendency of science is to generalize large groups of phenomena under binding laws, so it has come to pass that certain minds, of a highly speculative or mathematical type, have sought higher and higher generalizations to master larger and larger groups of phenomena until, they hope, the whole field of reference of a particular science can be brought under a single law. Such a mind is Einstein in our own time; such minds in the seventeenth century were Descartes and his contemporary, Pierre Fermat. This famous geometer thought that he had discovered the master key to all physical process in the principle that "nature always makes her movements along the simplest lines." Though modern physicists have found in this formula a useful expression of the principle of least action, some of Fermat's contemporaries, with a more experimental and a less speculative interest, criticized it as rather a moral than a scientific law, and as "a pitiable axiom by which no truth can be demonstrated." [1]

This last harsh judgment was expressed by Christiaan Huygens, who himself did enormously valuable work in physics. The scion of a gifted family of statesmen, poets and scholars, Christiaan was born at the Hague in 1629, was educated at Leyden and at Breda, and travelled extensively. Having at the age of seventeen discovered several laws of hydrostatics, he was hailed by Mersenne as a second Archimedes. His vast correspondence in Latin, French, Dutch, German, English, and Italian brought him into close relations with most of the leading thinkers of the day—among them Descartes, Boyle, Roberval, Mersenne, Fermat, Newton, Leibniz, Pascal, Chapelain, Bernoulli and Wallis. Chosen by Colbert as one of the charter members of the new *Académie des Sciences,* he migrated to Paris where he spent much of his time until the Franco-Dutch wars and the persecution of his fellow Protestants forced

[1] Fermat's law enunciated in 1657, *Œuvres*, ii, 255; criticism of Clerselier, 1662, *ibid.*, 465; criticism of Huygens, *Œuvres de Huygens*, iv, 71.

him to seek refuge again in his native land. While in Paris he came to know some of the great French writers, and he eagerly attended the plays of Molière and Corneille. Hampered by a sickly body, his powerful brain did the work of a giant in many fields, notably physics, mathematics, and astronomy. With all his triumphs he remained modest and gracious even until his quiet death in 1695.

Important additions to the theory of mechanics and some practical inventions are due to Huygens. Though Galileo had discovered the isochronous oscillation of the pendulum he did not apply it to the improvement of clocks. This was first successfully done by Huygens when he harnessed the driving force of the weight to the horizontal axis of the pendulum by a toothed canting wheel. This invention, perfected in 1657,[1] made an almost perfect clock possible for use on land, but was impracticable on the sea. And it was just on the sea that a highly accurate chronometer was desirable in order to find the longitude .So important was this problem to the East Indian and West Indian traders that the States General of Holland had tried in every way to stimulate the invention of a practical solution of it. Long negotiations with Galileo, who believed that longitude might be calculated by observation of the moons of Jupiter, ended in disappointment, for this method, though theoretically possible, is not sufficiently nice to be of practical value. As Huygens readily saw that the most accurate method of computing longitude would be the comparison of the time at noon as observed at sea with the time at some known longitude as kept by a precise clock, he labored hard to overcome the practical difficulties. He finally succeeded, at least in part, by substituting for the pendulum a balance-wheel worked by two springs.

The work, named *The Pendulum Clock*,[2] published in 1673, in which he set forth this mechanism, contained important sections on the descent of heavy bodies, the generation and measurement of curved lines, and the center of

[1] *Horologium*, Hugenii *Opera varia*, 1724, i, p. 1.
[2] *Horologium Oscillatorium, Opera varia*, i, 15.

oscillation of a compound pendulum. After approximating, in a general way, the idea of the conservation of energy, he carried further Galileo's experiments with balls rolling down inclined planes. More successfully than Galileo he tried to measure the speed of falling bodies by allowing a weight to slide down a taut string, carrying with it a strip of parchment on which a pendulum fitted with a pen-point should mark half seconds. By this means he made the nearly correct estimate that a body would fall 9.75 metres in the first second.

Huygens first spoke of what is now called "mass" but what he called "solid quantity." It is proportional to weight, but is not the same thing. It can be felt as the centrifugal force of a body revolved in a horizontal plane.

5. THE BAROMETER AND THE THERMOMETER

To Galileo again, the Anti-Aristotle, is due the disproof of another ancient and hoary maxim, that "nature abhors a vacuum." In his *Discourses on Two New Sciences* he tells how Sagredo had made a suction pump "which worked perfectly so long as the water in the cistern stood above a certain level, but failed to work below this level." His first thought, that the pump was out of order, yielded, on repeated experiment, to the conviction that water could not be raised by suction above 18 cubits (about 32 feet.). At that point the column of water would break of its own weight, like a heavy chain. Nature's supposed *horror vacui* was therefore very limited.

Galileo also showed that air had weight, though apparently he did not definitely take the step of attributing the rise of the water in a pump to atmospheric pressure. By pumping two or three times as much air in a bottle as it would ordinarily hold and then weighing it, he came to the conclusion that the specific gravity of air is about one four-hundredth that of water. It is now known to be about $\frac{1}{780}$ that of water.

Galileo's experiment with water was repeated with mercury and improved upon by Torricelli. Filling a long glass tube with mercury, closing one end with his finger and leaving the other end in a bowl of mercury, he found that the heavy fluid always stood in the tube at a height of about thirty inches above the level of the mercury in the bowl. This experiment he described in a letter [1] of June 11, 1644, which he illustrated with a handsome picture of his apparatus.

Torricelli's letter, briskly circulated in manuscript, came into the hands of the French scientist Mersenne and was by him shown to a youth of twenty-one who had already distinguished himself in mathematics and who was destined to win great glory in many fields. Blaise Pascal was born at Clermont-Ferrand in the southern central part of France. His father, Étienne, a noble and a government official, was a man of great piety but of so hot a temper that what he called "fraternal and evangelical corrections" of his friends appeared to them as virulent invectives, and that he boxed his children's ears with force sufficient to make them "jump three steps at a time." Nevertheless he gave them a good education and when he moved to Paris in 1631 and to Rouen eight years later, made his house a rendezvous for many of the most famous men of the time.

Stimulated by converse with Mersenne and Roberval, Blaise Pascal evinced extraordinary precocity, especially in the field of mathematics. Though he was sickly he burned with the love of glory and with the love of science which he was later, under religious influence, to abandon as an abominable concupiscence. Torricelli's letter fell into his mind like a fruitful seed, and he at once began to test for himself the new knowledge. In 1647 he published a treatise called *New Experiments with the Vacuum*,[2] with the purpose of proving once for all "that any vessel, however large, can be made empty of all matter known in nature and perceptible to the senses." His experiments with water and mercury were the same as those of the Italians; but he, following a hint

---

[1] *Opere di Torricelli*, iii, 187.
[2] *Experiences nouvelles touchant le Vuide, Œuvres*, ii, 43ff.

of Mersenne, now definitely explained the action of the fluid as due to the pressure of the air, and stated that the column of liquid in either case must weigh exactly equal to a column of air from the earth's surface to the top of the atmosphere.

This definite challenge to accepted doctrine called forth a loud chorus of protest and contradiction. Professor Jacques Pierius first entered the lists for the "plenists" with a Latin treatise on *Whether there is a Vacuum in Nature* in which he proved by arguments that would have satisfied anyone three hundred years earlier, that even the angels could not produce a vacuum, that only God could do so but that he would not, that mercury is a crazy bastard that does not know how it ought to act, but that God, to frustrate it and avoid the scandal of a vacuum, had attached to the mercury certain vapors which filled the upper end of Monsieur Pascal's tube.

But there were more serious attempts to explain away the new experiments. Some said that the rise of the mercury was due to capillary attraction; some that it was held to the top of the tube by invisible threads which anyone could feel pulling on his finger stopping the end of the tube; some that the rise was due not to air pressure but to a limited *horror vacui*. Pascal answered this last assertion by denying that nature could feel a horror of anything or any other passion, and by asserting that the old explanations of phenomena by "sympathy" and "antipathy" filled the ear but meant nothing. Never was the import of the new scientific challenge to the old scholasticism more clearly brought out than in his insistence that the explanation of natural phenomena could not be metaphysical, but must be mechanical.

The most serious of his opponents was Descartes, that hybrid of philosophy and science. On the one hand, with true scholastic logic, Descartes argued that a vacuum is an impossibility because it is inconceivable. If we say that a vessel contains a vacuum we are really saying that there is nothing between its walls, and if there is nothing between them they must touch,[1] which, in the case of Pascal's tube, is contradicted by our sight. On the other hand, he urged that the apparent vacuum must be filled with something because it transmits light, and light in Descartes' theory is a subtle body. The same argument might, to be sure, on the wave theory, prove that the so-called vacuum is filled with ether.

A further test of the theory of the air-pressure was so obvious that it occurred to Pascal and Descartes at nearly the same time, and led to an unpleasant controversy between them as to which thought of it first. This test was to try the height of the mercury on the top of a mountain and compare this with its height at the bottom. The experiment was carried out, at Pascal's request, by his brother-in-law, Florin Perrier, near Clermont on September 19, 1648.[2] Ascending the Puy-de-Dôme, a mountain which he estimated to be 3000 feet high from bottom to top—its top is 4800 feet above sea level—he took a barometer and found that the mercury fell three inches and one line as he ascended to the top, and that its height at various stages of the journey was proportional to the distance traversed, though another barometer, kept at the bottom for purposes of comparison, did not vary. During the next three years Perrier made experiments and kept records of the effect of the weather on the height of the mercury.[3]

These experiments vindicated Pascal's theory of air-pressure. He enforced it, and revealed new experiments in a *Treatise on the Equilibrium of Liquids*,[4] probably written in 1654, but first published in 1663 after the author's death. In this he definitely proved by an additional experiment that the height of the mercury in the barometer is really due to the pressure of the air. He found that when he placed a small tube of mercury in a larger tube the mercury would fall to the bottom when the air is exhausted in the outer

---

[1] Descartes: *Œuvres,* ii, 482, (1639).
[2] *Œuvres de Pascal,* ii, 349ff.
[3] *Ibid.,* 441ff.
[4] *Œuvres,* iii, 143ff.

tube. In this work he also propounded the law of hydro-statics which bears his name. He provided the cover of a water-tight vessel, full of water, with two tubes of different sizes, in each of which was fitted a piston. He then showed that the piston in the larger tube would bear a heavier weight than the piston in the smaller tube in the ratio of their cross-sections. Thus, if the diameter of one tube be ten times that of the other, and the area of the cross-sections therefore in the ratio of one hundred to one, a pound weight on the smaller piston will just balance a hundred pounds on the larger. This is a special case of the law of the lever and of the pulley.

Pascal's experiments excited wide interest throughout Europe. Even in the midst of the Thirty Years' War a German burgomaster found time to study and to improve upon them. Otto von Guericke was born at Magdeburg and studied law at various German universities, completing his education in science at Leyden and in the ways of the world by a tour in France and England. Soon after his return home the sack of Magdeburg by Tilly in 1631 drove him to seek service in the Swedish army. When he was finally able to return to his native city he entered the civic service, rising to the rank of burgomaster in 1646.

His passion for natural science led him to invent the air-pump in 1650 and the manometer in 1661. He recognized that no perfect vacuum could be obtained on earth, though he believed it to exist in the interstellar spaces.[1] How high a vacuum he obtained he does not inform us; but Huygens, who imitated and perhaps improved his pump, reduced the air in it to one one-thousandth of an atmosphere. That, how-ever, Guericke obtained a fairly high vacuum may be in-ferred from his most famous experiment, that by which, having placed in juxtaposition two nicely fitting hollow hemispheres, he exhausted the air within them and then showed that sixteen horses, eight harnessed on each side, could not pull them apart.

[1] Ottonis de Guericke: *Experimenta nova (ut vocantur) Magdeburgica de vacuo spatio*, Amsterdam, 1672, p. 84.

He discovered that a light would not burn in a vacuum, that animals could not live in it, and that sound is not propagated in it, for a striking clock in the cylinder remains mute. By means of an ingenious water-barometer Guericke measured the weight of a column of air at the surface of the earth at Magdeburg. His calculation that a column of air resting on a circular plane two-thirds of a Magdeburg ell in diameter would weigh 2678.1 pounds, each pound of the weight of sixteen imperial Thalers, is difficult to reduce to modern standards owing to the variety then prevalent in the weights and measures of Europe and especially of Germany. As near as I can calculate it, however, this would make the pressure of the atmosphere at land level about 13 pounds to the square inch, which is somewhat less than that verified by modern scientists (14.9 pounds to the square inch).

Presently England made her contribution to the new methods of weighing air. Indeed, the word "barometer" first appeared in the English *Philosophical Transactions* in 1665, where the invention of the instrument is patriotically but incorrectly attributed to "that Noble Searcher of Nature, Mr. Boyle." [1] Robert Boyle, the fourteenth son of Richard Boyle, Earl of Cork, was born in the south of Ireland and educated at Eton and in Geneva and Italy. When he returned to England he devoted his life to that research which, he tells us, provides man with his highest happiness. As a member of the new Royal Society at London and at Oxford he made many chemical and physical investigations, which he set forth in a style of such almost unexampled prolixity as to rob the reader of the "felicity" felt by the writer in making his experiments. [2] Besides studying nature he devoted much attention to theology.

Hearing of the air-pump made in Germany by Guericke he imitated it and started to investigate the pressure of the atmosphere. He noticed that a bottle filled with air and tightly sealed, left on the bottom of the receptacle of his air-pump, half filled with water, blew up as the air above the

[1] *Philosophical Transactions*, i, 153.
[2] Robert Boyle's *Works*, 6 volumes quarto, London, 1772.

water was pumped out. He also observed that a siphon ceases to work as the air becomes thin and that bubbles rise from the water in a vessel from which the air has been pumped.[1] He was probably right in explaining these bubbles as air dissolved in the water, for such bubbles will rise from ordinary (*i.e.* not recently boiled) water. The possibility that water will boil at low temperatures as the pressure goes down did not occur to him; and this phenomenon can only be produced with a very good pump, probably only with one better than his.

Boyle also observed that a candle would go out in a vacuum though gunpowder would burn, that an animal would die without air—though he was kind-hearted enough to revive the mouse used by letting in air as soon as it fainted away—and that even fish could not live in water in a vessel from which air had been pumped—though whether this was due to lack of oxygen or to the change in the pressure of the water it apparently did not occur to him to ask.

The most important discovery made in the course of his researches was not due to him but to his pupil Townley who rightly suggested that the cause of atmospheric pressure on the sides and top of a vessel was the expansive power, or, as Boyle called it, the "spring" of the air. Boyle set forth the theory that the air consists of, or abounds in, parts of such a nature that in case they be bent or compressed by the weight of the atmosphere or by any other body, they endeavor to free themselves from that pressure by bearing against the contiguous bodies that keep them bent. Boyle then enunciated the law usually known after his name, though sometimes by the name of Mariotte who independently discovered it a little later,—that the volume of air (or of any gas) varies inversely as its pressure.

An invention that excited less attention at the time, though ultimately as important as that of the barometer, was that of the thermometer. It had been suggested by Porta and realized, in an imperfect way, by Galileo. Filling a glass bulb as

---

[1] *New Experiments Physico-Mechanical touching the Spring of the Air,* 1660; *Works,* i, 1ff.

large as a hen's egg and fitted with a long narrow tube, with
air, he discovered that as the bulb was heated in his hand
the air would expand and some of it be driven out into a
bowl of water into which he had dipped the end of the tube.
Then, as the air in the bulb cooled again and shrank, the
water rose. This rough measurement of heat was improved
by his friend Sagredo who, in 1613, marked off the tube
into one hundred degrees. But this measurement was still
only relative; there were no fixed starting points either at
the upper or at the lower end.

6. CHEMISTRY

While physics was making giant strides into modern times
her sister chemistry still lagged in the Middle Ages. The
chief reason of this seems to be that the objects then studied
successfully by physicists—light, magnetism, gravity, energy, and atmospheric pressure—are more easily measured
by the instruments then known than are the far subtler and
more elusive phenomena of chemistry. What little advance
was made in this field was due to the valuable destructive
criticism that exposed the false doctrines of the alchemists,
and particularly the theory of Paracelsus and his followers,
the "spagyrics," that the original elements of all matter are
salt, mercury, and sulphur.

The seventeenth century saw a considerable increase of
experiment and no lack of theory. Until about the middle
of the century the interest centered in medicine; after that
time a more purely scientific interest was imported from
the neighboring realm of physics. The leader of the earlier
experimenters was the Belgian doctor of medicine, Jean
Baptiste van Helmont. His works are a mass of superstition, pedantry, and quackery, relieved by an occasional
flash of insight and by a laudable attempt to bring to notice
new phenomena. Among the several words he coined to express new ideas, only one has remained in common use. For
it is to him that we owe the word "gas," which he took
from the Greek word "chaos" already used by Paracelsus

to designate airy matter, and which he defined as "a spirit or wild exhalation which can be neither confined nor coagulated, belched forth from fomenting things as though it were an enemy to them, and often fatal to incautious bystanders. It is either mineral in subterranean caves—and this is called wild gas (*gas silvestre*) *par éminence,* or it is in the air like wind, or in vegetable matter, like that given off by fermenting beer and wine and by artificial effervescence, like the vapors exhaling from *acqua chrysulca* and other saline solutions." [1]

This cumbersome definition in itself shows the difficulty of grappling with a new subject. When carbon dioxide masqueraded as the wild and wicked "gas silvestre" it is no wonder that other chemical substances kept their incognito for some time longer.

The first scientist to study chemistry for its own sake was Robert Boyle, whose efforts, however, were successful only in refuting the two theories of the composition of matter then commonly held, the Peripatetic theory of the four elements of earth, air, fire, and water, and the Spagyric theory of the three elements of mercury, sulphur, and salt. His argument was set forth in a prolix work with a long title: *The Skeptical Chymist, or Chymico-Physical Doubts and Paradoxes touching the Experiments whereby vulgar Spagyrists are wont to endeavor to evince their Salt, Sulphur, and Mercury, to be the true Principles of Things,* published in 1661. [2]

The argument, cast in the favorite form of the dialogue, has little trouble in showing that neither of the older theories satisfactorily accounts for the observed fact that there are many more than three or four irreducible elements. Boyle's scepticism also attacked another theory then in vogue, that of explaining effervescence and other chemical phenomena like fermentation by alleging the natural anti-

---

[1] J. B. Van Helmont: *Opera Omnia,* 1707, Preface with glossary of words used by Helmont made presumably by his editor. Professor Wilder D. Bancroft of Cornell identifies "aqua chrysulca" with nitric acid.

[2] Boyle's *Works,* i, 458. And see T. L. Davis in *Isis,* 1926, viii, 71ff.

pathy of acid and alkali. In the first place Boyle objected
to the loose definition of an alkali as an anti-acid, which
he said would be like defining a man as an anti-lion; and
he further objected to assuming antipathy or sympathy between nonsentient beings. Not in vain had the physicists
taught him that the explanation of natural phenomena must
be a mechanical one.

But though Boyle brilliantly exposed "the illiterateness,
the arrogance, and the imposture of too many of those who
pretended to skill" [1] in chemistry, he was able to build up
much less than he tore down. It is a tribute to his foresight
rather than to his insight, that he was inclined to hold a
theory of matter not unlike the atomic hypothesis later
advanced by Dalton. This hypothesis he did not claim to
prove, but merely conjectured that it was "not impossible"
that matter might consist of small, ultimate particles of different original nature, which, by their mixture, give rise to
the various substances known to descriptive chemistry.
Boyle assumed that the many chemical elements are composed of small particles of primordial matter, and he explained their combination in fixed quantities by comparing
the atoms of one element to the blades of a knife and the
atoms of another element to the handles of the same sort
of knife: to make a knife of any given pattern only so many
blades would fit so many handles. While Boyle's scientific
imagination must be commended, his theory was patently
based not on experiments but on tradition. Since the time of
Democritus and Epicurus the atomic theory had been held
by a long succession of thinkers including Nicholas of Cusa,
Fracastoro, Ramus, Bruno, Gassendi, and Galileo.

The phenomenon of combustion is so striking that it
naturally engaged the attention of many observers. In 1630
a French physician named Jean Rey showed that the weight
of metals increases on calcination; in 1665 the Englishman
Robert Hooke concluded, on the basis of the experiment of
burning gunpowder in a vacuum, that saltpeter or something like it is necessary to combustion, and that the air

[1] *Works,* i, 354.

contains this substance. In 1674 John Mayow developed this theory a little further by comparing combustion with the oxidation of blood in the lungs.

The idea that heat is a movement of small round atoms was advanced by Descartes and adopted by Hooke, by Gassendi, and by Boyle. Boyle's vague conceptions of such a motion, which he thought might exist in heated or in magnetized iron, does not entitle him to be regarded as the discoverer of the fact that heat is molecular motion.[1]

[1] Boyle: *An Essay of the intestine Motions of the Particles of Quiescent Solids, Works,* i, 444ff. Descartes' words, written in 1639, in his *Œuvres,* ii, 485. On Hooke's definition see T. R. Gunther: *Early Science at Oxford,* ii, 1923, p. 2682. Gunther wrongly attributes to Hooke the discovery that heat is molecular motion.

CHAPTER IV

MATHEMATICS

I. THE CHARACTER OF MODERN MATHEMATICS

Mathematics may well claim to be the most original creation of the human spirit not only in the field of science but in
any field whatever. By a long course of logical argument it
has passed from the simplest operations of counting and
measuring to notions so remote from any agreeable to our
mental habits and to common sense and from any that can
be derived immediately by perception through the senses,
that they not only stagger the imagination but require a long
course of arduous training even to be understood. From
the invention by the early Egyptians of addition and multiplication, and from their discovery of the elementary laws
of "earth-measurement"—as the word "geometry" means—
to the conception of a universe in which the space and time
we know are but the four-dimensional surface of a fifth-
dimensional supersolid—this, surely, is the longest, the most
amazing flight of the human mind. This achievement, like
a great work of art or of poetry, impresses one the more
the more one thinks of it.

This being so, it is natural that in modern times mathematics should enjoy an immense prestige. It has conquered
the throne usurped by theology as queen of knowledge, and
has contested the claim of philosophy to be the *scientia
scientiarum*. Some idea that number is the key to the cosmos
was held by Pythagoras, and important additions to mathematical science were made by the Greeks. For many ages,
however, the knowledge slumbered, or at best was only
slightly improved by the Arabs. Beginning, however, with the
publication of Cardan's algebra (the *Ars Magna*) in 1545,

many important discoveries rapidly followed. The general causes of this sudden blooming of a long torpid plant were the same as those operative in producing the Renaissance of learning and of the other sciences. And the evident victories of mathematics in the fields of astronomy and of physics created a lively interest in that subject.

To the eager minds of the scholars of the Renaissance the writings of the Greeks offered much food for scientific, as for other, forms of thought. The first Latin translation of Euclid was published at Venice by Zamberti in 1505; thenceforward there were many translations of other works from the Greek and Arabic, and many commentaries written upon them, often by men distinguished for their own original work. By the year 1650 interest in the history of mathematics was keen enough to produce what can be called, without flattery, the first history of the science in a work by Gerhard Johann Voss: *De universae matheseos natura et constitutione*. After a disquisition on the certainty of mathematics and its importance for philosophy, he traced the history of the science, in its various branches. Arithmetic he thought originated with the Phoenicians, geometry with the Egyptians, and astronomy with the Chaldaeans. He added an interesting account of applied mathematics in its relation to music, optics, geodesy, astronomy, chronology and geography.[1] About the same time the Cambridge professor John Wallis devoted a part of his energies to writing the history of his discipline. First in his inaugural address (1649) [2] and then in his *Treatise on Algebra, both Historical and Practical* (1685), he traced the course of mathematical discovery from the time of Adam, whom he considered a genius for having invented number, through the antediluvian period, for which he used the admittedly suspicious testimony of Josephus, and so on to the Greeks and from them to his own day. Except for his account of the mythical age, and except for his desire to glorify himself

[1] G. J. Voss: *De Mathesi, Opera*, iii, 63ff.
[2] *Opera mathematica*, 1695, i, 1.

and his friends, Harriot and Newton, he wrote a commendable and excellent history.

From its rebirth in modern times till the present mathematics has been international. Among geniuses of the first order during the period under consideration, Cardan, Torricelli, and Cavalieri were Italians, Descartes, Pascal, and Fermat Frenchmen, Stevin and Huygens Dutch, Kepler and Leibniz German, Wallis and Briggs English, and Napier Scotch. Until near the end of the seventeenth century, when the first scientific periodicals were founded, their place was partly supplied by a voluminous and briskly circulated correspondence, of which collections were published occasionally. There was sufficient demand for books on mathematics to insure a market for a large number of text-books as well as for more ambitious treatises. Indeed, one of the striking features of modern science appeared thus early, in the vast number of men engaged in its pursuit and in the quantity of books that they produced. No brief history, which is necessarily confined to a few great names, can give an adequate idea of the bulk of the work produced. As in all ages, most of it was repetitious and elementary; genius, even in that age so prolific in genius, was the exception and not the rule.

2. RECKONING, DECIMALS, LOGARITHMS

The miraculous powers of modern calculation depend chiefly upon three inventions, the algorism, decimals, and logarithms. The algorism, or Arabic notation, when introduced into Europe during the later Middle Ages, for the first time allowed the four fundamental processes of reckoning to be conveniently performed; but as these processes were still laborious for large quantities, and as the spread of education, the growth of commerce, and above all the advance of science necessitated ever larger computations, much thought was applied to the invention of methods for rendering multiplication, division, involution, and evolution easier. Vast tables giving the products of multiplication and the quotients of division were published, but they were usually so cumbrous that little time was saved by their use. Napier, before he hit upon logarithms, invented a method founded on the arrangement of little sticks, called "Napier's bones," which, though it seems more tedious than the ordinary method, enjoyed some vogue. William Oughtred, an English clergyman, about 1622 invented the slide rule, which still has its uses. Pascal, at the early age of twenty-two, invented, in 1645, the first adding machine, and actually patented it. It looked like a long box, fitted with eight little wheels each marked with the ten digits, and representing respectively the units, tens, hundreds, and so forth up to the ten millions.[1] The turning of the wheels performed the process of addition. Leibniz spent some time in working on a similar arithmetical machine.[2]

But these mechanical methods proved far less effective in abridging labor than did the two inventions of decimals and of logarithms, the one made at the end of the sixteenth, the other at the beginning of the seventeenth century. Here and elsewhere, when we speak of the inventor of anything we mean not the first man to whom the idea ever occurred, but the man who made it a living and useful part of current thought. Even though earlier examples of the use of decimals have been found, Simon Stevin is rightly credited with their invention, for he first improved them to the point where their use became practical and hence popular. Among his many works on mathematics one of the most original was that published in Flemish in 1585 under a title meaning: *The Decimal, Teaching with unheard-of ease how to perform all calculations necessary among men by whole numbers without fractions.*[3] He began by defining the decimal as a sort of arithmetic using a geometrical progression with a ratio of $\frac{1}{10}$. He then explained his method of notation, which was far from being as simple as is the point now in use. He would put a zero in a circle over or beside the unit

[1] *Œuvres de Pascal,* ed. Brunschvicg et Boutroux, 1908, i, 296.

[2] *Sämtliche Schriften,* i, 346, (1673).

[3] *La Thiende de Simon Stevin, facsimile de l'édition originale plantinienne de 1585,* avec une introduction par H. Bosmans, 1924.

column, a "1" in a circle over or beside the column representing tenths, a "2" to designate the hundredths and so forth in the manner which can be most easily seen by the accompanying cut. The reason why he selected this notation was that the exponents represented the powers of .1, and so the calculator could tell, in multiplying decimals, how many decimal places there should be in the product by adding the exponents of the multiplier and multiplicand. Nevertheless, it was an unfortunate notation, not only because of its cumbrousness but because it was easily confused with

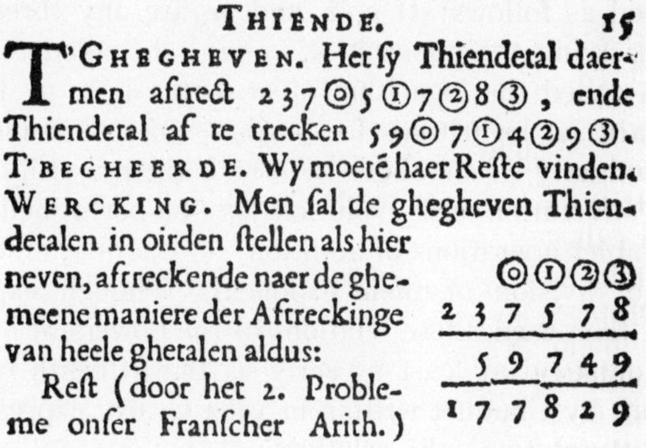

THIENDE.   15

T'GHEGHEVEN. Het fy Thiendetal daer-
men aftreَt 237⓪5①7②8③, ende
Thiendetal af te trecken 59⓪7①4②9③.
T'BEGHEERDE. Wy moeté haer Refte vinden.
WERCKING. Men fal de ghegheven Thien-
detalen in oirden ftellen als hier
neven, aftreckende naer de ghe-   ⓪①②③
meene maniere der Aftreckinge   2 3 7 5 7 8
van heele ghetalen aldus: 5 9 7 4 9
Reft (door het 2. Proble-   _____
me onfer Franfcher Arith.)   1 7 7 8 2 9

FIG. 2.—Showing Stevin's decimal notation. Reproduced from the facsimile edition of his *Thiende.*

algebraic notation of that time which had an entirely different meaning. The decimal point was first used in an English work of 1616.

Hardly less original than Stevin's numerical invention was the second part of his little book in which he advocated the decimal system of measurement in computing lengths and the volumes of liquids, in the coinage, and even in the division of a circle into degrees. While a large part of his program has been realized in reducing measures and coins to decimal standards, the change from the sexagesimal to the decimal division of the circle, though also advocated by his contemporary Vieta, has not been carried out. The brochure,

immediately translated into French and incorporated in a
larger work of the author on *Arithmetic*, and again translated into English in 1608, had a deserved success.

More difficult and surprising than the invention of decimals was the discovery of logarithms. And yet, like so many
great discoveries, it had been so thoroughly prepared for
and led up to that it occurred to two minds independently
at about the same time, though of the two, Napier is rightly
given the greater part of the glory, both for priority and
for theoretical superiority to his rival, Jobst Bürgi.

A logarithm is a particular class of function which may
be defined as follows: If a, x, and m, are any three quantities satisfying the equation $a^x = m$, a is called the base,
and x is called the logarithm of m to the base a. The immense value of logarithms for purposes of reckoning is due
to the property of numbers by which their multiplication,
division, involution, and evolution may be performed by the
much simpler operations of addition, subtraction, multiplication, and division of their exponents. Though exponents
were not then used, these relations of the powers of numbers
were understood at least as early as the fifteenth century,
for a work by Chuquet written in 1484 clearly expresses (in
a different notation) the relations:

$$a^m a^n = a^{m+n}$$

and

$$(a^m)^n = a^{mn}$$

Michael Stiefel in 1544 saw that the powers of numbers
could be expressed as a geometrical series with the exponents
in an arithmetical series and that this held good for negative
exponents, as in the two series:

-3	-2	-1	0	1	2	3
$\frac{1}{8}$	$\frac{1}{4}$	$\frac{1}{2}$	1	2	4	8

where the upper line represents the exponents of the powers
of 2 as written out in the lower line.[1]

[1] D. E. Smith in *Napier Tercentenary Volume*, p. 83.

The secret hidden in these relations, that they can be used for the purpose of simplifying calculations with large numbers, was first revealed to the world by John Napier (1550-1617) the "laird" or squire of Merchiston near Edinburgh. Born of a prominent Protestant family,[1] he took an active part in the affairs of kirk and state, and in 1593 accompanied a deputation of the General Assembly to King James and wrote him a stern letter advising him to purge his court of "papists, atheists, and neutrals." In 1593 he wrote *A Plain Discovery of the Whole Revelation of St. John*, which was much esteemed by the Protestant clergy at home and abroad.[2] In this he proved that the pope is Antichrist and that "the last trumpet and vial beginneth anno Christi 1541 and should end 1786" but that, as the world could not endure its terrors so long, the Last Judgment would come between the years 1688 and 1700. Napier also dabbled in the black arts, using divining rods to find hidden treasure and being credited with the possession of a familiar spirit in the shape of a black cock.

But with all his strenuous life of feud with neighbors and of studies in divinity, he devoted many laborious years to the perfection of his great numerical invention, on which he wrote two books, the one composed last being published by himself in 1614 under the title: *A Description of the marvellous rule of Logarithms*,[3] and the other *The Construction of Logarithms*, published posthumously in 1619. If we trust a letter of Kepler written in 1624, Napier had communicated his discovery to Tycho Brahe as early as 1594.

The name logarithm was invented by himself, as a compound of two Greek words, λόγος meaning ratio and ἀριθμός meaning number. Logarithms are, then, the "ratio-numbers" or, in his own words, "the numbers which divide equally proportional numbers or quantities." His illustra-

[1] A "Johannes Neaper" matriculated at St. Andrews in 1564. *Early Records of St. Andrews*, 1926, p. 271.
[2] For a German translation and German praise of it see Schelhorn: *De Vita Philippi Camerarii*, 1711, p. 181f.
[3] *Mirifici Logarithmorum Canonis Descriptio*, authore ac inventore Johanne Nepero Barone Merchistonii, 1614; First ed. at Cornell.

tion is that of two points moving along parallel lines in such a way that one of the points will cover equal spaces in equal intervals of time, while the second point, covering the same space during the first interval of time will thereafter cover only a certain proportion of the given space, differing from the space last covered by a fixed ratio, say ½. We thus have two series, one arithmetical and one geometrical. As his main purpose was to compute trigonometric functions (then the most laborious of all calculations), he thought of sines decreasing in a given ratio, and thus his two series went in opposite directions, one increasing and the other decreasing at the same time. The base he used was therefore $\frac{1}{e}$, the reciprocal of e, or the natural base.[1]

Even in the imperfect form in which Napier had left them logarithms represented the possibility of an immense saving of time in calculation and fully deserved the encomium in the dedication to the *Description,* which reads as follows:

> This new method of logarithms completely eliminates all difficulties inhering in the earlier methods of mathematical calculation, and is so adapted for relieving the weakness of the memory that by its aid we can in the' space of one hour solve more mathematical problems concerning sines, tangents, and secants than could before this have been solved in a whole day.

Within ten years the invention had been taken up by scientists in many lands. In 1620 Edmund Gunther published tables of the logs of trigonometric functions. In 1621 Cavalieri introduced logarithms to Galileo, and in 1632 published a book about their use in astronomy, called the *Directorium generale uranometricum.* Kepler also published a treatise on the use of logarithms "than which," he averred

there is nothing, except the knowledge of numbers, more admirable or useful for solving many problems of calculation, especially

---

[1] Mathematicians call e the natural base of logarithms because it is the easiest to use in analytical work; it is the sum of the factorial series

$$1 + \frac{1}{1!} + \frac{1}{2!} + \frac{1}{3!} \ldots = 2.71828 \ldots$$

in trigonometry, without multiplication, division, or extraction of roots by the usual long, laborious, and troublesome processes.[1]

Much the most valuable improvement of the system was due to Henry Briggs, professor of geometry at Cambridge, who was so filled with enthusiasm for the new discovery that he devoted most of his remaining years to exploiting it. He took as the new base 10, which is easier for ordinary calculation, though the natural base remains in use for analytical work. In 1617 he published a logarithmic table of the numbers 1 to 1000, the logs being calculated to 8 decimal places. In 1624 he published much more elaborate tables, with logs to 14 places for the numbers 1 to 20,000 and from 90,000 to 100,000. The gap between 20,000 and 90,000 was filled in by Adrian Vlacq in 1628. Logarithms had been fairly started on their usefulness. By halving the labor they have doubled the life of the astronomer and mathematician.

3. ALGEBRA

Algebra, the child of Diophantus of Alexandria, though born a Greek was given an Arabic name by his medieval guardians. The days of his youth were long, long days; for when he was handed over to the Italians of the Renaissance the backward child could do no more than solve quadratic equations. One cause of his backwardness was the extremely difficult language he was then obliged to speak; for mathematical notation was awkward and ill adapted to its purposes. What the development of instruments is to music, what the progress of experimental technique is to physics, *that* the invention of suitable symbols is to mathematics,— it is half the science. Now, when Luca Pacioli de Burgo published in 1494 the first treatise on algebra to be printed, he used no. (numero) for the known quantity in an equation, co. (cosa) for the unknown in the first degree, ce. (censo) for the unknown squared, cu. (cubo) for the unknown

---

[1] *Opera*, vii, 316ff.

cubed, p. for plus and m. for minus, so that the expression which we should write $3x + 4x^2 - 5x^3 + 2x^4 - 6a$, he wrote 3co.p.4ce.m.5cu.p.2ce.ce.m.6no. From the word *cosa,* literally meaning "thing" used for the unknown quantity, algebra came to be called the cossic art, and a convenient notation, called the cossic, was gradually evolved, chiefly by Italians and Germans. Michael Stieffel, equally celebrated as a mathematician and as a chiliastic preacher, introduced the sign for the square root. The Englishman Robert Recorde who wrote an algebra with the title *The Whetstone of Wit* (in Latin *Cos ingenii,* with a pun on *cos* meaning whetstone, and *cosa,* or the cossic art), is credited with the invention of the sign of equality ($=$), though it has recently been shown that he may have borrowed it from Pompeo Bolognetti. The signs $+$ and $-$ for plus and minus were perhaps first used by Johann Widmann of Eger. Bolognetti and others wrote the unknown as a number, signifying its degree, in a circle; thus (1) stood for x, and (2) for x^2. Gradually the letters of the alphabet took the place of the known and unknown quantities, Descartes being responsible for the convention that the early letters should stand for knowns and the letters near the end of the alphabet for the unknowns. In what follows the modern notation will be used even when it is not found in the original.

"The period of tentative systematic calculation with complex numbers was initiated by Cardan in 1545 in his algebraic masterpiece the *Ars Magna,*" says a great mathematician.[1] Hieronymus Cardanus or Girolamo Cardano or Jerome Cardan (1501-76) was born at Milan and educated as a physician at the universities of Pavia and Padua. The hardships of the sickly and illegitimate child, his precocity, vices, and superstitions, are piquantly described in his own memoirs. Though his dissipated life put obstacles at first in the path of his success as a physician he gradually won

---

[1] E. H. Moore in his presidential address before the American Association of Arts and Sciences at Cambridge, Mass., Dec. 26, 1920, as reported next day by the *New York Times.*

name and fame. He travelled to France, England and Scotland, but spent most of his life in northern Italy. His last years were darkened by the wickedness of his son, who was tried and executed for murder, and by a short imprisonment by the Inquisition for having cast the horoscope of Jesus Christ.

His many books, on physics, medicine, and mathematics, enjoyed much reputation at the time. Though his masterpiece, the *Ars Magna,* or *Great Art* (1545) expounds some discoveries that are not the author's own, it is now recognized as a valuable, and in some parts original, contribution to the progress of mathematics. The subject then agitating scientific thought in Italy was the theory of equations and particularly the solution of equations of higher degree than the quadratic.

The solution of the cubic equation, in a general form, had been discovered by Scipione dal Ferro, who was professor of mathematics at Bologna 1496-1526. But this solution, like many other achievements in science at that time, had been so jealously guarded from the public that the method had either been forgotten or never understood by others than the inventor. It was rediscovered by Niccolò Tartaglia, a man of wonderfully vigorous mind, though of deformed body. Educated not at the universities, but as a practical engineer, he made many discoveries which for long were neglected by the learned world because set forth in the vernacular. It was from him that Cardan learned the solution of the cubic equation under oath not to reveal it—an oath which, to the advantage of science but to the detriment of his own character for honesty, he promptly broke. Tartaglia's method, which is still used, is, in an equation in the general form $x^3 + mx = n$, for x to substitute $\sqrt[3]{t} - \sqrt[3]{y}$. In expansion the irrationals will disappear and give place to two new quadratic equations, which can easily be solved for t and y. From his pupil Ferrari, Cardan learned a somewhat similar solution of the biquadratic equation.

A bitter war of pens between Cardan and Tartaglia, conducted in the vernacular, at once scandalized, delighted, and educated the public.

Cardan's own work was no less remarkable than the work he borrowed, with frank acknowledgment, from others. He reckoned not only with negative but with imaginary (or, as he called them, "fictitious") numbers,—a path-breaking novelty. So new were even negative numbers to the thought of the time that the word "negative" was not applied to numbers with a minus sign until after Cardan's time. It was the Frenchman Pierre de la Ramée who about 1560 invented this use of the word negative, apparently because the grammatical rule that two negatives make an affirmative reminded him of the mathematical rule that the multiplication of two negative numbers produces a positive.

To Cardan we owe, in addition to the solution of cubic and biquadratic equations, which he took from others, the following advances: a recognition of the number of roots of a cubic equation and their connection with the coefficient of the quadratic member, the idea of the connection of the constant in an equation with its roots, an idea of the connection of the changes of sign in an equation with its roots, reckoning with imaginary quantities, and some work with series and the calculus of probabilities to be described presently.

While Simon Stevin added little to the theory of algebra, he invented, with his immense practical genius, a method of obtaining the roots of an equation of any degree by approximation. He discovered that if one substitutes for the unknown two quantities, one of which makes the total value of the equation positive and the other of which makes its total value negative, the root must lie between the two quantities substituted. Once we have started with any given quantities, we can continue to bring them closer and closer together, thus approximating with any required degree of closeness to the root, or at least to one root. This discovery was published in 1594 in an *Appendice Algebraique* of which the only copy known perished in the burning of the Louvain library in 1914.

François Viète, Seigneur de la Bigotière (1540-1603), commonly called Vieta, was the best French mathematician of the sixteenth century, and would perhaps have had more influence than he actually did—though this was considerable —had it not been for the bizarre and obscure jargon of newly coined technical terms in which he concealed his work. Born a Catholic in Poitou, he became a Huguenot and then later returned to the Catholic fold. Having studied and practised law he became successively Councillor of the Parlement of Paris and then *Maître des requêtes*, or examiner of petitions to the Council of State. One of his most valued public services was the deciphering of some Spanish dispatches written in cryptograph, which fell into the hands of the French government. He not only wrote many books on mathematics but published them at his own expense and sent them to scholars in his own and in foreign lands.

In 1593 he published a work on what would now be called algebraic geometry, *i.e.* on the solution of certain problems, as that of finding geometrical means between extremes, finding a fourth proportional, &c., by constructions with straight edge and compass. If this was not absolutely new, his application of it in certain instances was so, as was his "universal conclusion" that cubic and biquadratic problems can be solved geometrically by the interpolation of two mean proportionals, or by trisecting an angle. He introduced the word "coefficient" and recognized the dependence of the coefficients of an equation on its roots.

The Fleming Albert Girard (1595-1632), besides editing and commenting on the works of Stevin, published in 1629 a work entitled *Invention nouvelle en algèbre,* in which he showed that every equation has as many roots as the degree of its highest unknown, and that the roots can be calculated from the coefficients and constant. He also had a clear idea of the negative roots of an equation, and of their geometrical interpretation.

4. CALCULUS OF PROBABILITIES; MATHEMATICAL METHOD; THEORY OF NUMBERS

As a poor but dissipated youth Cardan was passionately addicted to gambling. From his need of reducing to a science the art of winning games of chance the calculus of probabilities was born. He reckoned the simpler cases of the likelihood of throwing given combinations in dice and of drawing given combinations of cards. How practical was his purpose is revealed by the fact that some of his directions were not strictly mathematical, but were doubtless as useful to the gamblers for whom he wrote as were his most scientific computations. The observation, for instance, that the chance of cutting any given card in a pack will be considerably increased if, naturally without mentioning it to the other players, one has previously extracted the card and rubbed it with soap, contributes rather to the art of the blackleg than to that of the mathematician.

About a century later the calculus of probabilities was revived in France for the same purpose of gambling. In 1654 when the Chevalier de Méré asked Pascal some questions about games of chance, the great moralist eagerly took up the problem with Fermat, and made many discoveries in choice and chance. Among other things he invented the arithmetical triangle, which can be extended to any desired size, but of which a small example follows:

1	1					
1	2	1				
1	3	3	1			
1	4	6	4	1		
1	5	10	10	5	1	
1	6	15	20	15	6	1

This triangle has the property of showing at a glance the number of chances of getting each one of several simple combinations, as in throwing a coin for heads or tails. If it is thrown 3 times there will be one chance in 8 of getting all heads, 3 chances of getting two heads and one tail, 3 chances of getting one head and two tails, and one chance of getting all tails, as represented in the third line. Much more complicated calculations are possible by the aid of the triangle, which also has properties unperceived by Pascal. It was later pointed out that the several lines represent the coefficients of a binomial expanded to higher powers, the first line representing those of the first degree, the second those of the square, the third those of the cube, and so on.

While he was in Paris in 1654 Huygens heard of the work of Pascal and three years later published a *Treatise on Reckoning in the Game of Dice*. He made the calculus of probabilities serve the needs not only of gamblers but those of more legitimate business in which the element of chance enters. Excited by reading John Graunt's *Natural and Political Observations . . . made upon the Bills of Mortality,* Huygens worked out tables of the expectation of life at different ages. In 1671 Jan De Witt, the great Pensionary of Holland, moved by the needs of a commercial nation in which all sorts of securities and of insurance were traded in, published a treatise on *The Value of Life Annuities in proportion to Perpetual Annuities*. From the tables of mortality he calculated that of every 212 persons 2 die each year from the ages of 4 to 53, 3 each year from 54 to 63; 4 each year from 64 to 73, and 6 each year thereafter until 80, beyond which age he assumed that no one, with exceptions so few as to be negligible, would live. On this basis he worked out carefully and correctly what would be the capital value of a life annuity at each age.

Progress in mathematics was made partly by the pursuit of old methods, partly by the invention of new ones, among which analytical geometry and the infinitesimal calculus must be counted as of the first importance. Among the old methods that of analysis, which went back to Plato, is defined by Vieta as "the assumption of what is required as though it were given, and following out its consequences to what is really given," [1] or, more simply,

---

[1] Vieta: *Opera,* p. 1.

by Oughtred,[1] as the process "in which by taking the thing sought as known we find out what we seek." The opposite process, synthesis, is defined by Vieta as "reduction of what is given, by following its consequences, to the end and comprehension of what is required."

Not content with accepting and exploiting the ancient principles, Pascal, that highly philosophical genius, wrote the first modern attempt at a philosophy of mathematics in a fragment on *The Method of Mathematical Proof.* Here he laid down seven propositions on the nature of definitions, axioms, and proof. He also discovered, or, if it were really known to Euclid, rediscovered the principle of mathematical induction with its two necessary steps in the proof of a general proposition, first to show that a certain proposition is true of a concrete example, and then "to show that if this proposition is true of the given example it must necessarily be true of the next example in the series."

Much work on the theory of number was done in the seventeenth century. Some idea of the subject had floated before the minds of certain ancient philosophers to whom the properties of numbers seemed mystical, and who therefore gave such names as "perfect number" to one which equals the sum of its divisors other than itself, and "amicable numbers" to those pairs each of which is equal to the sum of the aliquot divisors of the other. Even to the scholars of the Renaissance such properties seemed uncanny; we can read in Cardan much discussion of "magic numbers," where the reference is not to any supposed spell or charm in the number but merely to its primality, divisibility, or some such recondite but natural property.

Much more modern in viewpoint, though not much more helpful to thought, were Stevin's remarks on the philosophy of mathematics.[2] Arithmetic he defined as the science of numbers, and number as "that by which the quantity of everything is explained." All other numbers, said he, may

[1] Cajori: *Oughtred,* p. 20.
[2] *Œuvres,* i, p. 1.

be defined in terms of unity, but what unity is he could not explain, though he was as sure of it "as if Nature had told me out of her own mouth" what it is.

More profound was the work done on the theory of number, particularly during the years 1631-47 by Mersenne, Descartes, Pascal, and Fermat. Of them all perhaps Pierre de Fermat was the most richy endowed with genius in this particular line; and, though he published little, making known his work chiefly by correspondence, he won from his contemporaries the fame of being "the giant who has circumnavigated the mathematical globe and explored regions unknown to all others." Born near Toulouse he spent most of his life (1601-63) as Councillor of the Parlement of Toulouse. The son of a tradesman, he rose by the law, and perhaps partly by his scientific gifts, to the rank of the nobility. Of his public life little is known except that he protested against the unjust, and indeed savage, methods of collecting taxes in his province, and that an unfavorable report of his parliamentary activities was sent to Colbert in 1663. One would like to connect the two and to believe that the cause of the dissatisfaction of the government was the honorable one of his resistance to despotism. But it is true that his best energies were devoted not to administration but to mathematics.

Fermat is the father of the modern theory of number. Among many interesting theorems about primality and divisibility announced by him are such as that, though a square can be divided into two squares, a cube cannot be divided into two cubes, nor any higher power into two numbers of the same power.

But, if Fermat saw deepest into what is now called the theory of number, Pascal penetrated furthest into its philosophy. In addition to all that he had done on method, he first introduced two extremely important thoughts, of a highly philosophical character, into the world of mathematics. He first recognized that our decimal system of counting is a purely arbitrary thing, and can easily be replaced by an algorism with a number of digits less or

greater than ten—an idea first exploited after him by
Caramuel and Lobkowitz.[1] Moreover, Pascal was the first
to try to give a geometrical interpretation to four-dimensional space. It is probable (though certain scholars read
the idea into obscure phrases of ancient authors) that the
idea of a space of more than three dimensions was foreign
to antiquity. References to it are found in the schoolmen
of the fourteenth century, in Michael Stiefel, and in Descartes. But Pascal first considered it thoroughly. It is one
of those ideas far from human sense introduced by mathematical reasoning that have a fascination for the imaginative mind. One of the first to exploit it metaphysically was
the Cambridge Platonist Henry More, who, in his *Enchiri-
dion Metaphysicum* of 1671, declared that spirits have four
dimensions.[2]

5. TRIGONOMETRY; CYCLOMETRY; CONICS

When the word "trigonometry" was invented by Barthol-
omaeus Pitiscus in 1595, much work had already been done
in that science, but it had been regarded as a branch of
geometry. The great Copernicus in 1542 [3] summed up what
was known about the relations of the sides and angles of
triangles, and also delivered the first simple demonstration
of the fundamental formulae of spherical trigonometry. His
pupil, Georg Joachim Rheticus, published tables of sines,
tangents, and secants. Towards the end of the century
Vieta discovered the formula for deriving the sine of a
multiple angle. Napier discovered what are still known as
"Napier's rules," concerning the spherical right triangle.
The first logarithmic table of sines and tangents was constructed by Edmund Gunter. In 1670 James Gregory and

[1] Pascal: *Œuvres*, iii, 319, anno 1654.
[2] H. Wieleitner: *Zur Frühgeschichte der Räume von mehr als drei Dimen-
sionen*, and the note in *Isis*, vii, 486ff. Also H. Bosmans: "Sur l'Interpréta-
tion géométrique donnée par Pascal à l'espace à quatre dimensions,"
Annales de la Soc. de Science de Bruxelles, xlii, 1923, pp. 337-445.
[3] *De lateribus et angulis triangulorum, tum planorum rectilineorum tum
sphericorum*, Wittenberg, 1542. First ed. at Cornell.

in 1673 Leibniz independently discovered the series for the arc in powers of the tangent.

Much labor was wasted in the sixteenth and seventeenth centuries in discussing whether the circle could be exactly squared or not. Though it had long been proved that π is irrational, some scholars famous in other branches of learning damaged their reputations by claiming to have squared the circle exactly. Joseph Scaliger maintained the doubly false thesis that π is equal to the square root of ten, and that this is a rational number. John Hobbes engaged in a spirited controversy with Wallis and other mathematicians over this and other problems he claimed to have solved, a quarrel in which he distinguished himself equally by his mastery of invective and by the total absurdity of his mathematical paralogisms.

In the meantime Vieta had calculated the value of π nearly correctly as 3.14164075 . . . and in doing so had discovered the first infinite factorial series, which was luckily convergent. About the same time Adrian van Roomen calculated the value of π, by the old method of increasing the number of sides of an inscribed or circumscribed polygon, correctly to 17 decimal places, and a little later Ludolph van Ceulen calculated it correctly to 35 decimal places.

Among the other curves then investigated the one most discussed was the cycloid, the curve described by a point on a circle as the circle rolls along a straight line. Galileo had guessed that the area bounded by the cycloid and its base is three times that of the describing circle, but he could not prove it. This was done after his death by his disciple Torricelli and by the French mathematician Roberval. This triumph gave rise to one of those unhappy quarrels more characteristic of that time than of our own. Men did not then realize how common it is for two or more thinkers to make the same discovery at the same time. Moreover, in that age, when new truth was often communicated by letters circulated in manuscript, it was difficult to establish priority. The quarrel once started usually developed into an international affair, the French against the Italians and

(when Newton and Leibniz disputed) the English against
the Germans. Sometimes the accusation of plagiarism was
justified, but in no case less so than in the instance of
the cycloid, which attained great notoriety.

Among the peculiarities of sixteenth-century science
which have fallen into disuse was the habit of scholars
of proposing tasks to each other, either on a wager or for
a prize. Pascal took advantage of this custom to give a
wide publicity to the imagined grievance of the French
against Torricelli. In June, 1658, he offered a prize, anonymously, for the quadrature of parts of the cycloid; the
papers were to be in by October 1, and the judges were
to be Carcavy and Roberval. As the calendar then differed
by eleven days in England and France, and as there was
misunderstanding as to whether the competing papers must
have been received in Paris by the set date, or must merely
have been sent by this time, an acrimonious dispute between
the French judges and some English competitors followed,
though in the end the papers of Wallis and Wren were admitted. On November 25, 1658, the judges announced that
no one had won the prize and that only two proposed solutions, that of Wallis and that of Lalouvère, were worth
criticizing. The unhappy contest seemed to bring out the
worst side of all the competitors, for when Wallis later
published his paper, as the one submitted, he altered and
improved it. Accusations of unfairness and deceit were
made on both sides. In January 1659 Pascal published his
History of the Cycloid [1] under the pseudonym Amos Det-
tonville, in which he attributed the invention of the cycloid
to Mersenne and its quadrature to Roberval, in which he
accused Torricelli of plagiarism, and in which he added
some ugly and inaccurate charges against other scholars.
Replies and recriminations followed.

Among curves the conic sections have since antiquity
excited the interest of mathematicians. New truths were
added to the doctrine of them by the genius of Kepler,
who coined the word "focus" (suggested by the optical

[1] *Histoire de la Roulette, Œuvres* viii, 179ff.

properties of elliptical lenses) and who showed that the ellipse, the hyperbola and the parabola have each two foci, but that one focus of the parabola is "blind" or invisible, because at an infinite distance.

The idea of the infinite in geometry was fruitfully developed by Girard Desargues (1593-1662), an architect of Lyons. So remote were his ideas from those entertained by his contemporaries that all of them, except Pascal and Fermat, thought him crazy; these two and posterity recognized his genius. Following the suggestions of Kepler he showed that parallel lines might be supposed to meet in infinity, that a cylinder might be regarded as a cone with

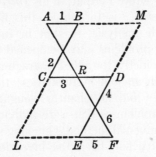

FIG. 3.—Pascal's Mystic Hexagram.

its vertex at infinity, and so on. His most original work, called *A First Sketch of a Method for understanding what happens when a Cone meets a Plane,* though published in 1639, has survived only in a manuscript copy by De La Hire. In it he showed that all conic sections may be regarded as circles seen askew, *i.e.* as projections of a circle. All properties of the conic sections may be deduced from this conception.

Pascal who, like the poet, precociously lisped in numbers, composed at the age of sixteen a treatise on conic sections. Notwithstanding its genius it was never published in full. The manuscript fell into the hands of Leibniz nearly forty years later, and for most of it we must rely on his account. Aside from Pascal's demonstration that a plane may inter-sect a cone in such ways as to form a point, a straight line, an angle, a circle, an ellipse, a parabola, or a hyperbola, and that all of these may be regarded as conic sections, his most original contribution was his discovery of the "mystic hexagram" (reproduced in Figure 3), and of the "theorem of Pascal" stating that if this hexagram is inscribed in any conic section the three points of intersection of the opposite sides are always in a straight line. From this theorem he claimed to have derived more than 400 corollaries.

6. ANALYTICAL GEOMETRY.

"My purpose," wrote Fermat, in his *Introduction to Plane and Solid Geometry*, "is to subject this branch of knowledge to a suitable analysis, so that in future a universal approach to such problems may be opened." In these words he expressed succinctly the chief characteristic of modern, as contrasted with ancient mathematics; the ancient sages, except Archimedes and Diophantus, sought the solution of each particular problem as if it were individual, the modern thinker seeks a universal method. One long step in the direction of universality had been the invention of algebra, a second stride in the same direction was the invention of analytical geometry. For this the main credit must go to Descartes, though Fermat independently seized and developed many of the new methods.

Nor was the idea the result of happy chance. So interwoven was it with the whole fabric of Descartes' thought that the publication of the *Geometry* as a part of the great philosophical *Discourse on Method* (1637) was natural and right. The very note of Descartes' mind and the key to the whole Cartesian system was the striving for the highest generality, for a perfectly universal method of thinking. In mathematics his idea, confided to his friend Beekman as early as 1619, was of a classification of all questions concerning quantity into a single, all-embracing science. Before his time geometry had been but an ensemble of diverse problems relating to continuous quantity; he first tried to classify all possible sorts of problems in it, and to find for each class general and exhaustive methods of solution. His success was great enough to justify his proud assertion that his geometry was as far beyond that of his predecessors as the rhetoric of Cicero was beyond the ABC of children.[1]

His first and most fruitful thought was that all problems of geometry can be given an algebraic interpretation, and every problem of algebra a geometric interpretation. In the earlier part of his *Discourse on Method* he criticized the older geometry as so bound by figures that it fatigued the imagination, and the older algebra as so subject to ciphers and to empirical rules that it had become an art to be mastered rather than a science to be cultivated. Resolved to take the best in each branch in order to correct the faults of the other, he found that he could represent any problem both by lines and by ciphers.[2]

The first of the three books into which the *Geometry* is divided treats simple figures the construction of which requires only straight lines and circles. Book II proceeds to the consideration of curves, of which some are very complicated, such as the conchoid of Nicomedes, the snail-shell (limaçon) of Pascal, the bow-knot (lemniscate), the cycloid, the epicycloid, the hypocycloid, and the trochoid. All of them, however, Descartes resolved into a series of algebraic equations.

The third book of the *Geometry* is on solids and super-solids—*i.e.* on the construction of problems in dimensions higher than the second. As Descartes showed that solid constructions, too, had their equations, he felt that he had theoretically solved, because he had classified, all problems in geometry. He demanded that all curves should be designated by the degree of their equation; for thus the problems connected with them could be most easily solved.

[1] *Œuvres*, i, 478.
[2] *Ibid.*, vi, 17ff.

CHAPTER V

GEOGRAPHY, BIOLOGY, ANATOMY

I. GEOGRAPHY

While, during the sixteenth and seventeenth centuries, astronomy and physics were not only collecting many new facts but were also colligating them in brilliant and daring generalizations, the other natural sciences, flooded with a wealth of fresh materials, were able to formulate only one new hypothesis of the highest importance, that of the circulation of the blood. But of the success of geography, biology, zoology, botany, and anatomy in accumulating and tabulating data there can be no doubt; nor of the fact that this success was due mainly to two factors, exploration and the microscope. What careful experiment and measurement had been to physics, *that* the voyages of daring travellers were to the sciences dealing with the surface of the earth and its inhabitants, human, animal, and vegetable; what the telescope was to astronomy, *that* the microscope proved to be to anatomy.

The heroic age of geographical discovery had, indeed, been the century preceding the year 1580. Before the voyages of Diaz, Columbus, Vasco da Gama, and Magellan, the world known to the European was only Europe itself, Northern Africa, Southern Asia and, vaguely, China, Japan, and Malaya. But within a single century following the discovery of the Cape of Good Hope (1486 or 1488) the Cimmerian darkness shrouding most of the globe had lifted and the continents and oceans as we know them had roughly taken their true shape, though with many a detail and some large unknown regions still to be filled in. If one looks at a map of the world drawn between 1580 and 1600, he will note that Europe is accurately known, and he will readily recognize the continents of North and South America and Africa, and most of the coast of Asia on the southern and eastern sides, as well as parts of the East and West Indies. True, the drawings of these lands and oceans are often grossly inaccurate, but the only parts of the globe left wholly blank are the northern part of Asia, the northwestern part of North America, and the region south of Africa, South America, and the East Indies. It was generally believed that this space was filled with a vast antarctic continent, of which the coasts were identified with Tierra del Fuego in one hemisphere and with Australia or New Guinea in the other.

Another century, and the knowledge of geography had again made great strides; the progress being due now rather to Dutch, English, and French explorers than to the Spanish and Portugese mariners of the earlier age. The knowledge acquired was in most cases intended to subserve commerce and the cost of obtaining it was defrayed by the great trading companies.

Thus, the determined efforts of Dutch and English to explore the North Polar regions was due to the desire to find a Northeast Passage over Asia or a Northwest Passage over America to the golden orient. In 1580 the English Muscovy Company sent out an expedition which got as far as, and a little beyond, Novaya Zemlya. Fourteen years later the Dutch dispatched Willem Barentszoon on the same errand. He not only pushed to the extreme north of Novaya Zemlya but wintered there—a feat hitherto unprecedented and not duplicated for a long time thereafter. Henry Hudson followed the same path before he made his more famous explorations on the northern coast of America, discovering the bay named after him, in which his mutinous crew turned him adrift in an open boat. He was followed by Baffin, who gave his name to a large tract of land, and by Luke Foxe, who published a map of the region and an account of it in a book quaintly entitled *North-West Fox, or Fox for the North-West Passage.*

The interior of North America was explored largely by the French fur traders and missionaries and by royal officers sent out to found a New France. Samuel de Champlain (1567-1635) sailed to the St. Lawrence in 1603; explored the Ottawa River, Lake Nipissing, Lake Huron, and the region to the south and east; while La Salle traced the course of the Mississippi and named the vast region west of it Louisiana in honor of his king.

As South America had been overrun by Spanish and Portuguese adventurers in the sixteenth century, less was done to map it in detail during the century following. The Jesuits, however, penetrated new regions about the Plata, in the southern part of Brazil, and in Peru. Nor were there lacking adventurers seeking El Dorado, and trying to duplicate the feats of Cortez and Pizarro; one of them, named Acuña, explored the Amazon, as had been done earlier.

So little was done to penetrate the interior of Africa that perhaps less was known of it to the men of the seventeenth century than to some of the then forgotten ancients. But Father Pedro Paez, taken prisoner in Abyssinia in 1588, made one important addition to knowledge when in 1613 he visited the Blue Nile and was thus enabled to give the true explanation of the Egyptian inundations, which had puzzled earlier generations, as due to excessive rains in the Abyssinian highlands during the wet season.

When, after the formation of the Dutch East India Company in 1602, the enterprising mariners of Holland and Zealand conquered the Spice Islands and established trading posts all over the East, exploration of the gigantic archipelago proceeded systematically. Ships of the Company as early as 1605 skirted the coasts of New Guinea and the northern coast of Australia. In 1616 Dirk Hartogszoon, taking a more southerly course than usual after leaving the Cape of Good Hope, came upon the island near the western coast of Australia still known as Dirk Hartog Island. But the greatest of the Dutch captains at this time was Abel Janszoon Tasman, who was born in 1603, entered the service of the Dutch East India Company in 1632 or

1633, and headed an expedition to the Far East in 1642. From the Cape he sailed to Mauritius and thence in a south-easterly direction until he struck the island now called after him Tasmania, but by him named Anthony Van Dieman's Land. Continuing eastward, he discovered New Zealand and other archipelagos, and eventually circumnavigated Australia, then called New Holland, thus proving that it was no part of the supposed Antarctic continent.

While the keels of the Dutch mariners were ploughing the seven seas, bold men, travelling on foot or on the backs of beasts of burden, were penetrating the vast and unknown interior of Asia. Some were adventurers, like Vincent Le Blanc and Thomas Coryat, who visited the far distant parts of the Orient in the footsteps of Marco Polo and often left accounts of their travels less authentic and valuable than his. Others were pioneers of the Muscovite power; a host of obscure officials and settlers who pushed the frontier farther and farther east, founding Tomsk in 1604, and thence marching on with such rapidity that by 1638 they had reached the sea at Okhotsk. Their efforts were supplemented by those fearless enthusiasts the Jesuits, men undaunted by any hardship or by any danger in their determination to plant the cross in every corner of the globe. As many of the missionaries were men of culture, intelligently interested in what they saw and capable of reporting it carefully, their relations are valuable geographical and ethnological documents. Among the most notable of these explorers of Asia were Fathers Benedict Goes and Father Antonio de Andrade, who both started, at different times, from Agra in India, where the Great Mogul then held his court. Father Goes went around the west end of the Himalayas to Turkistan and thence by caravan to China; Father Antonio crossed the Himalayas to Thibet. And others were stationed in China and generally throughout the East.

With considerable rapidity all this vast amount of new geographical information was incorporated into maps, which therefore exhibit, throughout the century, continually greater clarity, accuracy, and detail. Some of these maps were flat; some were globes. In this age flooded with new geographical knowledge a great advance in the art of cartography was also made. Particularly the doctrine of projection, or the method of representing a spherical surface on a flat page, was developed.

The most famous of the new projections tried was that still known by the name of the Flemish cartographer, Gerard Mercator (1512-94), who used it in an atlas published in 1569, though it had earlier been known to Spanish geographers. Mercator executed a famous survey of Flanders for military purposes and then proceeded to draw a map of the world, long lost but rediscovered in New York in 1878. This map, dated 1538, shows the influence of Ptolemy still dominant, but its successors improved upon it rapidly under the influence of enlarging knowledge.

Following in the footsteps of Mercator the German cartographer, Abraham Oertel, or Ortelius (1527-98) published an excellent and very popular atlas under the name *Theatrum Orbis Terrarum* in 1570. He sought to make "geography the eye of history," though it was not till Philip Clüver (1580-1622) made a careful comparison of ancient and modern descriptions of the earth that the foundations of historical geography were laid.

A superb *mappa mundi* in two hemispheres, based on the latest information of travellers for foreign parts and on the best surveys for European lands, was that drawn and engraved by Jodocus Hondius in 1611. The best charts and atlases of the time gave much information in addition to that of a strictly geographical nature. Thus, in 1592, Peter Planck published a great map, with the advertisement that in it

are set down more places, as well of both the Indies as Afrique, together with their longitudes and latitudes, than are to be found in either Mercator his map, or in any other modern map whatsoever. And this map doth show what riches, power, or commodities, or what kind of beasts both wild and tame, what plants, fruits, or mines any region hath, and what kinds of merchandise do come from every region. Also the diverse manners and qualities of the peoples, and to whom they are subject. Also who be the most mighty and greatest princes of the world.[1]

Even more information was given by a globe, called the Geocosmos, made and described by E. Weigel in 1672; this globe would show, as it revolved, the relative time of day and the season of the year in each locality, as well as its rainfall, prevailing winds, and volcanic eruptions. Indeed, geography was defined by Philip Clüver in 1624 as "the description of the whole earth so far as known to us"; and still more comprehensively by Bernhard Varenius in 1650 as "that part of applied mathematics which explains the state of the earth and of its parts depending on quantity, *viz.* its figure, place, magnitude, and motion, with the celestial phenomena, &c." If this definition includes matters now classified as astronomical, the author divides geography proper into three heads: 1, absolute, dealing with the form of the earth and the configuration of the land and water; 2, relative, dealing with latitude, longitude, and climate; and 3, comparative, describing the character of each particular region.

One of the last problems to be definitely solved was the exact size of the earth. It is said, indeed, that Eratosthenes in the third century B. C. had correctly calculated the circumference of the earth at about 25,000 miles, but this estimate had been reduced by his successor, Poseidonius, to about 18,000 miles, and this figure, much too small, had been accepted or but insufficiently increased by the geographers of the Renaissance. The standard text-book of astronomy, the *De Sphaera* of John Holywood (de Sacro Bosco) gave the circumference of the earth as 20,482 miles, and this figure is not far from the one probably accepted by Columbus and by other writers on the subject. If we except Eratosthenes, the first accurate measurement of a degree on a meridian of longitude was made by Jean Picard, a French savant, in 1669-70.[2] He began by measuring with great

[1] Stevenson, ii, 46.
[2] *Transactions of the Philosophical Society*, 1675, ii, 193.

care a straight line 5663 *toises* long between Sourdon and
Malvoisin in the north-west of France. Using this as a base,
by observation and triangulation, he calculated that there
were 57,060 *toises* to each degree. As a *toise* is something
over six feet, this works out to very nearly the true figure
of 69.5 miles. Picard's measurement had great importance
not only for geography but as giving Newton the necessary
datum for calculating the mass of the earth and the law of
gravitation.

The vast amount of new knowledge poured upon the
mind of Europe liberated and educated it to a totally fresh
evaluation of the earth, of society, and of institutions. The
discovery of the new world expanded the mind of Europe
as did the discovery of the new heavens by Copernicus and
Galileo. All knowledge had to be revised; all customs judged
by a novel standard.

The appetite of the masses for wonders fed eagerly
upon the tales of travellers. So vast were the numbers
of these, and so rapid their consumption, that they probably influenced the ideas of the masses more than any other
class of books. In England Richard Hakluyt published in
three stout folios (1588-1600) *The Principal Navigations,
Voyages, and Discoveries of the English Nation,* the prose
epic of the age and a vast storehouse of the history of
discovery and colonization. This was followed in 1625 by
a supplementary collection in four folios called *Purchas
his Pilgrims;* and in Germany a similar collection of *Travels
to the East and West Indies* was published in twenty-five
parts (1590-1634) by Dirk de Bry at Frankfort-on-the-
Main. While there was no similar collection in France,
there were in that tongue even more tales of voyages, and
there were many in Spanish and Italian. Some were wholly
fictitious, some embellished truth with fiction, but most of
them offered reasonably reliable information about the new
lands. They overemphasized the marvellous, they played,
by their descriptions of the nudity and the licentiousness
of savages, on the erotic appetites of their audience, and
they inclined to idealize the savage state as a Utopia of

liberty, toleration, and happiness. And yet, though they were read largely to satisfy other passions than the thirst for knowledge, they contributed enormously to educate and to enlighten public opinion.

They did this in various ways. In the first place the sheer wonder of the new discoveries inflamed the imagination of Europe with curiosity and awe and with a sense of glorious achievement. Though Rabelais satirized the tales of travellers in the allegory of Ouy-dire and his museum of incredible monsters, nevertheless he drew heavily upon the explorers to give color and substance to the voyages of Pantagruel. For those who could not read, elaborate pageants with exhibitions of American Indians or with actors dressed—or rather undressed—to imitate them displayed the wonders of the new world. After 1550 the literature of all Europe was filled with descriptions of or allusions to the new world. Tasso projected an epic on the discovery of America and, though he did not write it, introduced an episode on the same subject into his *Jerusalem*. His contemporary, Tommaso Stigliani, also planned such an epic but did not write it. The theater in both England and Spain celebrated the most remarkable of the adventures in exploration. Spenser alluded with awe to the many great regions lately made known, to the Orinoco and the Amazon, to Peru and "fruitfulest Virginia." Bacon wrote: "In our time many parts of the New World and all the limits of the Old World have been made known, and our stock of experience has increased to an infinite amount." In like tone Montaigne marvelled that:

Our world has just discovered a new world (and who will assure us that it is the last of its brothers since hitherto the demons and sibyls have been ignorant of this one?) a world as large and as well furnished as the old, but so young and childlike that we are still teaching it its A B C.

What most interested the average reader, as well as the poet and philosopher, were the descriptions of the outlandish and strange customs of the savages. There were two distinct schools of writers, those who represented the savage life as nasty, brutish and short, and those who idealized it as idyllic and utopian. The Jesuits who evangelized the Indians in Canada or in Paraguay often described their life as miserable, burdened with care and surrounded with terrors, their talk "such as swine and dogs would use," their morals as shocking, and their religion as devil-worship. In like manner some English settlers depicted the Indians as "a bad people, having little of humanity but the shape, ignorant of civility, of arts, of religion, and more brutish than the beasts they hunt, . . . captivated unto Satan's tyranny in foolish piety and bloody wickedness."

But this tone was on the whole exceptional. The majority of travellers who wrote authentic accounts of real journeys, and also the large number of pseudo-travellers who wrote romances about fictitious voyages, depicted the life of the savage as easy, without care, free, happy, innocent, and good. It is impossible to say when this idealization of the Noble Savage, which reached its climax in the eighteenth century, began. Certainly it can be found not only in the first explorers, in Las Casas, and in Pigafetta, and in Columbus, but in medieval writers, in Marco Polo and Mandeville, and in the classics. Does not Tacitus idealize the Germans, and Homer praise the "blameless Æthiopians"? In fact, the happiness of the simple life of nature as contrasted with the burdens and corruptions of civilization seems to be taken for granted in all ages, especially by satirists and moralists eager to read a lesson to their compatriots, or by the oppressed and weary longing to find in imaginary utopias a compensation for felt oppressions and miseries.

This tendency to idealize the remote and unknown takes different forms in different ages. In the sixteenth and two following centuries, it took the form naturally suggested by explorations of the new-found lands. Jacques Bouton in 1540 wrote that the Caribs of Martinique "lived at their ease in great leisure, entirely free to do or to say anything." Pigafetta, the companion of Magellan, informed the world that the Brazilian Indians "live by natural instinct, attain the age of 125 or 140 years, go naked, value conjugal fidelity, and are handsome, simple, and good." Paul Boyer wrote in 1644 that the Caribs "did not know what extortion, bribery and brigandage were; had no avarice, no covetousness, no calumny, no quarrels, no lawsuits, no legal pettifogging, no wantonness, no mendicancy, and not a scrap of lust." "We may call them barbarians," opined Montaigne, "judging them by the ideal rule of reason, but not judging them by ourselves, for we surpass them in every barbarity. Their war is as generous and noble as this human malady can ever be."

Not only was the idyllically happy and innocent life of the savages sung by Ronsard and by Jodelle and by many other poets, but political philosophers began to place in some new-found island the ideal state. Sir Thomas More's *Utopia* was but the first of many utopias to picture a perfect society somewhere in America or in the islands of the west. Indeed, until Galileo's telescope provided in the moon a still more remote situation for imaginary cities, the favorite place for such commonwealths was in America or in the Pacific Ocean. Presently men began to compare their own vices and miseries with the supposed happiness and virtue of the children of nature, and then to wonder what advantages their boasted civilization, culture, and religion had given them. There were strange searchings of heart as to the validity of the ancient traditions in laws, cults, and morals.

When colonies began to be planted, momentous problems in international law and in morals were raised. The right of Europeans to seize the new lands, to expel their inhabitants or to reduce them to slavery, was hotly debated. The use and profit of colonies was at first discussed and then proved by experiment. And when colonies had been planted they began to figure in the imagination of Europe as refuges for the oppressed and as ideal states redressing all the wrongs of an effete civilization. Even at this early date America became the land of hope and of opportunity. It appeared to the English settler as "the goodliest and most

pleasing territory in the world," and to the Dutch poet as
a second paradise:

> This is the land where milk and honey flows,
> This is the land where every sweet herb grows,
> This is the place where Aaron's rod now blows,
>   For this is Eden.[1]

If New Amsterdam was thus painted in the colors of
Eden, Virginia soon appeared portrayed in the tints of the
Earthly Paradise and New England with the epithets appropriate to Zion. And the colonists, while long cherishing
a love for the mother country, came to love their new
land far more dearly and, as men always do, to beautify
their own life with visions of ideal worth. For no mean purpose, they were sure, "God had sifted a whole nation with
choice seed with which to sow the wilderness."

2. ZOOLOGY AND BOTANY

From the newly found lands travellers brought back not
only knowledge of the configuration of the earth but descriptions of new flora and fauna, and often specimens of them.
From his first voyage to America Columbus fetched the
plumage of gorgeous birds as a gift to Queen Isabella. Many
questions were raised by the new facts, and there was much
anxious thought over such vital problems as whether all
these hitherto unknown species could have got into Noah's
ark, and whether each hemisphere had its own Adam and
Eve, and what to think of Aristotle and Pliny now that their
knowledge was shown to be so limited.

But there was more in the biological researches of the
sixteenth and seventeenth centuries than the incorporation
of new species into the old categories. There was an endeavor here as in other sciences to get rid of ancient superstitions and to see facts with clear eyes. Only those who
know the bestiaries of the Middle Ages can appreciate the

---

[1] A poem on New Amsterdam, 1659, printed in Vondel's *Lucifer*, transl.
by L. C. Van Noppen, 1898, preface, p. 23.

advance made by men who, uninspired and simple-minded as they seem to later generations, really tried to get accurate descriptions and pictures of the animals and plants referred to, and to study them with the desire primarily to know what they were like. For the great change was just this, the change from a moralistic to a scientific interest. The medievals cared not a whit to know anything about animals and plants for the sake of curiosity; they wanted to find in them something useful to the body or something profitable to the soul. They wanted folklore and they abhorred experiment. Besides including a large number of mythical beasts—dragons, griffins, cockatrices, basilisks, mantichoras, and phoenixes—in their menagerie, they had much to tell of the stag whose blood would dissolve pearls, of the lion born dead and coming to life after three days as a symbol of Christ, of the albatross feeding its young on its blood as a symbol of the eucharist, of the pelican that kills its young and then brings them to life with its blood as a symbol of redemption, and of the beaver that bites off its testicles when hard pressed by the hunter in order to give a practical lesson in the value of chastity to the sinner beset by that great hunter, the devil!

Compared with such legends the works of the later period were rational and scientific. They were, however, not entirely free from old superstitions, and they were encyclopaedic in scope rather than happy in classification. No general law of biological importance was discovered; the new facts were crammed into the old and faulty schemes of ancient classifiers. But there was a real and successful effort to get facts, and also to pay more attention to anatomy. Knowledge was thus deepened as well as broadened, even though it still suffered from subjection to teleological views, as in making the human body the standard to which all other types were referred, and in treating each special adaptation of a creature to its environment as a revelation of divine omniscience. There was no idea of morphological law, or of the necessary connection between the structure of an animal and its habits.

Of the many men who, about the middle of the sixteenth century, compiled Plinian encyclopaedias of zoology, only a few can be mentioned, or need be, for they were all much alike in method and results. Edward Wotton, a London physician and Aristotelian, published a work in ten books, *On the Differences of Animals,* in Latin, in 1552. His classification is that of Aristotle, into blooded and bloodless animals—two orders roughly corresponding to vertebrates and invertebrates. The former he divided into viviparous quadrupeds, reptiles, birds, and fish. Birds he subdivided into birds with toes, birds of prey, flying waterfowl, and wading water-fowl, including the ostrich in the last group.

Still more uncritical was Olaus Magnus, the Swedish Reformer, who wrote a *History of Northern Species* in 1555 in order to show that the fabulous animals of ancient writers had been rediscovered in the new world. To him we owe a romantic account of the glutton (or wolverine) and its incredible voracity, of a sea-serpent a mile and a half long (if German miles are meant its length would be seven of our miles), and of the octopus or giant squid so large that

> The pilot of some small night-foundered skiff,
> Deeming some island, oft, as seamen tell,
> With fixed anchor in his scaly rind,
> Moors by his side under the lee.[1]

The best of all the encyclopaedists was Conrad Gesner of Zürich (1516-65), who was given the name of "the German Pliny," though he far surpassed the Roman in knowledge and in thought. Educated at home, in Bourges, and at Paris, he spent most of his life teaching school in his native town, and writing numerous and voluminous works. Among these was a *Universal Dictionary* of ancient and modern

---

[1] It was from Olaus Magnus that Milton borrowed this description of the leviathan to which he compares Satan, in *Paradise Lost,* i, 201 ff. But the story of the whale mistaken for an island goes back to a bestiary of 1210.

biography, a work called *Pandects,* though it treated of grammar, dialectic, rhetoric, astrology, and geography as well as of jurisprudence, some theological tracts, and a work on language called *Mithridates.* But his best works were his *Catalogue of Plants* and his *History of Animals,* which latter appeared in five volumes (1551-87). In preparation for it he spent endless pains, travelling to see the animals, corresponding with learned men, reading widely, and searching for the best pictures as illustrations. Most of these were not original; one or two of the best were taken from Dürer, and some from books of travel. His description of each animal, which varies in length from a few pages to several hundred, is divided into eight parts; 1, the name of the animal in Hebrew, Arabic, Chaldee, Persian, Greek, Latin, Italian, Spanish, French, English, German, and Flemish; 2, the region where it is found and its appearance; 3, its actions including its voice, senses, food, sleep, diseases, method of reproducing and rearing its young, its health, and its dreams; 4, its habits and instincts; 5, its uses in hunting, drawing or carrying, doing tricks, and predicting the weather; 6, its use as food; 7, its use as medicine; 8, literary allusions to it and fables and proverbs about it —many of these last from Erasmus's *Adages.* So much useful information was given in this compilation that Cuvier called it the basis of modern zoology. That Gesner still included the bat among birds and the hippopotamus among fishes (or aquatic animals) rather proves the difficulties of classification at that time than the author's ignorance. He knew well that both the bat and hippopotamus are mammals, but he regarded their habitat, in the air and in the water respectively, as better criteria for classification than their anatomy.

After Gesner, the flood of knowledge from the new lands swelled into a larger tide and became accessible to scholars in the establishment of menageries in various European cities. Charles Clusius of Arras published *Ten Books of Exotic Wonders* describing the American humming birds, the cassowary, the dodo, and various strange beasts not recognizable from his data. José d'Acosta, a missionary to Peru, published a much read *History of the Indies* in 1590, in which he described the huge fossil bones of "Patagonian giants," and many species of living animals. The expedition best equipped for scientific exploration of the New World was that sent by Prince John Maurice of Nassau to Brazil in 1637. The naturalists in it, George Marcgrave, Willem Piso, and Jan de Laet, collected much information on humming birds, tapirs, llamas, and other exotic forms.

The exploration of the Far East also redounded to the benefit of science. Jakob Bontius of Amsterdam, who visited the East Indies 1627-31, brought back descriptions of the Javan rhinoceros, tiger, porcupine, and orang-outang—this last illustrated by a picture of a human female covered with hair. He also told of the amphisbaena, or two-headed snake, and gave a picture of it. How difficult, in fact, it was for Europeans to discriminate the true from the false in travellers' tales, is shown by two articles contributed to the *Journal des Savants* in 1674 and 1677, both purporting to be sober narratives of facts. One of them describes a unicorn—not a rhinoceros but the heraldic beast with a horn in the middle of its forehead—and the other tells of a tree with leaves which, when shed, walk around like butterflies. This error was probably based on the deceptive appearance of a flock of monarch butterflies during migration.

Ornithology and ichthyology were both advanced by Pierre Belon, who published a Latin work *On Aquatic Animals* in 1553, and a French work entitled, *History of the Nature of Birds,* with descriptions of them and their true portraits drawn from life in 1555. He classified birds into seven genera, and usually rejected fables about them. Neither he nor any of his contemporaries understood the migration of birds, which were thought to spend the winter hiding in holes, or sleeping under water. All aquatic animals—whales, seals, crustacea, molluscs, actiniae, and even the beaver and the hippopotamus—were then grouped together with fishes.

Insects were less understood before 1685 than were the

larger animals. About 1590 Thomas Mouffet (1553-1604) compiled from the previous works of Gesner, Penny, and others, and from his own observation, a work which he called *The Theater of Insects or of the smallest Animals* (*Theatrum insectorum sive minorum animalium*) which was not published until 1634, long after his death. In it he included the first known picture of an American butterfly— the Tiger Swallowtail—which he obtained from an explorer named White; in it he also described an insect named pyrigonum which can live in fire, in order to draw the conclusion that one must wonder at God's power in subjecting the fiercest element to the weakest animal.

Entomology as a science was really founded by Jan Swammerdam (1637-80), the son of an apothecary of Amsterdam, educated at Leyden, an intense, stubborn man and a devoted student of nature. His *General History of Insects* was published after his death in Latin (1685), and still later (1737) in much fuller form in Dutch and Latin as *The Bible of Nature*.[1] He showed that insects commonly pass through distinct stages from caterpillar or maggot to pupa and from pupa to the perfect form, and he classified them according to the rapidity and extent of their metamorphosis. With remarkable acumen he compared the insect metamorphosis to the change of tadpole into frog and to the changes observable in the human foetus, which is born of an egg and goes through the worm stage.

If biology was continually enriched and corrected by the study of the known orders of animals and plants, it was enormously extended by the discovery of those microscopic creatures later to be called protozoa, and of the still more minute organisms now known as bacteria. Both forms were discovered, or at least both were first carefully described, by Antony van Leeuwenhoek; the protozoa in 1673, the bacteria ten years later. Born of a good Delft family, in 1632, but not much schooled, he held various minor offices in his native city, while his independent means en-

---

[1] *Bybel der naturae* 2 v. Leyden, 1737-38; the Cornell Library also has the 1685 edition.

abled him to pursue scientific work. Though desultory and unsystematic, his observations and reports are interesting and careful. Most of his work appeared in the *Philosophical Transactions* of the English Royal Society, of which he was made Fellow in 1680. To this journal he contributed 125 papers, as well as 27 to the French Academy of Sciences, which elected him as corresponding member in 1697. He died in 1723.

In an early article in the *Transactions* he described the animalcula or living atoms "ten thousand times smaller than those drawn by Mr. Swammerdam, called water lice." These animalcula he discovered in rain water which had stood for some days in a barrel painted with oil on the inside. They are depicted as transparent balls which now and then put out horns and which move by wiggling a tail three times as long as their diameter. He later saw other forms of minute life in snow water, sea water, and in water in which pepper had been soaked and in the scrapings from his teeth. He estimated the size of these animalcula at one one-hundredth the diameter of a grain of coarse sand, and he described many of them so accurately that they can easily be recognized today.

Turning from zoology to botany we find much the same kind of advance made in the sixteenth and seventeenth century. Here, too, the moderns began by taking most of their ideas from the ancients, and were often misled into assuming that their masters had practically exhausted the field, had identified all existing plants and had learned all that it was possible to know about their structure. Even in the Middle Ages, however, there had been a little botanical investigation, chiefly with the purpose of ascertaining the medicinal qualities of plants and thus enriching the pharmacopoeia. The botanists of the Renaissance called the "herbalists" did excellent field work in observing and cataloguing the plants of Northern Europe, some of which, they found, were unknown to the ancient authors. Then came the flood of new species from beyond seas; then the attempt at classification, though this was not the work of one man so much as the inevitable conclusion of the observations of the affinities of plants made by many men; and finally came the deepening and broadening of knowledge due to the discovery of plant structure by the microscope.

Among the first to describe plants extensively from his own observations were Leonard Fuchs, whose *History of Stirpes* (*Historia Stirpium*, 1542) did much to clarify botanical terminology; the Englishman, William Turner, whose *New Herbal* appeared in 1551, and Conrad Gesner who published a *Catalogue of Plants* in 1542. In this he described more than five hundred plants not known to the ancients, grew many of them in his garden, and tested their medicinal qualities by eating them and rubbing them on his skin.

Work of a more thoughtful quality was done by Andrea Cesalpino (1519-1603), a professor at Pisa and physician to Pope Clement VIII. In his work *On Plants* (1583) he improved the system of classification. Whereas his predecessors had relied for classification entirely on the general appearance of the plants, Cesalpino tried to find a truer criterion in the development of seed and fruit. Though he wrote that he sought "those similarities and dissimilarities of form which are essential and not those which are merely accidental," he kept to the older division of plants into two great orders, trees and herbs. He still had the metaphysical notion that species, genera, and families of plants owe their resemblances to conformity to a Platonic archetype or idea; and he still believed in the spontaneous generation of plants. Like all his contemporaries he failed to recognize the sexuality of plants, and like them he wasted much time in discussing the seat of the plant's soul, or vital principle, which he found in the pith. With much insight, however, he recognized in the corolla, calyx, and cotyledons metamorphosed leaves.

The foundation of vegetable anatomy was laid by Robert Hooke, the discoverer of the cellular structure of plants. Hooke (1635-1703), the son of an English clergyman, though weak and sickly in body, burned to distinguish himself. Though he often claimed a priority for his own discoveries which is due to others, he occupied an important place in seventeenth-century science as an officer of the Royal Society and as the author of *Micrographia,* or some physiological descriptions of minute bodies, made by magnifying glasses, in 1667. In this he showed, among other things, that the structure of cork, of charcoal, and of other vegetable tissue, is cellular; indeed, he invented the name "cell" to designate the minute grains which he recognized as tiny hollow boxes. He estimated the number of cells in a cubic inch of cork as 1,200,000,000.

A further advance in plant anatomy was made by Marcello Malpighi, a modest, quiet, peaceful, and industrious professor of medicine at the University of Bologna. In 1668 he was made a Fellow of the English Royal Society, after having published some researches in its *Transactions.* His works on the *Anatomy of Plants* show that he was one of the first to discern the sexuality of plants, and also that he recognized the sack-like structure of the fibre. Moreover, he advanced the first good theory of the nutrition of plants, especially in comparing the function of the leaves to that of the lungs of animals.

3. ANATOMY AND MEDICINE

All biological studies were immensely enriched and deepened by the more careful cultivation of anatomy that began in the sixteenth century. Even before the application of the microscope the dissecting knife corrected and amplified knowledge to a surprising degree. Here, again, the extent of the advance made in the sixteenth century can only be appreciated by one in some degree acquainted with the anatomical work of the Middle Ages. The illustrations to books of medieval medicine, intended to represent the internal organs of the body, were presumably based on what someone—Aristotle or Galen—had once seen, but in the course of ages they had become so highly conventionalized and so remote from life that they look as if they were intended for the internal workings of wooden soldiers.

The first to make careful studies and good new drawings in large quantities was Leonardo da Vinci (1452-1519). With great pains in minute observation and with high artistic talent, he made hundreds of drawings of all the internal organs of man and woman and added to them some explanatory notes. But his work, beautiful as it is and valuable as it might have been, lay unpublished and practically unknown for four centuries, having been first revealed to the eyes of our own generation.

The first published work on anatomy in modern times that is of high value is therefore the treatise on *The Structure of the Human Body* by Andreas Vesalius (1514-64). This book, printed in the same year (1543) that saw the production of Copernicus' masterpiece, is a landmark in the history of science. The author, born in Brussels in 1514, educated as a physician at Louvain, Paris, and Padua, very early evinced an interest in the dissection of animals. When, after graduating as doctor of medicine at Padua in 1537, he was appointed professor there, he began teaching as a disciple of Galen, but innovated on the then customary method by making dissections before his students. When by this means he discovered many errors in Galen and other ancient writers, he conceived a scorn for them greater than they deserved, and proceeded to compose his own text-book of anatomy and to publish it at Basle. His illustrations, the works of minor contemporary artists, though not so good as and very different from the drawings of Leonardo— whom he has absurdly been accused of plagiarizing—were adequate, and his descriptions in the text far surpassed anything done up to that time. The preface lamented the evil state into which medicine had fallen since the "Gothic deluge," denounced the custom of leaving surgery to barbers, and emphasized the need for the study of anatomy as the foundation for the medical art. In seven books he treated the skeleton, the cartilage and muscles, the veins and arteries, the digestive and reproductive systems, the lungs, and the brain and head.

Soon after the publication of the *De Fabrica Corporis Humani* Vesalius was appointed court physician to Charles V. In 1564 he died while on a pilgrimage to the Holy Land.

Opposition to the new teaching developed among the adherents of the ancient masters. One man even tried to defend Galen by alleging that the human body had changed since Galen's time. If the thigh bones of modern men are straight and not curved as Galen had described them, this is due, he urged, to the modern invention of trousers. Vesalius was also attacked because he had demolished the old superstition, based on the biblical account of the creation of woman (Genesis ii, 21f) that the number of ribs is different on the two sides or in the two sexes.

But the work of Vesalius was followed up. Eustachio and Fallopia and others made important discoveries in the detail of human anatomy, and Volcher Coiter and Marco Aurelio Severino laid a good foundation for comparative morphology. Both of them, however, as well as Vesalius himself, were too much inclined to regard the human body as the standard and that of other animals as less perfect analogies or even imitations of the same.

The most important discovery in the field of anatomy was that of the circulation of the blood. Neither the ancients nor the medievals had any idea of this, or of the true function of the lungs. The first to notice and describe the *pulmonary* circulation of the blood was Michael Servetus, a Spanish physician burnt at the stake by Calvin for heresy in 1553. This talented and original, if somewhat eccentric, writer spoke thus in a work called *Errors concerning the Trinity* (1531): [1]

The vital spirit [*or*, the breath of life] takes its rise in the left ventricle of the heart, the lungs greatly helping to perfect it. It is a refined spirit, wrought by the force of heat, of a yel-

---

[1] Quoted in the *Encyclopedia Britannica*,[11] *s.v.* "Anatomy." My translation.

low color and of a fiery power, as though it were glowing with a purer blood, or were a vapor containing the substance of water, air, and fire. It is generated by the mixture, made in the lungs, of the inhaled air with a subtly wrought blood, which the right ventricle of the heart communicates. But this communication is made not, as commonly believed, through the middle portion of the heart; but with great artifice the subtle blood is drawn by a long duct through the lungs from the right ventricle of the heart. It is prepared by the lungs, made yellow, and poured from the arterial vein into the venous artery. Then in that venous artery it is purified of waste matter [*fuligo*, literally, *soot*] by the inhaling and exhaling of the air; and thus at last it is drawn from the left ventricle of the heart by means of the diastole, and is an apt substance to become the vital spirit. . . . Thus the spirit is conveyed from the left ventricle of the heart into the arteries of the whole body in such wise that what is finer seeks to go up to the higher parts where it is wrought still more, especially in a net-like fold at the base of the brain, where, from the vital fluid it begins to become animated, contributing to the proper reason of the soul.

It is worth while to quote this long passage in order to show just how much, and how little, is due to Servetus. With all his fantastic metaphysical ideas about the vital spirit,—ideas inherited directly from antiquity—it is plain that he had observed the circulation of the blood through the lungs, and no more. This idea was taken up and perhaps more clearly stated by two sixteenth-century anatomists, Realdo Colombo and Andrea Cesalpino.

But the discoverer of the circulation of the blood throughout the entire body was William Harvey of Folkstone (1578-1657). After taking his B.A. at Caius College, Cambridge, in 1597, he travelled on the Continent, studying medicine at Padua. Here he heard lectures by Fabricius of Acquapendente, and here he saw dissections in the anatomical theater, then new, and still standing today. His diploma of M.D., dated 1602, expresses high satisfaction with his work. Returning to England he was connected, as fellow and lecturer, with the College of Physicians, London, and

also with St. Bartholomew's Hospital. In this latter office
he gave free consultations under oath to prescribe such
medicines only "as would do the poor good," without regard
to the pecuniary profits of apothecaries.

As lecturer at the College of Physicians, he gave a course
on anatomy, the notes for which, dated 1616, have survived
and were published in 1886. In them he described the parts
of the body in Latin, with occasional digressions into the
vernacular to illustrate, with homely wit, some knotty
point. Thus, he compared the alimentary canal to the road
from St. Paul's to Leadenhall, one long and winding way
with many names; and he compared the shape of the stomach to a bagpipe. In these lectures he first spoke of the
circulation of the blood in the following terms:

It is proved by the structure of the heart that the blood is
perpetually transferred through the lungs into the aorta, as by
two clacks of a water-bellows [1] to raise water. It is proved by the
ligature that there is a transit of the blood from the arteries
to the veins; whereby it is demonstrated that a perpetual movement of the blood in a circle is brought about by the beat of the
heart.

In 1628 Harvey published his *Anatomical Dissertation
upon the Movement of the Heart*. The work, in Latin, was
printed, for some reason unknown to me, at Frankfort-on-
the-Main, and it was poorly printed. After a dedication to
Charles I, comparing the king to the heart of the body
politic, Harvey clearly and convincingly set forth his ideas
in seventeen chapters. He began with an apology for advancing new views against ancient authorities, and continued
by describing his methods of experiment, of which the most
important was the vivisection of animals, especially toads,
frogs, serpents, crabs, snails, and shell-fish. He also observed with a microscope the beating of the heart in the
"tail" of insects, and in the embryo of the chick. Immers-
ing the egg, divested of its shell, in tepid water, he could

[1] A water-bellows is a pump; a clack is a valve made to open one way
but not the other.

see, on the fourth or fifth day, a bloody point so small that it disappeared entirely on contraction and reappeared regularly on expansion; in this he recognized the rudiment of the already beating heart. Continuing with his main subject, he offered many proofs of the circulation of the blood, drawn partly from the anatomy of the heart and partly from the result of experiments with ligatures; whenever he bound an artery he found that the part nearer the heart filled with blood and the part away from it emptied, whereas exactly the opposite occurred in binding a vein. He concluded, therefore, that the fluid is sent out through the arteries and drawn back through the veins, making a continual movement "as it were, in a circle."

In 1618 Harvey had been appointed court physician and he remained a staunch Royalist throughout the Civil War. Indeed, he was near enough to the battle at Edgehill in 1642 to have watched it, but he became bored with it and turned for a more interesting occupation to reading a book. He travelled in Europe at various times.

In 1651 he published a second work, far inferior to the first, *On the Generation of Animals*. Of this it is sufficient to say that, though he beautifully described the development of the chick in the egg and of the embryo of deer (of which Charles I had allowed him to dissect a great number which he had hunted), he had the strangest lack of comprehension of the union of the male and female elements. He wrote: [1]

In the dog, rabbit, and several other animals, I have found nothing in the uterus for several days after intercourse.[2] I therefore regard it as demonstrated that after fertile intercourse . . . there are no remains in the uterus of the semen either of the male or of the female emitted during the act, and nothing produced by the mixture of the two fluids, as medical writers maintain.

[1] *Works*, 1847, 481.
[2] His observation was correct, though his deduction from it was wrong. The fertilized ovum does not descend to the uterus for several days after impregnation.

In highly speculative and completely mistaken vein he continued to set forth the idea that the male contributed only the "form without matter," impregnating the female by implanting in her a general immaterial idea, upon which she becomes the artificer of generation, producing a child much as an artist paints a picture or as a bird builds a nest of which she has no model.[1]

Harvey's discovery of the circulation of the blood, however, assured his eternal fame. It was hailed by his fellow-countryman and fellow-physician Sir Thomas Browne as greater than the finding of America; and by Joseph Glanvill, the clergyman of scientific tastes, as "the noblest discovery made by modern wit and industry in the economy of nature." There was, however, some reluctance in conservative quarters to accept it, until after Descartes has championed it. This philosopher, who saw in the circulation of the blood a valuable support to his mechanistic theory of the body, while recognizing some obligation to Harvey, tried, with his usual self-appreciation, to make good his own share to some credit in establishing so important a fact. His authority outweighed the adverse opinion of old-fashioned physicians who wrote against it.[2] In the next generation Molière could still satirize, in the person of Thomas Diafoirus, the ass who, studying medicine, has composed as his doctor's thesis, a book against the "circulateurs." Everywhere, however, Harvey won great renown. Cowley declared, in an ode to him:

> Harvey sought for Truth in Truth's own book,
> The creatures, which by God himself was writ;
> And wisely thought 't was fit,
> Not to read comments only upon it,
> But on th' original itself to look.

As Harvey had not seen the vessels by which the blood passed from arteries to veins, much remained to be done in filling out his work. Marcello Malpighi discovered the

---

[1] *Works*, 1847, p. 579. In this he followed Aristotle.
[2] Descartes: *Œuvres*, i, 263; ii, 501, 616; vi, 50; and Supplement vii.

capillary circulation in 1660-61 in a frog's lung. In one of his papers he described how he had seen under the microscope

> the blood forced and scattered by the pulse through the arteries into a network . . . of such a branching character that they proceed from the artery on one side and [are gathered] again into the vein on the other.

Malpighi also noticed the red corpuscles in the blood, which he took to be globules of fat.

Jan Swammerdam, who improved the technique of investigation by the invention of scissors so small and sharp that they could be used only under the microscope, and by making tubes as fine as bristles, also observed many anatomical facts and described them with an even greater accuracy than did Malpighi. He, too, observed the blood corpuscles (about 1667) and he tested experimentally the irritability of nerves and the response of muscles to stimuli.

Among the microscopists most of all was contributed, during this period, by Leeuwenhoek. In 1680, while examining under the magnifying glass the transparent tail of a tadpole he saw what he describes as the most delightful sight his eyes had ever beheld; namely, the vascular circulation:

> I saw not only that in many places the blood was conveyed through exceedingly minute vessels from the middle of the tail towards the edges, but I saw that each of the vessels had a curve or turning and carried the blood back towards the middle of the tail, in order to be conveyed again to the heart.

Leeuwenhoek also observed the corpuscles in the blood, and the cellular structure of hair, finger-nails, and other animal substances, and the spermatozoa in the semen of men, dogs, and other animals. What astonished him was the extraordinary number of the spermatozoa, of which he counted a thousand in a small quantity of man's semen, and estimated that in the milt of a single codfish there are

150,000,000,000 spermatozoa, or more than ten times the number of inhabitants that, as he reckoned, the earth would contain were all the land as thickly populated as the Netherlands. He quite rightly inferred that man develops from one of these little animalcula, though he imagined that he saw more than he really did of the likeness of the spermatozoon to the embryo about to be developed.

Until the latter half of the seventeenth century it was generally believed that living creatures, both animals and plants, are often generated "spontaneously" by slime, mud, and decaying flesh. When Shakespeare spoke of "the sun breeding maggots in dead dogs," [1] when Ambroise Paré,[2] the famous surgeon, described "big flies which had procreated themselves from the humidity of dead bodies and the heat of the sun," they but expressed the common belief. Some authors, indeed, went much further in the theory of spontaneous generation, as did Cardan who said that bees are bred from dead horses, hornets from dead oxen, and wasps from dead asses, and as did Thomas Mouffet, the entomologist who fancied that when bees are generated in the bodies of dead animals the king bee (as he called the queen) comes from the head, and the workers from the body.

The first experiments to test the theory were made by the Italian *littérateur*, Francesco Redi who, in a work *On the Generation of Insects* (1668), showed that no maggots are bred in meat from which flies have been kept. Even he, however, ascribed the generation of worms found in galls and other excrescences on plants to the soul of the plant. But, as Leeuwenhoek and other anatomists spoke against spontaneous generation, it came to be believed that there was probably no such thing.[3]

The benefit redounding to medicine from all this anatomical study was much less than one would naturally expect.

---

[1] *Hamlet,* II, ii, 201.
[2] F. M. Packard: *Life of A. Paré,* 1921, p. 243.
[3] See an article by the botanist Ray in *Philosophical Transactions,* 1671, i, 617.

The fact is that medicine failed to advance largely because it was still regarded as a trade to be learnt and as an art to be practiced for profit, rather than as a science to be cultivated for its own sake. It was common at that time for each successful physician to keep secret, or to sell for a high price, his methods, remedies, and instruments. Moreover, medicine was, to almost as great a degree as theology and law, crushed by the dead hand of the past. Throughout the sixteenth century there were furious, but fruitless, battles between the disciples of Hippocrates and Galen and the disciples of Avicenna and the Arabic writers. More because of the strong classical tendencies of the age than because of the merits of the question, the Greeks triumphed about 1550. But, as few more important questions had been decided than whether, in bleeding, a vein should be opened distant from the organ affected, as advocated by the Greeks, or near it, as maintained by the Arabians, the victory meant nothing for science. The few men, like Paracelsus, who tried to break the yoke of tradition and to found a new empirical school, were rather fantastic than sound in the original theories they advanced.

When, in the seventeenth century, new schools with scientific names arose, they were in fact founded less directly upon the work of scientists like Harvey than upon the metaphysics of Descartes and Gassendi. In overthrowing the authority of the Greeks and in substituting for it a metaphysics ostensibly allied with science, these philosophers caused the physicians of the following generation to look for a mechanical or chemical explanation of all natural phenomena, including those of disease. Thus there arose two new schools, the iatrochemical and the iatrophysical—this last also called by its extremists the iatromathematical— bitterly hostile to each other and yet equally helpless when confronted with a practical problem. The iatrochemists regarded physiological processes, particularly digestion, as fermentation; the iatrophysicists insisted that digestion is trituration and that all other bodily functions are mechanical in their nature. Too hasty generalization as to the cause of disease was accompanied by the advocacy of fantastic methods of treatment, also founded on supposed scientific analogies. Thus, Van Helmont insisted on the curative power of magnets.[1]

But in various respects the healthy influence of the experimental method made itself felt. Thomas Sydenham (1624-89), an eminent practitioner of London, rejected the *a priori* theories of the schools and relied solely on clinical observation. His theory, that disease, and especially fever, is nature's effort to expel morbific material from the system, had in it elements acceptable to later generations. In the meantime the teaching of medicine profited by the introduction of clinical instruction—an innovation due to Jan Heurnius of Leyden—and by the dissection, before pupils, of cadavers. The first permament theater intended for this purpose was built at Padua in 1594; and Rembrandt's famous "Lesson in Anatomy" showed Dr. Tulp demonstrating to his pupils the structure of the human body.

It is seductive, though perhaps fallacious, to see in some of the writers of this time an anticipation of the germ theory of disease. Girolamo Fracastoro of Verona in 1546 published a treatise on contagious diseases to prove that they are caused by living organisms endowed with the power of propagating themselves. His proof, in the lack of the microscope, is drawn from the striking fact that some diseases are carried by inanimate objects such as clothes, and that some are even infectious, through such articles, for a long time after they have been touched by the patient. A century later, in 1658, Athanasius Kircher, in a work called *An Investigation of the Plague* (*Scrutinium pestis*), stated that that disease, then endemic in Europe, was caused by minute "worms" which he had seen with magnifying lenses in the blood of sick persons. But, striking as are his words, his descriptions of these "worms" have led modern investigators to infer that what he really saw were not the bacilli of the disease, but pus-cells and rouleaux of blood corpuscles.

[1] *Opera,* 1707, pp. 700ff (written about 1650).

Among the various schools of the seventeenth century was one like that later called homeopathic, described by Milton in the preface to *Samson Agonistes* in these words:

In physic things of melancholy hue and quality are used against melancholy, sour against sour, salt to remove salt humors.

A certain practical advance was made by the introduction of new drugs, notably cinchona and ipecacuanha, from America.

Surgery perhaps advanced more rapidly than medicine during this period, though it still continued to be despised by regular physicians and to be practised by barbers and wandering charlatans. Nothing is more remarkable than the hatred shown by the regular physicians—Guy Patin, for example—for the apothecaries and surgeons who sometimes cured contrary to the rules patients who should rather have been allowed to die under the orthodox treatment. Throughout the seventeenth century there was fought a long battle by the surgeons for recognition by the University of Paris. But the utmost the barber-surgeons could obtain was a humble place subordinate to that of the physicians, with permission to attend lectures but not to give them nor to take medical degrees.

In excuse for this jealousy it must be remembered that surgery, in that day before antiseptics or anaesthetics, was extremely dangerous. A great improvement in method was made by a French barber-surgeon named Ambroise Paré, who got much practical experience in attending soldiers in the army. Besides inventing ingenious artificial limbs to take the place of those amputated, he improved the method of treating gunshot wounds. In order to prevent gangrene, wounds had hitherto been treated by something that must have been worse than death, the application to them of boiling oil. Paré found thorough cleansing of the wound with cool and emollient liquids far more effective. He also invented a better ligature to prevent hemorrhage. So slowly did medical knowledge spread in that day that the first mention of Paré's methods found in an English book dates nearly a century after he introduced them in France.

Among the other improvements in surgery deserving brief mention are the revival by Paré of the operation of podalic version in obstetrics, the introduction of the Cæsarian operation on living women by François Rousset, and a method of grafting flesh on injured parts attributed to Gaspare Tagliacozzi who first described it in 1597, though perhaps it had been performed by others some years earlier. Great interest was excited after 1650 by the transfusion of the blood, practised on animals by Desgabets and by Robert Boyle, and on human beings, as a method of treatment, by the French professor Denys in 1666. As some of the cases terminated fatally the operation was forbidden by the Parlement of Paris in 1668.

In popular estimation medicine was then ranked extremely low. Inveighing against it as more uncertain than the other arts, Montaigne,[1] according to his custom, played off the mutual contradictions of the doctors; they all differ, they all accuse each other of killing the patients and they are all, in this particular, and in this particular only, right. Three common practices of physicians, uroscopy, purging, and bleeding, were the butt of endless and not altogether undeserved sarcasm. The extravagant confidence in a naked-eye inspection of urine as a method of diagnosis is mildly satirized in a genre painting by Jan Steen,[2] and is mercilessly ridiculed by Molière.

This comedian, so sensitive to the foibles and vanities of every profession, and himself, as a consumptive, a sufferer from futile quackery, led a vendetta against the doctors in a series of plays as true to life as good caricatures ever are. In *L'Amour Médicin* he ranked medicine with flattery and alchemy as one of the three chief frauds practised upon men's credulity, and he exhibited the disagreement of the four doctors called in to treat Lucinde, and their common failure to discover her real malady. In his last play, *Le*

[1] *Essais*, II, xxvii.
[2] Now in the Corcoran Gallery, Washington.

Malade Imaginaire, he dealt a final savage blow at the doctors who had now, incensed by his sneers, become his professed enemies. "All the excellence of their art," he declared, "consists in a pompous rigmarole and in a special jargon which gives you words for things and promises for effects," and he proceeded to illustrate the truth of this censure by bringing on the stage the qualifying examination of a medical student, an examination conducted in dog Latin and in doggerel verse by the learned fools of the faculty. When one of them asks the cause and reason why opium puts one to sleep, the candidate, Thomas Diafoirus, makes the reply that has since attained a classic celebrity:

> Quia est in eo
> Virtus dormativa,
> Cujus est natura
> Sensus assoupire,[1]

whereupon the chorus of professors rapturously applaud:

> Bene, bene, bene, bene respondere;
> Dignus, dignus est intrare
> In nostro docto corpore,[2]

and continue to ask the candidate how to cure a number of diseases. No matter what the sickness is the young doctorandus has but one answer, held to be sufficient for all cases:

> Clysterium donare,
> Postea seignare,
> Ensuita purgare.[3]

[1] "Because there is in it a dormative virtue, the nature of which is to lull the senses."
[2] "A good, good, good, good reply; he is worthy, worthy to enter into our learned body."
[3] "Give an enema; then bleed; then give a cathartic."

CHAPTER VI

THE SCIENTIFIC REVOLUTION

I. THE PLACE OF SCIENCE IN SEVENTEENTH-CENTURY THOUGHT

The genius of seventeenth-century Europe brought forth many imperishable masterpieces in literature and art, subdued and colonized the other continents, and gave birth to liberty and popular government in the Netherlands, in England, and in North America. But the supreme glory of the seventeenth century—or, more accurately, of the hundred and fifty years beginning with Copernicus, Cardan, and Vesalius, and ending with Newton and Huygens—and the chief importance of that period in history, lies in its scientific achievements. Among all the brilliant discoveries of that age, none was more dazzling or ultimately more momentous than that of science itself. Not only did the scientific achievements of that epoch surpass all that previously had been done in the whole life of man upon earth, but these achievements now first began to teach men the power of the new instrument both in mastering and in understanding all things. Hitherto custom had been the sole guide, while religion, philosophy, literature, and art had been the chief intellectual preoccupations of men. Renascent in the sixteenth century, and vastly increasing in the seventeenth, science challenged and defeated other modes of thought and even the authority of custom itself. Naturally, the growth of a new mentality is gradual. There were some men who saw the vast import of the scientific revolution even then; there are some who do not see it even now. Among those to see it first were they whose eyesight was sharpened either by hatred and dread, or by love and enthusiasm; the churchmen who deprecated and opposed the revolution, and the scientists and thinkers who hailed and welcomed it. To the eyes of the masses and of their rulers the beginnings of the greatest revolution in history passed unnoticed, or at most furnished the matter for an hour's amusement or for some petty personal profit.

If one asks why it was that science should, just at this time, have taken so sudden and so vast a growth, the question, though infinitely intricate, can be partially answered. One must assume, as almost constant, the presence in Europe for many thousand years of a race gifted with intellectual curiosity and power. The genius of the Greeks in antiquity and the expanding mental capacities of the European races as a whole, may explain part, but only the smallest part, of the growth of science for a few centuries in ancient times, and again for the last few centuries. Changing conditions account for far more than do slow biological processes. The condition most favorable to the growth of science in the sixteenth and seventeenth centuries was the increasing number of men who were drawn into intellectual pursuits. Genius is like a fire; a single burning log will smoulder or go out; a heap of logs piled loosely together will flame fiercely. So it was that during the Middle Ages when anarchy prevailed, when communications were poor, and when books, the chief means of learning, were few, comparatively little was added to the sum of human knowledge. And that little, as it was in the tenth century, though it markedly increased in the twelfth and thirteenth, was less than it would have been but for the pessimistic, self-distrustful, other-worldly temper of the times.

But the establishment of strong governments, insuring at least domestic peace, the accumulation of wealth followed by the growth of a leisure class, the development of a secular, sanguine culture more eager to improve this world than anxious about the next, and above all, the invention of printing, making easier the storing, communication, and dissemination of knowledge, led naturally to the cultivation and hence to the advancement of science. The Renaissance

and the Reformation at first retarded and finally helped the
revolution. They harmed it provisionally by turning men's
thought and effort backward, to the classics or to theology;
they helped it, indirectly and finally, by breaking up many
of the medieval standards. Cloyed with barren imitations of
antiquity, sated with religious strife, men turned eagerly to
the new, fruitful, and generally safe paths of experiment and
of mathematics.

Once the ball had started rolling it gathered velocity
at a surprising rate. Every new discovery proved a key to
unlock a hundred doors. While some inventions, like the
telescope and microscope, improved the powers of vision,
others, like logarithms and the calculus, multiplied the
capacities of the mind, and all conspired together to furnish
not only better machinery for dealing with natural phenomena but an immense spiritual exaltation and mental
excitement, stimulating new efforts.

One can see a vast change in the temper of the educated
classes as the century rolls by. In the generation of Montaigne and Shakespeare science had little hold either upon
common affairs or upon the creative imagination. The
learned professions—medicine, building, the law, navigation
—were mastered as arts, not studied as sciences. The study
of political statistics had hardly begun. The greatest triumphs of the mind were then in the fields of art and letters.
The idea of natural law was absent from the popular mind.
But the generation of Newton and Huygens saw an enormous
change accomplished. There was then a distinct turn in the
direction of science, and above all a growing consciousness
of the achievements of the new instrument and of the possibilities of its future development.

This consciousness of the value of the new age can be
traced sporadically to the end of the sixteenth century when
Simon Stevin wrote that until 150 years ago men had lived
for nine hundred or a thousand years "like idiots or barbarians without letters or science," but that in the last century and a half they had discovered much in astronomy,

algebra, mathematics, and physics.[1] Pierre Bergeron began a *Treatise on Navigation* by pointing out that the last few centuries had discovered many things which had been unknown even to the ancients. Descartes argued that as science had given men the marine compass, printing, and the telescope, one might rely on it for continual improvement.[2]

Many generations have cherished the idea that they have at last arrived at a maturity or perfection unknown to their barbarous ancestors. In no age was this pride of achievement and consciousness of new glory stronger than in the seventeenth century. And this pride was founded not, as in the sixteenth century, on a religious revolution nor, as in the fifteenth, on a revival of learning, but on the new conquests of science.

Our century [wrote Campanella] has more history in its hundred years than had the whole world in the previous four thousand years; more books have been published in the last century than in the five thousand years before it; for it has profited by the recent inventions of typography, cannon, and the mariner's compass.[3]

Above all, Campanella urged elsewhere,[4] it is science that has given dignity to man, who is

a second god, the first God's own miracle, for man commands the depths, mounts to heaven without wings, counts its moving bodies and measures their nature. . . . He knows the nature of the stars . . . and determines their laws, like a god. He has given to paper the art of speech, and to brass he has given a tongue to tell time.

Like most of the philosophers of the seventeenth century Thomas Hobbes was deeply indebted to the new discoveries. Science, which he also called philosophy, he defined as "the knowledge of consequences and the dependence of one fact

[1] *Géographie*, Bk. i, def. 6, in *Œuvres*, 1634.
[2] *Œuvres*, ix, 309.
[3] *De Civitate Solis*, p. 459.
[4] Gardner: *Campanella*, p. 2.

upon another." Sciences he classified into natural and political, including in the former not only mathematics, physics, and astronomy, but also metaphysics (*philosophia prima*), ethics, poetry, rhetoric, and logic.[1] Astronomy, except for observations, he dated from Copernicus, physics ("natural philosophy or knowledge of the nature of motion") from Galileo, and human physiology from Harvey.[2]

Among other philosophers, Geulincx contrasted the rude and superstitious knowledge of the old writers with the sound, free and royal genius of the moderns who, by reason and experiment, have cut to the quick of nature.[3] Leibniz wrote: [4]

We have raised up a truly philosophical age, in which the deepest recesses of nature are laid open, in which splendid arts, noble aids to convenient living, a supply of innumerable instruments and machines, and even the hidden secrets of our bodies are discovered; not to mention the new light daily thrown upon antiquity.

Perhaps Leibniz was responsible for the declaration in the preface to the first volume of the *Acta Eruditorum* (1682) that the arts and sciences had now reached their zenith. Very similar was the opinion of Huygens who, after enumerating the discoveries of Galileo and others, continued:

What man, if he is not an absolute idiot, will not recognize the grandeur and importance of these discoveries? And what person initiated in philosophical studies will not see how brilliant a light this new knowledge has thrown upon our conceptions of nature and of the universe? Surely we should be grateful to the age in which we live for the knowledge of such important matters so recently acquired.[5]

Still more definitely in praise of the new instrument Roberval wrote [6] in 1647:

[1] *Leviathan, Works,* iii, 35, 72.
[2] *Elements of Philosophy,* 1655, *Works,* i, p. viii.
[3] *Quaestiones Quodlibeticae,* 1653, *Opera,* 1891, i, 73.
[4] *Sämtliche Schriften,* i, 30. (1669.)
[5] *Œuvres,* xiii, 438. (1685.)   [6] *Œuvres de Pascal,* ii, 49.

Logic can surprise or be surprised [in error]; moral philosophy changes, flatters, and wishes flattery, and is often reversed and, ruined by its enemies; but physics is all true though difficult to discover; it neither flatters us nor is capable of flattery; it annihilates chimaeras by its aspect alone as easily as light banishes shadows. . . . And mathematics has all the prerogatives of physics in being true, unchangeable, and invincible.

Robert Boyle wrote a defence of *The Usefulness of Natural Philosophy*,[1] which utility he found chiefly in the improvement of the mind and in the gratification of curiosity, but also in practical help and as a stimulus to devotion. Hitherto, he claimed, man had been like a spider in a palace, noting nothing of its architecture but only her own web, whereas now increased knowledge had begun to give man power and dominion over nature.

The international mission of science was expressed by Oldenburg in a letter to Huygens in these words:

I hope that in time all nations, even the less civilized, will embrace each other as dear comrades, and will join forces, both intellectual and material, to banish ignorance and to make true and useful philosophy regnant.

Otto von Guericke found in the contemplation of nature "the vestibule of celestial pleasure, the perennial jubilation of the mind, and the door of tranquillity."[2]

Joseph Glanvill, though otherwise remembered as a defender of the superstition of witchcraft, wrote several works on the advantages and glory of the sciences. In one of them, *Plus Ultra, or the Progress and Advancement of Science since the time of Aristotle* (1668), he championed the empirical method, the introduction of which he attributed to Bacon. In an *Essay on Modern Improvements of Useful Knowledge,* he opined that "no age hath been more happy in liberty of enquiry than this," and enumerated many discoveries made and steps taken from the invention of the compass to the institution of the Royal Society.

[1] *Works,* i, 1ff.   [2] *Opera,* Preface.

Though such eulogies of science might be quoted in large numbers, we must be content with one more, expressed with his usual felicity by Dryden, near the end of the seventeenth century:

> In these last hundred years . . . almost a new Nature has been revealed to us—more errors of the schools have been detected, more useful experiments in philosophy have been made, more noble secrets in optics, medicine, anatomy, and astronomy have been discovered than in all these doting and credulous ages from Aristotle to us.

Like all new ideas, that of the value of science spread from a narrow class to a wider and wider public. One can find, first in the poets and novelists, then in the rulers and nobles, and finally in the educated class as a whole, a growing enthusiasm for science until finally it came to be so much the vogue as to be affected even where it was not felt, and thus sometimes to make its professors ridiculous.

Compare the lack of interest in science and the total ignorance of it among the earliest and the latest poets of the period, and among those of the more advanced and of the more backward nations. In Shakespeare there are few allusions to scientific matters, and those few not very happy ones, as in the description of earthquakes as caused by a kind of terrestrial colic.[1] Hardly more felicitous are Spenser's references to atoms, or his allegory of the anatomy of the body.[2] In backward Germany popular science at this period remained folklore. Simplicissimus, in Grimmelshausen's famous novel, boasts of his knowledge of nature and to prove it tells how hens, partridges, swine, and bears eat plants as medicine, how storks give themselves enemas with their long bills, and how strangely cats conceive with pain but bring forth with pleasure.

But in Milton the number of the scientific allusions is only rivalled by the knowledge they reveal of the latest discoveries, particularly in astronomy and in geography.

[1] *Henry IV*, Part I, Act iii, Scene i.
[2] *Faery Queen*, Book ii, canto 9.

When the archangel Michael shows Adam the whole world,[1] or when Satan exhibits it to Christ,[2] a vast geographical prospect is unrolled before the eyes of the reader; and when Satan encircles the earth in his flight, his path is accurately traced on the latest maps.[3] And what interesting cosmical and chemical speculations are scattered throughout the great epic,[4] some of them doubtless echoes from antiquity, but others revealing an interest in the latest research! It is true that Milton, like the other deeply pious men of his time, subordinated science and all other matters to religion. Just as, in *Paradise Regained*, Jesus informs Satan that philosophy, art, and letters are useless, so in *Paradise Lost* Michael warns Adam to leave science alone and devote himself to higher things.[5] But the poet himself spent much of his life in the study of these denounced superfluities.

The fact is that by the time he penned his epics, the love of natural science, as Spratt wrote in 1667, was "so strongly aroused that there seemed to be nothing more in vogue throughout Europe." Science became fashionable; among its amateurs were many of high and of the highest station. The Grand Duke Ferdinand of Tuscany and his brother Leopold were fond of experimenting. That eccentric but intelligent queen, Christina of Sweden, corresponded with mathematicians and physicists. In France the Duke of Orléans, the brother of Louis XIV, had a laboratory "not," as Saint-Simon relates, "to make gold but to amuse himself with curious experiments." Prince Rupert, nephew of Charles I of England, dabbled in natural philosophy, and his cousin Charles II diverted himself in a "chymical elaboratory." Jan de Witt, Pensionary of Holland, not only patronized science, but invented chain-shot and wrote ably on statistics. It would be easy, but tedious, to add to this roster of royal

[1] *Paradise Lost*, xi, 388ff.
[2] *Paradise Regained*, iv, 44ff.
[3] *Paradise Lost*, ix, 62ff.
[4] The atomic theory, *Paradise Lost*, ii, 890ff; transmutation of metals, v, 439ff; creation vii, 322 to end; changes in the earth's axis due to the fall of man, x, 668ff.
[5] viii, 167ff.

names a long list of nobles who played with science and who occasionally, as in the case of Lord Brouncker, notably contributed to it.

Presently the passion for science spread throughout a much wider public. Evelyn the diarist was so much interested in physics that he proposed to found a retreat for persons engaged in research. Pepys, though he first learned the multiplication table when he was thirty, so diligently plied the microscope, the scotoscope (*camera obscura*), the dissecting knife, and the air-pump that finally he was elected President of the Royal Society.

In France, too, the educated were deeply interested in intellectual matters. Their republic of letters, like ancient Gaul, was divided into three parts: the literary province of Boileau; the philosophical and scientific province of Descartes, Gassendi, and Malebranche; and the historical, under Mabillon. Indeed, so necessary to the character of a gentleman did intellectual polish become, that when Monsieur Jourdain, the good bourgeois, aspires to enter a higher sphere than that in which he was born, the first thing he does is to hire a master to teach him logic and that science which treats of "the nature of the elements, metals, minerals, stones, plants, and animals, and the causes of meteors, the rainbow, meteorites, comets, lightning, thunder, rain, snow, hail, winds, and tornadoes." [1]

The ladies, too, became learned in these matters, and formed cliques, like the women's clubs of our own days, to enable those who were afraid to meet culture single-handed to hunt it in packs. With more zeal than knowledge they canvassed the latest views on the vacuum and the magnet, expressed their love for Descartes's vortices or for his "subtle matter," and announced important, if premature, discoveries, such as that of inhabitants of the moon. [2]

To meet the needs of this eager but ignorant public, books of popular science began to be written. Such was the treatise *On the Sphere* (*Della Sfera*) written in 1551 by

[1] Molière: *Le Bourgeois Gentilhomme*, II, vi.
[2] Molière: *Les Femmes Savantes*, III, ii.

Archbishop Alessandro Piccolomini of Siena in order to enlighten a lady. Similar in purpose and in method were the famous *Conversations on the Plurality of Worlds* published by Fontenelle in 1686. Such also was the book of *Mathematical Magic* written by John Wilkins in 1648. Such was Claude Gaspar Bachet de Méziriac's *Problèmes plaisants et délectables qui se font par les nombres,* published in 1612. Such was the work of the Jesuit Jean Leurichon, printed under the pseudonym of Van Etten in 1624, and called *Récréations Mathématiques,* a collection of ingenious problems on arithmetic, geometry, astrology, optics, telescopy, mechanics, and chemistry. It soon passed through seventeen French editions, and was translated into Dutch, German, and English.

Another French work, devoted partly to popular science, was that of Marin Mersenne entitled *Theological, physical, moral, and mathematical Questions; in which Every One will find Pleasure or Profit,* published in 1634. While it is true that this book denied the motion of the earth, the author yet imparted a good deal of valuable information.

Perhaps one of the best works on popular science published in English during this period was that of Sir Thomas Browne under the title *Pseudodoxia, or Vulgar Errors.* He set out to expose a large number of popular beliefs about nature, as that an elephant has no joints, and that the sight of a wolf strikes the beholder dumb. Incidentally, he communicated a good deal of scientific intelligence even where, as in allusions to the Copernican system and to the basilisk, he dared not come out squarely on the rational side of the question.

2. THE DEVELOPMENT OF SCIENTIFIC METHOD

Prior to the seventeenth century the word "science" in English, in Latin, and in the Romance languages, meant no more than "knowledge" in its general sense, and what is now called science was then known as "natural philosophy." But the more advanced thinkers, especially in France and

England, separated science from the larger and vaguer body of metaphysics and learning and began to give the word its modern significance. For, the word "science" acquired its modern connotation when it came to be felt that knowledge *par excellence,* man's truest and perhaps his only knowledge, is derived from the body of systematically collected, accurately observed and measured natural phenomena, colligated by general laws. The first author to use "science" in approximately this sense is perhaps Descartes; [1] usage confirmed and made this meaning more precise in the mouths of Pascal and his fellow workers; towards the end of the century the *Dictionary* of the French Academy defined "science" as "the certain and evident knowledge of things by their causes." Hardly before the eighteenth century did a similar change take place in the meaning of the English word, though Bacon's usage approximated it; and not until a still later period did the German "Wissenschaft" take the place of the older "Kunst."

The change in language records a change in thought not only as to the importance of science but as to its method and nature. Where ancient science had been largely metaphysical and speculative, modern science is empirical and objective. Ancient thinkers were obsessed with notions of form, substance, archetypes, and their mystic outgrowths; they were always either grubbing under ground to find out what made action act, or were soaring into the empyrean to glimpse the "idea" behind every class of phenomena. Modern science is content with observation and with the formulation of simple generalizations—those "laws of nature" of which Bacon said "we do not arbitrarily give them, but like faithful scribes we receive and write them down." [2] Galileo and others of his generation took science completely out of its metaphysical stage; never seeking final causes they were content with describing phenomena in their mutual relations. This is why modern science is so largely dependent on the development of experimental technique. Every improvement in the powers of observation yields a

[1] *Discours de la méthode, Œuvres,* vi, 18.   [2] *Prodromi, Works,* v, 182.

new harvest of facts. But it is a great mistake to imagine that the history of modern science is merely a history of the growth of experimental technique. Above all there is needed the genius to see and to formulate the bond between the phenomena, the natural law collecting many of them into a single manageable sheaf.

Kepler and Galileo may be taken as the founders of the new method and as the exponents of the modern mentality with its passionate interest in detailed facts and its equally passionate devotion to abstract generalizations. Prior to Galileo there has been little real experiment. The laws of nature were thought out *a priori,* or on the basis of an untested and insufficient experience. Telesio and Campanella explained nature "juxta propria principia," which might mean either "according to nature's own principles" or "according to the writer's own principles," but in either case amounted in practice to the same thing. Cardan and Della Porta did not even think out general principles, but conflated all sorts of traditions into an inconsistent mass of theory, while they handled experience in a way justly branded by Bacon as "a mere groping, which rather stupefied than informed them."

It was Galileo who first turned experience into experiment, that is, into a conscious manipulation of things in order to answer some definitely put question. Better, said he, to demonstrate a small truth than to discuss the highest matters exhaustively, without proving anything. Galileo first consistently asked the how and not the why of natural processes. For him, as for all modern scientists, the primary qualities of matter are size, shape, quantity, and motion, for no corporeal substance can be conceived without these qualities (rest being a form of motion). On the other hand, such qualities as sound, color, and taste, which depend on a percipient sense-organ, are secondary and adventitious.

In other words, science is measurement, and the true key to understanding nature is mathematics working upon the basis of data given by experiment. Galileo rightly declared that the book of nature is written in other letters than those of our alphabet—these letters being triangles, quadrangles, circles, spheres, cones, pyramids, and other mathematical figures.

Kepler saw and brilliantly expressed the same truth when he wrote, in April, 1597: [1]

As the ear is made to perceive sound and the eye to perceive color, so the mind of man has been formed to understand not all sorts of things, but quantities. It perceives any given thing more clearly in proportion as that thing is close to bare quantities as to its origin, but the further a thing recedes from quantities, the more darkness and error inheres in it.

Many men now began to declare, as did Boyle, that "Nature plays the mathematician," and like Leibniz, that "natural science is naught but applied mathematics." Descartes also glorified number as the key to all the arcana of the universe.

If mathematical measurement is the first principle of modern science, empirical observation is its second. The elder philosophers had been inclined to deduce natural phenomena from *a priori* principles; modern savants infer principles inductively from examining and comparing large numbers of particular examples. The inductive method, indeed, had been known to antiquity and to the Middle Ages. A clear explanation of the inductive method, together with the name, is found in Hugo of Strassburg's *Compendium of Theological Truth,* written about 1290 and often printed in the fifteenth and sixteenth centuries. He says: [2]

The philosophers have found a method of argumentation by induction: from many particular propositions they draw one universal conclusion. For example, thus: Socrates is an animal. Plato is an animal. Cicero is an animal. Therefore every man is an animal.

---

[1] *Opera,* i, 14, 1595).
[2] Codex lat. Monacensis 22224; facsimile in Arndt: *Schrifttafeln zur Erlernung der lateinischen Palaeographie*[4], 1904, Taf. 25.

In the sixteenth century Juan Luis Vives and Everard Digby both championed the experimental and inductive method of research; but it is to Francis Bacon that we owe the most impressive elaboration of the new way. This interesting man cultivated with high success, ending in tragic failure, the two very different fields of practical politics and contemplative philosophy. With a mind capacious of all knowledge, and proudly taking "all knowledge as his province," with a genius the most profound, penetrating and distinguished, with a mastery of language weighty, compact, and powerful, he turned aside from the exclusive pursuit of his vast philosophical ends to win, by every species of flattery and time-serving, such comparatively unworthy rewards as a peerage and the chancellorship. How, after attaining the highest place in the state, he was cast down from it by impeachment and conviction for taking bribes, and sentenced to a large fine and to imprisonment during the king's pleasure, is a tragedy too personal to require more than a bare mention here.

More interesting for our present purpose is the work of Bacon in cultivating and perfecting a new method and in extolling the prerogatives of research. His life-work was the promotion of the Great Renewal (*Instauratio Magna*), or the scientific renaissance which he also called the Greatest Thing Ever (*Maximus temporis partus*). The method on which he relied to bring this about was the inductive method, consisting of a wide collection of facts and observations of nature, the abstraction from them of their similarities, and the expression of these likenesses in general formulae. In the hands of a genius, who perceives what facts are significant and who is endowed with the power of generalization, the method is just that used, without Bacon's instruction, by his contemporaries Galileo and Kepler. But, for what he intended it to be, a universal instrument, powerful in the hands of the average man, the method proved to be nearly useless. Had nature been a closed finitude, so that all the data could be observed and classified, the system would have worked. But no mere catalogue of facts ever led to any important generalization. Science can only advance by asking questions of nature; that is, by framing and then testing hypotheses. This Bacon was neither able to tell others how to do, nor to do himself. As one reads his own attempts to apply his method, one is struck only by the ineptness and helplessness of the author, tossed without chart, compass, or rudder in a sea of miscellaneous notes. He spent years in observing and recording phenomena and then he classified them under some illusory resemblance. When he considered heat he grouped together not only fire, friction, manure, animal heat, and the heat produced by quicklime, but also the heat of acids and of pepper on the tongue. Under the general heading of "Swelling" he entered observations on gases, soap-bubbles, turkeys, insect bites, women's breasts, priapism, the pupil of the eye, ice, the apparent expansion of the stars on cold nights, and many other equally futile subjects.

One other severe criticism of Bacon's method must be made, and was made even in the seventeenth century: [1] and that is that Bacon ignored and undervalued mathematics. Thinking of science in the old way qualitatively, when it was becoming ever more and more quantitative, Bacon not only discarded the most powerful instrument for economizing thought, but missed the whole tonality of the modern age, the principle which lay behind the remarkable successes of his own contemporaries.

But though the constructive work on which he chiefly prided himself proved a total failure when put to the test of practice, Bacon's destructive criticism cleared away much of the accumulated rubbish of two thousand years. "The field of the mind must be levelled and freed from existing opinions to make it ready and apt to work upon what is then brought to it," he wrote, and he proceeded to level and wreck all the schools of antiquity and of more recent times in a most pitiless attack. He then pointed out the obstacles to truth in the constitution of the human mind, and classified the commonest sources of error in four groups:

[1] By Huygens in 1693; *Œuvres*, x, 404.

1. The Idols of the Tribe, or fallacies incident to human nature in general, as, the tendency to suppose greater order in nature than there is, and the tendency to support preconceived opinion by noting only confirmatory cases, neglecting the opposite; also the delusions of the senses and passions, and the belief that man is the measure of all things.

2. The Idols of the Cave, or errors due to the peculiar constitution of an individual, as, the tendency to derive everything from one prejudice or partiality.

3. The Idols of the Marketplace, created by the habit of mankind of mistaking words for things, of misapplying names and epithets, and so forth.

4. The Idols of the Theater, or fallacious modes of thinking resulting from the adoption of received systems and of erroneous methods of demonstration.

Whatever the incidental merits of Bacon's method may have been, his real service to the world lay in his proclamation of the glory and promise of science. That he was Lord Chancellor of England may have been, as his contemporary Harvey scornfully hinted, no guarantee of the soundness of his philosophy; but the position gave him an unequalled platform from which to preach his new gospel.

And that gospel was the need for cultivating natural science. Bacon became the chief herald of that habit of critical thought which has remade the world. It is hard for us to realize, after three centuries, how little science was then regarded; how much she suffered and languished under the fear of the orthodox, the contempt of the philosophers, the jealousy of statesmen, and the dense ignorance of the vulgar. Bacon resolved "to clear the way and as it were get silence, so that the testimonies of the dignity of learning may be heard better without railing of tacit objections," and he "resolved to free learning from the reproaches and revilings with which ignorance had loaded her." [1]

Bacon saw, more clearly than anyone had yet done, why the human mind had been a thwarted and ineffective thing

[1] *De Augmentis*, Bk. i, Works, 1861, ii, 100.

in the past. It was because natural philosophy had been introspective and traditional; because the schoolmen looked not at nature but at Aristotle and at their own minds. They were slaves to superstition and prisoners in the cells of their own logic. Science had been "corrupted by the mixing up with it of superstition and theology," for by the schoolmen error was not only embraced but apotheosized, in that they would endeavor to build a system of natural philosophy upon the first chapter of Genesis and the Book of Job.[1] And in the earlier ages the highest rewards were given, and every sort of assistance offered, to those who busied themselves with theology; [2] and none to those who read the book of nature. Such scholastic philosophy was not only completely bound by tradition, and engaged in framing subtle and intricate axioms and theorems to save the current practices,[3] but it was also fanatical and contentious, given to vain imaginations, vain altercations, and vain affections.[4]

Metaphysics had been barren, because the "mind had been turned inward on itself, like a spider weaving a web; for, having no power of going without its own boundaries, it wove webs of learning admirable for the fineness of the silk and workmanship, but frivolous and vain as far as any use is concerned." [5] Even the science of the Greeks was childish, fertile in controversies, but barren of results.[6] And the search for final causes, which had absorbed the whole energy of the Middle Ages, was as sterile as the nun dedicated to God.[7]

The state of the sciences was, then, not happy, nor greatly improved. A different road must be found and followed, and that road is simply the exploration of Nature. "There remains only one salvation and health: to begin the whole work of the mind over again from the beginning.[8] And

---

[1] *Novum Organum,* Bk. i, Aph. 65.
[2] *Ibid.,* Aph. 79.
[3] *Essays,* no. 17.
[4] *De Augmentis,* Works, 1861, ii, p. 112.
[5] *Ibid.,* 120ff.
[6] *Nov. Org.,* Preface, *Works,* i, 200.
[7] *De Aug.* iii, cap. 5.   [8] *Nov. Org.,* Preface.

there will be vast hope in the new method, for men know neither their riches nor their power; they overestimate their wealth, esteeming the known arts at an extravagant price, and at the same time they underestimate their powers, consuming their time in trifling occupations, and making no trial of the most important abilities.[1]

What would be the results of this new method? In part, "the relief of man's estate," "the service of human convenience," "fruit." Bacon proposed "neither the amplification of the power of one man over his country, nor the amplification of the power of that country over foreign nations, but the amplification of the power and rule of mankind over the world." It was "the restitution of man to the sovereignty of nature," "the enlarging of the bounds of human empire to the effecting of all things possible." And how richly, in this regard, has his wisdom been justified of her children! The triumphs of science, which were the paradoxes of that age, have become the commonplaces of ours. To enumerate all the inventions by which man has conquered time and space, has increased his wealth and comfort a hundredfold, has defeated his old enemies, and made nature the servant of his needs, would be a task both endless and superfluous. And even now we are but at the beginning of the establishment of the Republic of Man.

But Bacon's ends were not exclusively practical. Nobly he wrote: "Just as the vision of light itself is something more excellent and beautiful than its manifold use, so, without doubt, the contemplation of things as they are, without superstition or imposture, without error or confusion, is in itself a nobler thing than a whole harvest of inventions." "The human mind," said he again, "is like a mirror, capable of reflecting the whole world, and thirsting for it as the eye thirsts for light; passionately eager not only to see the changes and vicissitudes of time, but also ambitious to examine and explore the immovable and inviolable laws and

[1] Preface to the *Instauratio Magna, Works,* i, 199.

decrees of nature."[1] This was the chief end of science, which should be used not as a harlot for pleasure, nor as a maid-servant for gain, but as a wife for bearing children and for honest solace.[2]

Bacon has sometimes been reproached with having made no great discoveries himself. But if he discovered nothing else, he discovered science. If his inductive method proved a frail support, he did more than create a method, he first sensed the atmosphere in which invention flourishes. Science had been the Cinderella of the world's youth, doing the humble and thankless chores of mankind while her haughty sisters, Theology and Philosophy, had danced at the court balls. Once again the ancient fable came true; the cinder wench married the prince and became queen;—and Francis Bacon was her fairy godmother.

What he really expected from the great renewal is set forth in the fragment of a story, *The New Atlantis,* published in 1627. It is a Utopia; but differs from those of More and Campanella and Harrington in finding the best end to which society can devote itself not in various political and social aims, but in the advancement of research and increasing man's mastery of nature.

The author tells the tale of a visit to an imaginary South Sea island, and of seeing there the noblest foundation that ever was upon earth, called Solomon's House, the very eye of the kingdom, wholly dedicated to a study of the works and creatures of God. It was, in fact, a vast institution for scientific research, amply equipped with observatories and storehouses and laboratories in which one could "imitate and generate meteors, as snow, hail, rain . . . thunders, and lightnings." It was also endowed with zoological and botanical parks for the study and dissection of animals and of plants. The inhabitants of the New Atlantis have far outstripped the thinkers of other countries; they have discovered drugs to increase men's strength, and methods of conveying music to distant places, engines of swifter mo-

[1] *De Aug., Works,* ii, 101.
[2] *Ibid.,* p. 140.

tion than musket balls, machinery to make and break all
things, flying machines, submarines, clocks of perpetual motion, and many other marvels, including a house of deceit
of the senses in which feats of juggling produce apparitions
and illusions.

If it remained for later generations to bear witness how
true a prophet Bacon was, his own contemporaries were not
backward in acclaiming his merits. His influence on philosophy, in accelerating and organizing research, and in raising
the prestige of science, can be noted in every province of the
Republic of Letters. With one accord the forward-looking
men of the time turned against what Milton called the
"monkish mange" [1] of scholasticism, and the "idolisms,
traditions, and paradoxes" [2] of the ancient philosophy.
According to Joseph Glanvill [3] the Aristotelian philosophy
"teaches men to cant endlessly about *materia* and *forma,* to
hunt chimaeras by rules of art, and to dress up ignorance
in words of bulk and sound," whereas the modern empirical
philosophy "improves the minds of men in solid and useful
notices of things, helping them to such theories as may be
useful to common life, and searching out the true laws of
matter and motion."

In Italy Campanella welcomed the inductive method,[4]
and Malpighi wrote that wars and revolutions had done less
harm to the arts than the hitherto prevailing bad method of
study by reliance on authority rather than on first-hand
observation.[5]

Throughout the century many works on scientific method
were put forth by men each of whom was persuaded that
he had at last forged the key to unlock every door. Descartes
called his *Discourse on Method* "the plan of a universal
science which can raise our nature to the highest degree of
perfection." With the same purpose Tschirnhaus wrote his
Medicina mentis, the recluses of Port Royal, Antoine Ar-

[1] See A. H. Gilbert in *Studies in Philology,* xix, 152ff, 1922.
[2] *Paradise Regained,* iv, 234.
[3] *Skepsis scientifica,* 1665, Preface to the Royal Society.
[4] Blanchet: *Campanella,* 190.
[5] Malpighi: *Opera omnia,* p. 1.

nauld and Nicole, their *Art of Thinking*, Malebranche his *Search for Truth*, and Leibniz his several works on method.

Among the most suggestive remarks on method were those of Pascal prefaced to his *Treatise on the Vacuum*,[1] 1647. While admitting that antiquity should have great authority in matters of history and theology, he denied that it should have any in science. "But the misfortune of our own time," he continued, "is that we have many novel opinions in theology, unknown to the ancients, whereas in physics any new discovery is branded as false if it contradicts the received opinions."

3. THE SCIENTIFIC ACADEMIES

When an idea grows sufficiently strong it normally becomes embodied in an institution. As the religious thought of the first centuries of our era produced the church, the monastery, and the papacy, as the scholastic learning of the Middle Ages produced the university, so the scientific thought of modern times gave birth to the academy, or corporation dedicated to research. The origin of these societies is to be found in informal gatherings of men brought together by common interests. Only a few of the many clubs attained to fame or to permanent organization.

Baptista della Porta tells of an *Academia Curiosorum Hominum*, also called *Academia Secretorum Naturae*, which met at his house in Naples to help him perform the experiments recorded in his book on *Natural Magic*. The condition of admission to this club was that the applicant must have made some discovery.

Far more famous became the *Accademia dei Lincei*, which borrowed its name from the proverbial powers of the lynx's vision. Soon after it was founded at Rome by Duke Federigo Cesi in 1601, the habit of its members of keeping their minutes in cipher brought on it suspicions of conspiracy and magic sufficiently annoying to make it languish. Reorganized in 1609, it attained great strength when, on April

[1] *Œuvres*, ii, 129.

25, 1611, Galileo joined it. Among its rules were that no member of any religious order might be admitted, that no person could be accepted without having given evidence of scientific attainments, and that the members must not be slaves of Aristotle or of any other philosopher but must keep their minds "noble and free." The ambitious society planned to publish reports, to establish daughter societies in other cities, and to build a museum and laboratory, but most of these projects remained in abeyance. Some books of Galileo it did publish, but after his condemnation in 1633 the society, split by a schism originating in the members' divergent views of the Copernican system, pined away and finally died in 1657—to be revived three centuries later.

In that same year was founded at Florence, among Galileo's disciples, the *Accademia del Cimento* (or Academy of Experiment). This, too, originated in informal gatherings of learned men. On its organization it was given the powerful protection of Leopold, brother of the Grand Duke Ferdinand II of Tuscany, and its first president. So dependent was it on this patronage that when Leopold was given the cardinal's hat the society was dispersed, possibly at the suggestion of the pope. During its ten years of existence it conducted work of great value in physics, reports of which were published by the secretary Magalotti under the title *Essays in Natural Experiment made in the Accademia del Cimento*. Notable in these reports on the barometer, on the vacuum, and on heat, is the strict adherence to fact and the total abstention from anything faintly savoring of speculation.

Several similar societies sprang into being in Germany. One of the first was the *Societas Erneutica* (Society for Research) founded at Rostock by Joachim Jungius, professor of mathematics at the university there, for the purpose of "seeking truth in reason and experiment and freeing the sciences from sophistry, in order to get demonstrative certainty and to multiply useful inventions." The society, which was suspected of Rosicrucian purposes, lived only a few years.

More permanent, though more limited in aim, was the *Collegium Naturae Curiosorum* founded in 1652 at Schweinfurt by the physician Lorenz Bausch, with the purpose of advancing medicine and pharmacy by observation. Enlarged and reorganized in 1670, it began to publish reports entitled *Miscellanea Curiosa sive Ephemerides medico-physici* on the model of the *Philosophical Transactions of the Royal Society*. In 1677 the Emperor Leopold I became patron of the society, which ten years later changed its name in his honor to *Accademia Caesarea Leopoldina*.

A certain Christopher Sturm, who on a journey to Italy had attended meetings of the *Accademia del Cimento*, founded a similar society at Altdorf in 1672. Its chief purpose was to educate the public by doing experiments.

While the spontaneous and almost simultaneous rise of these clubs in all Western Europe shows that the same wind was blowing in them all, the Royal Society of England proudly claimed to be the daughter of Bacon, inspired and guided by his writings and modelling herself on Solomon's House in the *New Atlantis*. The first informal meetings which developed into the Society can be traced to about 1645; for about that year, Wallis relates, he became acquainted in London with "divers worthy persons, inquisitive into natural philosophy and other parts of human learning, and particularly of what has been called *New Philosophy* or *Experimental Philosophy*"; these men agreed to meet once a week in order to discuss physics, anatomy, geometry, astronomy, navigation, statics, magnetics, chemistry, mechanics, the circulation of the blood, and the Copernican hypothesis. The place of meeting, Gresham College, was an institution founded by the will of Sir Thomas Gresham in 1579 for employing seven professors to give lectures, one on each day of the week, on divinity, astronomy, geometry, physics, law, rhetoric, and music.

In the troubled years 1648-49 some of the London company withdrew to Oxford, but each of the two groups thus formed continued to meet regularly. The Oxford circle drew up a constitution consisting of eight rules for weekly meet-

ings at which each member in turn was expected to contribute a discourse or a demonstration. Minutes of the
meetings were kept until at least 1690, and some of these
have been recently published.[1]

But the larger and more important group remained in
London. Their meetings at Gresham College were interrupted in 1658 when the building was taken for barracks,
but were resumed in 1660 with the Restoration. As most of
the members were Royalists, and as the king amused his
leisure by playing with science, his interest was easily enlisted, so that in July, 1662, a charter was issued for the
incorporation of the body by the name of "The Royal
Society for Improving Natural Knowledge." Within the
next six or seven years several parcels of land in Chelsea
were conveyed to the corporation. The Society was given
the right to employ printers and engravers, to dissect
the bodies of criminals, and to correspond with foreigners
without molestation "on things philosophical, mathematical,
and mechanical." The first President was Lord Brouncker,
the highest in rank among the members. Ninety-six Fellows
were incorporated at once, and 309 were admitted during
the years 1663-86.

The purpose of the Society was to witness experiments,
to hear reports, and

to examine all systems, theories, principles, hypotheses, elements,
histories, and experiments of things natural, mathematical, and
mechanical, invented, recorded, or practised by any considerable
author, ancient or modern. . . . In the meantime the Society will
not own any hypothesis, system, or doctrine of the principles
of natural philosophy, proposed or mentioned by any philosopher ancient or modern, nor the explication of any phenomena
where recourse must be had to original causes (as not being
explicable by heat, cold, weight, figure, and the like, as effects
produced thereby); nor dogmatically define nor fix axioms of
scientifical things, but will question and canvass all opinions,
adopting nor adhering to none, till by mature debate and clear
arguments, chiefly such as are deduced from legitimate experi-

[1] By R. T. Gunther: *Early Science at Oxford*, iv, 1925.

ments, the truth of such experiments be demonstrated invincibly.[1]

How faithful to this empirical spirit were the labors of the Society can be read in every page of the *Transactions*. In order to facilitate experiment a considerable collection of instruments and also of curios was made. To further extend the usefulness of the Society, Sir Isaac Newton, about 1670 or a little later, drew up a plan for dividing the members into groups, given fixed duties in the examinations of books, papers, and experiments, and paid by the government. This scheme, which would have introduced some of the essential features of the French *Académie des Sciences,* was not carried out. But the Society did labor successfully to secure the rights of inventors, and also educated the public by inviting them to open meetings after 1673.

Especially after the publication of their *Philosophical Transactions* the Society attained international fame, and also made some enemies. That it gave further publicity to the scientific spirit, and raised its prestige among the vulgar is recognized as early as 1665 by Glanvill when he complimented the Society on having so "redeemed the credit of philosophy" that it would soon be accounted "none of the meanest breeding to be acquainted with the laws of nature and the universe." [2] In a further defence of the learned body he called it "a bank of all useful knowledge" which "had done more than philosophy of a notional way since Aristotle opened shop." [3] In 1670 Huygens called the Royal Society "an assembly of the choicest wits and finest intellects of Christendom"; [4] while Leibniz, when admitted in 1673, declared that the whole of Europe deferred to its authority.[5] John Graunt, the economist, spoke of the Royal Society as "his Majesty's Privy Council for Philosophy, and also his Great Council, his Parliament of Nature, with

[1] *Statutes,* ch. xi, quoted Ornstein, 131.
[2] *Skepsis Scientifica,* Preface.
[3] *Plus Ultra,* 1668.
[4] Huygens: *Œuvres,* vii, 11.
[5] Leibniz: *Math. Schriften,* i, 32.

three estates, viz. the mathematical, the mechanical, the physical." [1]

That the society should be attacked and ridiculed in certain quarters was inevitable. King Charles laughed mightily when he heard that his society spent its time in weighing air. In popular ballads their pendula were called swing-swangs, and their investigations of sheep-farming were derided as "the philosophy of cloth." One, Dr. Henry Stubbs, a Warwickshire medical man, complained that "the comical wits of the Royal Society" were negligent and false in relating experiments and in usurping those of others, and that they undermined respect for the Church of England and for the Universities." [2] Samuel Butler, the author of *Hudibras*, wrote a poem entitled *The Elephant in the Moon*, telling how a club of scientists was much excited by the discovery of an enormous animal in the moon, which turned out to be a mouse caught in the telescope. Though this satire was not published until nearly a century later, it was widely read in manuscript and furnished the argument for a poem by La Fontaine which appeared in 1678. [3] And early in the next century Jonathan Swift, in *Gulliver's Travels*, ridiculed the Grand Academy of Lagado, the members of which busied themselves with plans for extracting sunshine from cucumbers and for building houses from the roof downward.

Similar in some respects to the Royal Society, but with deep national differences, was its great rival the French *Académie des Sciences*. This, too, took its rise in the meetings of savants to make experiments and to communicate to each other their several discoveries. These meetings began perhaps soon after Étienne Pascal, the father of Blaise, moved to Paris, in 1631. In his salon met together with him and his precocious son, Mersenne, Roberval, Carcavi, Gassendi, Mydorge, and Desargues. The meetings continued weekly after the Pascals left Paris (1638), and were often

---

[1] C. Hull: *Economic Writings of Sir W. Petty*, i, 323.
[2] *Calendar of State Papers, Domestic*, 1670, p. 224.
[3] *Fables*, liv. 7, no. 18. Butler's poem in his *Posthumous Works*, 1759.

attended by distinguished foreigners. By 1660 the group had attained so much recognition that Colbert saw in it a useful instrument to improve and adorn the reign of his master Louis XIV. His first idea, to make it a part of the *Académie Française,* gave way to a plan for a more specialized group. The nucleus of the body now consisted of Carcavi, Roberval, Frenicle, Auzout, Picard, Buot, and Huygens; and of these the last named, a foreigner, drew up a program for the society, though it was not formally adopted as a constitution.[1] According to this:

the purpose of the society is to work for the perfection of the sciences and arts, and to seek generally for all that can be of use or convenience to the human race and particularly to France.

The work of the united savants was to be the study of astronomy, geography, chemistry, anatomy, and medicine, the invention of new machines and instruments, the rewarding of inventors, and the encouragement of exploration. Very significant were the aim of the society, as stated by Huygens, "to disabuse the world of all those common errors that have long passed for truth," and the provision that the meetings should never discuss religion nor affairs of state, and only when necessary metaphysics, ethics, history, and grammar.

In 1666 the Academy of Sciences was chartered, a room in the Royal Library was assigned it for meetings, 21 members were appointed and each given a salary of 1,500 livres (worth, in modern standards, about $3,000) per annum, and a fund for expenses. This governmental support is one of the main differences distinguishing the French from the English society. On the first official meeting, December 22, 1666, Carcavi explained to the members the intentions of the king, and they agreed to meet twice a week, on Wednesdays to discuss mathematics and on Saturdays to treat the natural sciences. They also agreed that no system should be allowed to dominate the academy.

[1] Huygens: *Œuvres,* iv, 325.

The minutes of the meetings, largely reported in the *Journal des Savants,* show that they devoted themselves zealously to all forms of experiment, that they examined inventions and books submitted to them, that they corresponded frequently with foreigners, particularly in London, and that they fitted out expeditions to the other countries of Europe and to the other continents.

If the king gave the members salaries it was not to allow them leisure to use or abuse as they saw fit. Much more than the English Society the French was a department of government, justified in the eyes of the rulers by its practical utility, and set definite tasks. Its fortunes rose and fell to some extent with the favor shown or withdrawn by the ministry of the day; so much so that as early as 1670 Huygens believed that the excessive demands upon the members for profitable works, the jealousies that had cankered the group, and its dependence upon the humor of the king and his ministers, would lead to its early dissolution.[1] Notwithstanding these handicaps, and notwithstanding the fact that the *Académie des Sciences* became the battle-ground for the rival theories of Descartes and his opponents, it survived all storms until the Revolution of 1789. Indeed, it not only survived, but at times did such excellent work that Laplace,[2] in 1796, was able to attribute to it in large part both the scientific advance made after its foundation, and the spread of the philosophical spirit throughout the whole French nation.

Two daughters of the London Society should not pass unnoticed. In 1684 the Dublin Philosophical Society was founded in imitation of the English group. It created a museum and botanical garden and published numerous scientific papers. Though never incorporated, a "private philosophical society" was started in Boston, Massachusetts, by Increase Mather in 1683. It consisted of "agreeable gentlemen who met once a fortnight for conference upon improvements in philosophy and additions to the stores of natural history."

[1] Huygens: *Œuvres,* vii, 12.
[2] *Système du Monde, Œuvres,* 1846, vi, 418f.

Though it did not survive much more than thirty years it is only one of several testimonies to the keenness of interest in science in the colonies. John Winthrop, Jr., of Connecticut (1606-76) and Colonel William Bird of Virginia were members of the English Royal Society. Winthrop brought with him to America what would then be considered a large private library, mostly on science, and corresponded with Hartlib, Hooke, Boyle, Newton, and Oldenburg.

4. SCIENTIFIC JOURNALS AND MUSEUMS.

Under the direction of the academies the organization of research proceeded apace. In an age lacking that vast apparatus for study accumulated during the last three centuries there was much to be done. The scholar at that time found it difficult to look up any particular subject, in order to make certain that he was not duplicating work already done. Descartes deplored the fact that what he called "mathematical history," by which he meant not the story of the science but a compendious and exhaustive account of all that had been done in the past, could not be found collected in one book, but must needs be sought in many scattered tracts.[1] Still harder was it for the scholar to keep abreast of recent discoveries in his own field. Epistolary correspondence supplied the chief means of communication between scholars, and though this was copious, international, and unrestrained even in time of war,[2] and though it furnishes for the historian a wonderful source, it was at best but a poor and restricted means of advancing and disseminating scientific information. Now and then collections of letters would be published—as the *Commercium Epistolicum* edited by Wallis in 1658, containing mathematical letters of Fermat, Frenicle, Digby, Wallis himself, and others. But in general the letters remained unpublished, and circulated in

---

[1] Descartes: *Œuvres*, Supplement, 1913, p. 3, letter of 1640.
[2] Which Huygens calls "a happiness in the unhappiness of war," in 1673; *Œuvres complètes*, vii, 278.

manuscript, among a narrow circle only. Most of the unhappy quarrels as to priority and the mutual charges of
plagiarism among scholars arose in *bona fide* misunderstand-
ings that would have been avoided had there been any
method of prompt publication.

The founding of scientific journals, therefore, came as a
boon not only to research but to the cause of international
good will. A generation after the beginnings of general newspaper and magazines, scientific periodicals were started in
France and England, both in the year 1665.

The first, by a few weeks, to be published, was the *Journal
des Savants* (or, as then written, *des Sçavans*), edited by
Denis de Sallo. The first issue appeared on January 5, 1665,
and thereafter one number came out at Paris regularly every
week. There was also a reprint at Amsterdam [1]—probably
unauthorized, but not regarded as piracy in the days before
international copyright. Though the original intention to
include political news was abandoned,[2] the journal encountered the hostility of the Jesuit and of the censor, which
forced de Sallo, a learned man and a member of the Parlement of Paris, to resign after four months as editor in favor
of a clergyman, the Abbé Gallois. The *Journal* proposed to
inform the public of "experiments in physics and chemistry,
new discoveries of useful and curious machines and inventions, observations of the sky, and of what anatomy finds in
new animals." In addition to original articles on these subjects, largely furnished by the members of the *Académie des
Sciences*, the journal offered book reviews, obituaries of
famous men, and news of the scientific world. About one
third of the articles were on history.

Two months after the first appearance of the French
journal, the English Royal Society began the monthly publication of its *Philosophical Transactions* under the editorship of Oldenburg (c.1626-78), a German who came to Eng-

---

[1] One volume of this, containing the years 1667-8, at Cornell, edited
"par le Sieur G.P."

[2] Spoken of in a letter of Perrier to Huygens, 1664, Huygens: *Œuvres,*
v, 92.

land as consul of his native town, Bremen, in the reign of
Charles I, became a tutor at Oxford, and distinguished himself by carrying on a wide correspondence with the learned
of all lands. In an introductory article he set forth the purpose of publishing these transactions as the advancement of
science and the benefit of mankind, to make known to the
world the results of the labors both of members of the Royal
Society and of other learned men in England and in other
countries, and thus to stimulate and encourage further exertions. While he declined to print anything on law or on
theology, he took a wide view of the natural sciences. He
furnished book reviews of excellent quality, often written
with humor as well as with learning, and he wrote just and
appreciative obituaries. Some of the articles were of a practical nature, as on the breeding of silkworms and on agricultural matters. Others were of a curious rather than
valuable character, as the account of a monstrous calf by
Robert Boyle, the description of some whale cubs caught
near Bermuda and which "were sharp behind but their heads
were pretty bluff," and the account of a woman, together
with her picture, who, though otherwise thin, had breasts
each measuring three feet in circumference. The contributions came even in the early years from all countries of
Europe and some (by John Winthrop, in 1670) from America. Many of the articles were of the highest scientific value.
Huxley hardly exaggerated when he claimed that, were all
other books destroyed except the *Philosophical Transactions*, "the foundations of physical science would remain
unshaken, and the vast intellectual progress of the last two
centuries would be largely, though incompletely, recorded."
Though most of the articles were in English, some were in
Latin; and Latin translations of some of the issues were
published in Germany and in Holland.

Next in importance to the French and English publications was the great German periodical called the *Acta
Eruditorum*, edited by Otto Mencke, a professor at Leipzig,
assisted by a learned body variously called *Collegium Gel-
lianum* and *Collegium Lipsicum*. Beginning in 1682, the first

series extended over fifty years, when a series of *Nova Acta* began. The *Acts of the Learned* aimed at a narrower public but covered a broader field than did the French and English periodicals. Written mostly in Latin, the journal appealed only to scholars, but it included departments of theology and jurisprudence as well as of science. The first volume contained 35 articles on theology, 16 on law, 66 on mathematics and natural sciences, and 51 on history, geography, and philology. Many of the contributions were of the highest value, the whole representing a record of vast achievement.

The first Italian scientific journal was the *Giornale de' Litterati di Roma,* edited by Angiolo Ricci, a corresponding member of the *Accademia del Cimento.* For twelve years, from 1668 to 1679, it continued publication at Rome, and was then continued as the *Giornale de' Litterati per tutto l'anno* at Parma till 1690, and at Modena 1692-97.

There was also an early scientific journal published at Copenhagen during the years 1673-80 under the title *Acta medica et philosophica Hafniensia.*

The first journal of avowedly popular science was the *Nouvelles de la République des Lettres,* published by the famous rationalist Pierre Bayle at Rotterdam for three years, 1684-87. When it stopped, its work was taken up by other magazines; and there soon sprang up throughout Europe a great variety of general and special scientific journals.

In many other particulars the equipment of science advanced rapidly throughout the seventeenth century. As early as 1594 Francis Bacon had pointed out that for the study of nature it would be necessary to have a botanical garden, a menagerie, a goodly cabinet (museum), and a still-house furnished with instruments (or, laboratory); [1] and in the *New Atlantis* he had broadly sketched the plan for such foundations.

Even in the sixteenth century, and perhaps earlier, there had been made collections of exotic plants and animals in

---

[1] *Gesta Grayorum, Letters,* i, 335.

various cities. The best botanical garden and menagerie were perhaps those at Paris; but such were also to be found in a number of other cities. Various libraries and schools made collections of natural curiosities, and procured pictures of others which had been examined but which could not be preserved. An advance in the technique of preservation was made by the discovery of Robert Boyle, about 1663, that organic substances can be kept free from decay and visible in alcohol. The foundation of the first great museum was laid by the gift to Oxford University by Dr. Elias Ashmole of his collection of natural curiosities in 1677. In order to house these and other similar property of the university the Ashmolean Museum was built and completed in 1683.

Along with other improvements, went the improvement of observatories. That built at Paris in 1667, and that erected at Greenwich in 1675, surpassed all previous ones in equipment, even the famous Uraniborg of Tycho Brahe.

PART II. THE HUMANITIES

PHILOSOPHY

I. PHILOSOPHY OF THE RENAISSANCE AND OF THE REFORMATION

Though it was discovered even in antiquity that man was, in his own esteem, the measure of all things, men have seldom been aware how anthropomorphic are all the creations of their minds. Even mathematics and the natural sciences bear deep marks of man's standards and interests, as when the decimal system of notation is chosen to make the number of arithmetical digits correspond to the number of fingers on the human hands, or as when astronomy is studied to compute time, as if the universe were a great clock. Nevertheless, in studying mathematics and the objects of the external world, men have attained an objectivity, a disinterestedness, not found in any of their other occupations. The reason is that in these limited fields man's curiosity, or wish to know the exact truth, does not ordinarily conflict with his other and much stronger passions and desires.

Far different is the case when men begin to study themselves, their own minds, customs, morals, religion, social institutions, politics, and history. Here the impulse of disinterested curiosity, though present, has generally proved all too feeble to overcome the enormous waves of emotion and self-interest surrounding and permeating the body of studied facts. That these emotions and interests are largely unconscious involves the most honest thinker in perils. The impulses of passion, the suggestions of the herd, the force of habit are so strong that they not only bend all thought

touching them in their own direction, but actually furnish
a large part of the data studied, which, however, seem to be
facts as hard and immutable as those of physics. Consequently, the social sciences and philosophy have been little
more than rationalizations of men's more or less unconscious wishes, the finding of reasons that may seem scientific
and convincing, for doing what the reasoner most wants to
do. And as wishes, like all else in the human mind, are
chiefly determined by habit, philosophy and the social
sciences have been mostly a justification of things as they
are, a discovery of new sanctions for old customs.

But, as the reasons and proofs are more short lived than
the habits and customs which fathered them, still other and
fresher reasons must be found by each succeeding generation. As economic and social changes give rise to new conditions and new customs, a new ethics and a new politics must
be invented to justify the interests and practices of groups
recently attaining power. And as science becomes a part of
man's thought and habit, that, too, must become an element
in his philosophy and politics.

This injection of a scientific interest and of a scientific
method has been the most important fact in the development
of the humanities in modern times. For philosophy it has
meant the change from a primarily religious to a primarily
physical or mathematical interest. Once the handmaid of
theology, philosophy now aims only at clarifying the fundamental ideas of the sciences, and at synthesizing them into a
connected vision of the totality of things, or rather of that
portion of the universe which man has thus far succeeded
in exploring. It has thus become, or has aimed at becoming,
the *scientia scientiarum*.

To the schoolmen of the later Middle Ages the chief function of philosophy seemed to be to reconcile the realms of
reason and of faith—Aristotle and the Bible. In the course
of the great debate on the ultimate reality, which divided
the Nominalists and Realists, Aristotelianism became so
closely entwined with orthodox theology that, as Descartes

complained, it was almost impossible to expound any other philosophy without appearing to contradict the faith.[1]

The Renaissance and the Reformation, though poor in original thought, brought in a wave of reaction against all things medieval, and especially against scholasticism and Aristotle, the god of the schoolmen. By the humanists Plato was adopted as the champion opponent of the Stagirite; by the Reformers the latter was denounced as a "damned heathen"; and the combined current of contradiction reached a high-water mark when, in the sixteenth century, Pierre de la Ramée advanced theses to prove that everything taught by Aristotle was false.

But the really new element in the philosophy of the time was furnished less by the humanists and Reformers than by the scientists. The great discoveries of Copernicus, Vesalius, and their followers, soon colored the thought of the age deeply with a new sense of the compulsion of natural law, culminating in a materialistic and mechanistic conception of the universe. Attempts were made, very crude at first, to apply to philosophy the inductive and mathematical methods which had proved so fruitful in the natural sciences. Philosophy tended to become naturalistic in content and geometrical in form.

The bankruptcy of the old scholasticism was followed by the complete skepticism of Montaigne and Sanchez, and this in turn by a new faith, a faith in the method of science to produce truth in the old and exhausted field of metaphysics. It proved difficult, indeed, to make metaphysics experimental: no telescope revealed God in the heavens; no microscope detected the soul in any gland or organ of the body. But introspection supplied premises and geometry an apparatus of deduction with which to work on them.

The new fact to be amalgamated with the old belief and assimilated into the new synthesis was the revelation of the immensity and uniformity of the universe. That nature is a great machine was borne into the consciousness of the age too strongly to be ignored even by those to whom such

[1] *Œuvres*, i, 85.

a conclusion was most repugnant. But did not human experience suggest that a machine, like a watch, is the expression of an idea? Could not the chasm between science and religion be bridged by some such postulate as this?

And, if so, was there not a gain to thought in the sweeping away of a vast rubbish of pseudo-science? All the old metaphysical explanations of particular properties of things by positing the existence in them of occult qualities were discarded in favor of a mathematical or quantitative explanation. If the book of nature is, indeed, written in mathematical symbols, it should be possible for the expert to read it. Less stress was now laid on the "essence" of a thing than on the process of its action. The laws of nature now came to be regarded as expressions of the quantitative relations of bodies and movements.

The philosophical implications of the new science burst on the world like a shower of meteors in the writings of Giordano Bruno (1548-1600), the champion of the Copernican hypothesis. The immense passion of his reckless and polemic rhetoric, displayed to equal advantage in Lucretian hexameters and in dithyrambic Italian prose, and his cruel martyrdom, have perhaps led posterity to overestimate his genius. His philosophy is nothing but the cosmological implication and the metaphysical justification of the Copernican astronomy in the conceptual terms of the fifteenth-century thinker, Nicholas of Cusa. But through all his writings runs the sense of liberation from the double tyranny of the senses and of tradition. Drunk with the new freedom of ranging through infinity, dazzled by the whirling maze of worlds without end scattered like blazing sparks through space, he poured forth a paean of breathing thoughts and burning words to celebrate the new religion of science.

"By the stars," he wrote, "we are moved to discover the infinite effect of an infinite cause, the true and living marks of infinite power, and to contemplate the Deity not as outside of, apart from, and distant from us, but as in ourselves and more within us than we are in ourselves." [1] In the vast

[1] *La Cena de le Ceneri,* dial. 1.

life of the universe he saw the flow of infinite Being, and
this Being he called God. Not absolutely consistent in his
pantheism he sometimes regarded God as immanent in the
universe and sometimes as outside of it as its cause. God and
the universe were, however, but two aspects of the same
thing, creative and created nature. Emphasizing the ubiquity
of Deity in all finite things, and the homogeneity of the universe, he abolished all distinction of worth between earth
and heaven.

Hardly less fundamental to his thought than the Copernican revelation of infinity was the atomic theory borrowed
from Democritus, Epicurus, and Lucretius. The *minima,*
indeed, from which he built his universe were not so
much a scientific hypothesis as the foundation of a theory
of hylozoism or universal vitalism. The *minimum* could be
regarded in three aspects, the geometrical as the point, the
physical as the atom, and the metaphysical as the monad.
Each monad is an atom-soul, containing the seed of life.
From Nicholas of Cusa Bruno had learned that God can be
found in the smallest as in the largest things; for, just as
the monad is the soul of the atom so God is the soul of the
universe, the monad of monads.

Such a conception of the Deity shocked other orthodox
contemporaries besides the inquisitors. Queen Elizabeth,
whom he adulated as the sun among the stars,[1] thought him
a faithless, impious and godless man;[2] and Kepler accused
him of having "converted God into the universe and reduced
him to circles and points."[3]

Very like Bruno in the circumstances of his life, in the
sources and principles of his philosophy, and in feeling the
hand of the Inquisition, was Campanella (1568-1639). Born
at Stilo in Calabria and baptized Giovanni Domenico, he
took the name Tommaso when he entered the Dominican
Order in 1582, possibly choosing the name to indicate that
he, like St. Thomas the Apostle, was a doubter. Accused of

---

[1] Bruno: *The Heroic Enthusiasts,* transl. by L. Williams, i, 171.
[2] *Opere di Galileo,* iii, 352.
[3] Kepler's letter of April 5, 1608, *Opera,* ii, 593.

ridiculing a papal excommunication, he was imprisoned by the Holy Office at Naples in 1591-2, after which he was allowed to study at Padua, though there also he soon got into trouble with the law on account of an alleged offense against chastity. His first work, entitled *The Harbinger of a Renovated Philosophy* (*Prodromos philosophiae instaurandae*), published in 1594, already announced his religion of naturalistic and humanitarian deism. His enthusiasm for liberty, spiritual and political, involved him in a plotted rebellion in Calabria in 1599, and when the conspiracy was crushed, he was incarcerated at Naples, because of sedition and heresy, for twenty-seven years, and four times tortured by the Inquisition. After recantation he was allowed to write; and as he confesses that he was driven to orthodox beliefs only by the whips of torment, we may safely infer that he masked his true views to some extent under a mantle of insincere conformity. The singular contradictions found in his works may be thus best explained. His numerous books of philosophy, politics, and science were largely written during his imprisonment. Freed at last from bondage he spent eight years at Rome (1626-34), still under the shadow of the Inquisition, and finally found in Paris a greater freedom and a welcome among the leaders of French thought.

A decisive element in the formation of Campanella's philosophy, as in Bruno's, was the new astronomy, though it came to Campanella rather from Galileo, for whom he wrote an apology in 1622. Long before that he had acknowledged his debt to the great scientist in these words:

All the philosophers of the world take laws from the pen of your honor, since, truly, one cannot philosophize without an ascertained system of the construction of the world, such as we have from you; and all things are doubtful as long as we do not know whether our words are mere words.[1]

Campanella felt that he could safely find in science a guarantee of the veracity of our impressions of the external

[1] "tanto che non sapemo s'il parlare è parlare," Letter to Galileo, 1614, *Opere di Galileo*, xii, 31.

world, for science taught him that the world is homogeneous and all of a piece. In knowing himself, therefore, man knows the outer world, and from his own feelings he can deduce the three prime factors of all reality, namely, power, knowledge, and will. These principles, found everywhere, are at full strength only in God; throughout nature they are found diluted by three forms of nonentity,—weakness, ignorance, and evil. And of imperfect things, not of God in his fullest power, come the various worlds: first the world of men and angels, then the mathematical world, then the corporeal world, and finally the empirical world bounded by space and time.

While the Italians strove to assimilate the new elements contributed by the Renaissance and by empirical science, transalpine thinkers devoted themselves rather to narrowly theological than to broadly metaphysical problems. Interest in the religious questions raised by the Reformation dominated the whole thought of Germany and deeply colored what poor philosophy she produced before Leibniz. In Jakob Böhme (1575-1624) the German idealists of the early nineteenth century have discovered the germ of a metaphysics not unlike their own. His style is maddening—a verbose, obscure German, full of fantastic words. The subtitle of his *Six Theosophic Points* (1620), namely, "An open Gate to all the secrets of Life, wherein the causes of all Things become known," is like the first and last lines of *Sordello,* as characterized by Tennyson, the only intelligible part of the book, but a lie. At length, however, the patient and determined reader discovers the glimmering of one great thought —that the primal cause of all things is Will. Medieval mysticism and philosophy had been intellectualistic; modern philosophy is largely voluntaristic. In making God primarily not reason but will Böhme was modern.

As Böhme was the most religious of philosophers, Francis Bacon was the least theological. So far removed is his materialism from the theosophy of Campanella and of Böhme, so few and slender are the threads connecting his worldview with any piety, that it may be doubted whether he

wished to be a metaphysician in any sense. And yet, as
passionate atheism is religious, so Bacon's passionate positivism evinces the emergence of a new or at least of a different conception of the ultimate reality. In limiting philosophy
to the knowledge of nature, in advancing the claims of
naturalism and empiricism, he was, almost in spite of himself, a philosopher. As a materialist he adopted the atomic
cosmology, and found "the moving principle of the original
atoms to be love, appetite, or incentive of primitive matter,"
which was blind like Cupid because "the appetite of the
world seems to have very little foresight." [1] Moreover, he
thought of matter as uncreated and indestructible, the sum
thereof as constant.[2] Even the souls of animals Bacon
thought to be purely material and the souls of men sus-
ceptible of scientific, *i.e.* materialistic, explanation.

2. DESCARTES

Philosophy is like a climber on the Mer de Glace, tied
in the middle of a rope at either end of which is a guide.
One of these guides is the scientist, a daring and active man
ever pressing forward vigorously to new and untried ground;
the other is Mrs. Grundy, a staid and cautious individual,
heavily ballasted with the *mores* and traditions of the group,
and extremely slow in her movements. For this reason the
trail of philosophy is always parallel to that of science; the
same ground is covered, only more slowly, and more reluctantly, for philosophy must make all possible compromises
with the inertia of mass opinion. It is therefore no accident
that, just as the stage was set in the early seventeenth century for a new era in science, a new age in philosophy also
was inaugurated. And the eras then begun both lasted three
centuries; science continued on the lines laid down by
Galileo and his contemporaries until the discoveries of radio-
activity and of relativity and of the quantum theory dealt
the cards for another round; philosophy remained pre-

[1] Bacon: *The Wisdom of the Ancients,* 1609, xvii.
[2] *Historia densi et rari, Opera* iv, 30.

occupied with the problems set by Descartes in 1637 until
William James inaugurated a new period with his essay
Does Consciousness Exist? in 1904.

For, what Bruno and Campanella, Böhme and Bacon
groped after, Descartes achieved, the incorporation into the
traditional mind of the age of some of the methods and
results of the new science. True, he was no more successful
than others in finding the absolute and the ultimate reality,
nor in proving the existence of God and of an immortal
soul, but he injected into the body of philosophy the first
strong dose of the scientific drug from which it has never
recovered since. He was able to do this because in his own
mind he united a catholic scientific curiosity with a genius
for generalization that made him one of the first mathematicians, as he was the first philosopher, of his generation.

René Descartes (1596-1650) sprang from the gentry of
Touraine. An education at the Jesuit school of La Flèche
(1604-12) left him in a curious state of mingled doubt and
faith. What he consciously learned, he tells us, was that
books have little to teach and that in philosophy everything
is doubtful. But what was suggested to him unawares was
the great body of the "truths" of the Roman Catholic religion; and so deeply were they imprinted on his mind that he
later made it the chief end of his philosophy to vindicate
them. After school days had ended he started out to read
the book of the world by travel, visiting Holland, Denmark,
and Germany, everywhere impressed by the variety of opinion and custom. After attending the coronation festivities
of the Emperor Ferdinand II (July-September, 1619) he
took service in the Bavarian army for one year and then
travelled in Italy and in Switzerland, leading the life of a
gay young spark, and even fighting a duel.

But under this exterior of dissipating pleasure a profound
revolution was working in his mind. On November 10, 1618,
in Holland, he met the physicist and mathematician Beeck-
man [1] who kindled in his mind the love of science. Just one

[1] Descartes: *Œuvres,* x, 22.

year later, November 10, 1619, while he was spending the
fall and winter in a little Bavarian town, he found much
leisure for meditation as he was shut up in the heated living
room of the inn, called in vivid metaphor "the stove." His
thoughts on philosophy filled him with "enthusiasm"—a
word then retaining its etymological meaning of divine
afflatus or inspiration—under the influence of which he discovered in three dreams the "foundations of a wonderful
science." The crisis, extraordinarily like a religious conversion, revealed to him the unity of knowledge and impressed
on him the mission of fortifying the human race by preaching a new philosophy. Just one year later, again, on November 10, 1620, he made another great discovery which was
perhaps the application of the geometrical method to philosophy.[1]

After 1628 Descartes lived mostly in Holland in order to
enjoy the freedom lacking in his own country. Though his
whole life was devoted to meditation and study so ardent
and severe that he described his house in Amsterdam as a
solitude, he was not too far removed from ordinary human
passions to love a mistress and a child, and to read *Amadis
of Gaul*. As his fame grew, he became extremely appreciative of his own originality and greatness, and correspond-
ingly sensitive to suggestion or criticism. Lack of courage
to express thoughts obnoxious to censure led him into insincere concessions and concealments; and a want of frankness in acknowledging his obligations to others brought on
him ugly charges of plagiarism which were mostly unde-

---

[1] *Œuvres*, x, 179; Milhaud 58ff; Cohen *passim;* Gilson in *Revue de
Métaphysique et de Morale*, xxviii, 551 (1921). The fact that Nov. 10
was Luther's birthday and that Descartes' "conversion" bears some resemblance to Luther's opens the way to a fanciful reconstruction of the
philosopher's experience as if it were influenced by the Reformer. It is
commonly said that Descartes learned much from the Rosicrucians, a society depicted by Valentin Andreae as one of mystical Lutherans devoted
to reforming science and religion. But Descartes says that he knew nothing certain of them (*Œuvres*, x, 193ff), and it is probable that the society
did not exist at this time elsewhere than in Andreae's imagination. Kuno
Fischer: *Descartes*,[5] 1912, 176.

served. In 1649, at the invitation of Queen Christina, he visited Sweden, where he died, under the combined rigors of the climate and of the queen's demands, in 1650.

In 1637 he published anonymously his *Philosophical Essays*, of which the first was the *Discourse on the Method of rightly guiding the Reason and of discovering Truth in the Sciences*. The other three essays, on *Dioptrics*, on *Meteors*, and on *Geometry*, were intended to serve as specimens of the application of this method. The *Discourse on Method* contains, in the form of an autobiography of the writer's thought, the essentials of his philosophy. Like so many other philosophers he begins by telling why all his predecessors had failed. As he held good sense and reasoning power to be approximately equal in all men Descartes attributed the failure of philosophy to attain a generally acknowledged body of truth to the wrong methods employed. He had early learned from books that there is no opinion so strange and incredible that some philosopher has not held it; and from travelling (and from Montaigne, though he does not say so) he had discovered that the customs of all nations differ so widely that each seems ridiculous to the others.

Vain, then, to look for truth in books or in men. Like a man who would pull down his house in order to build a better, Descartes resolved to doubt all things, to rid himself once for all of every opinion he had hitherto held true. But is this possible? Is there any axiom so self-evident that it cannot be doubted? Yes; he found one truth so firm and assured that even the most extravagant suppositions of the most determined skepticism could not shake it, the truth of his own existence. "I think, therefore I am"—this is the self-evident maxim to doubt which involves a self-contradiction.

Historians of philosophy have been at pains to find the source of Descartes' fundamental maxim in somewhat similar expressions of earlier philosophers, as Campanella. To Descartes himself was pointed out a kindred idea in Augustine's "even if I am mistaken, I exist"; [1] but he rightly claimed that this is a different thought, in its context, from his own, though he professed to welcome any support that Augustine might give. The author who really suggested his thought to him was doubtless Montaigne, who says in his *Apology for Raimond de Sebonde*: [2]

When the Pyrrhonian philosophers say 'I doubt,' they are presently taken by the throat, to make them confess that at least they know and are assured of this, that they doubt.

From his fundamental axiom as a starting-point Descartes believed that he could deduce a sound body of universal philosophy. This could be done, he asserted, only by the geometrical method, for only mathematicians had been able to reason certainly. And the essence of this method was that suggested by his own analytical geometry, to analyze all difficulties into their simplest elements, to receive at the start nothing as true but what is self-evident, to reason from the simple to the complex, and to make exhaustive tables of all things to be considered, so that nothing should be overlooked.

The first deduction he made from his primary axiom was that man is a being whose nature it is to think, and the second that those things conceived by the mind clearly and distinctly and, as it were, intuitively, are always true. Now, one of the clearest ideas in the mind is that of perfection, which can not be derived from anything corporeal, nor from the processes of one's own imperfect human mind. All our own ideas we might imagine to be creations of our own thinking. But the idea of a perfect being could have originated only from a being which itself possessed perfection. A man who finds that he has the idea of God can be sure that this

---

[1] "Si enim fallor, sum," *De Civ. Dei*, xi, 26. *Cf.* L. Blanchet: *Les Antécédents historiques de "Je pense, donc je suis,"* 1920.

[2] *Essais*, liv. i, ch. 12. That Descartes really knew Montaigne is proved by many similarities of their thought, by a direct reference in *Œuvres*, iv, 573, and by his borrowing the word "Essais" invented by Montaigne, as the title of his work.

idea, at least, is derived from a perfect being, and therefore
that God exists. Consequently, concludes the philosopher,
the fact that God exists is as certain as any of the truths of
geometry.

That this proof of God, which Descartes might have taken
from medieval thinkers, and which is commonly called the
ontological proof, failed to possess a geometrical rigor, is
demonstrated by the fact that it was rejected by many and
diverse schools of thought.[1] With Descartes, however,
though the felt need was doubtless that of vindicating the
current dogma, the ostensible use to which God was put was
to guarantee not a system of dogma but the reality of science.
For, the philosopher's proof of the existence of matter and
of the truthfulness of our knowledge of it *follows* the proof
of the existence of God and is dependent on that. Intuitions,
defined as "firm conceptions born in a sound and attentive
mind from the light of reason alone," must be truthful because it would be unworthy of God to deceive us. Hence our
deductions, if carefully made, must be equally true, for the
laws of nature rest on the will of God.

The eternal truths of mathematics [he wrote in 1630] have
been established by God and depend on him as much as do the
rest of his creatures. . . . God has established the laws of nature
just as a king establishes the laws of his kingdom. And there is
none of them which we can not understand if we apply our minds
to consider it, for they are innate in our minds, just as a king
would stamp his laws in the hearts of his subjects if he had the
power to do so. . . . They are eternal and immutable because
God is always the same.[2]

But, having postulated a divine guarantee of the trust-
worthiness of our mental processes, at this point Descartes
had to explain how error at all is possible—for that errors
exist can not successfully be denied by the most resolute
optimist. He answered the problem by saying that the irrational factor contained in a false judgment can not be found

---

[1] Leibniz: *Philosophische Schriften,* i, 221, (1677).
[2] Letter to Mersenne. *Œuvres,* i, 144.

in the realm of ideas, but only in that of the will, which employs its freedom by accepting or rejecting propositions for other reasons than their truth. The need for action, he explained, drives men to form hasty judgments of things of which they have no adequate knowledge, and so impatience and the desire for assertion pushes the finite spirit to affirm or to deny unclear ideas arbitrarily. This explanation of error had not only a plausibility drawn from mathematical analogy—for haste in doing a sum makes the process liable to error avoided by care and patience—but also the advantage of justifying God for permitting error by connecting it with free will. Error, like sin, is but the necessary implication of freedom.

Filled with the conviction of the supreme and comprehensive reality of spirit, Descartes was almost, but not quite, an idealist. All the qualities of matter—or what are commonly taken to be such—except one, he was willing to explain as subjective ideas. This single quality of matter resident in itself is extension. Our knowledge of matter always contains something true and clear and something unclear and deceptive. The true and clear part of our knowledge depends on those properties of matter which can be mathematically known, *i.e.* primarily extension, and derivatively the shape and motion of bodies. He proved this by arguing that a given body is not what we see or feel—for sensations are subjective—but what we think of. Now, as we can not think of bodies apart from extension, that is their only necessary quality; all other quantitative conditions are modes of extension. Hence bodies are extended things, just as souls are thinking, or conscious, things. In this radical dualism more than in almost anything else Descartes set the problem destined to engage and to perplex his followers for nearly three hundred years.

These ideas, all sketched in the *Méthode*, were elaborated in a much longer work published at Paris in 1641 under the title *Meditations on the First Philosophy, in which the existence and the immortality of the Soul are demonstrated*. Though in the second edition the words in the subtitle "immortality of the soul" were changed to "distinction of the soul and body," the dogmatic bias of the work is patent. In an introductory letter to the Sorbonne the author urged the necessity of demonstrating the truths of religion by philosophy rather than by theology, for, though believers are content to take the dogmas of religion on faith, unbelievers must be convinced. To convince them by natural reason, he added, is most needful, for neither religion nor morality would be left if the two fundamental doctrines of God and immortality are left unproved. In like apologetic tone he wrote to a friend: [1] that he did not lament the death of friends, nor fear it for himself because of

the consideration of the nature of our souls, which I think that I know very clearly must endure longer than our bodies, and which are born for pleasures and felicity much greater than we enjoy in this world. . . . And although religion teaches us much on this subject, nevertheless I confess in myself an infirmity which seems to be common to the greater part of mankind, namely that though we wish to believe and even think we believe strongly all that religion teaches us, yet are we not usually so touched by it as by what has been brought home to us by natural and clear reasons.

So far did his apologetic purpose take him that he advanced to the proof of other Christian and Catholic mysteries, claiming at one time that he could explain transubstantiation without a miracle.[2]

In 1644 he published a third great work which he had prepared many years before but held back through fear of condemnation by the spiritual authorities because of its Copernican principles. The *Principia Philosophiae* not only repeats the epistemology advanced in the other works, but endeavors to deal with the physical universe as a whole, mapping out the cosmos in the large and filling in many parts in detailed treatment of the solar system, of the principles of mechanics, light, and general physics. The work is

[1] *Correspondence of Descartes and C. Huygens*, p. 182.
[2] *Œuvres*, iv, 168.

not, as often represented, the framework in which future science was to move; rather is it the last of the great cosmic romances, of the family of the *Timaeus* of Plato and of the *De Rerum Natura* of Lucretius. Like them it is beautiful, even sublime in imagination; and like them it bears but slight relation to reality. The philosopher and the poet feel an urgent need for such comprehensive surveys of the universe; and therefore (as Voltaire said of God) if such things do not exist, they must be invented.

Descartes' method of procedure was anything but scientific, for he deduced all the laws of nature *a priori* from the infinite perfections of God. He criticized Galileo for seeking only the causes of particular effects without considering the first principles of nature. He eagerly studied the works of earlier and contemporary scientists, and here and there did good work in detail himself, as when he first correctly discovered the angle of refraction in optics. Even here, however, he annexed a fantastic explanation to his theory; and elsewhere, as in proving that light propagates itself instantly and in stating that a vacuum existed nowhere in nature except in Pascal's head,[1] he sadly erred.

Matter, he thought, consists of three sorts: the ordinary sort composing terrestrial bodies; a second sort consisting of extremely small particles, round or nearly round, and very subtle, which occupies the interstices of terrestrial matter and also composes the sky; and a third sort incomparably more subtle, with still smaller parts moving extremely fast and with no fixed form but taking the shape of the interstices left between the other kinds of matter. Between the subtle matter and ordinary matter there is no essential difference except in the size and shape of the particles; in fact, the subtle matter has probably been produced by the attrition of the larger bodies, as sand is produced by the grinding of stones.

This matter is in continual motion in a vast aggregate of whirlpools, or vortices, varying in size from extremely small ones to others so large that one of them carries the planets

[1] *Correspondence of Descartes and C. Huygens*, 256.

around the sun. That Descartes made a disingenuous use
of this large vortex to explain the solar system on Copernican principles while eluding the censures of the church
does not prove that he invented the whole theory for this
purpose.

While constructing and exhibiting a model of the universe
Descartes found his greatest difficulties in dealing with living creatures. Are they to be regarded as of a piece with
the rest of nature, as machines, or do they constitute an
exception? Here he drew a line not between animals, including man, on the one side and lifeless matter on the other,
but between man on one side, and all the rest of nature,
including animals, on the other. It would have been more
consistent with common sense to classify all living creatures together, but to do so would have been, in the philosopher's opinion, dangerous both to science and to morality;
to science as introducing contingency in nature (a prerogative reserved for man) and to morals as involving those who
eat or vivisect animals in a crime against rational creatures
like themselves. Moreover, if animals are rational, it would
be necessary to provide them with immortal souls.

Therefore Descartes regarded animals, except men, as
automata. Familiar as he was with the researches of Harvey
and of Vesalius, dissecting animals himself, and impressed
also with some remarkable mechanical mannikins made to
move and utter sounds by means of running water, he had
no difficulty in persuading himself that the acts of animals
are "reflex undulations" of machines run by heat and regulated by the triggers of various stimuli. Not only acts of
lust and hunger, but much more complicated matters, such
as the sagacity of dogs and the cunning of foxes, he thought
he could explain merely from the formation of their members.

The real break in the continuity of nature comes, according to Descartes, not in the phenomenon of life, but in Man,
who occupies a unique position as the one point of contact
between the two otherwise incompatible worlds of body
and mind. Men's bodies are machines or statues [1] created

---

[1] *De L'Homme,* first published 1664, *Œuvres,* xi, 119.

by God and endowed with a rational spirit. The seat of the mind Descartes put in the pineal gland—now thought to be a vestigial eye—in the brain because it is the only part of the brain not double, and because it is in a conveniently central position. Energy and direction are transmitted, he explained, from the pineal gland to other parts of the body by the animal spirits which flow along the nerves.

But, with his dualism which saw in consciousness and extension the two fundamental aspects of finite substances dividing them into two separate worlds, Descartes' hardest problem was to explain how thought can act on the body or how, *vice versa,* a motion of the body can act on the consciousness. In his judgment, this contact constituted a mystery or a miracle, and therefore it remained the principal subject of debate among his immediate disciples.

In a *Treatise on the Passions,* published in 1649, Descartes sketched the psychology agreeable to his general principles. "Passion" then retained its etymological meaning as the antithesis to action, the impression received by the mind from outward things as opposed to the acts of the will. "Passion" he defined more specifically as "a perception, sentiment, or motion of the soul, directly related to the soul, and caused, maintained, and fortified by some movement of the "spirits," *i.e.* of those vital spirits which act as messengers between the soul and the body. There are, in his scheme, six principal passions, with many varieties of each, namely wonder, love, hate, desire, joy, and sadness; of these, wonder is a uniquely intellectual passion; all the others are forms of desire. The function of a passion is to excite the soul to will the things for which the passion prepares the body. But, though the passions directly move the will, they should remain under its control. So closely does Descartes' theory of the mastery of the passions by the will resemble that set forth in the dramas of Corneille, that it has been conjectured that the philosopher must have derived his psychology from the poet. But the question of the freedom of the will was much in the air. Arminians and Gomarists, Jansenists and Jesuits, in the Netherlands and in

France, were hotly debating it; and the Jesuits, who had educated both Descartes and Corneille, strongly defended the freedom of the will and its ability to rule the passions.

The important thing to notice about Descartes is that here, as elsewhere, moral considerations decide the conclusions of his philosophy. His whole *Treatise on the Passions* is motivated by the desire to put the passions under the tuition of the will, which he thought could be done not directly but indirectly, by reflecting on the ideas of God, of immortality, of the extent of the universe, and of man's place in it. The *Treatise on the Passions* is a new form of Loyola's *Spiritual Exercises*. The supreme good for the individual, Descartes wrote in 1647, is a firm will to do right and the contentment produced thereby.[1]

Long before his death the fame of Descartes filled the whole Republic of Letters. Until Voltaire overthrew him, half a century later, in favor of Newton and Locke, he was the dictator of the learned and of the well-bred world. He made philosophy, for the first time, popular. Everyone read the *Discourse on Method*; even women, as Molière reminds us, became passionate partisans of his vortices and felt that, after reading him, they could no longer "suffer a vacuum." Cartesianism overthrew the Peripatetic philosophy, and gave laws to the scientist and to the theologian as well as to the metaphysician. The general opinion was that expressed by Constantyn Huygens, that the *Discourse on Method* was the best digested, ripest, and most savory piece of philosophy ever written.[2]

That fierce opposition should be aroused was a matter of course. The new opinion is always immoral, because morality is but inveterate custom. To some, the mechanistic explanation of nature appeared atheism; to some, even the attempt to prove the existence of God seemed to imply godlessness. When De Roy began to teach Cartesianism at Utrecht in 1642, the academy passed a decree that no philosophy but that of Aristotle should be permitted. The next

---

[1] *Œuvres*, v, 82.
[2] *Correspondence of Descartes, and Huygens*, p. 40.

year Gilbert Voet published a pamphlet comparing Descartes
to Vanini, who had recently been executed for atheism,
and adding: "while he seems to oppose the atheists with
Achillean arguments, he craftily and clandestinely infects
with the poison of atheism those too dull to detect the snake
in the grass."

Though the philosopher truckled to the Jesuits for their
good opinion, he truckled in vain. In 1640 the General Congregation of the Order forbade the teaching of the new
doctrine, and formally condemned thirty propositions in it.
In 1663 his works were put on the *Index of Prohibited
Books,* until corrected. In 1667 when his body was transferred to Paris a funeral oration was forbidden by the
authorities. In 1669 the chair of philosophy at the Sorbonne
was filled by a candidate who championed Aristotle against
Descartes, and when two years later the Archbishop of Paris
warned the four faculties of the University not to spread
doctrines like his which would disturb the church, the professors unanimously agreed to stop doing so. Bossuet, with
clear insight into the real rationalism of Descartes, took
alarm. All the philosopher's proofs of God and immortality,
said the eagle-eyed bishop, would not balance the evil he
would do the church, for he taught the people to admit only
what they could understand, and to reject what they could
not understand. "I see," he continued, "that under the name
of Cartesianism a great battle against the church is preparing." [1] At another time he wrote that while the religious
implications of Cartesianism should be strongly disapproved,
his scientific opinions might be legitimately treated as diverting subjects for conversations, though for himself Bossuet
held it beneath the dignity of the episcopal character to take
such matters seriously.[2] Perhaps at the instigation of Bossuet, and certainly with the approval of Louis XIV, a refutation of Cartesianism was issued in 1689 by Father Huet.

Nor was the French Catholic the only prelate to see

[1] *Correspondance de Bossuet,* iii, 370.
[2] *Ibid.* iv, 19f.

clearly the emancipating influence of Descartes, as the following quotation from an Anglican bishop will show:

The Cartesian [system] with his Corpuscularian Hypothesis, attempts to explain all the phenomena of nature by matter and motion; requiring only that God should first create a sufficient quantity of each, just enough to set him on work, and then pretends to do the business without his further aid . . . this hypothesis, I say, which, on the one hand contributed so much to free philosophy from the nonsense and tyranny of the Schools, yet on the other produced, while it was in vogue, many rank and irreligious materialists.[1]

In like manner Samuel Parker, Bishop of Oxford, wrote voluminously against Descartes, Hobbes, and Gassendi, whom he classed together as dangerous atheists.

On the other hand, Descartes found some support among theologians, and most of it in the quarter where he least expected it, at Port Royal. The great Jansenist Arnauld read a copy of the *Méditations* lent him by Mersenne, and accepted the greater part of it with delight while writing the author that he thought the method of doubt should be so stated as to give no prejudice to religion, and especially recommending that the words "since I know not hitherto the Author of my being" be amended by adding the words "or at least feign to know nothing." [2] The general opinion of the Jansenists was expressed even more favorably by Robert Desgabets, who wrote that Descartes' works were the most important since the publication of the Gospel and the best written in science for three thousand years.[3]

The Cambridge Platonists, too, accepted Descartes with enthusiasm; their leader, Henry More, writing the philosopher four letters filled with the warmest sentiments of admiration for his as a whole, but making some minor reservations.[4] Later, More changed his favorable opinion.

[1] Warburton: *Divine Legislation of Moses*, iii, 330. Written about 1750, published 1788.
[2] *Œuvres de Descartes*, iii, 334. Sainte-Beuve: *Port Royal*, v, 349ff.
[3] *Correspondance de Bossuet*, i, 223ff.
[4] *Œuvres de Descartes*, v, 236ff.

While Descartes' religious doctrines were hotly debated by the theologians, most of his scientific hypotheses were undermined by the progress of physics. Borelli, indeed, in a physiological work on *The Movement of Animals* (1680-81) adopted the mechanistic explanation of physiological processes. But Perrault (*Essais de Physique*, 1680) refused to regard the pineal gland as the seat of the soul, which he regarded as diffused throughout the entire body.

The most penetrating and yet friendly criticism of Descartes' science came from Christiaan Huygens. Praising the philosopher for rejecting all the old rubbish of "qualities, substantial forms, intentional species" and for substituting for it something clear and comprehensible, he yet characterized the cosmology of the *Principia* as a romance written with such realism as to make fiction pass for fact.[1] Elsewhere he wrote that Descartes was much more skillful in calculating by geometry what the laws of nature ought to be, than in discovering by experiment just what they are.[2] The current of opposition to a scientific method regarded as dogmatic rather than empirical grew until in the next century Voltaire could say that Descartes had set back the clock of science by fifty years.

But his geometry and one or two discoveries in optics remained inexpugnable. Of his more ambitious theories, that of vortices has had the strongest viability. Though already rejected by Huygens in 1690,[3] it was revived by James Clerk Maxwell and Lord Kelvin in the nineteenth century. As lately as 1923 Sir Oliver Lodge wrote: [4]

Probably the ether of space is absolutely continuous, though it may some day be found to have a texture which may be pictured provisionally as a number of vortices like spinning whirls in a continuous ocean of water or air.

Descartes' place in the history of thought and culture is very great. That his philosophy is no more final than any

[1] Huygens: *Œuvres*, x, 403f.   [2] *Ibid*, i, 218.
[3] *Ibid.*, ix, 386.
[4] "The Ether of Space," *Century Magazine*, 1923, p. 889.

other, that the edifice of his cosmology is falling into ruins, only proves that they share the mortality of all things. Perhaps his greatest glory is neither the metaphysics that set the problems for the thinkers of the next three centuries, nor even the wonderful geometry, but the work of popular education which taught the choicer spirits among the cultivated classes to admit only what they could understand. That the order of nature is invariable, that the scientific method is the proper approach to philosophy, that the life of reason is the chief hope and the chief glory of man— these are the truths inculcated by Descartes even though he could not with faultless consistency and at all times apply them himself.

3. HOBBES, THE CARTESIANS, AND SPINOZA

While the emotional bias of Descartes's rationalizations is patent to all eyes, that of Hobbes lies latent under a surface of apparent scientific objectivity and religious indifferentism. And yet Hobbes, no less than Descartes, Spinoza, and Locke, represented and rationalized the interests of a group very strong at that time, the group called in France the *Politiques*, dogmatically indifferent but anxious to find authority for religion, as a conservative and moral force, in the power of the state. On the other hand there appeared in Hobbes the strong interest in natural science characteristic of all the philosophers of his day. The attraction of the methods of natural science for thinkers in the seventeenth century is perhaps all the more impressive in the case of Hobbes because he evinced an even greater genius for blundering in mathematics and physics than for seeing clearly in politics and ethics.

Thomas Hobbes (1588-1679) learned the scholastic philosophy at Oxford, and unlearned it on a trip to the Continent in 1610, when he met Galileo and read the works of Kepler and Montaigne. As an atheist and a Royalist he felt more alarm than interest in the Civil War in England, fled to Paris in 1640, and remained there until 1651, when he judged it safe to return. At Paris he met many of the leaders of French thought. His first noteworthy book published was the Latin *De Cive* (*The Citizen*) in 1642. This was followed by the *Leviathan* in 1651, by *Questions concerning Liberty, Necessity, and Chance* in 1656, by the *Behemoth,* a history of the Civil War written in 1668, but not published until some years later, and by controversial tracts from the hand of the vigorous and pugnacious old man until his death at the age of ninety-one.

Hobbes's brilliant and original contributions to politics have so far thrown his other work into the shade that it is sometimes forgotten that his political theory is but an integral part of a comprehensive philosophical system. As a materialist who had learned from Galileo, Descartes, and Harvey that nature is a machine, he resolved to import the lessons of natural science into the psychological realm and to show that in the mind, as in physical phenomena, there is nothing but matter and motion. And he resolved to be a logical rationalist; to let not feelings, but only reason, rule.

He observed that human knowledge combines sensational and rational elements. When he showed, like Campanella, that perceptions are only the signs of unknown realities, his sensationalism turned into phenomenalism. Our knowledge, he urged, is but the discovery of the mind's own regularity, and the type of this creative activity of the mind is mathematical thought, in which the development of relations and connections is completely independent of the primary values of the elements dealt with. Thus Hobbes—reverting perhaps to the Terminalism he had learned at college,—concluded that all thinking is but a calculation with concepts which are merely the signs of things. The only test of truth possible in such a system is self-consistency. Though such a conception possesses a theoretical value as the germ of a logical calculus, for Hobbes its main interest lies in the practical conclusion that the construction of time and space in the mind develops from sensory perceptions, though their true reality is independent of these.

For Hobbes, therefore, the foundation of our knowledge of the external world is laid in mathematical and logical spontaneity, for only in the form of mathematics and logic is reality accessible to thought; hence all empirically felt reality consists of the perception of the body moved in time and space. But he added that a "body" might be of three sorts: a piece of matter, the body of a man, or an artificial corporation like the state. Thus by one daring definition did Hobbes transplant to the ethical and political world the method derived from natural science.

Nor did he flinch, as all of his predecessors and most of his followers have done. from drawing the logical conclusions of these drastic premises. As far as it was possible at that day he made psychology materialistic. It is true that his method, like that of all psychologists before J. B. Watson, was introspective, and hence to some extent falls under his condemnation of the moral philosophy of the Greeks as being but "the description of their own passions." But though he looked into himself "thereby to read the thoughts and passions of all other men," he saw no "spirits" or other occult qualities in his mind, but only the interaction of various forces. Even consciousness he made a function of matter. The state of the soul he explained solely by reference to the condition of the body. In fact he declared that the "immaterial substance" as used in psychology about a soul, and in theology about God, is mere nonsense. The whole of the mental life he built up on the foundation of the senses, declaring that "there is no conception in man's mind which hath not at first, totally or by parts, been begotten upon the organs of sense," and that "sense" is but "the motion in some of the internal parts of the sentient."

When other philosophers began to attack these shockingly materialistic principles they naturally found the vulnerable parts in Hobbes's body of doctrine in his errors in mathematics and in physics. Descartes went so far as to say that everything in physics proposed by Hobbes as his own was false.[1] Leibniz, while recognizing the wonderful penetration of part of his work,[2] attributed the strange weakness of other parts to mathematical ineptitude. Robert Boyle [3] wrote a refutation of Hobbes's physics in order to lessen the dangerous impression made by his opinions on important articles of religion, and Wallis exposed his mathematical paralogisms for reasons thus explained by him in a letter to Huygens: [4]

Our Leviathan is furiously attacking and destroying our universities (and not only ours but all) and especially ministers and the clergy and all religion, as though the Christian world had no sound knowledge, none that was not ridiculous either in philosophy or religion, and as though men could not understand religion if they did not understand philosophy, nor philosophy unless they knew mathematics. Hence it has seemed necessary that some mathematician should show him, by the reverse process of reasoning, how little he understands the mathematics from which he takes his courage; nor should we be deterred from doing this by his arrogance which we know will vomit poisonous filth against us.

Nevertheless, materialism made continual progress. The French Hobbes was Pierre Gassendi (1592-1650) a Franciscan teacher of mathematics at Aix and at Paris by profession, and a man of the world by temperament. After he had already been tinctured with the skepticism of Montaigne, his eyes were opened to the wonders of the new astronomy by Galileo, with whom he corresponded. At Paris he knew Hobbes and Campanella pleasantly, though his personal relations with Descartes were strained. Looking about for a great antique name under which to shield his principles he revived the fame and rescued the philosophy of Epicurus, a life of whom he published in 1647. Though there was much danger in this, Gassendi escaped punish-

[1] *Œuvres,* iii, 287.
[2] Leibniz: *Fragments Philosophiques,* ed. Couturat, 178.
[3] Boyle's *Works,* i, 186; *An Examen of Mr. T. Hobbes his Dialogus Physicus de Natura Aeris.*
[4] Jan. 1, 1659, Huygens: *Œuvres,* ii, 296.

ment because of his lip service to Christian dogma and because of his irenic temperament. While admitting all the Catholic dogmas as true in a higher sphere, he shut out from the realm of the human reason all properly metaphysical questions, in order to erect in this lower sphere a purely naturalistic interpretation of the world and of man. Matter he assumed to be atomic, uncreated and indestructible. All knowledge he thought to be derived from the senses, and all reasoning to be properly analytical.

The inevitable reaction against Descartes and Gassendi came with Nicholas Malebranche (1638-1715), who was educated at the Collège de la Marche, which he called the "university of Stageira" because of its devotion to Aristotle, and at the Sorbonne. Entering the Oratory in 1660, and ordained priest in 1664, he devoted himself entirely to meditation. With little taste for erudition, and a positive contempt for natural science, he cultivated entirely the moral introspection most profitable to the soul.

Men are not born [he wrote] to become astronomers or chemists, to spend their whole lives hanging on a telescope or chained to a furnace in order to draw useless conclusions from their laborious observations. . . . Men should regard astronomy, chemistry, and almost all other sciences as the amusements of a cultivated man, but we should neither be dazzled by their brilliance nor prefer them to the science of man.[1]

He was, however, convinced of the necessity of mathematics as a discipline to the mind.

He was also very religious, buttressing all his arguments with patristic authorities, and admitting that he preferred Moses to Aristotle and St. Augustine to the "miserable modern commentators of pagan philosophers." So strong is his apologetic interest that he thought Spinoza's doctrines should be rejected, even if his proofs seemed convincing, because of their horrible conclusions and impious consequences. His principal works were the *Search for Truth*

---

[1] *Recherche de la Vérité,* i, p. XV.

(2 volumes, 1674-5), some *Christian Meditations,* and *Conversations on Metaphysics.*

Investigating the relation of matter and mind, Malebranche expounded the two theories of "vision in God" and of "occasional causes." Mind and matter can not interact; their appearance of doing so arises in the fact that God is the source of both mind and matter, of our thoughts as well as of the laws of nature. "We see everything in God" means that God is the cause of our sensations (the Cartesian secondary qualities of matter) as well as of extension and motion (Descartes' primary qualities of matter).

The path of the innovator is hard. Thus Malebranche, who, from rational principles, proved to his own satisfaction not only the existence of God and the immortality of the soul but the divinity of Christ and all the other Christian mysteries, fell foul of the guardians of orthodoxy. "How I hate those philosophers," wrote Bossuet with him in mind, "who, measuring the designs of God by their own thoughts, make of him nothing but the author of a certain general order, from which the rest develops as it can." [1] And, accordingly, he eagerly welcomed refutations of this godless champion of God.

Among the many philosophers to exploit the mines of Cartesian thought, the mightiest was a Jewish lens-grinder of Amsterdam, who gave to modern metaphysics a new and decisive bent. The ancestors of Baruch (or Benedict) de Spinoza were Hebrews expelled from Spain and Portugal. He himself (1632-77) was born in Amsterdam and educated in the Hebrew literature and philosophy. The lessons, both of biblical criticism and of monistic metaphysics, which he imbibed from the writings of the Jewish medieval thinker Maimonides, he never forgot. But his education was expanded beyond that usual among children of his race and time, when he learned Latin from a German master, and a little Greek, some science, and the Cartesian philosophy from an ex-Jesuit free-thinker named Francis van den En-

---

[1] *Correspondance de Bossuet,* ii, 383. *Cf.* Bédier et Hazard, i, 309. Sainte-Beuve: *Port-Royal,* v, 362.

den. His Christian friends were chiefly Mennonites and Collegiants, small sectaries who laid the emphasis in religion on the spirit and not on the rites.

Under these strangely combined influences Spinoza became lax in attendance at the synagogue and even hostile to the ceremonialism of his cult. After various efforts to bribe him into conformity and silence the elders and chief priests of the synagogue cut him off from his people, cursed him with all the curses of the law, and called upon the Lord to destroy his name under heaven. Banished by this act from Amsterdam, after 1656 he lived in various Dutch towns, last of all in the Hague, supporting himself by grinding lenses for optical instruments. This occupation brought on, or aggravated, the consumption of which he died at the early age of forty-four.

His only book to be published during his lifetime was the *Theologico-Political Treatise* printed under the patronage of De Witt in 1670. The publication of his greatest work, the *Ethics*, was prevented by the hostility of theolgians until the year after his death, when it was printed with his *Political Treatise*, his letters, and a few minor works. A few other tracts have come to light since then.

The character of Spinoza is singularly beautiful in a lofty and consistent disregard of all but the one supreme moral good on which he had set his heart. Having early learned by experience, he tells us,[1] that all things encountered in common life are vain and futile; that on the one hand those things commonly dreaded have in them no evil except as they move the mind, and that on the other hand those things for which men usually spend their lives, namely money, lust, and honors, have in them nothing of intrinsic good; he set out to inquire

whether there was any true good capable of imparting itself and of affecting the mind to the exclusion of all else, whether in fact anything existed by the discovery and acquisition of which I might have continuous and supreme joy to all eternity.

[1] *Opera*, i, 3. (1882).

He found this good in the love of God—not the old tribal anthropomorphic Jehovah of his fathers, but the Being revealed by science, so he thought, as identical with the universe.

Though at first he found it hard to renounce the lusts of the flesh and the love of money and of honors, Spinoza at length attained the supreme good he coveted. Absorbed in his high intellectual passion, he soared far above all the lesser passions of earth to dwell in a more than Olympian calm on a throne above the stars from which he could contemplate all things *sub specie aeternitatis*. No human love seduced, no human anger ruffled him; except, indeed, when he felt a noble indignation against the assassins who murdered his friend and patron Jan De Witt, and whom he branded as "the last of the barbarians." He lived happy in poverty, in relative obscurity, and in failing health. Never was disinterestedness, selflessness, so measureless as his. Significant is it that whereas Descartes' philosophy was ego-centric—"*I* think, therefore *I* am,"—that of Spinoza was theocentric—"he is happy who lavishes love on the Lord our God," and "he who loves God aright must not demand that God should love him in return."

One can not understand Spinoza unless one realizes that he is the last of the Hebrew prophets. That he was cut off from his people is but the final proof of his mission, for when has Israel failed to stone the prophets and to crucify those who are sent unto him? His great work, characteristically called *Ethics*—for righteousness is of the Jew, and to this Jew the kernel of philosophy is a moral problem —is written in the grand style, worthy to take a place beside Isaiah and St. Paul. Strange indeed is the beauty of the style and typical of the new age, in that the new gospel is written in the language of mathematics, without rhetoric and ornament but with all the apparatus of definition, axiom, lemma, theorem, scholium, and corollary. But with this unusual and to the uninitiated forbidding material, Spinoza has erected a Doric temple through which blow all the winds of eternity.

Is this sublime and quiet temple also a tomb? Does it contain not the image of the living but the corpse of the dead God? The opposite answers given to this question by different philosophers and successive ages depend on the definition of God. To those who, like the average Christian and the average Deist of that day, need a personal, hearing, and loving God with whom they can be cozily at home, Spinoza seems to be, as Voltaire called him, a timid, little, long-nosed creature who sneaks up to the Supreme Being and whispers apologetically to him, "Excuse me, but I think that you do not exist." But to those who have outlived the old conception of the Deity, and who can nevertheless get something of the old thrill of religion out of the contemplation of nature, Spinoza seems to be, as Heine called him, "a God-intoxicated man."

For, the kernel of Spinozism is the doctrine that there is only one reality in the universe, one substance which may be called God and which is known to us under two of its attributes, extension and consciousness. Thus at one stroke Spinoza substituted for the dualism of Descartes a monism more in harmony both with his own inner needs —perhaps he found something of it in Maimonides—and also more answerable to the new demands of science. To make God all spirit, as the Cartesians had done, was to jeopard the reality of the material world, and to raise an insoluble problem as to the relations of mind and matter. But Spinoza, by placing the ultimate reality in a substance raised above the opposition of mind and matter, gave the best solution that had yet been given, perhaps the best that can be given by philosophy, to the problem of their interaction, as long as philosophy sticks to the concept of "substance" at all.

This led to pantheism. God was now regarded as immanent in all matter and in all thought, not as the cause of things, but as nature or substance itself, thing of things, and very thing of very things. Finite entities, be they bodies or spirits, are but modes of this infinite substance. The necessary relation existing between this substance and its modes is no longer the temporal relation of cause and effect, but the logical relation of premise and consequence —the relation existing between the nature of a curve and the algebraic equation expressing that curve. This substance, God or nature, said Spinoza, possesses an infinitude of attributes, each one of which is in itself infinite. But of this infinite number of attributes two only are known to man—consciousness and extension. These two forms in which God is revealed to man were not, for Spinoza, mere forms of ideas in the human mind, but were genuine aspects of the primal substance. Further, he argued, though the connection of finite things in God's being is original and necessary, our knowledge of this connection presents itself in two completely separate spheres. As these attributes are but aspects of the same substance, the connection of modes in one attribute (consciousness) must be the same as the connection of modes in the other attribute (matter). Hence the correspondence of body and mind. This theory, commonly called parallelism, rejects every form of mutual influence of mind and matter by dispensing with the need for such an interaction.

The corollaries of Spinoza's chief doctrine of pantheism, or the thorough identification of God and nature, imply the doctrine of necessity and determinism in the human will as in external nature, and also the rejection of teleology or judgment of value in science. Most impressive and arousing is his perfectly dispassionate analysis of the processes of the mind. He studied the passions, to quote his own famous phrase, not like previous moral philosophers "to reprobate or mock, but only to understand them . . . treating human actions and appetites just as one would treat lines, planes, and solids in a geometrical problem." [1] Candidly and thoroughly, but without cynical asperity, he tore away the masks of self-deception, and, like Hobbes, explained the passions as derived from the impulse to self-preservation. There are six primal passions in a trinity of opposites: pleasure and pain, love and hate, hope and fear. Will is but

[1] *Ethics,* Book III. *Opera,* i, 125. (1882).

"an appetite with the consciousness thereof," and is not free, being merely the name for the sum of the particular acts of volition, which are not desires but judgments.

The ethical ideal deduced from these premises is that virtue is reason, or sound judgment. Reason demands that every man should love himself and cherish the things that most contribute to self-preservation. Observation told Spinoza that a man's life partakes of the character of that which he loves. Those who love temporal things have a fugitive and transitory existence, but those who love eternal things partake of that eternity. Souls, he inferred, are mortal as they are united with the body, but immortal as they are united with God. This union with God by love is knowledge of God, which frees man from the world and is both liberty and salvation. The wise man is he who "loves God with that intellectual passion with which God loves himself." [1]

There is some truth in Hegel's judgment that "Spinozism is the high-water-mark of modern philosophy, and that we must take either that or no philosphy at all." Even those preferring the second alternative must bear witness to the amazing achievement of the Jew of Amsterdam. Deeply religious and strongly rational, he built a philosophy more honest than that of his French contemporaries and more acceptable to many than the ruthlessly destructive thought of Hobbes. Neither denying nor dissimulating the mechanistic implications of the new science, he succeeded in transferring to a conception of the universe compatible with the materialistic world-view all that immense store of emotion hitherto bound up with the idea of a personal God and with the idealistic morality of historic religion. Though his contemporaries, including Malebranche and Leibniz, denounced him as impious and illogical, he afforded to a later generation steeped in doubt but still craving the consolations of religion, the comfort of hearing the new concept of the material universe explained in the old terms consecrated by pious usage, and extolled with all the fire and fervor of the inspired prophet.

[1] *Ethics*, Part V, *Opera*, i, 272. (1882).

CHAPTER VIII

POLITICAL THEORY

I. THE ORIGINS OF INTERNATIONAL LAW

It is possible to hope that some day we may have experimental sciences of ethics and politics. But in the past
these studies have been little, if at all, more objective than
metaphysics; they have been concerned less with the patient
study of facts, than with justifying, often by singularly acro-
batic contortions of reason, masses of non-rational belief.
This simply means that in the life of humanity, propelled
by instinct and emotion rather than by reason, religion,
morals, and politics have been felt to be too important and
too delicate to bear the rough handling meted out to stars
and to atoms. But though men prefer the comfort of instinctive belief to the suspended judgment and dispassionate
coldness of science in these matters, they can not, nevertheless, be content to leave them alone, but must ever invent some elaborate rationalized justification of their customs and opinions. They must find some harmony between
their inherited beliefs and their acquired science; and still
more urgently do they feel the need of proving that their
interests are sanctioned by some noble, transcendental purpose.

The pressure put on students of politics and ethics to
make their conclusions conform to the interests of the group
to which they belong, is of two kinds, a coarser and a
subtler. In the first place any strong group, nation, or class,
will always have it in its power to reward the teachers
of doctrines agreeable to them, and to punish, suppress,
or slight the champions of new, or dangerous, opinions.
And, as there are always plenty of men corruptible by bribes

and amenable to pressure, a great mass of political writing is but a tissue of suborned evidence in favor of a powerful client. This pressure is so obvious that it was detected by the clearest-sighted political philosopher of the seventeenth century. Though Hobbes was convinced that the study of law should be as rational as mathematics,[1] he pertinently asked

If any man hath been so singular as to have studied the science of justice and equity, how can he teach it safely when it is against the interest of those that are in possession of the power to hurt him? [2]

And again, still more strongly, he averred that ethics are constantly disputed, while mathematical demonstrations are universally accepted, because in the first case men care not for truth but for their own profit:

For I doubt not, [said he] but if it had been a thing contrary to any man's right of dominion, that the three angles of a triangle should be equal to two angles of a square, that doctrine should have been, if not disputed, yet by the burning of all books of geometry suppressed, as far as he whom it concerned was able.[3]

So much subtler than this first kind of pressure is the second, and unconscious kind, that it has escaped detection until the twentieth century. Only recently has it been shown that man, being a gregarious animal, is extraordinarily liable to group suggestion. From the herd he receives the vast bulk of his beliefs and prejudices, which come to him with instinctive force, and seem generally to be *a priori* syntheses, needing no proof but their own self-evidence. Men of different nations and of different parties arrive at diametrically opposite conclusions on public questions, not because those of one group are less logical than

[1] *A Dialogue on the Common Laws of England, Works,* vi, 3.
[2] *Behemoth, Works,* vi, 212.
[3] *Leviathan,* bk. i, cap. 11, Works, iii, 91.

those of another, but because their premises are different, and these premises consist of beliefs that seem axiomatic to each disputant. Acceptance of works on politics is not due to their logic, nor even to the beneficence, humanity, and nobility for which they are praised, but largely to their appeal to the prejudices of a powerful group. The scientific interest, though present, and growing, has been subordinate to the practical interest.

The political theory of the seventeenth century, therefore, showed but little objectivity. As in metaphysics, so in political philosophy, whereas the form was often subjected to the mathematical method so valued for its success in the physical sciences, this form was little but a disguise for a more practical purpose, conscious or unconscious. The thought of the century was mainly taken up with three pressing problems: the creation of international law, the justification of the various parties in the English Civil War, and the discussion of the relation of French and Spanish absolutism to the rights of the Catholic Church. In each of these three questions there were various interests, and each major interest found apologists to proclaim its purposes in harmony with the eternal principles of right and reason. There is also just discernible during this period the beginning of statistics and economics—a small seed from which a true political science was destined to grow.

The conditions necessitating the creation of a new International Law arose partly in the Reformation. partly in the growth of Nationalism, partly in the commercial competition of maritime states in the newly discovered quarters of the globe. Medieval Western Europe had been bound into a compact community by the difficulties of communication with other continents, by the sense of an inherited common Roman culture embodied in the somewhat shadowy institution of the Holy Roman Empire, and by a lively sense of communion in the Roman Catholic Church. The regulation of international relations, and of the relations of state and church, though often rough and sordid in practice, was comparatively simple, and theoretically idealistic. But when the Reformation had broken the unity of faith, making Protestants and Catholics odious to each other under the names of heretics and idolaters, a series of religious wars broke out, evilly eminent in the history of the world for their atrocity and destructiveness.

The growth of nationalism also divided the commonwealth of Europe. Bursting the bonds of the old Roman imperial tradition, great national states arose, animated by an intense patriotism, and acknowledging no law but that of force. To secure order, to cultivate wealth, and to foster military power at home, and to expand to the limits imposed by the collision with equal or superior power abroad, were the laws of their being. Machiavelli was their prophet, and the "reason of state" their gospel—a maxim of policy expressing the idea that the public interest is above justice and humanity, that might makes right, and that the safety of the people is the highest law. At times conflicting with the idealistic motives of the religious wars, at times strangely combined with them into one policy, were the materialistic aims of the governments. The Thirty Years War, starting as an attempt to wipe out Protestantism by arms, evolved into a dynastic struggle for the secular interests of the powers engaged. It was the constant torment of Richelieu to be forced, as he often was, to bend the interests of the Catholic church to the exigencies of France's needs. And, besides the wars of religion, there were many wars of a purely and avowedly secular nature. "We are first Venetians and secondarily Christians" said the Venetian Doge who declared war on the Papacy. "Interest's the god they worship in their state," wrote Dryden of the Dutch, and added "states are atheists in their very frame.".

And, finally, the opening of new continents to European exploitation necessitated the formulation of new rules for dealing with the novel problems involved. At first the publicists debated the right of the Europeans to seize the lands of the natives of the East and West Indies; but when this had been settled by the whites in their own favor, more thorny problems arose in the dealings of the various colonizing nations with each other. Particularly was the right of one nation to exclude others from navigating portions of the ocean and from trading with certain quarters of the globe debated first by cannon and then by pens.

Just as the need for a new code of international intercourse became urgent, confidence in the authority of the church, to which men had been wont to appeal, broke down. In these circumstances, publicists and statesmen necessarily groped for some new authority binding on men of all religions alike, and they found it in the idea of a law of nature, or law common to all nations because founded on humanity and reason. This idea, as old as the Greeks, lay almost dormant during the Middle Ages, to wake to a new life in the sixteenth century. Not only by the Reformers, publicists, and rulers, but even by the poets,[1] the law of nature and of nations was invoked to supply the want of positive statutes governing the actions of states.

The first to formulate the new problems of international morality were the Italian Alberico Gentili (1552-1608) and the Spaniard Francisco Suarez (1548-1617), who groped after a law of nature and a law of nations binding on all men alike and revealed by reason.

A more thorough and successful attempt firmly to found and clearly to formulate international law was made by Hugo Grotius, commonly regarded as the father of this branch of jurisprudence. Born of good family at Delft, Grotius (1583-1645), with the precocity of genius, matriculated at the University of Leyden at the age of twelve, and, in contact with Scaliger, early attained proficiency in the classics, and also in philosophy, mathematics, astronomy, and jurisprudence.

His attention was soon directed to problems of international law by a commission from the Dutch East India Company to explain and defend their right to trade in the East and West Indies. At this early stage of Dutch maritime enterprise it was to the interest of the newcomers to protest against the vested rights and ancient monopoly of

[1] Spenser: *Faery Queen*, Bk, V, ix, 44; Milton: *Samson Agonistes*, 890.

Spain and Portugal in the distant seas. At the age of twenty-one Grotius composed a treatise *On the Law of Prize,* so remarkably thorough that it falls little short of being a code of international law in itself. As this work was much too large for the purposes of the East India Company, and as most of its material was later incorporated into his greater work, the author never published this treatise as a whole, but only one chapter of it, *On the Freedom of the Seas,* in 1608. This little tract ably argues, from biblical and other authorities and from the natural law of reason, that the sea is the common property of all mankind, incapable of private appropriation.

In 1616 Grotius was made Grand Pensionary of Holland and West Friesland. As the champion of the weaker party in the Arminian controversy, he incurred the hostility of Maurice of Nassau and of the Gomarists, and was imprisoned. Escaping to France he published in 1625 his great work on *The Law of War and of Peace.* For ten years he was employed by Sweden to represent her at Paris. Visiting Sweden in 1645, he died in the same year. Besides his works on jurisprudence he left many theological commentaries and treatises and a history of the Dutch war of independence.

The Law of War and of Peace begins with a thorough investigation of the source and validity of natural law. For the English word "law," Latin, French, and German have two words, "jus," "droit," and "Recht" for that law founded in common right, and "lex," "loi," and "Gesetz" for that law founded in statute. It is significant that Grotius prefers the words "jus naturale" to "lex naturalis" to indicate law's basis in right and reason rather than in the legislative act of God. The law of nature, he in fact expressly stated, is like the laws of mathematics and physics, inherent in reason and immutable even by God himself. The field for the action of this law of nature is society and the state, the former originating in man's social or domestic instinct, the latter in a mutual compact. To conserve society self-regard must be tempered by regard for others, and this tendency to social self-preservation is the source of natural law.

As this natural law governs every society, and not merely a particular state, it must govern that large society formed by the aggregate of all states or of humanity as a whole. Its sanction is found in the fact that any nation disregarding it will suffer and perhaps perish, and that all nations find it to their common interest to enforce it, just as all societies, even bands of robbers, are bound to recognize and to enforce good conduct among their members. And where has this law been formulated? Grotius is persuaded that it is instinctively recognized by mankind, and that it has been enunciated in the dicta not only of jurists and publicists but in those of poets and orators. Hence the vast mass of quotation, mostly from the Bible and classical authors, but also from modern treaties and statutes, is not the intolerable pedantry it at first seems, but a necessary re-enforcement of the argument. As Grotius was no legislator with authority to promulgate statutes binding on all nations, he was obliged to buttress his opinions by appeals to the authorities then generally recognized as valid. In order to make out a consistent body of natural right agreeable to his notions of humanity and reason, he was obliged to sift and choose his authorities. For he did not consider the practices of all peoples as equally cogent in proving the existence of a natural right. What he really did was to select the customs of European nations, and only the better practices of the more enlightened among these, as his criteria.

Much space he took in discussing whether any war can be just, and if so, what wars. His conclusion is that any war to repel an injury or to avenge an insult to God is just, but that a war for conquest, or to weaken a power increasing so as likely to become dangerous, or for any other cause, is unjust. As an alternative to war he suggested arbitration, as had been done by Erasmus, by Campanella and by others before him.

The third and last book of the treatise considered the

use of deceit in war, the treatment of captives, and restraints on the rights of slaughter, of devastation, and of pillage, and also expounded the rights and duties of neutrals. It was all inspired by the humane and rational purpose to reduce to a minimum the sufferings incident to arms.

Whether, as is sometimes stated, Grotius' work had an immediate influence in tempering the horrors of the war waged by Richelieu against La Rochelle and that waged by Gustavus Adolphus in Germany, and in humanizing the provisions of the Peace of Westphalia, it is certain that much that he first clearly advanced has become the admitted rule of international intercourse. Here, however, we must be on our guard against attributing to the influence of a book developments dependent on the material interests of the powers. Grotius never persuaded any power to act on his rules contrary to its own interests. His service, considerable enough, was but to see and to express what the common interests of the majority of European nations actually were.

That Grotius' pronouncements had no convincing power in quarters where they were repugnant to national interests, was at once proved by the attacks made on him by an Englishman. John Selden (1584-1654) combined in one capacious brain the accomplishments of a jurist, an antiquary, an orientalist, a statesman, and a wit. In 1618 he was commissioned by the English government to answer Grotius' *Freedom of the Seas,* for, though Grotius had aimed primarily at the commercial monopolies of Spain and Portugal, his arguments galled the neck of England, aspiring to be, and rapidly growing to be, the leading maritime power of the world. Selden's treatise, *On the Closure of the Seas,* though finished in 1618, was held back by officials who feared that certain of its expressions were not strong enough, until 1635. And yet Selden undertook to prove that the sea is not common to all men, but is capable of private dominion or private property like land, and that in fact the lordship of the seas adjacent to Great Britain was and had been an inseparable and perpetual appendant

of the British Empire.[1] To prove his first thesis he quoted
such texts as that of the Bible saying that God gave Adam
dominion over the fish, and to prove his second point he
quoted recent treaties in which other powers had acknowledged the maritime supremacy of England. His sources were
the same, his arguments as learned, as those of Grotius.
That modern law in this respect follows the Dutchman is
not due to the greater force of his arguments, but to the fact
that one nation, however powerful, has found it impossible
to enforce the monopoly she desired.

In 1640 Selden published a more comprehensive criticism
of Grotius in a work entitled *Of the Law of Nature and of
Nations according to the Teachings of the Hebrews*. Having
once remarked that he could not conceive what the law of
nature meant but the law of God,[2] Selden set out to show
that those writers who assumed that they could discover
the laws of nations by comparing the customs of all peoples
were on slippery ground. There can be no common law of
the world, he argued, except that which is prescribed to
mankind by their Maker, and this can be ascertained only
by consulting the historical records in the Bible. Twice, it
is therein set down, did God prescribe laws to all mankind,
once to Adam and once to Noah, and he also enacted a few
other laws expressly for mankind at large and not for the
Jewish race alone. Among these are the prohibitions of
idolatry, blasphemy, incest, theft, and eating a part of an
animal yet living,[3] and the injunction to civil obedience.

Though this work seems to modern readers hopelessly
antiquated in method, it appeared to many contemporaries
the authoritative Protestant statement likely to supersede
the Canon Law, being, as Milton put it, "a noble volume
more useful and worthy to be perused . . . than all those
decretals and sumless sums which pontifical clerks have
doted on." [4] This eulogy is the more remarkable in that

---

[1] "Imperium Britannicum," Selden: *Mare Clausum*, 1633, p. 225. On use
of the phrase "British Empire" in Tudor and Stuart times, see *Historische
Zeitschrift*, cxxxvii, 52.

[2] *Table Talk, Opera*, iii, 2041.

[3] *Cf.* Acts, xv, 20.   [4] *Prose Works*, ii, 148.

Selden, with his ironical joy in cracking ancient idols, spoke with little respect of some things reverenced by Milton, such as baptism and the authority of Scripture.

Skepticism similar to that of Selden as to the possibility of ascertaining the law of nature by the comparative method was expressed by Pascal [1] in a thought reminiscent of Montaigne:

They confess that justice is not in these [local] customs, but that it resides in natural laws, known in every land. Doubtless they would maintain this opinion obstinately if, among all the laws which chance has sown among humanity, they had found even one which was universal. But, as if to turn them to derision, the caprice of men is so diversified that there is not a single universal law. Theft, incest, the murder of parents and children have all been esteemed virtuous actions in some place or other. . . . Doubtless there are natural laws, but our beautiful corrupt reason has corrupted them all.

In spite of all criticism, the seed sown by Grotius grew, though it grew slowly. The word "international law," however, is said to have been coined much later by Bentham.

2. POLITICAL THEORIES OF THE ENGLISH COMMONWEALTH

If the growth of international intercourse and of world commerce necessitated the formulation of international law, the revolutionary changes which transformed European society in the seventeenth century set for the political theorists a new set of problems. One of the most marked notes of modern politics has been the gradual growth of democracy, the spread of civic power to larger and larger classes. The rise of the Third Estate, or the middle class of merchants, and the consequent curtailment of the privileges of priestly and noble classes, brought to the mind of all Europe a revolutionary ferment. In some countries the monarch became the ally and then the master of the bourgeoisie; in others,

[1] *Pensées,* ed Brunschwicg, no. 294.

the leaders of the third estate were able to call even the monarch to account.

The republican movement went furthest in the Calvinist lands of Britain, the United Netherlands, and New England, because Calvinism and capitalism were allies, and capitalism was the economic father of republicanism. The English Puritans bore the brunt of the struggle in Europe and America, after the Dutch War of Independence had deposed the Spanish tyrant and set up a Republic. In New England the Republican movement was fostered by conditions peculiarly favorable to equality and to self-government. In that Calvinist society the self-constituted, or Independent, congregation, was the primary aspect of each community, and the political organization was effected in conscious or unconscious imitation of the ecclesiastical. Moreover, America was destined to be republican because of the mere lack of materials for the formation of an aristocracy and because of the approximately equal distribution of wealth. The Mayflower Compact, the Fundamental Orders of Connecticut, and the Newport Declaration, all gave living examples of the foundation of states by contract between equal and free men, and all expressed, without reserve, republican principles. It is true that even in New England the middle-class settlers were no more intentionally democratic than they were in old England. The privileges of their class were all they really cared for. John Cotton who "employed his peculiar cares on the ecclesiastical constitution" of Massachusetts, thought that democracy was not ordained by God as a fit government, either for church or commonwealth, for, he asked, "if the people be the governors, who shall be the governed?" Consequently, religious and property qualifications were set up for voters in most of the colonies which nevertheless, as Clarendon clearly saw, were "hardening into republics" all the while. "We have drunk," wrote Roger Williams to Vane, "of the cup of as great liberties as any people we can hear of under heaven."

The example of America worked like leaven in the old country. New Englanders were received at first with

compassion as men "expulsed from their dearest homes by
the fury of the bishops," [1] and then with honor as pioneers
blazing the path to liberty. New Englanders took an active
part in all stages of the rebellion even until the final act
when one of them, Mr. Hugh Peters, of Salem, preached
the funeral sermon of the king, after sentence, taking his
text out of Isaiah: "Thou art cast out of the grave like
an abominable branch . . . as a carcass trodden under feet,
because thou hast destroyed thy land and slain thy people."

Men first *do*, and then justify their doings by philosophy.
All parties in the civil war put forward defences founded
on afterthoughts rather than acted on principles evolved
a priori. The supremacy of Parliament was vigorously asserted by its members and their class. Justification for its
acts were sought in history, particularly in Magna Charta
and in the supposed statute *De tallagio non concedendo*. An
antiquarian revival unearthed precedents, some well founded
and others spurious, to legitimate contemporary assertions
of liberty. The Common Law was declared by Sir Edward
Coke to be superior to the king. Selden spoke of kings as
"a thing men have made for their own sake, and for quiet-
ness' sake." In the *Declaration of the Parliament of England, expressing the grounds of their late proceedings and
of settling the government in the way of a Free State*, dated
March 22, 1649, the Parliamentarians set forth that kings
had been instituted by agreement of the people and were
accountable to the same. Nor did they shrink from a practical application of their belief, sending the king to the
block "as a malefactor . . . to teach all kings to know
that they were accountable and punishable for the wickedness of their lives." [2]

Though in that day, when the masses were monarchical
with all the instinctive force of custom, tradition, and inertia, it took signal ability to depose a king and signal
courage to punish him with death, the hardest task remained,
which was to reconcile the nation to the dominance of a

[1] Milton, *Prose Works,* i, 44, 187. (1641).
[2] Clarendon, xi, 224.

class still in a considerable minority. For, the Puritan revolution, like most others, was carried through not by a majority, but by a comparatively small, vigorous, and powerful, minority. Not only was the greater part of the national wealth, intelligence, and ability, in the hands of the rebels, but the religious cast of their minds gave to their aspirations a transcendental sanction. Conscious of being the chosen vessels of divine grace, kings by the election of Providence and priests by the imposition of God's hands, the Puritans always felt themselves to be an aristocracy, a small élite in this world and the "chosen few" in the next. Of their own mission they never harbored a doubt, and they bravely lived up to it. Their rise to power was not so much like a usurpation as like the advancement of able men taking their natural place in society.

But to the world at large the claims of their class did not seem so evidently right as they seemed to the Puritans themselves. To justify themselves they must appeal to eternal principles—and the great principle they discovered was that of liberty, or, of the liberties of Englishmen. The right of the individual to live his life and to enjoy his property within the limits fixed by known law was by them forever rendered secure. Both the Latin word "liberty," [1] and the Teutonic word "freedom," [2] are etymologically connected with words meaning pleasure, the fundamental idea of both being that liberty or freedom is the ability to do as one pleases. It is remarkable that the Puritans, who frowned on all carnal delight and on all frivolous amusements, should so passionately have idealized this doctrine of liberty,—which, after all, means nothing but pleasure—which liberty they found in the right to live one's own life, to say what one thinks, and to make and spend money, without unnecessary interference by the government. From king and lords they exacted security against imprisonment and punishment except by due process of law; while their class superiority to the masses was guaranteed by privileges, political and social, attaching to "the sacred right of property."

[1] liber, libet, libido.   [2] frei, froh, Freude.

In John Milton (1608-74) the Puritan Republicans found a mighty trumpeter of their claims. In his deep religious and political convictions, in his public spirit, courage, and temper, in his egotism, conscious pride in his own superiority and almost fierce determination to cultivate and discipline his powers and to exact from himself the uttermost, Milton was a typical Puritan. His father, a well-to-do London scrivener, early recognized his gifts, and gave him every opportunity to cultivate them. We can imagine him saying, like Jesus in *Paradise Regained* (i, 201):

> When I was yet a child no childish play
> To me was pleasing; all my mind was set
> Serious to learn and know, and thence to do
> What might be public good.

And in his own person he tells us that from early youth he aspired "to leave something so written to after times, as they should not willingly let it die."

At Cambridge University, on a journey to the Continent, in the London theaters, and in quiet study and retirement, he mastered all that was best in ancient and in modern literature. His early lyrics and pastorals show the depth of his religion, the extent of his culture, and the exquisite beauty of his poetic style. In another age Milton might have lived as retired and private a life as Tennyson or Wordsworth, cultivating poetry and piety alone. But when the Civil War broke out his whole being throbbed with the conflict. The ideal that gave consistency to a life of many apparent inconsistencies—for he was by turns monarchist and republican in politics, Anglican, Presbyterian, Independent and Individualist in religion—was devotion to liberty. From the first dawn of his reason to his death this was his "unchangéd mind." He refused to take holy orders because he saw that he who did so "must subscribe slave." When travelling in Europe he returned at once to England upon hearing that his "fellow-citizens were fighting for liberty." He lost his eyesight, as he proudly proclaims, "in liberty's defence, my noble task, with which all Europe rings from side to side."

Primarily, his ideal of liberty was found in rational self-government, something to be sought from within rather than from without, in sobriety of conduct and in integrity of life. But this implied free worship, free speech, free marriage and divorce, and freedom in general from the tyranny of custom, which "of all masters that have ever taught hath drawn the most disciples after him," and which, countenancing error, "would persecute and choose away all truth and solid wisdom out of life" were it not for "free reasoning." [1]

Milton's theory of freedom in church and state was set forth in a series of tracts, including, *The Reason of Church Government*, 1641; *Of Prelatical Episcopacy*, 1641; the *Areopagitica*, 1644; the *Eikonoklastes*, 1649; the *Pro Populo Anglicano Defensio*, 1649; *The Tenure of Kings and Magistrates*, 1649; and, in 1659, *The Ready and Easy Way to establish a Free Commonwealth, and the Excellence thereof compared with the Inconveniences of readmitting Kingship to this Nation*. These works, particularly the last which was argued with passionate vehemence, rendered him so obnoxious to Royalist vengeance that it is a mystery how he escaped the scaffold after the Restoration.

Milton's ideal of a state polity was a republic, which, he claimed, "is not only held by wisest men of all ages the noblest, the manliest, the equallest, the justest government, the most agreeable to all due liberty and proportioned equality, both human, civil, and Christian, most cherishing to virtue and true religion, but also, I may say it with greatest probability, plainly commended or rather enjoined by our Saviour himself." [2] Arguing that men are naturally born free, with the power of self-defence and self-preservation, he concluded that states had been founded by agreement, that kings and magistrates are elected deputies, without power save as it is delegated by the people

---

[1] *Doctrine and Discipline of Divorce, Prose Works*, ii, 73f.
[2] Matthew xx, 25f; Milton's *Prose Works*, ii, 306.

and with no title, in any case, to what the people can not delegate, namely sovereignty. The people have a right to choose and to change their government, and to depose and punish their kings. As means for preserving liberty Milton recommended dividing the nation into small republics with powers of local self-government, a supreme senate over all, a third part to be elected annually or at longer intervals, and the separation of the legislative from the judicial-executive power, allowing supremacy to the former. He had no liking for democracy, however, for to him the people were but "a herd confused, a miscellaneous rabble, who extol things vulgar," [1] and one main part of liberty was "the advancement of every person according to his merit" — or the career open to character.[2]

For proof of his propositions Milton argued from right reason, and quoted the Bible, ancient writers, Magna Charta, Hotman, and the *Vindiciae contra Tyrannos*, which he attributed to Beza, though it was almost certainly written by Duplessis-Mornay.

Naturally, Milton and the Independents considered a free church essential to the maintenance of political liberty. One of the pressing questions left by the Reformation was the relation of church and state. The Roman Catholic church had advanced the claim, acknowledged by all Western European states before the time of Luther, to be the final authority in matters of dogma and morals. When the Protestants seceded from her communion, they were soon obliged to define the nature and to discover the depository of religious authority. Two tendencies early manifested themselves, towards congregationalism and towards established state churches. Though Luther himself wavered, he finally decided that the civil government is charged with the duty of enforcing orthodoxy. That this made the civil government the final spiritual authority in matters of dogma was concealed from the Reformers by their belief in an objective standard in the Bible. In that book, to which they appealed,

[1] *Paradise Regained*, iii, 49ff.
[2] *Prose Works*, ii, 329.

they believed they had found a system of absolute truth
revealed so clearly that all good and sensible men would
interpret it as they themselves did; the function of the
civil authority was then merely to enforce this certain doctrine as expounded by pious ministers. But, in fact, the
power of interpreting implied the power of defining dogma.

When this was clearly seen, the doctrine of the *de jure*
subordination of the church to the state became known
as Erastianism, though it is not really found in the writings of Thomas Erastus, but was first clearly formulated
by certain Englishmen. If we ask, said Selden, whether
the church or Scripture is the judge of religion, we should
answer neither, but the state. This he thought necessarily
true even in Catholic lands like France and Spain. "The
pope is infallible," he asserted, "where he hath power to
command, that is, where he must be obeyed; so is every
supreme power and prince." [1]

While in England, as elsewhere in Protestant Europe, the
established church naturally represented the interests of
the governing classes, the sectaries dissatisfied with her,
and the classes unable to use the power of the state to
reform her, naturally attacked the union of church and
state, and expressed a preference for free churches with
congregational government. Such claims, put forward in
the first years of the Reformation by the Anabaptists, became strong in England towards the end of the sixteenth
century under the name of Brownism or Independency.

To combat them, and to defend the established church,
Richard Hooker (1553-1600) wrote his *Laws of Ecclesiastical Polity*, of which the first four books were published in
1593 or 1594, and the remaining books, poorly edited and
interpolated, posthumously. Not only the eighth book, expressly dedicated to proving that church and state are one,
and that the civil power has jurisdiction in ecclesiastical
matters, but the earlier books, on the authority of Scripture and on ritual, are saturated with the idea that peace is
only attainable by submission to authority, that the same

[1] *Table Talk, Opera*, iii, 2055, 2057, 2067.

natural laws founded civil and spiritual societies, and that to separate church from state is dangerous to the established civil order, and particularly to the privileges of the crown and of the nobility. It is notable that Hooker, starting from the same premises of the law of nature and of the foundation of society by contract, which were later used against the throne and church, should arrive at conclusions so different from those of the radicals.

The contrary view, that there should be a free church in a free state was defended by Milton in various tracts on church government published in 1641:

I am not of opinion [he wrote] to think the church a vine in this respect, because, as they take it, she can not subsist without clasping about the elm of worldly strength and felicity, as if the heavenly city could not support itself without the props and buttresses of secular authority.[1]

The allegation, he continues, "that the church government must be conformable to the civil polity . . . is the very maxim that moulded the calves of Bethel and Dan."

Next to Milton, though at a long distance, the most eminent representative of Puritan political theory is James Harrington (1611-77), a politician at first on good terms with King Charles, and then with the Republicans. His political ideas, less radical but more systematic than those of Milton, were set forth with much prolixity in his utopia, *The Commonwealth of Oceana,* published in 1656. In this, England appears as Oceana, Scotland as Marpesia, Ireland as Panopea, and Cromwell as Olphaus Megaletor, or Oliver the Magnificent. An ideal constitution is exhibited, assimilating the military to the political order (as had been done by Cromwell). The chief officers should be a Strategus (or General), an Orator (for civil government) and two censors; and the legislative power should be partly deposited in a senate, which should initiate legislation for the voters at large to ratify or reject. A national church is provided for and subordinated to the civil magistrates. One of Har-

[1] *Reformation in England, Prose Works,* i, 2, 34.

rington's most original suggestions is that political is dependent on economic power. Stability can be assured only by giving the franchise to property owners. The English rebellion he traced (with much plausibility) to the shift of property under Henry VIII when the monasteries were dissolved and a new aristocracy created and endowed with their lands. One of Harrington's suggestions for the preservation of liberty is that the government should be "the empire of laws and not of men."

While Milton and Harrington rationalized the interests of the Third Estate or bourgeoisie, triumphant in the Commonwealth, there arose a party far to the left of them, the proletariat, or, as they were called at that time, the Levellers. In the turmoil of civil war there came to the surface the claims of the vast masses of the poor to equal political rights and sometimes to equal property rights. In many earlier peasants' revolts such communistic and democratic claims had been put forward, but the risings had been suppressed by the upper classes, and the doctrines of equality were always regarded as either purely academic (as in More's *Utopia*), or as the wicked pretexts for the spoliation of the rich by rascals.[1]

During the troubled year 1647-48, in the Parliamentary Army, these democratic and communistic ideas were reborn. The ideals of equal opportunity for all and of universal manhood suffrage were put forward and argued on the ground of the law of nature and the law of God. Whereas Prynne and Hampden and Cromwell would have been content with the "rights of Englishmen," the Levellers appealed to the rights of man. The new party was brought forth in August 1647 by the issue of the supremacy of Parliament. The House of Commons, representing the propertied classes, had been exalted by possessors of the franchise in the war against the king. Now the Levellers, belonging mostly to

---

[1] See Spenser: *Mother Hubbard's Tale*, 1591. The Fox argues for community of goods by the law of nature, and takes his share of others' property by theft and fraud. Many of the Reformers wrote against communism.

the unenfranchised poor, accused the Parliament of exercising the same tyranny as did the king, and denounced the Common Law as the badge of slavery fastened by the Norman aristocracy on the Saxon masses at the conquest.

The chief representative of Leveller theory, as well as the most active leader of the party, was John Lilburne (c. 1616-1657) a man educated by reading the Puritan divines and Fox's *Book of Martyrs*. He early engaged in the printing of Puritan and seditious tracts in the Netherlands, was tried and cruelly punished by the Star Chamber in 1638, entered the Parliamentary army, fought bravely as a colonel, and devoted the rest of his life to championing the rights of the masses. In his numerous pamphlets he set forth that the Machiavellian policy of kings, lords, and clergy had deprived the people of their natural and national rights, freedoms, and immunities, that men are free and equal by nature, that governments have been instituted by compacts to preserve these rights, and that certain liberties are indefeasible even by the consent of the governed. In order to insure these rights against encroachments, the radicals drew up a written constitution, called *The Agreement of the People,* which, however, was never put in force.

Though the arguments of the Levellers were very similar to, and exactly as logical as, those of the moderate Puritans, they failed to carry conviction with men whose interests predisposed them to reject such appeals. The two parties came to blows, and the proletarian radicals were suppressed by the arms of Fairfax and of Cromwell. They soon came to regard the new Commonwealth, which had promised them so much and then failed them, with a hatred more bitter than that with which they had visited the old monarchy.

It must not be supposed that the innovators were the only party feeling the need of inventing principles to justify their interests. There was plenty of rationalization on the Royalist side also. One of the first to take up the pen in defence of the divine right of monarchs was King James, the Sixth of Scotland and the First of England. After having seen his mother first deposed by her own Scots and then beheaded by the Queen of England, he had been thoroughly, one might say drastically, educated by men whose learning he turned into pedantry and whose principles he came to abhor as restraints on his own conduct. Not content with acting, as far as he was able, on despotic principles, he preached them in season and out of season to his Parliaments, and wrote in their defence a book on *The True Law of Free Monarchy* (1598). This answer to his preceptor Buchanan's treatise on *The Constitution of Scotland* (1579) sustained a claim of the divine right of kings by arguments drawn from Scripture, from the laws of Scotland, and from the law of nature:

The state of monarchy [the royal author asserted] is the supremest thing upon earth; for kings are not only God's lieutenants and sit upon God's throne, but even by God himself they are called gods. . . . As it is atheism and blasphemy to dispute what God can do . . . so it is presumption and high contempt in a subject to dispute what a king can do, or say that a king cannot do this or that.

A far more brilliant attempt to justify despotism than any of which James was capable was made by Thomas Hobbes. For, Hobbes, influenced by the natural science of his contemporaries, and by the psychology to which he had contributed so much himself, went to the very root of the matter and grounded his apology for absolute government on an impressive theory of the origin and nature of society and of the state. Like most political philosophers he gathered his data more than he himself was aware from his immediate environment. The individualism shaping his theory of the self-sufficiency and autonomy of men in a state of nature was inherited from Puritan doctrine and from the common law of England. While the Civil War in England and the Fronde in France, threatening anarchy in both nations, filled him with horror, the strength of the French government and the brilliance of Parisian society excited his admiration. His ideas were exhibited in the Latin *De Cive,* written in 1642, revised in 1647, and translated into English as the *Rudiments of Philosophy,* and in the English *Leviathan,* published in 1651.

Founding his politics on his materialistic psychology, and on travellers' accounts of the ignoble savage, he imagined that men had originally lived in a state of nature which was not only ante-social but anti-social, for in it there would be no industry, no agriculture, no arts, no letters, no security, but a continual fear, so that the life of man would be "solitary, poor, nasty, brutish, and short." Man's egotism, coupled with the fact that all men are roughly equal in power, would produce a perpetual war of all against all, and would thereby defeat the very end, self-preservation, so passionately sought. In such a condition there could be no injustice, for "natural right is the liberty each man hath to use his own power, as he will himself, for the preservation of his own . . . life." But, as unrestricted exercise of this right proved to be suicidal, men soon discovered natural laws "or general rules found out by reason, by which a man is forbidden to do that which is destructive to his life,"—such laws as those enjoining peace, good faith, humility, gratitude, mercy, equity, modesty, and doing unto others as we would have them do unto us.

Having arrived at this point, men in a state of nature, said Hobbes, erected a commonwealth in order to get peace and security by enforcing the laws of nature, previously binding upon the conscience only. They did this by a contract conferring on one man, or one assembly of men, all their natural rights. "This is the generation of that great Leviathan, or, rather, to speak more reverently, of that mortal god, to whom we owe, under the immortal God, our peace and defence." And this corporation, the state,

is one body, of whose acts the great multitude, by mutual covenants, one with another, have made themselves every one the author, to the end that he may use the strength and means of them all, as he shall think expedient, for their common peace and defence.

The sovereign is therefore absolute; his acts cannot justly be accused by the subject, nor can he be justly punished by his subjects. Liberty exists in those matters which the sovereign sees fit to leave unregulated by law, except, indeed, that no man can be supposed to have abrogated his right of self-defence, and therefore none can be forced to kill himself or to put his life in danger by the sovereign's command. But no man has a natural right to property or to any other liberty to the exclusion of the sovereign power. Hobbes recognized the threefold division of states—monarchies, aristocracies, and republics—according as the sovereign is one man, an assembly of a part of the citizens, or an assembly of them all. He argued that monarchy is the preferable form.

With faultless logic Hobbes continued his disquisition by proving that the sovereign power is as supreme in spiritual as in temporal matters. In him at last we see the logical result of the Reformation theory recognizing the state as the final authority in religion. True, his ruthless reasoning shocked beyond measure the Christians of his time, for they still fancied that the authority of the state in ecclesiastical matters could be and was limited to the enforcement of dogma and discipline previously ascertained to be true and right by clear revelation, whereas he saw that the enforcement of a dogma did not depend on its orthodoxy, but its orthodoxy on its enforcement. For, Hobbes, notwithstanding his lip-service to the established religion, and notwithstanding his constant appeals to Scripture, which he cited as fluently as the devil in the wilderness, was embarrassed by no religious convictions. Religion to him was like any other social phenomenon, to be investigated by the scientist and to be utilized by the statesman.

The animus of his argument aimed to demolish the view held by many Protestants as well as by all Catholics, that the church has authority independent of the state. "Temporal and spiritual government," he protested, "are but two words brought into the world to make men see double and mistake their lawful sovereign." A church he defined as "a company of men professing the Christian religion, united in the person of one sovereign, at whose command they ought to assemble, and without whose authority they ought not to assemble." No appeal can be made to any authority, either to the Scripture or to miracles, against the religion established by the government.

Hobbes's effort to defend the royal power and the established church met with much the same reception from royalists and Anglicans that Descartes' efforts to prove the existence of God met with from theologians. Whatever his conclusions, his rationalistic method and inhumanly ruthless logic laid bare the quick and quivering nerves of true believers. Not until two centuries of speculation had accustomed men's eyes to bear the light without wincing, did Hobbes come into his own as a great political philosopher. Not that all the criticism directed against him by contemporaries was unfounded. When Sir Robert Filmer said that Hobbes's theory of a state of nature assumed that men "had all of a sudden sprung out of the earth like mushrooms," he laid bare one of the chief defects in a system lacking historical foundation. But the greater part of the revulsion against him was due to dislike of his method. In 1643 Descartes said of the *De Cive*:

The author writes more ably in moral philosophy than in metaphysics or in physics; nevertheless I cannot by any means approve either his principles or his maxims, which are very bad and very dangerous, in that he supposes that all men are wicked, or gives them a motive for being so. His whole purpose is to write in favor of monarchy, which could be done more advantageously and more solidly than he does, by taking more tenable and virtuous maxims.[1]

Leibniz, too, while admitting the "almost divine subtlety" of Hobbes, felt compelled to protest against principles which gave men license to do whatever they pleased, and which could be carried out only in the Utopia of Atheists.[2] Bishop

[1] *Œuvres*, iv, 67.
[2] Leibniz: *Sämtliche Schriften*, ed. Berliner Akademie der Wissenschaften, i, 89. Letter of 1670.

Burnet spoke of the *Leviathan* as "a very wicked book with a very strange title," which set up notions provocative by their novelty and boldness, and acceptable to the corrupt by their impiety.[1] In 1683 the royalist University of Oxford condemned as a "damnable doctrine destructive to the sacred person of princes, their state and government, and of all human society," Hobbes's whole theory of the origin of the state in contract, and of the nature of society as founded in the self-interest of the individual.

3. POLITICAL THEORIES OF CONTINENTAL WRITERS

As in the English, so in the Continental political theories, we see clearly reflected the interests and conditions of the states and parties in which they arose. Only, as there was nowhere else so violent a clash of party interests as in England, there was in other countries much less interest in political doctrines and much less produced on the subject. In some countries, indeed, as in the Spanish Netherlands, the censorship crushed nearly all political, and nearly all religious, thought. Here, where the clergy ruled supreme, they forbade either the printing or importation of books without their license, but they encouraged apologies for the existing government. In the realm of political theory absolute monarchy was defended by the Jesuits Lessius, in a work *On Justice and Law* (1621), and Scribani, in a tract entitled *Politico-Christianus* (1624).[2]

In brilliant contrast to this clerical tyranny stood the liberty and tolerance of the northern Netherlands, at least until the alliance of the house of Nassau with the Gomarists had reduced the country to a partial civil and ecclesiastical bondage. To her, as to an asylum, fled the persecuted of all lands, French Huguenots and English sectaries like the Pilgrim Fathers. In her strong arms scientists like Simon Stevin, scholars like Scaliger, publicists like Locke, and philosophers like Descartes found a refuge from the tyranny of their

[1] *History of my own Time*, i, 333.
[2] *Ibid.*, 510.

own countries, and much did they strengthen and adorn her whom they came to love as a second mother.[1]

This liberty, so advantageous to herself, came to be cherished by the Dutch, and consequently to be examined and justified by her philosophers. Grotius, while finding the origin of the state in compact, and while maintaining that the sovereign power is absolute and unlimited both in ecclesiastical and in civil matters, nevertheless tried to find a sphere for natural rights to both civil and ecclesiastical liberty. Internal acts (by which he meant opinions) could not be justiciable by the state; nor could the state punish as crimes acts not crimes by natural law, nor leave unpunished acts plainly criminal in the light of natural law and reason. Especially in matters of religion, he urged, no one can safely yield to the authority of another, nor can the state wisely regulate matters ecclesiastical without regard to the advice of the pious and learned pastors.[2] Here we see in Grotius the false premise adopted by the Reformers, and not rejected until Hobbes, that the laws of morality are like the laws of physics, rational, independent, and unalterable by the state.

Perhaps the soundest defence of civil and political liberty ever made was that advanced by the philosopher Spinoza. Here, again, however, he was but rationalizing the practice of the Dutch republicans, and the interests of the liberal party led by Jan de Witt, under whose patronage and at whose direct instigation he wrote. The *Theologico-Political Treatise*, concerned chiefly with religious liberty, was published in 1670; the *Political Treatise*, on civil liberty, not until the year after its author's death.

As in his metaphysics, so in his politics, Spinoza endeavored to start from scientific premises and to use mathematical methods.

I intend [he wrote] to investigate politics with the same freedom of mind with which we are accustomed to study mathematics. I

[1] *Cf.* Descartes' eulogy of the Netherlands, *Œuvres,* i, 204.
[2] *De Imperio Summarum Potestatum,* c. 1640. I use the edition (with a Catholic refutation) published in 1780.

have taken great care neither to mock nor to deplore nor to
reprobate human actions, but only to understand them, and to
regard human passions, like love, hate, wrath, envy, pride, pity,
and other commotions of the mind, not as vices of human nature,
but as its properties, which pertain to it as heat, cold, fair
weather, storms, and such things pertain to nature.[1] . . . For
a man, whether wise or ignorant, is a part of nature . . . and
does nothing, either from reason or from desire, except according to the laws and rules of nature.[2]

With this realistic bias Spinoza soon came into agreement
with the Hobbesian doctrine of the basis of society and of
the state. To him also natural right is identical with natural
power, self-preservation is man's controlling impulse, and
the passions are as much a part of man's nature and as
appropriate for securing his ends as is reason. As this results
in the war of all against all, the state is formed by contract
as an arrangement by which individuals seek their particular
good. But he differs from Hobbes in that his interest lies
not in proving the sovereignty of the state and the absolutism of the government, but in providing a rational basis for
the utmost individual liberty within the state. From the
very jaws of Leviathan, that earthly god of admittedly unequalled power, he draws an argument for individual liberty
so sound that it has carried conviction to readers of many
generations, and has become embedded in the texture of the
modern state.

By right and ordinance of nature [he began] I understand
nothing other than the rules of the nature of every individual
thing according to which we conceive every such thing as fashioned in its specific existence and action. Fishes, for example,
are fashioned to swim, and the big ones to devour the little ones;
fishes, therefore, have a sovereign natural right to obtain possession of the water, and the big ones to devour the little ones.[3]

---

[1] *Tractatus Politicus, Opera,* i, 282. (1880).
[2] *Ibid.* 285.
[3] Frank Thilly in *Chronicon Spinozanum,* 1923, pp. 88ff, quoting Spinoza.

Where, then, is the place for freedom in this philosophy of power? Just in this, that the state, like everything else, must act according to the laws of its being, and the primary law of its being is to secure the good of its members. To say that it has unlimited power to act contrary to this law, is as irrational as to say that a man has a right to go crazy. Just as that man most guided by reason is living up to the highest law of his being and securing his own supreme good, so that state guided by reason is most powerful and most in accord with the law of its being. The state has the power (in a certain sense) to deprive men of liberty, but it is irrational to do so. Not only is the grant of civil rights and of freedom of conscience consistent with the safety of the state, but their refusal is inconsistent with its safety. As an individual's power is limited by reason, so the sovereign power of the state is limited to such acts as make for the welfare of its citizens. And the chief condition of this welfare is freedom of conscience, of thought, and of expression.

This splendid defence of liberty came too late to save the cause of Dutch freedom, already declining under the reactionary tendencies of the Gomarist party and under the ambition of Willem of Nassau. No sooner was the *Theologico-Political Treatise* published than it was branded by the conservatives as "a wicked instrument forged in hell by a renegade Jew and the devil, and issued with the knowledge of Mr. Jan de Witt." Two years later the Grand Pensionary was murdered by the mob, and soon thereafter Willem III suppressed the book, which even Leibniz called "unbearably free-thinking."

Germany, torn by religious war, and absorbed in confessional controversy, produced less notable political theory than did any of the other great nations during this period. Though Samuel Pufendorf (1632-94) was unoriginal in his political thought, he enjoyed a wide vogue as combining into a consistent whole the variegated theories of earlier thinkers, particularly those of Grotius and of Hobbes. This Saxon jurist, educated, or, as he saw it, left uneducated, at Leipzig University, began life as a tutor and publicist, became professor at the University of Lund, royal historiographer at Stockholm, and finally privy-councillor to the Elector of Brandenburg. Among his philosophical, historical, and political works that *On the Law of Nature and of Nations* (1672) is perhaps the most important. This comprehensive treatise, beginning with an abstract definition of moral entities as "certain modes superadded to natural things and motions by understanding beings, chiefly for guiding and tempering the freedom of voluntary actions and for procuring a decent regularity in the conduct of life," goes on to lay the foundations of a science of ethics, and on that basis to raise a superstructure of law and politics. The author accepted the original state of nature and the origin of the state in contract not only as logical bases of government, but as probable conjectures of actual historical facts. Identifying the law of nature with that of nations, he asserted that this law has been revealed to mankind by reason.

In the Catholic South despotic monarchy was limited chiefly by the claims of the church to a large share in the government of the people. And even in the Spain of the Hapsburgs and in the France of Louis XIV memories of old liberties and examples of other free peoples kept alive a spirit of protest against the worst excesses of tyranny. In fact, in Spain, the rights of the church, fortified without and illuminated within as the sanctuary of popular liberties, found more ample expression in the writings of the sixteenth and seventeenth centuries than did the rights of the crown.

Juan de Mariana (1536-1624) studied at Alcalá and entered the Society of Jesus, dedicated as it was to the defence of the church and of the papacy. After teaching theology at Rome for eight years, and at Paris for five, he returned to Spain in 1574 to devote the remainder of his long life to the composition of historical and political works. Of the latter the most interesting is that entitled *The Education of the King,* published at Toledo in 1599. After considering the origin of society in man's social instinct, and after canvassing the various forms of government and giving

the preference to monarchy, Mariana proceeded to point
out the limits of the royal power and the guarantees against
despotism. The king is far from being free from law, and
in particular may decide nothing on matters of religion,
which should be left entirely to the church. Among the
limitations of the royal power which Mariana enumerated
elsewhere,[1] one is that the king shall levy no taxes without
the consent of the people and another that he shall not
change the weight or fineness of the coin without consent of
the people. The most interesting chapter of the *Education
of the King* is the sixth of Book I, on tyrannicide. Beginning
with a recital of the assassination of Henri III of France,
the writer continued by citing the authority of theologians
and of philosophers for the proposition that a conqueror
who had seized a land by force of arms might be killed by
anyone without a public decree, as a national enemy. If a
hereditary prince misgoverns, his vices should be borne up
to a certain point, said Mariana, but if they go to the degree
of ruining the state, pressure should be brought to bear upon
him to abdicate; if he refuses he should be declared a public
enemy liable to be slain by the sword by any private man.
And if there can be no such decree, nevertheless any man
brave enough to risk his own life for the freedom of his
country may win praise and glory by assassinating him. This
doctrine won greater force because the *imprimatur* of the
book stated that the work had been approved by pious and
grave men of the Jesuit order.

Before utterly condemning Mariana's doctrine of tyrannicide as contrary to humanity and morality, one should
remember, first, what little recourse there was for the oppressed in contemporary Spain. Despotism tempered by the
dagger was perhaps better than despotism free from the
fear of even this final recourse of the wretched. And, secondly, one should recollect how commonly political assassination was practiced at the time. Philip II himself had set
a price on the head of Willem of Orange, who perished by

[1] In a treatise on the *Debasement of Money* (*De la Moneda de Vellon*)
Obras, ii, 577, cap. 2 and 3.

the dagger in 1584; and in 1580 Pope Pius V sanctioned a plot for the murder of Elizabeth.

The same bias in favor of popular sovereignty as that exhibited by Mariana came out clearly in the work of his fellow-Jesuit Suarez. The interest of both was not really in popular liberty but in maintaining the rights of the church against the civil power. In the treatise *On Laws and God the Legislator,* Suarez investigated the origin of the state, which he found first in the social nature of man and secondly in the historical evolution of patriarchal government as depicted in the Old Testament. In a state of nature he found men equal, and their government a democracy. For the common good, however, they may delegate the sovereign power to one man or to a few men, and this delegation may be by tacit consent or by custom as well as by explicit compact. But in a monarchy the prince holds power only on the condition on which he receives it, namely that of exercising it for the common good. For private vices or even for tyranny he may not justly be slain by a private man; but he may justly be resisted either by one man or by a city, if he attack that man or that city, and this resistance may be carried to the point, if necessary, of tyrannicide in self-defence. And any prince may be deposed or executed by the people acting at the command of the pope.

The doctrine of tyrannicide excited much more opposition in neighboring countries than in Spain. Englishmen were required to take an oath "abhorring and abjuring as impious and heretical the doctrine and proposition that princes excommunicated or deprived by the pope may be deposed or slain by their subjects or by any others." In France the assassination of Henri III in 1589 and of Henri IV in 1610 made the theory acutely practical. The first murder was praised and the second was called for in an anonymous treatise published in 1590 entitled *On the just Authority of the Christian State against heretical and impious Kings.* Especially after 1610 a lively controversy arose on tyrannicide, and all books commending it were condemned and prohibited by the Parlement of Paris.

France was so tired of civil war and anarchy that she welcomed the strong despotism formed by Henri IV, Richelieu, and Mazarin, and culminating under Louis XIV. The successful suppression of the Fronde, that horrible parody of the English Puritan rebellion, inaugurated one of the most glittering periods of French history, which lasted until about 1685, when tyranny, bigotry, and foreign war prostrated the country.

The chief theoretical opposition to unlimited monarchy came from the church. The Italian Cardinal Bellarmine's tract on *The Power of the Pope in Temporal Things* (1610) advanced the thesis that while all power is ultimately derived from God, the people are the ultimate depositories of this power, and that "it is the consent of the people which sets up kings, consuls, and all other governments." In a commonwealth, he continued, all men are born naturally free and continue to be so until they transfer their sovereignty to a king or other ruler. Perhaps Bellarmine really thought democratic government the best; perhaps he was merely attacking the king in the interests of the pope, whose sovereignty, even in temporal matters, he defended. His book was condemned by the Parlement of Paris, which adopted as its own the words of the Bishop of Chartres in 1625, that

apart from the universal consent of peoples and nations, the prophets announce, the apostles confirm, and the martyrs confess, that kings are ordained by God, and not only that they are so ordained, but also that they are gods themselves . . . not in essence but by participation, not by nature but by grace.[1]

The battle between the royalists and the ultramontanists was carried on in the assembly of the States General in 1614-15.The Third Estate passed a fundamental law condemning tyrannicide and the doctrine that kings might be deposed. The clergy protested against this law, and, notwithstanding the support given by the court to the Third Estate, they succeeded in tabling it.

[1] Fouqueray: *Historie de la Compagnie de Jésus en France,* iv, 133.

For many years the struggle of king and pope over the so-called Gallican Rights of the French church colored all that was written on political theory in that country. The ablest defender of the royal power over the church was Jacques Bénigne Bossuet (1627-1704), also one of the chief champions of despotism as a theory of government. Born at Dijon, educated at the Jesuit school at Nantes and then at the College of Navarre at Paris, he gained rapid promotion in the church by his eloquence. As bishop first of Condon and then of Meaux, as tutor to the Dauphin, and as court preacher, he spent much of his life near the Sun-king by whose splendor his eyes were dazzled. While his histories and sermons have given him his chief fame, his works on theology and politics are by no means despicable.

Fairly worshipping kings, to whom he attributed a divine inspiration in matters of government, he published a defence of absolutism, originally written for the instruction of the Dauphin, under the title *Political Doctrine drawn from the Holy Scriptures*. By this authority he proved that monarchy is the most natural, the most common, the most ancient, and the best form of government, that no pretext justifies rebellion, that conquest gives the right of rule (though wars undertaken merely for the sake of conquest are unjust), and that wars of religion are right. The whole of history, ancient and modern, he interpreted according to this theory. The cause of the fall of the Roman Republic he found in the turbulence of the people jealous of their betters.[1] In the English rebellion and Commonwealth he saw nothing but a fearful punishment of God for the apostacy of the people.[2]

While courtiers gloried in monarchical power, France chafing under the chains of Louis' iron tyranny, dreamed of liberty. The expression of democratic or anti-monarchical doctrine, forbidden to her directly, came out in a disguised, almost pathetic way in the tales of travellers who beguiled her with stories of freer and happier peoples. No class of

[1] *Œuvres*, v, 475.
[2] *Œuvres*, iv, 575ff.

books was so popular in seventeenth-century France as were reports and romances of travel; and the remarkable thing about them is that most of them represented foreign and savage nations as free, innocent, and happy. Whether Baudier wrote of the *Court of the King of China,* or Garcilasso de la Vega described his native Peru, or Champlain published a thrilling narrative of exploration among the North American Indians, their readers eagerly devoured accounts of peoples living either in democratic equality or under a wise and benevolent monarchy limited by law. With these narratives, mostly highly colored by romance, and with truer histories of the republics set up in England and in New England and in the French Antilles (which revolted in 1644), the enslaved people nursed a spirit of liberty until at last the day of reckoning with their masters arrived.

The Italian, too, for the most part, languished under the double yoke of spiritual and temporal despotism. Campanella, who expiated a rash revolt by years in prison and by days on the rack, is a fit symbol of the mind of contemporary Italy. Abandoning, under the scourge of torture and in the tedium of fetters, hope of improving the condition of the world by rebellion, he came to believe that the Spanish world-monarchy, moderated and directed by the papacy, might be the divinely appointed means for bringing the peoples back to a golden age. Much the same ideal of a society directed for their own good by an absolute, though elected, spiritual and temporal ruler, is set forth in his most famous work, *The City of the Sun,* written about 1602, but not published until twenty years later. The City of the Sun is described as on an island on the equator, marvellously fortified with many walls and adorned with imposing buildings. The great ruler is called in their language Sol, which means Metaphysician or Philosopher being interpreted. He is elected for life by a college of magistrates named for life, and is chosen for his proficiency in history, metaphysics, and theology. His three chief assistants are called Pon, Sin, and Mor, or Power, Wisdom, and Love. If the model for the government of the City of Sol is found in the constitu-

tion of the papacy, the model for the life of the people is
found, except for, or perhaps including, their sexual promiscuity, in the monastery. Science is cultivated, education is
provided for, property is common, and reason is so respected
that no one is punished, by death or otherwise, until he is
convinced that his punishment is just. Women and children
are, as in Plato's *Republic*, held in common; but mating is
carefully directed by Mor, or Love, with a single eye to
eugenics, in order to secure the procreation of the best children. In all this Campanella but rationalized the interests of
the Catholic clergy, except that he borrowed the community
of women from Plato, and perhaps from the suggestion of
his own strong and unsatisfied passions. The nearest parallel
to the City of the Sun ever found in reality is the Jesuit
state of Paraguay.

4. ECONOMIC THOUGHT AND THE SCIENCE OF STATISTICS

Though Economics, like Politics, has been chiefly a
pseudo-science, more intent on finding reasons to justify
practices in accord with the interests of the group to which
the thinker belongs than with objective investigation, it may
best be considered by itself, for it is rather international
than national. Naturally and usually political thought is
colored by the conditions of some particular state, whereas
economic thought is that of a different group, often compris-
ing many nations. In the sixteenth and seventeenth centuries
all the nations of Western Europe belonged to one large
economic unit—with marked local differences, to be sure—
and therefore the political economy of the time was largely
similar in all nations.

It was founded on the interests of the rising merchant
class, in whose hands was concentrated much of the political
power and most of the wealth of the nations. In the modern
world money has been king, and his chief favorites and
ministers have been the great capitalists—*entrepreneurs*,
merchants, and manufacturers—who have been able to intercept for their own class the increase in wealth due to the

commercial revolution. The favorite argument intended to justify the encouragement of the import of gold and silver and the prohibition of their export was, throughout the seventeenth century, that drawn from the analogy of a private man. As that individual is rich who possesses much money, so it was thought that that nation was richest which held most gold and silver. This argument was stated by the Italian Serra in *A Brief Treatise on the Causes which Make Gold and Silver abound in Kingdoms where there are no Mines,* published in 1613. It was assumed in the *Treatise on Political Economy* by which Antoyne de Montchrétien in 1615 invented the name and laid the foundations of a new science. It was the guiding principle of Richelieu's protective tariff, sumptuary laws, and exclusion of foreign boats from French trade. It was clearly expressed in the maxim of Colbert that "manufactures will produce returns in money, which is the sole end of commerce and the sole means of augmenting the greatness and power of a state." It was elaborated by Thomas Mun in his book entitled *England's Treasure by Foreign Trade,* published in 1664, and containing the following sentences:

The ordinary means to increase our wealth and treasure is by foreign trade, wherein we must ever observe this rule—to sell more to strangers yearly than we consume of theirs in value. For, that part of our stock which is not returned to us in wares must necessarily be brought home in treasure. . . . Foreign trade is the great revenue of the king, the honor of the kingdom, the noble profession of the merchants, the school of arts, the supply of our wants, the employment of our poor, the improvement of our lands, the nursery of our mariners, the walls of the kingdom, the means of our treasure, the sinews of our wars, the terror of our enemies.

The earliest and crudest application of mercantile theory was in the absolute prohibition of the export of bullion. This eventually put traders to such difficulties that it was repealed in the commercial nations still following the mercantile policy in general. In 1682 Sir William Petty protested that the laws against the free exportation of money

are against the laws of nature and also impracticable; for we see
that the countries which abound in money and all other commodities have followed no such laws; and contrariwise that the countries which have forbidden these exportations under the highest
penalties, are very destitute both of money and merchandise.[1]

One particular problem investigated with great success
by sixteenth and seventeenth-century economists was that
of the debasement of the currency, the equivalent of the
modern issue of irredeemable paper. Copernicus, Bodin,
John Hales, and Suarez, each independently of the other,
discovered the reason why this should cause a violent rise
in prices even in the face of laws regulating prices. They all
saw the bad consequences of tampering with the currency,
Copernicus reckoning debasement as a curse to a nation
comparable with war, pestilence and famine, and Suarez
considering it an act unlawful for the most absolute monarch. Sir William Petty, with his usual insight, also saw that
depreciation of the currency is a tax on the creditor class.

Whereas a little economic theory may be found mingled
with the politics of Hobbes, Bodin, Pufendorf, and others,
a few writers devoted special treatises to the subject.
Among them one of the first and most comprehensive was
Antoyne de Montchrétien, whose *Treatise on Political
Economy* (1615) minted the name of the new science. In
general a cameralist or mercantilist, he attributed much importance to agriculture as well as to commerce. He was the
first, perhaps, to point out that labor is the source of all
wealth.

Far more valuable than the work of Montchrétien, perhaps, indeed, the most important contribution made to social
science in the seventeenth century, was an unpretentious
little tract entitled *Natural and Political Observations . . .
upon the Bills of Mortality,* by Captain John Graunt, published in 1662. It is another proof of the general fact that
idle curiosity is more likely to produce scientific results than
is any other motive whatever. For, Graunt really founded

[1] *Economic Writings of Sir W. Petty,* ed. C. H. Hull, ii, 445.

the science of statistics, the only reliable basis for any social science worthy of the name. Statistics in the social sciences take the place of experiment in the natural sciences. We do not artificially produce such phenomena as disease, divorce, suicide, and crime—however much some of our social arrangements seem calculated to encourage them—merely for the sake of experiment, but we do tabulate and compare the experiments made in these lines by society. And when this is done, the most startling results leap to the eye. The popular proverb about the superlative mendacity of statistics is wrong; but if the point of the comparison be in the degree of interest and not in the degree of veracity, one may correctly say that there are romances, grand romances, and statistics.

John Graunt (1620-74), who in idle moments of which he was rather ashamed discovered this new method, was a Cockney haberdasher who rose in wealth and influence in the city. As a pastime he collected the bills reporting the number of deaths from various causes, and published his *Observations* on them in 1662. The work won him election to membership in the Royal Society. His last years were clouded by misfortune.

By the simple process of comparing the records of the number of deaths from year to year, in London and in other towns, Graunt first discovered some of the most pregnant facts of demography. In the first place he noticed the regularity of certain social phenomena which appear to be, in their individual occurrence, the sport of chance. His own statement of this is:

Among the several casualties some bear a constant proportion unto the whole number of burials; such are chronical diseases and the diseases whereunto the city is most subject, as, for example, consumptions, dropsies, jaundice, gout, stone, palsy, scurvy, rising of the lights or mother, rickets, aged, agues, fevers, bloody flux, and scouring; nay some accidents, as grief, drowning, men's making away with themselves, and being killed by several accidents, &c, do the like.

The scientific and moral implications of this regularity, however, Graunt left for Quetelet and Buckle to point out.

A second fact universally found in vital statistics and first discovered by Graunt is the excess of male over female births. As men are more subject to death by war and accident than are women, Graunt showed that the numbers of those members of each sex capable of having children are approximately equal, and therefrom he deduced a natural sanction for monogamy.

Thirdly, Graunt discovered the high rate of mortality during the early years of life; and fourthly, the excess of the urban over the rural death-rate. Graunt's worst error in explaining the statistics with which he dealt was due to his imperfect apprehension of the law of large numbers. Finding much greater regularity in the proportions of deaths in the London bills than in those of smaller towns, he attributed this to the supposed fact that open towns are more subject to good and bad climatic influences, varying with the weather from year to year. In fact, the greater regularity is due solely to the larger numbers classified. But, with this deduction, Graunt's little tract remains one of the most surprising contributions ever made to social science.

Though less original than his friend Graunt—with the authorship or co-authorship of whose pamphlet he has been sometimes credited—Sir William Petty (1623-85) made important contributions to social science. Though born of a poor family in Hampshire, he won for himself an excellent education first in the Jesuit college of Caen (near which city he was shipwrecked) and then in Utrecht, Leyden, Amsterdam, and Paris. He taught anatomy at Oxford and music at Gresham College, and was later appointed physician to the army in Ireland. In this country he won fortune, political promotion, and a knighthood. While in London he joined the Royal Society. Among a number of pamphlets he wrote on medical, mathematical, political, and economic subjects, perhaps the most important are the *Treatise on Taxes*, published in 1662, and the *Political Arithmetic*, completed in 1676, widely circulated in manuscript, pirated in 1683, and published in an authentic edition in 1690.

Petty's chief merit as an economist lies in his recognition that social science, like natural science, must be quantitative:

The method I use [said he] is not yet very usual; for, instead of using only comparative and superlative words, and intellectual arguments, I have taken the course (as a specimen of the political arithmetic I have long aimed at) to express myself in terms of number, weight, or measure; to use only arguments of sense, and to consider only such causes as have visible foundations in nature.

As an economist Petty was a cameralist, distinguished from his precursors by his greater insight, originality, and suggestiveness. Much of his best work was founded on the bills of mortality and such other statistical material as was then obtainable. Even before Petty's time it had been pointed out—by Giovanni Botero in a book called *The Reason of State*, 1589—that population tends to increase faster than means of subsistence, and hence that the rate of increase of the one depends on the other. Petty added the idea that excess of population breeds war and that in a limited future time—which he put at 2000 years—the habitable earth would be overcrowded, with one person to every two acres of land. He thought it a rational conjecture that the total population of the world in 1682 was 320,000,000, which must have been a considerable underestimate.

Many historians and social theorists have noticed that trade during the Middle Ages lay largely in the hands of the Jews, and in modern times largely in the hands of Protestants, or, as Max Weber has put it, "Calvinism and capitalism go together." Petty noticed these facts, and others of a similar nature from India and Turkey, and stated as a general law that "the trade of any country is usually managed by the heterodox party." [1] How far this suggestive generalization can be substantiated, and upon what reasons it rests, would be an interesting subject for investigation.

[1] *Economic Writings*, 263.

CHAPTER IX

HISTORIOGRAPHY

I. THE CONCEPTION OF HISTORY PREVALENT IN THE SIXTEENTH AND SEVENTEENTH CENTURIES

The long debated question whether history is an art or a
science has drawn attention away from the more important
fact that history has usually been written with more urgent
and practical aims than the satisfaction of either the love
of beauty or the love of knowledge. History resembles the
cognate social sciences in rationalizing the interests of some
particular group, that is, in glorifying and justifying the
acts of the nation, family, church, party, or class to which
the writer belongs. In the sixteenth and seventeenth centuries the needs of three particular sorts of groups called
forth a supply of three particular sorts of history. The battle
of Protestant and Catholic following the Reformation gave
birth to church history; the rivalries of the several nations
stimulated nationalist histories; and the rise of parties in
the English Civil War produced party histories.

But, as running water purifies itself, so, to some extent,
does running thought. The longer and more deeply history
is studied, the more ardently it is cultivated, the more does
it tend to assert its own life, its own point of view. All historians profess, and most really aim at, an objective truth.
"Writers of history," said Sir Edwin Sandys at the turn of
the sixteenth and seventeenth centuries, "should know that
there is a difference between their profession and the practice of advocates pleading contrary at a bar." [1] So, even in
the stress of religious and political polemic a certain amount

[1] *Europae Speculum*, 1629, p. 98. I owe this reference to Prof. F. G.
Marcham.

of objectivity was attained and a very considerable amount of historical truth discovered and exhibited.

But those who sought the truth of history most earnestly were not yet ready to proclaim it a science. The tendency to make it an art, and to model it, as epic prose, according to the fashion set by the Greek and Roman writers, was very strong. The most important work on historical method written before Mabillon was the treatise of Gerard Johann Voss published in 1623 in Latin under the title: *The Historic Art, or, Concerning the Nature of History, and of Historical Method, and Rules for Writing History*. While the author proclaimed that his discipline is an art and not a science, he differentiated it nicely from the arts of literature, rhetoric, poetry and logic, and argued that its purpose is the memory of things. Truth he held to be the soul and foundation of history, and its chief profit he found in its moral and political lessons.

This pragmatic view was generally held at the time. Montaigne stated that histories are the best of all books for teaching the truth about man, both about his internal condition and about the accidents menacing him from without.[1] And to most of his contemporaries the chief value of the chronicles of the race lay in the practical lessons in morals and politics to be found in them. Kepler thought of history as an education of mankind in the knowledge of nature and of himself. Casaubon opined that "as ethical philosophy may be learned from biography, so political philosophy may be learned from history." Campanella found in history the basis of politics, ethics, oratory, and poetry. Most of the historians of the time justified their works on the ground of the great moral lessons taught by them. And those who disliked history attacked it by charging that it did not teach sound ethics. Sir Philip Sidney made the strange allegation, singularly inconsistent, one would think, with his highly moral purpose, that poetry and novels are superior to history just because in works of fiction the good are rewarded and

[1] *Essais*, II, x.

the bad punished, whereas in true narratives it is usually the other way.

The prevalent philosophy of history was religious and the prevalent scheme of periodization for universal history was taken from biblical and ecclesiastical chronology. For about two thousand years, it was thought, from Adam to Moses, the race lived in a state of nature; for about two thousand years the rule of the law promulgated to Abraham and his seed prevailed; and with the publication of the gospel began the third period which, it was believed, would also last about two thousand years.

A new periodization, and the beginnings of a new philosophy of history were offered by Jean Bodin, the French publicist, in his *Method for easily understanding History,* published in 1566. Not only did he coin the word "philosophistoricus" (which he applied to Philo), but he first tentatively sketched the outlines of a new and more fruitful study of the human record. He, too, divided the history of the world into three periods, of which the first two had lasted two thousand years each, but he made the criterion of his divisions not religious but racial. During the earliest period of antiquity Oriental peoples had dominated the world, during the second period Mediterranean peoples, and during the last period the nations of Northern Europe. As Bodin anticipated Hegel by this scheme, so he advanced ideas later commonly adopted about the influence of climate and geography, and he at least vaguely adumbrated the theory of progress soon to become prominent. Rejecting the then common assumption of a primitive golden age followed by degeneration, he thought of the story of the race as a constant ascent.

The great importance of the idea of progress in the history of culture is that its adoption marked a complete *volte-face* in the attitude of the race. There is no greater psychological contrast between modern men and their ancestors than that the earlier generations regarded the world as degenerate and destined to early destruction and that the more recent generations have regarded it as improvable and practically

certain of a long and brilliant future. The race, once back-
ward-looking, has become forward-looking. The change was
caused by the intellectual triumphs of modern times, at first
those in literature, art, and exploration, and then those in
science. The form in which the clash of the two views first
showed itself was naturally in the comparison of ancient and
modern achievements. Until the Renaissance was waning
almost everyone had deified the ancients and disparaged
the moderns. But in the sixteenth century one may find, in
addition to Bodin, a few men who dared assert that their
own generation had surpassed the Greeks and Romans in
civilization. Such were the Neapolitan jurist Scipione Capece
and the Tuscan philologian Sperone Speroni, both writing
about the middle of the century. Fifty years later the
poet Alessandro Tassoni compared ancient and modern literature to the advantage of the latter. The Englishman George
Hakewell and the Frenchman Saint-Sorlin adopted the same
view, the latter accounting for modern superiority by saying
that the descendants of the older generations had inherited
their wealth and added something to it. In this we see the
small beginnings of that battle of the ancients and moderns
that became so celebrated in the literature of the Enlightenment.

It was not the poets, however, but the scientists who were
most fully persuaded of the superiority of the later generations. "These be the ancient times, when the world is growing old," said Bacon; "our own age is more truly antiquity
than is the time which is computed backward, beginning
with our age." Pascal took up the parable and carried it a
step further:

Those whom we call the ancients [said he] were really new to
everything; whereas it is in ourselves, who have added to their
knowledge the experience of other ages, that we must look for
the antiquity which we revere in them.

Stating clearly for the first time a theory of progress, Pascal
set forth the comparison of men and bees which has become

so famous and has served so many writers on the philosophy
of history since his time. Bees make their combs now as
they have always done since the beginning, but men have
altered their ways of living because they have continually
stored up knowledge. Hence the life of the animals is static;
the prerogative of humanity is constant improvement.

But the seventeenth century was not yet ready to admit
the evolution of mankind according to natural laws. To
most men then, as to many still, man and his societies remained an exception to the rule of law, the field for the
sport of chance and the caprice of arbitrary will. In fact,
the most famous statement of this illusion ever made is the
remark of Pascal that "if the nose of Cleopatra had been
shorter, the whole face of the earth would have changed." [1]
A little more elaborate and less known is his expression of
the same idea in the following words: [2]

Cromwell would have laid waste all Christendom; the royal
family would have been destroyed and his own family established in power fòr ever, but for a little grain of sand that
lodged in his urethra. Even Rome was about to tremble before
him; but this little bit of gravel killed him, and in consequence
his family was cast down, peace made, and the royal family
restored.

Like so many theories of history this one is based on an
incorrect apprehension of the facts. Cromwell died not of
gravel but of a tertian fever.

The main fault to be found with Pascal's theory is that
it assumes that the essence of history lies in dynastic
changes. The fortunes of peoples were then thought to depend chiefly on the personal qualities of their rulers; that
the form of government itself is but the superficial expression of much deeper trends in society was an idea as yet un-
born. A few men, in advance of their time, but only a few,
protested, and protested in vain, against a purely political
and religious conception of history. Campanella thought that
the annalist should relate not only political changes and the

[1] *Pensées,* no. 162.   [2] *Ibid.,* no. 176.

occurrence of prodigies, but also "the manners of the age
. . . the food, medicine, and arms of the people, their
money, edifices, and inventions in the arts." [1]

Francis Bacon, with his supreme interest in science, called
for an intellectual history in these words: [2]

Surely the history of the world, if this part were lacking, might
be considered not unlike a statue of Polyphemus with his
eye put out, since that part of the image is wanting which
chiefly expresses the genius and character of the person. And
we conclude that such a history is lacking although we are well
aware that in the special disciplines of jurisprudence, mathematics, rhetoric, and philosophy there is an occasional mention,
and even some jejune accounts of the sects, schools, books, authors, and revolutions of these sciences; and we can also find
a few meager and fruitless treatises on the inventors of arts; [3]
but we assert, nevertheless, that a just and universal history of
learning has never yet been published.

Such a history, the author continues, should tell the origins,
progress, and migrations of the arts and sciences through
divers regions, and also their periods of decline, oblivion, and
rebirth. Such a history should describe the chief controversies and schools of thought, name the principal authors,
best books, universities, academies, circles, and orders of
scholars; it should explain the causes and effects of a
flourishing and of a languishing learning; it should discover
the accidents, times, and institutions propitious and those
hostile to culture,—as, the zeal for religion and the favor of
the laws. And finally such a history, by absorbing the arguments, style, and method of the chief books produced in
every epoch, should evoke the spirit and genius of each
successive age "as though rousing it by incantation from
the dead." Truly a noble and a comprehensive plan, but one
so far ahead of the time in which it was written that it has
not even yet been realized.

[1] *Rationalis Philosophiae* Pars V, 1638, p. 254.
[2] *De Augmentis,* ii, cap. 4.
[3] As, Polydore Vergil: *De rerum inventoribus,* 1536.

2. CHURCH HISTORY

One reason why it has never been realized is that the public has been vastly more interested in politics and in religion than in intellectual matters. Geometry and poetry can be safely left to take care of themselves; but God, the nation, and the party need zealous defenders against their detractors and enemies. During the sixteenth and seventeenth centuries the issue that most passionately stirred the masses was that raised by the Reformation. It was inevitable that both parties, appealing as they did to the authority of earlier ages, should diligently cultivate history.

Modern church history is therefore the child of the Reformation. Its purpose was not at first to investigate important and neglected phenomena, but to build arsenals in which each side might find weapons with which to attack the other. The natural result of so practical a purpose was to color and interpret all history with strong bias. In the most honest hands, the scale of justice was unconsciously depressed or elevated; by more passionate and less scrupulous partisans it was deliberately lightened with suppression of the truth on one side and weighted with suggestion of the false on the other. Some of the histories written by leaders, such as the memoirs of Knox, Bullinger, and Loyola, are so frankly apologies that they carry the antidote to their own virus. Others, like that of Nicholas Sanders, are little better than tissues of invented or too easily credited falsehoods; and still others, like that of Sleidan, make a notable effort to be fair to the enemy, and to tell facts exactly as they happened.

If the mutual animosity of Catholic and Protestant distorted history, their common lack of interest in, and their detestation of, all other religions except their own, greatly narrowed it. Orthodox Christianity, with its necessary preparation, ancient Judaism, was set apart as divinely revealed over against all other faiths and beliefs, which at best were "the beastly devices of the heathen" and at worst the direct inspiration of devils. Except for occasional flashes

of hatred, the history of the Greek mysteries and of Islam
was left in the outer darkness.

The philosophy of history held by both Protestant and
Catholic writers was that bequeathed by Augustine. God, it
was thought, had chosen a peculiar people under the Old
Dispensation, and a special church under the New, for
whose instruction and guidance he had raised up a series
of witnesses to the truth—prophets, apostles, and martyrs—
and to test whose faith he allowed the devil to inspire
heretics and persecutors. But, though both Catholics and
Protestants regarded history as a puppet show in which God
and the devil, by frequent direct interposition, pulled the
strings, and though both looked forward to a similar *dé-
nouement* of the drama in the exaltation of the true believers
and in the damnation of their enemies at the day of judgment, they differed as to what was the true and what was
the false church. The two pictures corresponded like the
seal and the wax, or like the photograph and its negative;
what was raised in one was depressed in the other, what was
light in the one was dark in the other. But the design was
identical.

Even with such a handicap of bias to weigh it down the
study of church history uncovered and ransacked a vast
body of new sources, and gradually learned from them the
lessons inculcated by the appeal to an objective standard.
Writing under the eye of vigilant critics, partisans reluctantly but necessarily abandoned the less tenable parts of
their respective claims. The critical dagger, sharpened
against an enemy, became a scalpel to cut away unsound
growths of legend and of pious fraud. With larger knowledge
came, though slowly, fairer judgment and deeper human
interest. In these respects the individual writers showed
marked differences. To condemn them all to the Malebolge
deserved only by the worst is undiscriminating.

Among the most industrious and most biased must certainly be numbered Matthias Flacius, called Illyricus from
his birthplace at Istria (1520-75). After teaching at Wittenberg he settled at Magdeburg, a city dubbed "our Lord

God's pulpit" by the strict Lutherans because of the purity of its doctrine. Besides various theological tracts he produced two historical works, a *Catalogue of Witnesses of the Truth who before our time cried out against the Roman Pontiff and his Errors* (1556), and, in collaboration with others, the *Ecclesiastical History* commonly called the *Magdeburg Centuries* (1559-74). This huge story of the church to the year 1300 aimed at making Protestant polemic independent of Catholic sources. Save for the accumulation of much material it deserves little praise. Frankly admitting that its prime purpose is to reveal God's blessings on the righteous and his punishments of the wicked, it is as much sunk in superstition as enslaved by prejudice. Its critical principles are worse than none, for the only criterion of sources used is their pro-papal, or anti-papal tendency. Miracles are not doubted as such, but are divided into two classes, those tending to prove an orthodox doctrine, which are accepted as true, and those supporting some papal institution, which are branded as "signal lies." The spurious correspondence between Christ and King Abgarus is used as not having been proved false, and the absurd legend of the female Pope Joan is never doubted. Still more discreditable to the authors' standards of truth are the incorporation in their tomes of the legends representing Hildebrand as a magician conjuring the devil by putting the consecrated host in the fire, and as first prophesying the death of the emperor and then seeking to fulfil his prophecy by dispatching assassins.

When, however, new truth was agreeable to the writers' bias, they were capable of discovering it. They performed an important service to historical criticism in first exposing as forgeries the series of documents now known as the Pseudo-Isidorian Decretals, accepted by all authorities between the ninth and the sixteenth centuries as genuine, but now universally abandoned.

While in general the strong anti-papal prejudices of the writers involved them in serious misinterpretations of the struggle between the popes and the emperors, their theological interests greatly narrowed their field. They filled their dreary tomes with mountainous discussions of doctrines, not worked into a readable whole by themselves, but frequently lifted in great chunks from their sources. Besides doctrine they also treated the ceremonies of the church, its polity, the chief teachers and bishops of each age, political changes, church councils, heresies, and other religions. Special sections were devoted in each book to the miracles and martyrdoms produced by the successive centuries. And even the passionate bias with which the Centuriators approached every subject could not often relieve the deadly dullness with which they endowed almost everything they touched.

The official Catholic counterblast to the *Magdeburg Centuries* was the *Annales Ecclesiastici* written at the order of St. Philip Neri by Cæsar Baronius (1538-1605). Their author, an Italian cardinal and librarian of the Vatican, early devoted his life to writing a history of the church to 1198, which was published in many folios from 1588 to 1607, and which has since been continued by various hands. Whereas Baronius's principles and criticism are little better than those of the Centuriators, his greater command of the sources and his warmer sympathy with his subject makes his work somewhat superior to theirs and usable in parts even now. The charges of dishonesty brought against him by partisans must on the whole be dismissed. In at least one instance he showed both candor and courage in abandoning the hitherto strongly defended Catholic position. The Donation of Constantine, though exposed by Valla in the fifteenth century, had still found general acceptance in Catholic circles, and had been defended by canonists and by Pope Paul V himself. Baronius, not without peril to himself, admitted the forgery.

Nevertheless, in more doubtful cases, his bias deceived him. His talent for switching the attention to a side issue and for tangling instead of clearing problems, made the Protestants regard him as "a great deceiver," though even the learned Casaubon found it difficult to refute him. The great French scholar could indeed expose certain faults, such as the acceptance by Baronius as genuine of the forged Sibylline Verses foretelling the birth of Christ, but the critic himself was too much hampered by dogma successfully to overthrow the historical edifice. Whereas Baronius' style is in some respects superior to that of the Centuriators, he adopted a worse method of presentation than theirs, ordering all events by years instead of by centuries.

Of more permanent value than either of the works just described has proved the great collection of sources known as the *Acts of the Saints* published by the Jesuits of the Spanish Netherlands. The work was suggested, some material accumulated, and two or three introductory studies published, by Father Héribert Rosweyde (1569-1629). Soon after completing his education at Douai he began collecting manuscripts, and laid the plan for a collection of hagiographa to be arranged according to the calendar. Undeterred by the warning of Cardinal Bellarmine that in the original biographies of the saints he would find many "inept, trivial, and improbable things more fit for laughter than for edification," he published a preliminary collection of the *Lives of the Fathers of the Desert* in 1615.

At his death he left his materials in the hands of Father Jean Bolland, from whose name the editors of the *Acta Sanctorum* have been commonly called the Bollandists. Bolland (1596-1665), born in the Duchy of Limburg, devoted the earlier years of his manhood to teaching in various Jesuit colleges, and his later life, with the assistance of several collaborators, to editing the great series. Two huge volumes, containing the lives of saints whose feasts come in January, appeared in 1643, those for February in 1658, and those for March, April, May, and June in different years from 1668 to 1709. With long interruptions the work has been continued till our own time, being still incomplete.

Its chief service to scholarship is that it gives access to a large body of original documents. Not only from the libraries of the Netherlands, but from those of all Europe, the editors collected and copied manuscripts. Those lives of

the saints which had been written in earlier ages they published as they found them; others they themselves worked
up from scattered sources. As their main interest was apologetic they developed criticism just to the point where it
would reject such miracles and other incidents as had by
that time come to seem ridiculous even to the faithful.
Other miracles, of a more edifying nature, were accepted.
Sometimes they would admit into their volumes acts which
they stamped as apocryphal or even as "absurdly fabulous."
So narrow is the path of orthodoxy that their pious work
was attacked by Catholic theologians and even, for twenty
years (1695-1715), prohibited by the Spanish Inquisition.

Bitterly as was the field of early and medieval church
history contested by Protestant and Catholic, that of the
Reformation was even more fought over. The first notable
work on the subject, Sleidan's *Religious and Political History of the Reign of Charles V*, was also, for at least two
centuries, the fairest. Though Johannes Sleidan (1506-56),
German jurist and diplomat, wrote as the official historian of
the Schmalkaldic League, he published his work just when
all Germans, sickened by religious wars, turned to the hope
of a lasting peace between the two confessions. Moreover,
his main interest lay in politics, which he saw to be in-
separably connected with the religious issue. In plain,
straightforward narrative, without deep reflection, he set
forth fairly and with copious quotations from the documents the diplomatic and theological side of the movement.
Though he was not above recording the trivial and the superstitious, and though he offered nothing on the causes leading
up to the Reformation, nor on the course of the development
of Protestantism, nor on the characters of the leaders, nor
on the life and thought of the people, he was better informed
on politics than was any of his immediate successors, more
fluent, more temperate, and more impartial.

In startling contrast to the superficial and pedestrian objectivity of Sleidan stand the brilliant style, penetrating
psychology, and marked, though peculiar, bias of Paolo
Sarpi, admired by Macaulay as the best modern historian

and denounced by Lord Acton as fit for Newgate prison.
Sarpi (1552-1623) was born at Venice and baptized Pietro,
a name which he changed to Paolo when he became a
Servite friar. Well educated and precocious, he mastered
much of the natural science of the day, and corresponded
with many thinkers and discoverers in all lands. Failing to
secure high promotion in the church, he entered into the
service of his country, which employed him on many important missions, and loaded him with equal responsibilities
and honors.

His devotion to the interests of Venice gave the tone to
his whole life and thought. While the great maritime republic
had remained Catholic during the Reformation, no government was more forward than was the Signoria to assert the
rights of the state over the church. For centuries the whole
life of the city had been one of conflict with the claims of
the papacy. If she resisted the seductions of Protestantism
it was not because of her love for Catholicism, but because
her mind was skeptical and her interest in theology slight.
To break with the faith of her neighbors would have exposed
her to the danger of confessional wars. But her determination was none the less strong to make religion subservient
to policy and to resist the temporal encroachments of the
Holy See.

Among all her cunning and able servants in carrying out
this policy none was equal to Sarpi. At every turn he defended the rights of Venice with a powerful pen. At his
advice the publication of papal bulls was forbidden in the
Republic; at his advice the interdict, that once mighty
weapon, was first resisted and then denounced in a lucid
and pungent tract; at his advice the religious orders refusing obedience to the Signoria were virtually expelled.

The victory of the "terrible friar" exasperated his Roman
enemies to such a point that they employed bravoes to
assassinate him. On October 5, 1607, he was attacked by
five murderers and left for dead. Fortunately he recovered;
and, on being shown by the surgeon the marks of the dagger
used against him, wittily punned: "Agnosco stylum Curiae

Romanae," that is: "I recognize the stylus [style, or stiletto] of the Roman Curia." Not only the populace, but the Signoria in an official account, agreed with Sarpi in blaming the pope and the Jesuits for instigating the crime. As the murderers took refuge in the papal states, and as they were not brought to justice, the public *démenti* of Paul V received little credence.

Sarpi used his recovered health in waging a fiercer war than ever with the pope. Though he was accused of being a Protestant, and though he undoubtedly helped the heretics, he continued to say mass and outwardly to conform to the Catholic rite. Apparently his real theory of religion was that it should be a matter of individual conscience only, leaving the regulation of all public acts to the civil government. Latent in all his thought is the modern conception of the secular state. Among his many important tracts expounding the implications of this conception are the following: *A History of Ecclesiastical Benefices,* a *Treatise on the Inquisition,* a tract on *The Right of Sanctuary,* and a pamphlet on the *Immunity of the Clergy,* each of which dealt a hard blow to one or another of the claims or weapons of the medieval church. He also wrote a defence of Venice's claim to dominion over the Adriatic. And he followed up his theoretical works with an extensive and brilliant correspondence with many of his most famous contemporaries.

In the light of all this polemic his greatest work, *The History of the Council of Trent* (1619), must be judged. Sarpi was a brilliant and also a somewhat unscrupulous controversialist in an age nowhere overburdened with scruples of delicacy. Though he probably did not write a Machiavellian tract attributed to him, recommending the use of poison as an ordinary expedient of statecraft, there would have been nothing in such advice repugnant to the manners of the time, nor to the practice of his Signoria, nor to Sarpi's own general political theory. Nor is his maxim "I speak falsehood never, but the truth not to everyone" that of the perfect historian. His *History* is a tract against papal tyranny and against Jesuitry and against superstition. "I hate superstition more than impiety," he wrote, "for the impious man hurts himself only, and does not try to propagate his opinions, whereas superstition is contagious, and he who is infected with it does his best to infect others." [1]

He began by a long introduction on the Reformation, mostly founded on Sleidan and extraordinarily favorable to the Protestants, with whom he had nothing in common except hatred of the papacy. In lurid colors he painted the history of the Council as an Iliad of woes. Medieval councils had been able to make good their claims to sovereignty in the church, but now at last, he set forth, a council, by Jesuit intrigue, and by every disreputable art of packing and of corruption, had been subjected to the papal yoke. The council had been called to heal the schism, but had made it irreconcilable. It had tried to confirm the legitimate authority of the bishops, but instead had reduced them to a harsher bondage than before. In short, Sarpi taught the world what the claims to guidance by the Holy Ghost were worth—the Holy Ghost which, as one of the members of the council put it, came in the mail-bags from Rome.

As a work of art Sarpi's *History* is the most attractive produced in Italy during the century. A subtle psychology, an animated style, and a warm enthusiasm for liberty and enlightenment make it delightful reading. Moreover it is packed with information which for a long time was obtainable nowhere else. The archives of Venice, enriched with those wonderful accounts sent regularly to the Signoria by its ambassadors in foreign lands, though kept closed to the public, were opened to the Servite friar, who took from them just what he chose. By many historians, among them Gibbon, Hallam, Macaulay, and Andrew D. White, Sarpi's work has been immensely admired. Ranke first pointed out serious errors in it, and a learned Catholic scholar has recently sought to shatter its credibility entirely. Father Ehses goes so far as to accuse Sarpi of arbitrary displacement and disarrangement of his sources in order to put events in a

[1] *Opere*, vi, 4.

deceptive light, and even of falsifying his account by quoting from sources which never existed. Here and there the historian appeals to a diary of Chieregato which has not been found and which Father Ehses asserts to have been invented by him. I have, however, discovered some support for Sarpi's assertions drawn from it in other sources, and I therefore believe it to have been genuine. My final judgment is that, whereas the Venetian historian's narrative was occasionally warped from the strict truth by bias, it generally conformed to the better standards of criticism and of accuracy prevailing when it was written.

The manuscript, for which no publisher could be found in Italy, was taken to London by Marcantonio de Dominis, formerly the Roman Catholic Archbishop of Spalato, but at this time a convert to the Anglican church. In 1619 Sarpi's work was printed at London under the name of Pietro Soave Polano, an anagram for Paolo Sarpi Veneto. Within ten years it was translated from Italian into Latin, French, German, and English. The Protestants hailed the work with great enthusiasm, Milton dubbing its author "the great unmasker of the Tridentine Council." The Catholics, wincing under the telling blow, put the book on the Index, and entrusted the Jesuit Sforza Pallavicino with the task of writing a counter-history.

In France the interest in the Reformation was keener than in Italy because of the large Huguenot population and the problem of religious peace. In 1680 the Jesuit Louis Maimbourg wrote a *History of Lutheranism* in a piquant style adapted to the tastes of the polite world. But his work was soon thrown into the shade by the masterpiece of Bossuet.

The eagle of Meaux served his apprenticeship by writing a *Discourse on Universal History* (1681) in order, as the sub-title put it, "to explain the Course of Religion and the Changes of Empires." Taking his philosophy directly from Augustine's *City of God*, Bossuet made a determined effort to prove from history the guidance of human affairs by Providence. For him the chronicles of humanity reveal the working out of a divine plan, which can be detected even in civil affairs, but is most plainly evident in the evolution of religion from the creation of Adam to the time when the author wrote. The work was divided into three parts. The first summarized the chief events of world history from the creation in 4004 B.C. to the conversion of Constantine. The only sources available were the Old Testament and the classical historians. As far as possible they were harmonized, but in case of conflict the authority of the Bible was preferred. Part II traced the course of religion, which was thought of as a consistent and divinely inspired unity from the beginning. The triumph of Christianity under Constantine the author considered miraculous, because paganism was supported by the senses, by vested interest, by ignorance, by tradition, by policy, and by philosophy. Part III investigated the causes of the Rise and Fall of Empires. The primary cause is found in the counsels of God and in his purpose to give practical lessons to princes; but the secondary causes can be traced, so that "the true science of history is to note in each age the secret dispositions which prepared for the great changes, and the important conjunctures which made them come to pass." The constitution and polity of the principal nations are described in what is perhaps nearer to a "histoire des mœurs" than anything before Voltaire.

Though the *Discourse on Universal History* is no contemptible work, it is far surpassed by its author's *chef d'œuvre*, the *History of the Variations of the Protestant Churches* (1688). The bishop's purpose was the practical one, frankly avowed, to convince the Protestants of the error of their ways and to bring them back into the fold of the church. He honestly believed, as he set forth in his preface, that if the Protestants but knew the true history of their origin, and the inconsistencies and even equivocations with which the Reformers had defended their doctrines, they would feel contempt for the Reformation and long for reunion with the Catholics. For, said Bossuet, truth is one; the Protestants are condemned out of their own

mouths by their mutual contradictions. With persuasive
iteration the moral was driven home that there is no certainty without a central tribunal, that one revolt leads to
another until all the bases of spiritual and of civil authority
are subverted. Luther is followed by Zwingli, Zwingli by
Socinus, Socinus by Arminius and Cromwell, and these in
turn by Libertines and Levellers, until atheism and anarchy
ensue.

In his use of sources Bossuet, writing largely for a Protestant audience, was careful and fair, but his learning was
insufficient. He knew no modern language but French, and
he avoided a large number of secondary works, including
some good ones, because he distrusted their tendency. On
the other hand he occasionally searched for unpublished
sources. His imagination was limited. He could not really
understand, much less sympathize with, either the German
character or the heretical aspiration for liberty.

More remarkable than his limitations was his real effort
to be fair. He could admit that some popes were bad, that
there was need of a reform, and that there was some good
in Luther. Luther, indeed, looms large in his history out of
all proportion to other men and to other factors in the
revolt. Nor is his characterization of Luther altogether bad,
much of the latter's personality as it leaves untouched.

Bossuet was quick to make the most of all charges that
might plausibly be brought against the Reformers. He
followed earlier, but mistaken, authorities in attributing
the protest against indulgences to the jealousy of the Augustinian for the Dominican order. He blamed Luther's permission of polygamy, and Zwingli's liberalism in admitting
the good heathen into heaven. He devoted a whole book to
refuting the Protestant doctrine that the pope is Antichrist. And, notwithstanding his own defence of the Gallican
Liberties, he reproached Luther for subjecting the church
to the yoke of the civil government.

3. POLITICAL HISTORY

The opinion of Bossuet, that "religion and civil government are the two points around which human affairs revolve," was shared by most of his contemporaries. They
cared nothing for economic or social history because they
saw little in the life of the common people worth recording.
But many of them wrote secular histories very different in
their point of view and interests from the church histories
just described. On the whole they offered much less that
was new than did the ecclesiastical historians. These narratives were animated by the desire to glorify the writer's
nation, and were influenced, though less deeply than were
the humanists of the earlier age, by classical models. To a
slight extent some of them were touched by scientific motives or methods. Many of the histories written at this time
were largely in the nature of personal memoirs and were,
therefore, like all autobiographies, to some extent apologies
for the author's life. In only one line did the secular historians of this period produce a new genre, in the Tory and
Whig histories called forth by the rise of political parties in
England.

Italian historiography, which had been the most notable
in Europe during the Renaissance, now languished under
the Inquisition. The establishment of the principate in
Tuscany put an end to the Florentine school so ably represented by Machiavelli and Guicciardini. Only in Venice was
it now possible to write freely on matters of divinity and
state, and only in Sarpi did seventeenth-century Italy
produce a great historian.

In Spain humanist historiography found a talented master
in the political theorist Juan de Mariana, whose *History of
Spain* was published in two volumes in Latin in 1592 and
1595, and then translated by the author into Castilian in
1601. Modelled on Livy, colorful, and interesting, it deserves at least the first half of the encomium lavished on
it by Ticknor when he called it "the most remarkable

union of picturesque chronicling with sober history that
the world has ever seen." The author's purpose was frankly
patriotic, first to free Spain from the reproach of not having
a classical historical work, and secondly to teach foreigners
"the principles and means by which Spain advanced to the
greatness which is now hers." Aiming no higher than at an
œuvre de vulgarisation, Mariana took his sources mostly
from the accessible earlier chronicles, and used them rather
uncritically, though he was not quite so credulous or so naïve
as he has sometimes been represented. His practice, however, of depending on literary sources for facts known to
him by experience, as in his account of the Spanish climate
and geography, would offer occasion for comment on his
lack of originality, were it not the all too common usage
among writers of every age and of every kind. Beginning
with the peopling of Spain by Tubal, a son of Japhet, immediately after the flood, he continued his story till the
conquest of Granada and the discovery of the West Indies
in 1492, which last event he considered "the most honorable
and advantageous enterprise ever undertaken by Spain."
Through his narrative he scattered moral reflections and
political maxims; but, though he occasionally praised a
king for restoring justice and good government, he rarely
or never betrayed that sympathy with liberty which one
might expect from the author of the *De Rege.*

Among the French secular historians of this period the
palm may be given to Jacques Auguste de Thou (1553-
1617) commonly known by his Latin name Thuanus. As
Privy Councillor to Henri III and Henri IV, and as President of the Parlement of Paris, he played a large part in
affairs. The *History of his own Time,* covering the period
1546 to 1607, to some extent partakes the character of personal memoirs, though it broadens its scope to survey the
whole of Europe. Apart from his personal interests, his
governing purpose was to expose the evils of religious war
and to advocate tolerance. Hating the Guises, to whose
private ambitions he attributed much that was worst in the
civil wars, he supported the monarchy as the best guarantee

of peace, while exhorting the monarch not to treat heresy by fire, sword, and exile, but to use gentler methods. Though written by a Catholic, the book was soon put on the Index because of its Gallicanism and liberality. Though de Thou has been accused of excessive timidity, he dared to brand the massacre of St. Bartholomew as "an outburst of fury unexampled in the annals of any nation," to paint in dark colors both its horrors and its dire effects, and to fasten the blame for it squarely on the shoulders of Catherine de Médicis. His principal sources were, for France, in addition to his own memory, public acts and speeches, and for other countries the best histories he could find and information furnished him by distinguished contemporaries like Camden. Writing in Latin, he perhaps disguised the spirit of his own age by throwing over it a dress cut in too classical a fashion.

Nevertheless, not only the dignity of Clio but her veracity suffered in the hands of the successors of de Thou who treated French history in various vernaculars. Enrico Caterino Davila (1576-1631), of noble Spanish descent, early became a page of Catherine de Médicis, and then as a soldier in the royal army fought through the wars of religion. When he left France and settled in Italy he published, in Italian, a *History of the Civil Wars in France,* which won rapid popularity (1630). Writing as a *politique,* his heroes were Catherine and Henri IV. Without interest in or understanding of religion he treated the Huguenots as merely a political faction.

A slightly different point of view found expression in the *History of France* published by François Eudes, commonly called de Mézeray (1610-83), who sympathized with the desire of the bourgeois class for strong government. As a *politique* he paid his respects to Catholicism only as far as good form required. His frankly expressed wish was to glorify the good kings (almost all French kings were good, in his opinion) and the heroes of France by conferring on them fame. Though he did not cite sources he claimed to base his work, which covered the whole story of France from the legendary Pharamond till his own birth, on the best authors and also on ancient and original charters. But above all he desired to write the beautiful new French style necessary to appeal to the cultivated class and to the *précieux*.

The two English historians who won fame in the early seventeenth century were at opposite poles in choice of subject, in treatment, and in temperament. The one was Sir Walter Raleigh, the gallant courtier, bold adventurer, and hardy explorer; the other was William Camden, the careful scholar and antiquary. Raleigh (c.1552-1618) wrote his *History of the World* while a prisoner in the Tower under indictment for treason; and perhaps he embarked on this new adventure "in the dark backward and abysm of time" because he was unable longer to explore the living world. Though he intended to cover the whole of man's life upon earth from the Creation till his own day,—making the latter part of his work chiefly a history of England— the task proved so heavy that he was forced to stop with the Roman conquest of Macedon in 146 B.C. His sources were few and easily accessible—the Bible, Herodotus, Xenophon, Thucydides, Plutarch, Polybius, and Livy, and among these his favorite was Plutarch. A little help was given him by the more learned Ben Jonson.

Raleigh's conception of history was a compound of the classical and the Puritan, for he said that the two main ends of history are "to teach by example of times past such wisdom as may guide our desires and actions," and to exhibit the workings of the divine plan of Providence, "how kings and kingdoms have flourished and fallen, and for what virtue and piety God made prosperous, and for what vice and deformity he made wretched."

The work is naturally a harmony of Jewish and of Greek and of Latin sources. Into his chronology he fitted not only the authentic events of the classical tradition, but the legendary adventures of the Argonauts and Tantalus and Œdipus and Pelops.

Here and there his history reflected the strong English love of liberty. James I was quite right, from his point of view, in threatening to suppress the book, which appeared in 1614, on the ground that it "was too saucy in censuring princes." Harsher judgments have rarely been passed on Edward II, Henry IV, Richard III, Henry VII, and Henry VIII, than can be found in a digression on English history in Raleigh's preface. But the same reason that made James hate the book made the Puritans love it; and from it many of them, including Milton, took their general notions of ancient times.

Purely patriotic was the purpose of William Camden (1551-1623) in investigating the antiquities of the British Isles. A Londoner by birth, educated in St. Paul's school, he studied some years at Oxford, but probably failed to graduate. Nevertheless, he became one of the deepest scholars of the day, devoting himself with diligence and success to antiquarian and historical lore. His first work, *Britannia* (1586) is a "chorographical description of the most flourishing kingdoms of England, Scotland, and Ireland," together with much material on early local history and with good maps. In this he also discussed the origin of the British nation, and related the stories, which he recognized as fabulous, of the settlement of Britain by Brutus, a Trojan of the family of Aeneas, in 1108 B.C. The manners of the ancient Britons, and the influence of the Roman, Danish, and Norman conquest interested him. The sources on which he drew were the early chronicles, personal inspection of remains, and a wide correspondence with the learned at home and abroad.

Camden's *Britannia* excited the admiration of scholars and the enthusiasm of patriots in equal measure. Casaubon and de Thou justly praised its accuracy, genius, diligence, candor, and judgment; while Edmund Spenser borrowed from it one of the most effective episodes in his epic, that in which Sir Guyon reads *Briton Moniments* and *Antiquity of Faery Land*.[1]

Camden next turned his attention to the most recent history of his country and wrote the *Annals of England and Ireland during the reign of Elizabeth*, which was published in

[1] *Faery Queen*, Book ii, Canto 9, vs. 59ff.

two parts, the first in 1615, the second after its author's
death, in 1625. While the work is scholarly it is far from
being impartial. The author wrote as a royalist, a conservative, and a member of the established church. Matters of
religion he found so ticklish that as far as possible he
handled them gingerly:

Although I am not ignorant [he explained] that war and politics
are the proper subjects of history, yet I neither could nor ought
to pass over ecclesiastical matters. There can be no divorce of
church and state; but as the church historian takes religion as
his special province, I have touched it only lightly.

Camden's services to the study of history were continued,
and his idea of what it should be was more clearly set forth,
in his endowment of a lectureship in history at Oxford in
1622. This was the first professorship in this discipline to
be established in England. The occupant was to receive £140
per annum, and his duties were thus set forth by Camden
himself:

It is my intention that (according to the practice of such professors in all the universities beyond the seas) he should read
a civil history, and therein make such observations as might be
most useful and profitable for the younger students of the university, to direct and instruct them in the knowledge and use of
history, antiquity, and times past . . . not intermeddling with
the history of the church or controversies further than shall give
light into those times which he shall unfold, or that author
which he then shall read, and that very briefly.[1]

It is significant of the change that came over the spirit of
England during the reign of James I, that whereas Camden's
purposes had been chiefly nationalistic, those of his younger
contemporary Selden should have been chiefly partisan. His
History of Tithes (1618) buttressed the authority of the
state in regulating ecclesiastical matters. His *History of*

[1] Allison: "The First Endowed Professorship of History," *American Historical Review*, xxvii, 1922, pp. 733ff.

Titles of Nobility, his tract on the *Privileges of the Baronage of England when they sit in Parliament* (1642), and many other historical monographs directly served the purposes of the popular party.

In the Civil War parties were born; and not long afterwards came that inevitable rationalization of the interests of the new groups, party history. In many respects this new genre resembled ecclesiastical chronicles more closely than the earlier political annals, for each author was bound to defend, not a family, patron, or nation, but a doctrine. And the temptation to warp the story was exactly the same to the political as to the ecclesiastical writer. Not that the party historians were more subject to bias than others; but their temptation was greater in that they felt obliged to represent the group to which they belonged not only as always good—which could easily be done, whatever the data—but as always consistent. Parties, which are essentially groups bound by the same material interests, often change their tactics and sometimes their principles, but they naturally always claim consistency in their actions. Not only did this appeal to tradition refract the clear ray of science, but it brought with it the almost irresistible tendency to view the earlier acts of the party in the light of its present struggles and program. But with all these faults party purpose made the page glow with new life and passion. Love and hate are sharp-sighted, and apt to command an energy and a devotion sometimes lacking to curiosity and to the strongest appetite for abstract knowledge.

Were Hobbes's *Behemoth* but a chronicle of the civil war in England, it might be considered the first of the party histories. But it is rather a disquisition on the causes of the conflict than a story of them, and even as a political discourse it is not profound. Blind as was the author to all economic and material causes, he found the sources of the great rebellion solely in religious controversies and in the study of Greek and Roman republicans. Having made might the criterion of right, and having justified the absolute authority of the *de facto* government, Hobbes was obliged to

show why the Commonwealth was not a true state to which
he, as a royalist, could yield ungrudging obedience. The
true state he had called the Leviathan, and made it a sort of
earthly god; for the false state he selected the name of
another biblical monster, Behemoth, which had commonly
been taken by the theologians as a symbol of the devil.

Not Hobbes, therefore, but Clarendon must be considered
the first of the great party historians, and one of the most
gifted in their long and brilliant line. Edward Hyde (1609-
74), created Earl of Clarendon in 1661, had in early life
been a member of the Short and of the Long Parliaments.
At first a moderate reformer, he became a royalist and fled
from England in 1645. Made Lord Chancellor at the Restoration, he was again obliged to retire to the Còntinent on
account of political intrigues in 1667. His *History of the
Rebellion and Civil Wars in England,* covering the period
1628-60, was written partly in his first exile (1646-47) and
partly in his second (1670-71). It was first published, in incomplete form, in 1702-04, and fully in 1888. Being largely
in the nature of memoirs it was based chiefly on the writer's
own recollections and on the documents he had been able to
collect during his public life.

Like most of his contemporaries, Clarendon failed to
notice economic and social changes; like many of the secular
historians he had little real understanding of the character
and motives of the Presbyterian and Independent Parties.
For him, the whole right and wrong of the rebellion depended on a question of constitutional law, and its causes
lay either in the inscrutable decrees of Providence or in the
incalculable folly, weakness, and wickedness of man.[1]

As he overestimated the influence of personality, it is
natural that his style, which is always clear and lively,
should attain its highest glow in some of his justly famous
portraits. Nor, though his bias is openly acknowledged and
even flaunted, do his portraits of enemies degenerate into
caricature. In fact, he is often as hard on the "folly and
weakness" of the king's advisers as he is on the "wickedness

[1] Book ix, 1f.

and malice" of his enemies. His picture of Hampden, while unfavorable, is not altogether a travesty, and his judgment of Cromwell is as follows:

> He was one of those men whom even his enemies were unable to vituperate without at the same time praising him; for he could never have done half that mischief without great parts of courage and industry and judgment. . . . As he had all the wickedness against which damnation is denounced and for which hellfire is prepared, so he had some virtues which have caused the memory of men in all ages to be celebrated; and he will be looked upon by posterity as a brave, bad man.

This characterization, so typical of the seventeenth century in its emphasis on moral good and evil as the mainsprings of action, but serves to remind the twentieth how useless are such ethical judgments for explaining the processes of society.

Comparable to Clarendon, even though somewhat inferior to him, were the two earliest historians of New England. Governor Bradford's *History of Plymouth Plantation* and Governor Winthrop's *History of New England* presented the apology of the Puritan party. Aiming at "a plain style with singular regard unto the simple truth of all things" the authors achieved, if not philosophical history, at least singularly vivid, honest, and trustworthy memoirs, written with that general elevation of tone and that slight tincture of prejudice and superstition common to most Puritan works.

A fine party history was produced in the Netherlands by Grotius to whom, when little more than a lad, the States General intrusted the important task of presenting the popular and national side of the war of independence. More mature work was completed by the "Dutch Tacitus," Pieter Cornelissen Hooft. Reading widely, using the archives, critically sifting his materials, and writing in a sententious and reflective style, he published a *History of Henri the Great* (Henri IV of France), 1626; a *History of the Miseries of the Princes of the House of Medici,* 1638, and a *Dutch History* (covering the period 1555-85) in 1642.

CHAPTER X

BIBLICAL AND CLASSICAL SCHOLARSHIP

I. BIBLICAL CRITICISM

One great province of history was, until recently, set apart from all others, partly because it required different methods of study from those applicable to other fields, and still more because it was regarded as more holy, or more heroic, than any other portion of the human story. Antiquity was known to our ancestors almost entirely from the biblical and the classical writers, the first invested with the halo of divine inspiration, and the second crowned with the laurel of un-approachable genius. Both the merits of the ancient writers and their defects made of the sources a medium strongly refracting the light of truth. In order to see clearly the facts of ancient history, the first necessary step was to examine thoroughly and fearlessly the documents, to establish the correct texts, to interpret, to criticize, to date, and to sift the genuine from the false. Philology, as it is now called, has ever been an important ancillary science to the historian; and in the seventeenth century philology, together with archeology, made some progress in the elucidation of ancient times.

The chief reason why biblical criticism, in that brilliant age, lagged far behind all other branches of learning, was that it had to contend with the strongest prejudices. Inveterate prepossession was an obstacle in the path of the natural scientist, but a small one compared to that opposing the rational critic of the Bible. Not only were religious passions excited by the confessional conflict to fury, but they were concentrated on the assertion of biblical infallibility. The Catholics, acknowledging the Bible and tradition as equal sources of divine truth, had defined their dogmas in a system recently perfected by the Council of Trent, and held to be unalterable and eternal. To the Protestant the doctrine of biblical inspiration was crucial, for to him the Bible was the sole guide for faith and morals, and the sufficient authority for attacking the Catholic tradition. The Bible was in fact, as Chillingworth declared it to be, "the religion of Protestants"; and as such it was to be revered, enjoyed, read, marked, learned, and inwardly digested, but never to be subjected to the solvent of free thought. To touch it was to lay profane hands on the ark of the covenant, a mortal sin. Thus it came about that the vast quantity of biblical exegesis poured forth from the pulpits was only to a tiny extent soundly critical. The preacher sought not to investigate facts with an unbiased mind but to find proof texts for his own dogmas and edifying lessons for his backsliding contemporaries. The fact that upon the same scriptural basis were reared numerous different superstructures of dogma may have done something mutually to discredit them all, but it helped very little towards the creation of a really sound historical criticism. The most important contributions towards the formation of such criticism were made not by the prolific Protestant commentators, but by the atheist Hobbes, the Jew Spinoza, and the Catholic Richard Simon.

One important discovery, was indeed made by a French Protestant professor at the college of Saumur, Louis Cappel (or Capellus). He found out that the square Hebrew characters, then regarded as primeval, were really Aramaic, having been substituted for the older pointed letters (now known as Samaritan) at the time of the Babylonian captivity. He further showed that the earliest Hebrew alphabet had contained consonants only and that the vowels, written as points above and below the line, were a later invention. This discovery was so fatal to the doctrine of verbal inspiration of the text that the most famous Hebrew scholar of the day, the elder Buxtorf, begged Cappel not to publish it. It was published, however, though anonymously, at Leyden in

1624, under the title *The Mystery of the Vowel-points Revealed* (*Arcanum Punctationum Revelatum*).

Though Cappel's position in regard to the vowel-points has been universally accepted by modern scholars, it met with little welcome among his contemporaries, least of all with the Protestant divines. Dr. John Lightfoot asserted that doubts about the verbal inspiration of the Hebrew text were refuted alike by common sense and by piety. The Puritan John Owen wrote a refutation of Cappel, suggesting that variations found in the manuscripts and versions did not discredit the true text, which God had carefully preserved somewhere, while allowing corruptions to creep in elsewhere in order to try the faith and exercise the diligence of students. This theory, however, was too much even for the pious credulity of the age. Samuel Fisher, in a vast work on the canon and text of the Scriptures which appeared under the title *Rusticus ad Academicos* (1666) poured scorn on Owen's suggestion in the following words: "Whence came this whiffle and whimsy within the circumference of thy figmentitious fancy?"

An important advance in the textual criticism of the Scriptures and in biblical scholarship generally, was made by the great *Polyglot Bible* published by a group of English scholars under the editorship of Brian Walton. This vast work, in six folios, while naturally using and generously acknowledging the labors of predecessors, among them chiefly the *Complutensian Polyglot* of the early sixteenth century, and the revision of this, commonly called the *Biblia Heptaglotta* published at Paris 1629-1645, marks a new stage in textual research, and also the peak of English cooperative scholarship in its own age. The printing, by Thomas Roycroft in London, 1657, is both sumptuous and accurate. The text of the Old Testament is reproduced in the Hebrew, Samaritan, Septuagint Greek, Chaldee, Syriac, Arabic, Ethiopian, Persian, and Vulgate Latin; that of the New Testament in the original and in several ancient versions. For the New Testament the text was founded on that of Estienne, and the best known codices were collated, the

Codex Vaticanus at Rome and the *Codex Alexandrinus* at London. The Vulgate was based on the Sixtine and Clementine editions, but was castigated by reference to better sources. In addition to the texts, there was a vast apparatus, including a table of ancient chronology prepared by Louis Cappel, descriptions and maps of the Holy Land and of Jerusalem; plans of the temple; treatises on Hebrew coins, on weights and measures, on the origin of language and of the alphabet, on the Hebrew idiom; an historical account of the chief editions and principal versions of the Scriptures; a table of variant reading, with an essay on the integrity and authority of the original texts; and other matter.

None of the biblical texts was much improved until the nineteenth century. Little attention was paid to the assertion of Jean Morin that the Samaritan and Greek versions of the Old Testament better represented the original than did the Hebrew Massoretic text. The Greek of the New Testament was practically that of Erasmus, somewhat castigated by Robert Estienne by the collation of fifteen manuscripts and of the Complutensian text. His edition of 1551 came to be known, from an advertisement of the printers, as the "received text," which still further enhanced its claim to authority. The version recognized as authentic by the Catholics was the Latin Vulgate. In order to have it in its utmost purity, Pope Sixtus V appointed a commission to revise it. Though the work of the scholars on this body was good, it was nullified by the pope, who went through the whole text, deleting most of the corrections, without regard to manuscript authority, in order to secure agreement with his own personal copy of the Bible, an Antwerp edition of 1583 without critical value. When the Sixtine recension appeared as the official revision in 1590, no wonder that Cardinal Bellarmine said that the procedure of the pope would incite the Protestants to say that he had corrupted the Scriptures with his own hand.

Turning from the textual to the higher criticism of the Bible, we find that the first fruitful work since the time of Luther was done by the Catholic Andreas van Maes, or

Masius. This Fleming, in an *Illustrated History of Joshua the Captain* (1574) advanced the opinion that Ezra, either alone or with the help of contemporaries, had compiled from ancient records not merely the Book of Joshua but other historical books, and that even the Pentateuch had been interpolated after Moses' time. The merit of Maes is that he first clearly recognized the composite character of large portions of the Old Testament.

A far more sweeping attack on the traditional views of the Scriptures is found in the *Leviathan* of Thomas Hobbes. The great atheist, without the courage to attack religion openly, and without the ingenuity of Gibbon to treat it with latent irony, professed to acknowledge the divine authority of the Bible, laughing in his sleeve all the while. Though his secret bias was strongly anti-Christian, he, like the Christian expositors, had a dogma to prove, which was hardly less fatal to really scientific purposes than was theirs. And yet, because he approached the subject from a new point of view, he was able to advance some theses which have found more or less acceptance with later critics. What he set out to prove was the theory that there had never been, either among the Jews or in early Christian times, a spiritual authority apart from the civil government. Whoever wielded the sovereign power over the Jews, the same, he said, had also held the supreme authority in matters of religion. Nor was there, Hobbes contended, any binding authority in Christianity until it was made the state religion of the Roman Empire, nor even any canon of the New Testament until it was defined by the Council of Laodicea, acting under imperial mandate, in 364. Nor yet, he continued, was there ever any authority to interpret the Scriptures except that set up by the civil government. Even the appeal to divine inspiration and to miracles must fail; for the Bible itself shows that of four hundred prophets consulted by Ahab all but one were imposters, and that at other times they were mostly liars (Jeremiah xiv,14). In short, the only test of a prophet's mission is his allowance by the civil ruler.

To prove these propositions Hobbes set out on a thorough

exploration of the books of the Bible, in order to ascertain the circumstances of their composition and the meaning of their messages. He easily proved that the Pentateuch was not written by Moses, that the book of Joshua was written long after his time, and that the books of Judges, Samuel and Kings are much later than the events they narrate. The book of Job "seemeth not to be a history, but a treatise concerning a question in ancient times much disputed, why wicked men have often prospered in this world, and good men have been afflicted." Hobbes was also right in asserting that the book of Psalms had been put in order after the return from Babylon, but he was too conservative in allowing that many of the Psalms were by David, and that parts of Ecclesiastes and Canticles were by Solomon. The books of the New Testament Hobbes accepted as genuine, for, said he, had they been falsified by later writers, the doctors of the church would have made them more favorable to the priestly as against the secular power than they were.

Somewhat similar conclusions in regard to the late date and composition of the Old Testament books were reached by Spinoza, who examined the critical problem at considerable length in his *Theological-Political Treatise* (1670). Doubtless he was much influenced by Hobbes, as well as by Maimonides, a rationalistic medieval interpreter of the Jewish Scriptures. But the thesis of Spinoza was entirely different from that of the English philosopher. Not to prove that religion had always been and always must be the servant of the civil power, but to prove that it had always been and always should be the minister of reason, was the pious and philosophical purpose of the righteous Jew.

Approaching the critical examination of the Scriptures more closely, he proceeded to lay down the correct rules for exegesis. Though all pretend to appeal to the Bible in order to learn its real meaning, all expositors really go to it, he complained,

anxious only to extort their own inventions and decrees from the Bible, and so to fortify them with divine authority. [On the

contrary we ought to study it without preconceptions, and to elicit
its meaning by] collecting the teachings of each book, arranging
them topically so that we may have for ready reference whatever can be found out about them; and then we ought to mark
all those which are ambiguous or obscure or which contradict
each other. And those sentences I here call obscure or clear the
sense of which is easily or with difficulty elicited from the context, not according as their truth is easily or with difficulty perceived by reason, for we are concerned only with the meaning of
the Bible, and not with its truth.[1]

After laying down this perfectly correct principle of
interpretation, Spinoza added to it the equally correct thesis
that in order to understand any book its purpose, date and
author must be known and its content thus explained historically and not otherwise.

Applying this method to the books of the Bible Spinoza
easily showed, from internal evidence, that the Pentateuch,
together with the books of Joshua, Judges, Ruth, Samuel,
and Kings, were written not by their supposed authors but
long afterwards. While he was correct in this claim, he was
too bold in asserting that all these books were written by
one author who was probably, though not certainly, Ezra.
This idea, which was not original with Spinoza, was based
on a verse (xiv.22) of the apocryphal II Esdras. The other
books of the Old Testament Spinoza believed to have been
written after the time of Ezra, perhaps after the time of
Judas Maccabaeus (who died 161 B.C.) The book of Job
he regarded as originally a gentile work, translated into
Hebrew. The Psalms, he said, were collected in post-exilic
times; the books of the Prophets were not written by themselves.

The excellence of Spinoza's critical method and the
correctness of some of his conclusions were lost upon a

[1] The sense of this fine passage has been destroyed in all editions but
the first and the last by the omission of the words italicized in the following quotation: "Atque eas sententias hic obscuras aut claras voco, quarum
sensus ex contextu orationis facile vel difficulter *elicitur, at non quatenus
earum veritas facile vel difficulter* ratione percipitur." *Tractatus Theologico-
Politicus,* cap. 2, *Opera,* ed. Gebhardt, 1925, iii, 100.

generation steeped in dogmatic prejudice. Even a philosopher so open-minded as Leibniz could write that the biblical criticism of Hobbes and Spinoza, if allowed, would overthrow the Christian religion.[1]

But even while the Jewish free-thinker was denounced his results were to some extent accepted and his method imitated by those few who had the ability to see clearly in these matters. Only seven years after the *Theological-Political Treatise* had seen the light, there was sent to the press an epoch-making work which denounced the impious conclusions of Spinoza while accepting some of his premises. This was the *Histoire Critique du Vieux Testament* by the French Catholic Richard Simon. He first clearly recognized the complicated processes of revision and change to which the sacred text had been exposed from the time of its composition until recently. The canonical books of the Old Testament, he said, had been handed on from generation to generation by a guild of scribes who had constantly re-edited and altered them. He thought that in the course of time the loose sheets on which the text was written became mixed, as can be shown by comparing the Samaritan version with the Hebrew. That such a process would destroy the theory of the verbal inspiration of the text did not disturb the author, for he hinted that the inspiration of the Bible is limited to matters of faith and does not guarantee inerrancy on other points, and he believed that for the Catholic the deposit of faith is sufficiently guarded by the church. His own words are:

The great changes which have come about, as may be seen from the first book of this work, in the copies of the Bible since the original autographs were lost, entirely destroy the principle of the Protestants and Socinians, who can consult only the copies of the Bible as they exist nowadays. If the truth of religion had not lived in the church it could not be found with certainty in books which have undergone so many changes, and

[1] *Sämtliche Schriften*, i, 148.

which have depended in so many things on the caprices of the copyists.[1]

The author followed the history of the text with a history of the versions, all of which he considered so incorrect as to be practically useless. In a third division of the work he pointed out many obscurities and difficulties in the interpretation of the sacred writings.

Notwithstanding Simon's belief that his conclusions would prove unacceptable only to heretics, his book did not escape the censure of the Catholic authorities. Even as it was being printed Bossuet heard of it, procured a table of contents and the preface, from which he concluded that the work was a "tissue of impieties and a bulwark of free-thought," that it would tend to indifference in matters of religion, would entirely subvert all religion and would "destroy the authority of canonical Scripture." Accordingly, he had the whole issue, of 1200 or 1500 copies, confiscated and burnt notwithstanding the licence to print.[2]

Nevertheless a pirated edition appeared in 1680; and a new edition, revised by the author, was printed, through the good offices of a Protestant scholar, at Amsterdam in 1685. Moreover the author continued to present his ideas to the public in a series of works including a *Critical History of the New Testament* (1689), a *History of the Versions of the Bible* (1690) and a *History of the Principal Commentators* (1693).

All these important and learned works excited considerable attention. The pirated edition of the *Critical History of the Old Testament* was early translated into English and became the subject of Dryden's famous poem, *Religio Laici* (1682). In this didactic rime by a free-thinker who was soon to announce his conversion to Catholicism, Simon was called a "matchless author" whose "weighty book" was the crabbed toil of years spent in sifting "Rabbins' old sophisticated ware from gold divine," a book

---

[1] R. Simon: *Histoire Critique du Vieux Testament,* 1685, Preface de l'auteur. I quote from the copy at Cornell.

[2] Bossuet: *Correspondence,* xiii, 308ff, 327.

Where we may see what errors have been made
Both in the copiers' and translators' trade:
How Jewish—Popish—interests have prevailed,
And where infallibility has failed.

The higher criticism of the New Testament was, at this
period, more conservative and less successful than that of
the Old. Hobbes, Spinoza, and Simon all believed that the
canonical Christian books were more authentic and reliable
than were the Jewish. Grotius, who published some elaborate *Annotations on the New Testament* (1641), sought only
to elucidate the simple verbal sense of the texts by adducing
parallels from the Greek and Latin classics. Though he
treated the Pauline epistles with special love, he had no real
insight into the world of Pauline thought.

Some light was shed on the Bible by the progress of
oriental studies. Indeed, several branches of science which
have long since doffed their ecclesiastical vestments were
then viewed almost entirely as ancillary to theology. This
"queen of sciences," as it was called in the Middle Ages,
still ruled over vast tracts of curious lore. In her service
John Selden produced the learned treatises, extremely valuable in themselves, on *The Hebrew Year,* on *The Sanhedrins
and Judicial Offices of the Jews,* on the *Syrian Gods,* and
many others. Half a century later (in 1685) J. Spencer
pointed out, in his treatise on the *Ritual Laws of the
Hebrews,* the resemblances between Jewish and heathen
rites.

The questions of the origin of language and of the alphabet were then almost always approached from the biblical
starting-point. The view naturally held was that the first
languages were created directly by God; the very first implanted in Adam and the others created by fiat at the Tower
of Babel. This general position, sustained in Brian Walton's
Polyglot (1657), was compatible with the recognition that
every language is in a state of perpetual flux; the changes
being due to the invention of new things for which new
words are required, and to contamination by other tongues.
This natural element in the creation of language was more

fully recognized in some words on the subject found in Simon's *Critical History of the Old Testament*. The invention of the first alphabet after the Deluge was variously attributed to Moses and to the Egyptians, and by Walton to the Assyrians. The fable of Cadmus bringing the Greek alphabet from Phoenicia was credited, while the derivation from it of all other European alphabets was recognized.

The interesting problem of ancient chronology, including the age of the world, was then solved almost entirely by biblical data. Whereas some Greek sages had thought of the past in myriads of years, and some of the Hindoo gymnosophists in crores of years,[1] the triumph of the Christian religion imposed the acceptance of the very limited Jewish chronology. According to the common Jewish era, the world was created in September, 3761 B.C. But this date, based on a computation of biblical evidence, was slightly changed by some Christian commentators under the dogmatic presumption that the world was intended to last exactly a week of millenia, or seven thousand years; during the first two thousand of which mankind had lived in a state of nature, and during the next two thousand under the Jewish Law. The succeeding two thousand, it was commonly believed, would complete the period during which the Christian Dispensation of grace prevails, after which the final millennium of Christ's kingdom upon earth would make its appearance. To this scheme Luther had given the sanction of his great authority. In 1541 he published a *Computation of Universal Chronology*,[2] placing the date of the creation of the world exactly 4000 B.C., and making the covenant with Noah, dated 2000 B.C., the dividing line between the first and second eras. This work, translated into English in 1576, had a vast influence in Protestant countries.

A more accurate estimate was attempted by Joseph Scaliger in his work on *The Restoration of Chronology* (1583). In the fifth book of this lucubration he calculated that the world was founded in 3949 B.C., and that man

---

[1] A myriad is ten thousand, a crore ten million.
[2] *Supputatio annorum mundi, Luthers Werke*, Weimar, liii, 1ff.

was created on the 23d of April of that year. He also suggested that the birth of Christ should be put in the year 4 B.C. of the vulgar era. Unlike the supposed creation of the world, this was a real historical event, though the data in the gospels are so diverse that modern scholars have given up its chronological determination. The vulgar era had been computed from Luke iii, 1 and 23, where it is said that Jesus was about thirty years old in the fifteenth year of the Emperor Tiberius. However, as Matthew connects the birth of Jesus with events in the reign of Herod the Great, who died in 4 B.C., it was evident, to those who accepted this narrative as historical, that Jesus could not have been born later than that date, which was therefore proposed by Scaliger as the true one. A slightly different calculation was made by Johann Kepler, who thought that Christ was born in 5 B.C., and that the world was created in 3992 B.C.[1] As Walter Raleigh, in his *History of the World* put the beginning of the Second Punic War in the year of Adam 3814, we may infer that he dated the creation in 4032 B.C. But he elsewhere hinted that the orthodox chronology was too short. Little different is the estimate of G. J. Voss who, in his *Epitome of Universal History* [2] (1622) selected the date 3946 for the creation.

Far more influential proved to be the chronology worked out by James Usher, Anglican Bishop of Armagh in the north of Ireland. His fancy was captured by the scheme of the three epochs of 2000 years each while his judgment was convinced that the birth of Christ had taken place in 4 B.C. In his *Annals of the Old and New Testament* therefore, (1650-54) he was able to inform the public with great nicety not only the year but the very hour of the creation of the world. This fell, he said, "at the beginning of the night before Monday, the 23d of October, 4004 B.C." Adam and Eve were both created on Friday, October the 28th; their first act was to celebrate and their second to consummate

---

[1] He published a tract *On the Year in Which Christ was Born* in 1606; and a chronological table called *Kanones Pueriles*, in 1620.

[2] *Opera*, 1698, iv, 1.

their marriage, with the blessing of the Almighty. Usher's dates for the creation and for the other events narrated in the Bible were inserted by an unknown editor into the margin of the Authorized Version of the English Bible, and soon obtained, in popular opinion, a quasi-canonical authority.

But this acceptance, being gradual, did not at first prevent other scholars from making different schemes. Walton's chronology, prefixed to his great *Polyglot,* dated the creation of the world 4103 B.C., but left a wide choice for the date of the Deluge, which he thought the Hebrews placed *anno mundi* 1356-57, the Septuagint translators *anno mundi* 2242 or 2262, and the Samaritans *anno mundi* 1307-8. Another estimate, contemporary with Walton, was that of Isaak Voss, who wrote a dissertation to prove that the world had been created before 5200 B.C.

This modest extension of the world's age was much less than demanded by certain rationalists who were moved to argue that the observed geological changes in the surface of the earth would have taken much more than 6000 years to accomplish, and also that the population of the world could not have increased, in the less than 4000 years since the deluge, to the amount at which it was estimated in the seventeenth century. A scientist named James Moore having come to believe, quite correctly, that England was at a remote period a part of the European continent, from this and other similar facts inferred that the age of the world was immensely greater than commonly believed, though he did not assert that the Scriptural account was false, but merely that the time therein had not been well computed nor understood.[1]

Those who argued from the large population of the world that it must be more than 100,000 years old were answered by John Graunt in 1662 and by Sir William Petty in 1683. The former, evidently forgetting the destruction of the earth's inhabitants in the great flood, argued that if the population had doubled every 64 years for the 5610 years

[1] S. Pepys: *Diary,* ed. H. B. Wheatley, 1903, ii, 38. May 1661.

since Adam and Eve, the earth might now have even more people on it than it has. The more careful calculation of Sir William Petty showed that if the eight persons emerging from the ark had doubled their numbers every ten years for the first century, the population of the world would have been 8000 one hundred years after the deluge; increasing somewhat more slowly thereafter it might well have reached 8,000,000 in 350 years, and 320,000,000 by the year of Christ 1682, a figure which just corresponds with what the author believed the total number of the world's inhabitants to have been.[1]

In inverse ratio to the fruitfulness of seventeenth-century biblical scholarship was the popularity and prestige of the Bible among the masses. This was due to the new translations made by the Reformers and their adversaries. Among these versions two, the English and the German, have taken their place as classics in their respective languages. The German translation of Luther has held its own from the time of its publication to the present, crowding out all rivals. More than any other work it created the literary language of the Germans, uniting them and training them in a noble and clear style. All the great German classical writers of the golden age were nursed on the language of the scriptures.

While Luther's version remained, because of its perfection and of his prestige, practically unaltered, the English Bible was a slower growth. The foundations were laid, in the age of the Reformation, by Tyndale and Coverdale, to whose genius must be attributed the greater part of excellence of most subsequent versions and revisions. And yet the singular felicity of the King James version, which may be regarded as the culmination of their labors, is due largely to the labors of several generations of scholars manipulating and polishing the same material.

Most of the revisions in the century between Tyndale and the Authorized Version were due, however, to dogmatic rather than to artistic or to scholarly needs. The Great Bible

[1] *Economic Writings of Sir W. Petty,* ed. C. H. Hull, ii, 388, 465.

of 1539 put a more Catholic sense on the style of Tyndale
and Coverdale. The Protestant leaders, exiled under Mary,
produced the Geneva Bible (1557-60) in order to harmonize
and interpret the Scriptures in a Calvinistic sense. Until the
King James Version this was the most popular English Bible,
being often reprinted, while the so-called Bishops' Bible,
though invested with the authority and representing the
views of the Anglican episcopate, found little acceptance.

The popularity of the Protestant versions forced the
Catholics to imitate them. This was done, in an English
translation, commonly called the Reims or Douai version,
made by Gregory Martin and other Catholic exiles and first
published, the New Testament in 1582 and the Old Testament in 1609-10. This version was made from the Latin Vulgate, defended in the preface as superior to the Greek original, and was strictly conformed to Catholic usage. In style
it differs wholly from all other English translations except
for a very few of its phrases adopted into the King James
Version. In it we find "the Parasceve" for "the day of preparation," "the Pasche" for the "Passover," "the feast of
azymes" for "the feast of unleavened bread," "the bread of
proposition" for "the shew bread," "prepuce" for "fore-
skin," and "didragmes" for the Greek coin translated "tribute" in the Protestant version of Matthew xvii, 24. The
Jesuit scholars also used the words "penance," "chalice,"
"host," and other Catholic ritualistic terms. Frequently we
find barbarisms incomprehensible without reference to the
Latin, as "he exinanited himself" (Philippians ii,7), "the
spirituals of wickedness in the celestials" (Ephesians vi,12),
and "what to thee and me, woman" (John ii,4). Most of the
differences from the Protestant versions departed further
from the original meaning of the text; but occasionally, as in
the "supersubstantial bread" of the Lord's prayer (Matthew
vi,11) the Catholic version represents more nearly the sense
of the Greek.

In order to put an end to the multiplicity of versions,
which bred doubt in simple minds, the Puritan John
Reynolds, President of Corpus Christi College, Oxford, pro-

posed to King James I the preparation of a new edition as an authorized and final standard. His majesty's interest having been secured, a large number of scholars was appointed to undertake the work, the whole board being divided into six sections, two of which met in Westminster, two in Oxford, and two in Cambridge. To each was assigned the revision of some part of the Bible, while the whole was again revised by a central committee of delegates from each section. The principles laid down for the guidance of the revisers were: to keep as closely as possible to the Bishops' Bible; to use proper names in the common forms; to keep the old ecclesiastical words such as "church" instead of "congregation" and the like used by Tyndale; to interpret the meaning of words with divers significations according to the opinion of the ancient fathers; and to use as few marginal notes as possible.

When the book was published, in 1611, the title-page stated that it "was appointed to be read in churches," and it soon became known as the "authorized version," though no legal authority for either the one or the other phrase has ever been discovered. What really gave it a monopoly for nearly three centuries was the rare excellence of its style. Many would agree with the learned Selden, who declared it to be the best translation ever made of any book in the whole world; few would dispute its title to be the first and greatest of English classics. Innumerable as are the testimonies to its beauty by literary critics, its highest glory is that it has formed the language of the Anglo-Saxon race, moulded their thought, inspired their art, and deeply tinctured their literature. Not only religious writers, like Bunyan and Milton, but distinctly profane ones, like Kipling, and avowed enemies of Christianity, like Swinburne, often secure their highest artistic effects by the use and abuse of biblical allusion.

That the French Bible enjoys no such pre-eminence as do the German and English Bibles is due partly to the fact that in France the Protestants were always in a small minority, but partly to the insufficient skill of the first Protestant translator. The version of Olivetan, published in 1535, though fairly adequate in Hebrew scholarship, was hastily done. Calvin found the style "rough and common," but while his own revision, and that of Beza, did not improve this feature of the work, they altered the sense of some passages from controversial considerations, much to the detriment of the version's accuracy.

While Olivetan remained, nevertheless, the Bible of the French Protestants for three centuries, several Catholic versions were produced, one of which was far superior to it in point of style. This was the great French translation by the Jansenists of Port Royal, the New Testament in 1667, the Old Testament in later years. The principal translator, Isaac Louis Lemaistre, commonly called De Sacy, was assisted by Arnauld, by Pascal, and by other famous Jansenists. Though they conformed their translation to the Vulgate, and compared it with the Protestant version in order, wherever possible, to differ from it, the work at first met with a hostile reception; De Sacy spent his last years in the Bastile, and Pope Clement IX prohibited his book. Nevertheless, its literary merit and its religious importance soon won it a place among the French classics of the seventeenth century, and a still larger place in the affections of the people. It was, indeed, the only Bible that secured popularity in any Catholic land. Though there were Italian and Spanish versions, both Catholic and Protestant, they languished in obscurity, at least during the seventeenth and eighteenth centuries.

But among the peoples of Teutonic or Anglo-Saxon speech and civilization the Bible was read, in the century and a half following Luther's translation, with more diligence and more attention than it has ever been read before or since. In all Christian countries at all times it has probably been the most read book; but in the age of the Reformation it combined something of the zest of a new discovery with an unequalled reputation for infallibility. That the Scripture, in all points essential to salvation, is clear and perspicuous, that its text is inerrant, perfect, and fully to be believed even in matters not pertaining to salvation, were the two points then insisted upon by all the Protestant leaders. Not only Calvin and Luther, but the Anabaptists and Socinians and those minor sects who represented the dissidence of dissent, appealed to the Bible as a perfect and sufficient guide to life. This attitude passed into bibliolatry; a superstitious worship of the book in which neither error of fact nor fault of style was allowed to be found. When the German scholar Joachim Jungius (1587-1657) pointed out that the language of the Greek Testament swarms with barbarisms, he was sharply reproved by the theological faculty of Wittenberg, and told that:

> To find solecisms, barbarisms, and poor Greek in the speeches and writings of the holy apostles, is to reflect on the Holy Ghost, who spoke through them; and whoever accuses the Holy Scriptures of barbarisms is guilty of no small blasphemy.

As every man with a rudimentary education could now read the book held to be so important to his eternal welfare, Bible-reading became the center of Protestant worship. Copious extracts were recited in divine worship; family prayers consisted partly of the reading of a chapter; and assiduous private perusal of God's Word was encouraged. Much of this reading became perfunctory, a matter of good form rather than of lively faith, for it was held to have beneficial effects from the mere doing of the task, and hence became the *opus operatum* of the Evangelicals. As the Bible was considered not only as inspired but as all-sufficient, to be "a man of one book" became the boast of many persons.

As studies pass into character it is natural to find a marked effect of this turning loose of a new source of spiritual energy. To the historian of civilization no question is more interesting, though few are more complex, than what was the exact effect of this new biblicism. The common assumption, hardly disputed even now, that the moral influence of the Bible has been wholly good, and that all that is needed to improve our society is to "spread the gospel" is not borne out by a candid study of history.

The problem is twofold: in the first place as to what the moral teaching of the Bible really is and in the second place as to how much this teaching formed morals and how much it merely sanctioned the ethic already developed by social and material forces. As to the first question, it is interesting to note that all great moral questions of modern times have been argued by an appeal to the Bible by both sides. Polygamy, the subjection of women, democracy, usury, slavery, and prohibition have been attacked and defended on biblical authority. As to the second question, while considerable influence must be attributed to the teaching of the inspired writers, it is probable, or certain, that they were often appealed to in ethical, as they were in theological, matters by men who were antecedently convinced of the rightness of their own dogmas and who sought only to find for them a divine sanction. The Puritans, particularly, studied the Bible with a zeal and diligence that wove into the pattern of their thought the threads of prophetic and of apostolic discourse. Something of the nobility of their style of speaking and acting, and something of their credulity, bigotry, and narrowness, must be attributed to their bibliolatry. Strong men they were, great soldiers, statesmen, and poets, but they were too cramped by formalism and literalism to be admirable moralists. Both their petty scrupulosity and ceremonialism and their larger vices of persecution and superstition can be traced in large part to their too assiduous reading of the Scriptures.

Some of the outward manifestations of their biblicism were harmless. To dress soberly and prudishly, to speak with a nasal accent, to snivel a little in prayer, to fill one's speech with "the abomination of desolation" and "the righteous judgments of the Lord," were affectations easily passing into a second nature. A more interesting manifestation of the same spirit is the abundance of biblical and other religious names suddenly blooming in the Calvinist churches. Even the Germans occasionally baptized their sons Ephraim and Gottlob and Immanuel, but the Puritans of Old and New England habitually called them either by some biblical name, as Abraham, Isaac, Joshua, Nathaniel, Rebecca, Deborah, Chileab, Peleg, and Maher-shalal-hash-baz, or by names with a religious meaning, as Faith, Mercy, Charity, for women, and for men Faithful, Faintnot, Hopestill, Praise-God, and Preservéd.

But if the accent and nomenclature of the Puritans were harmless affectations, other evidences of assiduous Bible-reading were decidedly noxious. Like all fetishes, the Bible was soon put to superstitious uses; the habit early took root among the Evangelicals, and has not yet entirely died out, of treating it as an oracle, by opening its pages at random, and deciding a vexed question by following the guidance of the first verse read. Even more detrimental to sound sense was the expectation of reading the future history of the world by study of the obscure enigmas of Daniel and of the Apocalypse. Not only ignorant exhorters, but famous scientists like Kepler, Napier, and Newton, attempted to expound the past history, the present condition, and the future state of mankind by investigating the dark oracles of the prophets.

A still more dubious feature of the bibliolatry of that age, and of this, was and is the narrow orthodoxy that treated the Bible as a text-book of science, and condemned in its name all the astronomy, cosmography, and natural history that seemed to contradict any part of it. The Thirty-years War of swords was hardly less devastating to the material resources of Germany than was the still longer war of sectarian pens destructive of her spiritual riches. No age in all German history is so barren as is the seventeenth century, in which the whole intellectual energies of a great people were absorbed in wrangling, with inconceivable bitterness, over trifling and absurd points of theology, as, whether the body of Christ is present in the communion wafer substantially or corporeally, and whether it is present by reason of the ubiquity of Christ or by the communication of his nature.

This savage squabbling of the sects showed how little perspicuous and convincing was the letter of the Bible to which all parties equally appealed. The sectarianism of the time was the one bad moral effect of the popularity of the vernacular Scriptures noted and condemned by contemporaries. That the Bible was the book of the heretics became a proverb not only with the Catholics but among all those established churches which essayed to set up a new orthodoxy. It was in vain for the ministers to prohibit the unlearned from interpreting the Word in novel ways. "After the Bible was translated," wrote Hobbes, "every man, nay every boy and woman, thought they spoke with God Almighty and understood what he said." Nowadays, wrote Walton in his *Polyglot*, "there is no fanatic and vagabond from the lowest dregs of the populace who does not advertise his own dreams as the Word of God"; and their numbers, he added, are like the stinging locusts who swarm in the cities, villages, camps, private houses, and pulpits of the land, and who— it is thus suddenly that the learned author changes his metaphors—blindly lead their blind followers into the ditch. "If bakers make the God of Catholics, shoemakers make the God of Protestants" declared Selden in his equal contempt for the Roman adoration of the host and the plebeian origin of the current Protestant theology. Great heresies and mischiefs, opined Dryden, followed Tyndale's translation of the Scriptures into the vernacular.

2. CLASSICAL SCHOLARSHIP

There is both a marked similarity and a marked difference between the position held by the Bible in the estimation of the sixteenth and seventeenth centuries and the position held by the Greek and Roman classics. During the later Middle Ages Aristotle had been worshipped as the master of them who know; during the Renaissance Plato and Cicero and, to a slightly less extent, some of the other ancient writers, were venerated as almost inspired authorities in philosophy and in ethics, and were imitated as the supreme masters of style. A good deal of this admiration of the ancients continued to exist throughout the later centuries, but it was confined to an ever narrowing group. Except by

a few humanists the authority of the classics was never regarded as quite equal to that of the Hebrew writers; and
among the mass of the people the Bible had a hold never
approached by any pagan poet or philosopher. None of the
vernacular translations of the Greeks and Romans ever com-
peted in popularity or in reputation with the new Protestant
Bibles. Moreover a large group of the intellectuals, still held
in bondage to the Scriptures, revolted from the yoke of
Cicero and Vergil, and sought to replace their language by
the various vernaculars. Their efforts were heartily seconded
by the reading public, who despised what they could not
understand, and who hated the aristocratic humanists for
their assumed airs of superiority.

In short, one of the great new forces of modern times,
democracy, exalted the position of the Bible, while it depressed the authority of the classics. The other great force,
science, which was to undermine the authority of both Bible
and classics, naturally attacked the weaker first, and began
to question Aristotle and Pliny and Ptolemy before it dared
to sit in judgment upon Moses and the Psalmist.

The idolatry of the ancient writers, Hebrew, Greek, and
Latin, had prevented impartial criticism of them. The first
great triumphs of scholarship, in the profane field as in the
sacred, came as the veneration for the writers studied began
to decline. Not till the middle of the eighteenth century was
a great work of biblical criticism produced; whereas some
of the most fruitful classical scholars of modern times lived
just at the decline of the Renaissance. The humanists of this
early period, which began with Petrarch and ended with the
Ciceronianus of Erasmus (1528) had studied the classics
with the purpose of imitating their style. The next period,
which began with the founding of the *Collège de France*
(1530) and closed about the end of the seventeenth century,
began to study the classics chiefly to learn their content
and to explain them historically. It was an era of multifarious erudition rather than of minute and exact criticism,
more concerned with Latin than with Greek, and domin-

ated chiefly by Frenchmen, many of whom, to be sure, were exiles from their native land.

Several of these great Frenchmen belonged to the family of Estienne, printers by profession and accomplished scholars by genius. Robert Estienne (1503-59) besides publishing a new edition of the Greek Testament, compiled a great *Thesaurus linguae latinae,* which remained the standard Latin dictionary for two centuries after its publication in 1532. Henri Estienne II (1531-98) even surpassed Robert as a lexicographer by producing the *Thesaurus linguae graecae* in five volumes in 1572. This work, aiming to explain all important Greek words by referring to every passage in which each is used by a classical writer, proved so excellent that it is still used in the nine-volume edition of 1829-63. As lighter *parerga* Robert wrote his *Traité de la conformité du langage françois avec le Grec* (1565), and his *Apologie pour Hérodote* (1566) pointing out, with satiric intent, the parallels between the strange stories related by Herodotus and the miracles accredited in the Roman church.

Two other great lexicons, published a century later, are due to the erudition of a Frenchman. Charles du Fresne, Sieur du Cange, published his *Glossarium mediae et infimae latinitatis* in three volumes in 1678, and his *Glossarium mediae et infimae graecitatis* in one volume ten years later. Du Cange was a French noble who studied law at Orléans, was admitted to the bar by the Parlement of Paris, and later became a treasurer of the royal government at Amiens. His legal studies in French charters drew his attention to the subject of medieval Latin of which he produced the first great dictionary, and the last, except for some augmentations of his work by later scholars. This truly marvellous repertory of medieval learning, still indispensable to the scholar, was made more useful by a prefatory history of the Latin language and its derivatives, and by supplementary treatises on various branches of medieval lore. Less important, though still valuable, were the glossary of medieval French, appended to the Latin lexicon, and the glossary of medieval Greek, published separately.

Though various other dictionaries and treatises on classical and Christian archeology were published during this period, none of them deserves mention here except the *Bibliotheca universalis* of Conrad Gesner of which the first part, published in 1545, is a bibliographical and biographical dictionary of all known Hebrew, Greek, and Latin writers, and the second part, which followed in 1549, is an encyclopædia of the arts and sciences.

None of the other scholars of that age made so great an impression on his contemporaries as did Joseph Justus Scaliger, whom they dubbed "the phoenix of Europe," "the light of the world," "the sea of sciences," "the bottomless pit of erudition," "the perpetual dictator of letters," and "the greatest work and miracle of nature." Born at Agen in the south of France in 1540, he was educated by his father, the famous scholar Julius Caesar Scaliger, in the love of truth and in the mastery of Latin, in which he soon attained a marvellous proficiency. To that he added a knowledge of Greek, Chaldee, Hebrew, Arabic, Syriac, Phoenician, Ethiopian, and Persian, as well as a considerable acquaintance with philosophy and mathematics. In fact he stood at the summit of universal philological knowledge to a degree never attained before and perhaps never since. His superiority to his rivals was due to the fact that he was more than a bookworm. In his study of texts he never lost sight of the solid body of facts for the knowledge of which the mastery of language alone is valuable. He despised the humanism of the Italians, who in their cultivation of style had forgotten matter, and hence produced prolix and insipid effusions of rhetoric, and nothing else.

To Italy, however, he travelled, in order to collect inscriptions and to examine manuscripts. Then he visited England, with eyes not bent on crabbed ancient texts, but open to all the interests of the present. The man who, while adding to stores of an immense erudition, noted the variety of English monastic chronicles, detected the absence of seigniorial jurisdiction in Britain, admired the merits of the Border ballads and the beauty of Mary Stuart, discovered that coal was used instead of wood in the north, and animadverted upon the indolence of the fellows in English colleges, and the prevalence of the sectarian point of view, was no pedant, but a man of the world and a keen observer as well.

Though educated a Catholic, his study of the Christian texts made him a Huguenot. His conversion, barring him from profitable employment in France, sent him first (1572) to Geneva, and later (1593) to the famous university of Leyden, at which he was given a research professorship without teaching duties.

Though his edition of the Latin lyric poets made of criticism a rational method, instead of the haphazard guesswork which it had hitherto been, Scaliger's greatest services to learning lay in his elucidation of ancient astronomy and chronology. In editing the *Astronomica* of Manilius, he first grappled with the problem of the ancient knowledge of astronomy; this problem he largely solved because, in addition to his wide reading in ancient authors, he studied the scientific works of Copernicus and Tycho Brahe.

A far more important work, which revolutionized all previous ideas of ancient calendars and of ancient dates, was his *De Emendatione Temporum* (*On the Restoration of Chronology*, 1583). The author set forth his purpose in the following words: [1]

I have nearly completed a work in which I expose the sloth of all our annalists who seem with one accord to have sworn the same oath, never to speak the truth. First I have explained the calendars of all nations, ancient and modern: of the Athenians, the Macedonians, the ancient Hebrews, the Chaldaeans, the Egyptians, the Persians, the Ethiopians, and the Armenians. For, by not knowing this not only historians, but all those who trust their authority, are at fault. Moreover I show . . . many other things by which the chronology of all ages, hitherto unknown, may become certain.

[1] J. Scaligeri: *Epistolae*, 1638, ep. 6, May 21, 1581.

The first four books of the comprehensive work survey the methods of reckoning time in all nations then known, from Persia to Mexico. The fifth and sixth books contain a repertory of historical dates. The section on the year of the foundation of the world, referred to above,[1] is the least valuable portion of the whole, for it merely shows that Scaliger was bound, like almost all his contemporaries, in the iron cage of his time. But when he descends from the mythical events of creation and deluge, he is on solid ground; and on this ground he built an imposing edifice of sound learning. The last two books contain further observations on the method of computing time, and on the improvement of the calendar.

In a second work Scaliger completed his contributions to chronology. As a basis for his outline of ancient history he selected the *Chronicle* of Eusebius, composed in the early fourth century. This work, when it left the pen of its author, consisted of two books, the first containing an epitome of universal history, the second chronological tables exhibiting in parallel columns contemporary events in several nations. But in the course of time the second book was lost in the original and was known only in the translation of St. Jerome, and the first book had apparently disappeared entirely. Scaliger, however, recognized the substance of the first book in a Greek monastic chronicle which he found in manuscript in 1602. From this and from Jerome he restored the content of the lost original—how perfectly was only revealed with the discovery of an Armenian version of the whole *Chronicle* in 1818. The results of his researches, making the most reliable foundation for ancient history ever laid up to that time, were published in a work called *Thesaurus Temporum* (*Repertory of Dates*) in 1606.

At one time it was fashionable to speak of Scaliger, Lipsius, and Casaubon as the "triumvirate of learning." But in truth the others were far inferior to Scaliger, who was not only the most richly stored intellect that perhaps ever gave itself to the acquisition of knowledge, but the first

[1] P. 289.

brilliant example of what scientific method could accomplish when applied, not to the slavish imitation, but to the elucidation of the classics. There is about his character something larger and nobler than can be found in either of his rivals. His superiority to them lay in the fact that, while they were accomplished masters of Greek and Latin, he was that and much more besides.

Justus Lipsius, scion of a distinguished family of scholars, was born in Brabant in 1547, and educated in the Catholic religion by the Jesuits of Cologne. When he began to teach at Jena he became a Protestant. For thirteen years (1578-91) he taught at Leyden; then turned Catholic again and was called to Louvain, on the somewhat tarnished fame of which university he cast a temporary luster. As· a grammarian, antiquarian, archeologist and critic, he won a high place in the esteem of the learned world. As a man he was a time-server, and a defender of witchcraft, of superstition, and of persecution. And this versatile turncoat affected Stoicism, and boasted that "all in Belgium are a troop of slavish minds, except myself, who bear in my heart the Catos, Brutuses, and Senecas, and who would succumb to death rather than to dishonor." [1]

Isaac Casaubon, the third of the "triumvirate" (1559-1614), was born at Geneva as the son of a Gascon Huguenot refugee. When his precocious talents secured him a professorship at the Genevan University, at the salary of $50 per annum and a room, he straightway married. His first wife dying two years after the wedding, he married again, this time the daughter of Henri Estienne the great scholar who was also the Royal Librarian of France. If, as seems likely, he hoped that this alliance would open to him the doors of the rich treasury of books, he was bitterly disappointed, for his father-in-law long proved as truculently monopolistic as did most of the librarians of that day.

After teaching for some years at Montpellier, he was called to Paris in 1599 by Henri IV, who was desirous of restoring the prestige of his decadent university. There

[1] Letter to Rubens, 1602; *Correspondance de Rubens,* i, 68.

he remained for eleven years, allowed to practice his religion, but plied with suggestions that he should join the Catholic church, and disingenuously entangled in a dispute on the eucharist in which he was forced, as a judge, to give an opinion that the Protestant disputant, Mornay, had misinterpreted some of his citations from the fathers, and that antiquity was on the side of the Catholics. Though this judgment was rather a proof of the honesty and soundness of his scholarship than of his approval of the Catholic cause, the cries of triumph with which the Romanists greeted what they took to be a vindication of their doctrine were extremely painful to Casaubon. His own views of religion led him to seek a *via media* between Protestant and Catholic, and presently to believe that he had found it in the Anglican church.

At Paris, however, he at last found the opportunity to study the 260 Greek manuscripts of the Royal Library. His whole life was devoted to the enjoyment and criticism of the classics, many of which he edited with valuable notes. With Scaliger a warm friendship, nourished entirely on epistles, sprang up. He listened with distaste to the theological disputes at the Sorbonne, remarking satirically that he had never heard so much Latin of which he understood so little, and that that was the place where men had disputed for four hundred years without deciding anything.

Wishing to leave Paris but unable to secure the royal permission, he rather fled than migrated to London, where he received a warm welcome from James I. Except that the kingly pedant wasted the scholar's time in talking learned drivel, Casaubon found much happiness in England, a liberal pension and leisure to work. Even here, however, he was unable to disentangle himself from the religious controversies which he detested. Urged to undertake the uncongenial task of refuting the errors of Baronius, he produced a rather futile volume at the expense of much precious time.

As an accomplished Grecian he won the unstinted admiration of his age. Of his best work, an edition of the *Characteres* of Theophrastus, Scaliger wrote:

Your new book made my mouth water; I was beside myself and unable to refrain from publishing abroad what your merit and my love require, although everything I can say is below the worth of your genius. . . . Everything about you delights me —your learning, your judgment, your style.[1]

Though a great scholar, Casaubon was hardly a great man. Self-distrustful and unhappy in his religious opinions, he was unable to bring to anything a judgment or a conviction superior to the authority of his beloved classics. He venerated the ancients so indiscriminately that he accepted their views as decisive on all matters, and their testimony, even to impossibilities, as authentic. He swallowed the alchemical fable of potable gold; he believed that the earth of Palestine worked magical cures because Augustine had said so; he believed, on the authority of Pliny and Hippocrates, that women sometimes turn into men; he credited stories of levitation and of spontaneous combustion. Nor was he tolerant of religious dissenters, urging the suppression of the Racovian Catechism and applauding the burning of the heretic Legett.

When the torch of learning dropped from the hand of the last of the "triumvirate," it was snatched up by Claude de Saumaise, commonly called Salmasius (1588-1653). Born in the north of France, educated at Paris and at Heidelberg, when converted to Protestantism he was called to Leyden in 1632, not to teach but "to shed on the university the luster of his name, to glorify it with his writings and adorn it with his name." Like his great predecessor Scaliger, he saw that in order to understand antiquity a knowledge of things was as important as the knowledge of books.[2] His main contribution to learning was his commentary on Pliny, especially on his geography. But he is chiefly remembered by posterity for his controversy with Milton on the execution of Charles I. Called to Sweden by Queen Christina, he soon

[1] Scaligeri *Epistolae,* ep. 35. May 7, 1594.
[2] C. Salmasii *Epistolarum Liber Primus,* 1656, p. 162; letter to Peiresc, 1635.

found the climate of the far north as fatal to him as it had just proved to Descartes.

While the study of the classics was pursued with such zeal and success, the language of ancient Rome continued throughout the seventeenth century to enjoy a prestige that was just beginning to give way to the claims of the various modern tongues. It was still the *lingua franca* of international science, of international diplomacy, and of the international church. While the canons of the Catholic hierarchy were couched in Latin, governments employed Latin secretaries—of whom Milton was the most famous—to draft diplomatic notes and treaties of peace. The universities still conducted their lectures and debates in Latin; and most scientists still preferred to write the one language that could be understood by their peers in all parts of Western Europe.

Like all tongues in use, Latin continued to grow and to change to meet the new demands made upon it. As in the Middle Ages the scholastic philosophy had warped and altered the tongue of Cicero, as the great humanists had again changed it to meet the literary needs of the fifteenth and sixteenth centuries, so the new science of the late sixteenth and seventeenth century changed it again. Construction and vocabulary were enriched, or sophisticated, by elements gathered from all quarters, ancient, medieval, humanistic, and vulgar. Every phase through which European culture had passed for fifteen hundred years had left some deposit in the language, which now contained elements of Greek, Spanish, German, French, Italian, and Arabic derivation. Nor was this all; the novel ideas to be expressed called for the minting of new words. Some of these neologisms were unhappy, as "omnilucentia" and "unomnia" (to mean the all-embracing, all-animating light) and the "alimota" (to mean things moved by impact from without) of Patrizi; and the almost untranslatable "toticipatio" and "comprincipitiatio" of Campanella. Others, notably the anatomical terms "pronervatio," "caritas," "articulatio," and "aniscalptor" coined by Vesalius, proved of permanent utility; indeed Vesalius, as the best writer of the new Latin after

Copernicus, has been dubbed the Erasmus of science. The utility of his terms, and of others in mathematics, justify their creation. Nowadays science has created its own international language of symbols. The Italian, Polish, German, and English scientists can now read each others' writings with ease because long usage and arbitrary convention have made the chief technical terms and symbols the same for all parts of the world. But at that time an international language was urgently needed if the French savant would comprehend the work of his Italian or English compeer. Bitterly did Kepler and other thinkers reproach those who abandoned the international tongue for the vernacular. And it must not be forgotten that Latin had one other great advantage; it had long been the bulwark of thought as well as its conductor. While a man wrote in the learned tongue, accessible only to a small class, he had generally been left free to say what he pleased. But the appeal to the masses was felt, by the conservatives, to be dangerous in science as it had been in religion. Erasmus had been left undisciplined to twit the church in Latin; Luther and Calvin, who spoke to the masses in their own tongues, were persecuted. So Copernicus and Kepler were left to convey their esoteric secrets to their disciples unmolested; Bruno and Galileo, who divulged them to the vulgar, were called to a terrible account.

With all these advantages making for the continued use of Latin, there were considerations outweighing them sufficiently to lead scientists, first in Italy, then in France, then in England, and lastly in Germany, to abandon it in favor of their respective mother tongues. The first of these reasons was that the old language, with all its stretching, was no longer adequate to the expression of the new ideas. The wine of the new thought, after distending the old sheepskin bottles to the utmost, burst them in sunder. Latin, which had once been a support to thought, now became a bond. The ancient tongue proved to be a great conservative force actively combating the new thought as well as wasting the student's time in the learning of words instead of allowing him to devote his best years to the study of things. These ideas were first expressed by Sperone Speroni, in an Italian *Dialogue on Languages* published in 1547. As Dante had long before championed the use of the vulgar tongue for poetry, so now Sperone advocated it for science. His argument was largely transferred into French by Joachim du Bellay's *Defense et Illustration de la Langue française.* While Galileo and Bruno began to write scientific Italian, Descartes defended the use of French in writing his *Geometry* by saying that those who employed their pure natural reason only would judge his opinions better than those who had been corrupted by idolatry of old books.

A second reason leading to the abandonment of Latin was the growth of a literate but not learned public interested in the things that were once the arcana of a small coterie. The battle between these democrats of culture and the opposing aristocrats of erudition was long and bitter. Humanism had fallen into deep disgrace; while mocking the crudity of the vulgar it was itself mocked by the leaders of the popular thought. No figure is quite so common, or quite so ridiculous, in the comedy of the sixteenth and seventeenth centuries, as is the pedant. The battle between the old and the new is the subject of Bruno's comedy, *Il Candelaio.* The pedant—the word first coined* in the sixteenth century— meets us in the *Commedia dell' Arte,* in the Holophernes of Shakespeare, in the Pancrace and Marphurius of Molière, and in a play of Cyrano de Bergerac. A constant source of fun at the expense of the humanists was the travesty of Latin appearing in absurd polysyllables such as Shakespeare's "honorificabilitudinitatibus." And the enemies of Latin won because those who could read only the vernacular became too numerous and too powerful to be ignored. Next to the wonderful advance of modern science the most remarkable fact about the history of the last four centuries has been the vulgarization of science. The first democracy to assert its rights was that of the Republic of Letters.

Notwithstanding the encroachments of the vernaculars upon Latin, and notwithstanding the mockery of humanism and pedantry, the classics continued to enjoy an enormous prestige. As some of them exercised an authority resembling, though it never approached, that of the Bible, so many of them were, during the sixteenth and seventeenth centuries, translated into the modern tongues for the enjoyment of the people. A few of these versions, notably that of Plutarch's *Lives of Famous Men,* translated into French by Jacques Amyot and thence into English by Sir Thomas North, are of surpassing excellence. The popularity of Plutarch in these new versions can hardly be exaggerated. On him, more than on any other author, was founded that ideal of ancient heroism, patriotism, and sententious wit that made of Greek and Roman history a standing lesson in ethics, politics, and *savoir vivre.* That the political life, philosophy, literature, and languages of the Greeks and Romans far outshone anything that modern nations could produce, was long accepted as a self-evident axiom. Almost the whole of modern literature is saturated with the thought and colored with the rhetoric and poetry of the ancients. Hundreds of writers expressed their admiration of the unapproachable beauty of the classic writers. Kings and nobles, cardinals like Barberini and millionaires like Fouquet, made great collections of antique statues, medals, and vases. The few scientists and poets who dared assert the superiority of modern to ancient times were overwhelmed by the mass of educated men, who still worshipped the authority of the ancients, even when they could no longer read their writings in the originals.

Like all idolatry, that of the classics proved, for good and for evil, a conservative force. How much the poets and orators and historians of modern times have profited by their education at the feet of the Greeks and Romans, is evident to all capable of judging such things. But the dead hand of the classics lay heavy upon the budding originality of many a genius. Aristotle and Pliny, almost as much as Moses and Job, set stumbling-blocks in the path of science. Many a superstition and many an outworn social abuse was sanctioned by Greek and Roman, as by Hebrew, example.

PART III. SOCIAL CONTROL

CHAPTER XI

EDUCATION

I. SCHOOLS

Over against the innovating forces of society, supplied by new inventions and discoveries altering the material and spiritual environment, all social institutions and arrangements stand in resistant conservatism. Partly as a matter of deep unconscious habit, partly in reasoned self-interest, every society, and particularly the ruling class in every society, dreads change and seeks to perpetuate the existing status in morals, politics, and religion. The three chief institutions for doing this have been the school, the church, and the state. To indoctrinate the child early with the prevailing world-view of the society and class in which he has been born, to enforce conformity in later life by the thunders of the priest and by the sword of the magistrate, has been the "wisdom of our ancestors" at every stage in their progress from savagery to civilization.

The school, indeed, has had a double task to perform. Not only must the existing moral, religious, and social ideas be firmly impressed on children, but that vast heritage of knowledge and skill accumulated by their ancestors must be handed on by each generation to its successor.

A large part of this knowledge and skill is handed on either unconsciously, like language, or by the method of apprenticeship. By living with the masters of a trade or profession, the child picks up, chiefly by imitation and practice, the craft of a guild, or proficiency in an art. A large part, also, of the child's education in morals and politics is unconsciously absorbed through herd-suggestion. To the schools and institutions of learning are relegated chiefly those matters of such general utility as to be needed by all men, or those matters requiring a more profound theoretical insight than can be imparted by mere contact with an expert. The universally useful arts of reading, writing, and arithmetic have been, for many centuries, the elementary occupation of the primary school; the learned professions the subjects which universities have taught, or for which the higher education has prepared. And in the moral and spiritual education of the child, the schools of all grades have supplied instruction in those branches of knowledge and culture deemed most congenial to the prevailing habits of the society and class from which the child comes.

But, however conservative and inert are social institutions, they do change, though reluctantly and slowly, under the compulsion of a shifting social environment. Education, like all else in a living world, evolves from age to age. As the mass of knowledge accumulates, as the skill required to pursue a given profession becomes more and more difficult to acquire, the process of technical education lengthens. Thus it is, also, that more and more subjects, once taught by apprenticeship, are taken over by the schools. Surgery, once handed down as a trade secret from barber to barber, wins a place, after a hard struggle, in the faculty of medicine. Engineering and architecture, mining and agriculture and "business" now find a place in the universities alongside of the professions of divinity, law, and medicine, to teach which the first universities were founded.

Moreover, reforms are constantly required in moral education by the altering world-view of any given society. The Catholic, the Protestant, and the secularist all have different ideas of what is most valuable in culture. The needs of an aristocratic society, regarding the liberal education of the gentleman as alone necessary, are very different from the needs of a democratic society, asserting the rights of all men to an equal share in the dividend of culture.

In modern times, the changes in education have been principally due to the triumph of science and of democracy. More and more, science has become not only increasingly necessary as a foundation for professional skill, but has come to be regarded as the most valuable instrument of culture. More and more, democracy has demanded and secured for the masses the opportunity for liberal education once open only to the favored classes.

In the sixteenth century education was still founded directly on the scholasticism of the later Middle Ages, modified considerably by the humanism of the Renaissance and by the theology and popular appeal of the Reformation and Counter-Reformation.

Hardly had the new ideals of humanists and Reformers incorporated themselves in the schools and universities, before still newer currents came to flutter the dove-cotes in academic groves. The rapidly growing science and novel philosophy of the seventeenth century began to knock at college gates too imperiously to be altogether denied admittance. And classes which had never demanded book-learning before began to clamor for it now. One of these classes was the aristocracy, the other the bourgeoisie. In the middle ages the nobles had signed their names with marks, proudly proclaiming that "being gentlemen they could not write." But when the humanists and better educated merchants had made them feel their crudity, they began to crowd into the older schools and to found new ones to meet their special needs. The privately founded German *Ritterakademien,* or "Young Gentlemen's Finishing Schools," aimed to bring up the children of the nobility and gentry not like pedants on crabbed Latin, but more liberally on history, geography, genealogy, heraldry, and politics, and more courteously on riding, dancing, fencing, drawing, painting and music. In England the same ideal was represented in the project of Sir Humphrey Gilbert for an academy to teach the sons of gentlemen refined manners and courtly accomplishments, and in an academy founded by the gentry at the close of the Civil War. And in France even more than elsewhere the pedant was the butt of ridicule by the advocates of the new courtly learning.

This ideal altered not only the curriculum but even the

dress and manners of professors and scholars. Both teachers and pupils at sixteenth-century universities had dressed and looked like clergymen even when they were not. Both professors and students at the seventeenth-century universities disguised themselves as gentlemen, even when they were not. And to give the final polish to the aspiring youth, a grand tour of Europe was undertaken at the end of his academic career.

Thus it was that new studies supplemented, though they did not entirely supplant, the curriculum based on the Bible and on the classics. The hold of the classics, indeed, was too strong to be shaken for centuries, but the more progressive minds of the early modern age began to speak of them with contempt. When Descartes learned that Queen Christina of Sweden was studying Greek, he expressed surprise that she should find pleasure in so poor a subject, and airily added that as a boy he had been crammed full of the stuff, but that since leaving school he had happily forgotten it all. And Leibniz, in fierce revolt against the still medieval scholasticism, proclaimed that there were only two classes of books with any value, those containing scientific demonstrations and experiments and those containing history, politics, and geography.[1]

At the other end of the social scale more and more of the common people demanded and gradually succeeded in securing an education. The cheapening of knowledge by the invention of printing slowly but surely opened to the aspiring and able proletarian the paths of learning. So far had this tendency progressed that Fynes Morison reported in 1600 that among the Germans all men even of the common sort could speak Latin and show some skill in arithmetic and music. Doubtless this was a great exaggeration, but it was a significant one.

In order to meet the needs of the time the governments had to take over the direction of education hitherto vested in the church. The intervention of the state was the first conspicuous effect on education of the Reformation. The

[1] *Sämtliche Schriften*, i, 417. Date 1673.

first Protestant city school was founded by the government of Magdeburg in 1524; and four years later the Elector of Saxony took over the general direction of schools in his territory. The most famous of the new state schools was that founded at Strassburg by Johann Sturm in 1538. Secular schools one cannot call them, for the subject most emphasized was that of religion, and next to that the classics. The combination of the two was happily described by Sturm in the phrase "wise and eloquent piety" as the purpose of education. The subjects taught were reading, writing, Latin, Greek, religion, and a certain amount of scholastic philosophy. The state schools of Germany became practically classical high schools, with much emphasis on the Lutheran catechism and on the Bible. Though the pay of the teachers was small and the social esteem in which they were held low, the intervention of the state marked some improvement in both these respects. The personnel of the teaching staff was no longer recruited, as it largely had been in the earlier period, from the refuse of the learned professions, but from the slightly higher class of candidates for the Protestant ministry who filled in a few years between theological school and a pastorate with teaching school.

In Calvinistic lands the new principles of democratic education bore fruit not less plentifully than in Lutheran countries. The stern, zealous, and clear-sighted Reformer of Geneva outlined for that little theocracy a system of elementary education for all children, which was widely imitated in Huguenot and Puritan lands. The Protestant schools of France emphasized the use of the vernacular, training in Greek as well as in Latin, and of course much Bible study and a severe moral discipline.

The Reformation in England transferred from the church to the state the charge of education. After the dissolution of the monasteries and the accompanying confiscation of ecclesiastical wealth, a vast number of new schools were founded, no less than 207 from the accession of Edward VI to the death of Elizabeth (1547-1603) and no less than 288 from the accession of James I to the Glorious Revolution,

(1603-88). Most of these were grammar schools, teaching, in addition to the three R's, Latin and religion. Most of them were recruited from the local parish. But the great endowed foundations, called "public schools" in England, continued to educate the children of the nobility and gentry in the classics. Some of these schools, like Winchester and Eton, were already old in the sixteenth century; other institutions like them were founded in that and in the following age. Such was the Charterhouse School, so called because its building had once belonged to the Carthusians, which was founded by a liberal bequest of Thomas Sutton in 1611. The statutes promulgated in 1627 directed that the forty scholars on the foundation should be "orderly and seemly dieted," and "cleanly and wholesomely lodged." Masters were directed to be moderate in correction and to observe "the nature and ingeny [ingenium, peculiar talents] of their scholars and to instruct them accordingly."

The education of the very poor was not altogether neglected, but was ministered to by a few charity schools, among which Christ's Hospital was the most famous. But as far as the state provided for the education of pauper children, it was to direct that they should be bound over as apprentices to learn a trade. This provision, which occurs in the Poor Law of 1601, was but one part of the attempt to deal with the problem of pauperism by drafting the proletariat into the army of labor required by the rising industries—a problem made acute by the commercial revolution.

As in other Protestant countries, so in England, the new state schools inculcated piety in the pupils and demanded orthodoxy of the teachers. Various laws of Elizabeth and of the Stuarts required schoolmasters to attend the established church. In addition to this the Act of Conformity of 1662 obliged all who taught in schools and universities to subscribe to a declaration that it is unlawful to take arms against the king under any pretext whatever.

Not in Old England, however, but in New England and in Scotland did the spirit of Calvinist democracy attain its perfect work in education. John Knox, like the other

Reformers, demanded that every church in every consider-able town should have a schoolmaster. As the kirk took the lead in educational matters it was natural that the Scotch Parliament should enact a law (in 1579) requiring that all teachers be approved by the ecclesiastical superintendents. Five years later they were required by law to swear obedience to the king. In 1616 the Privy Council issued a decree, ratified by Parliament in 1633, providing that every bishop might lay a tax on the land in his diocese, with the consent of the heritors and parishioners, for the support of a school. The petition of the kirk, in 1641, that every parish might have a primary school and every borough a grammar school, was in part given effect by the memorable law of 1646, which reads as follows:[1]

The Estates of Parliament, considering how prejudicial the want of schools in many congregations hath been, do therefore Statute and Ordain, that there be a school founded and a schoolmaster appointed in every parish (not already provided) by advice of the Presbytery; and to this purpose that the heritors in every congregation meet amongst themselves, and provide a commodious house for the school, and modify a stipend to the schoolmaster which fall not be-under 100 marks nor above 200 marks annually.

By this law primary education was made free to all; though it was not yet made compulsory to all. In order to extend the opportunities for higher education to the gifted poor students, the clergy began to found bursarships which opened the doors of the universities to classes generally excluded from them elsewhere.

New England took the final step in making primary education universal, not only free to all but obligatory upon all. Even allowing for the favorable conditions, the economic opportunity, the select, highly educated and deeply earnest character of the first immigrants, the pervading spirit of self-government and of stern resolution to preserve intact and to improve the finest gifts of civilization, it is truly

[1] *Acts of the Parliament of Scotland,* vol. VI, Part I, p. 554.

remarkable that the little band of settlers in Massachusetts, while still engaged in a mortal struggle with a savage wilderness and with hostile natives, should so early as they did provide for the education of their children. Within five years after the foundation of the colony of Massachusetts Bay, the Boston Latin School started on its famous career. Other towns, as soon as settled, erected schools, at first of their own accord, but soon at the command of the colonial government. The General Court in 1642 bade the selectmen of each town to examine all children and "take account especially of their ability to read and understand the principles of religion and the capital laws of this country."

Five years later the same body passed the famous law providing for the education of children in these words:

It being one chief project of the old deluder, Satan, to keep men from the knowledge of the Scriptures, as in former times by keeping them in an unknown tongue, so in these latter times by persuading from the use of tongues, that so at least the true sense and meaning of the original might be clouded by false glosses of saint-seeming deceivers, that learning may not be buried in the grave of our fathers in the church and commonwealth, the Lord assisting our endeavors:

It is therefore ordered, that every township in this jurisdiction, after the Lord hath increased them in numbers to fifty house-holders, shall then forthwith appoint one within their town to teach all such children as shall resort to him to write and read, whose wages shall be paid either by the parents or masters of such children, or by the inhabitants in general, by way of supply, as the major part of those that order the prudentials of the town shall appoint.

In these two laws, for the first time in history, a legislative body actually ordered that system of universal, compulsory, and state-supported education, which the more advanced spirits of the age had been demanding for a century. Within a very few years the other New England colonies, except Rhode Island, had followed the example of Massachusetts. The teaching, though no worse than the average in Europe, was not very good, being left largely in the hands of indentured servants. The first text-book used, the *New England Primer,* "taught millions to read and not one to sin," by selecting for the child's first literature examples and stories from the Bible, illustrated with quaint pictures and pointed with drastic morals.

While the Middle Colonies hastened to follow the good example of New England in providing free schools, the Southern colonies, with their royal governments, aristocratic society, and large numbers of slaves and indentured servants, lagged far behind, if not in the education of the masters' children, at least in providing for the poor. In 1670 Sir William Berkeley, the Governor of Virginia, thanked God that

there are no free schools, nor printing; and I hope we shall not have any these hundred years; for learning hath brought disobedience and heresy and sects into the world, and printing hath divulged them and libels against the best governments.

This happy condition of popular ignorance he labored sedulously to preserve.

While in Protestant lands the state took over from the church the direction of education, in Catholic countries the church continued to exercise this, as well as her other medieval functions. The instrument which reformed and revivified this ecclesiastical education was the Society of Jesus. The bull incorporating the society in 1540, mentions, among its other objects, "the education of children and other ignorant persons in Christianity." Loyola, though, or perhaps because, he had secured his own education late and with effort, laid great stress upon the importance of learning for his own followers. The constitutions drawn up by him, intended at first only for members of his own order, prescribed for them a thorough course in the classics, logic, natural and moral philosophy, metaphysics, and theology.

Very soon these schools—commonly called colleges—were opened to outsiders and made gratuitous. This cheapness of instruction, combined with its excellence, soon made the schools extremely popular; so that from the middle of the sixteenth to the middle of the eighteenth century the Jesuits almost monopolized education in Catholic lands, As they were subsidized by the various states, the cost of their schools was borne partly by the state, partly by the church, and partly by private endowment.

The first Jesuit school to be opened to the public was the Collegium Romanum in 1551; the second the Collegium Germanicum, also at Rome, in the following year. Under the vigorous leadership of Canisius the Society opened many schools in Germany in the last half of the sixteenth century, the largest of which was the one at Vienna, founded in 1558 with about 500 pupils, and growing to a thousand by 1623, as against one hundred or two hundred in the local university. In the Spanish Netherlands the Jesuits had by 1600 a school at Liège with 400 pupils, one at Saint-Omer with 450, and one at Douai with 1100. By 1626 they counted 13,195 pupils in Paris, and perhaps 40,000 altogether in France. And in all the other Catholic countries of Europe and America, as well as in some heathen lands, they had established numerous and flourishing colleges.

The curriculum was fixed by the *Plan of Studies* (*Ratio Studiorum*) drawn up by the General Claudio Acquaviva in 1586, and revised, in consequence of criticism by the Dominicans and of a reproof by the Inquisition, in 1599. This divided the course into elementary and secondary studies. The former devoted three years to the Greek and Latin grammars, one to poetry, and two to rhetoric. The secondary studies consisted of a three-year course in philosophy, the first year given chiefly to logic, the second to natural science, the third to metaphysics and ethics, all taught from Aristotle. For Jesuits and others intending to become clergymen, a four-year course in theology followed; it trained the students in the Bible and in the scholastic philosophy chiefly as represented by Aquinas.

The success of these schools was due partly to the fact that they first thoroughly absorbed and harmonized the humanistic and religious elements in the culture of the age.

Though the Jesuits set apart surprisingly little time for the formal teaching of religion they insisted on attendance at daily mass, at weekly sermon, and at monthly confession. The classics they taught extremely well. But the supreme triumph of their art was the perfection with which they imparted to each pupil just enough history, philosophy, and science to satisfy his curiosity without stimulating him to indulge in dangerous speculations. By a vaccination in free thought they prevented a dangerous attack of the disease in later life. Intentionally and successfully they discouraged originality, forbidding their teachers to dissent from Aristotle, except in points in which his teaching contradicts Christian doctrine, commanding them to praise and follow Aquinas, and drawing up a long list of questions considered too dangerous even to be mentioned in class.

In part their success was also due to the perfection of their pedagogical method. In 1619, long before any Protestants thought special training in pedagogy necessary, they began to teach the art of teaching. Less than on whipping —which, by a curious evasion, was done in their schools not by a member of the order but by a hired servant—they relied on rivalry and ambition to spur the pupils to their best efforts. Each scholar was pitted against a rival for mutual correction and emulation; contests were plenty, and were followed by distribution of prizes and of honorable titles. Wise, too, was the attention paid to bodily health and to recreation, at a time when such things were generally considered unimportant. Their best foundations were provided with neat dormitories, with a prison for offenders, with an ample playground, with classrooms for teaching music as well as other subjects, and sometimes with collections of birds and animals to instruct and amuse the pupils.[1]

As a proof of their success they could point to their many famous alumni. Molière, Corneille, Daniel Huet, Étienne Baluze, Scaliger, Descartes, Bossuet, Voltaire, and a host of other famous men studied at their feet. From many of these alumni their system won high praise. Des-

[1] John Evelyn: *Diary*, i, 32, Oct. 5, 1641.

cartes commended their method of teaching philosophy and their independent spirit in refusing to respect the rank and wealth, rather than the accomplishments, of their pupils. Their enemies, too, occasionally paid tribute to their art. "The excellent part of ancient discipline," said Francis Bacon, "hath been in some sort revived of late times by the colleges of the Jesuits, of whom I must say, *Talis cum sis, utinam noster esses.*"

On the other hand they had severe critics. In a polemic of Sarpi, alleging that the Jesuit masters "made sons disobedient to their parents, citizens disloyal to their country, and subjects undutiful to their sovereigns" there lies only the partial truth that among their enemies the Jesuits preferred the interests of the church to those of heretical parents and governments. In Catholic lands they inculcated the duty of passive obedience to the powers that be. In the Spanish Netherlands, in France, and in French Canada, they aimed first to make their pupils good Catholics, secondly to make them good subjects to the king, and thirdly to make them men of the world.

The true fault of their education was that it sacrificed the spirit of truth and candor to these ends. They cultivated memory and discouraged thought. They drilled boys in Cicero and in Aristotle, in expurgated classics and in carefully selected moderns, while they steadily set their faces against Galileo and Descartes. The virtues they sought to instill were "humility, obedience, purity, meekness, modesty, simplicity, chastity, charity, and an ardent love of Jesus and his Holy Mother"—but neither candor, nor self-reliance, nor love of truth.

2. UNIVERSITIES

The ancient universities of Italy continued to enjoy so much prestige that few new ones, and those insignificant, were founded after the middle of the sixteenth century. Bologna, the most famous of them all, had a large staff of about a hundred professors or lecturers, divided into two faculties, that of law, and that of arts, including medicine and a little theology. The subjects taught, and the number of professors of each, are as follows for typical years:

SUBJECT	1543	1600	1687
Faculty of Law, all told	37	41	53
Canon Law	15	20	20
Civil Law	20	18	24
On fiefs (De feudis)	1	0	3
On the art of the notary, or, on technical terms	1	1	3
On criminal law	0	2	1
On judicial practice	0	0	2
Faculty of Arts, all told	57	61	58
Medicine, theoretical and practical	15	18	16
On medicinal simples, or botany	1	1	1
Surgery	3	2	3
Astronomy, or meteors	4	1	2
Anatomy	0	2	11
Metaphysics	3	5	4
Physics	2	5	0
Logic	4	5	3
Greek and Latin	18	9	4
Art of writing, rhetoric	4	3	2
Mathematics	3	5	1
Bible	0	2	0
Theology	0	3	6
Casuistry and moral philosophy	0	0	4
Hebrew, Arabic and Chaldee	0	0	1
Total number of all professors	94	102	111

The Civil Law was taught from the Justinian Code, the Canon Law from the *Corpus Juris Canonici*. Medicine was taught chiefly from the works of Galen, Hippocrates, and the Arabians. Very notable is the increased attention to anatomy due to the great modern discoveries in that field.

Metaphysics and physics were both taught entirely from Aristotle and the ancients. Astronomy naturally languished in the age of Galileo's recantation; one of the two courses in that subject offered in 1687 was devoted to concocting an astrological almanac for the use of medical men. Remarkable, too, is the steady decline of Greek and Latin throughout the sixteenth and seventeenth centuries, and the introduction of courses in the Bible, in the scholastic theology, in the oriental languages, and in casuistry or moral philosophy. In 1687 one of the four courses in ethics was given in Italian; apparently the only lectures not delivered in Latin.

The large body of students in the school of arts was divided into two "nations" one of Italians and one of foreigners, each with its own Rector and its own statutes. As in the earliest times, so now, the Rector was elected and the statutes made, not by the faculty but by the students. The only power in the possession of the professors was the right of granting degrees. They maintained a fairly high standard for their Italian students, but graduated foreigners on very easy terms, remarking that when they got a pupil's money they could easily get rid of the ass by sending him back home. The greater part of the foreign students came from Germany.

Perhaps there was a little more freedom at Padua under the Venetian rule than at Bologna under the popes. The first prospectus of studies at Padua, published in 1629, shows that courses were offered in theology, in the Bible, in the *Metaphysics* of Aristotle, in Natural Philosophy, in Mathematics, in Classics, in Anatomy, in Medicine, in Surgery, and in Law. Though medicine was still taught from the books of Hippocrates and Avicenna, anatomy was taught by the dissection of corpses in a fine theater built for that purpose.

Of all the Italian universities that of Pisa was the most progressive even before the great Galileo illuminated it with his teachings. Courses in practical mathematics and in engineering were given there; and *there* was erected the first anatomical theater. This was copied at Pavia in 1552; and at Pavia surgery first won recognition, in 1655, as a subject of equal rank with logic, till then the premier science. Most of the other Italian universities lost their freedom and the best part of their intellectual life under the oppression of the Counter-Reformation. The professors were generally required to subscribe to a declaration of faith in the Catholic religion; and at Naples they were even obliged to supplement this by an oath to defend the doctrine of the immaculate conception, which, until 1854, was not a defined dogma of the church, but merely a pious opinion.

With the rise of the Spanish Empire to its apogee under Charles V and Philip II the universities enjoyed a period of great prosperity, but with the decline of the Empire under Philip III and Philip IV they, too, fell into decadence. In addition to fourteen universities founded before 1553, two more were founded in the sixteenth and one in the seventeenth century. The numbers at the universities rose in the sixteenth and declined in the following century. Salamanca reached the maximum number of students with 6778 in 1584, but shrank to 1995 in 1682. On the other hand Alcalá kept a steady average of about 2000 from 1550 to 1650, after which it declined to 1637 students in the year 1700.

Salamanca, the most famous as she was the fairest, of Spanish universities, boasted a faculty of seventy professors, distributed as follows: Canon Law 10; Civil Law 10; Medicine 7; Theology 7; Philosophy 11; Astrology 1; Music 1; Chaldee 1; Hebrew 1; Greek 4; Latin 17. The jurists were most highly paid, at the rate of 272 flourins (about $611) per annum in addition to board and lodging. The chairs were filled as they fell vacant by a competition in which the various candidates would give specimen lectures to be voted upon not by the professors but by the students. While some candidates owed their appointments to unworthy electioneering arts and particularly to lavish banquets given to poor students, others were chosen for their merits and their fame. The government of the university was partly in the hands of a Rector chosen for one year by the faculty, partly in the hands of a Master or Chancellor, representing the pope and charged with enforcing the statutes, directing studies, and judging criminal cases.

The decadence of the seventeenth century is directly traceable to the Inquisition. Books were rigorously censored, lectures supervised, and teachers who dared to advance anything novel smitten with the wrath of the church. The most famous case of heresy dealt with was that of Luis de León (1527-91) an eminent poet, an accomplished scholar, and professor of theology at Salamanca. Charged with heresy for making a new translation of the Song of Songs, which seemed to deprive it of its supernatural meaning, he was cast into prison for five years, subjected to the torture, and finally released with an admonition and restored to his chair at the university. Such was his sangfroid that he resumed his lectures at the point where he had been forced to drop them five years before, with the words "As I was saying at the last time."

But the other professors trembled and took such good care to trim their lectures to the required standards that few cases of heresy were found among them. Science particularly languished in bonds. After Stunica, a graduate of Salamanca, had been condemned for introducing the Copernican system into a commentary on Job, astronomy was taught from the books of Aristotle and Ptolemy, or sank to the level of astrology. Even anatomy, permitted at the Italian universities, was suppressed by the Spanish inquisitors. The anatomical theater, opened at Salamanca in 1568, was closed eight years later.

Education was further subjugated by the church when the Jesuits came to compete with and finally to vanquish the universities. The founding of the great Jesuit Imperial College at Madrid in 1625 drew from the older institutions of learning the sons of the aristocracy and many of the more ambitious youth of lower rank. Further competition, of a more respectable nature, was provided by the foundation of the Casa de Contratación, or school of navigation, at Seville. In this technical high-school mathematics, engineering, navigation, geography, cartography, and the construction of nautical instruments were well taught.

It must be mentioned, however, to the glory of Spain, that while she was still at the height of her powers she founded universities in the New World "for the service of God, the public welfare of the kingdom, and the protection of the inhabitants of the Indies from the darkness of ignorance." In 1551 Charles V founded a university at Lima, Peru, and two years later the Royal and Pontifical University of Mexico at the capital of that province. The courses given in theology, in law, and in the arts and sciences are judged to have been equal to anything offered at the universities in the English colonies before the nineteenth century. A third university was founded at Cordoba in the Argentine in 1613; and a fourth at the capital of Bolivia in 1624.

Like their sisters in Italy and Spain the French universities declined into impotent lassitude under the oppression of fanaticism and despotism. The proud University of Paris, who had once imposed her authority on church and state, who had shown the way to heal the Great Schism and who had raised the fame of French learning to the skies, bowed her head under the savage blows of the wars of religion, and exhausted her vitality in a struggle first with the Huguenots and then with the Jesuits. Since the foundation of the Jesuit Collège de Clermont, in 1563, the Sorbonne had taken a second place even in her own city.

When peace was restored to the kingdom by the genius of Henri IV, one of the first tasks of the king was to reform and strengthen the university. The Collège de Clermont was closed in 1595; and new statutes for the university were drawn up and promulgated in 1600. The most revolutionary thing about these statutes was their promulgation by the civil government instead of by the church. The secularization of education, due to the rise of the national states, though most marked in Protestant countries, took place also under Catholic and Most Christian kings. Great stress was still laid on orthodox piety, and much time devoted to religious study. To the great detriment of science orthodox opinions in intellectual matters were insisted upon. Philosophy and science were still in such servile bondage to Aristotle that when a few professors at Paris were infected with Cartesianism, the government at once sent the archbishop to warn them to abandon the novel doctrine. In 1624 the First President of the Parlement of Paris forbade a debate on the theses of three opponents of Aristotle after it had been publicly announced and after an audience of a thousand persons had gathered to hear it; at the same time the Parlement forbade on pain of death any scholastic attack on the ancient authors.

The war of the university with the Jesuits was renewed in 1618 when the Collège de Clermont was reopened; this school was now fostered by royal patronage to an ever growing extent until in 1682 it proudly changed its name to Collège de Louis le Grand. The struggle, which united all the French universities in a league against the new order, became extraordinarily bitter. The Sorbonne lost no opportunity of attributing the odious doctrines of tyrannicide and of ultramontanism to the Society of Jesus. Notwithstanding this advantage, and notwithstanding the ardent Gallicanism of the Faculties of Arts and Law, the Jesuits encroached more and more upon the prerogatives of their rivals.

Under these unhappy circumstances the universities languished. A few famous names among their faculties could not restore freedom to corporations bound hand and foot in civil and ecclesiastical chains. Not only did the universities fail to take any part in the expanding intellectual life of the time, but they used all their powers, as willing slaves, to oppose it. The Sorbonne condemned and refused license to almost all the important scientific works of the age, including Du Boulay's famous *History of the University of Paris*.

The same diseases that sapped the vitality of the Parisian

university attacked Louvain in the Spanish Netherlands in an even more virulent form. Exhausted by wounds inflicted in the religious wars, and starved on the Lenten diet of Spanish Catholicism, she devoted what little energy was left her to futile wars with Jesuitry and despotism. After the death of Justus Lipsius for at least two centuries no eminent scholar shed a ray of luster on her name; while she was forced to see a young rival in the North inherit her once proud position in the Republic of Letters.

This rival was the University of Leyden founded by the Dutch patriots to commemorate their first great victory over the Spanish army in the war of independence. The charter, couched in Dutch, and given at Delft, on January 6, 1575, though issued in the name of King Philip II, was authorized by Willem of Orange as Stadtholder and Captain General. Though Philip, as soon as he heard of the new institution, promptly forbade his subjects to attend it, he could not prevent its flourishing. The law passed by the prince and States General in May, 1675, provided for the erection of a primary department to teach Latin and Greek, and of a college with ten professors, two of theology, and one of medicine, one of law, one of logic, one of Hebrew and Greek, one of physics, politics and economics, one of mathematics, cosmography and chronology, and one of eloquence and history. All professors were required to subscribe to the articles of the Reformed faith. Expenses were met by an appropriation of 5000 guilders (about $2000) annually by the States General, and by assigning to the university the income of confiscated church property in the Rhineland.

Justus Lipsius, still a Protestant, was called in 1578 at a salary of 600 guilders, which was raised to 1000 guilders in 1591. Among the early professors were some other famous men, notably Scaliger, Arminius, and his chief opponent, Gomarus. One of the first acts of the Curators was to appoint a university printer and bookseller. This office was held first by the noted publisher Plantin, and then by the still more famous Louis Elzevir. In return for a modest salary the official printer was expected to publish all needed text-books and all treatises written by professors, to import for them all such books as they wanted from the Frankfort Fair, and, finally, to give a copy of every book he printed to the university library.

Announcements of the courses were published first in 1592 and thereafter frequently, but apparently not annually. The lectures of 1595 show that the usual subjects were taught from the usual ancient texts. But even then a botanical garden was started to assist the medical lecturers. By 1654, if not earlier, anatomy was taught by dissection, and a course in geometry was given in the vernacular. But in 1641 the Curators and Burgomasters—who together formed a body of trustees appointed by the government and not connected with the faculty—decreed that philosophy, natural as well as moral, should be taught from the works of Aristotle interpreted by ancient and not by modern authors; and in 1647, when Descartes complained to the same body that he had been defamed for atheism by some professors, they gave him the poor satisfaction of a decree forbidding the professors even to mention his name.

By 1681, however, a considerable advance in the curriculum is evident. Medicine was taught no longer exclusively from the ancients but also from dissection, from clinical diagnosis, and with due regard to modern discoveries. Physics and chemistry were both taught with demonstration and experiment.

Though torn by the Arminian controversy, and though suffering from the wars of their country—to sustain which the professors patriotically gave part of their salaries—the university grew rapidly in fame and numbers. The 800 students of 1600 grew to a body of 2000 sixty years later.

War, dogmatic religion, and state regulation proved as pestiferous to the German universities as to those in other countries. After the Reformation had weakened and divided the church, the universities became more and more organs of the state. No longer were they founded by papal bulls but by state charters. The professors, paid, appointed, and regulated by the government, became more and more like other civil officers. In this we see the dawn of what the Germans aptly call the "police-state," that polity in which every act is supervised, and almost every act "verboten" by the government. Its effect on the universities was particularly baleful. In addition to depriving the faculties of academic freedom, the new territorialism led to the idea that every petty state—and there were an enormous number of petty states in Germany—should have its own university, and should even forbid its subjects to go outside of their own city or principality for education. This caused the founding of a large number of new universities, most of which were unnecessary, and many of which proved not viable. Notwithstanding the fact that Germany had already a large number of universities in the year 1500, nine new institutions were founded in the sixteenth and nine in the seventeenth century.

Not less harmful than the attentions of the state proved to be the "rage of the theologians." Almost the whole intellectual life of the faculties of arts and of theology was absorbed in dogmatic subtleties and in confessional strife. And when at last the most devastating of all the wars of religion broke out, the universities, like everything else in Germany, were laid waste.

Under the oppression of the double yoke of state and church science languished. Only in the medical faculties did the new discoveries have the least place, and that a very small one. And the medical faculties were then despised in comparison with the faculty of law, which trained jurists for the bureaucracy, and with the faculty of theology which provided ministers for the church. In the college of arts the old authorities were acknowledged. Aristotle reigned supreme; and next to his treatises the almost equally archaic text-books of Melanchthon were held, in the Protestant schools, to be authoritative. And among the Catholics the most vigorous institutions were those which yielded, usually after a struggle, to the domination of the Jesuits.

Among the Protestant universities Wittenberg continued

to enjoy the prestige won during its early years by Luther and Melanchthon. Many famous foreigners—among them William Tyndale, John Rogers, Giordano Bruno, Alberico Gentile, Tycho Brahe, and Fynes Morison—wrote their names on her matriculation album. The old form of government, with a rector elected annually by the professors, continued. The faculty, compared to that of Bologna or Salamanca, was small. In 1591 it consisted of four professors of divinity, six of medicine, five of jurisprudence—which meant the Civil Law, for the Canon Law had been burned by the most famous of Wittenberg teachers—and one each of logic, history, rhetoric, Hebrew, mathematics, astronomy, poetry, and natural philosophy. These professors were paid from 100 to 600 gulden yearly, or from $56 to $336 at a time when money had ten times the purchasing power that it now has. The whole university was dominated by a narrow and aggressive spirit of Lutheran orthodoxy, intensified after 1592 by the requirement that all professors should subscribe to the Augsburg Confession and the Formula of Concord.

As a typical Catholic university, Vienna, after its reorganization in 1554, was the exact counterpart of Wittenberg in everything except its creed. The same curriculum of Aristotelian physics and philosophy, the same antiquated science, the same amount and quality of languages and history. But the theological faculty studied Lombard's *Sentences* and Patristics, instead of the Augsburg Confession and Luther's commentaries, as at Wittenberg.

It is impossible to estimate the numbers of the students at all the German institutions of higher learning put together. At Wittenberg, one of the largest, there were close to 2000 students during the latter half of the sixteenth and the first decades of the seventeenth century. Heidelberg and Marburg, which enjoyed the next greatest prestige in Protestant lands, were then much smaller, ranging from 300 to 600 students each.

While Germany was multiplying her universities England continued to remain satisfied with the two ancient and beautiful institutions of Oxford and Cambridge. There were, however, two new universities founded in the British Isles in the latter part of the sixteenth century, that of Edinburgh in 1582, and Trinity College, Dublin, in 1591.

As in other Protestant countries, so in England, the Reformation brought with it the violent transfer of much wealth and power from the church to the state. Energetic intervention of the government in university affairs began under Henry VIII, when Thomas Cromwell forced both Oxford and Cambridge to surrender their charters, bulls, and endowments to the king. The Royal Injunctions of 1535 also vigorously reformed the course of studies, by excluding Roman Catholic elements, pouring contempt on the scholastic philosophy, and "setting Dunce in Bocardo" —Dunce being Duns Scotus and Bocardo the Oxford prison. In place of these obsolete studies, the humanities were emphasized. In 1540 the first Regius professorships were created—a symbol of the secular revolution. To compensate the universities for their lost liberties, new colleges were founded from the spoils of the confiscated monasteries.

The reform was continued vigorously under Edward VI. The Injunctions and Visitors of 1549 completely recast the ancient trivium by discarding grammar in favor of mathematics, and remodelled the ancient quadrivium to include perspective and Greek. But natural and moral philosophy were still taught from the classic texts. The only concession to experimental science was made in the medical school, where each student was obliged to dissect two corpses and effect three cures before he could take his degree.

One of the chief cares of the government was to ensure the orthodoxy of professors and students. In 1553 Edward VI obliged all students admitted to the degrees of doctor of divinity, bachelor of divinity, or master of arts, to subscribe to the Anglican Articles of Religion. This law, not enforced by the Catholic Mary, was not only revived by Elizabeth, but extended to apply to all students over sixteen, and supplemented by a required oath to maintain the Act of Supremacy.

One of the first acts of James I was to give the universities the right of sending members to Parliament. In his reign and in that of his son new professorships of medicine, astronomy, history, and the oriental languages were founded. At this time Copernicus began to be studied as the only modern authority, along with the ancients, in astronomy.

Both universities suffered from Laud's despotic system of "thorough." The various subscriptions to creeds and laws were supplemented, after 1640, by the requirement of an oath recognizing the divine right of kings. While heresy was hunted out by spies, suspected teachers were dismissed.

Throughout the civil war both universities took the Royalist side. For this reason they were bitterly disliked by the extreme Puritans, who denounced them as "idolatrous high places," dens of drones, and nurseries of wickedness. Proposals to abolish them altogether and to erect new universities at Manchester and York were freely put forward. However, more sober councils prevailed. When the army of the Commonwealth took Oxford, in 1645, the Parliamentary government treated the great school generously. In 1649 an oath of allegiance to the Commonwealth was imposed on the Fellows, and those who refused it were ejected.

The Restoration brought little change in method of teaching to the universities. They continued to add to those glorious buildings which make them the fairest of the world's schools. In 1669 Oxford opened the Sheldonian theater, planned by Wren, and given by Dr. Gilbert Sheldon, the Archbishop of Canterbury. One who was present at the dedication described it as "a fabric comparable to any of this kind of former ages, and doubtless exceeding any at present." [1] With this judgment I hardly agree. The Sheldonian is one of the least beautiful of Oxford buildings.

Royalist as they were, Oxford and Cambridge held their religion even dearer than their king. Some tyrannical acts

[1] Evelyn's *Diary*, July 9, 1669; ii, 39.

of James II, who tried to violate the rights of both universities, were among the causes of his forced abdication.

In point of numbers Oxford and Cambridge grew and flourished mightily except for temporary depressions during the reign of Mary and during the Civil War. The highwater mark was reached early in the seventeenth century, when Oxford taught more than 2000 and Cambridge more than 3000 students at one time. Indeed, it has been shown that in 1630 one out of every 3600 Englishmen proceeded to Oxford or Cambridge, as against one in every 9000 in 1910. This calculation, however, does not take account of the fact that England then had only two universities, and now has many, the alumni of which would greatly raise the percentage of her college graduates.

Far from the seats of learning in old Europe there was founded, in the savage wilderness, a university destined to rival the greatest of them in fame, to be as rich in erudition and in science, and as prolific in great sons. It is a fact unexampled in the history of the world, and one that speaks more for the quality of the men who first settled Massachusetts than does anything else, that within six years after their settlement they should erect in their midst a university. The story of the foundation is told, with much charm, by a pamphlet published in 1643 under the title: *New England's First Fruits . . . in respect of the Progress of Learning in the College at Cambridge in Massachusetts Bay.*

After God [so the writer begins] had carried us safe to New England, and we had builded our houses, provided necessaries for our livelihood, reared convenient places for God's worship, and settled the civil government, one of the next things we longed for and looked after was to advance learning and to perpetuate it to posterity.

Accordingly the General Court in 1636 appropriated £400 to found "a schoale or colledge," to be located near Boston in a place then called Newetowne, the name of which was changed to Cambridge in 1638 in memory of the English university. For among the early settlers there was an extraordinary number of Cambridge graduates. In Massachusetts and Connecticut there was, during the first generation of immigration, one Cambridge graduate in every 250 of the population, and many Oxford graduates besides. This made a far higher proportion of university men than there was in the old country. The matriculation books of both Oxford and Cambridge, during the reigns of Elizabeth and the early Stuarts, swarm with names such as Washington, Hawthorne, and Emerson, destined to become more renowned in America than in England.

In 1638 the Reverend John Harvard, "a godly gentleman and lover of learning" who had emigrated to Massachusetts in 1637, died, leaving £700 and 260 books to the new college, which was thereafter called by his name. "After him," continues the author of *New England's First Fruits,*

another gave £300, others after them cast in more, and the public hand of the state added the rest: the college was, by common consent, appointed to be at Cambridge (a place very pleasant and accomodate). . . . The edifice is very fine and comely without, having in it a spacious hall (where they daily meet at common lectures and exercises) and a large library with some books to it, the gift of divers of our friends, their chambers and studies also fitted for and possessed by the students, and all other rooms of office necessary and convenient . . . and by the side of the college a fair grammar school for the training up of young scholars and fitting them for academical learning. . . .

Over the college is Master Dunster placed as President, a learned, conscionable and industrious man, who hath so trained up his pupils in the tongues and arts, and so seasoned them with the principles of divinity and Christianity that we have to our great comfort (and in truth) beyond our hopes, beheld their progress in learning and godliness. . . .

Over the College are twelve Overseers chosen by the general Court, six of them are of the magistrates, the other six of the ministers. . . .

The statutes drawn up in 1642 prescribe religious exercises, moral discipline, and a course of studies embracing logic, physics, politics, arithmetic, geometry, astronomy, Greek, Latin, Hebrew, history and botany. The first class of nine was graduated in 1642; and this was about the average number graduated annually throughout the century.

While it is plain that the universities of Europe and America did a great service to society, it is no less patent that they suffered generally from certain faults, of which the three that seem most striking to our generation were: 1, the lack of a healthy student life; 2, the lack of academic freedom; and 3, extreme conservatism which was unable to assimilate the new science, preferring the ancient diet of obsolete texts.

The student life of our ancestors suffered somewhat from class distinctions and still more from the lack of healthy recreation. Both professors and students were great respecters of persons. The rich young lord lived with horses and servants, had his examinations tempered by obsequious teachers and his lessons done for him by servile comrades. In debauch and riot he escaped the punishments visited on his comrades; in the distribution of honors, sometimes of the supreme honor of the rectorate, he was preferred to the most brilliant of his poor friends and to the most famous of his instructors. On the other hand, the poor youth lived miserably. At the endowed colleges he was fed on rotten eggs and sour wine; his hours were taken up with menial employments; and after graduation he had little chance of securing an entry into any learned profession or an appointment to any desirable office. He often sank into the condition of a vagabond. "Student hunger" (*hambre estudiantina*) was proverbial in Spain.

Nor were the boys, rich or poor, expected to indulge in any recreations. There were no athletics, no plays but those of Plautus and Seneca given as part of the instruction in the classics; card-playing, dice, games of all kinds, bear-baiting, and cock-fighting were forbidden. At Geneva, where Calvinistic rigor prevailed, some students were punished for indulging in a merry, but sober, dinner, or, as the record puts it, "being debauched from their lessons by eating capons."

The natural result of the repression of innocent pleasure was that youths found more dangerous outlets for their irrepressible good spirits. While toping, wenching, and gambling became favorite indoor sports, the place of the modern football game was taken by the glorious town-and-gown row. How fierce these sometimes were is almost incredible to those familiar with the gentle youths of our modern colleges. At Erfurt, when some students murdered a tavern-keeper for asking them to pay their bill, the enraged towns-folk started bombarding the dormitory with cannon. At Leyden bands of students paraded the streets at night breaking windows and frightening passers-by. At Paris their turbulence became so great that the Parlement had to threaten with the death penalty those who infested the highways in armed bands. At Salamanca in one riot two burghers were killed; and two students captured by the mob were in revenge inhumanly punished, one with death and the other with torture.

Compared with such outbursts, which, of course, were rare, the more frequent disorder in the classrooms and debating halls sinks into a minor matter, though it must have been annoying to the professors. To have one's lecture interrupted by catcalls, by the blowing of horns, by "indecent explosions," and by insulting gestures, was bad enough; to have one's gown spoiled by a well-directed hail of spitting was worse; to become the target for rotten vegetables, filth, and harder missiles was worst of all—but every one of these things is recorded more than once in the sober annals of deans and rectors of the sixteenth and seventeenth centuries.

But, after all, such conduct was exceptional. What hurt the universities far more was the bondage in which they were held by church and state. Neither professors nor students could call their souls their own, nor harbor unconventional opinions in any matter whatsoever. Practically everywhere they were forced to subscribe to creeds and to oaths of allegiance. Attendance at church was often compulsory; harsh and vindictive punishments were visited not only on those who refused the oaths, but on any who dared to disobey a royal command. While the Arminian controversy was raging in the Netherlands, the professors at Leyden were forbidden by the States General to write anything on it. Even in purely scientific matters the orthodox views were rigidly enforced. The governments of France and of the Netherlands forbade the teaching of the Cartesian and enjoined the teaching of the Peripatetic philosophy. The astronomer Mästlin was compelled by the academic senate of Tübingen to teach the Ptolemaic system, though he was a Copernican. When Isaac Dorislaus seasoned his lectures on Tacitus at Cambridge with hints of a preference for a republican to a monarchical government, he was suspended, then reinstated, then suspended again, and finally driven from the university.

Few, indeed, were the voices, even of philosophers or of radicals, raised against this tyranny. It was commonly thought that coercion of opinion in the interests of the ruling powers was a legitimate function of the state, and it was correctly believed that education was a powerful instrument in moulding opinion. Hartlib, the friend of Comenius and of Milton, wrote that the "readiest way to reform both church and commonwealth is to reform the schools therein." Hobbes insisted that the principal use to which universities should be put was to teach subjects their duties to their king. Leibniz spoke harshly of a plea for academic freedom, then called "liberty of philosophizing," which probably originated with Spinoza.

The third, and most fatal, disease of the universities was their addiction to obsolete philosophies and their consequent inability to assimilate the new science. How few of the great names of that marvellous age of science are connected with any university faculty! Neither Copernicus, nor Bacon, nor Boyle, nor Huygens, nor Leeuwenhoek, nor Swammerdam, nor Van Helmont, nor Kepler, nor Guericke, nor Fermat, nor Napier, nor Stevin, nor Pascal, nor Descartes ever taught at any school or university. And the fate of the few great men who, like Luis de León and Sanchez and Bruno and Galileo, did teach, was a warning to others.

Instead of a wholesome and stimulating diet of fresh truth the professors then fed the youths at their tables with an innutritious and nauseating broth concocted from the dry bones of long dead philosophies. There is much justice in the hard words of Milton, who said, they take "from young men the use of their reason by certain charms compounded of metaphysics, miracles, traditions, and absurd scriptures." At Cambridge, he complained, he had misspent his youth trying to digest "an asinine feast of sow-thistles and bramble," and in learning "sophistical trash."

With less turgid rhetoric and far deeper insight Bacon diagnosed the academic disease. All existing rules and customs, he pointed out, favored the old studies and opposed anything novel. The lectures and exercises were so arranged, said he, that it would not occur to any man to innovate, for he would consider it more professional, and find it more lucrative, to teach an old, recognized study than to start a new one. Even if professional jealousy and academic law allowed him to advance new ideas, it would dampen his ardor to find that no financial provision had been made for anything but the old courses.

"It is strange," he continued, "that amongst so many foundations of colleges in Europe, all are dedicated to professions and none left free to arts and sciences at large." Moreover, both the pay of the professors he thought insufficient to attract the ablest men, and the equipment of the institutions inadequate even in books, and much more in instruments for making experiments. Finally Bacon, in this as in his other criticisms far ahead of his age, detected the great weakness of research in his age in the lack of means of communication between universities.

What he wanted and proposed was endowment of research, the teaching of science, and the proper intellectual and material equipment for these purposes. His message re-echoed in the hearts of some of his contemporaries, but failed of realization for financial and traditional reasons. Descartes eagerly agreed that research is important, but added that its endowment on an adequate scale would tax the revenues of kings.[1] Torricelli advocated the study of science, and particularly of mathematics, as most conducive to truth, most profitable to religion, and most practically useful; but he added that any teacher who turned to science and away from the common studies would be considered melancholy mad. Much in the spirit of Bacon, and influenced by him, John Hall, of Cambridge, published in 1648 a remarkable tract on *The Advancement of Learning and the Reformation of the Universities.* After criticizing the obsolete methods, inefficient professoriate, and narrow curriculum of the universities, he continued:

Where have we anything to do with chimistry which hath snatcht the keys of nature from the other sects of philosophy by her multiplied experiences [*i.e.* experiments]? Where have we constant reading upon either quick or dead anatomies [*i.e.* corpses], or ocular demonstration of herbes? Where any manuall demonstration of mathematical theorems or instruments? Where is a promotion of their experiences [*i.e.* experiments], which if rightly carried on would multiply even to astonishment? . . . Where is there a solemn disquisition into history?

One reason for the defective teaching of science was the poverty of equipment in laboratories and in instruments. The then despised medical faculties made the most progress in procuring anatomical theaters and botanical gardens. But until the very end of the seventeenth century the faculties of arts and sciences had next to nothing of this sort. Before 1650 the whole scientific equipment of Oxford was limited to a few dials, astronomical instruments, and terrestrial and celestial globes. Several of the resident scholars provided themselves with private chemical "elaboratories." As time went on the universities gradually accumulated instruments and collections; one of the best of the early collections was that of Leyden.

[1] *Œuvres,* xi, 320.

Nor was the practice of endowing research wholly foreign to the age. Professorial duties at Oxford and Cambridge were so light, and the salaries there so relatively ample, that much original scientific work might have been done. Salmasius and Scaliger held honorary professorships at Leyden in order that they might devote their whole time to study. The Collège de Clermont endowed chairs, ranging in number from one to eight, for *Scriptores*, who were freed from other duties in order to read and write. As, however, they were expected to direct their energies to defending and ornamenting the church, they could hardly be called professors of disinterested research. Apparently their first appointment, in 1606, was due to the fact that the college had been closed by the government, leaving the faculty without teaching functions; but the appointments continued after the institution was reopened to pupils.

3. PEDAGOGICAL THEORY

If we turn from the destructive criticisms to the more positive ideas of reform prevailing among the contemporaries of Bacon and Milton, we shall find three demands frequently reiterated: that education be made more accessible and more practical for the poor; that it be made more liberal and courtly for the rich; and that it be made easier, pleasanter, and more interesting for all. The first two demands reflect clearly the currents of the age already operative in practice—for pedagogical like political theory as often follows as precedes the accomplished fact. The last demand embodied a discovery made afresh by every generation from the Greeks to the Americans—the discovery, namely, that compulsion is a far less powerful instrument for exacting work than is intellectual interest.

Veit Ludwig Seckendorf, William Dell, Samuel Hartlib, Andreae, Campanella, and a host of others clamored for a free, compulsory, and practical education of the poor, with special emphasis on scientific and technical subjects. Hartlib advocated establishing a college of agriculture. Sir William Petty wanted to have all children, rich and poor, taught a manual art or trade. Thomas Budd, an English Quaker who migrated first to New Jersey and then to Pennsylvania, drew up a very elaborate plan for training "each child in the art, mystery, or trade that he or she most delighteth in." Spinoza advanced the doctrine that the most profitable studies were moral philosophy for conduct, elementary medicine for health, mechanics for supplying conveniences to life, and above all the cultivation of methods to improve the mind.

On the other hand, there emerges in the pedagogical theory of the age a new and distinct idea of the education of the gentleman. Montaigne, saturated in classic authors though he was, reacted against the pedantry of the schools. Greek and Latin can be bought too dear, he averred; they should be taught naturally, as Latin had been taught to him;—he had been educated by a German tutor who could speak no French and who therefore always conversed with him, as a boy, in the Roman tongue. Philosophy should drop her forbidding and terrible mask to assume her natural guise of a gay and gentle guide to enjoyment. One learns to live, the essayist lamented, only by the time life has almost passed; many young men get the pox before they learn continence from Aristotle. The best education for the gentleman, he added, is intercourse with men, especially in travel; and next to that in history which is but intercourse with men of a former age.

Though Milton's *Treatise on Education* (1644) combines many currents of thought—Puritanical, humanistic, and democratic—it is chiefly a contribution to the theory of the liberal education of the leader, who should be fit "to perform justly, skilfully, and magnanimously, all the offices, both public and private, of peace and war." The sources of Milton's thought lay mainly in the classics, for a contemptuous allusion to "modern *Januas* and *Didactics*" shows that he scorned to read contemporary authorities. And the classics furnish the body of his curriculum; though with them he combines studies in science and in modern languages, now so necessary to the accomplished gentleman. Latin, Greek, geography, natural philosophy, astronomy, trigonometry, fortification, architecture, engineering, navigation, mineralogy, botany, meteorology, zoölogy, anatomy, ethics, Italian, politics, law, theology, physical exercises, military drill, and music are all crammed into an eight-year course between the ages of twelve and twenty. Having mastered these subjects, the author convincingly concludes, the young men "will be fraught with an universal insight into things."

The really modern element in Milton is his emphasis on *realia* rather than on languages. "Though a linguist," he argues, "should pride himself to have all the tongues that Babel cleft the world into, yet if he have not studied the solid things in them as well as the words and lexicons, he were nothing so much to be esteemed a learned man as any yeoman or tradesman competently wise in his mother dialect only." And in his last years he put into fine verse his weariness with mere book-learning:

> Who reads
> And to his reading brings not
> A spirit or judgment equal or superior
> (And what he brings what needs he elsewhere seek?)
> Uncertain and unsettled still remains,
> Deep-versed in books and shallow in himself,
> Crude or intoxicate, collecting toys.[1]

The pedagogical genius of the age was Johannes Andreas Comenius, by birth a Czech and by baptism a Moravian Brother. Suffering persecution for his faith, he wandered far, teaching school in twenty cities and publishing twenty books. From Bohemia he wandered throughout Germany; was called to England by Puritans who wished his services in reforming schools, and to Sweden for the same purpose by Chancellor Oxenstjerna. It is sometimes said, on the authority of Cotton Mather, that he was called to America

---

[1] *Paradise Regained*, iv, 321ff; cf. ibid. 285ff.

to be president of Harvard, but this has been doubted. If he were invited, he declined.

His first important work, the *Janua linguarum reserata,* or, *The Gate of Tongues unlocked* (1631) professes to be a new method of learning Latin. It contains a thousand phrases of easy Latin, so chosen as to give the child much information about the elements, the stars, the animals, the organs of the body, the arts, and trades. A considerable advance was marked in a recension of this, called the *Orbis sensualium pictus,* or *Illustrated World of Sensible Objects.* In this every sentence of Latin is illustrated by a picture. The idea of teaching young children by pictures is found before Comenius in Andreae and in Campanella; but Comenius first fully realized it.

His most important treatise, *The Great Didactic,* was published in Czech in 1632, in Latin in 1638, and in English in 1642. The full English title reads:

The Great Didactic, setting forth the whole art of teaching all things to all men; or, a certain inducement to found such schools in all parishes, towns, and villages of every Christian kingdom, that the entire youth of both sexes, none being excepted, shall quickly, pleasantly, and thoroughly become learned in the sciences, pure in morals, trained in piety, and in this manner instructed in all things necessary for the present and for the future life.

The comprehensive plan provided a "mother's school" in every family, an elementary public school in every district, a Latin school in every city, and a university in every kingdom or considerable province. Psychologically the method was based on the idea that the mind, hand, and tongue should be trained concurrently; the one to think, the second to do, and the third to interpret. Even from the earliest years the child should begin to know facts and to perform acts as well as to learn words. In physics the smallest infant could learn something about water, earth, air, and fire; in physiology something about the parts of his body; in astronomy the names and nature of the sun, moon, and stars; in geography the mountains, lakes, and rivers of his own region. And this method of combining manual training, practical understanding, and linguistic knowledge, should be continued from the lowest to the final stage of education.

Not the least original idea of Comenius was his demand for the equal education of girls and boys. Except for the most elementary instruction women were then generally thought incapable of learning and of culture. The contrary opinion of a few humanists, like Erasmus and Vives, had passed unnoticed; the example of a few learned women like Lady Jane Grey, Queen Elizabeth, Queen Christina of Sweden, and the Duchess of Newcastle, were held to be exceptions to the law of nature condemning women to ignorance. The Blue-stocking was heartily ridiculed by Molière who but represented the common opinion when he wrote:

Il n'est pas bien honnête, et pour beaucoup des causes,
Qu'une femme étudie et sache tant de choses;
Former aux bonnes mœurs l'esprit de ses enfants,
Faire aller son ménage, avoir l'œil sur les gens,
Et régler la dépense avec économie,
Doit être son étude et sa philosophie.

Women, of course, were excluded from the universities. At Oxford, in 1608, the question whether women were fit to hear lectures in moral philosophy was debated and voted in the negative. At Wittenberg, in 1595, it was even debated, and apparently left undecided, whether women could be called human beings, or not. Altogether exceptional was the plea of the Dutch philosopher Geulincx, to admit women to the higher education.

As a matter of practice poor girls were left wholly illiterate, while those of the higher classes received little instruction beyond reading, writing, religion, and good manners. Throughout Europe the co-education of girls and boys was the rarest occurrence even at the earliest age, and was forbidden by law in some places. In this matter, as in making education democratic, America led the way. The public schools were first opened on equal terms to both sexes at Meriden, Connecticut, in 1678.

4. LIBRARIES

As, for the last three thousand years and among civilized races, books have been the chief repositories of knowledge and the most powerful instrument of culture, libraries may well be reckoned among educational institutions, in the broad sense. Antiquity and the Middle Ages both made some large collections of manuscripts; the former mostly in public foundations, the latter mostly in the monasteries. But the invention of printing, by inundating Europe with millions of books, and the advent of the Reformation, by striking down the monasteries, necessitated the creation of new cisterns in which to store the precious flood of knowledge.

The largest collections of books were now made either by princes and potentates or by universities. The royal and pontifical libraries were at first so carefully guarded that they were almost useless to the public. Even scholars of the first rank were admitted only after securing the best introductions. Not only fear of losing treasures but the jealousy of the librarian eager to monopolize the advantages of his position operated to make many libraries rather the closed preserves of a favored few than the common property of all. Moreover, the historical sources in the archives were regarded as secrets of state, to be exploited only by friendly hands. In 1570 the pope forbade any one to copy a Vatican manuscript on pain of excommunication. From the first the universities were more liberal, making their stores accessible to foreign scholars as well as to their own members. The books were kept chained to desks convenient for reading. As this method of storing the books was best adapted to those of the largest format, librarians preferred folios and quartos. Sir Thomas Bodley would even seem to have tried to exclude octavos from his college library. The first library to keep books on shelves was that of Philip II at the Escorial. Finally, some municipal libraries were founded and opened freely to the public.

Until ravaged by the Thirty Years War Germany held the leadership in the number of books produced and stored. The greatest book mart in Europe continued to be the fair held at Frankfort every spring. Indeed, the catalogues of this fair give the most complete survey of European literature. Among the German princes who made notable collections of books were the Dukes of Brunswick, the Counts Palatine of the Rhine, and the Electors of Brandenburg. The library of Brunswick, at Wolfenbüttel, though the first to attain fame, was surpassed by the Bibliotheca Palatina at Heidelberg. The books in this, however, were sent to the Vatican when Tilly's troops sacked Heidelberg in 1622. Thirteen years after the end of the war the Great Elector of Brandenburg founded a library which soon acquired 20,000 printed books and 1600 manuscripts.

The Spanish kings during the seventeenth century made a great collection of books at the Escorial. They even preserved heretical and condemned books, though they kept them safely locked up in a room inaccessible to any but the licensers. Still more important was the Royal Library of the French kings, destined to become one of the greatest in the world. The curiosity of François I and of Catherine de Médicis added not a little to this aggregation of valuable books and manuscripts. Still more was it enlarged by Louis XIV, who in 1685 decreed that printers and publishers should give to it all copies of works licensed since 1652. This meant that from that date, or at any rate from 1685, every book lawfully published in France was acquired by the Royal Library.

The best library in Europe was at that time the property of the popes. It was first worthily housed by Sixtus V, who in 1588 erected a large building athwart the great court of Bramante in the Vatican. The fine library building, planned by Fontana, contained fourteen rooms on the second floor for the use of scholars, and on the third floor a great hall in which printed and manuscript books were stored. This hall—the Salone Sistino, seventy meters long, fifteen meters broad, and nine meters high—was well lighted, well equipped with closed cabinets to contain the books, and decorated with pictures more interesting historically than beautiful artistically. On the right wall eighteen frescoes depicted the œcumenical councils; while the pictures on the other walls presented the supposed inventors of the various alphabets, including Adam, Abraham, Moses, Ezra, and Queen Isis. Next to this hall was a large gallery, destined to house the libraries of the Duke of Urbino and that of the Count Palatine of the Rhine, when they came into the hands of the popes. John Evelyn, who saw the library on January 18, 1645, described it as "the most nobly built, furnished, and beautified of any in the world; ample, stately, light, and cheerful, looking into a most pleasant garden." His descriptions of the "emblems, figures, diagrams, and the like learned inventions" decorating the walls and ceiling recall so closely Campanella's account of the decorations of the chief palace in the City of the Sun as to make it certain that the Italian philosopher had the Vatican library in mind as his model, just as he took the papacy for his model for the government of his ideal state.

The first great library in Europe, except those of some universities, to be open to scholars, was the Ambrosiana founded by a bull of Paul V in 1606. Its patron, Cardinal Borromeo, tried to utilize it in the service of the church by appointing readers, both lay and clerical, to ransack its treasures.

Another prince of the church, Cardinal Mazarin, made his large library accessible to scholars a few year later. The credit for this must go largely to his librarian, Gabriel Naudé, whose *Avis pour dresser une Bibliothèque* (1627) won him merited fame. Naudé's taste was catholic enough to include the best authors in every department, the classics, the doctors of the church, the heretics, new scientific works, such as those of Kepler and Galileo, and dictionaries and other works of reference. During the Fronde the books were seized by the king; but on the restoration of peace the indefatigable cardinal began again to accumulate books. The Bibliothèque Mazarine is said to have contained 40,000 books at the time of the confiscation; whereas in 1672 it was estimated that the French Royal Library contained 35,000 printed books and 10,000 manuscripts.

By the end of the sixteenth century many universities had valuable collections of books. These were partly taken over from monasteries, partly given by patrons, and to a very small extent augmented by annual purchase. Wittenberg, after 1592, allowed thirty gulden (about $16) per annum for the acquisition of new books. Leyden began early to accumulate books and to loan them out to students and others. At Cambridge the chief library, before the foundation of a general collection by Humphrey Chetham in 1653, was that of Corpus Christi College, enlarged by a munificent gift from Archbishop Parker in 1578. The little parcel of 270 books given by John Harvard to the American university was augmented by a number of other early gifts. The catalogues show that theological books predominated, without excluding a number of others in classical, scientific, historical, and political fields.

But the greatest of university libraries, of that and perhaps of subsequent ages, was the one founded at Oxford by Sir Thomas Bodley who, after an education at Oxford and at Geneva, taught Greek for a while at his English alma mater. By 1602 he had collected more than 2000 books, had built a house for them, and on November 8 of that year opened it to the public. The first two printed catalogues are notable, that of 1605 as the first general catalogue of any European library, that of 1620 as the first completely alphabetical catalogue to be printed. When the number of books amounted to 6000, Bodley, who continued to labor for his foundation, thought the collection complete, and "wanting in nothing." What would he have said could he have foreseen the day when the Bodleian would contain more than 1,500,000 books? That it expanded to this enormous figure has been due chiefly to an act of far-reaching importance by the Stationers' Company, which, in 1610, granted to the Oxford library a copy of every book printed by its members. As this voluntary act was later turned into a legal obligation, almost every book printed in England since 1610 has been preserved, in one copy, at the Bodleian.

CHAPTER XII

RELIGION: THE CHRISTIAN CHURCHES

I. CATHOLIC AND PROTESTANT

The place filled by religion and superstition in the history of culture is a large one. By the impartial student no distinction can be made between the two that is of radical importance. Magic and religion are related phases of the same complex; they are merely different ways of approaching the mysterious forces of nature. Magic feels those powers as impersonal and therefore tries to manipulate or coerce them; religion feels them as personal and tries to conciliate or propitiate them. The emotional core of both is the thrill of awe or fear felt by man in the presence of phenomena transcending his powers of control or even of apprehension.

Religion soon becomes identified with the welfare of the group or of the individual. The most imperious of all man's spiritual needs is to glorify and beautify his own life. As most art and literature is flattery of man's passions, as most political theory is a justification of the existing polity, as most history and most law is influenced by the desire to extol the group to which the historian or legislator belongs, so religion is the supreme, instinctive effort of man to give importance to his earthly existence by connecting it with the vast forces of the universe. Bunyan's *Holy War,* depicting the universe as the theater on which Shaddai and Diabolus fight a desperate battle for the possession of Mansoul is a true type of all religion. Man sees his own shadow, like the specter on the Brocken, reflected and immensely enlarged against the clouds, and this gives him self-confidence and courage, mingled with awe, to fight manfully the battle of life.

And, more than this, religion is always one of the chief means of social control. The glorification of the life of the group in the dogma of religion has its counterpart in the sanctification of the custom of the group in the moral code inculcated by religion. That "religion is morality touched by emotion" is a perfectly true description of at least one important aspect of the subject. Religion, Kant rightly pointed out, consists largely in recognizing one's duties as divine commands.

On this basis of psychological endowment an immense variety of religions and of superstitions has been built up, corresponding to the intellectual and material needs of divers societies. The details of belief and of moral code are regulated by the general pressure of the intellectual influences and the ethical customs of the group. Thus, a change in the moral feeling or in the world-view of the group necessitates a change in religion.

The religious revolution of the sixteenth century, known as the Reformation, may be best understood as the natural, though unconscious, adaptation of religion to the needs of a new social situation. The individualism, the nationalism, the commercialism of the new age were all reflected in the Protestant church. But the revolution, though a mighty, was but a partial one. Europe was left, after two generations of Protestant propaganda and conquest, divided into two hostile camps. Speaking broadly, Catholic Europe was Latin, classical, monarchical, feudal, and aristocratic; Protestant, and especially Calvinist, Europe was Nordic, romantic, republican, plutocratic, and industrial.

In many essentials the two churches were alike. Both prayed to the same ethical and personal God, one substance in three persons; both accepted the doctrines of the incarnation, atonement, resurrection, and miracles of Christ; both read the same Bible. And that the great revolution which rent half Europe from the medieval church profoundly affected the other half cannot be doubted. The Catholic Reformation in many respects imitated the Protestant. Nationalism affected the Catholic states, especially France, in the assertion of the liberties of the local churches. Puritanism, the extreme form of seventeenth-century Protestantism, had in Jansenism its pale counterpart on Catholic soil. There were even men who still hoped, after a century of war, that the two faiths could be united. These plans for reunion, such as they were, generally emanated from Catholics who hoped that a few concessions, such as allowing the marriage of the clergy and giving the cup to the laity in communion, would suffice to bring the erring brethren back into the true fold. A French mystic poet, Alexandre Filère, illustrated his hope for church union by the strange and even indelicate allegory of *Hermaphroditus*, in which the naiad and the youth embraced so passionately as to grow into a single body. And a few years later Caspar Scioppius published with papal approbation a plan for leading the heretics back to the bosom of Mother Church.

However, the differences of the two confessions were felt keenly, while their similarities were overlooked. The literature of the age is choked with polemic, learned and popular, occasionally temperate but usually vituperative and bitter beyond all known examples. The best Catholic apologist was Cardinal Bellarmine, whose *Disputationes de controversiis Christianae fidei* appeared during the years 1586 to 1592. Quiet in tone and learned in content, this book aims to prove the identity of the modern Catholic faith with that of primitive Christianity. The best Protestant polemic was Johann Gerhard's *Confessio Catholica* (1634-37), which advanced the usual Protestant argument that his creed, and not that of his opponents, harmonized perfectly with the Bible. A comprehensive and highly vituperative attack on Catholicism was made by the Puritan Richard Baxter, in his work (1657) entitled: *The Safe Religion, or, Three Disputations for the Reformed Catholic Religion against Popery; proving that Popery is against Scripture, the unity of the Catholic Church, the consent of the ancient Doctors, the plainest reason and common judgment of sense itself.*

The French Huguenot Philippe Mornay had followed the same line of argument in his *Mysterium iniquitatis, seu historia papatus.*

A library could hardly contain the vast numbers of these wretched polemics, some of them logical enough in deducing their own theories from their own uncritically postulated premises, but most of them depending for their highest effects upon that common form of *ignoratio elenchi,* blackening the enemy's character. And the strife tainted much of the literature and much of the art of the day. Satire and caricature, called into the service of the warring parties, depicted the pope, on the one hand, or Calvin on the other, with the horns and hoofs of devils, or as animals or as loathsome monsters. These popular conceptions were circulated not only in the form of news-sheets and broadsides, but as medals struck in bronze or lead. Even the great poets, Spenser, Milton, and Vondel, lapsed into confessional polemic, and even the great artists misused their talents in the service of religious hatred.

The bitter war of pens was followed by the more horrible warfare of swords. The century between the outbreak of the Schmalkaldic War in 1546 and the end of the Thirty Years War in 1648 ran with rivers of blood shed in religious conflict. Civil war, partly caused by confessional animosities, and always exacerbated by them, devastated Germany, France, the Netherlands, and the British Isles, and exhausted the powers of Spain and of Scandinavia. If the conflict ended in a drawn battle between the two churches, that was due largely to the intermixture of secular with religious purposes. The Catholics, with the advantages of union and of greater resources, were unable to exploit their victories because of breaks in their own ranks resulting from the secular interests of the powers. Time and again Richelieu sacrificed, though with regret, the interests of his religion to those of his country. Even the papacy found itself in frequent conflict with the Catholic or with the Most Christian king, and was often virtually, if not nominally, the ally of Protestant princes.

And yet the Roman church could congratulate herself that she had survived the fiery trials of the Reformation and of the Religious Wars. If half her provinces had been torn from her, the remaining half were loyal, well disciplined, and powerful. Not for centuries had her spiritual forces been so fully mobilized. The definition of her doctrine and the reform of her morals by the Council of Trent (1545-63) had supplied her with arms of offence and defence against heresy. The Inquisition and the Index silenced all opposition to her in Catholic lands. And a new monastic order provided a disciplined and courageous army for defence and for fresh conquests.

In the general revival of Catholicism the papacy had less part than did other agencies. It is true that a temporary zeal for righteousness, born of fear, had seated in the Vatican some able and honest men, of whom one, Pius V, won the halo of canonized sainthood. But in the seventeenth century the reforming impulse had spent itself, to be succeeded by a spirit of intrigue in politics and of laxity in morals. The pope again felt himself to be an Italian potentate engaged in the diplomatic game with the other powers. Again, as in the Renaissance, he became a patron of art and of literature, though a bitter enemy to the new and dangerous science. Especially after that illustrious convert, Queen Christina of Sweden, took up her residence in Rome, the city became a brilliant capital of pleasure and of art.

But as a spiritual force the papacy again declined. Notwithstanding the apparent subjection of the Council of Trent to the papacy, the council had left undecided three problems which were to trouble the peace of the church for four hundred years. The first was the question whether the divine right of the bishops to govern the church was not equal or superior to that of the pope. The second was the standard of tradition, which, together with the Bible, had been defined as the source of truth. Was this tradition to be determined by the practice and precept of the pope, or in some other way, as by a general council? The third question was that of free will and predestination.

Nor was the church quite safe from further encroachments of nationalism, which had been so large an element in the Protestant Revolt. No sooner had the strong hand of Henri IV imposed peace upon Huguenot and Catholic than the old demand for the Gallican Liberties was revived. Under this name went the theory that in temporal matters the French church should be free from the pope and subject to the king. In 1594 Henri allowed the former Protestant and Parlementarian Pierre Pithou to dedicate to him some theses on the Liberties of the Gallican Church, strongly contending for the national as opposed to the papal control of matters affecting the French church. An infinite number of such liberties, he contended, can be proved historically, all depending upon two maxims: first, that the pope can not command in temporal matters, and second, that though the sovereignty of the pope in spiritual matters is recognized, yet even here it is not absolute, but is limited by the decrees of ancient councils recognized in France. He went on to prove that the kings of France had the right to summon national synods to make ecclesiastical laws; that the pope could not tax, nor dispense subjects from their allegiance, nor excommunicate officers for doing their duty, nor exercise criminal jurisdiction, nor force the acceptance of bulls without royal approval.

Similar claims were advanced again by Edward Richer in 1611, and by Pierre Dupuy in 1639. After long negotiations between the kings of France and the popes, Louis XIV incorporated in an edict of 1682 *Four Articles on the Liberties of the Gallican Church,* which were drafted by Bossuet and accepted by an assembly of French clergy, though condemned by the pope. These asserted: 1. That the successors of Peter have received from God power in things spiritual but not in things temporal, that they cannot depose monarchs nor absolve subjects from their allegiance. 2. That the decrees of the Council of Constance on the supremacy of a general council are valid. 3. That the papal power must be exercised in France in accordance with custom and former treaties. 4. That in matters of faith the decisions of the pope are binding until altered by the church (presumably in a general council).

Such claims were not pressed to their logical conclusion because pope and king found a common interest in upholding their respective despotisms against mutinous subjects. Outwardly the French church was splendid and powerful; inwardly corrupt and false. Bossuet and Bourdaloue adorned the pulpit with glowing eloquence, and a few saints illuminated the cloister with signal piety. But most of the clergy were ignorant, superstitious and morally unworthy; whereas a few of the higher ecclesiastics were monsters of vice. Such was the notorious Cardinal de Retz, a gay young duellist and Don Juan who, nevertheless, took holy orders. When elected, by family influence, Archbishop of Paris, he confessed, or boasted, that he determined in that office "to do evil intentionally; for this course, though beyond comparison the most criminal in the eyes of God, is doubtless the wisest from a worldly point of view."

Though far more bigoted and cruel than the French clergy, those of Spain were little more rigorous in sexual morals. There, too, the state made some effort to control the church. As elsewhere in Catholic Europe, so in Spain, the masses sank into a frightened apathy of conformity and superstition with little lively faith or moral earnestness.

In Latin countries the most religious men took refuge in mysticism and in works of charity. The best of the men of this type was Saint François de Sales (1567-1622), a Savoyard of good family, well educated at the Collège de Clermont in Paris and at the University of Padua, and later made coadjutor of the Bishop of Geneva. His efforts to convert Beza by offering him money and ecclesiastical preferment showed more zeal than judgment. His pious tracts and stories, inculcating the love of God and moral conduct, enjoyed much popularity. More practical was the work of Saint Vincent de Paul, who erected an asylum for foundlings and interested himself in the unhappy lot of galley-slaves.

Among the vast number of Spanish mystics—it is said

that there are 3000 writers of this school—the most famous were Saint Theresa, Saint John of the Cross, and Luis de León. In their writings one may read the rhapsodical outpourings of love and rapture, which they interpreted as marks of union with the divine, but which modern psychologists reckon as symptoms of hysterical disorders rooted in starved passions and in frayed nerves.

2. JESUIT AND JANSENIST

The defence of the Catholic church, its restoration to power and prosperity, and finally its government, were the work of a remarkable society, animated with the enthusiasm of the fanatic and disciplined with the severity of the soldier. Founded by the Spanish genius Ignatius Loyola, inspired by him with the ideal of conquest for the church, trained to the highest efficiency, and equipped with all the necessary weapons for the contest, the Company of Jesus from the first years after its foundation achieved the most extraordinary successes. With rare insight into the needs of the situation, Loyola had provided a constitution marvellously apt to develop and to use power. No special dress enjoined; fasting and asceticism so moderate as not to impair vigor; a rigorous selection of recruits from men of sound bodies and minds, and usually from men of the higher classes; ample education; an iron discipline; and a despotic concentration of authority in the hands of a single general —all these means made the Jesuits the embodiment of efficiency and of religious militarism.

With extraordinary zeal they addressed themselves to the three tasks of educating youth, of evangelizing the heathen, and of beating back heresy. Nothing is more remarkable than their versatility. They preached to naked savages on the Congo and on the Amazon, and they built churches and painted pictures for the most cultivated peoples of Europe. While some of them explored Asia and the Indies, others wrote libraries of apologetics, history, moral philosophy, and poetry, or labored to reconcile science and religion, for the age of Louis XIV.

But in no field were their combined courage, craft, and organization so victorious as in turning back the Reformation. Naturally the bull canonizing Loyola spoke of him as providentially raised up to combat that "foulest of monsters," Martin Luther! In the nick of time to prevent the defection of France and of the Spanish Netherlands, and to save much of Germany and all of Poland, they intervened and won back a large portion of the lost or imperiled territory. With heroic courage they braved the danger of death in England; with diabolic cunning they intrigued for the advantage of the church in the Holy Roman Empire. By force, when they could wield it, by craft and persuasion when they could not, by boundless zeal at all times, they consolidated and restored Catholicism throughout Europe. In all states subject to the popes they became a great power. Though their numbers were not large—amounting in 1626 to 1574 members in the Spanish Netherlands, 2283 in Germany, 2156 in France, and 2962 in Spain—they sat in the councils of kings and in the seats of authority. No wonder that a President of the Parlement of Paris addressed to them, in 1626, this eulogy:

You are great in the world, my fathers; you rule the larger and better part of the earth; you command the pulpits; you direct consciences; you mould youth as you please; and, what is more, you have the ear of almost all princes!

No wonder that they claimed that their zeal had been seconded by striking miracles! [1]

The self-confidence, not to say self-complacency, of the society reached its climax in the publication of a history of their first hundred years, the famous *Imago Primi Saeculi*, put forth in 1640 by the fathers of the Belgian province. The bulky book draws out an elaborate parallel between the life of Jesus and the life of the Society of Jesus: as Jesus,

[1] Father Fouqueray: *Histoire des Jésuites en France*, iv, 260, still, in 1925, believes in these miracles.

being in the form of God, had humbled himself to be born
in poverty, so Loyola, born a noble, had humbled himself
to mendicancy; as Jesus had waxed in stature and in favor
with God and man, so had the Society; as he had been
persecuted, so had his Company; as he had finally triumphed
in glory, so the Society had won great glory. The style of
the book, partly in rhapsodical prose, partly in lyrical
verse, is one of the most fulsome eulogy, representing the
Jesuits—to quote Antoine Arnauld's jest—"as born with
their cassocks on, pure, perfect, and good as angels."

But this society of pure and perfect young men—there
were few old Jesuits, the *Imago* explains, because they wore
themselves out in labors and dangers for the church—soon
earned the hatred of many Catholics as well as of most
Protestants. As early as 1577 a Dominican called them,
in public sermons, instruments of the devil, secret heretics, hypocrites, and Pharisees, so dangerous that he
crossed himself whenever he met one. Their foe Hasen-
müller's *History of the Jesuits* (1593) brings together a
mass of scandalous stories about them. That celebrated
forgery, the *Secret Counsels of the Jesuits* (*Monita Secreta
S.J.*, 1612) attacks them by revealing what purports to be
their secret instructions for wheedling gifts and legacies
from wealthy women. Paolo Sarpi proclaimed that "the
Jesuits have done all possible to bring about an universal
debauchery in the world." A French Libertine poet of the
early seventeenth century addressed them in a *Tableau
Satyrique* as a

> Société non point de Christ
> Mais bien plutôt de l'Antichrist. . . .
> Tygres cruels, affamez loups,
> Sauterelles, ordes, harpies,
> Du puits de l'abysme sorties,

while the English poet John Donne published an anonymous
pamphlet entitled: *Ignatius his conclave, or his inthroniza-
tion in a late election in hell.* Even from Catholic lands, like
France and Venice, they were expelled for some years,

whereas in Protestant countries it was widely believed that they were at the head of a great conspiracy to subjugate the world. Indeed, the Gunpowder Plot and other treasons were attributed chiefly to their agency; and in the law deposing James II "Jesuits and other wicked persons" were named as the subverters of the British constitution.

Behind all this opposition there was doubtless the envy of rivals and the fear of enemies; but there was something more. There was the widespread and not wholly unfounded belief that the Company was unscrupulous, prepared to sacrifice good faith and morality in the achievement of their ends. They were then widely accused, and are sometimes accused still, of acting on the principle that "the end justifies the means." If that maxim may be interpreted to mean that a pious end sanctifies any means to accomplish it, however criminal they may be, no just ground for imputing it to them can be found. The often quoted saying of Busenbaum, that "when the end is lawful, the means also are lawful," [1] is shown by the context to teach that, in accomplishing a lawful end, some means are, and some means are not, justified. Nevertheless it is true that the Jesuit doctors harbored many dangerous principles and excused many reprehensible practices.

Their works on moral philosophy gave enormous offence to the stricter parties inside and outside the Catholic communion. "No religion that I know of in all the world," said the Anglican Archbishop Tillotson, "ever had such lewd and scandalous casuists. . . . Their main business seems to be, not to keep men from sin, but to teach them how near they might lawfully come, without sinning." [2] Their purpose, however, in relaxing the demands of morality, was the pious one of extending the dominion of the church. Wishing to admit to the fold the largest possible numbers, and unable to make average men saints, they opened the doors of the church wide enough to include those

---

[1] H. Busenbaum: *Medulla theologiae moralis*, lib. 4, cap. 3, dub. 27, art. 2. I quote from the edition of 1654, p. 282.
[2] *The Golden Book of J. Tillotson*, ed. Moffatt, p. 77.

sinners whom more rigorous judges would have excluded. To
do this they perfected, though they did not originate, the
principle of probabilism and the art of casuistry. The work
was begun by the Spanish Dominican Bartholomeo de
Medina, who in a commentary on Aquinas (1577) expounded probabilism as the theory "that if any opinion is
supported by authority, it is lawful to follow it, even if the
opposite opinion is supported by better authority." That is,
for example, if most of the doctors of the church condemn
lying as always wrong, but if one doctor thinks it, in given
circumstances, lawful, the doubter may safely follow the
single authority against the consensus of opposite opinion.
In the application of this theory the Jesuits developed the
art of casuistry, or of deciding the general principles governing special cases. As easily as our writers of problem plays
they were able to show how comprehensible and pardonable,
in special circumstances, any act usually regarded as wrong
may be.

By this method the Jesuit confessors were able to argue
away all the crimes known to the laws of God and man.
"Behold the fathers who have taken away the sins of the
world" was the ironical greeting of their enemies. In their
works one may learn how the bankrupt, without sinning
mortally, may defraud his creditor of his mortgaged goods;
how the servant may be excused for pilfering his master;
how the gay young noble may justly kill his rival in a duel;
how the adulteress may rightfully deny her sin, even on
oath. Especially in two fields the Jesuits made notable contributions to ethical science. They developed the theory of
mental reservation and equivocation to the point where all
truth becomes impossible. In judging sexual sins they were
not only indulgent but so curious that their works are mines
of information about lubricity and perversion. The treatise
De Matrimonio, of the Jesuit Tomás Sanchez of Cordova,
has been called "an Iliad of impurity written at the foot of
the cross." The extreme laxity of their teaching became
unbearable and scandalous to the church, especially after
Pascal had exposed it. Among the sixty-five propositions

condemned by the Holy Office in 1679 were the following: that it is permissible for a son to rejoice in having killed his father; that it is permissible to use equivocation and mental reservation on oath, and to call God to witness a lie; that it is right to kill a calumniator, to steal in case of need, to procure abortion, and to commit adultery under certain circumstances.

It is significant, and highly instructive, to observe that the controversy of the Jesuits with the stricter moralists came to a head over the doctrines of free-will and predestination. As these doctrines played an enormous rôle in contemporary Protestantism, their full significance for the culture of the age can best be discussed in a later section of this chapter. But it is worth emphasizing here that exactly the same battle raged in both the Protestant and in the Catholic church. The party of strict morals, the Puritans and Jansenists, favored the high doctrine of predestination; the Libertines, the humanists, the Jesuits, and the common people argued for free-will.

Since the time of Augustine and Pelagius the controversy had been allowed to slumber until it was revived by Luther. The official doctrine of the church was Augustinian predestinarianism, which was held throughout the Middle Ages and apparently sanctioned by the *Roman Catechism* of 1566. But not in vain had Loyola exhorted his followers never to exalt the power of divine grace so much as to attenuate free-will; when Bajus, a professor at Louvain, issued 79 theses on the bondage of the will, they were promptly condemned in 1567 by a pope acting under Jesuit influence. In 1588 the Spanish Jesuit Luis Molina published his *Harmony of Free Will with Grace, Divine Foreknowledge, Providence, Predestination, and Reprobation*. When this was answered by the Dominican Domingo Bañes, the matter was argued at interminable length at first before the universities, then before the Spanish Inquisition, and finally before the Popes Clement VIII and Paul V.

The controversy was given a new and decisive turn by the intervention of Cornelius Jansen (1585-1638), bishop of

Ypres, a city in the Spanish Netherlands. Having imbibed at Louvain the Augustinianism of Bajus, he watched with intense interest the Synod of Dort (1618-19), and approved the high doctrine of predestination there asserted, though by heretics. Turning to Augustine for further light, he read through the voluminous works of the great doctor ten times, and then wrote his own large treatise entitled: *Augustinus, or, the Doctrine of St. Augustine on the health, sickness, and medicine of human nature.* In this work, which combines a certain Miltonic grandeur of style with a good deal of undigested pedantry, the author undertakes to prove, by a tissue of texts cited from his master, that there are two sorts of men and two sorts of divine grace, one for each. The common kind of grace is that given to man before his fall, and to men generally, sufficient to enable man to do right but not to determine him to do it. As man invariably fails to do good, his reprobation and eternal punishment is just. But there is a second and higher grace, given only to the elect, which not only enables but practically forces a man to do right; these elect are arbitrarily chosen and freely given salvation.

When the book was published in 1640, two years after its author's death, it was taken up by some French Catholic reformers, who were henceforth called Jansenists. They were the Puritans of the Roman Church, with the same high and stern morality, the same consciousness of being the elect, the same doctrine of predestination, the same return to primitive Christianity, the same intensification of theology and piety, as distinguished the English Puritans. So otherworldly and religious was Jansen that he utterly condemned, as abominable concupiscence, not only sensuality (the lust of the flesh) but scientific curiosity (the lust of knowing) and ambition (the lust of power). In this he represented an extreme reached only by a few Puritans. Unknown to themselves, the ethics of Jansenism and Puritanism were the expression of middle-class standards, as opposed to the looser practices of the aristocrat on the one hand and of the proletarian on the other. And Jansenism failed in France while Puritanism conquered in Holland and England, because the French bourgeoisie was weaker than the English. As the Fronde was an abortive brother of the English Commonwealth, so Jansenism was a sickly brother of the Puritan movement. The odds against it were too great in a people bound by political and ecclesiastical absolutism.

But, if it finally failed, it fought a noble fight. Into its bosom it drew many of the choice spirits of the time, Arnauld and Nicole, Pascal and Racine. So much did the battle engage, on the one side or the other, the best spiritual energies of France, that the greatest of literary critics has entitled his chief work "Port Royal."

Port Royal was the name of a convent of Benedictine nuns about eight miles southwest of Versailles. Here, in the early seventeenth century, was started a thorough monastic reform by Mère Angélique, a scion of the famous family of Arnauld. Her chief spiritual adviser, the Abbé de Saint-Cyran, was so much venerated for his sanctity that, on his death in 1643, handkerchiefs were soaked in his blood and his entrails divided as relics among his followers. In early life he had come to know Jansen and to conspire with him for a general reform of the church. Each of them saw in the Society of Jesus the chief instrument of the corruption both of the primitive theology and of the pristine morality of the church.

In 1626 the nuns moved from Port Royal des Champs (as the old convent was henceforth called) to a newly built cloister, also called Port Royal, in Paris. Some years after their removal the old convent became the headquarters of a society of earnest men, clerical and lay, who called themselves "solitaries." There they lived in meditation and prayer, in writing the lives of the hermits whom they imitated, and in intercourse so reserved and formal that, after many years of fellowship, they still called each other "monsieur."

Before Pascal joined them the most famous of the solitaries were some members of the family of Arnauld. Their ancestors had been Huguenots and famous lawyers and

their father had lately been in feud with the Jesuits. One of
the brothers of Mère Angélique, Robert Arnauld d'Andilly,
was deep in politics. The recently discovered fact that he
took a pension from that fomenter of ineffective revolutions,
Gaston, Duke of Orléans, partly accounts for the hostility
of the king and of Richelieu to the Jansenist cause. Another
brother, Antoine, commonly called "the great Arnauld,"
published in 1643 an immensely popular book of devotion
under the name of *La Fréquente Communion*. It is the first
appeal to the public by the pietists of Port Royal, a plea
for an inward and earnest religious life.

Momentous to the movement was its passionate espousal,
at this juncture, of the *Augustinus*. In 1642 Pope Urban
VIII condemned in general terms the doctrine of this book;
and eleven years later in the bull *Cum occasione* did it in
much more specific terms, picking out for particular animadversion five propositions containing the following assertions:
1, That certain commands of God are impossible even for a
good man to fulfil; 2, that divine grace is irresistible; 3,
that for meriting reward and punishment in a state of fallen
nature freedom from necessity is not requisite, but only
freedom from compulsion; 4 and 5, that it is semi-Pelagian
heresy to say that man can choose either to resist or to
accept grace, or to say that Christ died for all men and not
for the elect only.

As, both from conviction and from prudence, the Jansenists had always claimed to be loyal sons of the church, this
condemnation of their master apparently left them in the
awkward dilemma either of abandoning their darling doctrine or of repudiating the papal authority. Not for nothing,
however, had the great Arnauld been reared in a family of
lawyers. He soon discovered the famous distinction upon
which henceforth he and his fellows rested their cause and
reconciled loyalty to Jansen with obedience to the Holy See.
The pope was, Arnauld admitted, the highest authority in
matters of faith, infallible in his judgment of dogma. But
in matters of fact he could err, through misinformation, like
any other man, and often had erred in the past. The bull,

Cum occasione, therefore, was to be accepted for the doctrine it contained; the propositions it condemned were heretical. *But* it erred in attributing these propositions to Jansen, whose doctrine it had misinterpreted. This last assertion, though really a quibble, was plausible because the condemned theses were not taken word for word from the *Augustinus*, but were mere summaries of what was alleged to be his doctrine.

The question of fact was then appealed to the Sorbonne, which decided that the heretical propositions truly represented Jansen's opinions. Not only was Arnauld condemned, but the thesis he advanced, that the church could err in matters of fact, was denounced as destructive to her infallibility. And there, perhaps, the cause would have rested in a permanent Jansenist defeat, had it not been appealed to the general public in a series of powerful letters, published under the pseudonym of Louis de Montalte, but really written by Pascal.

This brilliant and famous scientist, having experienced a first conversion to religion in 1646, and a second more serious one late in 1655, and having now come to feel his love of knowledge and his love of glory as horrible bonds keeping him chained to the earth and remote from God, had retired to Port Royal. His restless mind soon found occupation in the battle of his school with the Jesuits and, as soon as Arnauld had been condemned, he began publishing those famous *Letters to a Provincial Friend* which, because of an eloquence equal to that of Bossuet, a wit rivalling that of Molière, and a lucidity of style unsurpassed in French prose, won lasting fame for the author and dealt a fearful blow to his enemies the Jesuits.

Of the eighteen letters only five, the first three and the last two, argue the Jansenist case. The core of the series is a trenchant attack on Jesuit moral philosophy. Having read deeply on the subject, Pascal stripped bare and mercilessly flayed the casuistry, the hypocrisy, the loose ethics and monstrous perversions of piety found in the teachings of his opponents. While they boast in the *Imago primi saeculi* that they are a society of angels, prophesied by Isaiah, with the spirit of eagles and the immortality of phoenixes, they have bent their whole energies, he charged, not on making men good and religious, but in stretching morals and religion to fit the practices of the worst men. By subtle distinctions, Pascal continued, they argue away all concrete sins and make piety easy for the most corrupt. As they palliate every crime, they are finally driven to take the position that nothing is sin except what is done for the sole sake of sinning. If one committed murder merely for the sake of being wicked he would be guilty; but as all murderers have some other motive, of interest, of honor, or of revenge, they are excused by the purity of their intention. Another telling attack is made by Pascal on the Jesuit definition of heresy. If pressed to give authority for their doctrines they will admit that these are not to be found in the Bible, in Aquinas, in the Fathers, in the writings of the popes or in the decrees of councils, and finally fall back on the mere power of numbers. "You must accept our formula," they told Arnauld in effect, "or else you will be a heretic, because we are in the majority and if necessary can bring enough men to win."

The letters gained immediate and wide recognition. Not only theologians but courtiers and ladies of fashion read them. The case was won at the bar of public opinion, if not in the Sorbonne and in the Royal Council. During the battle a strange element of superstition emerged. While the controversy was raging, in March 1656, the Jansenists produced a miracle. A girl with a tumor of the lacrymal gland, declared by the doctors to be incurable, was cured by applying to it a relic kept at Port Royal, a thorn from the crown of Jesus. Pascal himself was much moved by what he regarded as a sign of divine approbation of his cause; the Jesuits, too, accepted the fact of the miracle, but attributed it to the devil.

For some years the tide of battle favored the Jansenist cause. Various assemblies of the French clergy demanded a return to stricter morals. But the Jesuits stood by their guns, justifying their principles by further casuistry. Indeed, in a meeting of the parochial clergy at Paris, when Father L'Amy asked, as a test case, whether a priest, in order to avoid scandal to the church, would be justified in killing a woman who had boasted of being his mistress, the Jesuits present frankly admitted that the opinion that he would be justified must be defended as "probable." An answer equally characteristic of their methods was to get the letters put on the Index and publicly burned at Paris. But these answers did not convince Pascal. "If my letters are condemned at Rome," he wrote, "the thing that I condemn in them is condemned in heaven. Lord Jesus, I appeal to thy tribunal"; and again: "If the Jansenists resemble heretics by reforming morals, the Jesuits resemble them in evil."

The royal government espoused the cause of the Jesuits. Persecution waxed hot. The nuns of Port Royal, "as pure as angels and as proud as devils," were dispersed, and their schools closed. In 1668 the French Jansenist bishops signed a letter of submission to the pope couched in such general terms that it might be ambiguously interpreted. Louis XIV, eager to see harmony in the kingdom, proclaimed, in the next year, "the Peace of the Church." Long before this, Pascal had found rest in the grave. The great Arnauld turned his energies against the growing free-thought of the age, and against the frivolity of the court. "He continues," wrote Mme. de Sévigné in 1671, "to get more saintly and purer as he approaches death. He calls me a pretty pagan, chides me for making an idol of my daughter, and warns me that I am mad not to think of conversion."

Jansenism stirred the French mind as no religious controversy, not even the Reformation, has ever done. All the great writers of the classic age were drawn into the battle on one side or the other. Corneille, the disciple of the Jesuits, argued the cause of free will in his *Œdipe;* Racine, who spent his last years at Port Royal, replied with a history of the movement. The Libertines scoffed at both sides, and eventually profited by the battle in the church. Molière has a sneer for predestination in his *Fourberies de Scapin;* and

La Fontaine wrote a little satirical ballad to the casuist Escobar de Mendoza, thanking him for pointing out the velvet road to paradise.

Among the middle classes Jansenism lingered, as Puritanism lingered long in England, not as a dogma but as a moral tonic. Though smitten by renewed papal thunders, a few congregations of saintly men continued to cherish the ancient tradition. Finally, so many miracles were worked at the tomb of a Jansenist deacon in Paris, that the government closed the cemetery in 1732, and was satirized for its pains by a wit who wrote over the gate:

> De par le roi, défense à Dieu
> De faire miracle en ce lieu.

The Frenchman of the eighteenth century no longer cared who wrote the creeds of his church, if he could write its epigrams.

3. ARMINIAN AND PURITAN

While the Jansenist bore his defeat in quiet heroism, his Protestant counterpart, the Puritan, won striking victories. The Calvinism of the seventeenth century was a second wave of the Reformation, more powerful than the first, reaching its high-water mark about the time of the English Commonwealth, and thereafter ebbing. The different fate of Puritanism and Jansenism is due chiefly to the different economic and political environment of each. But among the forces that made for the Puritan conquest one was its ability to produce extraordinarily able leaders. The men who in Holland defeated and expelled the strongest military power in the world and set up a free Republic, the men who in England sent one king to the block and another into exile and put themselves into power, the men who planted in the American wilderness the seeds of a mighty commonwealth, were among the greatest soldiers and statesmen known to history. And their rising to what seemed their natural place at the top of society illuminated the world with immortal defences of liberty and beautified it with the marvellous art of Rembrandt and with the divine poetry of Milton. But their intense religion and their hostility to carnal pleasure made their rule irksome in their own days and a byword to posterity. Almost everyone, from the time of Ben Jonson to the present, who has aspired to wit and worldliness, has had a jibe for them.

Far be it from the historian to judge them, either to praise or to condemn, on any absolute moral standard. Their religion and their ethics, like those of every other group, were but the natural product of the economic evolution of their age. Protestantism, it must be repeated, was in one aspect but the religion of the rising bourgeois class. As the older privileged orders, clergy and nobility, decayed under the impact of new forces, the class which was able to shoulder its way into the front rank was that of the merchant. Calvinism and capitalism have been allies because Calvinism was but the religion of the bourgeoisie created by the rise of capitalism. The virtues and vices characteristic of Calvinism are the virtues and vices natural to the middle class. Industry, thrift, prudence, economy, restraint of manner, domestic virtue, are necessary to success in an industrial society; they are the virtues chiefly emphasized by Calvinism. Hypocrisy, greed, a narrow-minded and meddlesome hostility to pleasures, to the social graces, and even to art, are the vices most apt to flourish in the same soil.

At the center of Protestant ethics and religion lies the conception of "calling." As the Catholic ideal was to flee the world, so the Protestant ideal was to utilize it for moral growth. The typically godly life was no longer that of the monk, but that of the man diligent and faithful in the business of this world, especially in industry. In place of the old asceticism of pain came the new asceticism of labor. Everyday work was deemed the highest duty of all men, and the one most blessed of God. To make shoes, said Luther, is as spiritual as to pray and preach. George Herbert expressed the same thought in the words:

> A servant with this clause
> Makes drudgery divine;
> Who sweeps a room as to Thy laws
> Makes that and the action fine.

And Puritan books, with such titles as *Navigation Spiritualized, Husbandry Spiritualized, The Religious Weaver,* abounded.

The medieval attitude towards wealth and prosperity was reversed. Poverty was the blessing of the old religion, "apostolic poverty" vowed by every monk and friar. Riches was the blessing of the new, the evident sign of God's approval of work well done. "If God show you," wrote Richard Baxter, "a way in which you may get lawfully more than in another way (without wrong to your soul or any other), if you refuse this, and choose the less gainful way, you cross one of the ways of your calling, and you refuse to be God's steward." The Calvinist started the conception of business as social service. It was the Calvinist who opened all careers not so much to talents as to character. Rugged self-reliance and energy were both cultivated and rewarded in the new ethics.

This conception of a life lived "as ever in the great Taskmaster's eye" explains the Puritan attitude towards the amusements and pleasures of the ordinary man, towards the theater and games and dancing. These were but so many distractions from the real business of life. Above all things the Puritan loved work; his temperament without his creed survives in Bernard Shaw, who declares in *Who's Who* that his favorite diversions are "anything but sport." This is the temperament natural to the man whose work is creative enough to be interesting. Who has ever tasted the powerful wine of absorbing labor without finding that in comparison with it, all other pleasures, except, perhaps, those of love, are flat and insipid? That the Puritans lived a drab and unexciting life is a fable invented by their satirists. Their interests were so much vaster than those of the gentlemen about town that they escaped the notice of the latter altogether. King-baiting is a more exciting sport than bear-

378 RELIGION: CHRISTIAN CHURCHES

baiting; a civil war is the most absorbing of dramas; and subduing a savage continent a more thrilling adventure than the most unrestrained dance.

To those who made a business of pleasure, however, the Puritans who made a pleasure of business were extremely trying. The dramatists, especially, poured endless sarcasm on their scrupulosity. They could not indulge their appetite for roast pig, quoth Ben Jonson, without finding an absurd and hypocritical excuse for it, by alleging that it was done solely to profess their hatred of Judaism. They are the men, said Samuel Butler in *Hudibras,* who

> Compound for sins they are inclined to
> By damning those they have no mind to;
> Still so perverse and opposite
> As if they worshipped God for spite.

But if the Puritan could find moral edification in art or in recreation he was as ready as any one to allow it. Milton attended the theater and wrote a mask; he recommended physical exercises; and he loved music passionately.

Central to the Puritan's theology was the idea of calling in another aspect, in that, namely, of predestination. This doctrine which filled so tremendous a space in the life and literature of the sixteenth and seventeenth century has been often misunderstood as if it were a philosophical theory of determinism. To draw the parallel between the religion which exhibited man as helpless before God and the contemporary science which exhibited man as helpless before natural law is a specious but mistaken analogy. To say that tired civilizations like senile souls are apt to be deterministic, dignifying their fatigue as fatality, is a misreading of the facts; for the most energetic civilizations, as those of early Islam and early Protestantism, have been most predestinarian. With the idea, indeed, that predestination and determinism are the same, it is no wonder that many men have asked, with Morley: "How comes it that the fatalism implied in Calvinistic Protestantism has been the nurse of the most strenuous, energetic, active and independent natures in political history?"

The fact is that the doctrine of predestination bears little resemblance to modern determinism. The Protestant creeds repudiate with the utmost energy of language "the insane Stoical notion that all things happen by necessity, and that man does all things by constraint." [1] Any man, said Luther in defending the bondage of the will, can act as he pleases, milk the cow or not, as he chooses. He can even, added the Augsburg Confession, do acts of specious virtue and attain "a civil righteousness." The point emphasized was that what he did made no difference in his ultimate fate; if he were one of God's elect he might commit murders and adulteries without forfeiting his salvation; if he were not elect he might do the deeds of a Socrates or Regulus without escaping damnation.

In estimating the effect of the doctrine as it appeared to Calvinist eyes, we must remember that these men seldom harbored a doubt that they were the elect, the chosen few. As new men, crowding into the front ranks hitherto occupied by priests of apostolical succession and by nobles and kings of ancient lineage, they needed something to legitimate their pretensions. But what is apostolical ordination compared to the priesthood by the imposition of God's own hands? What ancient patent of nobility can vie with an eternal decree? Proud, exultant, fired with enthusiasm, they went out to break the ranks of their enemies and to tread upon the necks of kings. And so they were always, in their own eyes, a chosen people, an élite, a small remnant called by God from the general condemnation of the major portion of mankind. How small, indeed, were the ranks of the elect was set forth by the French Huguenot Pierre du Moulin, who calculated that only one person out of every one hundred thousand was called to eternal bliss: the rest God was pleased to pass by—that is, to condemn to eternal torment.

There were various schools of Calvinist theology. The "highest" doctrine is that called "supralapsarian" because it

[1] *Formula of Concord*, 1576, art. 2.

teaches that God by an eternal decree before the fall of man
had chosen his saints. The "sublapsarian" theory places the
decree after the fall of Adam, thus leaving a little free-will
to the first man, but involving in original sin all his descendants, except those specially chosen for redemption.

While this dogma of predestination proved highly com-
forting and stimulating to the elect, it excited opposition
amounting at times to fierce hatred among those who either
were not so sure of their own calling, or were more kindly in
their sympathy with the mass of mankind, especially as
among the damned the Calvinists included the good heathen,
most infants, and moral men of all persuasions save the
orthodox. If even Calvin himself had admitted that God's
eternal decree was dreadful, there were not wanting those
who asserted that it made God unjust, the author of sin, and
worse than the devil himself. The humanist found predestination irrational, the ruler and the pastor found it bad for
morals—for who would try to be good if it made no difference?—and the man of tender sympathies spoke of it as
cruel and of Calvin as

> The monster dread who from the poison chalice
> Pours out the drug of hell in unctuous malice
> And makes the gracious God a very fiend.[1]

The attack had begun in the early years of the Reformation and had continued with unabated zest until it developed
into a great theological battle in the Netherlands, the most
Calvinistic and also the most intellectually advanced of
countries. The leader of the new attack was Jacob Arminius
(1560-1609), an acute and learned, but not highly original
thinker. Born in Holland, educated at Basle and at Geneva,
and a traveller in Italy, he became first minister in the Reformed church at Amsterdam and then professor of theology
at Leyden. From the first days of the Reformation the
Dutch Calvinists had been divided into two wings, the Precisians or Puritans, and the Rekkelijken or Latitudinarians.

[1] Vondel (c. 1630) in a poem called "Decretum horribile," quoted in
preface to his *Lucifer*, p. 81.

The latter owed much to Erasmus, whose influence was strong in his native land, and much to Castellio and to Aconzio, early liberals and humanists. While refuting a tract of one of these liberals, Coornhert, Arminius began himself to have doubts about various dogmas, doubts which soon focused their hostile rays on predestination. What bothered him particularly was the thought that this doctrine seemed to make God the author of sin. The divergence of his views from those of the pure Calvinist may seem, to the non-theological eye, rather small. According to him, God decreed to appoint Christ as the Mediator to save all who should believe on him and to give them sufficient grace so to believe. God foreknew, but did not foreordain, who would be saved and who damned. Man had complete free-will before the fall, but now has it only by the assistance of divine grace which is, however, freely given to all who will stretch out their hands to take it. To Arminius' opponents his arguments and corollaries were more shocking than his main theses, for he asserted that Luther and Calvin had been mistaken, that man is justified by good works as well as by faith, that infants who die without sin would be saved, and that virtuous heathens would not be damned but rewarded with a fuller knowledge by which they might be brought to salvation.

Presently the United Provinces were in an uproar. The quarrel soon made plain the political and class divisions on which theological parties then usually rested. The Precisians, or High Calvinists, were the nationalists, advocating a strong centralized government, devoted to the house of Nassau, and committed to continued war with Spain. Their constituency was the merchant class, and their headquarters the commercial metropolis of Amsterdam. Over against them the moderate party, standing for a decentralized, provincial government, headed by the Republican Barneveldt, and desirous of peace with Spain, found its chief support among the old Dutch nobility and among the humanists and Erasmians of Rotterdam, Gouda, and Utrecht. The finer spirits, including Grotius and Barneveldt, were attracted to the

Arminian party, or else, like Vondel, were driven from the Protestant church to take refuge in the Roman communion.

While the controversy was raging Arminius died. An attempt of the States General to force the orthodox creed on his followers induced the Arminians to present to the States the famous Remonstrance of 1610 in which they defined, in five articles, their dissent from the prevalent Calvinism. When in the next years their opponents presented a Counter-Remonstrance defending the orthodox dogma the controversy waxed so hot that civil war was threatened. To avert this calamity the States General summoned a general synod to meet at Dordrecht, or Dort, as it is commonly called in English. The assembly met on November 13, 1618, and sat for six months.

An effort was made to give the synod a quasi-œcumenical authority by summoning theologians not only from the Netherlands but from England, Scotland, parts of Germany, and Switzerland. The membership consisted of 37 Dutch clergymen, 19 Dutch elders, 18 representatives of the States General, and 5 representatives of Dutch universities, in addition to 26 foreign divines. The synod was packed with high Calvinists, only two or three Remonstrants finding their way into the assembly. The leading members of the Remonstrant group, outside the synod, were summoned to its bar, not as equal participants in debate, but as accused heretics to plead their cause.

If the argument was violent, the conclusion was foregone. The synod, after condemning the five articles of the Remonstrants, branded them as introducers of novelties, disturbers of the church, and teachers of false doctrines. When the doctors came to draw up a creed, some differences of opinion became apparent. Their endeavors to get light from their much interested ally, James I of England, failed, for he was able to say only "I have not always been of one mind about it [predestination], but I will bet that my opinion is the best of any." In fact, the doctors promulgated a series of canons somewhat ambiguous as between the supralapsarian and sublapsarian views, asserting in one article that

"God would have done wrong to no one had he willed to leave the whole human race in sin, malediction, and damnation" because all men are tainted with Adam's sin, and in another article declaring that election had been made by God's free choice and good pleasure before the foundation of the world. But all the members were agreed that the test of orthodoxy was the opinion of the majority, whose decrees were considered practically infallible, though not declared to be so.

Nor did the stronger party scruple to enforce their views by the most drastic means. Maurice of Nassau, the political head of the High Calvinists, seized the leading statesmen of the Remonstrant party, put Barneveldt to death, and threw Grotius into prison. Two hundred Remonstrant preachers were removed, seventy retired, and eighty emigrated. On the crest of the wave of triumphant Calvinism a series of Puritanical laws were passed, enforcing the keeping of the sabbath and attacking plays and other amusements. As in England the playwrights retorted; Coster's *Iphigenia* and *Polyxena* scourged the prevalent orthodoxy, and Vondel's *Lucifer* held up the Protestant doctrine of the fall of man to execration, and represented the Dutch Puritans as false and hypocritical.

Time, the great healer, at last salved the wounds left by the conflict. Not only were Arminian preachers allowed gradually to resume their labors, but the Arminian opinion steadily won ground, not only in Holland but in all Protestant countries. Henry More, the Cambridge Platonist, wrote in 1663 that the private opinions of most Anglican divines resembled those of the Remonstrants; and when an English man of the world was asked what the Arminians held, he replied with equal truth and wit that they held all the best benefices in the country.

But this was in the last years of the seventeenth century. Earlier in that century Puritanism bore as full fruit in England as it had borne in the Netherlands. Indeed, its growth, its triumph, and its transformation are the most striking facts in the history of England during the seventeenth century. The Church of England, which had been Lutheran in doctrine under Henry VIII, and Bucerian and Melanchthonian under Edward VI, became strongly Calvinistic under Elizabeth. The confession known as the Lambeth Articles, drawn up by Archbishop Whitgift in 1595, set forth the purest Calvinism, and even Richard Hooker, the chief defendant of the Anglican polity against the Puritan attack, was able to call Calvin the wisest man that the church of God had produced since the age of the apostles. The leader of the Puritans in the Anglican Church during the reign of Elizabeth was Thomas Cartwright who, having studied at Heidelberg and visited Leyden, became professor of divinity at Cambridge. He made it his business to purge the church of the remains of Catholicism, both in ritual and government.

At the same time a strong party of separatists was founded by Robert Browne, the advocate of *Reformation without tarrying for Any*. His first ideas for a separate church were derived from the congregation of the Dutch exiles at Norwich. How much he and his friend Henry Barrow were influenced by the Anabaptists is uncertain. As early as 1567 they began to set up dissenting congregations in London, from which grew the great Independent church.

As elsewhere, so in England, the theological divisions coincided with political divisions, for both were based on the economic interests of different classes. The Puritan, or Parliamentary party, drew its main strength from the commercial classes of London and the Southeast; the Royalist, or Anglican, party from the aristocracy and gentry of the North and West. When battle was joined the Puritans won and established a Commonwealth.

One of the first problems to confront them was that of church government. Three plans were suggested: 1, Erastian, for erecting a Puritan State Church without toleration of Anglicans or of Anabaptists and controlled by Parliamentary lay commissioners; 2, Presbyterian, for a democratic church government by synods and general assemblies; and 3, Congregational, for allowing every church (excluding papists and Unitarians) to determine its own belief and practice. This last was the settlement actually adopted.

In order to reform the doctrine of the ruling church, a great assembly of divines was called at Westminster and sat, with intervals, for six years, from 1643 to 1649. In addition to theologians, some members of both houses of Parliament were given seats. As few Royalist divines were allowed to attend, the whole body was strongly Puritan. Apart from the controversy over the form of church government, the main effort of the Westminster Assembly was directed to make the doctrine, polity, and ritual of the prevailing church more Calvinistic. As in most other church councils, passions ran high and decisions were made by intrigue and force rather than by reason. "Plots and packing worse than those of Trent," sneered Milton; while Selden visited the synod "to see the wild asses fight in the arena, as the ancient Persians used to do." The Calvinistic *Shorter Catechism* promulgated by the divines in 1647 was well known by our grandfathers, though happily forgotten by most of us to-day.

It is, indeed, remarkable that dogma, on which the early Puritans laid so much stress, and which is still often mistaken for the essence of their ethos, should have proved the least durable of their contributions to culture. It was, in fact, like all dogma, but the surface (and hence the most conspicuous part) of a solid body of character. If Calvinism still lingers among the backwaters of civilization, it is not the most valuable or vital heritage of the Puritan. This lies in their contributions to civil liberty and to fair letters. England never quite forgot the lesson taught her by the Regicides; America still bears on every charter the stamp of her Pilgrim founders; world literature has been permanently enriched by the works of Puritan writers.

Of these John Milton was by far the greatest. The effort made by some modern critics to de-Puritanize him is born of their dislike of his theology and of their admiration for his poetry. In every line and lineament he was the typical Calvinist; his poems are as truly the monument of his Protestant environment as Vergil's epic is the glorification of ancient Rome, and Dante's *Comedy* the representative of Catholic medievalism.

While his education gave him an imperial command of literature, and a considerable tincture of science and art, it deepened and developed the convictions of an intensely devout nature. Even his early lyrics often glow with ethical, Christian, and Protestant purpose. In the style of the day he was not only Protestant but very polemically so; a school-boy poem of extraordinary power associates the pope and the devil as the arch-conspirators against the truth.

With the usual independence of the age in which every man was his own theologian Milton began to concoct his own body of divinity. Amid the turmoils of the Commonwealth he found time to write a long treatise on *Christian Doctrine,* which was not, however, published until nearly two centuries later. It is interesting as showing his full concurrence in the chief articles of Calvinistic Christianity, the extent of his reading, not only in the Rabbins and the Fathers and the Reformers, but in the writings of many minor sects, and the independence and eclecticism of his judgment on all but the chief articles of faith. To the very limits of orthodoxy, however, he inclined to pantheism in philosophy, to Arianism in soteriology, to Zwinglianism in theology, to millenarianism in eschatology, to individualism in church government, and to the allowance of polygamy and divorce in ethics. On the great question of predestination he, like so many others, tried to find a way to reconcile God's foreknowledge with free-will in men and in angels. What God wills is fate; some he has elected to peculiar grace; he foreknows the acts and fate of every man; and yet man is, or at least Adam was, free. Arminius Milton knew and rejected; his own language fluctuates between the supralapsarian and sublapsarian positions.[1]

The *Treatise on Christian Doctrine* is now interesting only as casting light on Milton's opinions, and these are

[1] *Cf.* Paradise Lost, ii, 558ff; iii, 102ff; 182ff; v, 236ff; 522ff; vii, 173; ix, 350ff; 1127ff; x, 43ff.

chiefly interesting as illuminating the sublime poems of his last years. *Paradise Lost* treats the very kernel of Calvinism, the fall of man and of the angels. It sings the Great Rebellion in heaven, the defection of Lucifer and his war with God,[1] the triumph of the Messiah, and the casting of the devils into hell. Then come the creation of the world and of man and woman, the temptation of Eve by the devil and of Adam by Eve, and their expulsion from the Garden of Eden. While the cosmology and supernatural machinery of the work is as dead as the cosmology and machinery of Homer or of Dante, the poetry lives eternal. Many critics have regarded it as "the greatest production, or at least the noblest work of genius, in our language," [2] and some have esteemed it "the beautifullest and perfectest poem that ever was writ." [3]

If *Paradise Lost* is the epic of Puritan Doctrine, *Paradise Regained* is the epic of Puritan Ethics. It is notable that Milton selects, in his scheme of man's redemption, not the death on the cross, but the scene of Christ's temptation in the wilderness. In Milton's Christ the Calvinist ideal of vocation, of doing resolutely the work for which one is appointed, is incarnated. Jesus is tempted with pleasure, love, learning, wealth, and fame, and puts them all aside so that he may follow resolutely the mission for which he is sent. Thus it is that the devil is foiled by him, and through him by all the elect and faithful ones.

The last poem, *Samson Agonistes,* is the allegory of the fall of the Puritan Zion in England and of its champion the author. For Samson, blind and captive, is Milton; the (Puritan) Chosen People are oppressed by the (Royalist) Philistines; but in adversity and defeat shines all the brighter the unconquerable mind, the indomitable will.

Second among the Puritan writers, though second at a long distance, was John Bunyan (1628-88). To this poor,

---

[1] During which artillery is invented by the devils—an idea found in Erasmus, *Epistles,* ed. P. S. Allen, ep. 1756, and in Spenser's *Faery Queen,* Bk. i, canto 7, verse 13.

[2] Addison: *Spectator,* no. 321, anno 1711.

[3] Burnet: *History of My own Time,* i, 284; also written 1711.

ignorant, and persecuted plebeian, life and religion bore a very different aspect from what they bore to the aristocratic, cultured, and famous leader of the people. Religion is always stratified by classes; some of its most striking divisions are horizontal rather than perpendicular. And yet it is essentially the same faith that inspired the patrician and the plebeian; only we see the obverse in *Paradise Lost* and the reverse in *Pilgrim's Progress*.

John Bunyan, a man of extremely low estate, belonged, like many of his class in that age, to one of the dissenting sects, but to one saturated in the main ideas of Puritanism. Before he was ten years old his dreams were interrupted and his waking hours burdened with the horrible fear that he was condemned to hell. Though his life was innocent, he reproached himself with using profane language and with ringing the chapel bell and playing tip-cat—a game about as immoral as football. After fighting in the Parliamentary army, his sectarian opinions and unseasonable zeal brought on him persecution at the Restoration. During the twelve years of his longest imprisonment (1660-72) he wrote his autobiography under the title of *Grace Abounding* (1666) showing that he had at last arrived at certainty of his salvation. But his fame chiefly rests on *The Pilgrim's Progress* (1678), the best allegory ever written, and on *The Holy War* (1682), the next best.

Pilgrim's Progress is simply the story of man's journey through life from the City of Destruction to the Celestial City. Its pictures of the Slough of Despond, the House Beautiful, Doubting Castle, the Valley of the Shadow of Death, Vanity Fair, the Delectable Mountains and Beulah Land, and its characters—Worldly Wiseman, Interpreter, Formalist, Talkative, the Man with the Muck-rake, Apollyon, Pope and Pagan, the Giant Despair, and Christian himself—have become household possessions. The Puritan idea of worldly seductions is expressed as nowhere else in the Fair set up by Beelzebub, Apollyon, and Legion,

wherein should be sold all sorts of vanity, and which should last all the year long. Therefore at this fair are all such merchandise sold as houses, lands, trades, places, honors, preferments, titles, countries, kingdoms, pleasures and delights of all sorts, as whores, bawds, wives, husbands, children, masters, servants, lives, blood, bodies, souls, silver, gold, pearls, precious stones, and what not.

What not, indeed? Was there ever another people which regarded not only fornication, pride, and lucre, but houses, lands, wives and children as but so much vanity compared to the solid values of piety and morality?

It is interesting to observe that Milton's epics and Bunyan's stories were written during the reaction against Puritanism that accompanied the Restoration. The most luscious fruits ripen in the frosts of late fall, though they would never have been formed but for the heat of summer. The causes of the fall of the hagiocratic Commonwealth were, like the causes of its rise, economic and political. Puritanism was commercial and republican; Anglicanism was agricultural and royalist. As Cromwell found out, when he tried Parliamentary government, his party was in the minority even when at the height of its power. The masses, like the nobility, were still conservative and easy-going in religion and morals as well as royalist in politics.

According to the common rule that reaction is proportional in violence to action, the swing of the pendulum against Puritanism went very far. The Clarendon Code, a series of laws passed 1661-65, broke the pretensions of the Calvinist party to political supremacy, reduced the quantity and sifted the quality of its religious and moral influence. The work of destruction was carried further by a school of satirists and dramatists who avenged themselves on the saints by bitterly attacking all pretensions to religion and morals as hypocritical.

Finally the equilibrium was re-established. Samuel Pepys, as little of a pietist as any, found that, after eight years of it, "the business of abusing the Puritans begins to grow stale and of no use, they being the people that, at last, will be found wisest." [1] Until now Calvinism has left a deep

[1] Pepys: *Diary*, viii, 92, Sept. 4, 1668.

impress upon the English middle classes, in their sabbath-observance, Bible-reading, prudery, and hostility to pleasure.

In America Puritanism, like democracy, grew and flourished after it had been temporarily defeated in England. The religions of the colonists were imported from Europe, along with the rest of their civilization. In Quebec to the north of the English colonies, and in Latin America to their south, Roman Catholicism was established. The colonies afterwards to become the United States were distinguished by the variety and generally by the intensity of their religions. Many of them were founded as asylums of refuge for persecuted sects. The Dutch Reformed Church continued in New Amsterdam after that settlement had been conquered by the English and renamed New York. Lutheranism came to the Middle Colonies with German and Swedish settlers. Anglicanism was established in Virginia; Catholicism was for a time the religion of Maryland; the Quakers founded Pennsylvania and soon welcomed to their bosom some of the small German sects. But the New England colonies were Puritan and Congregationalist. Three centuries after their first ancestors landed in North America, the people of the United States remain strongly religious, sectarian, and to a considerable extent Puritan.

For the spirit of New England has leavened the whole lump. In New, even more than in Old England, Calvinism found a congenial home. Piety, devotion to duty, hostility to frivolous diversion, a middle-class, democratic, and commercial ethics, flourished in the simple society of Massachusetts. Magnanimity and resolution stamped the character of the Puritan in the New World as in the Old. When the faint-hearted flinched before the hardships and dangers of planting the first colony in New England, William Bradford, the first Governor, replied, "that all great and honorable actions are accompanied with great difficulties, and must be enterprised and overcome with answerable courage."

A certain narrowness, a consciousness of divine guidance

in the smallest as well as in the largest matters, a slight tincture of superstition, qualified the wisdom and magnanimity of the New England Zion. Theology was the main interest, theocracy the natural government, of the chosen people. Calvinism was maintained according to the findings of the Synod of Dort, whose debates were eagerly followed by the Pilgrims during their sojourn in Holland. Antinomianism, the child of Luther's justification by faith only, but a child outdoing its parent in decrying good works, was sternly suppressed when it appeared, as it early did, in Massachusetts. But with all their limitations, the Puritans in the New as in the Old England were a great-souled society; next to their stern religion and to their fierce love of political liberty, nothing is more remarkable than the eagerness with which they cultivated learning.

Though New England, early conscious of her own independence of mind, never shared in the reaction against Puritanism that followed the Restoration in Britain, yet she saw a slight relaxation of the extreme rigor of the first generation about 1662. The establishment of the "Half-way Covenant" in that year, making it easier to "join the church," and dispensing with the necessity for a vivid personal experience of conversion, marks the beginning of the weakening of the theocracy and of the decline of interest in religion which was eventually to secularize even the American Zion.

4. QUAKER, SOCINIAN, AND LUTHERAN

In addition to the great national churches, Lutheran, Calvinist, and Anglican, there sprang up an enormous number of sects, or free churches. The tendency of Protestantism to split up into small groups is easily explicable by the element of individualism contained in it. When once an appeal from authority to private judgment has been made, there is no logical stopping-place until every man is his own doctor of divinity. In 1650 Thomas Edwards enumerated 180 sects, and doubtless there were, all told, many more. Almost all of them were as opinionated, intolerant, dogmatic, and bibliolatrous as were the established churches. The Unitarian and the Quaker were, at this period, almost as supernaturalistic and as anti-rational as were the Lutheran and the Catholic. The old epigram stating that Luther took the roof off the church, Calvin tore down the walls, and Socinus blew up the foundations,[1] is true only in the sense that one dogma after another was abandoned in the evolution of dissent.

Though all started from the same Bible, they deduced from it the most extraordinary variety of doctrines. Some of these doctrines were pure lunacy, as were those of a moonstruck person named Serles, tried for heresy in 1543 for asserting that the Virgin Mary was the moon and Christ the man in the moon, and that "as the moon was full at fourteen days, even so Mary was fully conceived with Christ when she was fourteen years old; also, that if one had looked in Mary when she was fully conceived with Christ, he should have perceived him in his mother's womb with a bush of thorns on his back."[2] From this extreme absurdity to the intelligible dogmas of other heresiarchs there is every variety and vagary of faith and ethics. Some took figuratively in the Bible what others took literally, and applied literally what others applied figuratively. Some were ascetic, some licentious, and many polygamous. A few were highly speculative and philosophical; most were hysterical, revivalistic, ranting, and "enthusiastic" in the older etymological import of that word, which literally means "filled with God."

Though the political tenets of the various sects varied as much as did their theological dogmas, many of them were communistic, and many actively revolutionary. For, religion was stratified by classes in that age even more than it is now. The sects everywhere appealed chiefly to the lowest classes. The proletariat was as characteristically Anabaptist, or

---

[1] Magna ruit Babylon: destruxit tecta Lutherus,
   Moenia Calvinus, sed fundamenta Socinus.
[2] *Letters and Papers of Henry VIII*, 1543, vol. 18, Part 2, p. 546.

Quaker, or Familist, as the middle class was Puritan and the upper class orthodox and established. The history of the sectarians is one of martyrdom and persecution. The work of the faggot and the fetter was supplemented by a campaign of ridicule, always a weapon ready to the hand of the rich and fashionable against the simple and uncouth. Not only the theology but the fair literature of the age swarms with sneers and satire directed against them. Jonson and Molière [1] brought them on the stage; Samuel Butler pilloried them in flowing verse. The most elaborate caricature is found in Dryden's *The Hind and the Panther*, in which we meet the Roman Catholic hind, the Anglican panther, the Independent bear, the Quaker hare, the Baptist boar, the Socinian fox, the Presbyterian wolf, and the atheist ape.

It would be unprofitable in a chronicle of culture to pursue the history of the Baptists, the Mennonites, the Collegiants, the Labadists, the Nicolaitans or Family of Love, the Diggers, the Seekers, and the numerous other sects which created small eddies in the stream of civilization. But one or two of the more important bodies must be briefly characterized.

The Quakers may represent the mystic wing of Puritanism, the spirit of which they in part intensified, in part modified. Their fortune was long imperilled, but ultimately assured, by their espousal of pacifism, or non-resistance to evil. They cultivated mysticism and the "inner light." As much as any Puritan they set their faces against luxury, ceremony, amusement, and pleasure.

Their founder, George Fox (1624-91), was a man of pure morals and great courage, combined with a perverse temper, eccentric habits, and a slightly disordered intellect. His journal, written in rhapsodical but ungrammatical English, reveals his self-assurance, his earnestness, his superstition. "He was as stiff as a tree and as pure as a bell" testified his jailers; but his stiffness was often as to absurdities, and his

---

[1] Ben Jonson: *Epicoene*, III, ii, 15, and *News from the New World discovered in the Moon*, p. 243f; Molière: *Le Bourgeois Gentilhomme*, IV, scene 11.

purity was directed against sports, plays, May-games, against idolatry as shown by saying "March" and "Monday" instead of Third Month and Second Day, and against "hat-honor," or removing the hat and bowing as marks of courtesy. Removing the hat, God had revealed to him, was an honor invented by man in the Fall of Adam, and condemned by the example of Shadrach, Meshach, and Abednego, who kept their hats on in the presence of Nebuchadnezzar (Daniel iii, 16). Fox believed that he sometimes worked miraculous cures, and at times he says, "I felt the seed of God sparkle about me, like innumerable sparks of fire."

After he had preached his gospel in England, Scotland, and America, his followers began a campaign against the churches, which they called "steeple-houses." These pacifists did not hesitate to brand the regular clergy as "serpents, vipers, children of the devil, sons of perdition, dumb dogs, false hirelings, liars, deceivers, ravening wolves, and cursed hypocrites." But they won from Cromwell the testimony that they were the only sect and people whom he could not win with gifts, honors, offices, and places.

Quakerism was fortunate in attracting men of higher gifts than its founder could boast. Robert Barclay and William Penn wrote eloquently and acceptably in defence of their tenets, and the latter founded that great American commonwealth called after his name, in which the Quakers and other persecuted and harmless sects found a refuge, and in which they have spread upon the pages of history a singularly honorable and consistent record.

One of the most bitterly hated and one of the smallest sects, but one which exercised an influence far beyond its own borders, was the Socinian or, as it was also called in the seventeenth century, the Unitarian. The founder, Fausto Sozzini (1539-1604), born at Siena, denied the doctrine of the Trinity, the deity of Christ, and the atonement. He accepted, however, the inspiration of the Scriptures, and the miracles, including the virgin birth of Jesus and his resurrection. The strong church founded by him in Poland, after flourishing for a few decades, succumbed to the powerful attacks of the Jesuits. After that the Socinians were a small and harshly persecuted body, but their writings, published in a large collection at Amsterdam in 1656, influenced many thinkers of other denominations. Many of the leading divines in the later seventeenth century were tinctured with their dogmas.

In the age following the death of Melanchthon less was contributed to the culture of Europe by Lutheranism, throughout Scandinavia and large parts of Germany the established church, than was contributed by some of the smaller free churches, or sects. Even before the Thirty Years War made the whole of Central Europe a desert, a blight seemed to have settled down on the intellectual and spiritual life of Germany. Doubtless the reasons for this are to be found in economic and political conditions more than in religious beliefs which, here as elsewhere, but followed the lead of material forces. In marked contrast to the internationalism of the Catholic church and the republicanism of Calvin's followers, Lutheranism became the handmaid of despotic monarchy. Calvinism idealized the money power by which it lived and conquered; Lutheranism idealized the princely power on which it was dependent.

Deprived of political liberty and unable to develop the great commerce and industry of Holland and Britain, Germany turned to inward speculation. All the force which the Puritan had spent in the practical matters of moral and social regulation went in Germany to dogmatic subtlety. All the extraordinary gifts of the German mind for philosophy and science, as revealed in the nineteenth century, were in this earlier age devoted to the exegesis and defence of subtle theological absurdities, and to ferocious polemics over hair-splitting distinctions. In this barren age of Protestant scholasticism the Bible became a set of proof-texts, and the writings of the Reformers, and especially of Luther, were canonized, and worked into elaborate systems of dogma.

The center of most of the controversies was the doctrine of the real presence in the eucharist. Luther had interpreted the words "This is my body" literally; Zwingli had taken them figuratively. Calvin tried to take a middle position but, as this is really impossible, most of his followers swung to Zwinglianism. In this particular issue Calvinism stood for the more rational view; the Lutheran doctrine of the real presence, commonly though erroneously called "consubstantiation," was based partly on an extreme biblicism, partly on an ultra-supernaturalism, and partly on the very individualism which in other aspects was one of the most modern elements of Luther's religion. For it seemed to him that some point of contact between the soul and God was necessary, and this he found most conveniently in the sacrament of the supper. While rejecting the outward, sensuous miracle of transubstantiation, he retained the inner miracle of faith, by which man, in his sin and weakness, could partake of the divine nurture.

To explain the real presence taxed his own ingenuity and that of his followers. To support an impossible absurdity, a number of doctrines were invented which a modern Lutheran has called "Christological monstrosities." The supposed ubiquity of Christ, his "multipresence," the blending of his natures, divine and human (*communicatio idiomatum*), were invoked to make intelligible an irrational dogma. But in proportion as the doctrine waxed incomprehensible the dispute grew bitter. The Calvinists called the Lutherans "flesh-eaters and corpse-eaters," and their sacrament "a Cyclopean godgobbling" (*Herrgottsfresserei*), and a Thyestean banquet; the Lutherans retorted by branding the Calvinists as Mohammedans, infidels and, still worse, rationalists. Both sides freely prophesied each other's damnation, and exulted in the prospect. The distressing thing about these controversies was that they seemed to absorb almost the whole mental energy of a great and gifted people. No one who has not studied the matter can imagine how numerous and how voluminous were the works of polemic divinity produced in Germany, but some idea of it may be found, by anyone with a taste for the cadaverous haut-gout of confessional war, in the volumes of Janssen, who has filled several hundred pages of his *History of the German People* with specimens of it.

As a reaction against all this was born, in the seventeenth century, the movement known as Pietism. Surfeited with dogmatic subtlety and fiery polemic, many people began to turn to a sort of practical mysticism; for even an unimaginative mysticism is better than a mindless orthodoxy. In the soft and sentimental hymns of Paul Gerhardt and in the *True Christianity* of Johann Arndt are found the first fruits of the new spirit.

But the real founder of Pietism was Philip Jacob Spener (1635-1705), a Lutheran pastor, first at Frankfort-on-the-Main, then at Dresden and finally at Berlin. His *Pia Desideria*, or *Heartfelt Longings for a Reform of the True Evangelical Church which will be pleasing to God* (1675) advocated Bible-study, frequent prayer, an active participation of the laity in religious exercises, devout demeanor, and a strict moral code.

Closely allied to Pietism was the Mysticism in which certain tired souls, among the Protestants as among the Catholics, found an asylum. The most influential of the German mystics of this period was Jakob Böhme (1575-1624) the cobbler of Görlitz. Though not learned he was deeply read in the mystical literature of the time, especially in the works of Paracelsus, Schwenckfeld, and Weigel. His *Aurora* (1612) brought on him the persecution of the Lutheran pastors, and his later writings gave occasion for his banishment. His great message, which reverberated in lands beyond Germany, was that God was all in all; the being in whom man lived "as did the fish in water." To him God was primarily Will, and was named by him the Unground, because he had no cause or "ground" outside himself. The proof of God's existence, and of some of the more specific Christian doctrines, as of that of the Trinity, Böhme held to be revealed by intuition, or instinctive faith, rather than by reason.

CHAPTER XIII

FREE-THOUGHT

1. NATURE AND AMOUNT OF FREE-THOUGHT

Though every age has had its skeptics, one age differs from another in the quantity and in the quality of its free-thought. The modern world has seen, in the last three or four centuries, a marked growth of skepticism and its ever wider diffusion among the educated classes, and has also seen the character of this skepticism change from a mild Deism, not very different in its tenets from Christianity, through various forms of agnosticism and pantheism, to a radical atheism.

Until the eighteenth century not only the masses but the great majority of the educated classes in Western Europe and America were believers. This is certain; but how far free-thought had really spread among the literate public of the later sixteenth and of the seventeenth century is almost impossible to say. True atheism, though not unknown, was probably extremely rare. Many Christian apologists, and some writers of more judicial temper, like Sir Thomas Browne, asserted that genuine atheism had never existed and is, indeed, impossible. The word, however, was applied not only to those who denied the existence of God, but to those who denied his personal or his ethical qualities, to Pantheists, Manicheans, Epicureans, and, in the heat of controversy, to Pelagians, Socinians, and Deists. Other terms, such as "esprits forts," "galants hommes," "rationals" or "rationalists," were coined in the seventeenth century to designate the dissenters from all Christian creeds. The word "libertine" has a curious history. It was first adopted by a quietistic sect arising in the Netherlands about 1530, who were anything but rationalists. But their doctrine of the inner light, analogous to that of the Quakers at a later date, made them assert a liberty from laws prescribed in the canons and Scriptures of the church. Driven from the Netherlands they took refuge in Geneva, where they soon came into conflict with Calvin. Calvin, indeed, first branded them with the stamp of "libertinism" in the modern sense, as if their name were derived "a libertate carnis," in his tract *Against the Furious and Fantastical Sect of the Libertines*. They became the leaders of the latitudinarian or libertarian opposition to Calvin. Finding protection with Margaret of Navarre, their name was adopted by all those in favor of religious liberty, and particularly by a school of French poets. As these men were often of lax morals, and as their enemies accused them of more laxity than they admitted, the name libertine gradually assumed the bad moral connotation it now has. In this chapter it is used only as synonymous with libertarian, or free-thinker.

The word "Deist," destined to so great a future, is first found in an *Instruction Chrétienne* by Pierre Viret, a Genevan Calvinist (1511-71) who coined it to designate Turks, Jews, and those men in Christian countries who believe in God but not in Christ. The neologism was adopted in English by Richard Burton in his *Anatomy of Melancholy* (1621), and began to attain currency in the last years of the Commonweath. Then, says Bishop Burnet, "many republicans began to profess deism. . . . They were for pulling down churches, for discharging the tithes, and for leaving religion free, as they called it, without either encouragement or restraint."

Though deism and atheism are logically direct opposites they are best treated together as being, in that age, both protests against supernatural, or revealed, religion. How far the revolt actually spread, at any given time, is difficult to say. As the open profession of anti-Christian opinions rendered the speaker liable to fearful penalties it was naturally avoided by the prudent. Few books were written, and still fewer published during their authors' lifetime, attacking the prevalent religion. A few brave fanatics like Vanini did this and paid the penalty; a few others, like Bodin, left to posterity manuscripts then reputed impious; but most of the radical dissenters were driven to various adroit artifices to sow the seeds of unbelief while the censors slept. To hint dislike, to hesitate a doubt, to insinuate skepticism was the art of Montaigne; loudly to profess orthodoxy and then to carry dogmas to extremes and thus reduce them to logical absurdities was the still higher art of Hobbes.

But in general we are obliged to write the history of free thought in that age largely from the testimony of its enemies. It is remarkable that so many works of apologetics should have been called forth to defend Christianity from its assailants; in fact, the very men who asserted that atheism never had existed nevertheless felt called upon frequently to refute it. Charges of atheism were freely bandied about, and laments over the growth of godlessness and other forms of "infidelity" were extremely common. But as the word "atheist" was at that time a bugaboo epithet, like "Bolshevist" or "communist" at present, polemics and exhortations against it can not be taken at their face value.

When Mersenne, in a work called *L'Impiété des Déistes* (1623) declared that there were 50,000 atheists in Paris, when Silhon asserted, a little later, that deism was the religion of the well-bred classes, when the Jansenist Nicole lamented (1671) that "the great heresy of the world is no longer Lutheranism or Calvinism, but atheism," one can only say that they immensely exaggerated the amount of "infidelity" existing, or, at least, appearing. Father Garasse in 1625 counted only five atheists in Europe, two Italian and three French. Other observers, however, like Fynes Morison, thought that the Italians had commonly little confidence in immortality.

Charges of widespread godlessness are fairly common in Elizabethan England. "Italianate Englishmen," said Roger Ascham, "are incarnate devils . . . for they first lustily condemn God, then scornfully mock his word, and also spitefully hate and hurt all well wishers thereof. . . . They

count as fables the holy mysteries of religion. They make
Christ and his gospel only serve civil policies." Lyly, in his
Euphues and his Ephebus, says that there were more atheists, more papists, more sects, and more schisms in Oxford
and Cambridge than in all Europe besides. In 1652 Walter
Charleton asserted that "England hath of late produced
and doth foster more swarms of atheistical monsters than
any age and any nation hath been infested withal." Stillingfleet in 1662 admitted that many "now account it a matter
of judgment to disbelieve the Scriptures, and a piece of wit
to dispute themselves out of the possibility of being happy
in another world." Sir George Mackenzie, known from his
persecuting zeal as "the Bloody Mackenzie," in bewilder-
ment asked "why the greatest wits are most frequently the
greatest atheists," and in like tone Glanvill complained
(1665) that it is "now accounted a piece of wit and gallantry
to be an atheist." A little later (1681) Archdeacon Parker
declared that "atheism and irreligion are now as common as
vice and debauchery" and that "plebeians and mechanics
have philosophized themselves into principles of impiety."
Tillotson asserted that "atheism hath invaded our nation
and prevailed to amazement."

Similar testimonies of the prevalence of skepticism in
Germany and the Netherlands abound. What they really
show is, not that it was becoming common, judged by the
standards of a later age, but that there was at first a perceptible, then a growing, and finally a fairly strong current
of unbelief among the more intelligent public. It is profitable
to inquire what were the main causes of this new development. They were mainly three.

2. CAUSES OF THE GROWTH OF RATIONALISM

The first cause was the warfare of the sects. The sight
of several churches mutually anathematizing each other's
dogmas, criminating and recriminating each other, and giving each other the lie, suggested to the puzzled seeker for

truth that possibly all of them were right in their mutual
accusations, though each false in its own claims.

One of the first to notice the effect of confessional wrangling in increasing skepticism was the English wit, Thomas
Nash:

> Another misery of pride it is, [he wrote] when men that have
> good parts and have the name of deep scholars, cannot be content
> to participate one faith with all Christendom but, because they
> will get a name to their vainglory, they will set their self-love
> to study to invent new sects of singularity. . . . Hence atheists
> triumph and rejoice, and talk as profanely of the Bible as of
> *Bevis of Hampton*.[1]

Half a century after this was written Thomas Fuller,[2]
the great divine and church historian, found in diversities
of religion a chief cause of atheism. It was soon noticed that
all sects, in fact all religions, appealed to like authorities
and claimed the same witness of miracle and martyr. "We
receive our religion," said Montaigne, "but according to
fashion. . . . Another country, other testimonies, equal
promises, like menaces, would imprint a contrary religion
in us." Can the same spirit, asked Charron, tell the Catholic
that the books of Maccabees are canonical and the Lutheran
that they are not? The first cause of atheism, said Bacon,
is division in religion. "If there is one main division it addeth
zeal to both sides," he explained, "but many divisions introduce atheism." Amidst a discordant jangle of hostile opinions
many men were driven to conclude, with Selden and Hobbes,
that the only practicable test of religious truth is force.

Some Christians felt the scandal of the sects very keenly.
Attempts at reunion of the churches were common. Apart
from the numerous proposals that this should be secured
by the Protestants re-entering the Roman Church, or that
the Dissenters should reunite with the established church,
there was one notable attempt to find a basis of dogma

---

[1] Thomas Nash: *Pierce Penniless's Supplication to the Devil,* (1592), ed.
J. P. Collier, 1842, p. 19f.

[2] *The Holy and Profane State,* Book II, chap. 6, 1642.

common to all Christians. Jacopo Aconzio, born in Trent, but living much of his life in England, published in 1565 a book called *The Stratagems of Satan,* to show that the divisions of Christians were due to the machinations of the old enemy of them all, and to propose that all should unite on a simple creed of belief in the triune God, in redemption by the blood of Christ, in baptism, in the Decalogue, in the resurrection, and in future rewards and punishments. Though this book enjoyed considerable popularity, going through eight Latin editions, and two French, two English, two German, and one Dutch version within a century, yet its program was never for a moment practicable.

And it was impracticable because the Christians were never able to lay aside their confidence each in his own creed, and their reciprocal animosities. This comes out most clearly in the work on the union of the churches by Arminius, as calm and independent a thinker as the Christianity of that age produced. He saw clearly and regretted keenly the evils of disunion which in the first place cast doubt on all religion and in the second place lead to deadly hate, war, and persecution; he attributed these schisms to Satan, and to man's vanity, blindness and sin. Though he called the sectarian spirit the curse of Christianity, he was able to propose as remedies only prayer, a general council, and mutual forbearance in calling other Christians harsh names. But he himself called the pope the adulterer, the pimp, the destroyer and subverter of the church, the false prophet, the antichrist, and the enemy of God. Nor did his followers submit to the decrees of the synod to which they had appealed.

For purposes of defence against the skepticism aroused by the warfare of the sects, the Catholics were on firmer ground than were the Protestants. One of the favorite charges made by the Romanist apologists against the Reformers, a charge which received its classic form in Bossuet's *Histoire des Variations des Églises Protestantes,* was that they had started the process by which all respect for authority and all belief in ascertainable truth would be exploded.

But the Catholic argument, that truth is one and that the Protestant sects were condemned by their mutual contradictions, finally operated to discredit the Catholics as well, for, to the candid inquirer, Romanism was but another of the hostile Christian parties.[1] And even the progress of unbelief has never availed to amalgamate the various churches.[2] Christian union remained in the state of pious aspiration in which it is found, for example, in a passage in Grimmelshausen's *Simplicissimus* [3] predicting that some day a German hero would arise to unite all states in a universal peace and all Christians in a universal church.

A second factor making for the growth of skepticism, somewhat analogous to the first, is found in the impact upon the mind of Europe made by the new knowledge of other peoples and of other religions. No works were so popular, during the two centuries following the discovery of America, as the tales of travellers describing the marvellous new lands and the strange peoples of the Far East and of the Far West. Some of them told of naked savages living in piety, virtue, and happiness, without priests, Bibles, or creeds. Along with the Noble Savage the Chinese Sage became the great critic of European faiths and morals. In India and in China were found, or imagined, cities more populous than European states, empires more powerful than that of ancient Rome, wealth beyond the dreams of occidental avarice, civilizations more polished than that of Greece, and religions more rational than, and as beneficent as, Christianity.

For the first time since the triumph of Christianity men began to suspect the narrow subjectivity of their own favorite prejudices. The arguments intended to convert the Jews, the refutations of the Koran published in the Middle Ages and in the Age of the Reformation, prove nothing but the passionate hatred of their authors for enemies not even understood. But when every ship brought in new tales of strange religions and outlandish customs, some men, at least,

[1] Burnet: *History of My own Times*, i, 335. (Anno 1660).
[2] *Ibid.* 467.
[3] Book III, Chap. 5.

began to see that their own little church was but a tiny part of a great world. "Is there any opinion so fantastical," asked Montaigne, "or conceit so extravagant, that custom and law have not planted it in some region?" Some nations sanctioned parricide and incest and human sacrifice; others had morals so austere that Christian ethics seemed, even to the Jesuit missionaries, less perfect than the heathen precepts and practices. That in general the Chinese and the savages were more moral than Christians was maintained by some writers. Disturbing, too, was the comparison of the heathen mythology with the Christian. Legends of miracles wrought by heathen sages, of virgins bearing children, of a chronology antedating the biblical by hundreds of thousands or even by millions of years, shook to their foundations the canonized myths of the church. Other inconvenient questions were: how could the remote continents have been peopled with such different races and each furnished with a peculiar flora and fauna after the Flood? How could savages go naked and unashamed after the fall of Adam? How could Indian women bear their children without pain—as it was widely reported they did—after the curse on Eve?

In short, many men began to say, with Spinoza, to the Christian doctors:

You believe that you have found the best of religions taught by the best of men. How do you know that they are really the best of all who have taught, teach, or will teach, other religions? Have you examined all religions, ancient and modern, of our countries, of India, and of all the world beside?

The third cause of the growth of modern skepticism, and the one which, though slowest to get started, proved most powerful in the end, was the rise of the scientific spirit. However much apologists may try to reconcile science and religion, and to prove that they do not and can not compete, the historical fact remains that the two have waged a relentless warfare in which faith has been driven back by knowledge from one fortified line to another, always retreating from a position declared to be vital until it is abandoned for another position now proclaimed as of strategic importance, but destined to be abandoned in its turn.

The hostility of reason and faith, loudly advertised by the Reformers and by the Council of Trent, was then so generally admitted that many proclaimed that a good Christian must rob his understanding of its authority. The judicious Bacon saw that atheism had flourished chiefly in learned times, that theology had been the chief enemy of natural science, that "all access to any species of philosophy, however pure, had been intercepted by the ignorance of divines," and that "science met a nasty and extremely stubborn adversary in excessive superstition and in immoderate religious zeal."

A fearful shock to the accepted Christian faith was given by the promulgation of the Copernican cosmology. Dean Inge, the learned theologian and popular essayist, has recently opined that the church of the twentieth century has not yet digested the Copernican theory; and from the first it was felt to be indigestible. "No attack on Christianity," wrote Jerome Wolf to Tycho Brahe in 1575, "is more dangerous than the theory of the infinite size and depth of the heavens." "Copernicism," wrote the poet Donne, "hath carried earth farther up from the stupid center, nor yet advantaged it, because for the necessity of appearances it hath carried heaven so much higher from it." Dean Wren, the father of Sir Christopher, called the Copernican system "a hellish suspicion." Descartes was attacked for making the universe infinite, which, the theologians declared, "is a theory difficult to reconcile with the prerogatives attributed by religion to man." He defended himself by alleging that he had not said "infinite," but "indefinite," that it honors God to suppose his works very large, that we do not understand all God's works, and that it is no longer reasonable to suppose that all things had been made for man.

Other apologists hastened to meet the attack of science. J. H. Alsted, of Frankfort, published a *Theologia Naturalis* in 1615, directed against "the atheists, epicureans, and sophists . . . who dare oppose science to revelation, reason

to faith, and nature to grace." Mersenne wrote a book entitled *The Truth of the Sciences* (1625) to prove that there
is no discord between science and religion, and can be none,
as both proceed from God. Glanvill, too, took arms against
those "who fancy that the knowledge of nature tends to
irreligion," and proved, to his own satisfaction, the agreement of reason and religion. Thomas Burnet wrote *The
Sacred Theory of the Earth* (Latin 1681, English 1684) to
reconcile the Copernican and the biblical cosmography, and
did it so satisfactorily that some minds, at least, found
pleasure in the thought of the new infinity. Of Burnet John
Evelyn wrote to Samuel Pepys:

> I am infinitely pleased with his thought concerning the universe
> (intellectual and material) in relation to this despicable molehill
> on which we crawl, and keep such a stir about it as if τὸ πάν
> (this *All*) were created for us little vermin. 'T was ever my
> thought since I had the use almost of reason.[1]

Other theologians, however, like Jansen, opined that the
investigation of the secrets of nature was not only unprofitable but wicked, while some pious scientists, like Van Helmont, attacked reason as the chief source of errors and as
inimical to religion. And the libertines, meanwhile, revelled
in the discomfiture of the divines, and even dared to mock
"Saint Augustine, that grand personage who assures us,
though his mind was illuminated by the Holy Ghost, that
in his time the earth was as flat as an oven, and that it
floated in the water like half an orange." Cyrano de
Bergerac, the author of the bold words just quoted, also
exploited, to the disadvantage of religion, the implications
of the Copernican theory.

In no part was the attack more trenchant than in the
application of the scientific method to the understanding of
religion and to the explanation of its phenomena by rational
and natural causes. Religions are like sphinxes, conquering
all who fail to guess their riddle, but falling into the abyss

---

[1] *Private Correspondence of S. Pepys*, 1926, i. 23.

when their enigma is once solved. One of the most important contributions of the Deists of a later age to the sum of knowledge was the erection of a religious science. Faint gropings towards this may be found in Bodin's *Hepta-plomeres,* and in Bacon's essay *Of the Vicissitudes of Things.* But it matured with startling rapidity in the hands of Hobbes, who tried, not unsuccessfully, to explain all religion as an evolution governed by natural laws. Religion first arose, he believed, from four sources: belief in ghosts, devotion to objects of fear, ignorance of secondary causes which led to the assumption of a First Cause, and augury, or the practice of prognosticating the future. There is no difference, Hobbes urged in the same secular and objective spirit, between one religion and another, or between religion and superstition. "Fear of power invisible feigned by the mind or imagined from tales, publicly allowed, is religion; not allowed, superstition." Moreover, Hobbes sketched a natural history of religion, according to the principle that any given religion decays when its beliefs become impossible, or when the insincerity of the priests teaching it becomes apparent, in their lives or actions, to the common people. In his heart an atheist, Hobbes argued against the possibility of miracles and against the doctrine of future rewards and punishments, and treated with supreme contempt those vast volumes of divinity "which fill our libraries and the world with their noise and uproar, but wherefrom the last thing we may expect is conviction." No wonder that the theologians foamed at the mouth as they railed against this method as "atheism, impiety, the destruction of Christianity and the subversion of all religion."

3. DEISM

Few men, however, went as far as Hobbes in the rejection of all piety. Not to end religion but to mend it was the aim of some thinkers who had outgrown the more obviously irrational dogmas of Christianity. Amid all the mutual contradictions of the sects, and in all the variety of differing religions they thought they could discern some elements common to all. Such elements, if found, would have a firmer foundation than had the accretions of positive dogma and elaborate cult based on accidental historical circumstances. This foundation of all religions lies, they held, in the nature of man; hence there is a natural religion and a natural morality to be derived from observation and study of the human mind, just as there are natural laws of astronomy and physics to be derived from study of the stars or of the elements. As science inculcated the lesson of universal law, it seemed reasonable that human nature, as well as inorganic nature, should come under its sway.

The articles of faith commonly thought to be natural and hence universal were: belief in God, belief in immortality, belief in the moral law, and belief in future rewards and punishments for good and for evil deeds respectively. As these ideas were really very widespread, they may well have seemed universal to the first students of comparative religion. Towards the end of the seventeenth century, however, it was discovered, or asserted, that there existed nations without some, or any, of these dogmas; and the question was then hotly debated whether such reports of atheistic savages were credible and how far, if substantiated, they invalidated the general "consent of mankind" hitherto assumed as the universal basis of natural religion.

The idea of a natural religion was a very old one, accepted by the church on the authority of the Bible. Until the promulgation of the Law on Sinai, or at any rate until God's covenant with Noah, mankind, it was held, had lived under an economy of natural piety. Some elements of this primitive faith, it was thought, survived among the heathen, and its fundamental articles could be discovered by the unaided reason. But it had been supplemented and superseded, in the theory of the theologians, by the positive revelations on Sinai and in Palestine. It was in rejecting these later revelations that Deism, as it came to be called, parted company with Christianity. According to the Deist's interpretation of history, the articles of Christian faith and morals either coincide with the articles of natural religion, and hence are superfluous, or sophisticate them with irrational accretions, and hence are superstitious.

The first noteworthy attempt to discover the common basis of all known religions was made by Jean Bodin (1530-96) whose *Colloquy on Secret and Sublime Matters*, commonly called the *Heptaplomeres*, though not printed until long after his death, circulated briskly in manuscript, enjoying a reputation for impiety far beyond its deserts. It is simply a conversation between a Jew, a Mohammedan, a Lutheran, a Zwinglian, a Catholic, an Epicurean, and a Theist about their various faiths, without a decision in favor of any. The obvious lesson, perhaps intended by the author, and sure to be drawn by the reader, was that there is little to choose between so many creeds, that there is something false in each, and something true in what is common to all.

A further step in building up the idea of a natural religion was taken by Campanella. Throbbing in every fiber with the glory of the new Galilean science, fettered and tortured by the Inquisition, he emitted from his dungeon a cry, half of exultation and half of agony, to summon all men to the new religion which he longed to found, and which he had reduced "to scientific truth." His *Atheism Vanquished* (*Atheismus triumphatus*, 1636) is a strange mixture of Catholic orthodoxy, mysticism, and rationalism, the first ingredient supplied by fear of the rack, the second by the author's passionate fervor, and the last by his scientific education. After speaking of the doubts cast on religion by the multiplicity of sects, and the growing suspicion that the church is but a tool of the state to overawe the masses, he advanced the theory that there is a primeval, natural religion, common to all men, though seen at its perfection (he prudently added) in Catholic Christianity. His deepest thought was that this religion is based in the laws of human nature, and that it can be found in every known faith. Among the twelve apostles of his cult he put not only Jesus and Moses, but Mahomet, Jupiter, and Osiris. Not only faith but morals he thought subject to natural law. He believed not only in God but in rewards and punishments in a future life. His *Con-*

quest of Atheism should have been called *Conquering Deism*.

But the "father of Deism" was Edward Herbert (1583-1648), created Baron Herbert of Cherbury in 1629, a man of the world, a diplomat, a Cavalier, a courtier, an original thinker and a poet himself as well as a brother of the greater poet, George Herbert. Free, fearless, and protected by his wealth, position, and title, he spoke openly and frankly what most men had dared only to whisper, and which some, like Campanella, had been forced to utter amid groans of agony. Lord Herbert's education at Oxford had been improved by converse with Grotius, Casaubon, and Gassendi, by versatile action, and by the composition of an amusing autobiography and an excellent life of Henry VIII. But his two great works were his treatise *On Truth as it is distinguished from Revelation, from Probability, from Possibility, and from Falsehood* (1624) and his posthumously published *Religion of the Heathen* (1663).

The former, an epistemological tract, intended to reconcile nature and grace, and to establish truth on a strong foundation, sought to prove, first that there is a truth coeval and coeternal with things, ubiquitous and self-evident, an abstract truth consisting of a sum of particular truths. Secondly, the author argued that this truth is found in the common sense, or innate notions, of mankind. But there are special degrees and kinds of truth, as certainty, probability, possibility, and falsehood. Among the most certain, because most universally accepted, common notions, he classed the belief in God, in man's obligation to worship him, in virtue, and in an immortality of condign bliss or of condign pain.

The second treatise, *On the Religion of the Heathen*, investigated these common notions more fully and empirically *a posteriori* instead of *a priori*. It began by repudiating the idea of the theologians that all men outside of their own little sects would be damned. Rather the author hoped to find means of grace and salvation for all mankind. What he actually found, by an examination of heathen cults, was that each of them contains some good elements and some bad ones. The good elements consist of the articles of faith in

God, virtue, and immortality; the bad elements, Lord Herbert thought, had been added by the impostures of ambitious or covetous priests. That among the fables invented by lying priestcraft he had in mind not only those of heathen religions is plain from his ironical examination of revelation. This supposed guarantee of truth, he cogently argued, can never have a universal validity, because any particular revelation has, as a matter of fact, proved convincing only to a small proportion of mankind.

In the second half of the seventeenth century the ideas of Lord Herbert received powerful support from several distinct quarters, and from that time they began, in fact, to spread rapidly. Though Spinoza denied that he had written anything to help "the bad cause of the Deists," his idea of a natural religion and a natural moral law was the same as theirs. His pantheism was more radical than theirs, but his passionate conviction that the fundamental articles of faith are those evident to reason, and his attacks on miracles, on revelation, and on the incarnation of Christ, profoundly impressed his more rational contemporaries. Urging that piety does not consist in believing absurdities, and that the light of nature is the truest revelation, he concluded that "the catholic religion, or the divine law proclaimed by the prophets and apostles to all mankind, is nothing else than the religion taught by the light of nature." The eternal validity of the decalogue and of the sermon on the mount, therefore, rests on their reasonableness. The ceremonial laws of the Jews he found human and worthless; while he attacked the fundamental article of Christianity in these words: "To say that God took on the nature of a man is as absurd as to say that a circle took on the nature of a square."

Similar ideas found their ways into the most liberal Christian thought. John Goodwin, the Arminian, after discovering many errors in the Bible, boldly asserted that the true Word of God is that "written in the hearts and consciences of men, before there was any copy of the word in writing."

Even the more conservative divines began to admit that

the true basis of religion is natural, however much revelation may have supplemented and explained it. According to John Tillotson, "all revealed religion does suppose and take for granted the clear and undoubted principles of natural religion."

At the same time philosophers began eagerly to search the accounts of non-Christian religions for notions common to all. Malebranche wrote a *Conversation between a Christian Philosopher and a Chinese Philosopher on the Existence and Nature of God,* to show that both agree in the idea of "a sovereign truth, wisdom, and justice subsisting eternally in matter." The current opinion of the natural religion of savages is brilliantly reflected in Dryden's *Indian Emperor* (1667), where the following conversation takes place between Montezuma, a Christian priest, and an Aztec priest:

Montezuma: In seeking happiness you both agree;
But in the search the paths so different be
That all religions with each other fight,
While only one can lead us in the right.
But till that one hath some more certain mark
Poor humankind must wander in the dark
And suffer pains eternally below
For that which here we cannot come to know.
Christian Priest: That which we worship and which you believe
From nature's common hand we both receive:
All, under various names, adore and love
One Power immense, which ever rules above;
Vice to abhor and virtue to pursue
Is both believed and taught by us and you.

Similar liberal ideas illuminate Dryden's *Religio Laici* (1682). After "submitting his opinions in all reverence to his mother church," the author rejects the idea that all mankind except Jews before Christ and Christians after him have been damned, and goes on to inquire what may be the grounds of the faith of other religions. His final conclusion is that "Deism, or the principles of natural worship, are only the faint or dying flames of the religion revealed to Noah."

The welcome accorded Deism by Christian apologists alternated between half accepting and wholly rejecting its principles. Nathanael Culverwell, the Cambridge Platonist, wrote a book *On the Light of Nature* (1652) to reconcile the mysteries of the gospels to reason; whereas Pascal stated that "Deism is almost as far from Christianity as atheism, its exact opposite."

4. THE WARFARE OF REASON AND RELIGION

Along such lines, then, the battle of the old faith and the new doubt was waged. But to call it a battle, after all, misrepresents it. Modern doubt is a slow growth. In every country we can see the gradual progress of the skeptical spirit, acquiring new forces from unexpected quarters, spreading from field to field, and coloring one mind after another with its own pure and luminous tint. Throughout the late sixteenth and seventeenth centuries in every Western European country north of the Alps and the Pyrenees it gathered strength, but most in France, the country of Montaigne.

For, the mind Michel de Montaigne was both the chemical retort in which the numerous constituent elements of modern doubt first crystallized and the reservoir from which much of it was supplied to the current of modern culture. The scion of one of the families then passing from the bourgeoisie to the nobility, Montaigne was born at his father's château in Périgord and given a remarkably thorough education in the classics and in the law. Living in the troubled period of the religious wars, he saw something of the court and of military service, travelled, and served for many years in various public offices at Bordeaux. In 1570, at the age of thirty-seven, he retired to his ancestral home and spent the leisure of a score of years in reading and in revery, and in writing his incomparable *Essays*.

They are one of the most original, as they are one of the most distinguished and characteristic, of all the literary creations of the modern mind. Even the name, so much exploited since, was invented by their author. Their style, which the author described as "comic and private," is that of desultory, but cultivated, conversation; their substance is delicate, insinuating, radical doubt—not bluntly asserted or acrimoniously argued, but hinted, suggested, administered like a drug in sugar-coated pills. For, the writer never affirmed or denied anything, but merely, as he put it, "juggled for company's sake, treating of idle subjects and frivolous discourses which he believed not at all."

After the fiery stimulants, compounded of brimstone and bigotry, offered by the polemic theologians, the gentle sedative of Montaigne's conversation comes like a draft of nepenthe or the fruit of the lotus. As we listen we can see him sitting in the study in his tower, his beloved books around him and a quiet garden in view of his windows; we can see his eyelashes droop and a subtle smile play upon his lips as he talks, apparently at random, "about that marvellously vain, various, and inconstant subject called man," and chiefly about the man he knew best, himself. So low is his tone, so aimless his choice of subjects, that at first one might think him a fool; but as one listens one is tangled in a cobweb of infinitely fine bonds. Those whose ears had been split by the tempest of the Reformation and the hurricane of religious wars, at first heard nothing; but while they sat with him, his words fell as thick and almost as silently as snowflakes, and left the world transformed into a *tabula rasa* of white doubt.

The sources of his skepticism were the sources of most modern skepticism—the multiplicity of sects and religions, the variety of strange customs, manners, and morals revealed by the new voyages, and the subversive conclusions of the new science. He saw in his boyhood that the Protestants had propounded more doubts than they had resolved, and that "the new fangles of Luther began to shake the foundations of ancient belief" and make men doubtful of all the articles of faith. Our religion, like our dress, is imposed on us by custom. All faiths use the same or similar arguments to support their pretentions. Nor can one see any differences in the morals of the various believers, unless, indeed, those of the Turks and pagans are better than those of the Christians. All sects fight each other with equal fury, except, again, that "there is no hatred so absolute as that which is Christian."

Piously hoping that he has set down nothing repugnant to the prescriptions of the Catholic Church, wherein he was born and out of which he purposes not to die, Montaigne proceeded to demonstrate that God is unknowable, for a man can not grasp more than his hand will hold nor straddle more than the length of his legs. Immortality is uncertain; the chief end of philosophy is to teach men to despise death, and meanwhile to live delicately. "It is as great folly to weep that we shall not exist a hundred years hence as it would be to weep that we had not lived a hundred years ago." Miracles are doubtful; even when they are reported by "that famous man St. Augustine" they are more easily explained by "ignorance, simplicity, malice, credulity, or imposture" than accepted as true. Prophecies have ceased; one can trust dice more than divinations.

Morals are as various and uncertain as creeds. The custom of one country violates all the prejudices and impulses of another. The Greeks burn their dead; the Indians eat them; the modern Europeans bury them; each people is equally shocked by the habit of the others. Some nations eat insects; some flesh, some vegetables; in some, one sex goes naked, in some the other, in some both, and in some neither; in some women go to war and bear rule; in some prostitution and even sodomy are sacred.

Nor can Montaigne find a sure hold in philosophy, for there is no opinion so absurd that it may not be found in some metaphysical work. The soul has been placed variously in the blood, the stomach, the eyelids, the brain, and in other parts of the body. Even the Pyrrhonists, who profess to doubt everything, cannot doubt that they doubt. Truth is a near neighbor to falsehood; the senses are deceptive, and the reason fallacious. Probability is as hard to get as certainty. If, in a large company, anyone says anything is impossible, someone else will say that he has seen that very thing. In short: "Is there anything that can be proposed unto you, either to allow or to refute, that cannot be considered as ambiguous or doubtful?"

Science is as uncertain as philosophy. Copernicus, having overthrown the old astronomy, may be in time himself overthrown. Paracelsus contradicts the old doctors only to pass out of fashion himself. Our theories are fantastical follies and dreams; reason is a toy and sport. Those who claim that nature is ruled by firm, perpetual, and immutable laws, which they call natural, refute each other, for they give these laws differently. "The effect of so many different assertions is an entire and perfect abdication of judgment." "Men have tried everything and sounded everything, but have found in this mass of science . . . nothing solid and firm, but all variety."

And in proportion as man is weak, he is vain:

Presumption is our natural and original disease. Man, the most calamitous and frail of all creatures, is yet the proudest of all. . . . This wretched and feeble creature is actually persuaded that the admirable vault of heaven, the eternal light of the torches over his head, the fearful tides of the infinite sea, were established and continued for so many ages just for his convenience and use.

Was there ever a house so thoroughly swept as was the study of Montaigne? His beneficent influence spread widely and flowed deeply through the life of Europe. For, not faith but doubt has liberated and humanized the modern world. The force which has blunted the sword of the crusader and thrown the rack of the inquisitor on the scrap-heap, which has dissipated the mists of superstition and broken the spell of outworn hocus-pocus has been the spirit of Montaigne.

Impossible to follow all its ramifications here. Pierre Charron (1541-1603) tinctured two works intended to defend religion with so much of Montaigne's skepticism that he was accused of attacking the faith. In one chapter, meaning to show that religion is no more uncertain than philosophy, he reduced them both to dubiety; in another, on the diversity of religions, he again unintentionally exhibited the weak points of what he meant to protect.

During the half-century that followed the publication of the famous *Essays* (1581) there flourished a considerable number of Libertine writers. Typical among them was Jacques de Barreaux, who believed in neither God nor devil, and who mocked the Jesuits and priests. His trial before the Parlement of Paris on the charge of blasphemy, and his banishment in 1625, together with the fearful punishment of death with torture inflicted on Fontainier and Vanini about the same time, put a temporary check on the expression of unchristian opinions. Vanini was the bravest and most outspoken of them all—an Italian atheist who was condemned in 1619 to have his tongue cut out and to be burned at the stake. No martyr ever died more courageously; he went to his dreadful doom boasting that, whereas Jesus had flinched from the cross, he would die like a brave man.

Among the apologists for Christianity Philippe de Mornay, Descartes, and Mersenne deserve mention, and Pascal and Bossuet brief notices.

Of them all the most interesting is Pascal, for he alone felt poignantly the antagonism of the new science and the old faith. Though there is nothing necessarily depressing in atheism or in agnosticism—creeds which have been held by many men with complacency and by some with all the exaltation of religious fervor—the conflict of faiths in a certain type of mind sometimes produces the bitterest pain. So it was with Pascal. No man of his age was more intensely religious in his nature and early convictions; no man was better able to feel the impact, on these convictions, of the new world-view. After he had read much science and philosophy and contributed notably to both, after he had devoted his great talents to purging the church of Jesuitry, he looked about for another task and found it in defending Christianity from the rising tide of indifference and atheism. This task he never brought to a conclusion, but the fragmentary material collected for the work, published after his death under the title *Thoughts* (*Pensées*) attained a singular

and various fame. They contain, indeed, the record of a
struggle between belief and doubt unsurpassed in tragic
grandeur in the annals of the human heart. The author had
read and accepted Copernicus, and had seen him condemned;
he had sounded the abysses of the universe and found them
empty; he had learned from Montaigne that all things are
doubtful; and from Descartes proof of the existence of
God only that God had been thrust, after creation, outside
the universe. Listen to this agonized cry:

This is what I see that troubles me. I look on all sides and I
find everywhere nothing but obscurity. Nature offers nothing
which is not a subject of doubt and disquietude; if I saw nowhere
any sign of a Deity I should decide in the negative; if I saw
everywhere the signs of a Creator, I should rest in peace in my
faith; but, seeing too much to deny and too little confidently to
affirm, I am in a pitiable state, and I have longed a hundred times
that, if a God sustained nature, nature should show it without
ambiguity, or that, if the signs of a God are fallacious, nature
should suppress them altogether. Let her say the whole truth or
nothing, so that I may see what side I ought to take.

Or to this:

Let man, then, contemplate the whole of nature in her lofty
and full majesty, let him extend his view above the low objects
which surround him. Let him consider this shining sun, set like
an eternal lamp to lighten the universe, until the earth appears
to him like a point in comparison with the vast circuit described
by that star, and then let him marvel that this vast orbit itself
is only a very small point compared to the circle of the stars in
the surrounding firmament. But if our sight stops at that point,
let our imagination pass beyond; she will weary of conceiving
before nature will weary of giving. All this visible world is but
an imperceptible line in the bosom of nature. . . . Nature is an
infinite sphere of which the center is everywhere and the circumference nowhere. But to present to man another prodigy just as
astonishing, let him search in the tiniest things he knows. A mite
offers him in its little body parts incomparably smaller, limbs with
joints, veins in these joints, blood in these veins, humors in this
blood, drops in these humors, vapors in these drops; finally let

him, dividing again these last things, exhaust his powers of imagination, and let the last object at which he arrives be that of our
present discourse. Perhaps he will think this the extreme of smallness in nature. I wish to make him see in this a new abyss. I wish
to depict for him not only the visible universe, but the immensity
which one can conceive in nature, all bounded by this epitome
of an atom. Let him see there an infinity of universes, of which
each one has its firmament, its planets, its earth, in the same
proportion as the visible world; in this earth animals and even
mites, in which he will find all that the mites he knows have,
and so on without end and without pause. Let him then lose himself in these marvels as astonishing in their smallness as the others
by their extent. . . . Thus he is suspended in nature between
two abysses of the infinite and the nothing. . . . Thus also we see
the sciences infinite in the extent of their researches, for who
doubts that geometry, for example, has an infinite number of
propositions?

And in these immensities how terrible is the condition of
man!

Imagine a number of men in chains, all condemned to death.
Every day some of them are put to death in sight of the others;
those who remain alive see their own condition in the fate of
their comrades, and, looking at each other with grief and without
hope, await their turn. This is a parable of the actual condition
of humanity.

The thoughtful mind cannot avoid framing some hypothesis, for even "to mock philosophy is really a philosophy,"
and yet he can never hope to attain truth, for, continued
Pascal:

Correctness and truth are points so fine that our instruments
are too blunt to touch them exactly. If the instruments get to the
point, they hide it and cover likewise the adjacent space, thus
resting more on the false than on the true.

Failing to find any support for faith in reason Pascal is
thrown back on two arguments both of which have become
famous. The first is that

The heart has its reasons which the reason does not know; we feel this in a thousand things. It is the heart that feels God, not the reason; and this is the essence of faith, that God is known to the heart and not to the reason.

The second argument is the celebrated wager. Pascal was familiar with the calculus of probability, and with the principle that a small chance of winning can be compensated by heavy odds in the stakes. Now, argued our Jansenist, faith in God is after all a great wager, in which the odds are so heavy that it would pay one to bet on his existence, even if the chances were greatly against it. For in case the Christian faith and promises are true we shall either gain or lose an eternity of bliss or of torment by accepting it; in case it is false we shall lose nothing more than this brief life by staking our fortunes upon it. Truly such a wager reveals a faith born of despair, a will to believe driven to its last ditch to make a stand against the assaults of doubt!

Nor was Pascal the only one to read aright the signs of the times. Behind the bigotry and cruelty of Bossuet lurked a great dread, the fear of progress and change, of the nascent spirit of the Enlightenment. He hated those who were

denying the work of creation and that of redemption, annihilating hell, abolishing immortality, stripping Christianity of all its mysteries and changing it into a philosophical sect agreeable to sense, by which all religions are made the same, the foundation of faith attacked, Scripture directly assailed, and the path opened to Deism, which is disguised Atheism.

In the Netherlands as in France the war between freethought and faith was waged. Here the Erasmian influence made for liberalism. The chief of Erasmus's followers, and "the prince of the libertines" was Dirck Volckertszoon Coornhert (1522-90), a versatile man of business and of letters, after 1572 promoted to the high office of Secretary to the Estates of Holland. In emphasizing the religion of the spirit, and tolerance, and in rejecting the dogma of predestination, he formed the connecting link between Erasmus and the Dutch Deists and Arminians. Hugo Grotius, too, worked in the Erasmian spirit to heal the differences between the churches, and wrote a short work *On the Truth of the Christian Religion,* intended to furnish arms to the Dutch navigators in their efforts to convert the heathen of the East Indies to the true faith.

The immense services of Spinoza in liberalizing religion have already been noticed. Though, by his caution and perhaps also by his early death, he escaped the hands of the law, his disciple and perhaps his friend, Adriaan Koerbagh, incurred persecution by publishing sundry skeptical opinions in a dictionary named *The Flower Garden (Bloemhof,* 1668). In some of his definitions he showed plainly that he believed neither in the Bible, nor in the deity of Christ, nor in magic, nor in angels, nor in devils.

Of the many signs of skepticism in the England of Elizabeth and of the Stuarts and of the Commonwealth only a few can be noticed here. The secular tone of the drama, the numerous charges of atheism, the frequent works of apology against free-thought, and the occasional punishment of those who denied the fundamental articles of religion, all show that there was, under the surface, a considerable current of unbelief.

And the same impression is given by a close study of the works of some men professing conformity. Bacon's lip service to the established creed, and his occasional arguments that Christian mysteries contrary to reason must be accepted on faith, scarcely veil the bold outlines of a rational mind. His much quoted saying that "a little philosophy inclineth man's mind to atheism, but depth of philosophy bringeth man's mind about to religion," sincerely expresses his theism, but still allows him to argue that too little belief is better than too much:

Atheism leaves a man to sense, to philosophy, to natural piety, to laws, to reputation, all which may be guides to an outward moral virtue, though religion were not; but superstition dismounts all these and exacteth an absolute monarchy in the minds of men.

Therefore atheism did never perturb the state . . . and we see the times inclined to atheism (as the time of Augustus Caesar) were civil times. But superstition hath been the confusion of many states.

Of all English writers the one nearest to Montaigne in spirit is Sir Thomas Browne. Though his *Religio Medici* (1642) professed to defend the author and his fellow practioners of medicine from the charge of irreligion commonly brought against them, yet he suggested so many doubts in the articles of faith, pointed out so many absurdities in the Bible, exhibited so many contradictions of the sects, and asserted so positively his right to an eclectic creed, taking what he chose, and leaving what he chose, that his thought must have unsettled many simple souls.

If Browne is a second-rate Montaigne, Henry More is an inferior Pascal. For he, too, and the group of "Cambridge Platonists" to which he belonged, felt the agonizing conflict of science and religion, of philosophy and faith. He often repeated the lines from Claudian expressing doubt whether the universe were ruled by a great governor, or whether all things went by chance. At one time a devoted disciple of Descartes, he later turned against him. He and his friends, became Platonists or, rather, Plotinists, for it was the late Neo-Platonists they admired, rather than their master. Like Pascal, More turned his arms against enemies on both the right and the left. His *Enthusiasm Vanquished* (*Enthusiasmus Triumphatus*, 1659) assailed contemporary prophetism, and his *Antidote against Atheism* (1652) attacked the growing skepticism.

The preface of the latter noted that "a loosening of the minds of men from the awe and tyranny of mere accustomary superstition . . . and a freer perusal of religion than in former ages," has carried many men from one extreme to the other. The two noteworthy features of his argument are, first, that he buttressed it with reasons drawn from the latest discoveries of science, as that the air-pump proves that there is a substance distinct from matter in the world, and, secondly, that he mingles it with a defence of the reality of the devil, witchcraft, and ghosts.

Another member of the same group, George Rust, later Bishop of Dromore, published an apology under the title *A Discourse on Truth* (1655), making many admissions damaging to his cause. For he argued, with an insight far in advance of his age, that truth is purely subjective:

Truth is a various and uncertain thing and changes with the air and climate—'tis Mahomet at Constantinople, the pope at Rome, Luther at Wittenberg, Calvin at Geneva, Arminius at Oldwater, Socinus at Cracow. [In short it is] a state mould committed to the keeping of some party that is in greatest favor, whereinto all opinions are cast . . . a piece of education, interest, humor, fancy and temper, an inveterate prejudice that is bred in our minds . . . an opinion first taken up and then reason sought out to maintain it.

CHAPTER XIV

SUPERSTITION

I. MYTHOLOGY

It may seem one of the most inexplicable paradoxes of history that the first great age of modern science should have been, at the same time, the darkest century of superstition. Not only among the ignorant masses, but throughout the cultivated classes generally, at the polished courts of Versailles and of St. James, in the pulpit and in the universities, in the very academies of science themselves, the germs of old superstitions not only lingered on, but flourished and produced epidemics of credulity and cruelty without a parallel in the history of the world. But a close examination will make the causes of this phenomenon plain. The first beginnings of an antiseptic skepticism frightened the maintainers of the old world-view into a passionate assertion of their dogmas by argument and into a fierce persecution of the doubters by force. In the Middle Ages there was little to disturb the quiet reign of superstition; since the Enlightenment there has been little energy left to the old ideas with which to rebel against the rule of reason; but the age of transition from one to the other was an age of conflict and of battle unto the death.

Some parts of the antique mythology seem harmless; some parts, transformed into poetry, seem beautiful. The fairies who then haunted the woods, the goblins who played tricks by the hearths, or turned milk sour in the dairies, or braided the horses' tails in the barns, live on for us as Queen Mab and Titania, as Ariel and Puck. The satyrs and wizards of the *Faery Queen,* the witches' sabbath as portrayed by Tasso, have lost most of their evil by losing

all their grewsome reality. Something of the old enchant-
ment still lies on the forlorn fairy-lands of Europe. In
the silver mists and purple distances of the Scotch Highlands one can still see the Weird Sisters crooning over
their cauldron; under the huge oaks and pines of the Black
Forest one can still catch the flutter of airy garments in
the chequered sunlight falling upon moss and fern; in the
lonely peaks of the Apennines or on the Brocken, one can
still hear, on windy moonlit nights, witches audibly ride
by upon their broomsticks, can see the specters dance in
the cloud-banks, and can feel the presence of the King
of the Willows (*Erlkönig*) and the Bride of the Wind in
the soughing of the leaves.

But the fairies and goblins had already become, in the
age of Shakespeare, creatures of the imagination, useful,
like the pagan deities, for furnishing machinery to plays
and atmosphere to poetry. Alchemy, too, had passed the
zenith of its fame. The alchemist depicted in the paintings
of Teniers or in the dramas of the time is but a poor
imposter playing upon the avarice of his dupes. So far
as faith in the possibility of transmuting metals at all per-
sisted, its votaries tried to give it a scientific explanation.

Even this was increasingly difficult. Bernard Palissy,
the French geologist, in his *Admirable Discourse on the
Nature of Waters and Fountains* (1580), denied the possibility of the transmutation of metals. The witch-hater
Binsfield, in a work designed to stimulate the action of the
law against witchcraft, spoke of alchemy as a foolish, but
innocent, delusion. A devastating attack on the superstition was made, upon the suggestion of an Erasmian *Colloquy*, by Ben Jonson. His comedy, *The Alchemist*, first
acted in 1610 and first printed in 1612, shows Subtle the
alchemist, Face his assistant, and Dol, a prostitute in league
with him, as playing upon the credulity of all sorts of fools.
Among his clients, Dapper the clerk and Drugger the
tobacconist hope to mend their desperate fortunes; Sir
Epicure Mammon is promised gold with which to indulge
his monstrous lusts; and some Amsterdam Puritans, named

Deacon Ananias and Tribulation Wholesome, seek the aid of magic to advance their political conspiracies. The satire had the truth of caricature. Among the Puritans who sojourned in Holland before sailing as Pilgrims to Plymouth, Jonathan Brewster searched for the grand elixir. Dr. Robert Child, the Remonstrant, born in England and living for a while in Massachusetts, dabbled in both alchemy and science. On the other hand, the "alchemical studies" of John Winthrop, Jr., first Governor of Connecticut, were really chemical rather than superstitious. These facts show that the line of research into natural marvels and investigation of the supernatural was in some places drawn very fine.

Far more lively was the faith in astrology, though this, too, was then abandoned in many quarters, not only by scientists and philosophers but by eminent theologians. But the common belief was that expressed by Tasso that "a comet, with ensanguined hair, doth realms upset and fierce diseases bring," [1] and by Spenser, that "a flying star . . . importunes death and doleful drearyhed." [2] Milton expressed his faith in astrology in *Paradise Lost,* and justified it, in his tract on *Christian Doctrine,* by citing the Star of Bethlehem. At the other extreme of religious opinion the Maréchal de Biron, who professed atheism, believed in astrology. Wallenstein was converted to the superstition by his horoscope cast by Kepler in 1609. The great mathematician Cardan cast horoscopes with perfect confidence, unshaken even by various signal failures and by the animadversions of the law. He proved that the whole career of Luther could be deduced from his horoscope, though he got the date of the heresiarch's birth wrong. He predicted for Edward VI a long and glorious reign a few months before the child's death; and his horoscope of Jesus sent him to the dungeon of the Inquisition. Another famous stargazer, John Dee, enjoyed a high reputation until his discovery that the stars ordained one of his disciples to change wives with him cast some doubts upon his good faith.

[1] *Jerusalem Delivered,* canto VII, verse 52.
[2] *Faery Queen,* Book i, canto I, verse 16.

When the progress of astronomy and particularly Tycho Brahe's investigations of comets had rendered the astrological superstition difficult of belief on the old grounds, there came forth, as there always do in similar cases, men who professed to find new reasons for the old faith, or who held simultaneously the double, and really self-contradictory, thesis that the conjunctions of the planets and the appearance of meteors were *both* natural and supernatural, governed by immutable laws and yet particular warnings of God's wrath. Giovanni Baptista della Porta, who refuted what he regarded as the demonic and supernatural elements of judicial astrology in his tract *On the Physiognomy of the Heavens,* and who mocked the same superstition in his comedy *The Astrologer,* nevertheless held firmly to the belief that the stars exercise a natural and ascertainable influence on human history. Campanella advanced the same thesis in his work on *Astrology,* "in which," he says, "it is treated as a natural science and freed from all superstition," and he devoted the last pages of his *City of the Sun* to predictions of future events on the basis of astrological calculations.

The most eminent champion of this view, though a champion troubled by many doubts and scruples, was Kepler. In the writing of almanacs, with predictions of events for the coming year, he found his surest means of making money, and at times he seems to have half excused, half accused, his practice in this regard as when he said that "as every animal had been given by nature some means of getting a living, so the astronomer had been furnished with astrology in order to enable him to live." Indeed, he added, as God often turns base purposes to good ends, as when he sanctifies concupiscence in matrimony, so he has made the curiosity of those who study the stars with superstitious purposes turn to the benefit of true science. And finally, he argued, there is real reason to believe in astral influences on human characters and events; the phases of the moon recur in the same period as does woman's menstruation; beer turns sour more readily under certain conjunctions of the planets. In fact, he concluded, there is such a natural correspondence between the macrocosm and the microcosm that those who reject all star-gazing as superstitious throw out the baby with the bath. In his own almanacs he carefully confined his prognostications to forecasts of the weather and to a few vague predictions about epidemics and politics.

Throughout the seventeenth century cultivated opinion was much divided and perplexed. A debate in Germany in 1609 revealed that one party held all astrology superstitious, and that the other party denounced such skeptics as "blasphemers, fools, contradictors of the truth, ignoramuses, cyclopes, mockers and despisers of God." In 1621 the question was debated at Oxford whether comets foretell changes in the state, and was decided in the affirmative. In 1681 John Evelyn, a man of the ripest culture, wrote:

We have of late had several comets, which, though I believe appear from natural causes, and of themselves operate not, yet I cannot despise them. They may be a warning from God, as they are commonly forerunners of his animadversions.

The same authority elsewhere relates that

that renowned mathematician Mr. Oughtred had strong apprehensions of some extraordinary event to happen the following year [*i.e.* 1656] from the calculation of coincidence with the diluvian period; and added that it might possibly be the conversion of the Jews by our Saviour's visible appearance, or to judge the world.

Increase Mather, a Boston Puritan of cultivated mind, in 1680 preached a sermon called *Heaven's Alarm to the World, wherein is showed that fearful sights and signs in heaven are the presages of great calamities at hand.* About the same time he wrote a treatise on comets to justify his opinion that "notwithstanding their proceeding from natural causes they may be portentous signs of evil events" and that "the great revolutions of the planets come to pass according to the ordinary course of nature, and yet they are wont to be attended with remarkable commotions in this lower world." The interesting feature of the treatise is its erudition. The author had read astronomers like Kepler and many scientific reviews in the *Transactions of the Royal Society,* to which, as well as to the Bible, he turned for guidance.

But, as the mind of most men cannot indefinitely entertain contradictory principles, the scientific world-view finally cast out the vestiges of superstition. That science won the final battle is certain; but she found allies in the laws of some governments and of the Catholic church. As the rulers found prophecies of revolution dangerous, acts against "fond and fantastical prophecies" were passed in England under Edward VI and under Elizabeth, and a much more comprehensive French law of 1628 forbade the insertion in almanacs of all predictions except those relating to the weather, to phases of the moon, and to eclipses, on the rational ground that whatever exceeds these limits is uncertain.

The church, having her own miracles and prophecies to defend, regarded those based on any other authority than her own as pagan or heretical. Hence the Spanish Inquisition in 1582 attacked astrology in its stronghold at the University of Salamanca, condemning it as a science and suppressing its teaching except in so far as it explained the natural influence of the stars on the weather, on disease, on public events, on agriculture, on navigation, and on nativities. While these exceptions might admit almost anything, a stronger position was taken by a higher authority when Pope Sixtus V published, in 1586, a constitution forbidding all methods of foretelling the future as deceptions of the devil, condemning the casting of horoscopes, incantations, divinations, and the casting of lots, and inciting bishops and inquisitors to proceed against persons practising such arts. The warning was reiterated in a bull of 1631 decreeing excommunication, death, and confiscation of goods for astrologers foretelling the death of the pope or of his kinsmen.

Independently of the church the more advanced spirits

of the age had already freed themselves from this superstition. Montaigne proclaimed almanacs lies and dreams deceptive, and condemned the predictions of astrologers, of fortune-tellers and of "the common interpreters of God's plans" as impostures. Bacon's famous essay on *Prophecy* explained the apparent fulfillment of predictions on three grounds: (1) "that men mark when they hit but never mark when they miss," (2) that many predictions are but probable conjectures, and (3) that "almost all of them, being infinite in number, have been impostures by idle and crafty brains merely contrived and feigned after the event passed." Descartes and Gassendi added the weight of their authority against belief in alchemy and in astrology. In fact, in cultivated French circles the body of opinion, after the middle of the century, was enlightened in this respect. While Molière [1] spoke with supreme contempt of those who believed there was any commerce between men and worlds separated from them by enormous distances, La Fontaine [2] proclaimed that in a universe governed by law astrologers and other charlatans are no more worthy of credence.

But even at the polished court of the Sun King there was one superstition tolerated or encouraged for its political value. From the Middle Ages the kings of France and of England had inherited the practice of touching scrofulous persons in order to cure them. When Henri IV was converted to Catholicism one of his first acts was to touch some hundreds of sick persons, the alleged cure of whom settled in many doubtful minds the legitimacy of the monarch. The idolatry of the throne under his son and grandson encouraged the same superstition and invested the ceremonial with a solemn and gorgeous ritual.

Nor did the change of religion in England alter the prevalent belief in the thaumaturgic powers of the throne. Edward VI purged the rite attending the touch of its Catholic elements, but continued to exercise it, as did Elizabeth and the Stuarts. The temporary eclipse of the monarchy in

---

[1] *Les Amants Magnifiques.*
[2] *Fables,* i, 13 (1668): *cf.* also *Fables* vii, 15 (1678).

the seventeenth century brought with it only a temporary eclipse of the superstition, for on the Restoration of the Stuarts the kings again began to touch the sick, and, according to the testimony of physicians and the panegyrics of courtiers, to heal them.

If the state had its own pet quackery, so did the church. At least, there was much in the religion of the time, both Catholic and Protestant, which is now regarded as superstitious. Not to mention the fact that ignorant priests often practised magic, the mass itself had become the center of a lush growth of credulity. Regarded as a fetish, or charm, the host was supposed to cure diseases and to bring good fortune to any enterprise, from a battle to a horse-race. The mass was applied, says a sixteenth-century author, "to soldiers in war, for fair weather and rain, for the plague, pox and such other diseases, for beasts sick of the murrain." [1] Whether the word hocus-pocus, first found in the seventeenth century, is really derived from the consecrating words of the mass "hoc est corpus" is uncertain, but if the etymology be not true, it is marvellously "well found."

The favorite form of Protestant superstition was the belief in special providences, or the theory that every event in public and private life is contrived by God for the warning, help, or edification of his own. Obvious miracles were no longer expected, but all classes and all sects looked for signs and portents. If a criminal was detected and punished, that was God's revenge for murder; if a profane young man fell sick, that was his punishment; if a battle was won by the right side, that testified God's approval; if it was lost, then (as the Massachusetts government wrote) "God spit in our face" to teach us a lesson. The parson's prayers drew down rain, and those of the flock stilled the tempest. God no longer divided the waters as he had done when the Israelites crossed the Red Sea, but he sent a fair wind to waft the Swedish army across the Baltic. Cromwell would

---

[1] *That answer that the Preachers at Basile made &c,* transl. by G. Bancrafte, 1548, preface. On the whole subject see my *Short History of Christian Theophagy,* 1922.

have been surprised had the sun stood still while he completed the rout of Marston Moor, but he wrote that the Lord had covered his retreat from Dunbar by putting a cloud over the moon. On the other side of the conflict, the Dean of Windsor attributed the unseasonable heat of January 1662 to God's anger because the regicides were as yet unpunished.

Particularly striking events were interpreted as portents and warnings from above. Increase Mather collected a large number of *Illustrious Providences* to show how God had made known his will by "such divine judgments" as "tempests, floods, earthquakes, thunders, strange apparitions, ... judgments upon noted sinners, eminent deliverances, and answers of prayer." Governor Bradford believed that an earthquake was a sign of the Lord's displeasure because the Pilgrims proposed to leave Plymouth. Governor Winthrop thought that during the Antinomian controversy, "God himself was pleased to step in with his casting voice, and bring his own vote and suffrage from heaven, by testifying his displeasure against the antinomian opinions and practices" by causing two women of that party to "produce from their wombs as before they had out of their brains, such monstrous births as no chronicle, I think, hardly ever recorded the like."

Nor was God the only author of remarkable events. Much was explained as due to the impertinent, but assiduous, activity of the devil. If the question who was the most important personage in the sixteenth or in the seventeenth century had been left to the suffrages of men then living, there is no doubt that the devil would have won by a large majority. He meets us as the ruined archangel in Milton's epics; as the protagonist in Vondel's play *Lucifer* and in many other plays then written on the fall of man; as the villain in Tasso's poem; as the tempter in the books and dramas on the Faust theme, and in Calderón's drama, *The Wonderful Magician;* and as the adversary in Bunyan and in the sermons of the time. He stirred up wars; he inspired crimes; he instigated the gunpowder plot and the execu-

tion of the king; he took counsel, if we may trust contemporary accounts, with the pope on the one hand and with
Cromwell on the other; he was the cause of most disease
and insanity, as well as of famine and of tempest, nor did
he consider it beneath him to frighten children by appearing to them in various ghastly forms.

To help him he had a vast legion of evil spirits, each
with his own appointed province. According to Milton
Moloch was the demon of hate, Belial of lust, and Mammon
of avarice. The Right Reverend Peter Binsfeld, Bishop-
Coadjutor at Trier, discovered that Lucifer instigated pride,
Mammon avarice, Asmodæus lust, Satan anger, Beelzebub
gluttony, Leviathan envy, and Beelphegor sloth. Other de-
monologists went into more detail, and found a devil, as
the Romans had found a tutelary god, for every petty act
of life. By their preachers the Germans were taught that
there was a curse-devil, a marriage-devil, a hose-devil, a
drink-devil, a hunt-devil, a usury-devil, a lazy-devil, a proud-
devil, a witch-devil, a money-devil, a dance-devil, and finally,
"the devil himself." The colonists in America, both French
and English, Catholic and Protestant, saw in the religion
of the Indians the worship of Satan. With him in person
the missionaries believed they had to struggle. *The Jesuit
Relation* of the mission in Canada ends with a chapter
entitled: "Of the reign of Satan in these countries and of
the divers superstitions there found as first principles and
fundamental laws of the state."

2. THE WITCH HUNT

While other superstitions seemed to decline demonology
grew and gathered strength throughout the sixteenth century until it culminated in the worst epidemic of blind
panic recorded in the history of the world. In all the chronicles of mankind there is no page so black at that recording
the mania of delusion, of horror, and of cruelty which, in
an age of science and of culture, swept over the most
civilized portion of the earth like a dreadful disease. To

irrational manias man is periodically subject because of the high suggestibility to herd opinion planted in the gregarious instinct. Once they are in full swing reason can do little to guide or check them. The few rational men who can still see the nature of their contemporaries' folly are mocked and persecuted, while any fanatical fool adding fuel to the flames of current passion is listened to, rewarded, and followed. But in order to reach the boiling point of herd mania, a particular idea must be fostered in favorable circumstances. In one age a financial speculation or national chauvinism will burst forth in uncontrollable and irrational madness; in another religious or superstitious fear will start the stampede.

The history of the rise and fall of the witch hunt is as clear as day; its causes, its symptoms, its crisis, and its cure are spread large upon the record. Certain elements in the superstition had descended from antiquity; both Hebrew and Roman law dealt with sorcery; both biblical and classical authors told of witches and demoniacs, of empusæ and lemures, of men changed into animals and of sexual intercourse of spirits and of mortals. Above all, the dread of unknown evil contributed to the hold of magic over the primitive mind. If a man wasted away with a mysterious disease, if a storm should do damage, or a blight ruin the crops, the first explanation that suggested itself to the primitive mind was that the evil suffered was the result of some hostile, spiritual force. "Maleficium," or the evil done by magical means, always constituted the burden of the witches' sin.

But the development of the superstition found by the folk-loreist in all primitive times into an elaborate system of demonology was due to the papal inquisitors of the fourteenth and fifteenth centuries, who discovered a new sect of devil-worshipping heretics, as they thought, in the witches, and to the seconding zeal and ingenuity of the schoolmen. A counterpart to the great edifice of theology reared by the divines of the later Middle Ages was the structure of a systematic demonology. Working partly on biblical data, partly with elements of popular superstition, they built up the theory that the devil was the ape of God, who imitated, but reversed and turned to blasphemy and evil, the ritual of divine worship. The diabolic cult was said to be celebrated in lonely places and on certain nights in a meeting called the sabbath, to which the witches were conveyed on broom-sticks or on demons in the form of animals. There they would renounce their baptism, trample on the host, parody the mass, worship the devil with loathsome and blasphemous ceremonies, after which the whole assembly of witches and evil spirits would indulge in wild orgies of lust.

The prime and crucial rite of Satan-worship was the apostacy from the Christian religion in a ceremony supposed to counteract the effect of baptism. The devil was alleged to scratch away the baptismal chrism, leaving on the body of his neophyte an anæsthetic spot recognized by the judges as the "devil's mark." He then rebaptized them, in his own name, or anointed them with a magic ointment composed of various drugs which enabled the converts to fly through the air. Sometimes a compact with the devil was sealed with the witch's blood, as in the tale of Faust. To compensate them for their loss of salvation the devil gave his disciples various supernatural powers of working evil to their fellow men. The witch was able, so the grave doctors taught, to provoke illicit love, to cause barrenness, to blast crops, to raise tempests, and to smite men and animals with disease. That certain persons really professed, either sincerely or fraudulently, to be able to do these things, lent plausibility to the charge of witchcraft in particular cases.

The witch has become a stock character in our fairy tales and in other fiction. English writers usually conceived her as an ancient beldam living in a lonely cottage by the woods, harboring a black cat, or other familiar animal, and gathering herbs by the light of the moon. But the writers of Continental Europe imagined her rather as a fair and wicked young woman. In the annals of the witch trials many of the victims were old crones, but many were wives and mothers in the bloom of womanhood, some were ladies in high station, some were fair and pure young girls, and some were men.

The number of women accused of witchcraft was much larger than the number of men—some contemporary authors guess that ten times as many women were brought to trial as men. The fact that women became witches more often than men was explained by the authors of the celebrated *Witches' Hammer* by alleging that women had less power to resist the wiles of the Evil One, a premise proved by deriving the word "femina" from the words "fides" and "minus," because, they said, *women* had *less faith* than men. Or, as the English divine Thomas Fuller put it,[1] witches are commonly women "because Satan knows that that sex is more liquorish to taste and more careless to swallow his baits" than the other.

Of course this rationalization only covered up the real reasons, which lay partly in the combined fear and contempt in which the female sex was then held, partly in the base passions of the jailers, notaries, and inquisitors. Woman, physically weak but mysteriously enchanting, has always found her defence in her charm and in her wit, and has been dreaded by man as endowed with dangerous power. And the celibates of the church had sublimated their desire for woman and their fear of her almost to madness in denunciation of her fearful attractions.

Along with this fear of women patent in the witch hunt, appears a hideous element of sexual perversion manifesting itself in obscenity and sadism. The profligacy of Martial or Boccaccio does not approach, the prurient gloatings of Escobar and Sanchez hardly equal, the mass of obscenity found in the protocols of the trials for witchcraft. Old women, young wives, maidens, and children of four or five were compelled to confess and describe wild orgies of lust and filthy rites of devil-worship. Nor were the inquisitors and torturers satisfied with listening. The

[1] *The Holy and the Profane State,* 1642, Bk. 5, chap. 3, "The Witch."

witch was stripped and indecently examined to be sure that
she had no charm concealed about her, or to discover the
anæsthetic spot called the devil's mark,—this last was done
by pricking her all over with needles. The hair was shaved
from her armpits and groin to deprive her of lurking-
places for charms. Cases are known in which the witch
was examined by women, but usually she was handled by
coarse men. When tortured she was commonly clothed in
a loose gown, but sometimes only in a pair of small breeches,
and sometimes she was naked. The judges, not ashamed to
record their deeds even in the torture chamber, have told
how women who did not quail before the pain would piti-
fully beg for a garment to protect their modesty.

The mere system of demonology would never have
produced its fearful harvest of madness and cruelty had it
not been supplemented by the efforts of the inquisitors to
stamp out what they regarded as apostasy, a crime worse
than heresy and a crime generally aggravated by murder
and demoniality (sexual intercourse of men and spirits).
Once this theory, together with the acceptance of denunciations of others by accused persons, was established, there
was no end to the hideous process by which, at last, almost
every suspect was convicted and put to death.

Proof was provided by superstitious tests or by confession wrung by torture. One test, not so much used as the
others, was the ordeal of water. This consisted of tying
the witch's thumbs and great toes together and throwing
her into a pond, on the theory that if innocent she would
sink, but that if guilty she would float on the water which,
offended by her renunciation of baptism, would refuse to
receive her. A commoner test was that already mentioned,
the search for "the devil's marks," usually conceived as
callous spots on the body, but sometimes as supernumerary
nipples by which the witch was supposed to suckle her
familiar imps.

But the main reliance of the judges was on confession
extorted by pain. The material of these confessions was
provided by questions put by the judges. These were pro-

vided in set forms, full of suggestions of the current demonology; and this method accounts for the similarity of the
confessions recorded. If the victim's memory failed, under
the stress of pain, she might be prompted or given a respite
to bethink herself.

It is impossible to exaggerate the excruciating nature
of the torments invented by men crueler than fiends—
fanatics and sadists as they were. Torture was then applied
also in other courts, but it was usually limited in amount.
The jurists, however, invented the theory of "excepted
crimes" of such heinous nature that they might be dealt
with by unlimited application of pain. In fact, the jailers
exercised a diabolical ingenuity in inventing modes of inflicting suffering. It is difficult now even to imagine the
torment, though the inquisitors have given us some help
in describing their deeds in detail and the shrieks, groans,
and bellowings of their victims. Some of the instruments
used can still be seen in old museums. The torturers plied
the scourge until the body was lacerated and flayed; they
stretched the limbs on the rack until every joint was loos-
ened; they applied red-hot iron and boiling liquids to every
tender part; they drove needles under the nails or pulled
them out with pincers; they struck the accused's feet in
iron boots and drove wedges between them until marrow
spouted from the crushed bones. One of the favorite tortures
was the strappado, which consisted in fastening the victim's
hands behind her back and raising her by a rope tied to
the hands and letting her hang until the shoulders were
dislocated. Though this torment did not work as quickly
as some of the others, in the end it proved fearfully effective.

In practically all cases the agony did its work. After
more or less of it the victim would confess anything to escape
the unendurable pain. The women bore the torment better
than the men; but at last even the strongest, in hysteria,
or in delirium, or in insanity, would give way. Some died
under the torture, in which case the procedure of the judges
was curious. Sometimes they issued a certificate of inno-
cence, as if that would atone for their murder; otherwise

they would swear that the devil had appeared and flown away with the soul of the witch, or had broken her neck. A few women, gifted with superhuman strength, outlasted the torment. The most famous of those who did so was Rebecca Lemp, of Nördlingen, who, after fifty-three applications of the torture, still refused to confess. At last, in sheer weariness, her judges let her go, after requiring her to sign an oath that she bore no malice and would not try to avenge herself for what they had done to her. In most cases death followed confession, often a painful death, though the pains thereof were lightened to the penitent. At the execution a summary of the witch's confession was read aloud; this process served to keep green the popular superstition, and to furnish new delusions and new accusations to the suggestible among the crowd of witnesses.

Accusations were demanded as a regular part of each victim's confession. Many a woman, who could remember from what she had previously heard of witchcraft, or who could invent from her own imagination the silly nonsense required by the court, who would tell how she had accepted the devil as a paramour, how she had flown through the chimney on a broomstick, how she had raised the last tempest and blighted the last crop, how she had killed a neighbor with an incantation, how she had prostituted one child to the devil and killed another with poison, yet stood aghast at the demand to tell which of her neighbors she had seen at the sabbaths. To name her judges and the rulers of the land was so common a device that it was recognized, by those same judges, as a diabolic trick; to denounce her enemies rarely satisfied the court; often not until the poor woman had named almost everyone she could think of was she freed from the fear of further torture by the sentence of death. As those whom she had named would in their turn be haled before the tribunal, and in their turn forced to confess, the horrible process became an endless chain of denunciation.

The mania would never have reached the height at which we find it in the late sixteenth and early seventeenth

centuries had it not been for other factors in the situation
than the development of demonology by the theologians and
the unlimited use of the torture by the inquisitors. There
can be little doubt that the Reformation, though at first
diverting the stream of attention into other channels, finally
contributed to the superstition. The zeal of the Reformers
heated the spiritual atmosphere, while their bibliolatry continually harped on the demoniacs of the New Testament,
on the witch of Endor, and on the injunction, "Thou shalt
not suffer a witch to live." Still more deleterious was the
influence of religious war, and its accompaniments of famine
and plague, for such make the depressive psychical conditions which predispose men to mental aberration and to
panic. Finally, the progress of liberating skepticism itself, in
its early beginnings, by frightening the obscurantists, drove
them to new exertions to prove and to vindicate their faith.

It is instructive to note that Germany, which suffered the
most from religious war during the seventeenth century, also
suffered the most from the witch hunt. Among the many
books and pamphlets on witchcraft which aroused the populace must be mentioned Fischart's translation of Bodin's
Démonomanie into German under a title meaning: *Concerning the liberated, raging Devil's army of possessed, mad
witches and wizards, spiteful conjurors, soothsayers,
necromancers, poisoners, spell-weavers, traitors, night-birds,
sight-destroyers, and all other kinds of magicians, and their
monstrous deeds: How they can be legally recognized, apprehended, stopped, discovered, investigated, examined by
torture, and punished.* The clergy of both religions threw
themselves eagerly into the holy work of exterminating the
worshippers of Satan, and the lawyers were not much behind them in zeal and learning.

The propaganda of word was followed by appropriate
action. The people of the Archbishopric and Electorate of
Trier, suffering from a series of bad harvests, turned to
extirpate the witches to whom they attributed the failure
of the crops. Wholesale arrests, trials, convictions and executions followed. In the words of a contemporary, "So

far did the madness of the furious populace and of the courts go in the search for booty and blood that at last scarcely anyone was left unsmirched by suspicion of this crime." In a group of little villages belonging to the abbey of St. Maximin near the city of Trier no less than 306 persons were executed during the years 1587-93 for this imaginary crime; in each of two villages only two women were left alive. The country was devastated as by pestilence or war. The most famous of the victims was Dietrich Flade, city judge, dean of the juristic faculty of the university, and privy councillor of the archbishop elector. That he was sacrificed to a conspiracy of his enemies is clear; and the cause of his denunciation seems to have been his hesitation as a judge in the extirpation of witches. At any rate, his death was thenceforth held up as a dreadful warning to those who opposed, or did not warmly second, the witch hunt.

In the bishopric of Würzburg an equally horrible outbreak of the madness swept away nine hundred innocent victims during the years 1623-29. Children of three and four confessed sexual intercourse with devils; boys and girls of nine or ten years old were burnt alive; among the wretched women who perished one was noted as the fairest and purest maiden of the city.

At Bamberg, the seat of another bishopric, during the years 1625-30 more than nine hundred persons were tried for witchcraft, and one bishop put to death no less than six hundred, among them some girls of eight, nine, and ten years old. In the little town of Gerolzhofen 99 witches were burnt in the year 1616 and 88 in the year 1617. At Fulda in the years 1603-5 250 persons were executed, besides many who died under the torture. In Mainz 60 were burnt in 1627, and in villages near by, 300. At Osnabrück 121 were burnt in 1583 and 133 in 1589. At Ellwangen 167 were burnt in 1612.

Exactly like an epidemic, the mania would appear in one place, grow to a climax and then die down, only to break out in some other district and there run a like course. In

Austria the most famous case proved to be one in which some evil priests had impersonated devils in order to indulge in obscene orgies with some frightened and deluded women. This rare, perhaps unique, example of a real celebration of the sabbath by fraudulent impostors, merited punishment, though hardly the fearful one with which all parties were visited. Besides several who died under the torture, or by their own hand, eleven men and women were burnt.

The statistics given in the last paragraphs are but a sample of a much larger number that might be drawn from the history of the mania in other parts of Germany, in Switzerland, and in Hungary. In Scandinavia the infection came late. No witches, as far as is known, were burnt in Sweden before the middle of the seventeenth century. But in 1669 one of the worst outbreaks of the madness afflicted Dalecarlia. Some children in this district told strange stories of their being carried off to distant wilds and some of them, doubtless under the stress of constant questioning, fell into paroxysms. A commission appointed to investigate the matter made it clear, by ample use of the rack, that the children had been bewitched. In the trials that followed 84 adults and 15 children were sentenced to death at the stake, and 128 children to be whipped once a week for a whole year before the church doors. Nor was this the end of the witch hunt. Wholesale executions took place elsewhere in Sweden throughout the rest of the century.

The witch hunt was started, or greatly stimulated, in England by the *Act against Conjurations, Inchantments, and Witchcrafts* passed by Parliament in the fifth year of Elizabeth. This act imposed the death penalty only when the sorcerer was charged with causing death; for the infliction of lesser injuries one year's imprisonment was decreed. In the reign of the queen 125 persons are known to have been tried for the crime, and 47 to have been executed. With the accession of James I the law was amended by making the practice of any kind of sorcery capital. The king himself had once been an ardent witch-hunter. Believing that he and his bride, Anne of Denmark, had been imperilled by storms raised by witchcraft, he caused a reputed magician, Dr. Fian, to be arrested, and then in person and "with great delight" he had assisted at his torture, of the most inhuman cruelty. He then published a *Dæmonologie* (1597), defending the superstition. His zeal was seconded by several other writers, among whom the most notable was the Puritan theologian of Cambridge, William Perkins, author of *A Discourse on the Damned Art of Witchcraft* (1608).

Though our lists are incomplete they show that at least thirty-seven persons suffered death for the crime of sorcery under James I. In the reign of his son, before the beginning of the civil war, only six witches are known to have been executed. The worst years of the witch hunt in England were those from the outbreak of the civil war to the end of the Commonwealth. This increase in persecution was due partly to the excesses of Puritan zeal, still more to the disturbed state of the country, and most of all to the efforts of Matthew Hopkins, the most successful of the witch finders. In the panic started by him in the eastern counties during the years 1645-48 nearly three hundred witches were tried, and the greater number of them sentenced to death. In 1649 a malignant hunt for witches afflicted the northern counties; in 1650 at Newcastle fourteen women and one man were hanged for the crime; and many other cases are known elsewhere.

Just what was the responsibility of Puritanism in this fearful epidemic of witch madness in England is difficult to assess; but that there was some connection between the religious crisis and the access of superstition can hardly be doubted. Calvin himself, though less credulous than Luther, and though denying the reality of the witch's sabbath and of the flight through the air, maintained firmly, on biblical ground, that witchcraft existed, that it was a crime, and that it should be punished with death. Those who denied these propositions he charged with "impudent blasphemy." And his followers, as is so often the case in great causes, emphasized the coarser and cruder sides of the master's message. During the middle years of the seventeenth century England passed through a fever of religious fervor, which superinduced many superstitious and other evil symptoms.

Nor were the lesser sects more enlightened than the greater churches. George Fox, thôugh averse to the darker side of the persecution, did not doubt the reality of demoniac possession or of witchcraft. When he healed a woman possessed of the devil, he warned the bystanders away "lest that which is in her get into you." [1] When he and his followers were accused of curing by witchcraft he of course indignantly denied it; and the charge made him more cautious in accusing others. He blamed those who threw overboard persons accused of raising storms by magic at sea. He dissuaded his followers from trusting fortune-tellers. But that he had some belief in witchcraft is plainly shown in a sermon published in 1657, of which a short extract may be quoted as a specimen of his argument and of his obscure and raving style:

A harlot, the mystery of witchcrafts, fells nations through her whoredoms, the mystery of it, and this hath gotten power over nations, whoredoms, harlot, well-favored, the witchcraft that fells nations and families, harlot, whoredom, is in the transgression.

After the Restoration the superstition rapidly abated, though the records, probably more complete for these than for earlier decades, show that nearly one hundred persons were tried and nearly twenty hanged during the years 1660-87. In one of these trials Sir Thomas Browne testified his belief in the reality of witchcraft, as he expounded more fully in his *Religio Medici*. He even accused of infidelity and atheism those who denied the existence of sorcerers. He answered the argument of the skeptics that those who do not believe in the devil never see him by saying that the devil is too wise to appear to infidels for by doing so he would convert them, whereas he already has them in his power through their heresy.

[1] *Short Journal*, p. 2.

Scotland, under the Roman law, dealt with witchcraft by torture even before she sanctioned the application of pain to those accused of sorcery by a special law passed in 1649. Commissions for trying witches issued in 1661 brought to light at least 150 cases. At this and at other times the clergy were the chief movers. One of the worst practices of their "subtle and privy inquisition" was their placing in the churches of boxes in which anonymous accusations might be cast by those afraid to appear publicly.

Among the English colonies in America only Massachusetts Bay and Connecticut suffered from the spiritual epidemic. The first crisis occurred during the years 1647 to 1663, during which fourteen persons in all were executed. The most eminent apologist for the persecution was the Puritan clergyman Cotton Mather.

Witch-panics plagued France more than they did Great Britain, though not quite so much as Germany. Sporadic outbreaks during the first half of the sixteenth century were followed during the second half by serious persecution beginning with the burning of seven sorcerers at Nantes in 1549. When the mania had already gathered considerable momentum it was aggravated by the publication in 1580 of a book called *De la Demonomanie des Sorciers* by Jean Bodin. That this man, who discovered important truths in politics and economics, who discussed religion with a cool skepticism, and who, as a member of the States General, pleaded for tolerance for the Huguenots, should have written this baleful apology for superstition and cruelty is a signal instance to prove that even the most rational minds are often open to the suggestion of herd opinion. In his preface Bodin insists that his belief in witchcraft is based not on hearsay, but on his experience as a judge. In courts of justice, he declares, where all the secret actions and thoughts and wiles of the human heart are laid bare, he has heard enough testimony, freely given without torture, to convince the most hardened doubter. In his opinion sorcery is the worst of crimes, meriting the severest of punishments, for it includes all the evil in heresy, sacrilege, murder and sexual perversion. The land which does not punish witches will be smitten by God's wrath with plague, famine, and war. Even if the crimes of the witches were purely imaginary, Bodin argued that they deserve punishment for their wicked intentions.

Under this stimulus persecution began with fearful energy. One single judge, Nicholas Remy (or, Remigius) boasted that during the fifteen years 1576-91 he had passed 900 sentences of death on witches. He had even condemned some children of seven to death, but later, on the advice of his colleagues, had commuted their sentence to the hardly more merciful one of having the infants stripped and scourged while walking around the stake at which their parents had perished.

It would be useless and harrowing to give all the statistics of similar cruelties. So deeply did the madness strike into the public mind that in 1623 a number of young girls announced themselves as possessed by the devil and begged to be exorcized. This epidemic impressed Jansen as a sign of the coming of antichrist. Among the alleged sufferers from sorcery in the same year was the boy Pascal, who fell ill in consequence, as was supposed, of a charm cast upon him by a witch, and was only restored to health when the curse was transferred to a cat.

Nine years later an epidemic of hysteria broke out among the nuns of Loudun, which was interpreted as possession by the devils Leviathan and Balaam. When the spiritual guide of the nuns had been put to death as a magician, the fiends were happily exorcized from the sisters by a corps of Jesuits.

Though a few famous cases of magic practised at court were tried in the reign of Louis XIV, the superstition abated its fury in his reign. In 1672 Colbert directed magistrates to receive no accusations of sorcery. Nevertheless a few persons were still tried and executed for this crime, though only seven in all after the year 1681.

Italy was less plagued with witch-hunters than were her northern neighbors, and she suffered from them most during the last years of the fifteenth and the first half of the sixteenth century. From the promulgation of the bull *Summis desiderantes* by Pope Innocent VIII in 1484, which started the whole dreadful persecution, to the founding of the Roman Inquisition in 1542, there were a number of trials for sorcery and some wholesale executions throughout Italy, mostly in the north. When the Roman Inquisition, after some hesitation, asserted its jurisdiction over this crime, it proved a moderating and restraining influence. The reasons for this were doubtless two: in the first place the passions of the inquisitors were wholly absorbed in stamping out heresy, and in the second place these judges were experts in taking evidence and thus able to perceive the utter flimsiness of the testimony on which innocent people were tortured and burnt. Throughout Europe the most skeptical and enlightened class were the lawyers, notwithstanding such eminent exceptions as Bodin, simply because they came into close contact with cases to which expert rules of evidence could be applied. So the inquisitors, cruel and fanatical as they were, had learned, by long experience in dealing with heresy, to sift false evidence from true. Heresy was a real thing, and could be proved or disproved; but imaginary crimes fared badly in the courts of the Holy Office.

Not only did the papal curia treat the witch-sabbath as a diabolical delusion without objective reality, but it put a wholesome curb upon the secular courts. A bull of Clement VIII in 1592, reserving to the papal treasury the fines from sorcerers which had previously gone to local corporations, took away one powerful incentive to prosecution and to conviction. There were no trials for witchcraft in Rome under Paul V (1605-21). This pope did something to mitigate the punishments and to reform the procedure in cases of sorcery, and his successor, Gregory XV, in 1623, issued an important bull confining the death penalty to those sorcerers who had committed murder, and imposing the milder punishment of prison on those who had, by magic, procured divorces, or produced sickness or impotence, or done damage to animals or crops. A further step in the direction of humanity, if not of skepticism, was taken by an instruction printed by the Roman Inquisition in 1657,[1] reforming many of the abuses in the trials of witches, even while still assuming the reality of their crime.

Like the Roman Inquisition, the Spanish eventually acted to restrain rather than to stimulate the superstition of the people. The prosecutions for sorcery before this court began in 1498, and continued to be fairly numerous until 1530, when the judges began to grow skeptical and to repress the noxious credulity of the ignorant. The worst outbreak of the mania, after 1530, occurred at Barcelona in 1610, when, of a large number of sorcerers tried by the Holy Office, six were relaxed to the secular arm for capital punishment, five died in prison, and eighteen others received severe chastisement. But, as these sentences shocked the better opinion of the public, the Supreme Council of the Inquisition appointed commissioners to investigate the subject of witchcraft thoroughly. Two several reports informed the Holy Office that the crimes of witches were imaginary, either invented under torture or hallucinations caused by the devil. In accordance with these advices the Supreme Council in 1614 issued an elaborate instruction to the judges which, while not denying witchcraft *in toto,* insisted upon strict and reasonable rules of evidence for proving it in any given case. After this there were very few punishments for sorcery in Spain, and the few cases celebrated in history, such as the supposed bewitchment of Charles II, and his exorcism, are examples not of superstition so much as of calculated political imposture. It is noticeable, however, that in Spanish America the Inquisition still found, throughout the seventeenth century, in the incantations practised by the Indians, material for a large number of trials and convictions for witchcraft. The best authority estimates that in the year 1650 alone the Mexican Inquisition tried 250 persons for the crime of sorcery.

[1] Cornell has perhaps the only printed copy in existence. The *Instruction* had been circulated in MS since about 1635.

At the close of this brief survey it would be interesting, were it possible, to offer some estimate of the total numbers of victims of the superstition; of the total numbers, that is, suspected, tried, tortured, punished, and executed for this imaginary crime. An estimate once accepted by Henry Charles Lea is that 100,000 persons were executed in Germany, and 30,000 were punished in Great Britain, for witchcraft. A German writer, Ohle, calculates that between 1575 and 1700 no less than a million persons were charged with witchcraft, of whom 25% to 30% were in Protestant lands. All these figures seem to be considerable exaggerations of the truth. I should guess that Protestant lands contributed nearer one half than one quarter or one third of the total number of victims. I should estimate the number of persons executed as witches in Great Britain as not more than 1000 all told. Doubtless the numbers were much larger in France, and still larger in Germany; nevertheless that in the latter country as many as 100,000 suffered death on this charge is hard to believe. But the truth is dreadful enough. When we consider the fantastic nature of the imputed crime, the utterly base and depraved nature of the mythology evolved, the elements of hysteria and mob panic, the unimaginable tortures inflicted and endured, and the large numbers of victims sacrificed, we must admit that no plague so ghastly as the witch hunt has ever afflicted our race.

3. PROTEST AND SKEPTICISM

Though it is impossible to read the chronicles of superstition without pity for its victims and without anger at its cruel devotees, it is important to remember that neither pity nor anger will explain the causes of a mania like the witch panic any more than they will explain the causes of a typhoid epidemic or of cancer. The historian's function is not to award praise and blame, nor compassion and admiration, but to understand the social conditions which gave rise to the phenomena of a given process. The causes of the rise of witchcraft have been explained; the cause of its fall is as plain as day to any careful student of culture. The force that killed it was the spirit of science with its revelation of a new world of law and of reason in which there is no place for either magic or devil. The noxious germ of superstition can no more flourish in a world flooded with the light of science than can the germ of tuberculosis flourish in the beams of the sun, even though a few germs linger on and develop sporadically. The greatest triumphs of science have been not its material achievements, wonderful as these are, but the diffusion of the bright light of knowledge and the consequent banishment of ghosts and bugaboos created by man's fear of the dark.

It is true that the scientists were not always, though they were often, the most enlightened men of their generation in casting off the inherited credulities. They did not always feel the full implications of even their own discoveries. This is, however, naturally explained by the fact that most of them were specialists, creative and revolutionary in their own fields, but for that very reason conventional and conservative in all others. The mind intensely absorbed in mathematics or in astronomy has neither time nor interest left for careful study of religion and politics. Such men accept the bulk of their mental furniture and habits as they accept the fashion of their clothes and the ordering of their daily life. It is often, though not always, left to others to feel and to point out the implications of the new thought in other fields. Thus, in England, it was the lawyers, and not the members of the Royal Society, who first, as a class, became doubters of witchcraft. Public opinion was as a whole becoming more skeptical and enlightened, and the lawyers, being in the most intimate contact with trials for witchcraft, first largely felt and applied the lessons of the new spirit in that particular case.

Even before the triumph of the scientific spirit there were a few men skeptical enough to doubt the superstition, just as long after its triumph there were a few men credulous enough to defend it. Among the first of the great doubters was, of course, Montaigne. Nowhere do his skepticism and his irony show to better advantage than in the eleventh essay of his third book of *Essays,* in which he deals, though only by way of excursus, with the subject of sorcery. He had read Bodin's *Démonomanie,* he had investigated, both as a magistrate and as a curious traveller, cases of alleged magic, and had come to the conclusion that they were all either fraud or hallucination. It is easier, he says, to believe that a man lies than that he has been transported in twelve hours from one end of the earth to the other. It is easier to believe that a witch is mad than that she has flown through the chimney on a broomstick. One miracle, bruited all over France, proved to be a prank of young people counterfeiting ghosts. When one hears a marvel one should always say "perhaps." And to put men to death one needs more than the flimsy evidence of suspicion and forced confession.

The next great French doubter, Gassendi, tried an experiment to test the reality of witchcraft. A drug prepared by one sorcerer was administered to four others; under its influence they fell into a deep sleep, on awakening from which they declared that they had been attending a sabbath. As their bodies had been under observation the whole time, it was obvious that their excursion had been purely imaginary. While not denying the miracles of the Bible, Gassendi expressed the belief that modern witchcraft is a pure delusion, a cheat, or a dream.

The Italian scientist Cesalpino, investigating the rôle of demoniac possession in disease, concluded that magic is imposture. Campanella also wrote a long treatise to explain that science is the only real magic. Superstitious magic is false science, an attempt to master nature by a short and easy road rather than by careful observation and thought. "For, unskilful and base men," said he, "weary of the labor of research, have sought from the devils a short road to those things which they cannot really do but which they pretend that they can do."

In Germany the path of the skeptic was made hard by the witch-hunters, who counted doubt of witchcraft the worst of heresies. Cornelius Loos, a professor at Trier, wrote a work attacking the superstition, but before he could publish it he was seized, imprisoned, and forced to recant his "errors." Among these was the denial that witches could be transported on broomsticks, that they could have sexual intercourse with devils, and that their confessions were forced from them by torture.

Loos had been much influenced by Johann Weyer, a native of the Netherlands who studied medicine at Orléans and practised it in Rhenish Germany. In a book on *The Tricks of the Devils* (1563) he cautiously sought to show that old, feeble-minded, stay-at-home women sentenced for witchcraft were victims simply of their own and of other people's delusions. As a Christian he dared not deny the existence of the devil, but as a philosopher he denied the possibility of corporal union of spirits and mortals, and as a physician he attributed some of the delusions of the witches to the effects of such drugs as belladonna and henbane. As a humane man he protested, too, against the exceeding cruelty of the judges and accused them of iniquitous extortion. Though the book ran through six Latin editions in twenty years and was translated into French and German, it was put on the index of prohibited books in 1570, and elicited from Bodin the opinion that the author was a true servant of Satan.

An effective answer to Weyer was produced by Martin Delrio. This Flemish Jesuit, who studied at Paris, at Douai, and at Louvain, and who taught at Valladolid and at Louvain, published, under the name of *Disquisitions on Magic* (1599), the most learned defence of this superstition ever written. Even this obscurantist, however, bore unconscious testimony to the slightly rising rationalism of his age. While fully convinced of the reality of the compact with Satan, he rejected as improbable certain magical powers attributed to witches, and as uncertain the water proof and the pricking proof. But the thoroughgoing skeptics he assailed with both ridicule and menace, asserting that denial of the reality of witchcraft is heresy, and pointing to the fate of Loos and of Flade as warnings to rash doubters.

It is not remarkable that some men who still believed in witchcraft, or who did not dare to deny it, should have been shocked by the inhumanity of the trials. The most famous and effective of several protests was a book which appeared in 1631 under the title: *On the Criminal Procedure against Witches, a Caution,* by an Unknown Catholic Theologian. For eighty years the secret of its authorship was known to few; but it was then discovered by Leibniz that the writer was a Jesuit named Friedrich Spee, known also as a poet. During the height of the persecution he had served as a confessor to condemned witches, and among the very many victims to whom he administered the last consolations of religion, he became convinced that not one had been justly condemned. The horror of this discovery and the sight of the fiendish tortures by which confession had been wrung from innocent women turned his hair prematurely white, and drove him to raise his voice, though cautiously, against the iniquities of the courts.

Admitting the existence of witches, he asserted that their number had been greatly exaggerated by popular rumor, and that many innocent victims had perished. The ferocious persecution had "laid waste whole countries more than war ever did, but had accomplished nothing towards the extirpation of sorcery," which flourished most where the persecution was most savage. Against this ferocious procedure he then entered a protest. He riddled the method of procedure, by which persons were arrested on mere suspicion, and by which the presumption was held to be against the accused; but most of all he denounced the rigor of the torments, which, he cried, would wring confession of witchcraft or of any other crime from prelates or from monks, from the pope or from the saints, nay, from the very executioners and judges themselves.

Slowly, slowly, in the face of theological argument and in spite of judicial rack, skepticism spread. As the light of science brightened and diffused itself among the public, books like those of Weyer and of Spee took on new meaning and cogency. And as tortures were relaxed, evidence failed, and the noxious superstitions nourished on it began to wither. The Great Elector of Brandenburg led the way by reforming the procedure and mitigating the punishments for witchcraft in Prussia. The juristic faculty of Mainz, to whom a case was referred in 1674, dared to speak for humanity and reason.

At last, even though the public was as yet far from enlightened, some minds had become completely rational. Such minds resemble the mountain peaks on which the sunrise breaks while the lowlands still lie in darkness. Such was the mind of Spinoza, clear, cold, calm, and brilliantly illuminated. In a chapter on Devils in his *Short Treatise* (1660) he declared that "such a wretched thing could not exist even for a moment." In a correspondence with Boxel he affirmed that stories of ghosts and specters are on a par with tales of centaurs, hydras, harpies, satyrs and griffins, utterly incredible. To Oldenburg he wrote:

I have taken miracles and ignorance as equivalents; for those who try to prove the existence of God by miracles, try to prove an obscure thing by one more obscure.

Finally, in bad luck he saw clearly one of the chief psychological factors predisposing to superstition. When men are prosperous they are rational, but when they fall into misfortune they trust to childish omens, or betake themselves to still more childish remedies in magic.

Turning from the European Continent to England we find the most brilliant and thorough attack ever made upon the witch superstition in a book by a Kentish squire and jurist, perhaps a justice of the peace. Reginald Scot, having his attention drawn to the subject by a particularly notorious imposture, made a painstaking study of the subject both by attending witch trials throughout England and by reading many authors on the subject, of whom he catalogues two hundred and thirty-five. His conclusions were cogently set forth in a book published in 1584, under the title: *The Discovery of Witchcraft, wherein the lewd dealing of witches and witch-mongers is notably detected, the knavery of conjurors, the impiety of enchanters, the folly of soothsayers, the infidelity of atheists, the pestilent practices of pythonists, the vanity of dreamers, the beggerly art of alchemistry . . . is opened.*

The bulky work, written not only with sound and rational judgment, but in a lucid English style, pointed out that witchcraft is "contrary to nature, probability, and reason, and void of truth and possibility." The author exposed, in a series of narratives, the utter flimsiness of the charges and of the evidence on which poor old women were done to death. To wilful imposture and to illusion he attributed the origins of the superstition, for which, with calculated partisanship, he blamed the Catholic church. In explaining away the biblical evidence, he interpreted the performance of the witch of Endor as ventriloquism, an exegesis for which he had the support of the Septuagint translation of the Old Testament.[1] Finally, as the possibility of magic could not be completely disproved on empirical grounds, he attacked it *a priori* by arguing that spirits and bodies are in two categories, unable to act directly upon each other.

Though it was long before the English public was prepared to deny witchcraft as categorically as had Scot, there are evidences that even in the crisis of the superstition during the Civil War there were men who suspected that many, if not most, of the accused were really innocent. The famous William Harvey, being called upon to examine some suspected old women for the marks supposed to stigmatize them, reported that they had nothing peculiar about them and so had them acquitted. Thomas Fuller, the Prebendary of Sarum and ecclesiastical historian, admitted that many

---

[1] I Sam., xxviii, 7. The words translated in the King James Version, and also in the Geneva Bible, which Scot read, "woman having a familiar spirit" are translated in the LXX by ἐγγαστρίμυθος, (ventriloquist), and in the Vulgate by "mulierem habentem pythonem," which shows where he got the "pythonists" of his title.

were unjustly accused of witchcraft and that the crime,
though proved by the Bible, was nowadays rare.

Passing over various evidences that public opinion was
becoming more enlightened, we come to the completely
skeptical mind of Hobbes, who, in two separate chapters
of the *Leviathan,* labored to prove that fairies, ghosts, demons, and apparitions are creatures of the fancy only,
taught to the common people, or at least not confuted, by
priests, "to keep in credit the use of exorcism, of crosses,
of holy water, and of other such inventions of ghostly men."
In Hobbes, however, as also in Selden, we find the disturbing opinion that, though witchcraft is no real power, yet
those who profess to practise it are justly punished for their
malice.

The growing skepticism of the public so alarmed the
obscurantists that the ablest defences of the superstition
were written during the period of growing enlightenment
between the Restoration of the monarchy and the Revolution. Henry More, the Cambridge Platonist, in his *Antidote
to Atheism,* argued at great length that storms are raised
by incantations, that Weyer was unreasonable in doubting
the power of devils, that witches have been seen by eye-
witnesses to ride on broomsticks, that the story of the Pied
Piper of Hamlin is an authentic case of magic, and that the
story of a witch who declared she had been married to
Satan for thirty years "was neither any figment of priests
nor delusion of melancholy."

More remarkable than the lingering superstition in a
professional theologian is the defence of the obsolescent
belief by a member of the Royal Society, who may aptly
be compared with the defenders of spiritism still to be
found among the eminent scientists of our own days. Joseph
Glanvill published *Some Philosophical Considerations touching Witches and Witchcraft* in 1666, republished it as *A
Blow at Modern Sadducism* in 1668, and again republished
it, expanded, as *Sadducismus Triumphatus* in 1681. He began by stating that the greatest wonder of an age of wonders
is that "men otherwise witty and ingenious are fallen into

the conceit that there's no such thing as a witch or appari-
tion, but that these are creatures of melancholy and superstition, fostered by ignorance and design." This skepticism,
suggested by the devil, leads logically, in the author's opinion, to the denial of the existence of spirits, of immortality,
and of God. Atheism, said he, not bold enough to declare
itself, attacks the outworks of religion as sadducism, or
the denial that spirits exist. The argument, founded in the
Bible, was chiefly buttressed by a collection of tales of
ghosts and witches, all of which were accepted with a credulity truly remarkable.

Glanvill's work proved more important as a symptom
than as a remedy for the growing skepticism. The hobgob-
lins were flitting in spite of his valiant summons. Fewer and
fewer grew the trials, and still fewer the convictions. As a
class the lawyers and justices of the peace displayed the
most enlightened disbelief, while the clergy still clung to the
ancient credulity. More and more the gentry and especially
all pretenders to philosophy and wit began to deride the
old wives' tales that had struck terror into the hearts of
their grandfathers. But another half-century of advancing
science and of enlightened propaganda was needed to break
the spell that had lain so long and so balefully upon the
mind of the civilized world.

CHAPTER XV

PERSECUTION AND TOLERANCE

I. THE PRACTICE OF PERSECUTION

Like so many other social phenomena, persecution has a psychological and biological foundation. For a gregarious animal the herd instinct, implying uniformity of action and conformity to the group mind, has a high survival value. If even animals expel the eccentric, men in the lowest stages of civilization allow no divergence whatever from group custom and opinion. Not only in matters of religion but in politics, morals, manners, and fashions, absolute conformity to the prevalent standard is enforced.

Like other instincts and passions, the herd instinct with its passion for uniformity has varied in its manifestations under changing social conditions. The task of the historian is to explain the causes of these variations in intensity and in forms of manifestation. In one social group religion, in another nationalism, in another racial feeling, in another economics, and in another fashions in dress and manners will be the chief objects of animadversion. In one age the passions aroused by persecution will be allowed their fullest sway; in another they will be put under the tuition of reason and under the restraints of interest and of fear.

For two hundred years after the burning of the first Protestant martyrs (1523) religious persecution and confessional war raged as they have never done before nor since. In some respects the tidal wave of bigotry and hatred resembled the mania of the witch hunt. Both were outbursts of passion and unreason occurring in the first great epoch of modern science and enlightenment. And the causes of the rise and fall of the observed phenomena are plain. Religion then occupied a far larger place in the thought of civilized nations than it does now. In its social functions the church has now been supplanted largely by the state; in its intellectual aspects the scientific world-view has largely taken the place of the religious. But throughout the earlier Middle Ages there had been too little dissent to allow much persecution. The growth of free-thought and heresy in the later Middle Ages had caused the church to found the Inquisition and to wage bloody wars against the Albigenses and against the Hussites. But these sporadic rebellions were as nothing compared to the Reformation. *Then* so much of Europe seceded from the Roman communion that the peoples were divided into two camps not unequal in strength, each animated with a fierce hatred of the other, and each fighting, in its own opinion, for its life.

Religious zeal was seconded by political and even by some intellectual and moral forces. Church and state were so intimately connected that any defection from the established church seemed to imply treason to the state. Protestant kings thought it unsafe to allow those who acknowledged the supremacy of a foreign authority in the pope to remain in their lands; Catholic kings dreaded the *imperium in imperio,* such as that set up by the Huguenots in France. And indifferent publicists and statesmen urged that, for the sake of public peace, if not for the purity of the faith, only one religion could be permitted in a state.

Moreover, it was felt that religion, as a conservative force, furnished a useful moral restraint upon the passions of the populace. During the seventeenth century the argument began to be advanced that, even if Christianity were false, it should be maintained as the necessary bond of society. And, finally, the whole age instinctively dreaded the intellectual and moral anarchy which, it was wrongly believed, would follow the overthrow of supernatural guides. That in the warfare of the sects all religion would be subverted, and therewith the only guarantee of absolute truth and of future happiness would fall to the ground, was apprehended and was dreaded with all the instinctive fear of mankind for the unknown.

The theory of the Catholic church has always been consistently intolerant. The chief apologist for the theory of intolerance during the late sixteenth century was Cardinal Bellarmine, who proved from imperial law, from canon law, from the Bible and from natural reason that the church has the right and duty of putting heretics to death. The execution of heretics, he argued, saves many souls and even profits the heretics themselves inasmuch as the longer they live the worse they would get and the heavier would be their punishment in hell.

To cope with the new situation arising from the Protestant rebellion Pope Paul IV founded the Roman Inquisition in 1542. Authorized to invoke the aid of the secular arm to punish culprits with death, confiscation, or prison, it judged heresy, some forms of vice, witchcraft, and the forgery of papal bulls. Even at Rome it found considerable combustible material, putting to death, for example, seven heretics in 1595, seven in 1596, and six in 1600. Among the victims of the last year of the century was Giordano Bruno, who dared to say to his judges, "Perhaps you pronounce sentence against me with greater fear than I hear it." Apart from the sentences of death, there were many milder, but rigorous, punishments. The fear of the tribunal sat so heavy on the populace that an English traveller in Rome in 1600 reported that "the least idle word against the pope, the church, or religion, will draw a man into the Inquisition, where he will lie long time close prisoner." Though the records of the Inquisition at Rome are less sanguinary during the seventeenth century, they include some capital sentences, and some famous trials. Campanella felt the rack, and Galileo either felt or barely escaped it.

In other Italian cities the Roman Inquisition found much more to do than in the papal capital. At Venice there were nearly nine hundred processes for heresy during the sixteenth century. In Sicily, during the years 1547-51, it punished 207 penitents, most of them for blasphemy, big-amy, or sorcery. In Naples in 1561 it butchered 88 Waldenses in one day, of whom seven were burnt alive, and the others strangled. Though hated by governments and peoples throughout the peninsula, it was rarely successfully resisted. It is noteworthy, however, that in 1593 the grand duke of Tuscany assured free exercise of their religions to all foreigners, Protestants, Jews and even Turks, resident in the commercial cities of Leghorn and Pisa.

Far more terrible was the record of the Spanish Inquisition, the very name of which has passed into a byword for cruelty and fanaticism. Founded in the reign of Ferdinand and Isabella to deal with Jews and Moors who, having been converted, had relapsed, it soon grew into a power able and often willing to defy both king and pope. That, far from being a political instrument, it was almost independent of the state, has now been proved. Though the crown never lost the power of appointing the Inquisitor General, all other appointments were made by the Supreme Council of the Inquisition. It controlled its own finances, it punished criticism of itself, it could inhibit the action of other courts and could be inhibited by none, its officers were inviolable and exempt from military duty.

Its jurisdiction extended only to those who had once been baptized, and only over certain crimes, of which heresy, blasphemy, unnatural vice, seduction in the confessional, and sorcery were the most important. Annually it promulgated an Edict of Faith requiring all persons, under fearful spiritual and temporal penalties, to denounce heresy and other crimes against religion. By making delation a pious duty and every man a spy, it terrorized the whole population.

The annals of its procedure and punishments are one long record of diabolical cruelty. Endless delay and browbeating to break the spirit of the accused would be followed by torture, theoretically limited in amount but in practice applied until the human frame could bear no more without dissolution. The accused was not confronted with his accusers nor told the nature of his crime, but was simply urged to confess. An advocate was given him simply to betray him. All classes, even the clergy, were subject to the Holy Office; nor was there any privileged age except that of the tenderest childhood. Men and women of ninety, boys of fourteen and girls of twelve, young mothers and women with child, were stretched on the rack, and sent to the stake. Acquittal was almost, though not quite, unknown.

Penalties included reprimand, objurgation, the social stigma of wearing a special dress called the *sanbenito,* exile, scourging, imprisonment, the galleys, and the stake. Heretics who recanted were strangled before being burnt; the obstinate or relapsed were burnt alive. The ecclesiastical officers did not execute the victims themselves, but relaxed them to the secular arm; that is, turned them over to the secular authorities, who were allowed to exercise no discretion, but were obliged, under pain of excommunication, to execute.

If anything could be wanting to complete the horror it was furnished by the festive spirit of the butcheries. The *Auto da Fe,* or act of faith, was a favorite spectacle offered to the people on high feast days or on gala occasions, such as the celebration of a royal wedding or christening. Vast crowds gloated over the agonies of the victims or were edified by the untimely end of the misbelievers.

As there were few Protestants in Spain, the Inquisition found its chief work in keeping in the strait and narrow path those Jews and Moors who had, usually under compulsion, submitted to baptism. The persecution of both religions was exacerbated by race hatred. The Jews, except those who accepted conversion, had been expelled, amid scenes of massacre and pillage, in 1492. Those who had remained at the cost of apostacy continued to be harassed by vexatious laws and by popular prejudice. The least vestige of their racial habits, such as the refusal to eat pork, was regarded as ground for suspicion of heresy and was punished by the Inquisition as such.

The Moors, or Moriscos, being more numerous, caused more trouble. Guaranteed the enjoyment of the Mohammedan religion on the conquest of Granada in 1492, they were nevertheless vexed with harsh laws and burdened with heavy taxes intended to crush them. Goaded by despair into a rebellion (1568-71) they were cut down in large numbers by the Spanish troops, or sold into slavery. But those who survived constituted a standing provocation to bigotry and racial prejudice so vexatious that the government finally decided, in 1609, to expel them from the country. The proposals of the clergy that they should be sent to sea in ships to be scuttled in mid ocean, or that they should be deported to Newfoundland and left to perish there, were too expensive for adoption. The greater part of the 600,000 exiles took refuge in Africa, though a few found homes in other European countries. The barbarous act of expulsion was applauded by Lope de Vega, by Calderón, and even by Cervantes, and was undoubtedly approved by public opinion. But materially and spiritually the country suffered by the loss of the most laborious and of the not least intelligent element in her population.

Apart from this act of wholesale persecution it is difficult to estimate the numbers of victims of bigotry. Henry Charles Lea, the leading authority on the Spanish Inquisition, says that statistics are not sufficiently complete to allow an accurate calculation of the numbers punished by the Holy Office. But the extant figures show that a steady stream of blood flowed throughout the whole sixteenth and seventeenth centuries. The records of the inquisitorial court at Valencia, for example, name 643 persons relaxed and 3104 tried during the year 1485-1592. And there were a number of other tribunals throughout the country. But after the expulsion of the Moriscos and the crushing of the few heretics— Protestants, mystics, and illuminati—produced by Spain, there was little combustible material left. Persecution died slowly down, not because of the growth of tolerance but because of the elimination of all forms of heterodoxy.

In the Spanish colonies of the New World the Inquisition was introduced at various dates; in Peru in 1570, in Mexico in 1571, and elsewhere later. As the natives were exempt from its jurisdiction and as the Spanish conquerors were practically all good Catholics, foreigners furnished the larger number of those tried and punished for heresy. In 1574, for example, thirty-six English Protestants were sentenced by the Mexican Inquisition, three to the stake and the rest to scourging and the galleys. In the seventeenth century, except for a spasm of activity from 1643 to 1658, persecution died down in Mexico, partly because the Holy Office was hampered by poverty, partly because there were few persons left liable to suspicion.

In the Spanish Netherlands, once the scene of the holocausts of Alva, the last heretic to suffer death for his faith was an Anabaptist buried alive in 1597. Prior to this the Protestants had been practically exterminated there, and an active persecution, though not unto death, kept them from attaining any foothold in the now purely Catholic provinces.

Eventually, the French showed themselves as capable of wholesale persecution as were the Spaniards. But for a long period the intolerant spirit of the Catholics was held in check by the strength of their opponents, the Huguenots. When Protestantism first appeared in France a series of persecuting laws and the establishment of a special tribunal, commonly called the Burning Chamber, to enforce them, supplemented by frequent outbreaks of mob violence and of massacre, made the history of the innovators one of martyrdom. When, nevertheless, the numbers of the Huguenots continued to grow, and when the collisions of the two faiths precipitated civil war, the government began to temporize. Catherine de Médicis and her minister, Michel de l'Hôpital, headed the party known as *politiques*, who were indifferent in religion and willing to do anything to secure civil peace. The result was that for thirty years short intervals of freedom of conscience alternated with periods of fierce persecution. The government being too weak either to enforce a policy of toleration on the Catholic party, or to crush the Huguenots completely, tried first one course of action and then the other. After the extensive massacre of St. Bartholomew's Eve (1572) had failed to exterminate the Protestants, civil war wasted the whole country, until a truce was finally imposed by the strong king, Henri IV.

Originally a Huguenot, Henri sacrificed his religious convictions, such as they were, in order to give peace to his country. But, though he became a convert to Catholicism, he determined to grant freedom of conscience to the Huguenots. That he was able to do this, against the strenuous opposition of the Catholic party, was due solely to the fact that the country was prostrated by civil war and to the fact that all sober men saw that the Huguenots, though in a minority, were too strong to be crushed. Henri was therefore able to enact the Edict of Pacification, commonly called the Edict of Nantes (1598).

The principle of this law, elaborated in ninety-one public and fifty-six secret articles, was the concession of liberty of conscience and of public worship to the Huguenots under such guarantees as would ensure the respect of each party for the rights of the other. Both parties were to have equal civil rights and equal permission to erect schools, and each was to be free from laws enforcing religious observances contrary to its principles. But Protestant worship was limited to a certain number of towns and bailiwicks. In order to enforce the edict a mixed court, consisting of ten Catholic and six Protestant members, was instituted; and, as a further guarantee of the rights of the minority, two hundred towns were left in the hands of the Protestants, with the power to maintain garrisons in them.

During the reigns of Henri and of his successor, Louis XIII, the terms of the edict were well kept. But there were some ominous signs of growing bigotry. The expulsion of the Jews in 1615, the declaration putting the kingdom under the special protection of the Virgin Mary in 1638, the reduction by Richelieu of the strongest Protestant town, La Rochelle, all showed the inclinations of the government.

The rule of Cardinal Mazarin, troubled by the Fronde and hampered by the minority of the king, observed the terms of the Edict of Nantes, which was solemnly ratified, for the last time, in 1656. But, with the enormous growth of the royal power following the majority of Louis XIV, the winds of persecution again arose until they burst in violent tempest. The sufficient explanation for this change of policy lies not in the temper but in the power of the Catholic party. As long as they were weak they were tolerant; when they had gained the support of a mighty army and of an imperious monarch, and when their rivals had lost ground by the hazards of eighty years of inferiority, they began again to persecute.

In 1651 the General Assembly of the French Catholic clergy petitioned the king to "abolish the unhappy liberty of conscience which destroys the liberty of the children of God." In 1659 a series of persecuting edicts began to appear, edicts forbidding the Protestants to sing too loudly in church, to engage in various trades, to teach school, to print books maintaining their religion, to assemble for any purpose but worship, and to do many other things.

These means proving insufficient to suppress Protestantism, the horrible persecutions known as the dragonnades began in 1680. Troops of dragoons were quartered in the houses of Protestants with permission to abuse them in every way, by destroying their property, torturing their persons, and raping their women, until they should be converted to the true faith.

Finally, in 1685, the Edict of Nantes was revoked by a law ordering the destruction of the Protestant churches, prohibiting all heretical meetings for divine worship, and expelling heretical ministers from France, but forbidding all other Protestants to leave the country, prohibiting heretical schools, and ordering that all children of Huguenots be baptised by Catholic priests. This terrible edict was supplemented by others depriving Protestants of civil rights, declaring illegal all marriages not celebrated by a Catholic priest, disinheriting Protestant heirs of Protestants, and finally ordering that all children of Huguenots be taken from their parents at the age of five years and given to their Catholic relatives, if they had any, or else to other Catholic families named by the courts.

In spite of the punishment of the galleys meted out to Huguenots caught leaving the kingdom, no less than 200,000 succeeded in getting away. In them France lost, and her rivals gained, a large number of persons above the average in intelligence and character. Some of the descendants of those who remained kept their faith against all the terrors of the law for many generations.

Though this policy of persecution shocked Protestant Europe, it was applauded by the servile courtiers and blind bigots of France. La Bruyère, La Fontaine, Mme. de Sévigné approved; Fénelon taunted the converted Huguenots with cowardice; and Bossuet burst forth into the following paean:

> Let us publish abroad this miracle of our days; let us pour forth our hearts on the piety of Louis; let us push our acclamations to the sky, and let us say to this new Constantine, this new Theodosius, this new Marcian, this new Charlemagne, "This is an act worthy of your reign, and its true glory; through you heresy has ceased to exist; God alone has done this miracle."

Somewhat similar to the history of toleration in France was the history of toleration in Germany, except that the dark periods in the one happened to be the light periods in the other, and the era of religious war in one was the time of confessional peace in the other. Analogous to the Edict of Nantes were the two great instruments known as the Peace of Augsburg and the Peace of Westphalia which formed the basis of the public law of the Empire for two centuries. In neither of them was religious liberty recognized as a right, but in each of them a measure of toleration was granted as a necessary expedient.

The Religious Peace of Augsburg (1555) imposed a truce between Catholic and Lutheran states until union of the two faiths should be achieved. In the meantime the government of each state was allowed to choose between the Roman Catholic faith and the Augsburg Confession. All other confessions were barred, including the Calvinist. But, though the governor of every state was thus given the choice between at least two alternatives, his subjects were obliged to conform to his creed on the principle famous as "who rules a region prescribes its religion" (*cujus regio ejus religio*), or else to emigrate. Catholics in Lutheran lands and Lutherans in Catholic lands were to be punished in no way save by banishment; and the hardship of this provision was greatly modified by the fact that there were so many states of each faith that no German Catholic or Lutheran would have to travel far before he reached a community of like-minded believers.

The limitations of the Peace of Augsburg are patent. It gave freedom of choice only to princes and governors, and to them freedom of choice between two churches only. Expediency and not theoretical preference for freedom of conscience are written large on the terms of what was, in fact, nothing but a treaty between hostile coalitions. Nevertheless, like so many laws passed on the same principles of opportunism, the Peace of Augsburg met the exigencies of the situation by actually keeping the public peace for more than sixty years. Within the various states there were frequent violations of the provisions of the treaty, both in favor of more liberty than the law allowed and to the prejudice of the minimum liberty prescribed by law. Laws condemning to death heretics outside the two recognized churches were constitutional and common. On the other hand, Calvinists were in some states allowed an extra-legal toleration. In 1609 the Emperor Rudolf gave to dissidents in Bohemia the Imperial Letter (1609) which has rightly been called the most liberal decree of the seventeenth century. But the concessions in this of liberty of conscience to nobles and towns were not adhered to either by Rudolf or by his successors, and persecution broke out fiercely again in a few years.

Sporadic breaches of the peace on both sides finally led to the outbreak of the appalling religious conflict known from its duration as the Thirty Years War (1618-48). As is so often the case in war, those who sowed the wind reaped the whirlwind; for, once the conflict was started in Germany, foreign powers, especially Sweden and France, took advantage of her distracted state to trample her to earth. At the end of thirty years of battle, of pillage, of famine, and of the epidemics following war, Germany emerged with a population reduced by a quarter, and with most of her wealth, spiritual as well as material, wiped out. In extensive districts civilization itself disappeared to make room for barbarism. The fetid pages of *Simplicissimus* reflect the misery, the crime, the despair, of a society from which all elements of order and decency were torn by the ravages of war.

After heart-breaking delays the Peace of Westphalia finally put a stop to warfare and allowed Germany to convalesce. The articles of the treaty dealing with religion provided for recognition of three cults, the Catholic, the Lutheran, and the Reformed. Lutherans in Catholic lands and Catholics in Lutheran lands, who had been allowed public worship in the year 1624, were to be tolerated and put at no disadvantage in civil or commercial rights. But except for this the prince was allowed to choose the religion of his land, and to suppress all other forms of worship. Dissenters, however, within the limits of the three recognized communions, were to be allowed to emigrate.

This toleration, though so limited, aroused the wrath of Pope Innocent X. In the bull *Zelo domus Dei*, he protested against the permission to Protestants of the exercise of their religion as prejudicial to the Roman Church, and declared the pertinent articles "null, void, invalid, wicked, unjust, damned, and reprobate."

In the face of papal opposition toleration continued to broaden in Germany even beyond the limits prescribed by the public law of the Empire. Brandenburg, under the guidance of the Great Elector Friedrich Wilhelm (1640-88), though a Calvinist state, allowed not only Lutherans but Catholics free exercise of their religion.

Like Germany, Switzerland was a confederacy of autonomous states, and, like Germany, she allowed each state, or canton, to determine its own faith. Occasionally war broke out between the two confessions, or massacres were perpetrated by the adherents of one or of the other creed.

The Scandinavian countries, early converted to Lutheranism, tolerated no faith but their own. Catholic priests were banished from Denmark and from Sweden on pain of death and Catholic laymen were put under severe restraints. The conversion of Queen Christina to Catholicism was followed by her abdication and by the enactment of more rigorous laws than ever against all dissenters from the established Lutheran church.

The aristocratic constitution of Poland, guaranteeing every noble a large sphere of liberty, permitted the rapid spread of dissent. By 1555 the sects—Lutheran, Hussite, Calvinist, Anabaptist, and Unitarian—had become so numerous that they abolished the jurisdiction of the ecclesiastical courts. The still further growth of the sects, after this loosening of restraint, laid upon the always feeble government the task of keeping the peace between them. This was provided for by the law known as the "Dissenters' Peace" passed by the Diet of Warsaw in 1573. In this the dissident nobles promised on their faith, oath, honor, and conscience never to impose any penalty, either of death, of prison, of confiscation of goods, of exile, or of infamy, on any one for differences in religious faith and practice. This law gave complete religious liberty, but only to the nobles, who were allowed to force upon their serfs their own cult. Thus it was that the lower classes were marched from Catholic pillar to Protestant post and back again without daring to rebel or even to protest. Such as it was, however, the peace was loyally observed by King Stephen Báthory, though he summoned the Jesuits to support a pacific Catholic propaganda. Under his successor, Sigismund III (1587-1632), however, the Jesuits completely triumphed and again lit the fires of persecution, at first against the Unitarians, and then against the other Protestant sects.

On the map of Europe, so dark with persecution, one small country shines, in the light of large religious liberty, almost white by contrast. The influences which made the

Dutch Republic the most tolerant of European countries during the seventeenth century were three. In the first place the inhabitants were divided not unequally between the Catholic and the Protestant faiths, thus creating that equilibrium of force which is one of the most potent conditions making for tolerance. Secondly, Holland, as the most commercial of states, felt the advantages and even the necessity of tolerance most strongly. Finally, of all nations the Dutch were then the most cultivated, the most open to the new science and philosophy, and the most skeptical or indifferent.

Even in the Dutch Republic perfect liberty of conscience did not prevail. The foundations of a large toleration were, however, laid by a decree published at Antwerp by Willem the Silent in 1578 with the purpose of uniting all his countrymen in the war of independence against Spain. This provided that "in the matter of religion everyone shall remain free as he shall wish to answer to God; so that no one shall trouble anyone else, but each man may serve God according to the understanding given him." The Union of Utrecht, which in the following year became the constitution of the seven seceding provinces, recognized the power of each province to regulate religion, but quite clearly recommended toleration of Catholics. Though some persecuting laws were passed against them, they were in practice usually left unmolested. A brief outbreak of intolerance following the Synod of Dort exiled the Arminian clergy, but in a few years the wave of bigotry spent itself and the Remonstrants were allowed to return. In fact, with few exceptions, no pressure was put upon any Christian of any sect. Holland became the refuge for the persecuted of other lands and profited enormously by her liberality. Even she, however, punished the expression of anti-Christian views. In 1668 Adriaan Koerbagh, the Deist, was sentenced to a heavy penalty, which was commuted, on his recantation, to ten years' imprisonment.

Though less enlightened than the Dutch Republic, England indulged her religious passions more moderately than did most of her European neighbors. Persecution under the reign of Henry VIII and Edward VI varied from moderate rigor to mildness. The Catholic restoration under Mary was marked by the execution of nearly three hundred Protestant martyrs. With the Anglican settlement under Elizabeth moderation again reasserted itself. The first seventeen years of the queen's reign were free from persecution, but the war with Spain, coupled with Catholic plots against the throne, and even against the life, of the sovereign, led to the banishment of Jesuits in 1585 under pain of death as traitors. This was followed six years later by the act against Popish Recusants, declaring that Catholics, as rebels and spies, should be obliged to remain within five miles of their homes on pain of forfeiture of their goods.

Under the operation of these laws 189 Catholics, of whom 128 were priests, suffered death for their faith under Elizabeth, and to them should perhaps be added 32 Franciscans who died in prison. But the contrast of the 221 victims in the forty-five year reign of the Virgin Queen with the 290 martyrs in Mary's five years is less important than the changed purpose of the government. Under Mary the executions were for heresy, under her sister for treason. It is true that church and state were closely allied; nevertheless the distinction is plain. Cecil put men to death, not because he detested their dogma, but because he feared their politics. Even while putting Jesuits to "the bloody question" and illegally torturing them, he felt called upon to explain that he punished them not for anything relating to "their supposed consciences," but only for their political opinions on the power of the pope.

Notwithstanding the provocation given by the Gunpowder Plot, persecution of Catholics relaxed under the early Stuarts. The laws against Jesuits, seminary priests, and popish recusants remained in force, but violations of them were no longer punished by death, but only by fine and imprisonment. Catholicism was now regarded by the government as "tolerated vice." In fact, two Unitarians burnt at Smithfield in 1612 were the last to suffer death for heresy in England.

But, though the actual infliction of capital punishment for erroneous opinion became happily obsolete, it was at least threatened by a severe ordinance passed by the Long Parliament in 1648. This declared that those who deny God, his ubiquity or foreknowledge, or the doctrine of the Trinity, and those who publish heresies about Jesus Christ, or who deny the authority of Scripture or the resurrection, shall be guilty of felony, and shall be punished by perpetual imprisonment, until they find sureties for good behavior, for the first offence, and by death for the second offence. Furthermore, those who preach the doctrines of the papists, Quakers, Episcopalians, or Anabaptists, or who maintain that "man is bound to believe no more than his reason can comprehend" were to be sentenced to prison until they should find surety or renounce their errors. During the Commonwealth further intolerant laws were passed against atheists, antinomians, papists, and Arminians. These laws, however, were laxly enforced by Cromwell, who personally desired wide toleration, and who practically extended it to the Jews. Such liberal action was denounced by Baxter as "soul-murder."

The triumph of the Anglican church at the Restoration was followed by the enactment of severe laws against all dissenters, Protestant and Catholic. Various statutes prohibited the meeting of sectarians in conventicles under penalty of fine, prison, and transportation to America. The Act of Uniformity imposed the Anglican Articles of Religion on all clergymen, deans, readers in the universities, and schoolmasters. Two thousand clergymen who refused to subscribe were deprived of their livings. It is significant, however, of the gradual progress of opinion that in 1677 the writ *De heretico comburendo*, by which so many heretics, since the time of Wyclif, had been burnt, was abolished by law.

Though capital punishment was no longer regarded as appropriate for heresy, heretics were still considered too dangerous to the state to be allowed participation in civil and political rights. The Test Act excluded from public office all who would not take the oaths of allegiance and supremacy and who would not communicate according to the Anglican rite. This was reenforced by a special act disabling papists from sitting in either house of Parliament, a law justified by Archbishop Tillotson on the ground that Catholicism was more mischievous than irreligion, and that papists were less trustworthy than pagans. How little the Catholic opinion which most fiercely resented these discriminations was itself tolerant may be gathered from Dryden's poem *The Hind and the Panther,* in which, while denouncing the Test as "a poisonous, wicked weed," the author extolled the Inquisition, which had preserved the happy regions of Italy and Spain from the ravages of the heretics.

The brunt of English intolerance was borne not by Englishmen, but by the Irish. The race hatred endemic ever since the conquest by Strongbow and Gerald of Windsor was inflamed by the injection of a religious element at the time of the Reformation. The civil war waged in Ireland contemporaneously with that in England laid the country waste before it was completely crushed under the booted heel of Cromwell. Sir William Petty, the most careful statistician of the age, a man long employed in Ireland, calculated that between the years 1641 and 1652 out of a population of 1,466,000, there had perished by sword, plague, or famine artificially produced, no less than 504,000 Irishmen, and 112,000 persons of English extraction. Besides these, many youths and maidens were sold into bondage to the American and West Indian colonies. The anti-Catholic laws, more rigidly enforced than in England, and against a large population, practically made the exercise of the prevailing religion a crime.

The Reformation in Scotland was followed by the enactment of severely persecuting laws, but by very few executions. In 1567 the Scotch Parliament authorized the Confession of Faith as an infallible doctrine; and in the same year prohibited the celebration of mass under the penalty of banishment for the second and death for the third offence for all who willingly heard it. In 1587 Jesuits were banished on pain of death, and the estates of all other "enemies of religion" were confiscated. In 1598 it was "statute and ordainit that all his Highness' subjects should embrace the religion presently professed" under heavy penalties; and in the same year the punishment of treason was threatened against those who entertained or received Jesuits or trafficking priests.

During the Commonwealth and after the restoration of the monarchy the laws against papists, re-enacted, were supplemented by a series of acts aimed at Protestant dissenters. The meetings of Quakers and Baptists were prohibited; the death penalty was provided for denial of the Trinity; while refusal to have children baptized, and withdrawal from the kirk, were punished by fine.

If we turn from the blood-drenched soil of the Old World to the virgin forests of the New shall we find a greater degree of religious liberty? On the western coast of the Atlantic a fresh start was made in building states. In these new societies men had shaken off many of the trammels still binding the older countries. In America the material conditions of life made for democracy and civil liberty. But, as the colonists brought their religion and their laws from the Old World, we shall find a strange mixture of the new and of the old. Colonies planted as political or commercial enterprises reproduced closely the institutions and spirit of their parent state. Beside these there were some few plantations settled by sectarians persecuted in their own country, who, not daring or not caring to persecute in their turn, at last realized complete religious liberty, and with it complete separation of church and state.

The French and Spanish colonies supported the Catholic church and persecuted all other religions. What the Inquisition accomplished in Mexico and Peru was achieved by the royal government in Quebec. Preaching and persecution made the atmosphere as stifling as in old France. Perhaps even more than in France the soldier and the priest gave the tone to the whole of society. In the Dutch colony of New Amsterdam, on the other hand, though the Reformed church was established, most dissenters, except Catholics, were tolerated, and so were Jews.

The first of the English colonies, Virginia, founded as a commercial and political venture, established the Anglican church and enforced conformity by banishing dissenters. As the New England colonies, Plymouth and Massachusetts, were settled by men fleeing from persecution at home, they might have been expected to allow complete religious liberty. That they did not do so can be explained by the contemporary history of England, with which they kept in close touch. The bulk of the immigrants came over during the years 1630-40 from the Puritan party, which, though in a minority when they emigrated, soon became, in the Commonwealth, the dominant party. The Congregationalists of New England thus began to feel themselves a state church, and to persecute dissenters exactly as did the established church, Presbyterian or Anglican, at home. And when the Restoration again put the Puritans at a disadvantage in England, Massachusetts had grown to such strength and to such an assertion of liberty and self-government, that she was ready to act as an independent state. In the matter of religion she had every excuse that can palliate, though none can extinguish, the guilt of persecution. To have tolerated the Episcopalians would have been not merely to welcome the Prayer Book and vestments and prelacy, but to have admitted men who had persecuted in England and who would have persecuted in America, when they had grown strong enough. Those who had built the citadel of Zion in Massachusetts were determined to keep the Philistines out.

Nor was there, from the first, the least sentiment in favor of religious freedom among the men who faced the hardships and dangers of the wilderness not to make an asylum for all men but to build a home for themselves. Nathaniel Ward, an immigrant clergyman, who published *The Simple Cobbler of Agawam* in 1645, declared that "to authorize an untruth, by toleration of state, is to build a sconce against the walls of heaven, to batter God out of his chair." Thomas Shepard preached that " 'T is Satan's policy to plead for an indefinite and boundless toleration," and Uriah Oakes denounced religious freedom "as the first-born of all abominations." Increase Mather, the most influential of the Puritan divines, told the General Assembly in 1677: "Sinful toleration is an evil of exceeding dangerous consequence," but he added: "It were better to err by too much indulgence than by too much severity. . . . There are other ways to suppress heretics besides hereticide."

It was natural, therefore, that, immediately after the settlement of Massachusetts, a state church should be established, the ministers of which were paid by public funds and attendance at which was obligatory upon all. The franchise was restricted to church members.

Very early, indeed, the colonial government was called upon to deal with heresy. When Mrs. Anne Hutchinson advanced some antinomian opinions, the general synod of 1637, branded them as heretical, blasphemous, erroneous, unsafe, unwholesome, and tending to disturb the peace. She and her followers were banished.

Still more drastic was the persecution of the Quakers, two of whose missionaries, arriving in 1656, were promptly deported, while a law was passed threatening flogging and imprisonment for "those cursed heretics" in future. When some of the brave sectaries came to Massachusetts in the years 1659 and 1660, five of them were condemned to death and four actually hanged on Boston common. This harsh act, however, shocked public opinion and almost caused an insurrection. Increase Mather himself little approved it, arguing that banishment rather than death is the appropriate punishment for heretics.

Among the dissenters banished from Massachusetts the most famous, Roger Williams, at first an Independent and later a Seeker, having become convinced that all persecution is wrong, determined to found a state which should be a refuge for all persecuted for conscience' sake. His plantation at Rhode Island, strengthened by the followers of Anne Hutchinson, sought and obtained a charter in 1644. The purely democratic government enacted three years later a code of laws insuring complete religious liberty. The new charter obtained from the king after the Restoration (1663) affirmed "full liberty in religious concernments" and provided that "no person within the said colony at any time hereafter shall be molested, punished, disquieted, or called in question for any differences of opinion in matters of religion." Moreover all Christians, not excluding Catholics, were given full civil rights. Nor was there any established church.

Somewhat less complete, but still very broad, was the religious liberty obtaining in Maryland. Here, too, we find a society founded as a refuge for an oppressed sect, in this case for Catholics. Lord Baltimore, the proprietor of the colony, though himself a Catholic, admitted Christians of all denominations freely. Knowing that he would not be allowed by the English government to persecute Protestants he granted full liberty to all Christians, though excluding other religions than Christianity. In 1649 the Maryland Assembly enacted a decree ensuring full religious liberty to all Trinitarian Christians. It stated that

since coercion in matter of religion has often produced harmful consequences . . . nobody in this province professing to believe in Jesus Christ shall from henceforth be anyways troubled, molested, or discountenanced for or in respect of his or her religion, nor in the free exercise thereof.

But the same act imposed the penalty of death and confiscation of goods on deniers of the divinity of Jesus or of the doctrine of the Trinity, and other punishments, such as fines and whippings, on blasphemers of God or of the Virgin Mary and on profaners of the sabbath.

The reign of liberty, such as it was, did not last long. No sooner had the Protestant Puritans attained a decided majority than they passed, in 1654, an Act concerning Religion, excluding from toleration papists and Episcopalians. After the Restoration the Baltimore family, reinstated in the proprietorship of the province, reintroduced toleration as it existed under the law of 1649.

The last of the colonies confessionally free from the beginning was Pennsylvania, founded as a refuge for the Quakers. The Great Law of 1682 provided that

> no person now or at any time hereafter being in this province, who shall confess and acknowledge Almighty God to be the creator, upholder and ruler of the world, and that professeth himself obliged in conscience to live peaceably and justly under civil government, shall in any wise be molested or prejudiced for his or her conscientious persuasion or practice.

Thus, atheists were excluded from toleration, and only Christians were allowed to vote. In practice little countenance was shown to Jews or to Catholics.

Relieved by a few brilliant exceptions to, and a few partial mitigations of, its persecuting principle, the history of the sixteenth and seventeenth centuries is in general one of blood, cruelty, and bigotry. The causes of this outburst of fanaticism having been explained, it remains to say a few words about its effects. What were the results, for humanity and for civilization, of this long régime of phlebotomy and cautery? For any particular nation the result was often the loss or gain of elements which were merely transferred from one country to another. The Jews and Moors expelled from Spain, the Huguenots fleeing from France, and the Puritans emigrating from England, but carried from a native to an adoptive home the elements of intellectual and moral strength and weakness inherent in their characters. But, if in many cases the gains of one country balanced the losses of another, there can be no doubt that the race as a whole and Western civilization as a whole, suffered considerably from the long reign of persecution. On the race the effects were undoubtedly dysgenic. The witch hunt, atrocious as it was, probably resulted in no deterioration of the stock, because the victims were largely past the age of child-bearing, and because those who were younger were for the most part rather below than above the average in character and mind. But the victims of persecution for conscience' sake were often among the choicest elements in the population. Though there were among the heretics some mean and narrow, and a few freakish and fanatical persons, the persecuted were as a whole superior to their persecutors in intellect and character, as they were above the average of their fellow-citizens in wealth and culture. From the groups of dissenters persecution sifted out those with the most courage and moral earnestness for the worst punishments. Year in and year out resolute men of independent minds were sent to the stake or to perpetual prison, and the racial stock impoverished by their sterilization.

The effects on civilization were more rapid and more decisive than the effects on the race. To eliminate independence of mind, to stamp out variations from the conventional pattern of thought, to discourage liberty in all its forms, could not fail to retard the progress of culture. In those lands, like Spain, where persecution did its perfect work, the Middle Ages were prolonged. In those lands, like Germany, where religious forces were equally divided and equally hostile, mutual slaughter uprooted the very foundations of civilized society. The most progressive countries were those in which relative tolerance prevailed.

2. THE THEORY OF TOLERANCE

So firmly were the principles and practice of persecution woven into the fabric of law and social life that it must pass as one of the most astonishing of revolutions that at last almost complete religious freedom has been won. The herd instinct for compelling conformity has not been rooted out; but its objects have been changed and its violence tamed. The heresies of the twentieth century, so far as they provoke forcible suppression, are economic, political, or moral. Indeed, in most civilized countries, a man would suffer more inconvenience from adopting an eccentric costume, or by violating some irrational taboo, than he would by proclaiming his atheism. And even in times of excitement the hand of power now laid upon the anarchist and the pacifist is far less cruel and bloody than it was formerly when it smote the heretic and free-thinker.

For this great change there were two causes, or two classes of causes, one material, the other intellectual. The material cause was the proved damage done to the temporal interests of society by persecution and religious war and the proved advantages of toleration. The experience of the Middle Ages had seemed to show the success and expediency of persecution. When the Albigenses succumbed to the sword of the Norman baron and to the stake of the Dominican friar, peace was restored both to France and to the church. When the Lollards were extirpated, England rejoiced that one more cause of civil war had been eliminated. The Hussites, though not crushed, were reduced to a harmless local sect. The persecution of the Jews may have impoverished the intolerant country in the long run, but it enriched the exchequer for the moment; for, as one king expressed it, the Jews were like sponges which, when they had sucked up the fluid wealth of the people, could be conveniently wrung into the royal treasury.

But the wars of religion and the wholesale massacres and expulsions following the Reformation obviously ruined nations and exhausted states. "Lucretius the poet," cried Bacon,

when he beheld the act of Agamemnon that could endure the sacrificing of his own daughter, exclaimed "Tantum religio potuit suadere malorum!" What would he have said if he had known the massacre in France or the powder treason of England? He would have been seven times more atheist and epicure than he was.

And Bacon wrote before the Thirty Years War, the massacres in Ireland, and the revocation of the Edict of Nantes had shown the worst that confessional hatred could do. Then, indeed, as the church historian Seckendorf admitted, men began to doubt the worth of the Reformation, or of religion in any form, if it produced such fruits.

Not only the horror of the slaughter but its uselessness

now stared men in the face. All the persecution and warfare of a century left the equilibrium of the religious balance almost unchanged. That neither Protestant nor Catholic were strong enough to crush the other was the obvious conclusion of both sides. And so, what neither the common ground of the Christians in doctrine, nor their vaunted love of God, nor their enlightenment by the Spirit could produce, was finally wrung from their mutual and bitter hatred.

As it became plain that persecution wasted the material and human resources of the state, it also was learned from experience that tolerance was economically profitable. The great commercial state of Holland flourished by allowing free trade in spiritual goods as much as by the free importation and exportation of more ponderable commodities.

In addition to the material reasons urging tolerance, there was a group of purely intellectual forces which in the long run proved even more effective. The truce imposed by the exhaustion of all parties could be nothing more than a truce as long as all parties harbored the evil passions of bigotry and of the *odium theologicum*. The religious peace imposed by skepticism and indifference proved permanent because it sapped away the interest of the public in those matters once held to be vital. The change was gradual, nourished by many sources. Most important of all was the growth of science and of the scientific spirit. The religious world-view with its biblical mythology and cosmology and with its scheme of eternal salvation so fearfully urgent and so fearfully doubtful, gave place to the scientific world-view with its boundless universe unvexed by the petty dogmas of the priest. Moreover, the lesson of science was the supremacy of reason, the lesson that truth cannot be implanted by force but must be recommended by persuasion.

Long before the mind of the race had fully assimilated the lessons of science, it was prepared for them by a variety of considerations emerging from the new conditions. The same forces which made for the birth of the theory of natural law and of natural rights in politics insinuated the conviction that freedom of conscience is a natural right. The comparative study of the various sects of Christianity and of the various cults of the heathen obliterated petty differences and expanded the realm of tolerated dogmas.

Like all great changes, this from persecution to tolerance was gradual. The reasons for the new liberty were apprehended and studied and built into a theory before they induced statesmen to incorporate such liberty in the laws and constitutions of states. Not until the eighteenth century did tolerance win its way into public opinion and policy. But in the seventeenth century, and even earlier, there were men in advance of their fellows who saw clearly the forces which would one day make religious liberty universal.

Among the groups to advocate tolerance most heartily were naturally the persecuted sects. Usually, though not universally, the Anabaptists, the Socinians, the Quakers, and the other small sects urged a policy by which their own position would have been so much improved. If there were some who, while their backs were smarting with the lash of the inquisitor, still prayed that other dissidents, more radical than they, might be visited with the same or severer punishment, there were others who proclaimed that compulsion is useless and that cruelty is repugnant to the spirit of Christ. Indeed, as in all great debates between Christians, the authority of the Bible was pleaded by both sides. If the gentle benevolence of Jesus was urged as an argument for tolerance by Castellio, the example of "all godly reforming magistrates spoken of by Scripture . . . pulling down false worship," was set forth by Increase Mather to justify persecution.

In the end, the theory of the separation of church and state, adopted by the Independents and by the German school of natural law, and reduced to practice by some American colonies, proved to be more effective than the pleas for mercy advanced by unhappy dissenters. It is significant that religious and political freedom flourished in the same soil. The Levellers of England and the democrats of the American colonies chiefly developed the theory of religious liberty based on the complete separation of Christ's kingdom from the kingdoms of this world.

It is natural to expect, and it is instructive to observe as a fact, that the expression of the theory of religious freedom should progress furthest on the soil which was already the freest. In Spain there was no liberty even to express the desire for it. In Italy an attack on the Inquisition could be made only by a man like Sarpi, safe in the protection of a powerful and anti-clerical government. And in France, before the Revocation of the Edict of Nantes, few pleas for tolerance could find a printer.

Montaigne, indeed, with his supreme art of indirectly sowing the seed of doubt, observed that "it is overvaluing one's own conjectures to cause a man to be put to death because of them," and added that liberty might not, in practice, foment division, but might blunt the edge of opinion, which is sharpened by rarity, novelty, and difficulty. His contemporary, De Thou, wrote the history of the wars of religion to show how baleful are the effects of persecution. Pascal saw clearly that force could put terror, but not true religion, into the heart, and that "the Inquisition and the Society of Jesus are the two scourges of truth." But the only open and avowed plea for complete liberty written by a Frenchman before the suppression of the Huguenots was a tract by Basnage de Beauval, called *Tolérance de Religions*.

Almost the only idea of tolerance obtaining in Germany before 1687 was one modelled on the religious peace of Augsburg or on the peace of Westphalia. It is vain to search the various tracts on politics and religion, such as that of Pannonius, for more than a plea to tolerate the great churches and to keep the peace and maintain the public faith between them. But in 1687 Samuel Pufendorf, inspired by the example of the Elector of Brandenburg, published an important treatise on *The Relation of Religious Liberty to Civil Life*, advocating tolerance of dissent on the grounds of natural right and of expediency.

From the Dutch Republic emanated several distinguished pleas for liberty of conscience. Among the small band of

Erasmians inheriting the liberalism of the great Rotter-damer Dirck Coornhert took the lead by publishing, in the late sixteenth century, a number of tracts assailing the murder of heretics as a crime, and pleading, from a clear head and a Christian heart, for a broad latitudinarianism. Erasmian, too, was the scholar in politics, Hugo Grotius, who used his vast influence, at home and abroad, to point out the advantages of liberty for the welfare of the state. The popular opinion was perhaps best represented by the poet Constantijn Huygens, the father of the great scientist, who satirized the bigot for trying to inculcate faith by force and love by hate.

More humane than the plea of the Christian, broader than the argument of the statesman, loftier than the dream of the poet, were the views of the philosopher touched with the spirit of science. From that empyrean sphere of thought where he habitually dwelt, Spinoza sent down to earth a revelation of the glory of free opinion that makes all other treatments of the subject seem petty and opportunist by comparison. In his *Theologico-Political Treatise* he mar-velled that those professing the religion of love should so hate one another; he proved that dogmas can neither hurt nor help true religion, which is nothing else than morality revealed by the light of nature; he pointed out the ineluct-able subjectivity of opinion and of religious taste, so that what edifies one man will move another to mockery. And, finally, he showed that "liberty of philosophizing can not only be permitted with safety to religion and civil order, but that such liberty cannot be taken away without detriment to civil order and to religion itself"; for, he added,

seditions excited under the guise of religion arise directly from this cause, that laws are passed regulating speculation, and opin-ions are condemned as crimes. . . . If the law animadverted on deeds only, and left words unpunished, under no legal pretext could similar seditions arise, nor could controversies ever turn into riots.

If Holland and some of the American colonies were freer than England, it happened, nevertheless, that the great cause of liberty of conscience was more debated in England than elsewhere. There, the great revolutions and the constant strife of parties and of sects laid bare the arcana of the state and uncovered the very foundations of society. In the course of the debate all arguments were advanced: that of expediency by the statesman, that of natural right by the political philosopher, that of indifference by the latitudinarian and free-thinker.

The extent and limits of Francis Bacon's tolerance were determined by his views of the good of the state. His essay on *Unity in Religion* proposed to seek this desirable end without too great rigidity on the one hand or too great laxity on the other. Though unity must not be secured by violation of charity, persecution he thought not allowable "except it be in cases of overt scandal, blasphemy, or intermixture of practice against the state." Seditions and conspiracies under religious guise must be ruthlessly crushed; but except in these cases persuasion is the only proper weapon of the church. His tolerance therefore extended to papists, but not to Anabaptists and "other furies," who intermixed, he said, dangerous political with unsound theological doctrine.

While the statesman was laboring to extend the bounds of toleration for the good of society, certain churchmen were endeavoring to enlarge the fold of the established religion to accommodate within its walls the largest number of Christians possible. This was the hope of Hooker, who would even have allowed heretics to grow in the church side by side with the orthodox, like the tares beside the wheat, and of Chillingworth, who went so far as to argue that persecution itself is schismatic, as rending the unity of the all-comprehensive national church. Chillingworth, therefore, wished for "such an ordering of the public service of God, that all who believe the Scripture and live according to it might, without scruple, or hypocrisy, or protestation against any part, join in it."

When these hopes for unity were shattered by the growth

of sectarian opinion and by the outbreak of civil strife ending in the subversion of the throne and of episcopacy, the problem of religious liberty became more acute than ever. The policy of the Commonwealth, to tolerate the larger Protestant communions, but to punish free-thinkers, papists, and some of the extremer Protestant sects, was reflected in the pamphlets of a large number of writers. John Owen and the anonymous author of *The Ancient Bounds of Liberty of Conscience* (1645) and John Milton and Jeremy Taylor all labored to show that a certain amount of toleration, strictly limited in accord with their own special preferences, is according to the law of God and of nature.

Though Milton wrote a *Treatise on Civil Power in Ecclesiastical Causes, showing that it is not lawful for any power on earth to compel in matters of religion,* and though one of his poems scathingly arraigns the "New Forcers of Conscience under the Long Parliament," yet he would exclude from tolerance the Roman Catholic church both because he considered it idolatrous, and because he asserted that "it is less a religion than a priestly tyranny armed with the spoils of the civil power which, on pretext of religion, it hath seized against the command of Christ himself."

While Milton was urging the cause of limited toleration under the Commonwealth as a member of the dominant Republican party and of one of the Puritan churches, Jeremy Taylor argued the same cause from the very different position of a persecuted adherent of "prelacy." So directly, indeed, did his *Discourse on the Liberty of Prophesying* spring from the "necessities of the time" that, when the Anglican church was restored to power, he retracted all his liberal opinions. The *Discourse,* however, remains an able indictment of the unreasonableness of prescribing other men's faith and of the iniquity of persecuting differing opinions. Broad-minded enough to admit that "all Papists, Anabaptists, and sacramentaries are not fools," and that "among all those sects there are very many wise and good men, as well as erring," Taylor argued that the truths

necessary to salvation are few and simple, and that variations in creed and cult are usually in non-essentials. To the
Bible and reason he appealed to justify both the extent of
his advocated toleration, and its limits, which were set by
considerations of morality and political expediency:

Whatsoever is against the foundation of faith, or contrary to
good life, or the laws of obedience, or destructive to human society
and the public and just interests of bodies politic, is out of the
limits of my question and does not pretend to compliance or
toleration.

From the uneasy position of the persecuted also the
Quakers continued to cry out against application of force to
spiritual matters. William Penn's *Great Cause of Liberty of
Conscience Debated and Defended* (1670) protested that,
just as public opinion was becoming more tolerant, persecution of dissenters became more rigorous. Such persecution,
he argued, is unchristian, unscriptural, against "the privilege
of nature and principle of reason," and "a contradiction to
government in the nature of it, which is justice, in the execution of it, which is prudence, and in the end of it, which is
fidelity."

Penn's plea was warmly seconded by his fellow-Quaker
Barclay, who, among his *Theses Theologicae,* set forth the
following axiom:

It is not lawful for any whatsoever, by virtue of any authority
or principality they bear in the government of the world, to
force the consciences of others; and therefore all killing, banishing, fining, imprisoning, and other such things, which men are
afflicted with, for the alone exercise of their conscience, pro-
ceedeth from the spirit of Cain, the murderer, and is contrary to
truth.

A surer guarantee of religious liberty than could be
exacted by persecuted sects is to be found in the growth of a
secular and indifferent opinion among those who were, at
heart, either beyond or very near to the outer bounds of

Christianity. The cultured, learned, and skeptical Selden opined:

> 'Tis a vain thing to talk of a heretic, for a man can think no otherwise than he does. In the primitive times there were many opinions. One of these being embraced by some prince and received into his kingdom, the rest were condemned as heresies, and his religion . . . said to be orthodox.

Naturally Selden was for complete toleration except for those "who pretend conscience against law" to plot against the state. Selden's opinion was exactly that of Hobbes; and was nearly that of Matthew Clifford and of Henry Robinson.

A slightly different note was introduced into the debate by two writers of the Commonwealth, James Harrington and John Goodwin. Harrington connected religious liberty with democracy, "a commonwealth being naught else but the national conscience." Goodwin urged that "freedom of conscience is a natural right, both antecedent and superior to all human laws and institutions whatever: a right which laws never gave and which laws never take away."

Not from England, however, nor from the Dutch Republic, but from America came the first thoroughgoing, radical plea for religious liberty, with no shrinking from the logical implications which had staggered less resolute champions. It is for this reason that the little tracts of Roger Williams must be reckoned among the world's great books. In the quality of their thought and emotion they surpass all the arguments for religious liberty written during the seventeenth century except the treatise of Spinoza, and they antedate Spinoza by a quarter of a century.

Though published in London, the works of Williams were written from his American experience as an immigrant who had originally settled in Massachusetts and had been expelled thence in 1635 on account of his unorthodox opinions, chiefly those on oaths and on tolerance. His fame rests equally on his plantation of Rhode Island as the first religiously free state in the world, and on his defence of his principles in three tracts: *Queries of Highest Consideration,*

The Bloody Tenent of Persecution, and *The Bloody Tenent yet more Bloody,* the first two published in 1644 and the third a few years later.

Writing as a devout Christian, his first proposition is that "the blood of so many hundred thousand souls of Protestants and Papists, spilt in the wars of present and former ages, for their respective consciences, is not required nor accepted by Jesus Christ, the Prince of Peace," and his second proposition is that persecution is unwarranted by Scripture. To a modern reader, however, far more telling and original is his thesis that "all civil states with their officers of justice in their respective constitutions and administrations, are proved essentially civil, and therefore not judges, governors, or defenders of the spiritual state of worship." To Williams a church is but a group of individuals united for a purpose which is of no more concern to the civil magistrate than the purpose of any other group, such as a trading company. State and church are each sovereign in their own domains; their union is fatal to both, for it "denies the principles of Christianity and of civility." There is no more a specifically Christian government than there is a specifically Christian trade, medicine, or fishery. Even morality, as far as it is regulated by law, should be kept separate from the religious holiness demanded by the church.

Most impressive of all the pages written by Williams are those in which he accepts the full logical consequences of his principles. All writers before him, and most of those after him, at least for a long time, while asserting the principle of religious toleration, made so many exceptions to the rule of liberty as to make it worthless. To tolerate all beliefs, except those of the papists, or of the Unitarians, or of the atheists, had been the demand of less courageous champions of freedom. But Williams dared to assert, "It is the will and command of God that . . . permission of the most paganish, Jewish, Turkish, or Antichristian consciences and worships be granted to all men in all nations." The excuses of those who pretend that they are not persecuting religious opinion but punishing blasphemy or idolatry are exposed as false.

Still somewhat hampered by his pious postulate that correct faith is necessary to salvation, Williams labored not a little to prove that the true church cannot be hurt by the propinquity of flourishing false cults. Such an argument, which really led to the maxim, "let us go to heaven our way, and let other people go to hell their way," profoundly shocked a generation conscious of the duty of every man to be his brother's keeper. But as the future was with Williams, it is from posterity that he, like other men in advance of their times, has reaped his meed of fame.

CHAPTER XVI

LAWS

I. THE SPIRIT OF THE LAWS

One of the best tests of the quality of the civilization of any given people at any given time is the code of laws enacted and enforced. For, like all other manifestations of social life, the laws are the natural outgrowth of that body of convictions, sentiments, and prejudices which make up the public opinion of a particular era; and, far more plainly than in the case of other social phenomena, the changes of public opinion from age to age and from year to year are written in the statute books and in the records of the courts. Even so, some allowance must be made for the conservatism of all modes of social control. The laws lag always a little behind the prevalent public opinion, just as that lags behind the changes implied in the advance of science and in the evolution of technology and of the economic structure.

Throughout the sixteenth and seventeenth centuries the spirit of the laws reflected very clearly the religious bias of the age and the interests of the governing classes. Crimes were commonly classified as those against God, those against the prince, and those against private persons. In an age of faith it seemed highly necessary to the welfare of society to prevent and punish affronts to the divine majesty. Among the crimes most severely repressed were therefore heresy, blasphemy, sacrilege, and sorcery; and among felonies or misdemeanors penalized because they were held to violate the commands of God were such things as working on Sundays, eating on fast days, and various sexual offences such as the seduction of nuns, marriage between a Christian and a Jew, and sodomy and incest. Even in the punishment of other crimes the religious element was present. The preambles of statutes against theft and murder speak of these acts not only as tending to "the great annoyance of the commonwealth," but also as incurring "the high displeasure of God." "Those greatly err," says the French publicist, Bodin,

who think that penalties are established only to punish crime. I hold that this is the least of the benefits accruing therefrom to the state, but that the greatest and chief benefit is the appeasement of the wrath of God, especially if the crime is directly against the majesty of God.

Nevertheless, the secularization of law, so marked in later ages, began to be noticeable in the period following the Reformation. In Protestant countries the Canon Law disappeared in the flames kindled by Luther. In all countries the right of the church to try clergymen and to try certain types of crime committed by laymen tended to decline. Benefit of clergy was abolished in one statute after another; while the right of sanctuary was restricted or totally abolished.

The foundation of all secular law on the continent of Europe was the *Corpus Juris Civilis* of Justinian. About the time of the Renaissance this great code superseded the native laws, of Teutonic origin, not only in Latin countries but in Germany, in Scotland, and in Scandinavia. For this there were both sentimental and practical reasons. In the age of scholasticism and in that of the rebirth of the classics Justinian was to the lawyer what Aristotle was to the philosopher and the Bible to the theologian. From the most practical standpoint, the Roman law served the purposes of society emerging from a natural into a capitalistic economy, and from a feudal into an absolutist polity. Codified in the last age of the Roman Empire, emphasizing the rights of property and the despotic power of the prince, the *Corpus Juris* met the needs of a society struggling with economic and political anarchy far better than did the primitive laws of the Saxons and of the Salic Franks. Moreover the very fact that it was *one*, whereas the codes of the barbarians were many, made it a natural and convenient authority for universal appeal. And, once generally adopted, it was deified as all legal, moral, and political systems tend to be deified by the groups living under them. Leibniz found in it a profound and elegant demonstration of the laws of nature and of reason.

In England and her colonies the place of the Roman Code was taken by the Common Law, constructed from decisions in the king's courts. The insularity of England, the popular element in her government, and the legal and political talents of her ruling class, enabled her to evolve a native system of justice superior in many respects to that of Rome herself. Among the great judges who developed the Common Law, the highest place must be assigned to Sir Edward Coke, a man of mean character but of consummate learning and of much genius. In the common law, to the study of which he devoted his life, he found "the artificial perfection of reason, gotten by long study, observation, and experience."

In addition to the Justinian Code and the Common Law numerous statutes and ordinances supplied the needs of justice and adapted the legal system to the changing demands of public opinion. It is remarkable that even in that age, when new statutes were so few in comparison with recent legislation, they should have been felt as too many. Montaigne advised that laws never be changed, lest the compact edifice of public polity be pulled down by its would-be menders. "Laws are usually worse in proportion as they are numerous," wrote Milton; while many reformers proposed to simplify the laws and to reduce their number by codification. Such a reform was, indeed, enacted in the Netherlands in 1570 and in France and Spain in the seventeenth century, and proposed, though not enacted, in England under the Commonwealth.

Compared with the treatment of criminals both in the Middle Ages and in very recent times the justice of the sixteenth, seventeenth, and eighteenth centuries was distinguished by its savage cruelty. Torture was used both in extracting confession and in punishment. The prisons were hells on earth; punishments were frightful. Scourging, mutilation, blinding, racking, burning, and boiling made the punishment of even minor offences worse than simple death; and when death was inflicted it was often made as painful as possible. In order to strike terror in the populace execution and torture were made public spectacles. Public opinion approved this cruelty, and even gloated over the grewsome sight of it. When Ravaillac, for regicide, was plied with redhot pincers, and then pulled limb from limb by wild horses, a vast crowd shouted its ferocious joy, and threatened to lynch the priest who, by absolving him, would have delivered his soul from hell.

Under the ancient German codes most crimes were punished by fines; and nowadays all but murder and treason are punished by prison or fine. But in the age of transition death was inflicted, in a gradation of painful forms, for a large number of felonies. Among capital crimes were homicide, *lèse majesté*, heresy, sorcery, sacrilege, theft, counterfeiting, smuggling, falsifying weights and measures, refusal to take up a public service, adulteration of food, perjury, various sexual offences, damage to property by night, arson, breaking prison, removing landmarks, and attempting suicide.

The chief reason for the ferocity of the penalties was the weakness of the machinery of justice. It is generally true that a strong government is a mild one, and that a weak administration of the laws tries to make up for its inefficiency by its cruelty. Punishments, like betting odds, are weighted in inverse proportion to the probabilities of loss. In the Middle Ages, justice for the lower classes had been mainly a personal matter between the landlord and the serf; while it could only be enforced against the powerful at the cost of a petty civil war. But as the new, capitalistic society emerged with its need for order but without the means for enforcing it, the readiest method to secure it that occurred to the judge and legislator was the threat of fearful pains.

In all countries the police was contemptible, the streets were left in perfect darkness at night, the judges were commonly corrupt, and the laws were respecters of persons. While a dreadful vengeance was visited on the poor criminal who happened to be caught, the rich thief would bribe the constable or judge, and the noble murderer would plead his privilege or his clergy and escape without a scratch. The satire on French justice in Racine's play *Les Plaideurs* depicts with equal force and truth the suborning of false witnesses, the corruption of judges, and the sadistic delight of the old magistrate in inflicting torment.

With the improvement of methods of dealing with the criminal public opinion became more humane. Indeed, there were always men like Montaigne, Johannes de Greve, Von Spee, and Governor Bradford of Plymouth Plantation, to protest against the barbarity of torture and the absurdity of inflicting it to procure true confessions. Early in the seventeenth century prisons were improved in Rome, Berne, Basle, and Lübeck; while new laws in many lands frequently sought to limit the amount of torture and the number of crimes to which it could be applied. The great reform of the criminal law in the Netherlands in 1570 forbade the use of torture, as a means of extracting confession, except in the case of heinous crimes and except when the proof was clear without it.

By far the most humane code of the seventeenth century was that adopted by Massachusetts, originally drawn up in 1641, and supplemented year by year by acts of the General Court. The legislators, while appealing to Magna Charta and other great English statutes and to the Common Law for precedents, greatly improved the criminal code as then obtaining in the old country. But they were still hampered by an excessive veneration for the Jewish legislation of the Old Testament. According to the laws of 1641, when very many offences were punished with death in England, the following crimes, and they only, were capital: idolatry, witchcraft, blasphemy, murder, bestiality, sodomy, adultery, kidnapping, false witness with the purpose of taking away a man's life, and treason. Eight years later rape and the undutiful behavior of children over 16 towards their parents were added. But the last named could hardly have been intended for use; for the law could only be put in motion by the parents of the wayward child and, in addition to that, they had to satisfy the magistrates that they had given their child no palliative cause for striking, cursing, or disobeying them.

The Massachusetts code of 1641 forbade all "barbarous, inhumane, and cruel punishments," though allowing whipping to the number of forty stripes, while seventeen hundred were sometimes inflicted in England. The same code provided:

No man shall be forced by torture to confess any crime against himself nor any other unless it be in some capital case where he is first convicted by clear and sufficient evidence to be guilty. After which if the cause be of that nature, that it is very apparent there be other conspirators or confederates with him, then he may be tortured, yet not with such tortures as be barbarous and inhumane.[1]

If such limitation of the use of torture fall short of modern ideas, nevertheless it was a long step in the right direction. And the humanity of the New England Puritans becomes yet more apparent when we read their laws for protecting women, children, strangers, servants, and dumb animals; for, almost alone among the legislators of the seventeenth century the Massachusetts General Court forbade "any man to exercise any tyranny or cruelty towards any brute creature which are usually kept for man's use." [2]

2. THE BLUE LAWS

While the repression of certain antisocial acts, such as murder and theft, has been the necessary business of government in all ages and in all societies, the regulation of morals

[1] W. H. Whitmore: *The Colonial Laws of Massachusetts,* 1889, p. 43.
[2] *Ibid.,* p. 53.

in many respects has varied widely with time and place. Morals, as the *mores* or customs of a group, though founded in the economic conditions and in the intellectual culture of the particular society, tend to be exalted by the members of the group into eternal rules of right and wrong. But, as every great economic or intellectual revolution alters the habits of society, it changes also their ethical ideas and then their laws. The statute-books of the sixteenth and seventeenth centuries are crowded with laws intended to meet the situation arising from the Reformation, from the Commercial Revolution, and from the intellectual revolution caused by the invention of printing. To sanction the religious prejudices, with their ethical corollaries, of the Reformation, both Protestant and Catholic, the several governments enacted many statutes dealing with such matters as blasphemy, sabbath-breaking, and amusements;—these are commonly called "the blue laws." To enforce the economic interests of the newly powerful merchant class, and to break the morale of the other classes, numerous ordinances and acts which may be conveniently grouped together as "sumptuary laws," though some of them dealt with other than strictly economic matters, were spread upon the statute books. And, finally, the censorship of the press became a matter for copious government regulations.

Nowadays the blue laws are sometimes regarded as one of the most regrettable of the many unfortunate peculiarities of the Puritan mind. Recent English and American historians, who know little but the annals of their own countries, have delighted to pick out the most crabbed laws and to quote the most rancorous of Cavalier libels in order to paint the Puritan drab. When they find a Connecticut law forbidding a man to kiss his wife on Sunday, or an English law abolishing the theaters and substituting seasonable meditation and prayer as the recreation suitable for a Christian man, when they read in Braithwait that the Puritans hung their cats on Monday for catching mice on Sunday, they jump to the conclusion that the men of the Commonwealth and the early settlers in New England were unique in their zeal for taking the joy out of life. But a comparative study shows that such laws were as common in Lutheran and in Catholic as they were in Calvinist lands. They were but the natural sequel to the Reformation, Protestant and Catholic; nor were they anything altogether new. In this, as in so many other respects, the great religious revolution of the sixteenth century was but a revival and an intensification of the medieval spirit.

Hence we find the French and Spanish kings, Lutheran margraves, and the popes themselves as hostile to frivolity and to some forms of art as were the Long Parliament and the General Court of Massachusetts. Bossuet and Pascal scourged the theater as soundly as did Prynne. Sixtus V and other popes made and enforced laws against gambling, obscenity, gossip, sabbath-breaking, and blasphemy more draconic than any enacted at Westminster, at Edinburgh, or at Boston. Whether, in forbidding bear-baiting, the Puritans objected to the pain given to the bear or to the pleasure given to the spectators, their scruples were shared by several of the popes. If the theater was not suppressed at Rome, it was hampered by restrictions of its subject-matter and by other regulations, such as those prohibiting women from acting and limiting the hours at which plays might be given.

So far, indeed, were the blue laws from being a specially Puritan creation, that the only reasoned and general objections to them that I have found were voiced by eminent Puritans during the reign of the saints in England. In private matters, Milton argued, every man has the right to be a law unto himself. "Retain only those laws," he urged,

which are necessary, which do not confound the distinctions of good and evil, which, while they prevent the crimes of the wicked, do not prohibit the innocent freedoms of the good, and which punish wrongs without interdicting lawful things only on account of the abuses occasionally associated with them. For, though the intention of law is to check vice, liberty is the best school of virtue, and affords the strongest encouragements to its practice.[1]

[1] Milton: *Second Defence of the English People, Prose Works,* i, 293f.

In like tone Harrington advocated the foundation of two national theaters, one for tragedy and one for comedy, and argued against restraining dancing and other amusements on the ground that

to tell men they are free, and yet to curb the genius of a people in a lawful recreation to which they are naturally inclined is to tell a tale of a tub.[1]

Typical of the blue laws were those punishing blasphemy. In 1564 Pope Pius IV chartered the Spanish Society of the Most Holy Name for the purpose of stamping out the practice of taking God's name in vain, and his successors promulgated drastic laws against it in the Patrimony of Peter. In 1566 Philip II decreed ten years in the galleys to profane swearers, in addition to previous penalties, which had been mild. This law failing to stamp out the practice entirely, the penalties for blasphemy were further enhanced in 1655 and in 1656.

The French legislation of the sixteenth century frequently animadverted upon "swearing, cursing, blasphemy, imprecations and other villainous oaths against the honor of God." A comprehensive decree of the Parlement of Paris in 1647 punished blasphemy of God, the Virgin Mary, or the saints, by cutting off the lips and piercing the tongue, and, it is suggestively added, "by death if it happens to follow." Many examples of sufferers under this law, practically all from the lower classes, are known.

The laws in England, passed during the Puritan ascendancy, were much less severe; even the act of 1650, marking the culmination of the movement to suppress blasphemy, punished it only by fine. Scotland began in the middle of the sixteenth century to legislate against "grievous and abominable oaths, swearing, execrations, and blasphemation." This was punished by imprisonment until 1649, when blasphemy complicated by heresy was made capital, whereas prison continued to be the fate of those who were guilty of "swear-

[1] *Oceana*, 220f. (1656).

ing, scolding, and other profanities." Similar enactments can be found in Germany, and in other countries.

If the laws against Sabbath-breaking were stricter in Great Britain than elsewhere, this was rather a national than a confessional difference. The revival of an intensely serious type of religion and the growth of aversion to amusement led in all countries to a new emphasis upon the observance of public worship and other pious duties. The Council of Milan (1573) complained of the profanation of Sunday by open markets, sports, and theatrical performances. Ten years later the Council of Reims forbade the faithful to participate in dances, public fairs, or stage plays on Sundays. The Council of Narbonne in 1609 protested against the profanation of the Sabbath by dancing, singing, hunting, hawking, feasts, or revelry. Several of the popes and some national governments in Catholic countries, notably in the Spanish Netherlands, enforced attendance on divine service.

As Luther, with his habitual candor, had stated in his *Catechism* that the strict observance of the Sabbath, or Saturday, was a bit of ceremonial law binding on no Christian, his followers usually permitted themselves to indulge in Sunday recreation, and even in work, after they had discharged their religious obligations by attending church. Calvin began, and his Puritan followers in England continued, to identify the Christian Sunday with the Jewish Sabbath, which finally resulted in that spiritual desert known as "the Lord's day" in Britain and America. Like all moral customs the observance of Sunday was deeply rooted in the psychology of the group in which it arose. It was the middle-class moral earnestness characteristic of the Puritan that led him to devote six days of the week to relentless labor in his "vocation," and the seventh day to an equally relentless cultivation of his spiritual nature. But he rationalized his sabbatarian practice by an appeal to the decalogue, by the assertion that the Fourth Commandment is a part of the moral, and not of the ceremonial law, and by the further argument that the Christian First Day of the week is the equivalent of the Jewish Seventh Day. The labored proof of this position was first perfected by Dr. Lancelot Andrews in lectures given at Cambridge in 1585, though not printed until 1650. At first this view was adopted only by the Puritan party, and was contraverted by the Anglicans, and by King James I who, in his *Book of Sports* (1618) proclaimed the right of the people to indulge in most of their accustomed pastimes on Sunday. Eventually, however, the Puritan program was adopted by all parties. The Anglican Jeremy Taylor, in a section devoted to the subject in his *Holy Living,* declared it to be the duty of the Christian to abstain from all ordinary work, and from all recreation, on Sundays, and to devote the day wholly to religious exercises.

Legislation on the subject seriously began in a law of the first year of Charles I (1625) declaring that "the holy keeping of the Lord's day is a principal part of the true service of God," and forbidding the "frequenting of bear-baiting, bull-baiting, interludes, common plays, and unlawful exercises and pastimes" on Sunday under penalty of the stocks or of fine. Two years later a "further act for the reformation of sundry abuses committed on the Lord's day" forbade carriers, drivers, carters, and butchers, to work or trade on Sunday. A still more stringent ordinance of 1644 forbade all unnecessary work and all recreation such as "shooting, bowling, ringing of bells for pleasure, masks, wakes otherwise called feasts, church-ales, dancing, games, sport, or pastime whatever." This law was re-enforced in 1650, and re-enacted in a different form, prohibiting work rather than play, after the Restoration, in 1677.

More forward than her southern sister, Scotland began legislating on the Lord's day in 1551, prohibiting "gaming, playing, passing to taverns and ale-houses, selling of meat and drink, and wilful remaining away from kirk in time of sermon." This law, with variations, was repeated at sundry times during the sixteenth and seventeenth centuries. Similar laws were enacted and enforced in the American colonies.

In the hostility of the pious to the theater and in the governmental regulation of it are to be found mixed motives. In part, the Reformers were moved by the occasional indecency of the plays, and the rulers by fear of an instrument used for political and religious propaganda. If these had been the only motives for censoring the drama its regulation would be analogous to the supervision of the printing press. But beneath and beyond the desire to repress obscenity and dangerous doctrine lay the deep aversion of the religious man, whether Catholic or Protestant, to any form of pleasure as a thing perilous to salvation. And when the battle was joined it was rendered fierce and mortal by the use made of the stage to ridicule its pious enemies.

While the popes tolerated plays, as they tolerated brothels, they hampered them by severe rules. The Synod of Milan ordered the clergy to "denounce and curse plays and spectacles and similar diversions without ceasing." St. Carlo Borromeo wrote a tract on *Dancing and Spectacles* to advocate the repression of both on church festivals and the licensing of the drama by ecclesiastical censors. At the behest of the church Venice expelled her comedians in 1577, and in 1611 the Roman Inquisition forbade women to act, and prohibited the impersonation of the clergy. Even sacred plays, a means of edification in the Middle Ages, were frowned upon. While Borromeo advocated their restriction, Pope Urban VIII forbade their being given in convents.

Though the theater in Spain was carefully licensed, and though *autos sacramentales* had long edified the public by the depiction of scenes from the Bible and from the legends of the saints, the theater was savagely denounced by Mariana [1] as the corrupter of morals. Plays were entirely suppressed during the years 1598-1600, after which they were allowed under rigid licensing.

The fondness of the French court for the drama encouraged its cultivation at Paris. Players were licensed by various acts of the government which aimed only, in a law of 1641, to repress indecency. But, particularly after Molière had pilloried hypocrisy in *Tartuffe* the devout declared against the theater. Even Pascal, the most brilliant philosopher and scientist in France was able to say, about 1659:

[1] *De rege*, Lib. III, cap. 16.

All great amusements are dangerous for the Christian life; but among all those which the world has invented, none is more to be feared than comedy. In it the representation of the passions is so natural and so delicate that it moves and begets them in our hearts, especially the passion of love; and the more chaste and good it makes love appear, the more dangerous it is.

Much harsher was the condemnation of the stage by the professional ecclesiastics. Harlai, the profligate archbishop of Paris, denied Christian burial to the body of Molière, while Bossuet declared that

The plays of Molière are full of impieties and infamies. . . . In them virtue and piety are always ridiculed and corruption is defended and made agreeable. Even the tragedies of Corneille and Racine are pernicious to modesty, as Racine recognized when he gave up play-writing. . . . Corneille's sole aim is to make his heroes serve love and beauty.[1]

In the Dutch Republic, where the stage was often a vehicle of religious propaganda and of political satire, it fell under the reproof of the Precisians as "a school of idleness, a mount of idolatry, a relic of paganism," and as leading to sin, godlessness, impurity, and frivolity.

In Puritan England the battle between the church and the theater was fought to a finish. In the first year of Elizabeth a censor was appointed to eliminate "unchaste, uncomely, and unshamefaced speeches" from the drama, and a little later a law was passed forbidding playwrights to meddle with matters of divinity and state. In 1574 the city council of London banished theaters from the city limits with the explanation that they fostered incontinence, frays, theft, extravagance, and "the uttering of popular, busy, and seditious matter," and were therefore "a great provoking of the wrath of God and the ground of all plagues."

In the reign of James I the battle waxed hot and furious between Puritan-baiters like Ben Jonson on the one side

---

[1] *Correspondance*, vi, 256; *cf.* his *Maxims on the Theater*, *Œuvres*, x, 753.

and scourgers of the theater like Prynne on the other. This hot gospeller attacked the stage as "sinful, heathenish, lewd, and ungodly." Even Bacon lamented the moral unprofitableness of the modern theater. And though a few Puritans like Milton could still defend tragedy as "the gravest, moralest, and most profitable of all other poems," yet even he confessed that it had fallen into "small esteem or rather infamy" under the reign of the saints. The closure of the theaters in 1642 was made permanent by the famous ordinance of 1648 "for the utter suppression and abolishing of all stage-plays and interludes," which declared them to be "condemned by ancient heathens and much less to be tolerated amongst professors of the Christian religion," and to be "the occasion of many and sundry great vices and disorders, tending to the high provocation of God's wrath and displeasure which lies heavy upon this kingdom." It therefore ordered all theaters to be pulled down or rendered unfit for spectacles, and all players to be punished as rogues. [1]

Much the same spirit of hostility to pleasure animated the attempts of the Reformers, Catholic and Protestant, to repress other forms of amusement, such as games, dancing, and bear-baiting. In 1567 Pope Pius IV, declaring that bull-fights and similar contests of beasts had been introduced by the devil, forbade them in the states of the church, admonished the clergy not to attend such spectacles, and exhorted princes everywhere to abolish them. Though eight years later Gregory VIII relaxed the penalties for giving bull-fights in Spain, his successors continued to repress them in Italy.

In France the blue laws were directed against gambling more than against other forms of diversion. In 1577 Henri III promulgated an edict prohibiting "minors and other debauched persons" from playing dice and cards in taverns, and six years later followed this by a crushing impost on these instruments of gaming which, it is stated, no longer

---

[1] L. Hotson: *The Commonwealth and Restoration Stage*, 1928, has shown that a good many plays were given surreptitiously during the Commonwealth, and that Sir William Davenant used the theater for the presentation of opera.

gave rise to innocent amusement but fomented "cheating, fraud, deceit, expense, quarrels, murder, debauch, ruin and perdition of families."

The moralists across the Rhine were less shocked by gambling than they were by the dances which one of them, the Lutheran parson Melchior Ambach, characterized as "mad, wild, crazy, raging, frivolous, unchaste, salacious, whoreish, and rascally." In excuse for this intemperate language it must be remembered that some of the dances then favored were boisterous romps in which the girls were hugged, kissed, and whirled about so giddily that their skirts—to quote another preacher—"flew up above their waists and sometimes above their heads." Nevertheless it is interesting to note how much more liberal and sensible was the opinion of the Puritan divine, John Cotton, of Massachusetts. "Dancing," said he, "yea, though mixed, I would not simply condemn. . . . Only lascivious dancing to wanton ditties. . . . I would bear witness against as a great stimulus to lust." [1]

Merry England, even before she became infected with the Puritan spirit, began to reprove and to repress the amusements of the vulgar. An act of Philip and Mary (1555) took away the licences from houses for bowling, tennis, dice, and cards, on the ground that these clubs became centers of conspiracy. Partly to encourage archery, and partly to prevent frivolity, the laws against gaming and sport became more severe under the Puritan régime. After the Restoration it was thought necessary to pass an act "against deceitful, disorderly, and excessive gaming." In Scotland and in America cards, dice, May-day games, and excessive hilarity of all sorts were forbidden. Scotland sought to restrain betting on horse-races by enacting that all winnings above one hundred marks in the space of twenty-four hours should be forfeited to the kirk. (The Scottish mark was a coin worth a trifle more than an English shilling.)

---

[1] The German opinions quoted in Janssen: *Geschichte des deutschen Volkes,* vol. VIII, p. 476; Cotton's opinion in T. J. Wertenbaker: *The First Americans,* 1927, Plate X.

3. SUMPTUARY LAWS

In addition to the blue laws passed primarily from religious and moral motives, many statutes were spread upon the records of the age of the Renaissance and of the Reformation with the purpose of enforcing the political and economic interests of the ruling classes. It is important to note that a great change in the purpose of these laws came as a consequence of the progress of the commercial revolution and of the rise of the middle class at the turn of the sixteenth and seventeenth centuries.

Many of these laws were sumptuary in the strict sense of the term. A paternal legislation then sought to regulate the private life of every citizen in minute detail, prescribing the fashion of his clothes, the number of courses at his meals, how many guests he might entertain on festive occasions, how long he should be permitted to haunt the tavern, what games he should be allowed to play and what songs to sing, how he should betroth himself, how dance, how part his hair, and when he should go to bed. For some of these laws no reason can be found except sheer conservatism, the prejudice against novelty and new fangles which is strong at all times and was stronger then than it is now. Another powerful motive was the desire to preserve class distinctions. To make the vulgar know their places it was deemed necessary to define the dress and diet of every rank. Economic motives also played their part. According to the doctrine then prevalent it was held to be to the advantage of the state to encourage saving. Luxury, especially when it took the form of consuming foreign imports, was regarded as deleterious and immoral. Certain clothes were prescribed in order to help the native wool trade, or fish was commanded to be eaten on certain days even in Protestant countries in order to support the merchant fleet.

These laws begin to appear on the statute books about 1300, and lasted in England until 1604, and in some other countries much longer. The popes (Sixtus V, for example, in 1586) forbade extravagant expense in clothes, banquets, and weddings. The French law of 1549 reformed the apparel of all classes, according to rank, in order to "avoid expense in superfluous things." But evidently the French of that age found that "la superfluité est chose très nécessaire," for the re-enactment of the law over and over again, down at least until 1660, proves how difficult it was to enforce it.

In Germany numerous and stringent laws prescribed to each class its dress, and for every variety of entertainment the maximum of expense and luxury to be permitted. The Scotch Parliament forbade the use of cloth of gold or silver, inordinate use of spices, "confections and drugs," and superfluous banqueting. One act, providing that "it be lauchful to na wemen to weir [clothes] abone [above] their estait except howries" was not only "apprevit" by King James VI, but endorsed with his own royal hand, "This acte is verray gude."

The numerous sumptuary laws enacted in England began to be attacked in the reign of Elizabeth, and were consequently repealed by an act of the first year of James I. This is one of the most remarkable, though one of the least noted, signs of the end of the Middle Ages and of the advent of modern times. The rise to power of the merchant class blurred the distinctions of rank based on birth or calling, and began to substitute for them an aristocracy of wealth. The rich, untitled men began to feel that they should be allowed to make their habit as costly as their purse could buy. And, if permission to dress according to wealth flattered their pride, the new economy of spending rather than of saving ministered to their interests. To the medieval theorists it seemed that wealth was increased by saving; to the modern merchant the wealth of his class, at least, seemed to depend on selling. While Bodin still thought it necessary to restrain private expenditures in the interests of the state, statesmen like Burleigh and philosophers like Spinoza began to proclaim, for different reasons, that regulations of luxury are vexatious and unsound.

Another sign of the triumph of the spirit of capitalism may be found in the numerous laws of all countries punishing mendicancy and forcing sturdy vagabonds to work. The new capitalist ethics, furthest developed in Calvinism, regarded idleness as a mortal sin, poverty as a proof of demerit, and prosperity as a chief sign of God's blessing. To be faithful to his calling was the highest duty of the middle-class Puritan; to succeed in it was his condign reward. Moreover the capitalist needed laborers, and to draft them into his factories he was willing, in the England of Edward VI, to sentence sturdy vagrants to slavery, and in all parts of Europe to force them to work for regulated wages. The harsh nature of these acts and their extraordinary number prove the difficulty found in all countries of coping with the new problems caused by the rise of capitalism, and also prove the progress of the capitalist mentality which in this, as in all similar cases, first established new customs, then recognized them more or less grudgingly in laws, and finally exalted them in ethics and sanctified them by religion.

In nothing can the struggle between the new ethics of capitalism and the old ethics of feudalism be traced more clearly than in the changed views of usury and of the just price. In the Middle Ages money had been scarce, and what little there was of it was in the hands of the Jews and not of the clergy and nobility. Naturally the church denounced filthy lucre as the root of all evil, and the noble scorned it as a low thing, unnecessary to a landed gentleman, and tainted with vulgarity. Founding their doctrine on the Bible and on Aristotle the medieval economists had declared that all commodities have a just price, which should not be raised in time of scarcity, and that all interest on money is immoral. But after the coming of capitalism and the rise of a class owing its power to wealth, and its wealth to free command of borrowed money and to the free manipulation of prices, both the medieval doctrines were bound to melt away.

One can trace the exact time of change most exactly in the English statute book. A law of Edward VI declared all usury (that is, all interest on money) "by the word of God prohibited as a vice most odious and detestable," and therefore made it unlawful. An act of the thirteenth year of Elizabeth repealed the act of Edward as having proved to be "the utter undoing of many gentlemen, merchants, occupiers, and others," and therefore declared usury up to 10% per annum not sinful, but lawful. In 1624 lawful interest was reduced to 8%, and in 1651 to 6%. Along with these laws went numerous others sanctioning the new practices of capitalism, such as insurance, and relaxing the laws against debtors, as was made necessary by the increase of investment and of commercial loans. During the Commonwealth, especially, new laws released innocent bankrupts from prison, and the first law of limited liability—though it was not so called— was passed in 1662. A somewhat similar progress of legislation is observable in Scotland and on the European continent.

It is notable that clerical opinion retained the medieval ethics long after they had been abandoned by statesmen and parliamentarians. Pope Sixtus V condemned usury and commercial loans in 1586; and Clement VIII in 1605 exhorted the civil officers to help the Bishop of Ventimiglia to extirpate usurious practices. The Puritan Henry Smith condemned all interest on money as theft, and the Rev. John Cotton lectured against the false principle "that a man might buy as cheap and sell as dear as he could." Bacon, however, would allow usury as a necessary concession to men on account of the hardness of their hearts. Other statesmen followed the lead of the merchant with more enthusiasm, and at last the divines were converted to the new philosophy of wealth. "You may labor in that manner," said Richard Baxter, "as tendeth most to your success and lawful gain, for you are bound to improve all your talents."

4. CENSORSHIP OF THE PRESS

Among the novel social conditions that seemed to cry most loudly for governmental intervention was the growth of the habit of reading. Perhaps no invention in all history,

except that of the alphabet, has so altered the cultural environment of humanity as has that of typography. As knowledge is power, the art that cheapened knowledge vulgarized
power. When the arcana of the priest and clerk were exposed
to the gaze of the public they no longer imposed upon the
public. The conflict of opinions and parties were henceforth
argued not before a small, privileged, professional, and
sacerdotal coterie, but before an ever expanding body of
readers. And as the literate opinion of the world became
the supreme court before which all causes were pleaded and
by which they were decided, the press, as the moulder of this
opinion and judgment, became the most powerful instrument
of education and of propaganda in the world.

With eyes sharpened by fear for her threatened authority
and by jealousy for her invaded privileges, the church led
the way in curbing the press. The first edict for licensing
books to be printed was issued by the Archbishop of Mainz
in the city of Gutenberg in 1485. A few years later Pope
Alexander VI and the Fifth Lateran Council extended the
institution of papal censorship throughout Christendom. The
first list of prohibited books was that promulgated by the
English government in 1526, drawn up by Wolsey and
other prelates to obviate the dangers of Lutheran infection.
A more extensive list, prepared by the University of Louvain, was issued with the emperor's authority in 1546.

In the same year the Council of Trent prohibited the
printing without licence of anonymous books and of books
on religion. When, in 1557, the Roman Inquisition issued a
long list of books to be publicly burnt, *that* might be considered the first *Index of Prohibited Books*, but the first
document to bear that name was issued by Paul IV in 1559.
It divided forbidden books into three classes, those of authors totally condemned, those of writers erring only in
some works, and anonymous books. A long list, intended to
be complete, was added. Three years later the Council of
Trent again took up the matter, and in fulfilment of their decree Pius IV promulgated an extremely thorough Index,
prohibiting the faithful on pain of excommunication from

reading books condemned by popes or councils prior to 1515, versions of the Bible, the works of heretics, obscene literature, and treatises on magic.

In order to enforce her decrees the church made offending booksellers liable to heavy penalties at the bar of the Inquisition; and in order to keep the Index up to date, Pius V instituted a special Congregation, which has issued more than forty *Indices Librorum Prohibitorum,* and which still condemns dangerous books and authors almost every year. One of the duties of the Congregation was to prepare also an *Index Expurgatorius,* or list of passages to be deleted from books which might then, so corrected, be read. This task proved so delicate and onerous as to tax the powers of several university faculties. The only *Index Expurgatorius* ever issued by the Roman Congregation was one prepared in 1607, dealing with 51 authors.

At this point it is pertinent to inquire just what were the results of the efforts of the church to "protect her flock from poison and to give them salubrious fodder," as Sixtus V put it, by selecting their reading matter for them. It is not too much to say that most of the important works of modern science, philosophy, and learning, and not a few of the chief products of Catholic piety, have been forbidden by the church as dangerous to the faith of her children; and that, in addition, many of the ornaments of fair letters have been tampered with in order to protect the sensitive pride of ecclesiastics or the squeamish prudery of priests. These are serious accusations, but they may easily be substantiated by anyone who takes the trouble to glance through the *Indices.* Confining ourselves for the present to books produced before 1687, we shall find the following works prohibited in whole or in part, in perpetuity or with the proviso "until they be corrected": Among books on religion most versions of the Bible are forbidden to the faithful, together with not a few of the fathers of the church, and, of course, all works of Protestants and of other heretics, the writings of the Jansenists and of the Quietists, of many mystics, moral theologians, and dogmatists. Among philosophers we shall find the names of Bruno, Ramus, Montaigne, Bacon, Charron, Hobbes, Campanella, Malebranche, Descartes, Spinoza, Telesio; among historians Burnet, Fox, de Thou, Baronius, Guicciardini, and the Magdeburg Centuriators; among political scientists Botero, Gentili, Grotius, Suarez, Sarpi, Mariana, Hotman, Machiavelli, Buchanan, Bodin, and Marnix; among scholars Salmasius, G. J. Voss, I. Voss, Usher, Casaubon, Scaliger, Walton, Selden, R. Simon, Erasmus, H. C. Agrippa; among scientists Copernicus, Galileo, Pascal, Cardan, Mercator, Recorde, Paracelsus, and many anatomists. Among poets and novelists prohibited or expurgated were Milton, Dante, Murnar, Rabelais, Marot, Castiglione, Sir Thomas More, and Boccaccio. It is instructive to notice that Dante was expurgated for his reflections on the papacy contained in the *De Monarchia* and in the *Divine Comedy*, and that Boccaccio was expurgated not chiefly for his indecency but for his satire on the clergy. Thus, his tale of the seduction of an abbess was rendered acceptable by changing the nun into a countess; and the story of a priest who led a woman astray by impersonating the angel Gabriel was altered merely by turning the priest into a layman masquerading as a fairy king.

While the pious Catholic is still convinced that the services of the *Index* in preserving the faith of the flock inviolate outweigh whatever temporal disadvantages accrue to science and to literature, the philosopher will find in the mere list of names mentioned above, to which a vast number of others might have been added, a telling indictment of the church's wisdom. That servile faith, bigotry, and obscurantism have been fostered, and that science, philosophy, and liberty were long sorely hampered in Catholic lands is due to the *Index* even more than to the Inquisition. The censorship, said Sarpi truly, is a dagger drawn against all writers. "The expurgating indexes," said Milton, "rake through the entrails of many an old, good author, with a violation worse than any that could be offered to his tomb."

Independent of the Roman *Index*, but like unto it, was the censorship in Spain. Early in the sixteenth century the

Spanish Inquisition asserted the right of condemning old books and of licensing new ones, and, though Charles V in 1554 confined the duty of issuing licences to the Royal Council, the Inquisition retained the right of denouncing heretical books, and occasionally even presumed to issue licences. The interests of the church were consulted in a savage decree of the royal government forbidding, under penalty of death and confiscation of property, the keeping or selling of any book condemned by the Inquisition, or the publishing of any work without first submitting it to the Royal Council, or the circulation of any manuscript without permission. This law, first promulgated in 1558, and confirmed in 1627, remained unrepealed until the time of the French Revolution.

Under its authority of guarding literature from heresy the Spanish Inquisition issued various indices of its own. Enormous labor, and not a little controversy, followed the attempt to expurgate authors not totally condemned. Any fool or bigot could find matter dangerous to his neighbor's faith in any book no matter how wise and good; consequently when the Edict of Faith demanded denunciations of heretical passages in literature, these denunciations came in in such numbers as to overwhelm the theological professors who were drafted for the service of correcting their betters. Though years of labor were spent in preparing the expurgatorial indices issued in 1584, 1612, 1632, and 1640, none of them was thorough enough to suit the extremists. How earnestly the expurgators took their task may be seen from the single example of Erasmus; the list of passages to be deleted or altered in his works occupies fifty-nine double-columned, closely printed folio pages.

It is interesting to observe that the Spanish and Roman indices differed considerably. Works included in the one were sometimes omitted from the other, not only from inadvertence but even from mutual jealousy. Galileo's name never appeared in the Spanish *Indices,* which on the other hand, tampered with Shakespeare and Cervantes. In the English College founded at Valladolid in 1589, there are preserved copies of the First and Second Folios of Shakespeare's *Plays,* the second of which has been expurgated by the censor Guillen Sanchez. This gentleman cut out *Measure for Measure* entire, presumably for its satire on hypocrisy, and deleted from other plays a few passages reflecting on Catholic monarchs or praising Protestant rulers. From Don Quixote was stricken a passage designated as "impious" because of its disparagement of perfunctory works of charity. It is remarkable, however, that a passage faintly satirizing the censorship by representing the curate and barber examining the books of chivalry belonging to the ingenious hidalgo and relaxing them to the secular arm of the housekeeper to be burnt, escaped the vigilant eye of the Inquisition.

Though kept entirely under the control of the royal government the censorship in France was as rigid as in Spain or in Italy, and as much directed against heresy. The laws against printing or importing heretical books passed in the reign of Francis I were strengthened in the reign of his son by various edicts, of which one, promulgated in 1557, forbade the importation of condemned books under penalty of death. Other edicts forbade the printing or selling of any book on religion not licensed by the Sorbonne. In 1609 the drama was put under the supervision of a censor, who was to be, however, not an ecclesiastic but the attorney general. While the religious purpose of the censorship was never lost sight of, the political purpose became more and more pronounced. The decree of 1630, regulating the book-trade of Paris, declared that "experience has shown the kings of France how prejudicial to the state is the liberty of the press." During the Fronde the regulation of the press fell into abeyance sufficiently to allow many pamphlets to cater to the heightened public interest in politics, and to present the views of the various parties in the civil war. But in 1649 a severe and comprehensive decree of the Parlement of Paris prohibited the printing and selling of unlicensed books and pamphlets. So alarmed was the government by the rise of newspapers that in the years 1660 to 1665 all of them were suppressed except the semi-official *Gazette de France* and the insignificant *Mercure Gallant*. Even the *Journal des Savants,* founded in 1665 and devoted entirely to scientific and historical subjects, soon fell under the animadversion of the government and was for a time suppressed.

Not less rigid was the regulation of the press in most of the other countries of Europe. The Spanish viceroys in the Netherlands ordered the destruction of all plays and songs reflecting on the Catholic religion, appointed prototypographers or Head Printers to license books, drew up expurgatory indices, and denounced the severest penalties against those who should sell, or even read or possess, heretical and scandalous literature.

In the Northern Netherlands, after their secession, there was more liberty than elsewhere, and more than the theologians liked. The Synod of Dort spent some time in considering methods of strengthening the censorship against heretical and atheistical books. But, except in times of excitement, so lax was the supervision of the press that Amsterdam and Leyden became the great publishing centers for all the liberal writers of every country. Scientists smitten with the censure of the *Index,* heretics of the extreme left, daring philosophers, and political exiles, all found in the Netherlands publishers for works unprintable at home. Galileo's *Dialogue on the New Sciences,* the tracts of Socinus, the treatises of Descartes, the lucubrations of Richard Simon, Locke's *Letter on Tolerance,* are only a few examples of the many famous foreign works printed in the Netherlands. And from the clandestine press, connived at by the authorities, poured forth so many French journals banned at home, that the ordinary name for newspaper in seventeenth-century France came to be *Gazette de Hollande.* The first English newspapers were also printed in Holland. Nevertheless, even there some decrees forbade the printing or importation of scandalous and seditious books.

The comparative freedom of the press in Germany was due not to the liberal intentions of her princes but to their divided and weakened rule. While Catholic states rigidly imposed the *Index of Prohibited Books* upon their subjects, and while most Protestant states evinced considerable zeal in suppressing books which they regarded as unsound or seditious, among so many principalities and free cities it was usually not difficult to find one which would allow the publication of any given book. The famous fair at Frankfort remained the center of Europe's book-trade, and the pecuniary profits derived from it doubtless biased the authorities in favor of liberal press laws. In Germany as in Holland many books of foreign origin were published, including the only complete editions of the works of Sir Thomas More ever published, and the first edition of Harvey's treatise on the circulation of the blood. From the date of Gutenberg's invention down to the beginning of the Thirty Years War Germany printed more books than did any other country.

Particularly interesting is the history of censorship in England because in that country was issued the first and the noblest defence of the freedom of the press ever written. While the early Tudors had punished the publication of treasonable, seditious, heretical, and blasphemous books as a crime, the later Tudors found a readier instrument for regulating the press than the courts had proved to be in the incorporation, in 1557, of the Stationers' Company, with wide powers to monopolize and control the printing trade. The instructions issued by Elizabeth forbidding the publication of books without licence from privy councillors, or bishops, or chancellors of the universities, or archdeacons, or any two of them, were re-enforced by a law of 1581 making the printing, writing, or publication of seditious books felony without benefit of clergy. Under this law a peccant printer was hanged, drawn, and quartered in 1584.

In order further to facilitate the repression of objectionable literature, two detailed ordinances were issued by the Star Chamber in 1586 and 1637. The first limited the number of printers to a few resident in London, Oxford, and Cambridge, and required a licence for all books, except those printed for the queen's service, to be obtained from the archbishop of Canterbury, or the bishop of London, or two chief justices, or the chief baron. The ordinance of 1637, with similar purpose, was far more elaborate in its scheme of licensing, in prohibiting the importation of unlicensed books, and in protecting copyright.

The disorders of the Civil War allowed, and the growing interest of the public in politics and in confessional controversy encouraged, the publication of vast numbers of polemic books, pamphlets, and journals. To meet the situation thus arising and to obviate what were called "the great late abuses and frequent disorders in printing many false, forged, scandalous, seditious, libellous, and unlicensed papers, pamphlets and books, to the great defamation of religion and government," the Long Parliament promulgated an ordinance in 1643 strictly forbidding the publication of any book or pamphlet without licence obtained from certain officers named in the text.

As a protest against this ordinance there promptly appeared, without licence, a famous defence of the liberty of the press, remarkable not only as a masterpiece of style and of persuasion, but as a symptom of the change of public opinion in its most advanced lines. Hitherto, apparently, readers, so far from resenting the selection of their literature by the authorities in church and state, had generally regarded strict press laws as necessary bulwarks against errors which they had been reared, largely by the operation of those very laws, to detest. The poet Spenser, for example, Puritan though he was, had depicted error as a dragon vomiting out "books and papers" amid a "flood of poison horrible and black." [1] But a half century of religious and political controversy had taught the wisest and boldest of the Puritans to see in a free press the strongest ally of truth in her everlasting battle with error.

Borrowing his title from "the old man eloquent" Isocrates, whose *Areopagiticus* (as is the form of the word in Greek) is a plea to the Athenians to renounce servile innovations and to return to the free constitution of their ancestors, Milton called his pamphlet *Areopagitica: A Speech for the*

---

[1] *Faery Queen*, Bk. i, Canto i, stanza 20.

Liberty of Unlicensed Printing, and selected for his text or motto a verse from Euripides.

> This is true liberty, when freeborn men,
> Having to advise the public, may speak free.

While pleading with the Parliament to repeal their recent ordinance, the writer admitted that it is a matter of public concern to keep a vigilant eye upon books, for they

> are not absolutely dead things but do contain a potency of life in them to be as active as that soul whose progeny they are. . . . A good book is the precious life-blood of a master-spirit, embalmed and treasured up on purpose to a life beyond life.

Nevertheless, he continued, a history of the censorship—for which he chiefly blamed the Inquisition and the Council of Trent—shows that it is inexpedient to shelter people from erroneous and even from vicious doctrines:

> I can not praise [he wrote] a fugitive and cloistered virtue, unexercised and unbreathed, that never seeks out and sees her adversary, but shrinks out of the race, where that immortal garland is to be run for, not without dust and heat. . . . That virtue which knows not the utmost that vice promises to her followers, and rejects it, is but a blank virtue, not a pure.

If we regulate printing, he argued, we must also regulate all pastimes, as music, dancing, and eating—and this conclusion, though it would not have been unacceptable to some Puritans, seemed absurd to Milton. Furthermore, he urged that licensers are generally more ignorant than the authors they judge, that the submission of a book to a censor is an affront to learned men, and a discouragement to them to teach with authority. If error is dangerous, he added, the learned are in more danger than the vulgar, nor does any man know all the truth. Liberty of argument is the nurse of all great wits, and so, he concluded:

Let truth and falsehood grapple. Who ever knew truth put
to the worse in a free and open encounter? Her confuting is the
surest suppressing. . . . She needs no policies, nor strategems,
nor licensings to make her victorious. These are the shifts and
defences that error uses against her power.

But the argument, eloquent as it is, failed to convince
those in power, though they were of Milton's own party.
Ever severer ordinances and acts were issued by Parliament
in 1647, 1649, and 1653. These were chiefly directed against
the publication of "Diurnals, News, or Occurrences" by the
"Malignants," as the Royalists were called.

With the Restoration the old system of licensing was
revived in a law of 1662 which declared that "the regulation
of printers and printing presses is a matter of public care,"
and that "many evil disposed persons have been encouraged to print and sell heretical, schismatical, blasphemous,
seditious, and treasonable books and pamphlets." This
statute provided that all books must be licensed, those on
the law by the Lord Chancellor and other judges, those on
history and politics by the Secretary of State, those on
heraldry by the Earl Marshall or King of Arms, and all
others by the Archbishop of Canterbury, or the Bishop of
London, or the chancellor of one of the universities.

The spirit of the Scotch laws on the subject is well
summarized in the Act of 1599, which declared that

In all well governed commonwealths it is expressly prohibited that
any subject take upon hand to write, print, or publish any books
in whatsoever discipline or science, but especially invectives or
libels, defamatories, histories, chronicles, or annals . . . without
his majesty's licence.

In the matter of the freedom of the press the New World
was no more advanced than was the Old. A seventeenth-
century Governor of Virginia thanked God that there were
no presses to corrupt the manners of the settlers in that
colony. The first press in British America was set up at
Cambridge under the supervision of the president of Har-

vard College. As he failed to exercise sufficient vigilance to satisfy the demands of the theocracy, two licensers were appointed in 1662 without whose consent nothing could be printed. Twelve years later the General Court of Massachusetts granted permission to set up presses elsewhere than in Cambridge, and, to meet the dangers of an expanding book-trade, added two licensers, of whom Increase Mather was one, to the two formerly appointed.

PART IV. THE SPIRIT OF THE TIMES.

CHAPTER XVII

MORALS AND MANNERS

I. MORALS

The task, once assumed by the theologian, of discovering and proclaiming the laws of right and wrong, has now been taken over by the psychologist and sociologist. To the historian falls the humbler duty of recording the infinite variety of moral practice and of ethical theory. There is no act, however repugnant to the prejudices of one society, which has not been tolerated and encouraged in some other community; there is no act, however socially deleterious it may appear to be, that has not at some time and in some place, been tolerated and encouraged. Homicide, though commonly reckoned the chief of crimes, has nevertheless, been tolerated and praised in some forms by many societies—in war, in human sacrifice, in the duel, in head-hunting, in the vendetta, in tyrannicide, in avenging the point of honor. Every conceivable form of sexual relations, every conceivable form of holding property, has been regarded in some society at some time as the only righteous one. To insist further upon these contrasts would savor of satire rather than of history. Not to ridicule human inconsistency, but to explain the moral changes in human nature as due to the alterations of social conditions, is the province of the chronicler of culture.

One of the most marked changes in the seventeenth century was in the attitude of the public in regard to duelling. In the old feudal society private war between nobles had rarely been regarded as a crime. But with the rise of the merchant class, preferring commercial to combative competition, duelling began to be condemned and severely repressed. Decrees of the Council of Trent and bulls of the popes denounced it. A papal bull of 1592 deprived those who died in a duel of Christian burial, and another bull of 1660 threatened duellists with excommunication, the anathema, malediction, perpetual infamy, and loss of privileges, in addition to imprisonment and other temporal punishments, including, in extreme cases, death or the galleys. But even these penalties did not quickly suppress a custom which was, in Italy, often associated with family vendettas, such as the one between the Montagues and Capulets, made famous by Shakespeare.

In France, an aristocratic and military society allowed private combats. The nobles boasted of their prowess, the ladies encouraged its exercise by granting their favors to the brave, and the clergy excused those who defended their honor by a variety of casuistical arguments. The number of single combats was so large that a courtier of Henri IV estimated, or counted, four thousand men who had perished in duels during a period of eighteen years. Finally the government intervened. An edict of 1609 made duelling punishable by death and confiscation of goods, and established a court of honor to arbitrate disputes. This proving ineffective another edict was promulgated in 1626 by Richelieu and was so stringently enforced that at last the number of single combats began to decrease, though they did not entirely vanish.

Far less military and more commercial than the continental monarchies, the nation of shopkeepers across the Channel suffered less from the curse of private warfare than did they. But even in England duels were not unknown, nor without some justification in public opinion. Selden wrote a history of the duel, defending the practice as a necessary method of revenging non-justiciable wrongs.

The wild manners of the Scotch nobles were restrained by a law of 1600, declaring that the king and Parliament

considering the great liberty that sundry persons take in provoking each other to singular combats upon sudden and frivolous occasions, which has engendered great inconveniences within this realm, statute and ordain, that no person in time coming without his Highness's licence fight any singular combat under pain of death and movable gear escheat.

The same worship of physical prowess that respected the duellist found ample expression in the general exaltation of war. Statesmen like Bacon thought that "for empire and greatness it importeth most that a nation do profess arms as their principal honor, study, and occupation"; [1] kings like Louis XIV declared that "Conqueror is the noblest and loftiest of titles," and erected arches of triumph to commemorate their victories; poets like Dryden, while weaving the laurel crown of verse for the hero's brows, declared in sober prose that "all other greatness in subjects is only counterfeit; it will not endure the test of danger; the greatness of arms is only real; other greatness burdens a nation with its weight, this supports it with its strength." [2]

But along with these examples of warlike feeling, which might be multiplied *ad libitum*, there are a few signs that the ethics of pacifism had already won a few converts. Milton denounced men as worse than devils for "levying cruel wars, wasting the earth each other to destroy"; declared that patience and heroic martyrdom were nobler themes of poetry than was "the long and tedious havoc of fabled knights"; lamented that "manslaughter should be held the highest pitch of human glory"; asserted that great conquerors should be "destroyers rightlier called and plagues of men"; and proclaimed that "Peace hath her victories not less renowned than war." [3]

Though with less eloquence than Milton's, Leibniz denounced wars among Christians as both impious and foolish. He was wise enough to point out to Louis XIV that his career of conquest would unite all nations against him, and fond enough to think that he could, by this argument,

[1] *Essay,* XXIX.
[2] Preface to *Annus Mirabilis,* 1666.
[3] *Paradise Lost,* ii, 496ff; vi, 501ff; ix, 28ff; xi, 695ff; *Paradise Regained,* iii, 71ff; *Sonnets* XV, XVI, XVII; *Elegia Quarta,* 71ff.

divert the royal foe of his country from the conquest of Germany to the conquest of Egypt.

Few transvaluations of moral values have been greater than that following the emancipation of women in the twentieth century. Until the cheapening of knowledge and the economic results of the industrial revolution set them free women of all past ages have been held in subjection. But the conditions of their slavery varied with the attitude of society towards sex. The great wave of asceticism accompanying the rise of Christianity denounced the pleasures of love and degraded women. The theory that the church exalted woman because the church worshipped the Virgin Mary is no more true than would be the assertion that Christianity exalted the Jew because Christians worshipped Jesus. Nor can it be said that chivalry, which made gallant love the sport and business of the noble, did more than gild the chains of the weaker sex. The Reformation, by abolishing sacerdotal celibacy, by secularizing marriage, and by exalting wedlock, instead of virginity, as the typically godly estate, did much to restore a healthier view of woman and of sex, even though many reformers reviled women for tempting them beyond their strength.

In the sixteenth century, therefore, various strands of inherited prejudice and custom crossed one another. The churchmen continued to proclaim, in the language of the English Prayer Book, that the purpose of marriage was not to "satisfy men's carnal lusts and appetites," but that it was ordained for the procreation of children, as a remedy against sin, to avoid fornication, and for mutual society, help, and comfort. Most churchmen thought that most women were "fond, foolish, wanton flibbergibs . . . evil-tongued, worse-minded, and in every way doltified with the dregs of the devil's dunghill." [1]

The middle-class view of woman restricted her sphere to the household, and inculcated on her the duties of submission to her husband, of chastity, of sobriety in dress,

---

[1] Sermon of Bishop Aylmer before Queen Elizabeth, quoted by Powell, p. 147.

of keeping house, and of suckling babies. This view was set forth in a popular poem of Jakob Cats, called the *Marriage Ring,* and in a treatise named *The Perfect Wife* by Luis de León, which shows an intimate knowledge of women surprising in an Austin friar. But the most famous exposition of the view that woman was made for man and is his inferior is found in the poems and prose works of Milton, most strongly perhaps in the lines

> Therefore God's universal law
> Gave to the man despotic power
> Over his female in due awe,
> Nor from that right to part an hour,
> Smile she or lour.[1]

This view was not particularly Puritan but was shared by all confessions and all nations. Thomas Fuller, the Anglican prebendary and ecclesiastical historian, says that the good wife "commandeth her husband in any equal matter by constant obeying him," but "never crosseth him in his anger." [2] Woe to her if she did! The laws and public opinion of most countries then sanctioned the corporal chastisement of wives. The amount of this practically depended entirely on the husband's judgment. The English law, that he might use no stick thicker than his thumb, very slightly limited his power, and such as it was was evaded by some brutes who "put a rod in pickle," that is, soaked it with salt and vinegar in order to make the wales more painful. It is one of the glories of New England that she first began to prohibit the degrading chastisement of women. The Massachusetts laws of 1641 provided that "Every married woman shall be free from bodily correction or stripes by her husband, unless it be in his own defence upon her assault." Virginia, on the other hand, provided a special stool in which any woman whose clacking tongue and scan-

---

[1] *Samson Agonistes,* 1053ff; *cf. Paradise Lost,* viii, 540ff, ix, 233ff, and *The Doctrine and Discipline of Divorce,* Bk. II, chap. 15.

[2] Fuller: *The Holy State and the Profane State,* chap. 1, "The Good Wife."

dalous gossip caused suit to be brought against her husband, should be ducked once for every five hundred pounds of tobacco recovered from him in damages.

The upper-class, or courtly, attitude towards women still held much of the fantastic woman-worship of chivalry. Indeed, the position of woman at court was necessarily better than elsewhere in that she could hold the highest position in the land. At one time women ruled as queens in England and in Scotland and as regents in France and in the Netherlands. At court they entered into all intrigues and played a prominent rôle in politics. Women who could not manage their own property, or make wills, or even assert their right to control their own children in common life, found themselves at court, as the mothers, wives, or mistresses of kings and ministers, powerful to sway the destiny of nations. Nor was it only political power that they found in the court, but they found there also opportunity, elsewhere denied, to cultivate their minds. The few learned and accomplished women of the period were queens or ladies of high rank— a Jane Grey, an Elizabeth of England, an Elizabeth of Bohemia, a Christina of Sweden, a Duchess of Newcastle.

As very few women could be queens, and not a vast number, in proportion to the population, could be kings' mistresses, marriage remained the only career open to the majority. Though some divines, including Luther, Melanchthon, Cajetan, Beza, and Bishop Burnet, certain philosophers like Bruno and Campanella, and certain poets like Milton, thought polygamy lawful, the laws of church and state continued to enforce, and public opinion to approve, monogamy. While the Catholic church kept her preference for celibacy, she found much trouble in suppressing, through the Inquisition, the opinion widely spread even in Catholic lands, that the married is better than the virgin state. The Protestants exalted marriage as necessary to man's virtue and as a wholesome discipline to his temper. From the first the Reformers regarded marriage as a civil contract rather than as a religious sacrament. Civil marriage, first practised in Holland in 1580, was soon adopted in Puritan Britain and

America. A form of trial marriage, known as "handfasting," was allowed in Scotland. Betrothal was so binding a contract that perfect liberty was allowed the engaged couple by law in Sweden and by custom in some other countries. The custom known as "kweesten" in Holland and as "bundling" in New England permitted engaged couples, or even lovers before betrothal, to go to bed together with their clothes on, or without them, provided a sheet separated them. Children were usually betrothed by their parents at an early age, and sometimes the marriage ceremony was performed between mere infants, not followed by cohabitation until the legal age, which was 14 for boys and 12 for girls.

Though the Catholic theory proclaimed that lawful marriage is indissoluble except by death, the practice of the church made it easy for a person of influence to obtain annulment of his marriage by finding some flaw in its legality. Protestants allowed full divorce for adultery. Milton advocated the granting of divorce for irresistible antipathy, or, as it is now called, "incompatibility." "What an injury is it after wedlock," he exclaimed, "not to be beloved? what to be slighted? what to be contended with in point of rule, who shall he head?" And again,

Christ himself tells us who should not be put asunder, namely those whom God hath joined, a plain solution of this great controversy, if men would but use their eyes; for when is it that God may be said to join? . . . Only then when minds are fitly disposed and enabled to maintain a cheerful conversation.

But, though the English law of 1653 did something to make divorce easier, it remained for America, the most Puritan of lands, to practise, in this respect, the precepts of the most Puritan of poets.

In all societies and in all ages there has been found a considerable amount of extra-legal sexual enjoyment branded as vice. The definition of vice, and the severity of its condemnation, has varied from time to time and from place to place. In the sixteenth and seventeenth centuries harsh

punishment of vice by laws went along with general con-
donation of it, in its commoner forms, by public opinion,
though the opinions, if not the practices, of different classes
varied widely. What the Puritan denounced as adultery
the Cavalier boasted of as "good fortune."

Sodomy was made a capital crime by a law of Edward
VI re-enacted by Elizabeth, and was punished with death
also in New England, in France, in Spain, and in Germany.
Rape was commonly punished by death, unless expiated
by marriage of the violator and his victim. Adultery was
made capital by the Saxon law of 1543; but was more lightly
punished in Italy, even by the popes. An English law of
1650, and a Scotch law of 1581, made adultery a capital
crime; and the magistrates appointed to draw up a code
of laws for Massachusetts recommended the penalty of
death for this crime. Incest was frequently punished with
death.

"The filthy vice of fornication" as the Scotch law called
it, was punished there by ducking "in the deepest and foulest pool of water in the town," and in England by three
months in prison for the first offence and in America by
fine or whipping. One particular form of vice, the seduction
by priests of their female penitents, gave much concern to
the Inquisition. It was so common that the judges acted
on the presumption that every priest would solicit the chastity of every young woman confessing to him, but to prevent
scandal to the church it was punished secretly and leniently.
To reduce the dangers of the confessional there was invented, in 1547, the closed box within which the priest
should sit and hear the confession of his penitent through
a small window, instead of having her, as previously, kneeling at his knees. Though resisted by the clergy, the use of
this apparatus was made obligatory by the Roman Ritual
in 1614. Nevertheless, seduction and minor acts of lubricity
continued to stain the relations of priests with the women
of their flocks.

Prostitution was commonly tolerated on the theory, expressed by St. Augustine, that harlotry is a remedy for

worse forms of vice. Now and then, however, brothels were closed by national or town governments. Notable for its ferocity is an edict of Louis XIV of 1684 condemning all prostitutes found with soldiers within five miles of Versailles to have their noses and ears cut off. This rigorous act came with special grace from a king whose passing amours were innumerable, and who spent many nights, with different mistresses, in the dormitories of the maids of honor.

With all these savage laws against sexual vice there went a much milder judgment of it by public opinion, at least in certain quarters. Probably the amount of sexual passion has been pretty constant in all generations, and the limits of its indulgence not very different in different societies. Preachers have always painted conditions as black as possible, as did the Lutheran theologian Andreas Musculus who declared that "Sodom and Gomorrah and the Venusberg itself are child's play compared to the immorality prevailing" in Germany. In many royal courts a sort of promiscuity, occasionally tempered by murder but unvexed by the laws, prevailed. One of the propositions very frequently detected and punished by the Inquisition was the contention that fornication is no sin. While under the Puritans vice was suppressed, or hypocritically dissembled, at the Restoration it rather flaunted itself. The gentlemen of the later comedy are represented as debauchees who run through the vices of the town, fine women are depicted as mercenary jilts and secret adulteresses, and marriage is held up to ridicule as being for women "worse than excommunication." "To talk of honor in the mysteries of love," says one of Wycherley's characters, "is like talking of heaven or the Deity in an operation of witchcraft; just when you are employing the devil it makes the charm impotent." Nor was this profligacy confined to the court. Samuel Pepys has studded his priceless journal thickly with records, slightly disguised by the intermixture of French and Latin and Spanish words, of the numerous women with whom he "did what he would."

So intimately connected are all phases of social life that a history of the use and abuse of alcoholic beverages, if written with philosophy and insight, would lay bare many of the economic and cultural vicissitudes of the race. To imagine that the consumption of large quantities of wine, beer, and spirits indicates moral depravity, and that their prohibition is a noble experiment dictated by a lofty sense of duty, is the illusion of the temperance reformer or the claptrap of the politician. The use of drink has depended on geographical, economic, social, and cultural conditions, just as have all other customs. Drunkenness is the vice of cold and damp climates, found more among the Teutonic than among the Mediterranean peoples, more in Europe than in America. The first great prohibition movement arose in Arabia. Heavy drinking is more characteristic of an aristocratic than of a democratic and industrial society. To be habitually "as drunk as a lord" one must have leisure and means to devote to the avocation. "If whiskey interferes with your business, give up your business" is a proverb flavored with irony only in a nation of business men. Temperance, like thrift, is the virtue of the middle and laboring classes, because it is necessary to success in money-making. Again, the amount of indulgence in drink depends somewhat upon the relations of the sexes. The more the pleasures of love are permitted by social conditions and encouraged by public opinion, the less will the pleasures of the bottle be sought or even tolerated. Mohammed and his followers, who filled their harems on earth with many women and peopled paradise with houris, strictly forbade the drinking of wine. The Greeks, who extolled drunkenness as due to divine possession were addicted to vices flourishing in a purely masculine society. When Montaigne observed that drunkenness was decreasing and wantonness increasing in his lifetime, he bore witness to the growing feminization of society. Finally, ages of great poetry and art have deified such pure sensations as may be won from alcohol and narcotics; ages of industry and science have preferred such mental stimulants as caffeine.

In the sixteenth century potations were always large and often excessive. In the seventeenth century a check was put on drunkenness by the larger admission of women into masculine society in France, and by the growing power of industrialism and Puritanism in England. In Germany the amounts of beer and wine consumed, particularly by the nobles, stagger credibility. The vast ton of Heidelberg, the 26,000 casks of wine stored in the cellars of the Saxon electors, aptly express the tastes of the princes and of their retinues. To drink fourteen beakers of wine to welcome a guest, and twenty more at dinner, was but an ordinary day's work; on great occasions the Saxons celebrated, at a place well named "Schweinitz," competitive contests in swilling (*Wettsaufen*) which often ended in nausea, in delirium tremens, in prolonged sickness, and sometimes even in death. In 1601 Landgrave Moritz of Hesse and the Elector Palatine founded an Order of Temperance to cure the nobility of the vice of drunkenness, and it was held to be extremely severe because it allowed its members only fourteen goblets of wine a day.

Serious efforts were made by the Puritans to restrain excessive potations, though even their most rigid moralists did not demand total abstinence, but thought "drink in itself to be a good creature of God, to be received with thankfulness," and "only the abuse of drink to be from Satan." Laws against inordinate tippling and haunting taverns were passed by the English Parliament in 1603, 1607, 1610, 1624, 1625, and 1627, by the Scotch Parliament in 1617, and frequently by the American colonial legislatures.

2. MANNERS

Manners, which are morals in small matters, also have much to tell of the social conditions from which they spring. Nothing has improved them so much, in point of kindness and candor, as has the rise of democracy. The politeness which was once, as the etymology of the words "courtesy" and "courtly" indicates, confined to the highest ranks has now been diffused through the masses. There is no more striking difference between our age and all its predecessors than that human beings are no longer born into a class and chained down to it. It is true that our plutocracy is still largely hereditary—90% of the great fortunes in England have been inherited, and even in America more money is inherited than made by each generation—but these fortunes tend to be divided and dissipated in a few decades.

Not so with the class distinctions of the sixteenth and seventeenth centuries. Even then, of course, any career was open to very exceptional talents; but that Cromwell made himself autocrat of England, and that a few base-born men attained peerages and bishoprics, does not disprove the general proposition that society then set rigidly in classes. At the top was the monarch, sacrosanct and despotic, asserting in loud tones his divine right, and claiming to be, in his own person, the state. Around the Sun King—as the representative monarch of the period was called—revolved the great nobles and prelates and officials, satellites who borrowed their glory from him. Below them was the vast mass of the people, whose honest work was despised as servile, and whose necessary contributions to the support of the state were branded as badges of infamy. At least, this was true in most European monarchies; but much less true in Holland and England, and still less in America.

The social as well as the political guidance of the peoples fell into the hands of the nobility. Prominent and successful merchants and lawyers could satisfy their aspirations for influence and position only by acquiring a title. The capital and the salon became the centers of culture and the arbiters of good form. The country squires remained coarse and clownish, though proud of their families and ready to assert their privileges. The clergy, except for the noble recipients of high preferment, was regarded as a plebeian class. Neither in Catholic nor in Protestant lands were there many learned, or even many well educated priests, nor were most of them patterns of Christian virtue. Many were dependents and toadies of the great, poor "Levites" as they were called, who asked the blessing on the squire's table from the enjoyment of which they were largely excluded, and who often married a menial, if not a cast-off mistress, of their patron.

More important was the learned class which now began to assert itself. Scientists, writers, artists, scholars, professors, and journalists, were highly esteemed as ornaments to courts and as guests at nobles' houses. Literary and artistic dilettantism became the fashion. Particularly in Paris, in Rome, in Amsterdam, and in London there grew up a society almost as much interested in books, in pictures, in the drama, and in science, as in dress, in cosmetics, in gallantry, and in snobbery.

Even at royal courts manners were rather ceremonious than refined. Like the art of the time they were baroque, admitting of startling contrasts of ornament and of the grotesque. An elaborate etiquette attended court functions, including the dressing and undressing of the king and queen. But in moments of relaxation the king would raise his cane to his ministers, or lapse into buffoonery or obscenity; the queen would swear at, spit at, slap, pat, or tickle her courtiers as suited her mood.

Not in the courts of Versailles and Whitehall, but in the *salons* of wealthy and cultivated ladies grew up a more exquisite refinement of manners than had hitherto prevailed even in the Italian cities of the Renaissance or in the Provençal courts of love. The cause of this refinement has often been sought in the influence of women, now more largely admitted to society than earlier. But a deeper cause must be found. Women have always existed; and their influence, in unchanging social conditions, should be constant. What has given them their larger sphere of action in modern times has been the growing wealth and the growing cultivation of male society. Woman became the chief object of conspicuous expenditure, the chief exponent of the ostentatious leisure of a newly wealthy class. And the growth of interest in literature, in art, and in science provided richer materials for culture than did the former exclusive interest in sport, in the bottle, and in the chase.

To these influences may perhaps be added another in the growth of the comforts and conveniences of the household. The ladies in the old romances were always looking out of the castle window, because there was little else for them to do by way of amusement. The dungeon of the old château was too dark, cold, and poorly furnished to offer much inducement for the holding of balls and other social gatherings. Nor should it be above the dignity of history to note that modern delicacy and refinement, not to say prudery, depend largely on the improvements of modern plumbing. The bathrooms of our ancestors were cold and unprovided with running water in stationary wash-bowls and tubs; their toilet apparatus was not only extremely noisome and unsanitary but also much less private and convenient than is ours. The first attempt to improve these conditions was made by a wit, poet, and courtier of Elizabeth, who explained his project to the world in a Rabelaisian pamphlet with the punning title *The Metamorphosis of Ajax* [1] (1596).

But as it was yet two centuries before the excellent suggestions of Sir John Harington were widely adopted, there continued to be a good deal of coarseness in the manners and a good deal of obscenity in the conversation of even the higher classes. Not only were plays and novels and the ordinary conversation of men and women more or less interlarded with words and allusions now banished from decent usage, but the sermons of divines and the exhortations of moralists frequently went to the very limits of frankness in describing and denouncing the sins of the flesh, or even in vituperating the writer's enemies. Milton defended his own use of an obscene expression on one occasion by alleging the examples of the "famousest Greek and Roman orators," of the "tart rhetoric of Luther," and of God himself as reported in the Bible.[2]

A revolt against coarseness in all forms and an assiduous

---

[1] A jakes is a water-closet.

[2] *Apology for Smectymnuus;* among the texts of the Bible cited is I Kings, xiv, 10.

cultivation of good manners and of correct speech is found
in the famous *salons* of Paris in the early seventeenth century. The best known of them is the *salon* of the Marquise
de Rambouillet. Among the wits who frequented her
at-homes were many men of learning and of literary fame
and many a *bel esprit*. The great entertainment of these
gatherings was conversation, which now came to be esteemed
as the "greatest pleasure in life and almost the only one,"
and as "the bond of society and the best means of fostering
not only politeness but also sound morality and the love of
glory and of virtue." And in the gentle art of conversation
women, according to La Rochefoucauld, outshone the men.

Next to conversation the preoccupation of this feminized
society was love—a curious, fantastic, long-drawn-out flirtation known as gallantry. It was no longer considered
proper, by the well-bred girl, "to begin with marriage" nor
even, as her father in Molière's play reminds her, with
concubinage. The lover must know how to bring forth beautiful sentiments, to exude the sweet, the tender, and the passionate, to write *billets-doux* and madrigals, and to endure a
long discipline of caprice, jealousy, rivalry, and despair.
So enormously complex and precise did the rules for co-
quetry become that Ninon de l'Enclos called the ladies of
the new school "the prigs of love." But what might they have
called Ninon de l'Enclos with her hundred paramours?

Though there were some Don Juans at the French court,
as elsewhere, there were also many of the most exquisite
types of refined and cultivated character. No more charming
picture of a woman's life has ever been painted than that
seen in the letters of Madame de Sévigné. Full of affection for her children and of delicate consideration for
her other correspondents, these famous epistles report without malice or much scandal the gossip of the court, draw
pictures of d'Artagnan and of Fouquet and of the adored
king, tell of the writer's life on her estate and of her love
for nature, for the songs of the birds, for the triumph of
May, for the odor of the honeysuckles, and for the beauty
of the harvest moon. Moreover, these letters abound in the

nice literary judgments of one who loved Tacitus and Tasso and Rabelais and the writings of her own contemporaries, whose eyes were open to all forms of poetic beauty, and whose pen was capable of criticizing her favorite authors in purest French.

From Paris the new taste for refinement spread to the provinces. Everyone who made a small fortune bought an estate and began to call himself "de la Souche" or by some similar title derived from it. The *nouveau riche* soon discovered his noble or royal blood, and found heralds willing to make him, for a thumping price, a coat of arms and a genealogy reaching back to Priam. To the scions of really old families and to the initiates in the mysteries of the Hôtel Rambouillet these parvenues seemed ridiculous. Nothing delighted the Parisian audience more than the satire of George Dandin the peasant who marries above his class, or of the Comtesse d'Escarbagnas, the provincial who apes the manners of the capital, or of M. Jourdain, the tradesman turned gentleman who thinks that "there is nothing so fine as to frequent the company of great lords," and who hires a dancing master, a fencing master, a singing master, and a philosopher to prepare him to enter the *beau monde*.

In London, too, the influence of France, and the growth of a wealthy and leisured class, led to the cultivation of the new elegance. "The complete gentleman," says Sir Fopling Flutter, "ought to dress well, dance well, fence well, have a genius for love-letters, an agreeable voice for a chamber, be very amorous, something discreet, but not over constant." The complete lady, according to a character of Ethredge's, should be mistress of the arts of affectation and of flirtation, "teaching you how to draw up your breasts, stretch up your neck, thrust out your breech, play with your head, toss up your nose, bite your lips, turn up your eyes, speak in a silly soft tone of voice, and use all the foolish French words that will infallibly make your person and conversation charming."

As important in the history of manners as the *salons* were the clubs that gathered in the coffee houses, newly established to promote the enjoyment of coffee, tea, chocolate, and tobacco. The last named narcotic, introduced into Europe from America in the latter sixteenth century, soon became enormously popular. It was celebrated as "divine tobacco" and "our holy herb nicotian" by the poets, extolled as an excellent medicine by some physicians, and denounced by some moralists, among whom was James I, as dangerous to the health and to virtue. The new beverages, introduced into Europe from Asia and America in the early seventeenth century, soon became so necessary to the majority of the people that they caused a marked change in social manners. To enjoy themselves to the full most companies need a stimulant; but whereas alcoholic beverages rather dull the wits while prodding the emotions, the soft drinks sharpen the wits and promote the pleasures of conversation. London was soon filled with coffee houses in which men gathered to chat and to hear and read the news. Macaulay describes them as follows:

Every rank and profession, and every shade of religious and political opinion, had its own headquarters. There were houses in St. James's Park where fops congregated, their heads and shoulders covered with black or flaxen wigs, not less ample than those now worn by the Chancellor and the Speaker of the House of Commons. . . . Nowhere was smoking more constant than at Will's. That celebrated house, situated between Covent Garden and Bow Street, was sacred to polite letters. There the talk was about poetical justice and the unities of time and place. . . . There were coffee houses where the first medical men might be consulted. . . . There were Puritan coffee houses where no oath was heard and where lank-haired men discussed election and reprobation through their noses; Jew coffee houses where dark-eyed money-changers from Venice and Amsterdam greeted each other; and Popish coffee houses where, as good Protestants believed, Jesuits planned, over their cups, another great fire, and cast silver bullets to shoot the king.[1]

So popular did these rendezvous become that they soon alarmed the government. A proclamation suppressing them,

[1] *History of England,* i, 335.

as hotbeds of conspiracy and of scandal, in 1675, caused such an outcry that it was almost immediately withdrawn, and its place taken by regulations holding coffee-house keepers responsible for the conduct of their patrons.

From London and Paris the new standards of manners and of culture sifted slowly through the provinces and to other countries. Not least of the civilizing influences in the world is easy communication. This has steadily improved in modern times. Perhaps the English turnpike acts of 1663 and the following years had as much to do with the history of culture as did many a more famous law. Travel, which had once meant "travail," now came to mean the opposite —rest, recreation, and refinement. The grand tour became popular. With the establishment of the post offices in the sixteenth and seventeenth century communication became easier and more frequent. When Mme. de Sévigné said that she always felt like thanking the postillions for carrying her mail, she but expressed the obligations of the whole of cultivated society.

3. ETHICS

Just as political theory rationalizes the public institutions of a particular group, just as theology and philosophy rationalize the prevailing religious habits, so ethics, or the theory of morals, rationalizes existing social custom. Men have an incurable tendency to glorify their own herd and to justify its ways and thoughts by finding for them authority in the laws of the universe, either divine or natural. The antidote to this excessive anthropomorphism is found in science. Impelled by disinterested curiosity and disciplined by scientific pursuits in its gratification, men at length learn to study themselves and their passions and social arrangements objectively.

Considered historically ethical theory has constantly changed under the action of two processes. As customs change it must find justification for the new practices in the old world-view; as the world-view changes it must find new reasons, consistent therewith, for old practices. To anyone who admits this it becomes plain that the vast change from medieval to modern morality is the inevitable concomitant of the contemporary social and intellectual changes. The growth of wealth, of luxury, and of science, the shift from an other-worldly to a this-worldly interest, and the secularization of thought, all left a deep impress on moral practices and then on ethical theory.

The most noticeable of these changes have been the following: 1. The shift from an ascetic to a hedonistic attitude, from a bias against pleasure to a bias in its favor. 2. The substitution of a scientific for a religious rationalization of morality. 3. The abandonment of a transcendental for a utilitarian sanction for conduct. 4. The breaking down of authority by reason, involving the change from a glorification of the virtue of faith to a suspicion of its demerit. 5. The alteration of man's view of himself from an idealistic to a realistic one. Doubtless these movements overlap, and probably they do not exhaustively cover the field, but they sufficiently indicate the major trends of modern ethics.

The changes, of course, came slowly, and at different times in different *milieux*. The medieval attitude still survived largely in the seventeenth, as it still survives somewhat in the twentieth, century. The churches then extolled the virtues of faith, denounced pleasure, and tenaciously insisted upon the supernatural sanction for the moral code. That no life could be good, that no man could be saved, without divine grace appropriated by faith, was common ground for all creeds. That pleasure, and especially sexual pleasure, is a sin, was proclaimed by Catholic and Protestant alike. The Romanist exalted celibacy and deprecated all sexual acts, even in marriage, except with the purpose of procreation. The Puritan, said Hobbes, thought there were no sins except carnal lusts and vain swearing. The Anglican Jeremy Taylor advised husbands and wives not to yield to "high and violent lusts," nor to "passionate applications of themselves to the offices of marriage." All parties of Christians extolled sobriety, temperance, humility, and blind faith, and all denounced the effort to inquire into the secrets of God or to fathom divine mysteries as impious, or at least as fearfully dangerous. The Protestant, however, was distinctly more modern in his view of vocation. While the Catholic found his highest opportunity to serve God in solitude, meditation, and prayer, the Protestant found it in labor and in thrift. Asceticism was the life-work of the pious Catholic; work to the point of pain was the asceticism of the Protestant. Not to abandon the world but to subdue it is the Protestant ethics, which is, therefore, far more than the Catholic, oriented with reference to the things of this life.

While the Protestant compromised with the new moral forces, the free-thinker fully accepted them. To unravel the braided cord of law, religion, and ethics, which had bound the medieval mind, separating each from the other and breaking the conceptual presuppositions to which all had been tied, was the work of the Italian philosophers and English moralists of the late sixteenth and of the seventeenth centuries. These moralists did for ethics what the Deists a little later did for religion; they loosed it from its traditional moorings in dogma and bound it to the laws of nature as revealed by science.

Among the first of these radical moral philosophers was Giordano Bruno, whose tract on *The Heroic Passions* aims to prove the independence of religion and virtue, and to find for the latter a natural social sanction. Denying the virtues of asceticism and of chastity, and rejecting the Christian ideal of passive faith, Bruno raised the concept of virtue to that of an active life dedicated to the progress of material civilization. His contemporary, Telesio, also argued for natural, as distinguished from religious, morality, and proposed a utilitarian criterion of conduct in the instinct of self-preservation.

In the far more thorough treatment accorded to the subject by the British philosophers was at last established, on sound psychological foundations, the concept of a natural, scientific standard of conduct. Of course, their work was

not born fully matured; the relativity of all morals was
not fully apprehended. They still held to the belief in an
absolute and eternal ethics; in a standard of right and
wrong founded in the law of nature, and discoverable by
reason as the laws of physics are discovered. Analogies were
also drawn by them between the laws of morals and the
laws of the state. As the ideal of the English Commonwealth
was a strongly regulated society, and as the ultimate sanction of its government and polity was seen to be the army,
it is quite natural that the greatest contemporary moralists
should find in force the ultimate sanction of right and wrong.

With his accustomed boldness and originality Hobbes outlined the first consistent and well grounded system of natural
ethics. Deducing his moral theory from his psychology he
defined passion as "the interior beginning of voluntary
motion" and will as "the last appetite in deliberation" when
different passions balance one another. All passions he fitted
into a comprehensive scheme of six fundamental forces, of
which three—pleasure, love, and desire—are attractive and
three—pain, hate, and fear—repellant, and all passions he
reduced, with remarkable penetration, to the instinct for
self-preservation. On this foundation he built a structure of
purely utilitarian and hedonistic ethics. The will he thought
not free nor did he allow any criterion of right for the individual except self-interest. Society, however, he thought
justified in rewarding as good those actions which promote,
and in punishing as evil those actions which damage, the
welfare of the group.

Even before Hobbes gave precise expression to the idea
of a natural law of morality other British moralists were
working towards it and trying to reconcile it with their
theology. "God," said Milton, "hath created a righteousness
right in itself against which even he cannot do." [1] But the
ripest fruit of the new ethical field was grown by the Cambridge Platonists. Horrified by the sensualism, utilitarian-
ism, and realism of Hobbes, and yet unsatisfied with the
bluff positivism and dogmatic rigor of Puritanism, Cudworth,

[1] *Doctrine and Discipline of Divorce,* 1643, bk. 2, chap. 4.

Henry More, and Cumberland tried to find a basis for ethics
in natural law. Starting with a parallel between ethics and
mathematics Cudworth made moral laws the necessary consequences of the interrelation of spirits, as geometrical laws
are the necessary consequences of the interrelations of
bodies. Henry More completed the psychological analysis
of Hobbes by adding to his rational calculus of pain and
pleasure an affective, emotional motivation. According to
his scheme the sense of right and wrong is a particular
"boniform faculty" of the soul, acting directly on the will
and not through the love of pleasure or the dread of pain.
Cumberland's chief contribution was a criticism of Hobbes's
hedonism as too crude; for it he would substitute a eude-
monism in which a large element is the love of others—
or altruism, as it later came to be called.

The development of a new ethics in France was closely
connected with the growth of free-thought and of the revival of the antique. Montaigne's eclecticism was half
stoical, half epicurean. But he still idealized virtue and
disliked the growing realism and cynicism of his time:

Our judgments are sick [he complained] according to the de-
pravation of our morals. I see the greater part of the wits of my
generation exerting much ingenuity to obscure the glory of the
beautiful and generous actions of men of old, giving them some
base interpretation and finding for them vain causes and occasions.[1]

When the French philosophers began to erect an ethical
system on a naturalistic basis, they found the readiest instrument in the doctrine of Epicurus. Gassendi, who wrote
a life of Epicurus and revived his metaphysics, also appealed
to his authority to prove that happiness is the sovereign
good and chief goal of all human actions. Virtue, therefore,
seemed to him to be nothing but prudence, or, as it was
later dubbed, "enlightened self-interest." Happiness, however, he thought could be found not in sensual pleasure but
in wisdom, in mental repose, and in "the pleasures and trans-

[1] *Essais*, liv. i, no. 37, 1580.

ports of joy caused by the study of mathematics." To these
constituents of happiness, indeed, he added the knowledge
of God, nor can this concession to religious claims be considered hypocritical. The paradox of reconciling the ethics
of Epicurus with those of Christ had been championed by
no less famous humanists than Lorenzo Valla and Erasmus.[1]

If Gassendi provided the metaphysical foundation of the
libertine morals that flourished among the French nobility,
François de la Rochefoucauld applied his principles to particular lines of conduct, thus doing for the free-thinkers
what the casuists had done for the Catholics. This complete
and accomplished representative of the ancient *noblesse* discovered his ethical system less in philosophers than in observation of the life around him and in a comparison of the
ideal of virtue professed and the reality of vice practised,
at Versailles. The court had developed a moral system based
on its customs and biased by its interests; La Rochefoucauld simply added the suitable doctrine. The code really
practised at court and by the nobles generally was not that
of Christian precepts, but that of the laws of "honor." The
gentleman of honor might cheat a tradesman but not another gentleman, must pay a gambling debt but need not
pay a commercial debt, might lie to a woman but never to a
man. In fact, like all moral codes, that of "honor" was
based upon the narrow self-interest of the class practising
it. The laws of honor bore the same relation to the laws
of the land that luxuries did to necessities; they were the
monopoly and pride of the aristocrats. And in this respect
the gentleman of honor was but too prone to believe that
if he might have the luxuries of life he could get along
without the necessities.

What struck La Rochefoucauld about the conduct of
men in general, and of "the best people" in particular, was
its total repugnance to the principles still inculcated by the
church. The gallant who boasted of his good fortunes with

---

[1] Valla: *De voluptate ac vero bono,* 1519; Erasmus: "The Epicurean,"
Colloquies, 1533; Preserved Smith: *A Key to the Colloquies of Erasmus,*
1927, p. 55.

women and of his duels with men, who spent his life in
drinking, gaming, and merry-making, still heard at church
adultery and murder branded as wicked and the pomps and
vanities of the world and the lusts and sinful desires of the
flesh denounced as the snares of Satan. Not unnaturally
an extremely low view of human nature prevailed among
the preachers. In fact, human nature has always been regarded with sour looks of suspicion by the professional moralists who first give it a bad name in order to hang it later.
It was not sheer impudence but the irony of simple truth
when La Rochefoucauld described his *Moral Reflections*
(commonly called his *Maxims,* 1665) as "a concise system
of ethics conformable to the thought of several fathers of
the church." Augustine, so much discussed by the Jansenists, had, like La Rochefoucauld, regarded self-love as the
mainspring of man's actions; but what had made the saint
weep, made the courtier laugh.

The subtlety of the duke's method lies in his penetration of the disguises of selfishness; his exploration, as he
called it, of "the many unknown lands of self-love." Like
an earlier Freud he discovered the importance of the unconscious. He knew that "our virtues are nothing but vices
in disguise" and that "what frequently prevents us from
abandoning ourselves to one vice is that we have several,"
and that "hypocrisy is the act of homage rendered by vice
to virtue." Like all innovators in the field of morals he
shocked his first readers, but he contributed not a little
to the transition from the medieval to the modern ethics.[1]

[1] It has recently been argued, cleverly but not quite convincingly, that
the crux of Shakespearean tragedy lies in the conflict between the old,
romantic ethics of feudalism and the new, realistic ethics of Machiavelli.
Shakespeare's heroes, according to this view, are idealists defeated by hard
facts. See W. Lewis: *The Lion and the Fox,* 1927.

CHAPTER XVIII

LITERATURE

The word "literature" may be used in two senses, a broad and a narrow one. In the broad sense it includes everything ever written: poetry, fiction, history, science, school exercises, bills, checks, statutes, newspapers, tabloids, and advertisements. In the narrow sense it comprises only that part of what is written that has artistic merit, that part which is called in French and German, and which should be called in English, "fair letters." Exactly what this is is hard to define. Not only are there infinite degrees of beauty, but there are a vast number of diverse judgments. Historical studies of the whirligig of taste have shown that aesthetic judgments are as relative, as subjective, as changeable as are moral and political opinions. There is no style that has not been alternately admired and disliked; no author among those most commonly praised who has not been, at some time and by some able critic, decried. Nevertheless, some books have stood the test of time better than others. That which has appealed to the greatest number of expert critics for the longest time may be defined for our purposes as the best.

Style rather than subject-matter is the preservative of books. In the subjects they treat the most beautiful works differ little from the most ordinary. Great works of science are the only original and creative products of the press as far as thought and subject-matter are concerned, and few of them have a high artistic value. Poetry, fiction, and popular philosophy chiefly harp upon the commonest and most trite of themes. For, literature may be considered as a long soliloquy of the race talking about itself. All human interests are reflected in literature, and in about the proportion in which they are widely distributed. Some men are interested in religion, some in politics, some in art and science, some in history, some in food, some in drink, some in children, and some in many other things. Almost all men are interested in sex, which therefore furnishes the matter for many books. All persons are interested in themselves and those who cannot satisfy their egotism in reading about themselves directly and by name, find a vicarious pleasure in identifying themselves imaginatively with some hero, historical or fictitious. All the plays and novels dealing with human fate and many chronicles and biographies minister to this taste. Practically all men are interested in their immediate group or herd, and most of them are convinced of the superiority of the laws, morals, manners, gifts, and talents of their own group, and of the superlative excellence of their own race, country, religion, party, and class. Literature flatters these predilections by extolling the habits of the group to which it appeals, and also by criticising and depreciating the standards and achievements of other groups. Such interests reflected in books are constant, but the depiction of society varies as society itself changes. In this chapter a few masterpieces of fair letters will be evaluated as a reflection of the change from a medieval to a modern interest.

I. THE OLD ROMANCES

The medieval mind long wandered, like a knight in pursuit of adventures, in the forest of its own imaginations, or, like a crusader, in the desert of oriental enchantments. The forest was well stocked with game of dragons and great serpents; it was infested by ogres and giants; it was haunted by fairies and magicians and witches and gnomes, and by all manner of spiritual vermin. It was as full of lost maidens as are our newspapers—maidens of miraculous beauty, guarded by monsters or kept prisoner by recreant marauders, or simply sitting by the shore of old romance, ready to reward with their hands the knight who is always amorous and frequently insane for love. The oriental desert, too, was full of adventure, for *there* lived the paynims and other miscreants who worshipped Termagant and Mahound, and who needed to be convinced of the truths of Christianity, as St. Louis remarked, by being cloven to the middle. And in that far land of sand and ruin and gold there was always, too, the lady weeping her life away by a tideless, dolorous inland sea, until the predestined knight should serve and win her.

Equal with the ladies, or even superior to them, God was to be served by the errant soldier: his Holy Grail to be followed in the West and his Holy Sepulchre to be redeemed in the East. For, "God and the ladies" were almost always joined in the devotions of a medieval knight; and, with all the childishness of the troubadour's adventures, and with all the childlikeness of his faith and love, there was something noble, as there almost always is in childhood, be it of the individual or of the race. The world has been enriched by the ideal of chivalry, the code of honor of the belted knight. Though it was but an aristocratic code of morals, recognizing no duty to the base-born, still it upheld the worthy ideal of doing courtesy to one's equal, of rescuing the unfortunate in distress, of fleeing treason, of telling no falsehood, and of keeping vows made in religion and in love. And the beauty of chivalry saturates the old *chansons* and the epic cycles.

As manners changed, tastes changed with them. While dragons seemed to be dying out, policemen and mercenary soldiers were multiplying, and with their new firearms were giving much more annoyance both to the good knights and to the miscreants than the older breeds of monsters had ever done. While the man of the world, in the polished epoch of the Renaissance, found the old stories ridiculous, the stern moralists of the Reformation, Protestant and Catholic alike, discovered that they were immoral, and hastened to replace "their impure filth and vain, fantastical fabulosity" by supplying new translations of the Bible, or by legends of the saints. Roger Ascham, the tutor of Queen Elizabeth, declared that the whole pleasure of *La Morte d'Arthur* "stood in two special points—open manslaughter and bold bawdry." When St. Theresa of Spain severely condemned the old books of chivalry, the Catholic reformer, Luis de León added that men filled with the spirit of God would shun the tales by the vanity and indecency of which their souls were continually poisoned. Nay, more, the very governments began to proscribe the old romances by which, as the Cortes of Castile declared in a law of 1538, "much harm is done to men, boys, young girls, and others, and many are seduced by them from the true Christian doctrine."

But the poets who loved the stories still sought to make the old material acceptable to the taste of the time by moralizing it, and by carefully expelling from it those ancient crudities which were now condemned, on grounds of taste, by the humanist critics. Among those who most assiduously studied the religious, moral, and artistic demands of the new age, two were supreme, the Catholic Tasso, and the Protestant Spenser.

Torquato Tasso (1544-95), like his age, was educated by the Jesuits and passed his life in terror of the Inquisition. Nor were the chains of the Counter-Reformation the only bonds that galled his sensitive nature. As a humble pensioner of the great he found at the court of Ferrara first a refuge and then a prison until the gloom of melancholy madness turned his asylum into one for the insane. Incessantly he labored to rid his poems of all suspicion of heresy, and to polish the style, in the baroque taste of the period, until he made it so ornate that Galileo compared it to a museum of curiosities.[1]

At the early age of thirty he had completed the *Jerusalem Delivered*, a noble epic, though not, as Voltaire pronounced it, superior to Homer. In it are found both imitations of the Greek and Latin authors, and, much more richly, of the machinery of the medieval romances. Even the subject, the First Crusade, was not a novel one for treatment in a *chanson de geste*. The whole, however, is colored by the spirit

[1] *Opere di Galileo,* ed. nazionale, ix, 69.

of the Counter-Reformation; by the endeavor, that is, to moralize the old material and to turn it to the profit of the church.

The hero, Godfrey de Bouillon, is discovered besieging Jerusalem. The intricate adventures of the Christian and Moslem knights, fighting, going on long pilgrimages, falling in love, deriving help on the one side from God and the angels and on the other from the devils, fill twenty books of mellifluous verse. There are councils in heaven and conclaves in hell; there are female warriors, and plenty of wizards and enchanters; there are battles of angels and demons; there is an expedition to the Fortunate Islands of the West; and finally there is the assault of the Holy City and the victory:

> Thus Godfrey triumphed, and as still for him
>   The setting sun sufficient daylight shed,
> Without a pause, to freed Jerusalem,
>   Christ's blest abode, the conquerors he led;
> Nor yet laid down his blood-stained mantle, he
>   Sped to the temple, where, with beaming brow,
> He hung his arms up, and on bended knee
>   The great tomb worshipped, and performed his vow.[1]

The Protestant counterpart to the Catholic epic of chivalry and of the church, is Edmund Spenser's *Faery Queen*. The author (c. 1552-1599), born in London and educated at Cambridge, was a typical Englishman in his royalism and in devoting part of his life to the pacification of Ireland; he was a typical man of his age in his Puritanism and in his love for poetry. Besides many minor poems, he composed an epic romance twice as long as the *Iliad* and more than three times as long as *Paradise Lost*. In its vast extent, boundless and uncharted as the fairy-land it describes, the reader is sure to get lost, and is not unlikely to fall into a voluptuous slumber in one of its many enchanted dales. Here, as in Tasso, are the old subject matter and the old machinery of the medieval romances, with improve-

[1] Closing stanza of the *Jerusalem Delivered*, transl. by J. K. James.

ments borrowed liberally from their modern Italian imitators; but here is a much more conscious and carefully thought-out allegory to moralize the whole. By this method even the most naked descriptions of the temptations of the Bower of Bliss, or of the adventures of Hellenore with the satyrs, could be made to contribute to the reader's moral education; and the senses might be titillated while the conscience was soothed. But, as the author's heart was truly in his allegory, his realistic method of ethical instruction won the approval of the greater poet and sterner Puritan, John Milton.

"The general end of all the book," says the author, "is to fashion a gentleman or noble person in virtuous or noble discipline; which, for that I conceived should be most plausible or pleasing, being colored with an historical fiction, I chose the history of King Arthur." The twelve books planned —of which only six were written—were designed to display an allegory of the twelve virtues, and with the moral purpose go a Protestant polemic and a patriotic exaltation of England and of her queen Elizabeth, who is cast for the part of Glory in the abstract and for that of Gloriana, the queen of Fairy-land, in the concrete. So determined is the poet to attribute every excellence to his patroness, that he even, under an obscure veil, ventures to flatter the daughter of Henry VIII and Anne Boleyn on her birth and parentage. In the story of the chronicles of Elfland, Henry VII appears as Elficleos (*i.e.* The Famous Elf), his son Arthur as Elferon, and his son Henry VIII as Oberon. Elizabeth's mother, called Chrysogonee, *i.e.* "Gold-born" or "new gold," with a play upon "Boleyn" and "bullion," is said to be the daughter of Amphisa, which, being interpreted, means the "separation," or great divorce of Henry from Catharine of Aragon.[1]

Book I relates the adventures of the Red Cross Knight, or Holiness who, as St. George of England, or possibly Henry

[1] Such at least is my own interpretation of the intentionally much veiled passages, book ii, canto ix, 75 and book iii, canto vi, 4. Spenser uses "bullion" in the sense of "fresh gold," in bk. iii, canto i, 32.

VIII, fights with the magician Archimago (the pope), slays the foul witch Duessa (Mary Queen of Scots or the Catholic church) and finally marries Una (the church of England). Sir Guyon, or Temperance, in Book II, and Britomartis or Chastity, a woman warrior in Book III, vanquish the many enemies of their virtue. Book IV contains the legend of Cambel and Triamond, or Friendship; and Book V under the title of Artegall or Justice, relates the recent history of the death of Mary Queen of Scots, of the wars of religion in the Netherlands and in France, and of the administration of Lord Grey de Wilton as Governor of Ireland. In the sixth book, called Sir Calidore or Courtesy, the vast and formless, but sweet and sensuous, allegory winds to its end.

If the old romance in Italy and England was rejuvenated by a bath in the fountain of poetry, it wilted in Spain under the sirocco of ridicule. These romances had perhaps been more popular in the Iberian peninsula than elsewhere; and new ones continued to be produced even to the beginning of the seventeenth century, notwithstanding the criticism and opposition of mystics like Luis de León, of Reformers like Valdés, and of scholars like Vives and Oviedo. In Spain, too, there had been attempts to make the old knights march to the music of the new religious tune; Hieronym Sempere had depicted Christ as the Knight of the Lion, Satan as the Knight of the Serpent, and the Apostles as the Paladins of the Round Table, in his story of *The Celestial Chivalry of the Fragrant Rose.*

Even while Sempere wrote, the ancient knight-errant received his death-blow at the hands of a man whose own life was more adventurous than that of many heroes of fiction. Miguel de Cervantes (1547-1616), a born daredevil and soldier of fortune, learned in the hard realities of war and of captivity how hollow were the bombastic pretensions of an Amadis or a Roland. It is likely, though not quite certain, that he served with Alva in the Netherlands, in the bloodiest and bitterest struggle of the century in which the victories of the Spanish troops were ever and again rendered fruitless by the cruelty of the Spanish Inquisition and by the heroism of the Dutch. After a year's service, the turbulent soldier returned to live the hardly less strenuous life of a swashbuckler at home. For a brawl he was sentenced to have his right hand cut off and to banishment. Escaping before the first part of the sentence could be inflicted, he enlisted in the navy, and saw, at the battle of Lepanto (Oct. 7, 1571) a signal triumph of the Spanish fleet over the Turks. Four years later he was captured by Algerian pirates, and spent five years of Moorish slavery in thrilling attempts to escape and in not less exciting adventures with the fair sex, until he was finally ransomed and sent home. As his left hand had been shattered in battle, he devoted his right hand to literature, and set out on his last and greatest quest, in the course of which he met and laid low all the knight-errants of the Middle Ages.

Even if we do not agree with Macaulay that *"Don Quixote* is incomparably the best novel ever written," we must admit that it is incomparably the most famous. Almost at once its hero attained such international renown that his figure and his quests are still familiar to everyone, and that his name has given an adjective to most of the languages of Europe. He is depicted as a Spanish gentleman, living plainly on a small estate, but thinking highly in terms of the romances of chivalry. These he read incessantly during long periods of leisure, until, at the age of fifty, his "fancy was filled with enchantments, quarrels, battles, challenges, wounds, wooings, loves, agonies, and all sorts of impossible nonsense." Crazed with these ideas, he imagined himself a knight-errant, and, taking an aged hack named Rocinante for his charger, a country lass named Dulcinea del Toboso for his lady, and a yokel named Sancho Panza for his squire, he set out in search of adventures.

Then comes the fun. Mistaking inns for castles, and their keepers for nobles, Quixote lodges in them and dedicates his arms; or he fancies that the serving-wenches are highborn ladies dying for love of him while, true to his Dulcinea, he virtuously and rhetorically declines the advances they never thought of making. He assails windmills as giants and flocks of sheep as armies of paynims; he attempts to free prisoners from the police, thinking them Christian captives in the hands of caitiffs. Knowing that a true knight must suffer for his ideals, he recks little of the many sound drubbings he gets, and, when he loses most of his teeth in one encounter, he even adopts as a proud sobriquet the title of "The Knight of the Rueful Countenance." He does, indeed, lament the diabolical invention of gunpowder, by which a detestable age has robbed the champions armed with sword and spear of the chance of distinguishing themselves.

And in this wild-goose chase after a long-vanished world, tripping up against realities at every step, turning somersaults and cutting capers in his shirt to prove that he, like Orlando, has gone mad for love, he yet keeps his mind fixed on his lofty but impracticable aim of righting every kind of wrong, and of esteeming perils and material loss or gain as nought compared to loyalty and devotion. Quixotry is not merely absurdity; it has something noble in it, too.

Don Quixote the idealist, is admirably set off against Sancho Panza the practical man, full of common sense, of proverbial wit and wisdom, who loves good eating and drinking and above all plenty of sleep. Though he only half believes in the provinces and islands which his master promises him in the kingdom to be conquered, he follows him still, as the practical man always does eventually follow the visionary, grumbling and complaining, hesitating and often turning back, casting a cold douche of homely sense on every vision and on every fantasy, and yet following to the end.

Cervantes' novel stands as do few other works of literature at the end of one epoch and the beginning of another. It abolished the pretensions of knighthood throughout Europe as Luther had abolished the claims of the priesthood throughout the North. It rang the knell of chivalric affectation as *Tartuffe* rang the knell of hypocritical affectation a little later. It was immensely popular, not only in his own country but elsewhere. In the land of Spain's chief enemy

there are many allusions to it by contemporaries, and perhaps several imitations. The lost play *Cardenio,* (1613) by
Fletcher and Shakespeare is said to have been based upon
it; and the extant *Knight of the Burning Pestle* (1607) is
either based on it, or else arrives at the same result by
ridiculing independently the same romances as those Cervantes had in mind.[1] In either case it bears witness to
the bankruptcy of the old ideals, and to the readiness of
the world for new ones.

2. THE NEW DRAMA

The reason why the old romances drooped and languished
was that the world they portrayed had passed away. Chivalry and feudalism succumbed to gunpowder and commerce.
The twilight shadows of romance were dispelled by the
light diffused through the printing of many books. The
discoveries of a new world substituted the quest of the
kingdoms of America for the quest of the kingdom of God,
the hunt for gold for the search for the grail.

In the new society the interest of man in himself
changed its quality. The medieval had been naïve, childlike,
objective, thinking of himself as a member of a class, or
gild, or nation, or church. Last of all he discovered himself
as an individual, even as the last familiar object that a child
discovers is himself. Consciousness of object is followed, in
reflection, by consciousness of subject. This awareness of
self, consequent upon the expansion of the ego by the acquisition of new wealth and of new knowledge, and by pride
in great exploits, is the essence of the individualism so
often noted as one of the characteristics of the Renaissance.
Man became more than previously curious of his own heart,
eager to explore his own passions, anxious for tidings from
the realms of life.

The charts of the newly discovered inner world were

---

[1] On this play by Beaumont and Fletcher see the edition by H. S.
Murch (*Yale Studies in English,* no. 38); *Cambridge History of English
Literature;* C. M. Gayley: *Beaumont the Dramatist,* 1914, pp. 72ff.

found in the stage-plays, its Columbus in Shakespeare.
Though the drama of the sixteenth and seventeenth centuries had its roots in the past, its astounding growth made
it a practically new thing. England alone produced about
435 comedies during the half century from 1592-1642, as
well as a large number of tragedies. And vast numbers of
plays were staged in the other countries of Western Europe.
In Spain and in England the drama attained maturity earlier
that elsewhere; then in the Netherlands, and finally in
France. Germany, though barren of great dramatic genius
at this time, produced many Shrovetide farces and other
plays, secular and sacred. Italy gave birth to a small but
exquisite literary drama, and also to the popular *Commedia
dell' Arte*, in which only the plot was sketched, to be filled
in by dialogue and comic business largely invented *ex tem-
pore* by the actors, usually stock characters such as the
Lover, his Lady, the Braggart, and the Pedant.

The common characteristics of all these plays (except
a few devoted to the portrayal of sacred subjects) is that
they give an almost completely secular, an almost completely mundane and, compared with all previous forms of
fiction, a highly realistic picture of life. The supernatural
machinery which had so heavily weighted all earlier epics
and tragedies and *chansons* and most novels and tales,
was not, indeed, completely absent, but it was so subordinate
to the main purpose of the play as to be insignificant. Compare Dante at the beginning of the Renaissance with Shakespeare at the end. Heaven, Purgatory, and Hell constitute
for the one the whole of the argument; for the other they
are almost non-existent. The theme of the one is theology;
of the other humanity. *The Divine Comedy* is a message
from the other world; the Shakespearean drama is the
gospel of this world. Dante's poem resembles the night; all
is darkness and terror and mystery here below, but the
heavens are revealed in light. Shakespeare's poetry shines
like the noon-day sun, blotting out the stars and planets
of the sky, but illuminating the earth with splendor and
discovering all its features in a blaze of light.

The new interest, wholly concentrated in man, was not yet turned to science or to philosophy. The people were sufficiently concerned with "matters of divinity and state" to make it worth while for the government to forbid playwrights to touch upon these themes; but all the signs show that the heart of the matter, for the spectators as for their greatest dramatist, lay not in adventitious or outward circumstances, but in the interplay of passions and in the mystery of character and of fate.

The popularity of Shakespeare is due partly to the fact that his whole interest was concentrated on those passions which are common to all men. In an age of religious strife he cared little for creeds. In a nation gifted beyond others with political ability the poet cared nothing for politics. The contemporary of Galileo and Kepler, of Gilbert and Bacon, took no thought of the marvellous triumphs of science. Even his allusions to nature betray an utter indifference to her mysteries and no very high appreciation of her beauties. He knew only the folk-lore of the birds and flowers, not their natural history. In him we read of the jewel in the toad's head, of the camomile as growing faster the more it is trodden upon, and of the polity of the bee-hive in a passage which as an apologue may be allowed some merit, but which as a study of nature is simply grotesque. But in the knowledge of the most universal passions, of the sex-complex, of the herd-complex, and of the ego-complex, Shakespeare is unrivaled. He studied them all with a rare objectivity, an ability to put himself in the position of his characters which makes him the most veracious and penetrating of reporters.

His unequaled gift of language is in part the secret of his genius, in part the gift of his environment. He wrote the current Elizabethan English, more poetical and emotional than is the language of today, full-bodied, highly colored, honied, sensuous, and drastic, full of conceits and quips, not a little inclining to the baroque in its love for strong effects and for gorgeous ornament. Words were both his instrument and his environment; he loved them as the artist loves his medium and as the sailor loves the sea.

Though the industry of several generations of scholars has at last lifted the veil which long hung over the incidents of his life, there is little in the outer career to satisfy the eager questionings of the worshipper of his genius. Born in 1564 in a tradesman's family at the little village of Stratford-on-Avon, educated in the grammar school, he left his native place young and perhaps partly on account of an early and unhappy marriage. He went to London, where he lived for many years as actor and playwright. In this profession he won the patronage and friendship of the great, wealth, fame, and a coat of arms; all of which he apparently valued chiefly for the consequence they gave him in his native village, to which he retired to spend a few years of rest before his death in 1616.

While in London he wrote two narrative poems, a series of sonnets, and either wrote or collaborated in nearly forty plays. These plays show little originality of plot; more than half are based upon previous plays, and the rest are nearly all founded upon earlier novels, or on Plutarch's *Lives,* or on the English chronicles. Many of them scintillate with wit and glow with humor, nearly all of them contain flights of imagination and of powerful poetry. But their supreme excellence is the study of character as revealed in the stress of passion and in the storms of fate. Love is portrayed from all points of view: as pleasure in *Venus and Adonis,* as base lust in *Lucrece,* as a social problem in *Measure for Measure,* as true love in a variety of forms. The witty courtship of Beatrice and Benedict in *Much Ado,* the plaintive, silent passion of Viola in *Twelfth Night,* the ecstasy of youthful devotion in *Romeo and Juliet,* the mature ardor of Anthony and Cleopatra, the heart-break of Troilus, the jealousy of Othello, exhaust the forms in which sexual desire can be psychologically studied.

One thing interested Shakespeare more even than love, and that was fate, fate as an individual thing, as the destiny of man wrought out by character and circumstance in this life and not carried by the dooming gods to the regions of another world. Every man is confronted with the problem of the best course of action to pursue in the typical vicissitudes of life. Does the ruthless man, striding over all obstacles to the object of his ambition fare best, or does the more scrupulous and thoughtful man succeed better? The poet works out both alternatives in a series of dramas. Titus Andronicus, Richard III, and Macbeth are strong, ruthless men, who in the end ruin everything and turn life into a hell, even for themselves, by their very successes. Brutus (in *Julius Caesar*) and Hamlet are scrupulous, good men, who fail only less tragically than the bold, bad men have done.

And finally, whether strong or weak, man is the sport and prey of forces over which he has no control. In Shakespeare's drama, as on the theater of real life, character is part of destiny but not the whole of it. The terrible sufferings of Lear rejected by his daughters, of Timon repulsed by his friends, of Coriolanus exiled by his country, are due less to the faults of each man's character than to the unworthiness of what he most loved. On the other hand, fate is sometimes merciful. It is kind to Antonio and Bassanio in *The Merchant of Venice*, it smiles in *The Midsummer Night's Dream* and in *The Tempest*. Griefs are overcome and temporary estrangements end in reconciliation and joy in *Pericles*, in *Cymbeline*, and in *The Winter's Tale*.

While Shakespeare's appeal is so universal and his genius so powerful that he has become a sort of secular Bible throughout Christendom, the stars of his fellows have paled their ineffectual fires before his sun. While he was, in Jonson's often quoted tribute, for all time, they were for an age; few of their plays are now widely read and only one [1] still holds the stage. But of their own age they have much to tell. Their interests were often more special than were Shakespeare's; they reflected local conditions and transient fashions. Tragedy they painted in the strong, crude colors

[1] Massinger's *A New Way to Pay Old Debts*. I saw Walter Hampden give it on Nov. 11, 1922.

of blood, crime, and incest; comedy in the gaudy hues borrowed from the manners of "a lubrique and adulterate age."

In political and religious matters many of the dramatists, though bound by laws and watched by the censor, took a stronger stand than did Shakespeare. Cyril Tourneur called one of his plays *The Atheist's Tragedy,* and Marlowe dramatized the story of *Faust,* that parable, so characteristic of the spirit of the time, of the man who risked and lost salvation for the power to know everything, to do everything, and to enjoy everything, in this world. In other plays the superstitions of witchcraft and alchemy were ridiculed; and the devil was called, in the title of one of Jonson's comedies, an ass, a comic butt for the wits of cleverer men.

Though the prevailing tone of the drama was royalist, there were some playwrights daring enough to warn the prince who began "to swell with pride and to disdain the commons' love," that he would "better lead a private life than rule with tyranny and discontent." [1] A new sympathy with the middle and even with lower classes is reflected in such plays as *The Shoemaker's Holiday* by Dekker (1600), *Eastward Ho* by Chapman, Jonson, and Marston (1605), *A New Way to Pay Old Debts* by Massinger (1525-6), and *The Jovial Crew* by Brome. In the first two of these plays the virtuous apprentice wins the hand of the wealthy citizen's daughter, though she is wooed by earl and gentleman. *A New Way to Pay Old Debts* scourges the tyranny of the newly powerful moneyed class. Through the capitalistic revolution the merchant had just won the leading position in the state, and harsh use of his upstart power made him intensely hateful to the people. Massinger pilloried him in the person of Sir Giles Overreach who corrupts justice, evicts tenants, exacts usury, and grinds the faces of the poor. Ben Jonson, in *Every Man Out of His Humor,* expresses a similar scathing judgment of the monopolist Sordido who maintains that dearth is wholesome for the state in killing off and reducing to order the superfluous or licentious members of the teeming working class.

[1] George Peele, *Edward I,* lines 276ff.

So far afield do the dramatists go in search for a subject that even the new scientific interests are brought upon the stage, as in Jonson's *Magnetic Lady* and *News from the Moon,* and the tales of travellers to the New World are exploited, as in *The Tempest* and in *Eastward Ho.*

Each of the principal dramatists had his own preferences and his own manner. Christopher Marlowe (1564-1593) who enjoyed a reputation among contemporaries for atheism [1] and debauchery, dressed in turgid blank verse tales of blood and horror: the career of the conqueror Tamburlaine, the crimes of the *Jew of Malta,* the *Massacre at Paris* (of St. Bartholomew), the reign of *Edward II,* and the already mentioned *Doctor Faustus.*

Ben Jonson (1573-1637) turned from romance to realism and from kindly wit to savage satire. Not shrinking from exhibiting the deformity of the times, he presented on his stage a series of characters, each "in their humor," defining "humor" as

> some one peculiar quality [which]
> Doth so possess a man that it doth draw
> All his affects, his spirits and his powers
> In their confluctions, all to run one way.

His stage is crowded with a large variety of knaves, fools, hypocrites, pimps, and whores. In Jonson's world Volpone, the nasty, rich, old miser, is courted by legacy-hunters; Fastidious Brisk and Sir Amorous La-Foole ply the pastime of seduction; the expectant nephew of a rich old uncle cheats him by carrying him to Epicoene, a boy dressed as a girl; and Zeal-of-the-Land Busy and Win-the-Fight Little-wit cant about religion.

A blither, if more distant, world is created by Francis Beaumont (1584-1616) and John Fletcher (1579-1625). As the truest followers of Shakespeare, with whom they once

[1] This reputation for atheism is confirmed by recently discovered letters published in the *London Times Literary Supplement,* 1921. The story of his death, in a tavern brawl, has been set forth by J. L. Hotson: *The Death of Christopher Marlowe,* 1925.

or twice collaborated, they produced a succession of plays in the style popularized by him; some of these plays were written jointly, though not so many as used to be supposed.[1] They portray a courtly and idyllic scene.

As Spain was England's great rival, in the age of Elizabeth and the early Stuarts, for empire, so, also, she contended with her for the palm of dramatic composition. Though the two nations were hostile in religion and very different in government and in polity, it is remarkable that the drama of both reflected much the same new interest in man, doing and suffering. "For," says Cervantes:

the drama places before us at every step a mirror in which we may see vividly displayed what goes on in human life; nor is there any similitude that shows us in more life-like fashion what we are and what we must come to, than do plays and players.[2]

The drama did, indeed, in its golden age, depict every aspect of Spanish life. There were historical melodramas called "comedies of noise" (ruido); "cloak-and-sword plays" dealing with the upper bourgeoisie or lower aristocracy; palace plays putting kings on the scene; comedies of character; comedies of manners, and satires; pastoral pieces; picaresque comedies; mythological and sacred plays and "autos" treating the mystery of transubstantiation with allegorical *dramatis personæ*. These last appealed to the deep religious interests and passions of the audience; the others catered to the newer human interest in secular affairs.

Though the drama, as in England, did not know the bondage of the unities, and feared not to represent an infant in the first act as a grown man in the second, nor to change the scene from Europe to America or Asia,[3] and though, as

---

[1] According to the *Cambridge History of English Literature,* VI, ch. 5, of the 52 plays passing under their joint names, only 8 or 9 are really the work of both together; 1 is by Beaumont alone; 15 by Fletcher alone; 22 by Fletcher and some other dramatist; and a few by neither.

[2] *Don Quixote,* Part II, chap. 12.

[3] See Cervantes' strictures on this in *Don Quixote,* Part I, chapter 48. His censure is exactly that expressed by Ben Jonson in the prologue to *Every Man in his Humor,* and by Sidney in *A Defence of Poesie.*

in England, it mixed comedy and tragedy, producing a new form compared by its exponent and defender to the Minotaur,[1] it was, far more than in England, under the influence of certain conventions and of strong national prejudices and loyalties. The conventions descend from the Latin comedy and are in part due to the incurably romantic illusions of the heart about love. Among these conventions is that of having a heroine of absolute physical and moral perfection; and a hero with no fault except possibly a little too sensitive irritability on the point of honor, and a little too great propensity to sacrifice himself with generous rashness —a propensity nearly always foiled by the resourceful dramatist. Among the purely literary conventions may be reckoned the absence of mothers—for it can hardly be supposed that mothers were rarer in Spain than elsewhere—and the abundance of old, cross, widowers as the necessary butts of the children's and servants' pranks. Many of the Spanish dramas, moreover, are deeply tinctured with religion, or with patriotism, or with royalism, or with all of them.

Of the patriotic plays Cervantes' great melodrama *Numantia* may stand as the extreme type. The vast stage represents the siege of the Spanish city Numantia by the Romans and its defence to the last man. The *dramatis personæ* include both armies, citizens of every description, and supernatural beings like War, Famine, Disease, Fame, the River Duero, and a Demon. The ardent fanaticism of Spain is typically exhibited in Cervantes' play *The Picture of Algiers,* representing a Christian captive repulsing the advances of a Moorish lady on account of her religion, and preferring to her a Christian slave-girl, with whom he at last escapes to freedom.

As a dramatist Cervantes was surpassed by Lope Felix de Vega Carpio (1562-1635) called "a prodigy of nature" because of the unequalled extent of his literary output. He claimed to have composed 1500 comedies and 400 one-act pieces called *"autos";* of which more than 450 comedies and

[1] Lope de Vega: *The New Art of Writing Plays,* Eng. transl. by W. T. Brewster, 1914.

more than 50 *autos* have been printed. In addition to these he wrote long epics in the style of Ariosto and of Tasso, and many lyrics; he fought in the Armada and engaged in several duels; and he lived a life of libertine pleasure at court, not much changed by his ordination as priest in 1613.

While his countrymen rejoiced in his brilliant style, grace, gaiety, polished prosody, and sententious eloquence, he himself professed to write only to please the common people, and felt called upon to apologize for doing so:

> To vulgar standards then I square my play,
> Writing at ease; for, since the public pay,
> 'Tis just, methinks, we by their compass steer,
> And write the nonsense that they love to hear.[1]

The variety in the comedies lies simply in the fable; the characters and the motivation are very similar in many of them.

"The cloak and sword play," Lope's own invention, depicts the every-day life of the Spanish gentleman, and the intrigues of people who wore their hearts on their sleeves and carried their hands on the hilts of their swords. The point of honor, the code of genteel society, demanded that they run their rapiers through the man who trod on their toes or through the wife who polluted their beds. Such a play was *Punishment without Revenge* (*El Castigo sin Venganza*), showing the Duke of Ferrara sentencing his adulterous wife and incestuous son to death. Such a play is *The Star of Seville;* [2] the sad tale of the loves of Sancho Ortiz and Estrella, of the slaying of the lady's brother by her lover, and of her entrance into a nunnery.

Many of the dramas fall into the class known as "comedies of noise" (*ruido*), designed to celebrate the glory of Spain and of her kings. It is the very stamp of the new age that the strong royalist tone pervading these dramas is founded upon devotion to the king as the protector against

---

[1] Lope de Vega: *The New Art of Writing Plays,* Lord Holland's translation.
[2] Doubtfully attributed to Lope.

the injustice, violence and tyranny of a depraved and vicious nobility, and that is quite compatible with a considerable feeling for popular liberties. Springing from the bourgeois class then first coming into power, Lope championed the rights of the people against the encroachments of aristocrats, and nearly always depicted the king as the protector of the humble. Thus, the play called *The King the Great Judge,* displays Don Tello the wicked lord, seizing and carrying off a peasant girl with whom he is in love, but later forced by King Alfonso VII of Castile to give her back to her poor lover, Sancho. The same alliance of king and people forms the plot of *Fuente Ovejuna.* The peasants of the town so named are oppressed by Fernan Gomez de Guzman, Knight Commander of the military order of Calatrava. He flogs their men and abducts their women until the people rise and slay him, proclaiming their allegiance to Ferdinand and Isabella, who appear in the end as their protectors.

Many of the plays, founded upon the history of Spain, glorify her arms and empire. One of the most interesting of these, *The New World Discovered by Christopher Columbus,* brings on the stage a vast number of characters including Columbus, his brother, the kings of Portugal and of Granada, Ferdinand and Isabella, Gonsalvo de Cordova, some American Indians, and a variety of mythological persons such as Providence, Imagination, Christianity, Idolatry, and the Devil. Not only the discovery of America, but the conquest of the Moors in 1492, is acted out; and the whole is unified under the point of view of the triumph of the true faith through Spanish blades.

Many of the one-act *autos* treat religious themes, such as the *Holy Sacrament,* the *Prodigal Son* and other biblical stories, the *Antichrist,* the *Triumph of the Church over Heresy* (in which Luther appears), the *Inquisition,* and the lives of the saints. Many of these short pieces, also, are historical and patriotic; some are mythological (as one on *Venus and Adonis*); and some are pure farces.

A younger contemporary of Lope, commonly known as Tirso de Molina (1571-1648), evinced much talent for play-writing. His subtle, psychological method of approaching his subject colored even his treatment of religious matters. The play called *Lost for Lack of Faith* (*El Condenado por desconfiado*) [1] dramatizes the arguments, so passionately debated in the age of the Reformation, for and against justifiscation by faith. In the play a hermit famous for good works, but weak in faith, is damned, while a criminal strong in faith is saved. But the strong element in the drama lies not in its subject but in a profound study of different temperaments.

Tirso's fame, however, rests chiefly upon his creation, from older materials, of the type character Don Juan, in the play entitled *The Libertine of Seville and the Stone Guest* (*El Burlador de Sevilla y convidado de piedra*). The villain of the piece is a wicked lord, a rake, gambler, and blasphemer, who caps the climax of his crimes by killing in a duel the father of his deeply wronged wife. The stone statue of the dead man, mocked by Don Juan, comes to life to strangle the villain, whose soul is promptly taken to hell. Don Juan Tenorio is the most universal type, except Don Quixote, produced by Spanish fiction, a type imitated by Molière, Mozart, Byron, Mérimée, Bernard Shaw, Rostand, and many other writers.

Note: This survey of seventeenth-century literature is very incomplete. Chapters on the drama—French, Dutch, Spanish and English—after 1636, and on the rise of the modern prose style, have been postponed to the second volume.

[1] If it be indeed Tirso's, which has been doubted.

CHAPTER XIX

ART

I. ITALIAN ART

The mind of Europe, during the sixteenth and seventeenth centuries, is perhaps reflected even more clearly in her art than in her literature. To those who can read them the painting and architecture of the baroque school in the South and of the Dutch realists in the North tell in every line the form and pressure of the time that give them birth. Europe was divided artistically along the same frontiers by which it was divided racially and religiously. The secular art of the South was aristocratic, its religious art Catholic; the subject matter of this art was the heroic and ideal, its inspiration in the past, and its style baroque. The secular art of Holland was democratic; its religious art Protestant; the subject matter of this art was the every-day and commonplace, its inspiration in the present, and its treatment realistic.

In its artistic tradition the baroque was founded both on the Gothic and on the Renaissance; in its sociological and cultural relations it expressed the two new forces of the Counter-Reformation and of Absolutism. In its sacred branch it discharged the mighty task of realizing and consolidating a Catholic reform of art, of emphasizing the aesthetic and emotional side of religion. In the secular field it ministered to the pomp and pride of princes. To both church and throne it lent effulgence.

From the Renaissance the baroque painters and architects took their consummate technique and their senuous element; from the older medieval artists a certain supersensuous ideal. As the Counter-Reformation had been a revival of medievalism, with a few modern improvements, so the sacred art of the age sought to recapture the deep feeling of the Middle Ages and to drive it home into the hearts of men by technical means superior to those wielded by the medieval artists. The result was a union of the transcendental and the natural. Particularly in Spain, but also in other Catholic countries, the artist used the resources of a studied treatment to arouse the strongest possible emotions in the beholder. Thus was naturally evolved that exaggeration which is a marked characteristic of baroque, and which revealed itself in the exuberance of ornament, in the emphasis of gesture, in the continued *fortissimo* of color and *prestissimo* of movement. In striking composition, in piquant detail, they sought that "strangeness of proportion" without which, said Francis Bacon,[1] "there is no excellent beauty."

Moreover, they sought to enhance the effect of each art of painting, sculpture, and architecture by a harmonious and grandiose combination of them all. Large dimensions, profuse ornament in the same style, skillful arrangements of lighting, of spacing, and even of landscape gardening and of town-planning, raised and exaggerated the effect of the whole. In color was sought a unifying as well as a pleasing element.

The influence of the church was not altogether positive. The prudery of the Catholics surpassed that of the Puritans. The Council of Trent forbade the nude in religious paintings, and hired "the breeches painter" to make Michelangelo's *Last Judgment* decent. Moreover the church still feared the pagan element in art so much that Pope Sixtus V systematically destroyed ancient statues and exorcized the stones taken from old Roman pilasters to furnish a pedestal for the statues of some apostles. "What the barbarians spared the Barberini have destroyed" was written of Pope Urban VIII. Recognizing that the age had become more sophisticated, the church frowned upon certain of the old legends too naïvely set forth in pictures. The regulations for painters digested from the prescriptions of the Council

[1] *Essay xliii,* "Of Beauty," 1612.

of Trent by Molanus in 1573 really impeached much of the
medieval simple-mindedness while seeking to revive, nevertheless, medieval earnestness. Nor were these rules dead
letters. The Inquisition summoned to its bar famous painters, like Veronese, on the charge of filling their pictures with
nude, or with ridiculous figures. On the other hand the
church encouraged the production of orthodox art, in which
she found so powerful an ally. The Academy of St. Luke
was founded by Clement X in 1670 to encourage painters
and sculptors in the cultivation of the edifying.

The princes of the church, like the princes of the world,
put no prudish restrictions on the paintings ordered by
them. Cardinal Odoardo Farnese, who employed Carracci
to paint for him the *Triumph of Bacchus and Ariadne,* the
Rule of Love on Earth and the *Rule of Love in the Sea,*
was typical of many others in his licentious tastes.

Italy, as was natural, first developed the baroque style
which spread from her to the rest of Europe. With her there
was no violent break with the Renaissance; the cool light
of Botticelli's morning was followed by the splendid noon of
Raphael and Leonardo and Titian and Michelangelo, and
in the seventeenth century by the gradually lengthening
shadows of a clear afternoon. Though painting remained the
leading art, and the one that gave the tone to its sisters architecture and sculpture, it was in building that the new
style first crept in. The architects started with the aim of
developing further the Renaissance ideas of space and ornament; they tried to make the effect of size colossal, and
that of ornament richer and more complex. They essayed a
more powerful unification of the total effect by emphasizing
the chief space; they sought also to enrich the language of
form by planning a more regular and organic decoration.
Many of the famous Roman villas were built at this time;
their straight lines were broken by corners or bay-windows;
the pillars and pilasters were multiplied in number; the
gables were broken up; and the effect of the house was
enhanced by surrounding it with a trim and congruent
garden.

But the highest effects of Italian baroque in architecture as in painting, were achieved in the service of the church. Above all cities Rome became the capital of the new style. So numerous were the new buildings of this age that medieval and Renaissance Rome was transformed into the baroque city which it remained until the twentieth century. The most famous of all early buildings in this style is the Jesuit church at Rome called *Il Gesù*. The square front and slim dome in the rear make a striking and unified effect on the exterior, but the triumph of the architect is the grandiose and rich spectacle that greets the eye of him who enters. Beyond the high, broad nave with rounded roof looms the ample apse; mighty rows of pillars, a gigantic entablature, a skillful lighting from above, all enhance the impression of vast space. Great masses of colored marble and a profusion of gold ornament in brackets, festoons, balustrades, and bas-reliefs dazzle the vision. As the eye turns upward to the painted and gilded ceiling it seems to see crowds of moving figures, the heavens opening, wild angels holding golden suns, and a vast tumult of movement, light, and color. So skilfully are the arts of architecture, painting, and sculpture harmonized, that each beam of light falls upon some form of bronze or of lapis lazuli, or upon an altar once decorated with one of Rubens' splendid paintings. Such, at least, is the first sight of the church; but the jaded senses recoil afterwards from effects so obviously calculated as to seem insincere; and the mind rebels against the too evident suggestion of propaganda and resents the apparent lack of sincerity, which appears so plainly in many of the Jesuit creations.

In this age was completed the cathedral church of the popes, St. Peter's. Begun in the fifteenth century, it was the work of a series of great artists—among them Bramante, San Gallo, Raphael and Michelangelo. After the dome was completed, in 1590, Cristoforo Roncalli, commonly called the Knight of Arpino, was employed to decorate the interior by paintings of angels and of saints. When the façade was finished, in 1612, two side towers were started, though later abandoned, and the leading sculptor of the time, **Bernini,** employed to add ornaments. On November 18, 1626, 174 years after the first plan had been made, the great church was consecrated by Pope Urban VIII. That it is massive, gigantic, imposing, and, in its own way, quite beautiful, but that it cannot compare in charm with the best cathedrals of the Middle Ages, is the judgment of most modern critics. After all, there is something conveniently symbolic in the fact that, as the church had declined in power and in spiritual wealth, so also the churches became poorer and less lovely.

Even more than architecture, Italian painting came not only into the service but into the servitude of the church. Art in the hands of Giotto and Raphael had been an ally of religion, but a free ally asserting her own rights. But in the Counter-Reformation, with the censor to tell her what not to do, and with the Jesuit to tell her what to do, art sank into an ignoble bondage. In her decadence she dwelt on the ecstasy and rapture of sickly saints, or on the physical tortures of ghastly martyrs. A race of eclectic epigoni, without the genius or spiritual fire of the great masters, could do naught but imitate and recombine the various manners of the high Renaissance: the tragic grandeur of Michelangelo, the charm of Raphael, the chiaroscuro of Correggio, and the color of Titian.

The decline was gradual. Tintoretto (Jacopo Robusti, 1518-94) deserves by his power in treating the problems of space and atmosphere to be reckoned the last of the great masters; but on the other hand a close study of his canvases reveals that his highest effects depend not so much on any original quality as on the successful eclecticism that combined Titian's color with Michelangelo's form. In Veronese's (Paolo Caliari, 1528-88) gorgeous decoration of wall and ceiling, in the religious and mythological work of the Carracci the decline of originality went on in the Counter-Reformation, until Caravaggio (1565-1600) inaugurated what might almost be called a Counter-Renaissance, in his rebellion against the purely imitative, and in his proclamation of nature, of nature even in her brutal and ugly manifestations. But Caravaggio, too, was a man of his age; he guided art along the paths of asceticism to the representation of miracles, visions, and martyrdoms.

Guido Reni (1575-1642) the most talented as he is still the most popular Italian artist of the seventeenth century, brought painting fully back into the academic tradition. His best work, the *Aurora,* a fresco in the Rospigliosi palace at Rome, embellishes a commonplace idea with the resources of perfect technique, of a brilliant palette, and of an artistic composition. Among his mythological and religious pictures are found very few portraits:—the famous one called *Beatrice Cenci* being neither a portrait of that tragic heroine nor even a genuine work from the brush of the master.

After Guido the best of the Italian painters was Salvator Rosa (1615-73), who delighted in the gruesome and the sentimental. While his battle-pictures filled with carnage, and his religious pieces depicting such subjects as *Saul and the Spirit of Samuel, Jeremiah in the Pit, Daniel in the Lion's Den,* and *Jonah,* are traditional, his landscapes are new in Italian art. Far from the realism of the Dutch landscape-painters, he depicted by preference desolate beaches and romantic caverns and wild spots filled with warriors, beggars, spirits, and apparitions, all treated in a sentimental composition.

2. SPANISH ART

The same energy that made Spain the leading Catholic power of the world showed itself in her art. The militant patriotism and the fierce fanaticism so repugnant to the soft Italian nature were the breath of the Castilian's nostrils. The Society of Jesus, the *auto-da-fe,* and the Index were the darling children, either native or early adopted, of the Hispanic soul. Next to the church the throne, symbol of empire, was the shrine of the Castilian's worship. Spanish art, whether architecture or sculpture or painting, was almost altogether courtly or ecclesiastical. How characteristic of it is the scarcity of the nude that played so large a rôle in the art of Italy and of Flanders! In the breast of the Spaniard the love of woman and the thirst for pleasure, in fact all passions and all preoccupations, were subordinated to his sense of duty to his God and to his king.

On the southern declivity of the Sierra de Guadarrama, Philip II and his architect Herrera erected (1563-84) a palace, dark and grandiose like the Spanish character, gigantic like the Spanish Empire. Built of gray granite and covered with slate, the Escorial looks like a part of the mountain from which it sprang. The vast quadrangle with its towers encloses a space divided into sixteen courts and partly filled with a domed church and with other buildings. All the courts, all the 86 staircases and all the 2673 windows are exactly in the same style—a unity of conception nowhere else found on so large a scale. But behind the might of the bald five-storied façade the chief halls and the church lack no charm of pleasant line, of noble articulation, and of congruous ornament. Close to the church are the royal chambers; of which one, the bedroom, looks by a window into the sacred edifice—fit expression of the piety of the Catholic king!

None of the churches built in the sixteenth or seventeenth centuries are as characteristic or as imposing as the palace. Many of them, after the middle of the seventeenth century, were built in the half-gothic, half-baroque style known, after its chief exponent, as Churriguerism. The limit of this style was perhaps reached in the sacristy of the Carthusian monastery at Granada, every inch of which was carved with elaborate filigree or crowded with a giddy profusion of figures.

And what figures of the Saviour and of the saints! No effort was spared to make them living to the eye of the believer. The sculptors, regardless of beauty and intent only on religious emotion, put crystal eyes into their statues' heads, made pearly tears run down their cheeks, and painted streaks of blood on the crucifixes and the martyrs' wounds. Here, and in the Spanish religious pictures, we see as nowhere else the gruesome tortures of the holy ones, the ecstatic nightmare of their visions:

The flesh that the live blood faints in, the leavings of racks and
    rods;
The ghastly glories of saints, dead limbs of gibbeted Gods.

It is the irony of fact that Spain should have learned from a Greek the art so remote from the Hellenic spirit. Domenico Theotocopuli, commonly called El Greco, was born in Crete about the middle of the sixteenth century, studied painting in Venice under Titian, and came to Toledo in 1575 or 1576 to live there until his death in 1614. Strongly temperamental as he was, forcing everything, like an impressionist or an expressionist, into the mould of his own artistic vision, he yet put on all his pictures the stamp of the Spanish Reformation. In the enraptured *Annunciation* (at Budapest), in the flickering, lambent flame of the Holy Ghost outpoured at *Pentecost* (Madrid), in the mysterious *Apocalyptic Vision* (owned by Zuloaga), one sees the peculiarly spiritualized forms of the mystic's dreams. In the gray visages of his long-faced, long-nosed, long-limbed men, we see deep eyes glowing with the arid beauty of a soul burnt in the fire of fanaticism.

After the Greek, the "Little Spaniard"—Jusepe de Ribera, called Lo Spagnoletto (c. 1588-1652)—exhibited a further stage in the Catholic evolution. Though he lived part of his life in Naples, he was a true Spaniard at heart, depicting with fervor the asceticism of hermits and the sorrows of penitents. The terror of the Last Trumpet convulses the face of his *St. Jerome:* pain, humiliation and stubborn resolve stare from the eyes in the small, convict-like head of *St. Bartholomew* in the hands of his torturers. On the other hand ecstasy beams in the warm, golden light bathing the lovely form of the kneeling St. Agnes in the picture illustrating her legend. Exposed to the crowd naked, the beautiful Christian girl had found her modesty miraculously protected by an angel with a covering sheet. The picture of the *Angel*

and Shepherds of Bethlehem (in the Brooklyn Museum)
suffuses a pretty idyl with warm religious emotions.

That full-blooded, strong, and hard Spaniard, Francisco
Zurbaran (1598-1662) devoted his talents chiefly to the
depiction of fanatical monasticism or of the triumphs of the
Christian armies over the infidels. The picture (now in Berlin) of St. Bonaventura showing St. Thomas Aquinas the
crucifix as the source of all wisdom realistically portrays two
monks in an access of pious emotion. The fine *Battle with
the Moors* (in New York) shows the Virgin and Child sur-
veying the battle-field with exultation.

While El Greco and Zurbaran appealed to the stern
virtues of the militant Christian man, other painters found
a more congenial field for the exercise of their talents in
fostering the softer piety of female devotion. Perhaps the
race, under the combined influences of culture and luxury,
and under the oppression of despotism, priest-craft, and
defeat, was itself becoming slightly effeminate. At any rate,
after the Moor and the Jew had been expelled, and after
the obstinate heretic had been consumed in the fires of the
auto-da-fe, under Jesuit tuition there grew up an art mar-
velously apt to kindle men's piety through their senses, to
nurse a sentimental and unquestioning devotion to the
church.

The master of this style was Bartolomé Esteban Murillo
(1617-82), born in the Andalusian city of Seville to set
forth on canvas the visions and the ecstasies of women.
Progressing from the cold style to the warm, from the warm
to the vapoury, he depicted with ever growing ardor the
love of Mary and the happy transports of the saints. In
his efforts to represent the *Immaculate Conception of the
Virgin*—a dogma hardly capable of pictorial treatment—he
raised a mortal to the skies; in his illustrations of the legends
of the saints he brought the angels down to earth. An almost
sensual glow of loveliness warms the features of the Puris-
sima as she stands, the Queen of Heaven, on the crescent
moon, surrounded by cherubs as was Cytherea by the Loves.
On another canvas Mary is depicted as a tiny baby sitting

on the midwife's arm, with an expression of rapt astonishment and devotion, surrounded by a happy crowd of earthly god-parents and of attendant angels, and bathed in an atmosphere almost like the clouds of incense in a gorgeous church.

Familiar and yet sentimentalized is the conception of the legends of the saints as set forth in *The Charity of St. John of God*, in the *St. Elizabeth of Hungary*, and in the *Angels' Kitchen*. In the last named, St. James having forgotten in prayer the culinary duties assigned him, the officious angels come down and supply his place, thus saving the brothers from a burnt meal and him from a scolding. Particularly congenial to Murillo's genius was any scene of tenderness expressed by an embrace. As *St. John the Apostle* lifts the body of Jesus from the cross, as *St. John of God* supports the sick beggar, as *St. Anthony of Padua,* with evident transport, takes the child Jesus to his bosom, many a deep chord of sympathy vibrates in the heart of the spectator. This note of sensuous devotion, so congenial to many secret or unacknowledged emotions in the devotee's heart, made the artist immensely popular in his own day, and for long after, but has brought on him the severe condemnation of critics unsympathetic with this type of piety. Historically it lays bare the artificial, almost professional seduction practised by the Jesuits of the seventeenth century. Not only to frighten men into conformity, but also to allure them into devotion was the policy of the church.

Besides his religious paintings Murillo spread on his canvases many studies of beggars and gamins of the street. Charming the little rascals often are, as they pick lice from their clothes or hair, or as they eat melons, or gamble; but they were not painted, like the peasants of the Dutch school, as genre studies in the life of the common people. Beggary in Spain, like deformity and idiocy, is a privileged thing; poverty in Catholic lands is "apostolic," and alms-giving a high virtue. While Northern Europe at this time was forcing mendicancy into the work-house, and suppressing vagrancy by harsh if salutary laws, Spain was still employing her beggars to stimulate the generosity, and to exercise the piety, of the rich.

While the majority of Spanish painters dedicated their best talents to God, the greatest of them, Diego Rodriguez de Silva y Velasquez (1599-1660) devoted his matchless genius almost wholly to Caesar. Though born, like Murillo, in Seville, he found his home not there but chiefly in the court. After his genius became known he was at first loaded with menial duties as gentleman usher to the king, was then appointed royal commissioner to buy paintings in Italy, and was finally decorated with the honorable, if onerous, insignia of Grand Marshal.

The secret of his art lies partly in his perfect technique, partly in his objective temperament. He was the first painter to use oil as his sole medium; his predecessors had used tempera in general with a little oil to give lustre when required. Velasquez's drawing was extraordinarily free and correct, his mastery of perspective faultless, his lighting as clear as the day, and his color soft and splendid. Moreover he shared with Shakespeare the gift of suppressing his own personality in his perfect sympathy with his subject. He, almost alone of the major artists, painted not what he felt, still less what he imagined, but only what he saw; and he saw only what was there.

This almost greatest of painters took almost the meanest of subjects. Most of his efforts went to portray the degenerate race of the Spanish Hapsburgs and the repulsive creatures, dwarfs, monsters, and idiots, with whom they delighted to fill the court. The decadence of Spanish power is partly explained when one sees, in Velasquez's canvases, that the most intimate associates of the monarch of half the world were hydrocephalic dwarfs and cunning fools chosen for some deformity of mind or body, gorgeously dressed and given in derision such names as *Don Juan of Austria, The Geographer, The Philosopher*, and *Æsop*.

From no less than forty portraits Philip IV's lack-lustre eye looks out; his pale face and frail body showing plainly the signs of hereditary taint and of enervating pleasures.[1] With all their pride and all their wealth the Spanish Hapsburgs were a melancholy race. Even the children, rigid in their stiff clothes and court manners, look unhealthy and unhappy. Of course there is no satire in the artist's purpose, which was but to flatter and to please. But here, as is often the case, simple fidelity to nature proved slightly caricaturesque. Even with these unpromising subjects the artist sought not in vain to make a pleasing picture. The little prince, *Don Baltasar,* sitting proudly on a Spanish jennet, gallops along over the heather with scarf floating to the wind, while behind him are seen the snowy peaks of the Guadarrama like pearls against a brilliant, azure sky. The *Infanta,* too, a child in enormous hoop-skirts, holding a pink rose in her hand, makes a pleasing effect in her gray and silvery dress contrasted with her pale golden hair. And the group picture of the maids of honor, *Las Meninas,* is charming.

When he had a good subject Velasquez could rival Holbein or Titian as a master of expression and of facial beauty. His portrait of himself depicts, with self-evident truth, a singularly noble, handsome, and intelligent countenance. His portrait of *Innocent X* reveals the ruddy face of the astute Italian.

Fortunately, the court did not demand only portraits of its inmates. The glory of the Spanish arms is celebrated in the historical painting commemorating the *Capture of Breda* from the Dutch in 1625. In the foreground the Spanish general Spinola receives the keys of the town from the Dutch commander; to the right bristles the forest of Spanish spears, to the left gleam the pikes and halberds of the vanquished, and in the distance the town itself is seen in the midst of a smiling landscape.

If Christian subjects were seldom attempted by Velasquez, his treatment of the pagan mythology that filled the canvases of Italy and Flanders is so realistic and simple that it gives,

[1] One fine portrait of Philip and one of Innocent X by Velasquez are now at Fenway Court, Boston.

as in many of his portraits, the impression of irony. In *Los Borrachos (The Topers)*, he humorously paints Bacchus as a plump, pretty youth sitting half-naked on a winecask surrounded by six Spanish peasants clothed in the garb of their country, and with a nude faun in the background.

Even more humorously he depicted a genre scene in the fine canvas called *The Forge of Vulcan*. The god of fire is nothing but a village blacksmith with four cyclopes, who are nothing but day-laborers, assisting him. Into his shop comes that handsome youth Apollo, all agog to tell him of his wife Venus' infidelity. The news is reflected in the amused smile of Apollo, in the evident dismay of Vulcan, and in the gaping curiosity of the assistants.

Another magnificent canvas, *The Tapestry Weavers*, exhibits a scene from Spanish life without the excuse of a mythological title. In the highly lighted background the splendid tapestry hangs; while five working women weave or spin in the darker foreground. Such pictures as these, with their sound, healthy peasant types, reveal the foundations of Spain's greatness as clearly as the courtly and ecclesiastical art explains the causes of her decay.

3. BAROQUE ART IN FLANDERS

When the bloody war of independence waged in the Netherlands slackened towards the close of the sixteenth century and halted in a twelve-year truce in 1609, the ten southern provinces remaining subject to Spain and to the Catholic Church were left by the court of Madrid under the nearly autonomous rule of their archdukes. Enjoying the blessings of peace, they regained, even in their servitude, some of the wealth and polish that had formerly placed them in the front rank of European civilization. But the course of events had turned all their purposes backwards, and had made all their thoughts reactionary. Their abounding energies, barred from following, with their northern brethren, the new religion, the new republicanism, and new ideals in art, expended themselves in the effort to give fresh life to the

old forms of monarchy and aristocracy, to restore the church
to her ancient power if not to her pristine purity, and to
copy the art of the Italian Renaissance.

Unlike the Spaniard the Fleming was no fanatic. Reluctantly and without passion he espoused the causes of king
and of church. He built no empire; he founded no Society
of Jesus, and would have preferred to have had no Inquisition. But the stream of his full life, damned up and turned
aside from its natural channels, inundated the field of art
and made it blossom like the garden of Eden. The flowers,
it is true, were of no new variety; they were the off-
spring of the seed sown in Italy a hundred years before.
To change the metaphor, the sun of the Renaissance set in
Antwerp, and set in a splendid flame of gorgeous color. It
was the culmination, the glory of the baroque style; the
imitation not of nature but of the masters; and not only
their imitation but the exaggeration and intensification of
their style. The art of Antwerp was not only imitative and
exaggerated, but it was almost purposely unreal and romantic. The men of Brabant wanted not their own life reproduced in painting, but something better. They demanded,
and their artists created for them, a world free from the
sordid realities of poverty, of political slavery, and of
thwarted spiritual yearnings; they created an imaginary
world in which everyone is rich, noble, and distinguished;
every man a hero, every woman a paragon of voluptuous
beauty, and every moment a dramatic crisis.

Never did Belgium produce such great painters as in the
first century after her separation from the Northern Netherlands; never did she show such zeal in building churches as
in the period of the Counter-Reformation. The architecture
of these, in the baroque or "Jesuits' style" imitated the
Italian models, but at the same time adapted the new
buildings somewhat to local conditions. The principles of the
rising school were laid down by the great master Jacques
Franquart of Brussels in his *Livre d'Architecture,* published
in 1616. Many of his churches have survived, though his
chef d'œuvre, the Jesuit church at Brussels, has been de-

stroyed. The leading Flemish artist set the stamp of his approval on the new style in words worth quoting for the aesthetic judgments conveyed in them.

In our country [wrote Rubens] we see the style of architecture called barbarous or Gothic becoming obsolete and gradually disappearing; and we see men of taste introducing, to the great ornament of the country, that style of architecture that is possessed of true symmetry and which conforms to the rules established by the ancient Greeks and Romans. Examples of this are the magnificent churches just built by the Venerable Company of Jesus at Antwerp and at Brussels.[1]

Not in architecture, however, but in painting, was the baroque style to attain its perfect maturity. Its consummate master was the writer of the above words, Peter Paul Rubens (1577-1640), the very note of whose life, as of his art, is an exuberance, a fecundity, and a facility hardly found elsewhere. Born in Siegen and baptized a Protestant, he was brought as a child to Antwerp and reconciled to the Catholic church. His professional education, begun too early to allow him to have much book learning, was continued by eight years of travel, mostly in Italy, but also in Spain. Returning to Antwerp, he soon became the favorite and darling of princes; he was employed in high diplomatic missions and courted by the monarchs and great ones of the world; he was ennobled; he won wealth and distinction in many fields. And he left more than two thousand two hundred paintings ascribed to his brush. Even making large allowance for the known fact that many of these were painted by his pupils and assistants, and only retouched or finished by him, still the residue of his output is almost unequaled. And what pictures! Huge compositions most of them are; vast surfaces crowded with figures and filled with detail.

The quality of his output is as exuberant as its quantity. Without subtle thought or delicate feeling he poured on his

[1] *Correspondance*, ii, 422, May 29, 1622.

canvas a riot of movement, a stream of bright color, a blaze of light, a torrent of sensual pleasure. He loved everything that could delight the eye or stimulate the sense; he loved rich clothes and jewels and the joy of motion, and above all he loved women. Very many of his subjects are mythological; for the old stories that had lost their savor to the fresher, more realistic feeling of Velasquez or of Rembrandt, still offered the best excuse for filling the canvas with Venuses and Dianas, with nymphs and goddesses and heroines in distress. Never so much in distress, to be sure, but that they seem happy and certain of rescue; even Judith smiles on Holophernes' head, and Andromeda on the dragon. Beautiful they all are; fair-haired and white-skinned and red-cheeked and plump of thigh and full of breast. Rubens found his best models in his own wives; in pretty Isabella Brant whom he married in 1609 and who died in 1626, and in Helen Fourment whom he married four years later. Carried away, at the age of fifty-three, with love for this beauty of sixteen, he filled several canvases with her likenesses, both richly dressed and in the higher adornment of her lovely nudity. She is Venus in the *Judgment of Paris,* she is *Diana surprised by Actaeon;* and she is the nymph lustily embraced by the satyr in that apotheosis of desire aptly called *The Sacrifice to Venus.*

Rubens' interest in the antique mythology and history was not due solely to the opportunities it gave for erotic subjects; it was largely due to admiration of its heroism. The *fable convenue* then passing as Greek and Roman history presented the story of the Hellenic cities and of the Latin race as a series of episodes in a tale of glory. Like the humanists before him and like the French dramatists after him, Rubens depicted scenes from ancient legends as lessons in patriotism and in virtue. The story of *Decius Mus* in eight cartoons, that of *Constantine* in twelve, and many single illustrations of fables or of authentic chronicles reflect the struggles and triumphs of strong men posing as heroes. Their athletic forms, their valiant bodies, their arched eyebrows and noble attitudes show the world as it ought to be rather than as it is.

Not only ancient worthies but modern monarchs were idealized by Rubens beyond all recognition. High station supplied the want of every virtue, for Rubens (like God in the epigram of the French *marquise*) thought twice before he damned a person of quality. Fulsome flattery has never so strained all the resources of art to make visible the divinity hedging a monarch as it did in the magnificent series dedicated by Rubens to the *Apotheosis of Marie de Médicis*. In twenty-one magnificent canvases, most of which can now be seen in one of the great rooms of the Louvre, this ill-tempered and narrow-minded woman is depicted as a goddess, whose happy destiny was woven by the Fates, whose birth was surrounded by the deities of Olympus, whose education was supervised by Minerva, whose marriage with Henri IV was arranged by Jove and Juno. When she crosses the sea nymphs and tritons guard her vessel; when she is crowned all earth and heaven attends; when she is left a widow and regent of the kingdom the blessings of her rule are expressed by the opulent charms of a multitude of symbolic figures. Even her battle with her son and her flight from court are turned into occasions for eulogy of her maternal and royal virtues. Similar, though shorter, series of pictures deify the memories of Henri IV of France and of James I of England.

The artist, like so many of his generation, was not only blinded by the purple, but was dazzled by gold wherever he saw it. His portraits express the dignity of rank rather than scrupulous fidelity to truth. His landscapes are the pleasant parks of the rich; his festivals and bacchanals are the orgies of voluptuaries in a land of heart's desire; his great hunting scenes of the lion, the boar, the crocodile, and the hippopotamus are the sports of heroes imagined rather than witnessed.

It is highly significant that Rubens' religious pictures should exhibit exactly the same style and taste as do his secular subjects. The Catholic Reformation, so passionately felt in Spain, and strong enough to crush the Renaissance in Italy, in Flanders rather succumbed to than vanquished the secular temper of the age. If men could not be made saintly or devout, it was something to make them conform outwardly; for the beauty of holiness an effective substitute, in attaching hearts to the church, might be found in the beauty of art. The new or renovated churches in the baroque style demanded pictures suitable to their giant altars. Rubens' best religious pieces, painted for such churches as the *Gesu* at Rome, and for the Cathedral and Jesuit Church at Antwerp, solved to perfection the problem of a decorative art congruous with the architectural surroundings. The brilliant lighting, the perspective seeming to burst the bounds of space, the gaudy color, the dramatic composition, delighted the eyes of the worshippers and struck their hearts with admiration, and sometimes with terror or with love.

Lacking in conviction but armed with wonderful technical resources, the Flemish genius painted scenes from the Bible and legends of the saints with as much facility as he had depicted pagan legends and the glories of monarchs. One and the same style set forth the *Assumption of the Virgin* and the *Apotheosis of James I*, the *Ascension of Elijah* and *Apollo driving his Car*. Not a Christian but a heathen sentiment animated the best of the new church pictures; certainly Venus and not God was glorified in the stories of Susanna and Bathsheba and Mary Magdalene exposing their naked charms on the canvases of the Flemish master.

The judgment of a secular generation will perhaps applaud Rubens in pursuing the ideal of earthly beauty as certainly more attainable and possibly more desirable than that of heavenly beauty. Where he really suffers is not in comparison with any medieval or Puritanical asceticism, but in contrast with his contemporary Rembrandt, whose quiet but deeply felt treatment of religious story makes Rubens' composition seem theatrical, his gesture a pose, and his color garish. But the world would be poorer without variety; two opposite styles may each produce objects of worth. Not to disparage Rubens but to explain the temper of his age and country, it must be pointed out that the secularization of religious art begun in the Renaissance was carried by him to its logical conclusion; that when the church called in the painter to aid her, she incurred the fate of every power that calls in an ally stronger than itself.

What the public wanted was a pageant or a sensation; something to dazzle the eye or to thrill the nerves. The two paintings, *The Elevation of the Cross* and the *Descent from the Cross* in the Antwerp Cathedral, exhibit a mighty and beautiful Christ, a group of powerful, half-naked men in tense attitudes; a splendid nobleman on a fine horse, and some fair women and children. The *Adoration of the Magi* is elsewhere presented as a great festival, a royal ceremony of kings in costly clothes, of Herculean burden-bearers, of a retinue of horses and camels, and, almost lost in the crowd, the lovely baby who is the center of it all.

The dramatic passes into the horrible in such pictures as *Judith with the head of Holofernes,* or the *Martyrdom of St. Livinus,* whose tongue has just been torn out and offered to a dog. The drastic presentations of hell and damnation in the various *Last Judgments* remind one of Loyola's injunctions in the *Spiritual Exercises* that the initiate should endeavor to bring hell before his imagination as vividly as possible, to see the length and breadth of the fiery lake, to smell the brimstone and to hear the wailings of the damned, to taste the bitterness of their tears and to feel the worm of conscience. These pictures, and the others setting forth the miracles of St. Ignatius and of St. Francis Xavier witness the extent to which the Jesuits had won the mind of Catholic Europe. Other pictures exhibit the triumph of the eucharist over heresy, idolatry, and blindness, and the *Victory of the Inquisition over Heresy.* Even the details of this composition (dated c.1626) reveal something of the history of the time; for Luther lies prostrate on the ground of his ravaged country, while Calvin, much alive in Holland, Britain, and Switzerland, still continues to defend his doctrine.

Two of Rubens' pupils carried on his art in different spheres: Jordaens in the tavern, Van Dyck in the court.

Jacob Jordaens (1593-1678) of Antwerp, more original, racier, more reckless than his master, coarsened Rubens' art in endeavoring to surpass it. Finding among the middle classes an even more Gargantuan appetite for pleasure than prevailed among the aristocracy, he set himself to celebrate, to exaggerate, all the joys of the senses: to paint the fruit more luscious, and the wine a richer red, to throw a perfume of pleasure on every act of life, and to gild the golden, laughter-loving Aphrodite. Everything in his pictures eats and drinks, everyone makes love, almost everyone laughs. His compositions, aptly called *Fertility* and *Abundance* pour torrents of light on the voluptuous forms of nymphs and satyrs luxuriating in an exuberant harvest of fruits and grains. Like Sancho Panza, Jordaens loved meat and drink and popular proverbs, many of which are illustrated by his genre pieces. Like Rabelais he would have loved to be king; though the only king he depicted is a tipsy reveller, a jolly old soul with his pipe and his bowl, and with his boon companions and his women. All his pictures, genre subjects like the *Satyr in the Peasant's Family*, mythological subjects like the *Festivals of Venus and of Bacchus,* religious pieces like *Susanna in the Bath,* are hymns to the senses. Vulgar he was, and coarse; but brilliant with the desire of the earth and flushed with the joy of living. It is, as one likes to take it, either the moral of his story or the irony of the human comedy, that this devotee of gluttony and revelry and lust should, when cloyed and sated towards the end of life, have become a Calvinist in a country where it was dangerous to be one.

If Jordaens inherited Rubens' joyous sensuality, another pupil, Anthony Van Dyck, (1599-1641) fell heir to his courtly tastes and position. Disliking coarse carousing, he loved the refinement and distinction of palaces; and he loved the high-born ladies who sat to him for portraits. Born in Antwerp, trained by Rubens, he travelled to Holland and to France, and spent long years (1621-7) in Italy and still longer years (1620-21, and 1632-41) in London. His religious pictures reflect the influence of his master, as well

as of Veronese and of Titian, in their haughty refinement
and in their baroque taste. Though his portraits are famous,
and are undoubtedly his best works, they achieve success
rather by reflection of aristocratic distinction than by revelation of character. As the dresses became richer, the composition more picturesque, and the color more splendid, the faces
gradually set into a kind of mask; the masculine type, particularly, became so fixed as to give the artist's name to the
then fashionable pointed beard.

4. THE BIRTH OF THE MODERN SCHOOL IN HOLLAND

Nearly allied as were the Dutch and Flemings in race and
in their earlier political tradition, the war of independence
and of religion had torn them so far apart that anyone who
crossed the border from the Southern to the Northern Provinces stepped into another world. The United Netherlands,
tiny in extent and population, but powerful, rich, free, and
civilized, developed a new type of life and with it a new
art totally different from all that had gone before and in
every point the antithesis of the art of Brabant. The Dutch
painters consulted not tradition but their eyesight; they
imitated not the masters but nature as they saw it. All that
vast and burdensome convention that forced the southern
painter to select only the heroic and specious, or at least
the dramatic and striking, was discarded by the men who
first saw and first ventured to depict the beauty of the common. Life is not, after all, entirely or even chiefly a succession of thrilling moments, of theatrical gestures and of perfect epigrams, ending in a glorious death. The average
populace is not composed of heroes, saints, martyrs, and
beauties, nor of gods, goddesses, satyrs, and angels; not even
of monarchs and patricians.

The Dutch artist was tired of kings; and he was equally
tired of professional saints and of attitudinizing heroes.
Thus he developed the new style of painting originally called
"le genre bas," and afterwards simply "genre," the depic-

tion of low life, of some scene from the ordinary activities of the common people.

It is highly characteristic that the Dutch should have cared so little for historical pictures; and for battle-pieces not at all. The people that had won such military glory as can be compared only to that of Greece when she defied the Persians; the people that had beaten back the sword of Alva and the battalions of Louis XIV, that swept the English channel with their fleets and planted their colonies in every quarter of the globe, did not wish to commemorate these triumphs in their monuments. Two or three pictures—one by Rembrandt and one by Terborsch, for example—celebrate the signing of the Peace of Westphalia (1648); but even these are not very successful. War, with all its gory victories, seemed horrible to the Dutch. What they fought for and what they won and what they beautified in the paintings of their artists was their own little country and their own small homes and polders. Looking at the paintings of this land and school is like looking in at the windows of the seventeenth-century; through them we see every aspect of Dutch domestic life, and of the Dutch land. In them we see the dunes and woodland glades in the misty sunlight; we see the sea and the dykes and the windmills and the paddocks filled with cows and swine and horses; we see the kermis with its jolly crowd of merry-makers; we see many taverns and cottages and the interiors of neat drawing-rooms as well as of kitchens and of butchers' shops. And we find many portraits of happy, healthy burghers and peasants with an occasional artist or surgeon or burgomaster or captain; and we see groups of the various companies and guilds and committees and clubs in which the citizens loved to combine.

In architecture as in painting the Dutch developed a highly original style to meet the needs of their new type of civilization. Few new churches were built, and those few of a severely simple pattern, for what the Protestant required was a lecture-hall and not a monument of art. The typical products of the Dutch style were docks, magazines, stores, mercantile exchanges, bourses, hospitals, banks, schools,

guild-houses, clubs, town halls, and, last but not least, com-
fortable private houses. The first example of the new style
is the Town Hall of Utrecht, completed about 1545, and
there are many other examples still standing, such as
the Meat Market at Haarlem, the Cheese Market at
Alkmaar, and the Town Hall (later royal palace) at
Amsterdam.

To decorate their public halls and their private homes the
Dutch cultivated with consummate success two arts, gardening and painting. The passion for tulips in the garden and
the passion for pictures in the house made the homes of the
Hollanders the most beautiful in the world. Evelyn noted
with amazement that common burghers would often spend
£2000 or £3000 for pictures, and that every man's house was
full of them, "especially landscapes and drolleries, as they
call these clownish representations".[1] For it was their own
homely life that they loved and that they adorned with
such consummate genius that, in the hands of their artists
a serving wench became as fascinating as Marie de Médicis
or as Diana, and the flayed carcass of an ox as interesting
a study as the flayed body of a martyr.

The first great Dutch painter, Franz Hals (c. 1580-1666),
devoted himself chiefly to portraiture in which he attained
a new realism and a new power of putting the sitter into
living personal relationships with the beholder. In his works
we see the Dutch burghers in their habit as they lived;
sometimes in single portraits as in that of *Hille Bobbe,* the
old witch with the owl on her shoulder, or in that of *The
Bohemian Girl,* or of *The Cavalier.* Sometimes there will be
groups of two as in *Junker Ramp and his Sweetheart* (New
York), or *The Smoker and his Girl.* Hals began that series
of group portraiture so common among the later masters. In
his pieces we see large societies or committees at banquets or
deliberating; such as *The Archers of St. George* at Haarlem;
such as the group of five women *Trustees of the Old People's
Home* at Haarlem. Almost all his subjects are so cheerful
that one may study in them every type of laughter from the

[1] *Diary,* i, 20, Aug. 13, 1641.

boisterous good humor of the reveller to the seductive smile of the harlot and the fatuous grin of the fool. Like a modern photographer, he asked all his patrons to "look pleasant".

The originator of genre, and one of its greatest masters, was the Fleming Adriæn Brouwer of Oudenaarde (1608-40) who lived long enough in Holland to come under the influence of Hals and of Dutch thought. He exhibits the very life of the common people, and mostly their coarse pleasures, drinking, smoking, eating, gambling, and laughing in the tavern. Adrian van Ostade delineated the merrymakings of the peasants at village fair and wineshop; but also their routine work—as in *Slaughtering a Pig*—their growing prosperity, and their love of music. With perfect truth he depicted them just as ill-favored, rowdy, and jolly, as they were in life. Another Fleming by birth and residence but Dutchman in style and feeling, was David Teniers the Younger (1610-90). Preferring cities to villages, civilization to nature, he became the genre painter of the polite world. He shows us the kermis and the middle-class house. His *Dutch Kitchen* (New York) exhibits the carcass of an ox hanging up, the pans, jars, and cooking utensils of the time, with a woman in a red jacket working over a large vat, and a dog to keep her company.

One of the elements introduced by the Dutch school into art is humor. Gerard Dou of Leyden (1613-78) rarely failed to focus the foibles of his citizens—the dentist, the schoolmaster, the fiddler, the herring-monger, the astronomer, the doctor, the cook, or the maid-servant—in a comic light.

But of all the Dutch painters good old Jan Steen (c. 1626-79) had the readiest laugh and perhaps the hottest blood. Life was to him an eternal kermis; jollity and laughter the subjects most worthy of serious attention. Born in Leyden, he matriculated in the local university with the object of escaping the tax on beer, exemption from which was one of the privileges then enjoyed by the students. While an undergraduate he imbibed more liquor than Latin; and he learned less of life from his masters in the lecture hall than from his mistresses in the tavern. When, in later life, he

became more moral and religious, his early experiences—
as in the case of other powerful preachers—lent point to
his satire. Now he depicts *St. Nicholas' Festival,* dear to
children, or *Twelfth Night* with its gay ritual. Again, in a
Hogarthian vein he satirizes the vices of brawling, drunkenness, or sloth; making his meaning quite plain by inserting
some little symbol or *memento mori* among his happy
revelers or idlers, some symbol like a pig eating roses or a
miniature gallows hanging from the walls.

A cooler temperament and wide travelling made Gerard
Terborch (1617-81) less characteristically Dutch than were
the other genre painters. His pictures, portraying the life
of the upper middle class, are anecdotal, or even historical.
His *Erat sermo inter Fratres* introduces us to a handsomely
furnished room in which four men sit conversing at a table,
while two others stroll around the room looking at the
ornaments. Terborch also painted a large group picture to
commemorate the negotiations between Holland and Spain
at Münster in 1648 which resulted in the final recognition
by Spain, in the Peace of Westphalia, of the long since
accomplished fact of Dutch independence.

Not less new in sentiment and perhaps more beautiful in
subject than the genre pictures were the many landscapes.
In the dunes of Flanders seen in Brouwer's works; in the
scenery of the Rhine and Meuse reflected by Albert Cuyp
(1620-91); in the peace and quiet of the City of Delft seen
from a distance by Vermeer (1632-75), are reproduced
different aspects of the same charming land. Vermeer loved
also the interiors of rooms, which he painted with the
fidelity of a photographer and with the vision of an artist.

Jacob van Ruisdael (1635-81) succeeded in combining
in an even higher degree a photographic realism and a poetic
fantasy and inspiration. If the melancholy Jacques had been
as great an artist as he was a poet he would have thus
depicted for us the Forest of Arden. More than any other
painter, except Rembrandt, Ruisdael mingles spiritual values with earthly ingredients. His trees and hills, his clouds
and sky, even his windmills are drenched with an ineffable

peace and quiet. And he could at times touch the heart with a deeper awe. In the picture called *The Jewish Cemetery* (Dresden) he has shown, in the dim light of a gathering storm, the waste of man's works encroached upon by time, and beside them the eternity of nature in the trees that grow quietly from generation to generation and in the mountain brook that goes on for ever.

Though the genius of Meyndert Hobbema (1638-1709) was early choked by the cares of a state office unfortunately presented to him at the age of thirty, he, too, has left us wonderful landscapes, full of light and air and space. Many of the outdoor painters introduced animals into their works, and a few of them soon found in the animals the principal object of study. The white nags of Wouwerman (1619-68), the splendid bulls and cows and swine of Paul Potter (1625-54), the game painted by Jan Weenix (1640-1719) open up a whole new world hitherto neglected by the haughty artist.

Not only Holland but the whole of Northern, Teutonic, and Protestant Europe found the supreme expression of her genius in Rembrandt Harmensz van Rijn (1606-69). Born at Leyden in a house overlooking the Rhine from which he takes his name, brought up in a middle-class burgher family, steeped in the stirring memories of the famous siege by the Spaniards, educated at the university where he matriculated at the age of fourteen, living after 1631 at Amsterdam, the metropolis of Holland and the first commercial city of the world, he was in all things the chosen representative of the Dutch blood and of the Dutch civilization. Confessionally, he was reared not only as a Protestant but as a Mennonite; that is to say, he belonged not to one of the established churches—Calvinist or Lutheran—but to one of the dissident Anabaptists sects, intensely biblical and simple in their doctrine, and proletarian in their constituency and social outlook.

After his marriage with Saskia van Uylenburgh in 1634, he lived for eight years in the sunlight of love and prosperity, until her death began a series of misfortunes that overclouded his whole later life. Unwillingly to marry again because of the provision in Saskia's will that his interest in her property should terminate with that event, he took as mistress Hendrickje Stoffels, thereby bringing on himself the censure of his church and ostracism from decorous society. As his art was not popular enough with the fat burghers to win him a livelihood, he fell into poverty, ending in bankruptcy in 1656. Poor, overwhelmed with domestic bereavements, despised and rejected of men, he remained true to his art. "A pious soul esteems honor before wealth", he wrote; and again, "When I give rein to my spirit, it is not honor that I seek, but freedom".[1] And so, in his dark little room, he continued to paint and to engrave those pictures that have ever since been the delight and the wonder of the world.

If many of his portraits are of himself, they were prompted less by vanity than by self-study. He posed before the glass; he grimaced, he touseled his hair, assumed rich clothes and a foppish expression, and tried all methods of lighting, in order to surprise the secret of his own personality. And he did surprise it; for that face, like his art, is outwardly homely and vulgar, and yet saturated with the rarest genius and insight. Such are all his other portraits; realistic and imaginative; they tell us all there is in the sitter's life, even if that be only that there is not much to tell.

Like his contemporaries, Rembrandt painted some groups. One of the most famous, characteristic of the scientific interests of his countrymen, represents the *Anatomical Lecture of Professor Tulp*. Grouped around a cadaver stand the famous savant, grasping some muscles of the corpse's arm in his forceps, and seven eager listeners to his learned exposition. Even more famous is the painting of a squad of the civic guard under Captain Banning Cocq, popularly but incorrectly known, because of its deep shadows and dark colors, as *The Night Watch*. Bright light falls only on

---

[1] "Een vroom gemoet acht eer voor goet"; "Als ik mijn geest uitspanning wil geven, dan is het nit eer die ik zoek, marr vrijheit," quoted by H. Kaufmann: "Rembrandt und die Humanisten von Muiderkring," *Jahrbuch der Preussischen Kunstsammlungen,* Band 41, 1920, pp. 46ff.

the captain dressed in black, on his lieutenant in yellow and
on a little girl in light blue. All else is cast into shadow with
a glint of red and gold; and all is instinct with the thrill
of life, and with military bustle. Another group, *The Syndics
of the Cloth-makers Gild,* brings before our eyes the very
spirit of Dutch industry embodied in the substantial merchants, in their black suits and white collars, sitting around
the table richly covered with a bright red Smyrna rug.

Rembrandt also painted and engraved landscapes in a
tenebrous night, and genre pieces,—as *The Old Woman cutting her Nails* (New York) and the etching of *The Golf-
players.* Some of his subjects he took from story, as the
Faust, and a few mythological pictures. The best of his
nudes, called *Danae,* shows a comely Dutch woman lying
on cool white linen and a deep orange-red coverlet, while the
room is further decorated with green hangings, gold and
amber carvings on the bed, and a greenish-blue carpet. The
whole is pervaded not by the spirit of antique classicism,
but by the timeless spirit of the bridal bed. Some other
mythological subjects treated by Rembrandt look like paro-
dies and were probably meant as such. The *Rape of Gany-
mede* depicts not a handsome youth happily sailing to
heaven, but a squalling, bawling brat snatched up by the
eagle in a comic travesty of the classical mythology that
had so long held all Europe, and that still held most of Europe, under its sway. Neither the heroic spirit of Rubens'
pictures, nor their nudity, greatly interested Rembrandt. He
had, indeed, an eye for the erotic, as for everything else in
life, but it was the erotic of the commonplace, half ashamed
and half shamelessly obscene.

In landscape he achieved wonderful distinction. His great
Mill, now in the Widener collection in Philadelphia, displays
a large windmill on an eminence with bright sky to the right,
and dark clouds on the left, and a river and a few figures
in the background. While there is no great effect of distance,
and little striking color, the chiaroscuro and the suggestion
of a particular atmosphere are marvellous.

It is the glory of Protestantism to have produced poetry

like Milton's, music like Bach's, and pictures like Rembrandt's. For it is from Protestant biblicism and laicism that the inspiration of the Dutch artist is drawn. Though not personally a very pious man, he was able to see and to reveal the spirit of the popular religion as few other men have done. Discarding altogether the heathen and Renaissance manner of Flemish ecclesiastical painting, the artist of Amsterdam exhibited in all its outward ugliness and in all its inward beauty the life and aspirations of the weary and the heavy laden who came to Christ to find rest for their souls. He painted and etched no more, or few, legends of the saints, for he preferred stories from Scripture, and he interpreted these stories in terms of contemporary Dutch manners. The Old Testament worthies are dressed as Jews of Amsterdam; the apostles and evangelists as Mennonite preachers. His little paintings, and still more his etchings, did not decorate baroque churches, but found their way into many a humble and pious home. Impossible in this brief review to do more than mention such great conceptions as *Paul in Prison, Judas before the High Priests, The Presentation in the Temple,* and the many scenes from the life of Samson.

Rembrandt painted Jesus as a humble laborer or preacher, not as an Adonis or Hercules. Take for comparison of the old style and the new, *Christ at Emmaus,* as painted by Rubens and by Rembrandt. The Catholic shows us a smiling landscape, a beautiful Savior with pathetic look and theatrical gesture, and the two disciples one overcome with a thrill of horror and one protesting his obsequious devotion. The Protestant conceived the scene as a small, dark room, in the twilight, with three poor men sitting at a table, none of them handsome or demonstrative, but all of them transformed by a hidden and yet deeply felt, spiritual power. So, in the contrast of expressions in *The Tribute Money,* in the seduction of Potiphar's wife and Joseph's chastity; in *Abraham entertaining the Angels*—who look like carpenters with wings of their own make—even in the *Raising of Lazarus,* there is nothing theatrical, but much that is deeply felt and strongly expressed.

When the occasion demanded it Rembrandt could put into his burin or his brush more passion and more horror than could any one else. The Crucifixion has rarely been so deeply felt as in his etching of 1653. In the storm and the earthquake the lurid light pours down like a cloud-burst on the awful and sublime spectacle of the Crucified; it illuminates with a ghostly glare the women fainting near the cross and the Jews fleeing in panic to the horror of the outer darkness. No less wonderful, in very different ways, is the *Annunciation to the Shepherds,* a wild dance of cherubs in the sky and a stampede of frightened cattle below; or Abraham as a wealthy burgher sending away his fat maidservant Hagar and her chubby child, while his good Hausfrau Sarah watches with malignant satisfaction from a window. The deeply felt *Presentation in the Temple* shows Mary and Joseph in the shadow and Simeon kneeling in ecstatic light, while two onlookers, gleaming in dull gold, seem to act as witnesses to the great fact that the Savior of the world is born.

It is fitting that Rembrandt should have reached the height of his sacred art in depicting the parable of the Prodigal Son. The beautiful story had been a great favorite in the sixteenth and seventeenth centuries, especially in Protestant lands, where the younger son had been interpreted to mean justifying faith and the elder son barren works. The fable had been dramatized many times—in Germany of the sixteenth century at least twenty-seven times—and had often inspired painters. They had generally represented the gay Prodigal wasting his substance with pretty harlots, or tending the swine, or sometimes returning, still handsome and attractive, to receive in a graceful attitude the forgiveness of a benignant and dignified father. The Dutch Mennonite, —who often treated the subject, and whose best painting of it is now in Leningrad—shows us the son as an ugly, brutal man, in all the squalor of his misery, and yet not so besotted with his recent life with the harlots and the swine but that he wants something better; for there is on his dimly lighted face that dumb longing for love and comfort that feels the tragedy of its own muteness. As he kneels, the father puts his arms over the boy's shoulders as if he were feeling him, for the old man cannot trust his eyes to believe the good news of his son's return, but must get his hands on him and his arms around him, as well.

5. FRENCH CLASSICISM

Outside of the Netherlands, Spain, and Italy, Europe produced little of artistic value during this period. Germany, exhausted by dogma and war, could do nothing but imitate first the Italian and then the French taste. Heidelberg Castle was indeed a splendid and grandiose building—now a ruin— in the baroque style. The Zwinger at Dresden, now housing one of the greatest of the world's picture galleries, witnesses the even more florid fashion of the French rococo. England, too, succumbed to the half-baroque, half-classic style brought back from Italy by Inigo Jones (1572-1651) who erected some churches and the fine banqueting house of Whitehall, still preserved.

Possibly the Puritan temper of England was averse to art; and even in France the greatest of the Jansenists denounced painting as vanity in that "it draws admiration by resemblance to things of which one does not admire the originals".[1] But art certainly suffered more in France at the hands of the neo-pagans than at those of the Christians. An intense and servile admiration of the classics, so clearly revealed in the French drama, affected to approve in art only the ancients and their modern imitators. Molière expressed the prevalent horror of the "Gothic ages which had made war on the polish of civilization", and the prevalent desire that painting should imitate antique sculpture. In the same poem the great comedian discloses the other burden that then oppressed French originality, that of an absolute monarchy. Louis XIV was, according to him, the only infallible judge of the arts; and Louis himself harbored no doubts on the

[1] Pascal: *Pensées,* ed. Brunschvicg, 1904, no. 134 (c. 1660).

subject. He, and his ministers, Mazarin and Colbert, regulated art and regimented letters as they did their army and their revenue.

The French Academy of Painting and Sculpture, founded as a voluntary society in 1648, was given a charter and a subsidy by the king in 1655. Sixteen years later the Academy of Architecture was founded. These institutions, intended as nurseries of the young arts, became rather old ladies' homes for the ancient and indigent muses of Greece and Rome. For, in logical France, the baroque style justified and rationalized itself by appealing on the one hand to the authority of the classics, and on the other to the philosophy of Descartes. The French theorists sought to reduce everything to universal rule. Malebranche defined beauty as "imitation of order", and opined that the

visible world would be more perfect if the seas and lands made more regular figures; if, being smaller, it could support as many men; if the rains were more regular and the fields more fertile; if, in a word, it had fewer monstrosities and less disorder.[1]

With this preference for regularity, few Frenchmen could share the love of Mme. de Sévigné for natural scenery, and for "the mountains charming in their excess of horror." Far more typical of the age was the description of Niagara Falls by Father Hennepin, the first white man to see it. He depicted the waters as "falling from a horrible precipice, foaming and boiling after the most hideous manner imaginable, and making an outrageous noise and dismal roaring more terrible than that of thunder." [2]

Who would wish to introduce so horrible a thing into a picture? Certainly not Claude Lorrain (as Claude Gelée, 1600-82, was called) who knew how to tame even wild landscapes and to make happy household pets of the mountains and the seas. Claude, indeed, found his landscapes, as

---

[1] *Méditations Chrétiennes, Œuvres*, ii, 43.
[2] Father Hennepin saw the falls in 1678; his description of them, from the *Nouvelle Découverte*, 1697, reprinted in *Harper's Literary Museum*, 1927, p. 165.

he found everything else worth imitating, in his ideal of the classic world of ancient Rome. Though he has been thrown unduly into the shade by his more brilliant disciples, Gainsborough and Turner, he has won the admiration of fine critics, among them Goethe, who justly praised him for combing "the highest truth with no trace of actuality".[1]

Claude's contemporary, Nicholas Poussin, (1594-1665), also found his inspiration in the classics. Like his fellow-Norman, Corneille, he deified ancient and early Christian Rome, finding in classical mythology or in early Christian legends the worthiest subjects for his attention. The clarity, the unified composition, the delicate Racinean sentiment of his art are pleasingly French as well as obviously Latin.

Not in painting but in architecture did the genius of the French monarchy at its apogee express itself most fully. France in the seventeenth century became the most powerful and the most polished nation in the world. The center of France was the Sun King around whom all the other powers in the state revolved, if, indeed, the state was allowed to have any part except the monarch who is reputed to have said, "l'état c'est moi". To express the towering majesty of their monarchy and to satisfy their large appetites for pleasure and for pomp, the Bourbons erected the largest and most expensive, though far from the most beautiful, palaces in the world.

The Louvre, an ancient château, was enlarged first by Louis XIII, and then again by his greater son, whose directions to the architect "Above all, don't show me anything small", well expressed the spirit of his reign. Two great wings, those along the Seine and along the Rue de Rivoli, were added in half their present length, when the completion of the plan was abandoned for the greater project of building a palace at Versailles.

The new château, begun in 1668, grew to enormous size in order to gratify the pride of the king and to furnish ample accommodations for the many fêtes with which he loved to entertain his numerous court. The great Gallery

[1] Eckermann: *Gespräche mit Goethe,* April 10, 1829.

of Mirrors was completed in 1684 and the two vast wings a few years later. The main gallery is 250 feet long, furnished with Gobelin tapestries and with carved silver chairs, inlaid cabinets, and other pieces in the "Louis XIV style". The gardens and artificial lakes with fountains, flowers, shrubbery and a park added greatly to the usefulness and splendor of the whole.

The great pile, now rather cold and lifeless, was a magic palace when the magician who created it was there. The whole of Europe was astonished at the unequalled splendor of the court, with its lavish festivals, its crowd of nobles and ambassadors, its troupes of artists and poets all bent on exalting the majesty of the great king. Louis was an aesthete and an actor, great chiefly in knowing how to play, with dignity and conviction, the splendid part for which he had been cast. The palace is the great symbol of despotism. It corrupted all the petty kings in Europe by setting them to emulate the ostentation and the display of the master. It played an important part in imposing French taste and French dominion on the rest of Europe. And it ruined the French people. The prodigious cost was wrung from the commons in cruel taxation and in yet harsher forced labor, under which many lives were sacrificed. Even the army, that darling and dreadful toy of kings, was robbed to enable the monarch to flatter his overweening pride and to glut his insatiable lust for pleasure as he ministered to them in the grandiose palace of Versailles.

EPILOGUE: THE CHARACTER OF THE AGE

The Age of the Great Renewal, falling between the Reformation and the Enlightenment,[1] has as marked a style and character as has any century in history. But because it has lacked a convenient name it has been less envisaged as a whole and less described as a unit than have some other eras. What largely determined its intellectual progress were the conflicts of ideals fought out in it; what makes it important for posterity were the creations, positive and negative, of its spirit; what gives it unity and coherence is the baroque style which distinguishes all its achievements.

Though the warfare of nations in that epoch of patriotism was bitter and momentous, it was less important for the history of culture than were the numerous conflicts of ideals, each founded, to be sure, on a solid material base.

In the first place, there was the strife between liberty and despotism. The great alignment between Protestant and Catholic divided two types of civilization, each of which desperately tried to subdue the other. And within each of the great churches there were several parties and various internecine wars. Even more important in the history of culture was the mortal strife between authority and reason, which manifested itself in several forms: in the battle between science and religion, in the struggle of skepticism with superstition, and in the conflict between the partisans of the ancients and the followers of the moderns, between Latin and the vernaculars, between ancient example and recent experience. In none of these many battles of the spirit was

[1] *I.e.* from about 1588 to about 1688, from the Armada to the English Revolution; or, if one prefers, from the beginning of the Shakespearean to the beginning of the Newtonian epoch. In all but its scientific achievements the half century following the publication of the *De Revolutionibus* of Copernicus (1543) belongs to the Age of the Reformation.

a decisive victory scored for either side; but it is noteworthy that the progressive and liberal side of each conflict
won a larger and securer place, forecasting the completer
conquest by reason and liberty in ages yet to come. The
world was safer for the republican, for the Protestant, for
the heretic, for the skeptic, for the scientist, and for the
"modern" in 1687 than it had been in 1588.

In the midst of these conflicts were brought forth some
of the more important creations of the human spirit. Many
eras have contributed to the sum total of civilization, but
few have given more than has the age of the Great Renewal.
Not only from the economic and political standpoint but in
its intellectual aspects the expansion of European power in
the far lands overseas was one of the most important factors
in the formation of the complex of modern culture. The
daring ships which, in quest of wealth and empire, sailed
to all unknown coasts, brought home as many exotic ideas
as precious materials. Above all, the planting of the English
colonies in North America was destined to prove one of the
most momentous events in the history of the world. The
spirit of America is still stamped by the seal of the seventeenth century, and her vast population is still guided and
governed by the children of those who sought her shores
before 1687.

In the realm of politics proper the establishment of liberty,
popular government, and party rule in England, America,
and the Netherlands, the imposing edifice of French absolutism, the creation of international law, are largely the
work of the seventeenth century. Nor, in assessing the balance of debit and credit, must one forget the negative aspect
of the rise of France, England, and the Netherlands to the
joint hegemony of the world. The same period that saw
their expansion, saw also the marked decline of the Empire
and of the Papacy, of Germany, of Italy, and of Spain.

New forms of religion evolved under the stress of fresh
cultural and material conditions. The foundation of many
sects, the beginnings of Jansenism, Arminianism, and Pietism, fall within the late sixteenth or within the seventeenth

century; most powerful of all, Puritanism set its seal on the government, the laws, the morals, the whole character of Calvinistic lands.

The most momentous of all the gifts of the Great Renewal to humanity was the gift of modern science. Whether for good or for ill—and I believe for good—whether as the new salvation or as the new superstition, science has moulded the whole life of the modern world. With equal steps the vast material achievement and the rapid conquest of the scientific spirit have advanced. All modern production of wealth, all material conditions of contemporary life, depend on the knowledge of nature acquired by science. But more than that, religion, politics, philosophy, art, and literature have capitulated to science or at least receded before her. There is no department of human activity today untouched with the spirit of experiment and of mathematics. In this vast change, the Great Renewal played a momentous part. Not only was it the first great age of science—always excepting the Greek—but its achievements were probably greater than those of any other equal period of time. Sober and competent judges, like Mr. Alfred North Whitehead, have given it as their opinion that "a brief, and sufficiently accurate description of the intellectual life of the European races . . . [since 1700] . . . is that they have been living upon the accumulated capital of ideas provided for them by the genius of the seventeenth century".[1]

All periods stamp their creations with their own particular seal. No one can deny that the age of the Great Renewal moulded all its acts and all its monuments in the grand style. Probably no age of the world, not even the fifth century B.C., has equalled it in the solidity of substance and in the perfection of form of its best creations. That Shakespeare is the greatest of poets, that Milton is second to him in English, that the classic age of French literature is that of Corneille, Molière, and Racine, and the classic age of Spanish literature that of Cervantes, is commonly admitted. Less known, except to their own countrymen, are the Dutch

[1] *Science and the Modern World*, 1925, 55f.

and Polish poets who made the seventeenth century the golden age of their respective nations. Italy, it is true, had slightly passed her apogee, and Germany had not yet produced her classics, but much of the poetry of the seventeenth century is the greatest ever written. The baroque painting of Spain and the Netherlands will bear comparison with that of the Italian Renaissance. In architecture, according to the taste of our generation, the new style marked a decline in beauty from that seen in the Gothic cathedrals.

What is true of the literature and art of the period is true also of its other creations. Since Burckhardt pointed out the connection of art and political theory in the Italian Renaissance, we have been able to see the aesthetic style of political creations. Certainly the monarchy of Louis XIV, the Dutch Republic, the English Commonwealth, and the colony of Massachusetts Bay, resemble majestic poems, the first Corneilleian, the second Vondelesque, the last two Miltonic. And the same is true of at least the major religious developments of the age. The Jansenists and the Puritans were able to express their ideas in an artistic form that has often had a greater vitality than the substance of their doctrine.

And so one might show that many of the greater works of the age, the philosophy of Descartes and Spinoza, the history of Sarpi and Clarendon, the treatises of Galileo and of Huygens, and many other books in various fields, were written in a form as beautifully adapted to their matter as it is possible to conceive. Such judgments are not to be driven home by argument. The deeds of that age were not done in a corner; they are open to all to be seen and appreciated; and the most convincing proof of their greatness is that the more they are studied the more artistic they appear.

In casting up the debit and credit of the age, one must not forget, of course, the horrible wars, the cruel persecutions, the Draconic laws, the mad superstitions, that disfigured it. They were all due to the conflict of the old and the new, the eternal warfare of reason with stupidity.

Behind both the good and the evil manifestations of the

age lay a philosophic absolutism and a certitude of conviction now lost. Even those men who had shaken off some prejudices and particular beliefs retained the conviction of the eternal and absolute validity of truth and duty. It is this that gave such ferocity to the wars of creeds, and that also lent so much sublimity to the poetry and philosophy of the age. A conviction of the dignity of man and of the worth of his acts still illuminated human thought. Heroism, great tragedy, intolerance, and epic poetry were all more possible then than they are to the generation prone to regard the story of the race as "a discreditable episode in the life of one of the meaner planets".

Perhaps, among the major conflicts of the age, and underlying all its creations and all its thought, should be mentioned the conflict between reason and emotion, between prose and poetry, between form and matter. Behind lay the centuries of poetry and of emotion; ahead lay the age of enlightenment and of prose. In the battle of the two and in the balance of the two in almost perfect equipoise lies the secret of the Age of the Great Renewal.

BIBLIOGRAPHY

CHAPTER I. INTRODUCTORY

WORKS ON THE GENERAL HISTORY OF THE PERIOD
1543-1687

W. C. Abbott: *The Expansion of Europe,* 2 vols., 1918.

R. Nisbet Bain: *Scandinavia,* 1905.

C. A. and M. R. Beard: *The Rise of American Civilization,* 2 vols., 1927.

C. L. Becker: *The Beginnings of the American People,* 1915.

P. J. Blok: *History of the Netherlands,* English transl., 4 vols., 1900ff.

B. Bretholz: *Geschichte Böhmens und Möhrens,* 3 vols., 1922ff.

Cambridge Modern History, vols. 3-5, ed. Ward, Prothero, Leathes, 1902ff.

C. E. Chapman: *A History of Spain,* 1918.

E. P. Cheyney: *A History of England from the defeat of the Armada to the death of Elizabeth,* 2 vols., 1914, 1924.

B. Croce: *Storia della età barocca in Italia. Pensiero, poesia, e letteratura, vita morale,* 1929.

J. Dierauer: *Geschichte der Schweizerischen Eidgenossenschaft,* vols. 3 and 4, 1907, 1912.

J. W. Draper: *History of the Intellectual Development of Europe,* 1863.

R. Dyboski: *Outlines of Polish History,* 1925.

B. Erdmannsdörffer: *Deutsche Geschichte 1648-1740,* 1892.

A. Guerard: *The Life and Death of an Ideal: France in the Classical Age,* 1928.

W. C. Hazlitt: *History of the Venetian Republic,* 4 vols., 1860.

A. Huber: *Geschichte Oesterreichs*, 1896.

M. M. Knight, H. E. Barnes, F. Flugel: *Economic History of Europe in Modern Times*, 1928.

M. M. Kowalewsky: *Die Ökonomische Entwicklung Europas*, 7 vols., 1901-14.

K. Lamprecht: *Deutsche Geschichte*, vols. 5, 6, 1895.

E. Lavisse: *Histoire de France depuis les origines jusqu'à la Révolution*, Tome VI (1598-1643) par J. H. Mariéjol, 1905; Tome VII (1643-85) par E. Lavisse, 1906.

F. S. Marvin, ed.: *Progress and History*, 1916.

D. Ogg: *Europe in the Seventeenth Century*, 1925.

V. L. Parrington: *Main Currents in American Thought*, vol. I, 1927.

L. von Pastor: *Geschichte der Päpste*, 13 vols., 1886-1928.

L. Pfandl: *Spanische Kultur des 16. und 17. Jahrhunderts*, 1924.

H. Pirenne: *Geschichte Belgiens*, Band IV (1567-1648), 1913.

S. F. Platonov: *A History of Russia*, 1926.

J. H. Randall, Jr.: *The Making of the Modern Mind*, 1926.

L. von Ranke: *The Popes: Their Church and State in the Sixteenth and Seventeenth Centuries*, 2 vols., 1845.

A. von Reumont: *Geschichte von Toscana*, vol. I, 1876.

M. Ritter: *Deutsche Geschichte im Zeitalter des dreissigjährigen Krieges*, 3 vols., 1889-1908.

W. S. Robertson: *History of the Latin-American Nations*, 1923.

Preserved Smith: *The Age of the Reformation*, 1920.

H. O. Taylor: *Thought and Expression in the Sixteenth Century*, 2 vols., 1920.

G. M. Trevelyan: *England under the Stuarts*, 1904.

T. J. Wertenbaker: *The First Americans*, 1927. (History of American Civilization, ed. A. M. Schlesinger and D. R. Fox, vol. 2.)

S. Young: *Portugal Old and Young*, 1917.

CHAPTER II. ASTRONOMY

GENERAL WORKS

E. W. Brown, H. A. Bumstead, F. Schlesinger, H. E. Gregory, L. L. Woodruff: *The Development of the Sciences,* 1923.

W. W. Bryant: *History of Astronomy,* 1907.

A. E. Burtt: *The Metaphysical Foundations of Modern Science,* 1925.

F. Dannemann: *Die Naturwissenschaften in ihrer Entwicklung und in ihrem Zusammenhange,*² 4 vols., 1922.

P. Duhem: *Le Système du Monde,* 5 vols., 1913-17.

F. M. Feldhaus: *Ruhmesblätter der Technik,*² 2 Teile, 1924-26.

E. Goldbeck: *Der Mensch und sein Weltbild,* 1925.

W. Libby: *An Introduction to the History of Science,* 1917.

W. T. Sedgwick and H. W. Tyler: *A Short History of Science,* 1917.

H. S. Williams and E. S. Williams: *A History of Science,* 5 vols., 1904.

1. COPERNICUS

Nicolai Copernici: *De Revolutionibus Orbium Coelestium Libri VI,* Nuremberg, 1543. (Copy of first edition at Cornell.)

Copernici De Revolutionibus orbium coelestium, ed. Societas Copernicana Thornensis, 1873. (Contains Rheticus: *Narratio Prima,* and other illustrative material.)

Inedita Coppernicana, ed. M. Curtze, 1878. (Contains the *Commentariolus* of c. 1530.)

J. L. E. Dreyer: *Tycho Brahe,* 1890.

L. Prowe: *Nikolaus Coppernicus,* 3 vols., 1883-4.

Tychonis Brahe Dani Opera Omnia. ed. J. L. E. Dreyer, vols. 1-8, 10-13, 1913ff.

2. KEPLER

W. W. Bryant: *Kepler*, 1920.

W. von Dyck: "Nova Kepleriana," 4 articles in the *Abhand-lungen der Bayerischen Akademie der Wissenschaften, Math.-Naturwissenschaftliche Abteilung*, vols. 25 Heft 5 and 9; 28 Heft 2; 31, Heft 1, 1912-26.

G. M. Jochner: *Briefwechsel zwischen Wolfgang Wilhelm von Neuberg und Kepler* (Historische Politische Blät-ter, cxli).

J. Kepler: *Opera Omnia*, ed. C. Frisch, 8 vols., 1858-71.

J. Kepler: *Unterricht vom heiligen Sakrament des Leibes und Blutes Jesu Christi*, reprinted in Theologische Stu-dien und Kritiken, 1904.

A. Müller: *J. Kepler*, 1903.

3. GALILEO AND THE ACCEPTANCE OF THE COPERNICAN HYPOTHESIS

L. Bell: *The Telescope*, 1922.

W. W. Bryant: *Galileo*, 1918

G. Bruno: *Opere, pub. da* A. Wagner, 3 vols., 1820.

G. Bruno: *Opere Italiane*, 3 vols., 1907-9.

E. A. Burtt: *The metaphysical foundations of modern physi-cal science*, 1925.

T. Campanella: *Apologia pro Galileo*, 1622.

M. Cioni: *I Documenti Galileiani del S. Ufficio di Firenze*, 1908.

J. J. Fahie: *Galileo, his Life and Work*, 1903.

J. J. Fahie: "The Scientific Works of Galileo," in C Singer: *Studies in the History and Method of Science*, ii, 1921, pp. 206ff.

A. Favaro: *Adversaria Galileiana*, 4 series, 1916-21.

A. Favaro: *Galileo e l'Inquizitione*, 1907. (The documents of Galileo's Process, now reprinted in vol. 19 of the National Edition.)

A. Favaro: *Galileo Galilei*,[2] 1912.

A. Favaro: *Scampoli Galileiani*, 24 series, 1886-1915.

Galileo Galilei: *Opere. Edizione Nazionale*, ed. A. Favaro, et alii., 20 vols., 1890-1909.

G. Gentile: *G. Bruno e il Pensiero del Rinascimento*, 1921.

A. H. Gilbert: "Milton's Text-book of Astronomy," Papers of the Modern Language Association, 1923.

M. Mersenne: *Les nouvelles pensées de Galilei . . . traduit de l'Italien en François*, 1639.

G. Monchamp: *Galilée et la Belgique. Essai historique sur les vicissitudes du système de Copernic en Belgique*, 1892.

A. Müller: *Der Galilei-Prozess*, 1909.

L. Olschki: *Galilei und seine Zeit*. (Geschichte der neusprachlichen wissenschaftlichen Literatur, Band 3), 1927.

G. B. della Porta: *Magia Naturalis*, XVII, cap. 10 (I use the edition of 1593).

A. Rhode: *Die Geschichte der Wissenschaftlichen Instrumente vom Beginn der Renaissance bis zum Ausgang des* 18. Jahrhunderts, 1923.

R. Delorme Salto: "Copérnico y los astronomos españoles," *Revista de España*, vol. 138, 1892.

Gli Scienziati Italiani, dall' inizio del medio evo ai nostri giorni. Repertorio biobibliographico, diretto da Aldo Mieli, vol. 1, 1921.

C. Singer: "The Invention of the First Optical Apparatus," in C. Singer: *Studies in the History and Method of Science*, ii, 1921, pp. 385ff.

V. Spampanato: *Vita di G. Bruno*, 1921.

D. Stimson: *The Gradual Acceptance of the Copernican Theory of the Universe*. 1917.

A. D. White: *A History of the Warfare of Science and Theology*, 2 vols., 1896.

F. Wieser: *Galileo als Philosoph*, 1919.

E. Wohlwill: *Galilei und sein Kampf für die copernicanische Lehre*, Band i, 1909. Band 2, 1926.

CHAPTER III. PHYSICS

<small>SOURCES, IN ADDITION TO THOSE PREVIOUSLY LISTED
UNDER CHAP. II:</small>

Robert Boyle: *Works*, 6 vols., 1772.

*Correspondence of Descartes and Constantyn Huygens
1634-45*, ed. L. Roth, 1926.

R. Descartes: *Œuvres, pub. par C. Adam et P. Tannery*, 13
vols., 1897-1913.

Galileo: *Dialogues concerning Two New Sciences*, transl. by
H. Crew and A. de Salvio, 1914.

W. Gilbert: *De Magnete et magneticis corporibus et de
magno magnete Tellure*, 1600.

W. Gilbert: *On the Loadstone and Magnetic Bodies and
on the Great Magnet, the Earth*. Transl. by P. F.
Mottelay, 1893.

Ottonis de Guericke: *Experimenta nova (ut vocantur)
Magdeburgica de Vacuo Spatio*, 1672.

J. B. Van Helmont: *Opera omnia*, 1707.

C. Huygens: *Œuvres complètes*, pub. par la Société Hol-
landaise des Sciences, 1888ff. As yet 15 vols.

C. Hugenii: *Opera Reliqua*, 1728, 2 vols.

C. Hugenii: *Opera varia*, 4 vols., 1724.

C. Hugenii: *Opuscula posthuma*, 2 vols., 1728.

B. Pascal: *Œuvres*, pub. par L. Brunschwicg et P. Boutroux,
8 vols., 1904-14.

G. B. della Porta: *De Miraculis Rerum Naturalium libri iv.*,
1560.

G. B. della Porta: *Magia Naturalis*, 1597.

S. Stevin: *Œuvres mathématiques*, augmentées par A.
Girard, Leyden, 1634.

E. Torricelli: *Opere*, ed. da G. Loria e G. Vassura, 3 vols. in
4, 1919.

<small>LITERATURE:</small>

F. Auerbach: *Entwicklungsgeschichte der modernen Physik*,
1923.

E. Bloch: "Das chemische Affinitätsproblem geschichtlich betrachtet," Isis, viii, 119.

H. Crew: *The Rise of Modern Physics,* 1928.

J. Chevalier: *Pascal,* 1922.

E. Gerland: *Geschichte der Physik . . . bis zum Ausgange des achtzehnten Jahrhunderts,* 1913.

V. Giraud: *La Vie héroïque de Blaise Pascal,* 1923.

G. Hanotaux: *Histoire de la Nation Française.* Tomes XIV et XV: Histoire des Sciences en France, 2 vols., 1924-25.

A. Heller: *Geschichte der Physik,* 2 vols., 1882.

K. Lasswitz: *Geschichte der Atomistik vom Mittelalter bis Newton,*[2] 2 vols., 1926.

A. Maire: *Bibliographie générale des œuvres de Blaise Pascal,* 5 vols., 1925-27.

M. Marie: *Histoire des Sciences mathématiques et physiques,* vols. 2 and 3, 1883-4.

Irvine Masson: *Three Centuries of Chemistry,* 1926.

H. Metzger: *Les Doctrines chimiques en France du début du xvii à la fin du xviii siècle,* 1924.

G. S. Milhaud: *Descartes Savant,* 1921.

P. F. Mottelay: *Bibliographical History of Electricity and Magnetism.*

Pattison Muir: *A History of Chemical Theories and Laws,* 1907.

S. Stevin; biographies of him in *Nieuw Nederlandsch Biografisch Woordenboek,* iv, 815ff, 1921; and in *Biographie Nationale* (de Belgique), xxiii, 888ff, 1924.

J. M. Stillman: *The Story of Early Chemistry,* 1924.

G. B. Stone: "The Atomic View of Matter in the XVth, XVIth, and XVIIth Centuries," Isis, x, 1928, 445ff.

C. M. Taylor: *The Discovery of the Nature of the Air and of its changes during breathing,* 1923.

S. T. Thompson: *Gilbert of Colchester,* 1891.

E. T. Whittaker: *A History of the Theories of Æther and Electricity from the Age of Descartes to the Close of the Nineteenth Century,* 1910.

CHAPTER IV. MATHEMATICS

Sources, in Addition to Those Listed Under Chapters
II and III

Isaac Barrow: *Mathematical Works,* ed. W. Whewell, 1860.
I. Barrow: *The Geometrical Lectures,* translated by J. M.
    Child, 1916.
Hieronymi Cardani: *Opera Omnia,* 10 vols. Lugduni, 1663.
B. Cavalieri: *Geometria indivisibilibus continuorum nova
    quadam ratione promota.* First ed. 1635, second ed.
    1653.
B. Cavalieri: *Trigonometria plana et spherica,* 1643.
G. Desargues: *Œuvres,* ed. par N. G. Poudra, 2 vols., 1864.
R. Descartes: *La Géometrie,* transl. by M. Latham and
    D. E. Smith, 1926.
P. de Fermat: *Œuvres,* publiées par P. Tannery et C. Henry,
    5 vols., 1891-1922.
Philippe de La Hire: *Mémoires de mathématique et de phy-
    sique,* 1694.
F. Vieta: *Opera Mathematica,* ed. F. à Scooten, 1646.
G. J. Voss: *De Mathesi, Opera,* iii, 1699.

Literature in Addition to That Previously Cited:

W. W. R. Ball: *A Short Account of the History of Mathe-
    matics,* 3 ed., 1901.
H. Bosmans: "Simon Stevin," *Periodico di Matematiche,*
    vi, 1926.
A. von Braunmühl: *Vorlesungen über Geschichte der Trigo-
    nometrie,* 1900.
L. Brunschvicg: *Les Étapes de laPhilosophie mathématique,*
    1912.
F. Cajori: *A History of Mathematical Notation,* Vol 1,
    1928.
F. Cajori: *History of Mathematics,*[2] 1919.
F. Cajori: *The Early Mathematical Sciences in North and
    South America,* 1928.

F. Cajori: *William Oughtred,* 1916.

M. Cantor: *Vorlesungen über Geschichte der Mathematik.*
Band II [2] (1200-1668) 1900; Band III (1668-1758),
1898.

L. E. Dickson: *History of the Theory of Numbers,* 3 vols.,
1919-23.

Anne and Elizabeth Linton: *Pascal's Mystic Hexagram,*
1921.

L. Olschki: *Geschichte der neusprachlichen wissenschaftlichen Literatur,* 3 vols., 1914ff.

D. E. Smith: *A History of Mathematics,* 2 vols., 1923-25.

J. Tropfke: *Geschichte der Elementar-Mathematik in Sys-
tematischer Darstellung,*[2] 6 vols., 1924.

H. K. Wieleitner: *Die Geburt der modernen Mathematik.*
I Die analytische Geometrie, 1924.

H. K. Wieleitner: *Geschichte der Mathematik.* II Teil: Von
Cartesius bis zur Wende des 18. Jahrhunderts,[2] 1921.

H. G. Zeuthen: *Geschichte der Mathematik im 16. und 17.*
Jahrhundert, 1903.

CHAPTER V. GEOGRAPHY, BIOLOGY, ANATOMY

GEOGRAPHY: SOURCES.

F. Bacon: "Of Plantations," *Essays,* xxxiii, 1625.

Epistulae Ortelianae, ed. J. H. Hessels, 2 vols., 1887.

R. Hakluyt: *The Principal Navigations, Voyages, Traffiques
and Discoveries of the English Nation,* 12 vols., 1903-5.

G. Mercator: *Atlas sive cosmographicae meditationes,* 5
parts, Duisburgi Clivorum, 1585-95.

G. Mercator: *Atlantis Pars Altera.* Geographia nova totius
mundi. Dusseldorpii, 1595.

M. de Montaigne: *Essais,* I, 31, II, 6.

Monumenta Cartographica, ed. F. C. Wieder, vol. 1, The Hague, 1925.
Purchas his Pilgrimes, 20 vols., 1905-7.

GEOGRAPHY: LITERATURE.

R. Almagia: *L' "Italia" di G. A. Magini e la cartografia dell' Italia nei secoli XVI e XVII,* 1922

G. Atkinson: *Les Relations de Voyages du XVII* ᵉ *siècle et l'évolution des Idées,* 1925.

G. Chinard: *L'Exotisme américain dans la littérature française au XVI* ᵉ *siècle,* 1911.

G. Chinard: *L'Amérique et le rêver exotique dans la littérature française au XVII* ᵉ *et au XVIII* ᵉ *siècle,* 1913.

S. Günther: *Geschichte der Erdkunde,* 1904.

E. Heawood: *A History of Geographical Discovery in the Seventeenth and Eighteenth Centuries,* 1912.

G. B. Parks: *Richard Hakluyt and the English Voyages,* 1928.

O. Peschel: *Geschichte der Erdkunde,*[2] ed. S. Ruge, 1877.

E. L. Stevenson: *Terrestrial and Celestial Globes,* 2 vols., 1921.

C. Wessels: *Early Jesuit Travellers in Central Asia,* 1924.

BIOLOGY AND MEDICINE: SOURCES.

J. B. Canano: *Musculorum humani corporis picturata dissectio,* ed. H. Cushing and E. C. Streeter, 1926.

Conradi Gesneri: *Historiae Animalium,* 2d ed., 5 vols., 1617-21.

Conradi Gesneri: *Opera Botanica,* ed. C. C. Schmiedel, 3 vols., 1751-71.

G. Harveii: *Opera Omnia,* a Collegio Medicinorum Londinensi edita, 1766.

G. Harveii: *Praelectiones Anatomiae Universalis,* ed. by the Royal College of Physicians, 1886.

Wm. Harvey: *An Anatomical Dissertation upon the Movement of the Heart.* Facsimile reproduction and translation of the original, 1894.

Wm. Harvey: *Works,* English translation, 1847.

A. van Leeuwenhoek: *Ontledingen en Ontdekkingen, vervat in verscheide brieven geschreven aan de wijt vermaarde Koninglijke Wetenschapzoekende Societeit tot London,* 3 vols., 1696ff.

A. van Leeuwenhoek: *Opera Omnia,* 4 vols., 1722.

M. Malpighi: *Opera Omnia,* 2 vols., 1687.

M. Malpighi: *Opera Posthuma,* 1697.

S. W. Mitchell: *Some Recently Discovered Letters of W. Harvey,* 1912.

F. Redi: *Esperienze intorno alla generazione degl'insetti,* 1688.

F. Redi: *Experiments on the generation of insects,* tr. M. Bigelow, 1909.

F. Redi: *Opere,* 9 vols., 1809-11.

J. Swammerdam: *Bybel der naturae, of, Historie der Insecten,* 2 vols., 1737f. (English translation, as *The Book of Nature, or, History of Insects,* 1758.)

J. Swammerdam: *Historia Insectorum Generalis,* 1685.

J. Swammerdam: Tractatus physico-anatomico-medicus de respiratione usuque pulmonum. In quo praeter primam respirationis in foetu inchoationem, aëris per circulum propulsio statuminatur, attractio exploditur; experimentaque ad explicandum sanguinis in corde tam auctum quam diminutum motum in medium producuntur. Leiden, 1667. *Opuscula selecta Neerlandicorum de arte medica.* Fasciculus sextus quem curatores miscellaneorum quae vocantur *Nederlandsch Tijdschrift voor Geneeskunde* collegerunt et ediderunt, 1927. Reprint of the original edition of Leiden 1667, with Dutch translation

A. Vesalius: *De Fabrica corporis humani,* 1568.

BIOLOGY AND MEDICINE: TREATISES.

J. M. Ball: *Andreas Vesalius, the Reformer of Anatomy,* 1910.

M. Bourbier: *L'évolution de l'ornithologie,* 1925.

A. H. Buck: *The Growth of Medicine from the earliest times to about 1800,* 1917.

620   BIBLIOGRAPHY

J. V. Carus: *Geschichte der Zoologie bis auf J. Müller und C. Darwin*, 1872.

F. J. Cole: *The History of Protozoology*, 1926.

J. G. Curtis: *Harvey's Views on the Use of the Circulation of the Blood*, 1915.

G. Favaro: *Gabrielle Falloppia*, 1928.

F. H. Garrison: *An Introduction to the History of Medicine*,[4] 1929.

R. J. H. Gibson: *Outline of the History of Botany*, 1919.

R. T. Gunther: *Early Science at Oxford*, vol. 3, 1925.

K. W. F. Jessen: *Die Botanik der Gegenwart und Vorzeit in kulturhistorischer Entwicklung*, 1864.

A. C. Judson and others: *A Memorial Volume to Shakespeare and W. Harvey*, 1917.

G. Keynes: *A Bibliography of the Writings of W. Harvey*, 1928.

Paul de Kruif: *Microbe Hunters*, 1926.

J. G. de Lint: *Atlas of the History of Medicine*, 1926.

W. A. Locy: *The Growth of Biology*, 1925.

E. R. Long: *A History of Pathology*, 1928.

L. C. Miall: *History of Biology*, 1911.

H. Morley: "Gesner," in *Clément Marot and other Studies*, 1871.

E. Nordenskiöld: *The History of Biology*, transl. by L. B. Eyre, 1928.

W. Osler: *The Evolution of Modern Medicine*, 1921.

F. R. Packard: *Guy Patin and the Medical Profession in Paris*, 1925.

F. R. Packard: *The Life and Times of A. Paré*, 1921.

J. von Sachs: *Geschichte der Botanik vom 16 Jahrhundert bis* 1860, 1875. (English Translation, revised, 1890).

C. Singer: *A Short History of Medicine*, 1928.

C. Singer: *The Discovery of the Circulation of the Blood*, 1922.

C. Singer: *The Evolution of Anatomy*, 1925.

U. Viviani: *Vita ed opere inedite di Francesco Redi*, 1924.

R. B. H. Wyatt: *William Harvey*, 1924.

CHAPTER VI. THE SCIENTIFIC REVOLUTION

SOURCES:

Accademia del Cimento: *Saggi di naturali esperienze fatte nell' Accademia del Cimento e descritte dal secretario* 1666. (In Neudrucke von Schriften . . . über Meteorologie, 1897; and better in Opere di L. Magalotti (who was the secretary), ii, 1806.

Acta Eruditorum, Lipsiae, 1682-1731; *Nova Acta,* 1732-76; *Supplementa* 1692-1734; *Nova Supplementa* 1735-57; Indices 1782. 115 vols.

F. Bacon: *Works,* 10 vols., 1861.

Theodorus de Bry: *Collectiones Peregrinationum in Indiam Orientalem et Indiam Occidentalem,* 25 parts, 1590-1634.

Correspondence of Hartlib, Hooke, Oldenburg . . . .with Gov. Winthrop of Connecticut, ed. R. C. Winthrop, 1878.

Glanvill: *On Modern Improvements of Useful Knowledge,* 1675.

Glanvill: *Plus Ultra; Progress and Advancement of Science since the Days of Aristotle,* 1668.

Joseph Glanvill: *Skepsis Scientifica,* 1665.

R. T. Gunther: *Early Science at Oxford,* iv, The Philosophical Society, 1925.

Histoire de l'Académie Royale des Sciences . . . avec les Mémoires de mathématique et de physique . . . tirées des Registres de cette Académie, many volumes, Paris, 1777ff. (Contains the proceedings of the Académie from 1666, somewhat abridged).

Journal des Sçavans, 1665ff.

Letters and Life of F. Bacon, by J. Spedding, 6 vols., 1862.

Thomas Spratt: *History of the Royal Society,* 1667.

The Philosophical Transactions of the Royal Society from their commencement in 1665 *to* 1800, abridged, 1809ff, 215 vols.

TREATISES:

J. Bertrand: *L'Académie des Sciences et les Académiciens de 1666 à 1793*, 1869.

T. Birch: *History of the Royal Society of London*, 4 vols. 1766-67.

C. D. Broad: *The Philosophy of F. Bacon*, 1926.

J. Caillat: "La Méthode scientifique selon Pascal," Revue d'histoire littéraire, xxx, 1923, 129*ff.*, 273*ff.*

Cambridge History of English Literature, vol. viii, chap. 15.

W. Frost: *Bacon und die Naturphilosophie*, 1927.

A. H. Gilbert: "Milton and Galileo," Studies in Philology, xix, 1922, 152*ff.*

A. C. Howell: "Sir Thomas Browne and 17th-century Scientific Thought," Studies in Philology, xxii, 1925, 61*ff.*

T. B. Macaulay: *Essay on Bacon.*

F. Masson: *Robert Boyle*, 1914.

M. Ornstein: *The Rôle of the Scientific Societies in the 17th Century*, 1913.

J. Walter: *Die Kaiserliche Akademie der Naturforscher zu Halle*, 1927.

C. R. Weld: *History of the Royal Society*, 2 vols. 1847.

E. Wolff: *Francis Bacon und seine Quellen*, 2 vols., 1910-13.

CHAPTER VII. PHILOSOPHY

SOURCES:

Jakob Böhme: *Epistles*, reprinted from the 1649 Edition, 1886.

Jakob Böhme: *Signatura Rerum* . . . translated from the High Dutch, 1651.

Jakob Böhme: *Six Theosophic Points and other Writings*, translated by J. R. Earle, 1920.

Jakob Böhme: *Werke*, hg. von Schiebler,[2] 7 vols., 1861f.

Jordani Bruni: *Opera Latine conscripta*, ed. Fiorentino, 3 vols., 1879-91.

Giordano Bruno: *Opere Italiane*, 3 vols., 1907-9.

Tommaso Campanella: *De Monarchia Hispanica,* 1653.

Campanella: *Atheismus triumphatus,* 1636.

Campanella: *De sensu rerum et Magia,* 1620.

Campanella: *Disputationum in quatuor partes suae Philosophiae Realis libri,* 1637.

Campanella: *Lettere inedite,* ed. D. Berti, 1878.

Campanella: *Philosophia sensibus demonstrata,* 1591.

Campanella: *Philosophiae Realis partes quinque,* 1638.

Campanella: *Universalis philosophiae libri xviii,* 1638.

The Correspondence of R. Descartes and Constantyn Huygens, ed. L. Roth, 1925.

René Descartes: *Œuvres,* pub. par C. Adam et P. Tannery, 13 vols., 1897-1913.

P. Gassendi: *De vita, moribus et doctrina Epicuri,* 1647.

P. Gassendi: *Syntagma Philosophicum,* 1658.

P. Gassendi: *Three Discourses of happiness, virtue and liberty* . . . translated out of the French, 1699.

A. Geulincx: *Opera philosophica,* ed. J. P. N. Land, 3 vols., 1891-3.

T. Hobbes: *Opera philosophica quae Latine scripsit omnia,* ed. G. Molesworth, 5 vols., 1839-45.

T. Hobbes: *The English Works,* ed. Sir W. Molesworth, 11 vols., 139*ff.*

N. Malebranche: *Fragments philosophiques inédits et Correspondance,* ed. J. Vidgrain, 1923.

N. Malebranche: *Méditations Métaphysique et Correspondance,* ed. F. Feuillet de Conches, 1841.

N. Malebranche: *Œuvres,* ed. J. Simon, 4 vols., 1871, 1884.

Spinoza: *Correspondence,* transl. by A. Wolf, 1928.

B. de Spinoza: *Opera, ed. J. van Vloten et J. P. N. Land,* 2 vols., 1882.

Spinoza: *Opera,* im Auftrag der Heidelberger Akademie der Wissenschaften, hg. von C. Gebhardt, 4 vols., 1925.

Spinoza's Short Treatise on God, Man, and his Well-being, transl. by A. Wolf, 1910.

TREATISES:

X. Atanassievitch: *La Doctrine métaphysique et géométrique de Bruno*, 1923.

L. Blanchet: *Campanella*, 1920.

L. Blanchet: *Les Antécédents historiques de "Je pense, donc je suis,"* 1920.

W. Boulting: *Giordano Bruno* (1917?).

G. S. Brett: *A History of Psychology*, vols. 2 and 3, 1920-21.

Baron Cay von Brockdorff: *Descartes und die Fortbildung der kartesianischen Lehre*, 1923.

L. Brunschvicg: *Le progrès de la conscience dans la philosophie occidentale*, 2 vols. 1927.

E. Cassirer: *Das Erkenntnisproblem in der Philosophie und Wissenschaft der neueren Zeit,*[3] 3 vols., 1922f.

G. E. G. Catlin: *Thomas Hobbes as philosopher, publicist, and man of letters*, 1922.

J. R. Charbonnel: *L'éthique de G. Bruno*, 1919.

J. Chevalier: Descartes, 1921.

Chronicon Spinozanum, ed. Societas Spinozana, 3 vols., 1921-3.

A. Espinas: *Descartes et la Morale*, 2 vols., 1926.

K. Fischer: *Descartes,*[5] 1912.

K. Fischer: *Geschichte der neueren Philosophie*, 10 vols. 1897-1910.

J. Freudenthal: *Spinoza: Leben und Lehre,*[2] 1927.

G. Gentile: *Giordano Bruno e il pensiero del Rinascimento*, 1920.

A. Georges-Berthier: *"Le mécanisme cartésien et la physiologie du xvii ᵉ siècle,"* Isis ii, 1914 and iii, 1920.

H. Gouhier: *La vocation de Malebranche*, 1926.

H. Höffding: A *History of Modern Philosophy*, English transl. 2 v., 1900.

L. Kuhlenbeck: *Giordano Bruno, seine Lehre von Gott, von der Unsterblichkeit der Seele und von der Willensfreiheit*, 1913.

Maledictus oder Benedictus: Spinoza im Urteil des Volkes und der Geistigen bis auf Constantin Brunner, 1924.

R. McKeon: *The Philosophy of Spinoza,* 1928.

E. Namer: *Les aspects de Dieu dans la philosophie de G. Bruno,* 1926.

L. Roth: *Spinoza, Descartes, and Maimonides,* 1924.

G. de Ruggiero: *Modern Philosophy,* English trans. 1921.

V. Salvestrini: *Bibliografia di G. Bruno,* 1925.

G. Sortais: *La Philosophie moderne depuis Bacon jusqu'à Leibniz,* 2 vols., 1920-22.

V. Spampanato: *Giordano Bruno,* 1921.

V. Spampanato: *Sulla soglia del Secento: Studi su Bruno, Campanella,* &c., 1926.

F. Thilly: *A History of Philosophy,* 1914.

F. Tönnies: *Thomas Hobbes' Leben und Lehre,*[3] 1925.

F. Ueberweg: *Grundriss der Geschichte der Philosophie.* III Neuzeit. 10te Auflage hg. von M Heinze, 1907.

E. T. Whittaker: *A History of the Theories of Æther and Electricity from the age of Descartes to the Close of the Nineteenth Century,* 1910.

W. Windelband: *Die Geschichte der neueren Philosophie in ihrem Zusammenhang mit der allegmeinen Kultur und den besonderen Wissenschaften,*[4] 1907.

W. Windelband: *Die neuere Philosophie* (Kultur der Gegenwart. Theil I, Band V: Allgemeine Geschichte der Philosophie), 1909.

CHAPTER VIII. POLITICAL THEORY

Sources, in addition to those mentioned for Chapter VII.

J. B. Bossuet: *Œuvres Complètes,* 12 vols. 1845-46.

Bossuet: *Correspondance,* 14 vols. 1909-23.

T. Campanella: *La Città del Sole,* ed. E. Solmi, 1904. (Also printed in the *Realis Philosophia,* and translated into English, with omissions, in *Ideal Commonwealths,* ed. Henry Morley, 1893.)

T. Campanella: *Lettere,* ed. V. Spampanato, 1927.

A Declaration of the Parliament of England, expressing the grounds of their late proceedings and of settling the present government in the way of a Free State, March 22, 1648-9.

J. Dmochowski: *N. Kopernika Rozprawy o Monecie*. (Latin and German texts and Polish transl. of Copernicus's *Monetae cudendae ratio*). 1925.

Grotius: *Briefwisseling*, ed. P. C. Molhuysen, 1928.

Grotius: *De Imperio Summarum Potestatum*, 2 vols., 1780.

Grotius: *De Jure belli et pacis*, ed. with abridged translation by W. Whewell, 3 vols., 1853.

Grotius: *De jure belli et pacis*, text and transl. by F. W. Kelsey, 2 vols., 1925.

Grotius: *De Jure praedae commentarius*, 1868

Grotius: *De Mari libero*, 1633. (English transl. by R. Van D. Magoffin, 1916.)

Grotius: *De Origine gentium Americanarum dissertatio*, 1714.

H. Grotius: *Epistolae ineditae . . . ad Oxenstiernas*, 1806.

H. Grotius: *Epistolae quotquot reperiri patuerunt*, 1687.

H. Grotius: *Opera Omnia Theologica*, 3 vols., 1779.

Grotius: *The Jurisprudence of Holland*, text and transl. by R. W. Lee, 1926.

J. Harrington: *The Commonwealth of Oceana*, 1656. (The same, ed. Liljengren, 1924).

Richard Hooker: *Works*, ed. J. Keble, 3 vols., 1874.

James I: *Political Works*, ed. C. H. McIlwain, 1918.

[Lilburne?]: *A Defence against all arbitrary Usurpation or Encroachments either of the House of Lords or of any other, upon the Sovereignty of the Supreme House of Commons*, 1646.

J. Lilburne: *The Second Part of England's New Chaines Discovered*, 1649.

J. de Mariana: *De Rege et Regis Institutione*, 1605.

Mariana: *Obras*, ed. F. P[i] y M[argall], 2 vols., 1864, 1854.

J. Milton: *English Prose Works*, 2 vols., 1826.

Milton: *Poetical Works*, numerous editions.

Milton: *Prose Works,* ed. by J. H. St. John, 5 vols., 1848-53.
Antoyne de Montchrétien: *Traicté de l'Œconomie Politique,* ed. T. Funck-Brentano, 1889.
Thomas Mun: *England's Treasure by Foreign Trade,* 1664. New ed. for Economic History Society of Oxford, 1928.
Sir W. Petty: *Economic Writings . . . together with Observations upon the Bills of Mortality more probably by Captain John Graunt,* ed. C. H. Hull, 2 vols., 1899.
The Petty Papers, ed. the Marquis of Lansdowne, 2 vols., 1927.
Pufendorf: *Briefe an C. Thomasius,* ed. E. Gigas, 1897.
S. Pufendorf: *De Officio hominis et civis,* new ed., 2 vols., 1927, with English transl. by F. G. Moore.
S. Pufendorf: *Of the Law of Nature and Nations,* done into English by B. Kennett, 2 vols., 1729.

TREATISES:

J. W. Allen: *History of Political Thought in the Sixteenth Century,* 1928.
G. E. G. Catlin: *Thomas Hobbes as Philosopher, Publicist, and Man of Letters,* 1922.
G. N. Clark: "Grotius and International Law," in *The Evolution of World-Peace,* ed. F. S. Marvin, 1921.
W. A. Dunning: *A History of Political Theories from Luther to Montesquieu,* 1905.
A. Gemelli: *Scritti Varî pubblicati in occasione del terzo centenario della Morte di F. Suarez,* 1918.
R. G. Gettel: *History of America Political Thought,* 1928.
G. P. Gooch: *The History of English Democratic Ideas in the 17th Century,* 1898.
L. Gumplowicz: *Geschichte der Staatstheorien,* 1926.
L. H. Haney: *A History of Economic Thought,*[2] 1920.
P. Harsin: *Les doctrines monétaires et financières en France du XVIe au XVIIIe siècle,* 1928.
F. J. C. Hearnshaw, ed.: *Social and Political Ideas of some great Thinkers of the Sixteenth and Seventeenth Centuries,* 1926.
F. E. Held: *Andreae's Christianopolis,* 1914.

628   *BIBLIOGRAPHY*

J. O. Hertzler: *History of Utopian Thought*, 1923.

R. Hönigswald: *Hobbes und die Staatsphilosophie*, 1924.

P. Janet: *Histoire de la Science Politique dans ses rapports avec la morale*,[3] 2 vols., 1887.

J. Jastrow: "Kopernikus' Münz- und Geld-theorie," *Archiv für Sozialwissenschaft und Sozialpolitik*, xxxviii, 1904, 734ff.

W. S. M. Knight: *The Life and Work of H. Grotius*, 1925.

J. Laures: *The Political Economy of Juan de Mariana*, 1928.

D. Masson: *Life and Times of Milton*, 6 vols., 1859-80.

F. Meinecke: *Die Idee der Staatsräson in der neueren Geschichte*, 1924.

C. E. Merriam: *History of American Political Theory*, 1903.

T. C. Pease: *The Leveller Movement*, 1916.

J. C. Rager: *The Political Philosophy of the Blessed Cardinal Bellarmine*, 1926.

H. Rommen: *Die Staatslehre des F. Suarez*, 1927.

G. de Ruggiero: *History of European Liberalism*, Eng. transl. by R. G. Collingwood, 1927.

E. K. Sanders: *Bossuet*, 1921.

D. Saurat: *La Pensée de Milton*, 1920. (Enlarged by author and translated as, *Milton: Man and Thinker*, 1925).

H. Sée: *Les Idées Politiques en France au XVII*ᵉ *siècle*, 1923.

C. E. Vaughan: *Studies in the History of Political Philosophy*, 2 vols., 1925.

H. Vreeland: *H. Grotius*, 1917.

A. D. White: "Grotius" in *Seven Great Statesmen in the War of Humanity with Unreason*, 1910.

G. A. Wood: "The Miltonic Ideal," in *Historical Essays by Members of Owens College*, Manchester, 1902.

CHAPTER IX. HISTORIOGRAPHY

ORIGINALS.

Acta Sanctorum. Antwerp, 1643ff.

C. Baronii, O. Raynaldi, et J. Laderchii: *Annales Ecclesiastici, denuo excessi ab Thenier,* 37 vols., 1864-83.

J. Bodin: *Methodus ad facilem historiarum cognitionem,* 1566.

Jacques Bénigne de Bossuet: *Histoire des Variations des Églises Protestantes,* 1841.

Bossuet: *Discours sur l'Histoire Universelle, Œuvres,* 1846, vol. 3, pp. 10ff.

William Bradford: *History of Plymouth Plantation,* 1856.

W. Camden: *Britain, or a chorographical description of the most flourishing kingdoms, England, Scotland, and Ireland,* 1637.

Camden: *The History of Queen Elizabeth,* (English translation of *Annales rerum Anglicarum et Hibernicarum regnante Elizabetha*), in W. Kennet: *Complete History of England,* ii, 1719.

Guglielmi Camdeni et illustrium Virorum ad G. Camdenum Epistolae. 1691 (with supplement in *English Historical Review,* July 1919, p. 407.)

Enrico Caterino Davila: *Istoria delle guerre civili di Francia,* 1630.

Matthias Flacius Illyricus: *Catalogus Testium veritatis qui ante nostram aetatem pontifici Romano eiusque erroribus reclamarunt,* 1562.

[Flacius Illyricus et alii:] *Ecclesiastica Historia, integram ecclesiae Christi ideam . . . complectens . . . secundum singulas centurias. . . . Per aliquot studiosos et pios viros in Urbe Magdeburgica,* 13 vols., 1562ff.

T. Hobbes: *Behemoth: The History of the Causes of the Civil Wars in England, Works,* vi, 161ff.

Edward Hyde, Earl of Clarendon: *History of the Rebellion and Civil Wars in England,* ed. W. D. Macray, 6 vols., 1888.

Louis Maimbourg: *Histoire du Luthéranisme*, 1680.

Juan de Mariana: *Historia general de España*, 9 vols., 1783-96. (English translation by J. Stevens, 1699.)

François Eudes de Mézeray: *Histoire de France depuis Faramond jusqu'à maintenant*, 3 vols., 1643-51.

Sforza Pallavicino: *Istoria del Concilio di Trento*, 1656-57.

Sir Walter Raleigh: *A History of the World*, 1628.

Paolo Sarpi: *Opere*, 8 vols., 1761ff.

Sarpi: *Lettere*, ed Polidori, 2 vols., with supplement by Castellani, 1863-82.

Neue Briefe von Frà Paolo Sarpi, ed. K. Benrath, 1909.

Jacobi Augusti Thuani: *Historiarum sui temporis libri cxxxviii*, 7 vols., 1733.

G. J. Vossius: *Ars Historica, Opera*, iv, 1699.

J. Winthrop: *History of New England*, ed. J. K. Hosmer, 2 vols., 1908.

TREATISES:

K. Benrath: *Paul Sarpi, ein Vorkämpfer des religiösen, ein Bekämpfer des politischen Katholizismus* (Schriften des Vereins für Reformationsgeschichte, Heft 100), 1910.

J. B. Bury: *The Idea of Progress*, 1920.

G. Cirot: *Mariana Historien*, 1905.

H. Delehaye: *The Work of the Bollandists*, 1923.

S. Ehses: "Hat P. Sarpi für seine Geschichte des Konzils von Trient aus Quellen geschöpft die jetzt nicht mehr fliessen?" *Historisches Jahrbuch der Görresgesellschaft*, xxiv, 299ff, xxvii, 67ff, 1905-6.

A. Fasulo: *Fra Paolo Sarpi*, 1923.

E. Fueter: *Geschichte der neueren Historiographie*, 1911.

A. Rampolla Gambino: *Fra Paolo Sarpi*, 1919.

G. Hardy: *Le "De Civitate Dei" source principale du "Discours sur l'histoire universelle,"* 1913.

A. Rébelliau: *Bossuet Historien du Protestantisme*, 1892.

E. K. Sanders: *Bossuet*, 1921.

A. D. White: "Sarpi" in *Seven Great Statesmen*, 1915.

CHAPTER X. BIBLICAL AND CLASSICAL SCHOLARSHIP

1. Biblical Criticism

Sources:

Jacobi Usserii Armachani: *Annales veteris et novi testamenti.* Editio nova, 1741.

The Bible. Translated according to the Ebrew and Greeke, and conferred with the best Translations in divers Languages. London, 1608. (A reprint of the Geneva Bible, in my possession, commonly known as "the Breeches Bible" because of the translation of Genesis iii, 7: "they made themselves breeches.")

The Holy Bible . . . translated out of the original tongues . . . by his Majesty's Special Command. (The "authorized version," first printed in 1611).

Biblia Hebraica Samaritana Chaldaica Graeca Syriaca Latina Arabica. Edited by G. M. Le Jay, J. Morin and others, 9 vols., Paris, 1629-45.

Biblia sacra polyglotta complectentia textus originales Hebraicum, cum Pentateucho Samaritano, Chaldaicum, Graecum, versionumque antiquorum Samaritanae Graecae LXXII interp., Chaldaicae, Syriacae, Arabicae, Æthiopicae, Persicae, Vulg. Lat. . . . ed. B. Waltonus. 6 vols., London, 1657.

T. Hobbes: *Leviathan,* 1651, chap. 33.

M. Luther: *Supputatio annorum mundi. Werke,* Weimar, liii, 1ff.

J. Selden: *De successionibus ad Leges Ebraeorum,* Lugd. Batav., 1638.

J. Selden: *De Dis Syris.* Lipsiae, 1668.

R. Simon: *Histoire critique des principaux commentateurs du Nouveau Testament,* 1693.

R. Simon: *Histoire critique des versions du Nouveau Testament,* 1690.

R. Simon: *Histoire critique du Nouveau Testament,* 1689.

R. Simon: *Histoire critique du Vieux Testament,* 1685.

B. de Spinoza: *Tractatus Theologico-Politicus. Opera,* ed. Gebhardt, 1925, vol. iii.

G. J. Voss: *Historiae Universalis Epitome, Opera,* 1698, iv.

Isaak Voss: *Dissertatio de vera aetate mundi. Quâ extenditur Natalis mundi tempus annis minime 1440 vulgarem aeram anticipare,* 1659.

TREATISES:

E. von Dobschütz: *The Influence of the Bible on Civilization,* 1914.

E. McQ. Gray: *Old Testament Criticism,* 1923.

C. R. Gregory: *Die Textkritik des neuen Testaments,* 3 parts, 1900-09.

C. R. Gregory: *Canon and Text of the New Testament,* 1907.

D. Lortsch: *Histoire de la Bible en France,* 1910.

C. B. McAfee: *The Greatest English Class. A Study of the King James Version of the Bible,* 1912.

A. Monod: *La Controverse de Bossuet et de R. Simon,* 1922.

A. W. Pollard: *Records of the English Bible,* 1911.

N. Schmidt: "Early Oriental Studies in Europe," *Journal of the American Oriental Society,* vol. 43, 1923.

A. Schweitzer: *Geschichte der Paulinischen Forschung,* 1911.

H. Preserved Smith: *Essays in Biblical Interpretation,* 1921.

2. CLASSICAL SCHOLARSHIP

SOURCES:

S. Cyrano de Bergerac: *Le pedant joué, comédie,* ed. H. B. Stanton, 1899.

I. Casauboni: *Epistolae,* ed. T. Janson. 2 vols., 1709.

C. Du Fresne, Dominus Du Cange: *Glossarium Mediae et Infimae Graecitatis,* 1688.

C. Du Fresne, Dominus Du Cange: *Glossarium Mediae et Infimæ Latinitatis.* Editio nova a Léopold Favre. 10 vols., 1883.

H. Estienne: *Thesaurus Graecae Linguae,* 5 vols., 1572.

R. Estienne: *Thesaurus linguae latinae,* 1532.
C. Salmasii: *Epistolarum Liber Primus,* 1656.
J. Scaliger: *Autobiography,* transl. by G. W. Robinson, 1927.
J. Scaligeri: *Epistolae,* 1638.
J. Scaligeri: *Opus novum de Emendatione Temporum,* 1583.

Treatises:

E. Drerup: *Homerische Poetik,* 1921. (History of the Homeric problem, beginning with the 16th century.)
L. Olschki: *Geschichte der neusprachlichen wissenschaftlichen Literatur,* 3 vols., 1913-27.
M. Pattison: *I. Casaubon,*[2] 1892.
M. Pattison: "J. Scaliger," *Essays,* 1889, i, 132ff.
H. T. Peck: *A History of Classical Philology,* 1911.
A. Roersch: *Juste Lipse,* 1926.
Sir J. E. Sandys: *A History of Classical Scholarship,* vol. ii, 1908.

CHAPTER XI. EDUCATION

Sources:

J. M. Anderson: *Early Records of the University of St. Andrews,* 4 vols., 1926.
F. Bacon: *De Augmentis Scientiarum lib. ii; (Works,* 1861, ii).
Sir T. Bodley: *Letters to T. James,* ed. G. W. Wheeler, 1926.
Bronnen tot de Geschiedenis der Leidsche Universiteit, ed. P. C. Molhuysen. (Rijks Geschiedkundige Publicatien, vols. 20, 29, 38.), 3 vols. 1913ff.
Comenius: *Orbis sensualium picti Pars i (ii),* 2 vols., 1745-46.
Comenius: *Pansophiae Prodromus,* 1644.
Comenius: *The Labyrinth of the world and the paradise of the heart,* by J. A. Komensky, ed. by Count Lützow, 1905.
J. A. Comenius: *The Great Didactic,* English transl. by M. W. Keating, 1896.

Comenius: *Triertium Catholicum.* Facsimile reproduction, with introduction by G. V. Klima and L. Z. Lerando, 1922.

U. Dallari: *I Rotuli dei Lettori Legisti e Artisti dello Studio Bolognese dal 1384 al 1799,* 4 vols., 1924.

M. Fourier: *Les Statuts et Privilèges des Universités françaises jusqu'en 1789.* Tome 4, 1894.

W. Friedensburg: *Urkundenbuch der Universität Wittenberg,* 2 vols., 1926.

R. T. Gunther: *Early Science at Oxford,* 4 vols., 1923.

R. T. Gunther: *The Diary and Will of Elias Ashmole,* 1927.

Harvard College Records: Corporation Records 1636-1750. (Publications of the Colonial Society of Massachusetts, vols. 15, 16), 2 vols., 1925.

J. Milton: *Of Education,* 1644.

M. de Montaigne: *Essais,* liv. I, nos. 25, 26.

G. Naudé: *Avis pour dresser une bibliothèque,*[2] 1644.

New England's First Fruits, 1642, reprinted in *Harper's Literary Museum,* 1927, pp. 87ff.

G. M. Pachtler: *Ratio Studiorum et institutiones scholasticae Societatis Jesu.* (*Monumenta Germaniae Pedagogica,* vols. 2, 5, 9, 16), 4 vols., 1887-94.

Statuti e Ordinamenti della Università di Pavia dall' anno 1361 all' anno 1859, 1925.

B. de Spinoza: *Tractatus de intellectus emendatione.* (*Opera,* i, 6ff.)

A. Thorbecke: *Statuten und Reformationen der Universität Heidelberg vom 16. bis 18. Jahrhundert,* 2 vols., 1886.

TREATISES:

M. Alcocer et alii: *Anales Universitarios: Historia de la Universidad de Valladolid,* 4 vols., 1918-22.

C. Borgeaud: *Histoire de l'Université de Genève,* 2 vols., 1900-1904.

C. Compayré: *Histoire critique des doctrines d'éducation en France depuis le 16ᵉ siècle,* 1885.

E. P. Cubberley: *The History of Education,* 1920.

BIBLIOGRAPHY 635

E. G. Dexter: *A History of Education in the United States*, 1904.

L. van der Essen et alii: *L'Université de Louvain à travers cinq siècles*, 1927.

G. Dupont-Ferrier: *Du Collège de Clermont au lycée Louis-le-Grand*, 2 vols., 1923.

V. de la Fuente: *Historia de las universidades, colegios y demás establecimientos de enseñanza*, 4 vols., 1884ff.

J. G. Gardiner: *Harvard*, 1914.

H. Hermelink und S. A. Kaehler: *Die Philipps-Universität zu Marburg*, 1927.

A. Hessel: *Geschichte der Bibliotheken*, 1925.

T. Hughes: *The Great Educators: Loyola and the Educational System of the Jesuits*, 1892.

C. Jourdain: *Histoire de l'Université de Paris au XVIIᵉ et XVIIIᵉ siècle*, 2 vols., 1862-66.

J. Kvačala: *Die pädagogische Reform des Comenius*, (*Monumenta Germaniae Pedagogica*, 26, 32), 2 vols., 1903.

H. Leser: *Das Pädagogische Problem in der Geistesgeschichte der Neuzeit*, 1925.

Sir C. Mallet: *A History of the University of Oxford*, 3 vols., 1924ff.

G. Meyer: *Die Entwicklung der Strassburger Universität aus dem Gymnasium und Akademie des J. Sturm*, 1927.

E. Morel: *Bibliothèques: Essai sur le développement des bibliothèques publiques*, 2 vols., 1909, 1908.

J. B. Mullinger: *History of the University of Cambridge*, 3 vols., 1884ff.

F. Paulsen: *Geschichte des gelehrten Unterrichts auf den deutschen Schulen und Universitäten vom Ausgang des Mittelalters bis zur Gegenwart*. Dritte Auflage von R. Lehmann, 2 vols., 1919-21.

G. Reynier: *La Vie universitaire en l'ancienne Espagne*, 1902.

E. C. Scherer: *Geschichte und Kirchengeschichte an den Deutschen Universitäten*, 1927.

K. A. Schmid: *Geschichte der Erziehung vom Anfang bis auf unsere Zeit*, 5 vols., 1884-1902.

G. H. Turnbull: *Samuel Hartlib*, 1920.

C. F. Thwing: *A History of Higher Education in America*, 1906.

F. Torraca, G. M. Monti, R. F. di Candida, N. Cortese, M. Schipa, A. Zaro, L. Russo: *Storia della Università di Napoli*, 1924.

CHAPTER XII. RELIGION, THE CHRISTIAN CHURCHES

SOURCES:

A. Arnauld: *Œuvres complettes*, ed. Hautesage, 43 vols., 1783ff.

Acta et scripta synodalia Dordracena ministrorum remonstrantium in Foederato Belgio, 2 vols., 1620.

Acta synodi nationalis Dordrechti habitae. Hanoviae, 1620.

J. Arminius: *Opera theologica*, 1629.

J. Arminius: *Works*, translated by J. Nichols, 3 vols., 1825-75.

R. Baxter: *Reliquiae Baxterianae*, 1696.

R. Baxter: *The Saints' Everlasting Rest*, ed. W. Young, 1907.

W. Bradford: *A dialogue, or third conference between some young men born in New England and some ancient men which came out of Holland and Old England, concerning the church and the government thereof.* (Proceedings of Massachusetts Historical Society, xi), 1871.

W. Bradford: *History of Plymouth Plantation*, ed. W. J. Davis, 1908.

J. Bunyan: *The Pilgrim's Progress from this World to that which is to Come*. (Innumerable editions.)

S. Butler: *Hudibras*, 1663.

G. Fox: *A Journal*, 1694.

G. Fox: *Autobiography*, ed. R. M. Jones, 1903.

G. Fox: *The Short Journal and Itinerary*, ed. N. Penney, 1925.

Imago primi saeculi Societatis Jesu, a provincia Flandro-Belgica ejusdem societatis repraesentata, 1640.

J. Milton: *Works*, 8 vols., 1851.

C. Mirbt: *Quellen zur Geschichte des Papsttums und des römischen Katholizismus*,[4] 1924.

A. F. Mitchell and J. Struthers: *Minutes of the Sessions of the Westminster Assembly of Divines*, 1874.

P. Mornay: *Mysterium Iniquitatis, seu historia papatus*,[3] 1662.

B. Pascal: *Lettres provinciales*, ed. H. F. Stewart, 1920.

B. Pascal: *Œuvres*, pub. suivant l'ordre chronologique, par L. Brunschvicg et P. Boutroux, vols. 1-8, 12-14, 1904ff.

St. Vincent de Paul: *Correspondance, entretiens, documents*, pub. par P. Coste, 14 vols., 1920-25.

W. Penn: *Select Works*, 2 vols., 1771.

Praestantium et Eruditorum Virorum epistolae ecclesiasticae et theologicae, ed. P. van Limborch, 1704.

S. François de Sales: *Œuvres*, 19 vols., 1892ff.

P. Schaff: *The Creeds of Christendom*,[4] 3 vols., 1877.

H. Smith: *Sermons*, 1675.

G. L. Turner: *Original Records of Early Nonconformity under Persecution and Indulgence*, 3 vols., 1911-14.

J. Winthrop: *A Short story of the rise, reign, and ruine of the Antinomians, Familists, and Libertines that infested the churches of New England*, ed. C. J. Adams, in *Antinomianism in Massachusetts Bay*, 1894.

J. Winthrop: *History of New England*, ed. J. K. Hosmer, 2 vols. 1908.

TREATISES:

L. W. Bacon: *History of American Christianity*, 1897.

M. L. Bailey: *Milton and Jacob Boehme*, 1914.

M. Blondel, L. Brunschvicg, H. Höffding, J. Chevalier, J. Laporte, F. Rauh, M. de Unamuno: *Études sur Pascal*, 1923.

H. Böhmer: *Die Jesuiten*,[4] 1921.

H. Bremond: *Histoire littéraire du sentiment religieux en France, depuis la fin des guerres de religion jusqu'à nos jours,* 6 vols., 1916-22.

J. Brodrick: *The Life and Work of Blessed Robert Francis Cardinal Bellarmine,* 2 vols., 1928.

J. Brown: *J. Bunyan,* revised by F. M. Harrison,1928.

J. Brucker: *La Compagnie de Jésus 1521-1773,* 1919.

L. Brunschvicg: *Le génie de Pascal,* 1924.

C. Burrage: *The True Story of Robert Browne,* 1906.

C. Burrage: *The Early English Dissenters in the light of recent research,* 2 vols., 1912.

J. Chevalier: *Pascal,* 1922.

B. Duhr: *Geschichte der Jesuiten in den Ländern deutscher Zunge,* 4 vols., 1907ff.

B. Duhr: *Jesuiten-Fabeln,*[2] 1892.

W. K. Ferguson: "The Place of Jansenism in French History," *Journal of Religion,* vol. 7, 1927.

H. D. Foster: "Liberal Calvinism: the Remonstrants at the Synod of Dort," *Harvard Theological Review,* vol. 16, 1923.

H. Fouqueray: *Histoire de la Compagnie de Jésus en France,* 5 vols., 1910-25.

A. Gazier: *Histoire Générale du mouvement janseniste,* 2 vols., 1922.

J. W. Graham: *The Faith of a Quaker,* 1920.

A. Harnack: *Dogmengeschichte,*[4] vol. 3, 1910.

A. W. Harrison: *The Beginnings of Arminianism,* 1926.

G. B. Harrison: *John Bunyan,* 1928.

W. Heatherington: *History of the Westminster Assembly of Divines,* 1843.

H. Heppe: *Geschichte des Pietismus und der Mystik in der Reformierten Kirche, namentlich der Niederlaender,* 1879.

C. M. Jacobs: *The Story of the Church,* 1925.

R. M. Jones: *Spiritual Reformers of the 16th and 17th Centuries,* 1914.

R. M. Jones: *The Story of George Fox,* 1925.

J. M. F. Laporte: *La Doctrine de Port-Royal,* 2 vols., 1923.

M. A. Larson: *The Modernity of Milton*, 1927.

H. Leuba: *Kalvinismus und Luthertum. Band I. Der Kampf um die Herrschaft im protestantischen Deutschland*, 1928.

A. Maire: *Bibliographie générale des œuvres de B. Pascal*, 5 vols., 1925-7.

D. Masson: *The Life and Times of Milton*,[2] 7 vols., 1881-96.

J. McCabe: *A Candid History of the Jesuits*, 1913.

A. C. McGiffert: *Protestant Thought before Kant*, 1911.

A. de Meyer: *Les premiers controverses Jansénistes en France*, 1917.

K. B. Murdock: *Increase Mather, the foremost American Puritan*, 1925.

L. von Pastor: *Geschichte der Päpste*, vols. 7-13, 1920-28.

A. F. S. Pearson: *Church and State: Political Aspects of Sixteenth-century Puritanism*, 1928.

A. F. S. Pearson: *T. Cartwright and Elizabethan Puritanism*, 1925.

E. A. Peers: *Studies of the Spanish Mystics*, 1927.

F. J. Powicke: *Richard Baxter*, 2 vols., 1924-27.

O. Ritschl: *Dogmengeschichte des Protestantismus*, 4 vols., 1908-27.

H. K. Rowe: *History of Religion in the United States*, 1924.

C. A. Sainte-Beuve: *Port-Royal*,[4] 6 vols., 1878.

E. K. Sanders: *Saint Francis of Sales*, 1927.

D. Saurat: *Milton, man and thinker*, 1925.

W. F. Schirmer: *Antike, Renaissance, und Puritanismus*, 1925.

F. Strowsky: *Pascal et son Temps*, 3 vols., 1907-8.

R. H. Tawney: *Religion and the Rise of Capitalism*, 1926.

E. Troeltsch: *Aufsätze zur Geistesgeschichte und Religionssoziologie*, 1925.

E. Troeltsch: *Die Soziallehren der christlichen Kirchen und Gruppen*, 1912.

J. Tulloch: *Rational Theology and Christian Philosophy in England during the 17th Century*,[2] 1874.

CHAPTER XIII. FREE-THOUGHT

Sources:

J. Acontius: *Satanae stratagematum libri VIII*, ed. W. Köhler, 1927.

F. Bacon: *Essays* (many editions), especially no. 16 of *Atheism*, 17 of *Superstition*, and 58 of *Vicissitudes of Things*.

S. Cyrano de Bergerac: *Œuvres diverses*, 2 vols., 1681.

S. Cyrano de Bergerac: *Histoire comique des états et empires de la lune et du soleil*, ed. L. Jordan, 1910.

Sir T. Browne: *Religio Medici*, 1642.

T. Campanella: *Atheismus triumphatus, seu Reductio ad Religionem per scientiarum veritates*, 1631.

P. Charon: *Les Trois Vérités*, 1593.

P. Charron: *La Sagesse*, 1601.

J. Dryden: *Religio Laici*, 1682.

J. Ganvill: *Scepsis Scientifica*, 1665.

H. Grotius: *De Veritate religionis Christianae, cum notulis J. Clerici*, 1809.

Lord Herbert of Cherbury: *Autobiography*, ed. S. L. Lee, 1886.

Lord Herbert of Cherbury: *De causis errorum*, 1656.

Lord Herbert of Cherbury: *De Religione Gentilium*, 1700.

Lord Herbert of Cherbury: *De veritate prout distinguitur a revelatione, a verisimili, a possibili et a falso*, 1656.

Lord Herbert of Cherbury: *Poems*, ed. G. C. M. Smith, 1923.

F. Lachèvre: *Le Libertinage au XVIIe Siècle*, 12 vols., 1907-25. (The first volume contains *La procès du poète T. de Viau;* the later volumes contain the works of De Barreaux, Saint-Pauvin, Claude le Petit, Baron de Blot, J. Dehénault, Cyrano de Bergerac, G. de Foigny, D. Veiras, C. Gilbert, and others.)

Malebranche: "Entretien entre un Philosophe Chrétien avec un Philosophe Chinois sur l'existence et la nature de Dieu," *Œuvres*, ii, 319.

M. de Montaigne: *Essais.* Many editions; there is an old English translation by Florio, and a modern one by G. B. Ives.

H. More: *Philosophical Writings,* ed. F. J. MacKinnon, 1925.

Philippes [sic] de Mornay, Sieur du Plessis-Marly: *De la Vérité de la Religion Chrestienne, Contre les Athées, Epicuriens, Payens, Juifs, et autres Infideles,* 1581.

B. Pascal: *Pensées, ed. L. Brunschvicg,* 3 vols., 1904.

Treatises:

G. Atkinson: *Les Relations de Voyages du XVIIe siècle et l'evolution des Idées,* 1925.

F. von Bezold: "J. Bodins Colloquium Heptaplomeres und der Atheismus des XVI. Jahrhunderts," *Historische Zeitschrift,* Band 113, 1914.

Biographical Dictionary of Modern Rationalists, 1920.

H. Busson: *Les Sources et le développement du Rationalisme dans la littérature française de la Renaissance,* 1922.

F. Gentile: *Pascal. Saggio d'interpretazione storico,* 1927.

E. H. Leuba: "Die Bekämpfung des Atheismus in der deutschen Lutherischen Kirche des XVII. Jahrhunderts," *Zeitschrift für Kirchengeschichte,* Band 43, 1924.

F. Mauthner: *Der Atheismus und seine Geschichte im Abendlande,* 2 vols., 1920f.

F. J. Powicke: *The Cambridge Platonists,* 1928.

J. M. Robertson: *A Short History of Freethought,*[2] 2 vols., 1906.

C. C. J. Webb: *Studies in the History of Natural Theology,* 1915.

CHAPTER XIV. SUPERSTITION

Sources:

P. Binsfeld: *Commentarius in titulum Codicis Lib. IX. de Maleficis et Mathematicis,* 1605.

P. Binsfeld: *Tractatus de Confessionibus Maleficorum et Sagarum,*[2] 1605.

J. Bodin: *De la Demonomanie des Sorciers,* 1580.

H. Boguet: *An Examen of Witches,* tr. by E. A. Ashmin, and ed. by M. Summers, 1929.

G. L. Burr: *Narratives of the Witchcraft Cases, 1648-1706,* 1914.

G. L. Burr: *The Witch-persecutions,* 1897. (University of Pennsylvania Translations and Reprints, vol. 3, no. 4).

A. Caesalpinus: *Daemonum investigatio peripatetica,* 1580.

T. Campanella: *De Astrologia Libri VII,* 1630.

T. Campanella: *Del senso delle cose e della magia. Testo inedito italiano,* ed. A. Bruers, 1925.

T. Campanella: *De sensu rerum et magia,* 1620.

M. Delrio: *Disquisitiones Magicae,* 1599-1600.

G. Fox: *A Declaration of the ground of error and errors, blasphemy, blasphemers and blasphemies, and the ground of inchantings and seducing spirits and the doctrine of devils, the sons of sorcerers, and the ground of nicromancy, which doth defile witches and wizards,* 1657.

J. Glanvill: *A Blow at modern Sadducism in some philosophical considerations about witchcraft,* 1668.

J. Glanvill: *Sadducismus triumphatus, or Full and Plain Evidence concerning Witches and Apparitions,* 1681.

James I: *Dæmonologie,* 1924.

B. Jonson: *The Alchemist,* ed. C. M. Hathaway, Jr., 1903.

J. Kepler: *Die Astrologie des J. Kepler: eine Auswahl aus seinen Schriften,* hg. von H. A. Strauss und S. Strauss-Kloebe, 1926.

J. Kepler: *Zwei wiederaufgefundene Prognostica auf die Jahre 1604 und 1624,* 1910. (Baierische Akademie der Wissenschaften, Phil.-Hist. Klasse, XXV).

Increase Mather: *Heaven's Alarm to the World,* 1682.

I. Mather: ΚΟΜΗΤΟΓΡΑΦΙΑ, *or, A Discourse concerning Comets,* 1683.

I. Mather: *An Essay for the Recording of Illustrious Providences*, 1684. (ed. by G. Offor as *Remarkable Providences*, 1890.)

M. de Montaigne: *Essais*, liv. 1, no. 32, and liv. 3, no. 11, "Des Boiteux."

News from Scotland, declaring the damnable life and death of Doctor Fian, 1591. (New ed. 1924).

B. Palissy: "Discours admirable de la nature des eaux et fontaines," in *Œuvres*, ed. B. Fillon, 2 vols., 1888.

W. Perkins: *Discourse of the damned art of witchcraft*, 1608.

G. B. della Porta: *Della celeste Fisionomia*, 1616.

G. B. della Porta: *Lo Astrologo* in *Commedie*, ed. v. Spampanato, 2 vols., 1910-11.

R. Scot: *The Discovery of Witchcraft*, ed. B. Nicholson, 1886.

L. M. Sinistrari: *De la Démonialité*, 1876. (French translation of the original Latin text. An English translation by Montague Summers has been issued in 1928).

[F. Spee]: *Cautio criminalis, seu De Processibus contra Sagas . . . Auctore incerto theologo Romano*, 1631.

J. Weyer: *De Praestigiis Daemonum*, 1563.

TREATISES:

M. Bloch: *Les Rois Thaumaturges*, 1924.

G. L. Burr: *A Witch-Hunter in the Book-Shops*, (The Bibliographer), 1902.

G. L. Burr: *New England's Place in the History of Witchcraft*. (Proceedings of the American Antiquarian Society), 1911.

G. L. Burr: *The Fate of Dietrich Flade*. (Papers of the American Historical Association, 1891).

G. L. Burr: *The Literature of Witchcraft* (Papers of the American Historical Association, iv, 237-66.)

T. de Cauzons: *La Magie et la Sorcellerie en France*, 3 vols., no date.

A. Graf: *Il Diavolo*,[3] 1890.

G. L. Kittredge: "Dr. Robert Child, the Remonstrant," *Transactions of the Massachusetts Historical Society,* xxi, 1919.

G. L. Kittredge: *Witchcraft in Old and New England,* 1929.

H. Kopp: *Die Alchemie,* 2 vols., 1886.

W. E. H. Lecky: *History of the Rise and Influence of the Spirit of Rationalism in Europe,* 2 vols., 1910.

A. Lehmann: *Aberglaube und Zauberei, von den ältesten Zeiten bis in die Gegenwart, Dritte deutsche Auflage nach der zweiten umgearbeiteten dänischen Auflage übersetzt und . . . ergänzt von D. Peterson,* 1925.

W. Notestein: *A History of Witchcraft in England, 1558-1718,* 1911.

G. Roskoff: *Geschichte des Teufels,* 2 vols., 1869.

W. G. Soldan und H. Heppe: *Geschichte der Hexenprozesse,* neu bearbeitet und hg. von M. Bauer, 2 vols., 1911.

CHAPTER XV. PERSECUTION AND TOLERANCE

SOURCES:

[Anonymous]: *The Ancient Bonds of liberty of conscience tenderly stated, modestly asserted, and mildly vindicated,* 1645.

F. Bacon: *Essay III,* "Of Unity in Religion."

F. Bacon: *The Wisdom of the Ancients,* 1609.

W. Chillingworth: *The Religion of Protestants a safe way to Salvation,* 1637.

M. Clifford: *A Treatise on Human Reason,* 1674.

J. Goodwin: *Theomachia, or the grand Imprudence of men running the hazard of fighting against God in suppressing any Doctrine or Practice,* 1644.

J. Milton: *A Treatise of Civil Power in Ecclesiastical Causes,* 1659.

J. Milton: Of *True Religion, Heresy, Schism, Toleration,* 1673.

J. Milton: *On the Forcers of Conscience under the Long Parliament.* In *Poems.*

M. de Montaigne: *Essais,* II, no. 19; III, no. 11.

J. Owen: *Of Toleration and the Duty of the Magistrate about Religion,* 1649.

Stephanus Pannonius: *De circulo operum et judiciorum Dei, et de ratione ineundae pacis inter omnes Christianos qui illum Deum Triunum invocant,* 1608. (In, M. Goldast: *Politica Imperialia,* 1614).

L. von Pastor: *Allgemeine Dekrete der römischen Inquisition,* 1913.

W. Penn: *The Great Case of Liberty of Conscience . . . debated and defended,* 1670.

B. de Spinoza: *Tractatus Theologico-Politicus,* (in *Opera,* 1880, i, 367ff).

J. Taylor: Θεολογία ἐκλεκτική, *or, A Discourse on the Liberty of Prophesying, with its just limits and temper.* (In *Works,* ed. R. Heber, 15 vols., 1822, vol. 7.)

R. Williams: *The Bloody Tenent of Persecution for the case of Conscience,* ed. S. L. Caldwell, 1867.

R. Williams: *The Bloody Tenent yet more Bloody by Mr. Cotton's attempt to wash it white. in the blood of the Lamb,* 1652.

TREATISES:

J. B. Bury: *A History of Freedom of Thought,* 1913.

M. Freund: *Die Idee der Toleranz im England der Grossen Revolution,* 1927.

A. J. Klein: *Intolerance in the Age of Elizabeth,* 1917.

J. Kühn: *Toleranz und Offenbarung,* 1923.

H. C. Lea: *A History of the Inquisition in Spain,* 4 vols., 1906-7.

H. C. Lea: *The Inquisition in the Spanish Dependencies,* 1908.

W. E. H. Lecky: *A History of the Rise and Influence of the Spirit of Rationalism in Europe,* 2 vols., 1865.

F. Ruffini: *Religious Liberty,* transl. by J. P. Heyes, 1912.

CHAPTER XVI. LAWS

SOURCES:

Acts and Ordinances of the Interregnum, ed. C. H. Firth and R. S. Rait, 3 vols., 1911.

The Acts of the Parliament of Scotland, printed by command of his Majesty George III, vols. 3ff, 1814.

Bullarum Diplomatum et Privilegiorum Sanctorum Romanorum Pontificum Taurinensis editio, 24 vols., Neapoli, 1882.

The Colonial Laws of Massachusetts, reprinted from the edition of 1660 with the supplements of 1672. . . . also the Body of Liberties of 1641. . . . W. H. Whitmore, 1889.

The Colonial Laws of Massachusetts, reprinted from the edition of 1672 with the supplements through 1686. . . . W. H. Whitmore, 1887.

Elenchus librorum omnium tum in Tridentino, Clementinoque Indice, tum in aliis . . . prohibitorum, . . . per F. M. Cappiferreum digestus. Romae, 1632. Bound with two supplements: *Index librorum prohibitorum per Patres a Tridentina Synodo electos*, 1596, and *Librorum post Indicem Clementis VIII prohibitorum Decreta*, 1624. (Cornell University Library.)

Groot Placaat-Boeck vervattende de Placaten Ordonnatien ende Edicten Van de . . . Staaten Generaal der Vereenighde Nederlanden. Ed. C. Cav et al. 1725, 10 vols.

W. W. Hening: *The statutes at large; being a collection of all the laws of Virginia from the first session of the legislature in 1619*, 13 vols., 1819-23.

Indices Librorum Prohibitorum. (Various editions; one in Sarpi's *Opere*, 1763, iv, 431ff.)

Klein Plakkatboek van Nederland: verzameling van ordonnantiën en plakkaten betreffende regeeringsvorm, kerk en rechtspraak (14e eeuw tot 1749) door A. S. de Blécourt en N. Japikse, 1919.

Nederlandtsche Placcaet-boeck: vvaerinne alle voornaemste placcaten, ordonnantien. . . . 2 vols., 1581, 1644.

Ordonnancien, statuten, edicten, en placcaten, ghepubliceert in de landen van hervvaerts-ower, van vveghen der Keyserlicker & Conijnglicker Majesteyten, 2 vols., 1559, 1629. (Laws of Flanders).

Recueil Générale des anciennes lois françaises, par Isambert, Decrusy, Armet, Tomes, 13ff, 1828ff.

The Statutes of the Realm, printed by command of his Majesty George III, vols. 4, 5, 1819.

TREATISES:

F. E. Baldwin: *Sumptuary Legislation and Personal Regulation in England*, 1926.

C. L. von Bar: *A History of Continental Criminal Law*, transl. by T. S. Bell, 1916.

H. J. A. Baudrillart: *Histoire du Luxe privé et public*, 4 vols., 1873.

C. Calisse: *A History of Italian Law*, transl. by L. B. Register, 1928.

C. Dejob: *L'Influence de la Concile de Trent sur la Littérature et les beaux-arts*, 1884.

C. A. Duniway: *The Development of the Freedom of the Press in Massachusetts*, 1906.

A. Esmein: *A History of Continental Criminal Procedure*, transl. by J. Simpson, 1913.

A. Esmein: *Cours élémentaire d'histoire du droit français*,[4] 1901.

K. Fullerton: "Calvinism and Capitalism," *Harvard Theological Review*, xxi, 163ff, 1928.

F. Helbing: *Die Tortur: Geschichte der Folter im Kriminal-Verfahren aller Völker und Zeiten*, 2 vols. (1912?)

W. S. Holdsworth: *A History of English Law*, 9 vols., 1924.

L. Hotson: *The Commonwealth and Restoration Stage*, 1928.

R. Huebner: *A History of Germanic Private Law*, trans. by F. S. Philbrick, 1918.

M. M. Knappen: *Richard Greenham and the Practical Puritans under Elizabeth*. (Unpublished, Cornell thesis, 1927, in typescript at Cornell University Library).

G. H. Putnam: *Censorship of the Church of Rome*, 2 vols., 1906.

F. H. Reusch: *Der Index der verbotenen Bücher*, 2 vols., 1883,

R. H. Tawney: *Religion and the Rise of Capitalism*, 1926.

CHAPTER XVII. MORALS AND MANNERS

SOURCES:

This chapter has been based on the general literature of the sixteenth and seventeenth centuries, including the drama, the memoirs, the diaries, the letters and other works of moralists and of satirists. It is also partly based on the laws, for editions of which see the last chapter. Also on

J. Milton: *The Doctrine and Discipline of Divorce*, 1643. *Works*, ii, 73ff.

La Rochefoucauld: *Réflexions Morales*, 1665. (Many editions under the name of *Maximes*).

Jeremy Taylor: *The Rule and Exercise of Holy Living*, (*Works*, iv).

TREATISES:

T. F. Crane: *Italian Social Customs*, 1920.

G. Fagniez: *La femme française et la sociéte dans la première moitié du 17ᵉ siècle, 1929.*

E. Fuchs: *Illustrierte Sittengeschichte*, 1909.

J. E. Gillespie: *The Influence of Oversea Expansion upon England to 1700*, 1920.

F. Jodl: *Geschichte der Ethik,*[2] 2 vols., 1906-12.

M. Magendie: *La Politesse Mondaine et les Théories d'Honnêteté en France au XVIIe Siècle*, 2 vols. (1925).

C. L. Powell: *English Domestic Relations, 1487-1653*, 1917.

H. R. Stiles: *Bundling; with more about bundling* by A. M. Aurand, Jr., new ed. 1928.

H. D. Traill: *Social England*, 6 vols., 1894-6.

E. Troeltsch: *Gesammelte Werke*, iv, 374ff, 1925.

CHAPTER XVIII. LITERATURE

A. C. Bradley: *Shakespearean Tragedy,* 1904.

Sainte-Beuve: "Don Quichotte," *Nouveaux Lundis,* tome 8, 1864.

The Cambridge History of English Literature, 14 vols., 1907-17.

F. I. Carpenter: *A Reference Guide to Edmund Spenser,* 1923.

Lope de Vega Carpio: *Obras, publicadas por la Real Academia Española,* 20 vols., 1890-1918.

Lope Felix de Vega Carpio: *The New Art of writing Plays,* tr. by W. J. Brewster, 1914.

Miguel de Cervantes: *El ingenioso hidalgo don Quixote de la Mancha,* many editions of the original, and English translation by J. Ormsby, ed. by J. Fitzmaurice-Kelly, 4 vols., 1901.

Miguel de Cervantes: *The Exemplary Novels,* transl. by N. Maccoll, 2 vols., 1902.

E. K. Chambers: *The Elizabethan Stage,* 4 vols., 1923.

W. Creizenach: *Geschichte des neueren Dramas,* 6 vols., 1893ff.

B. Croce: *Ariosto, Shakespeare, Corneille,* Eng. tr. 1921.

Morel-Fatio: "Le 'Don Quichotte' envisagé comme peinture et critique de la societé espagnole du 16e et 17e siècle." *Études sur l'Espagne,* 1895.

J. Fitzmaurice-Kelly: *History of Spanish Literature,* 1904.

J. D. M. Ford: *Main Currents of Spanish Literature,* 1920.

C. M. Gayley: *Beaumont the Dramatist,* 1914.

C. M. Gayley: *Representative English Comedies,* 3 vols., 1913ff.

V. C. Gildersleeve: *Government Regulation of the English Drama,* 1908.

H. Hallam: *Introduction to the Literature of Europe in the fifteenth, sixteenth, and seventeenth Centuries,* 3 vols., 1837-9.

C. H. Herford and P. Simpson: *Ben Jonson,* 3 vols. as yet, of which the first two contain his life; the others will contain his works, 1925ff.

B. Jonson: *Masques and Entertainments,* ed. H. Morley, 1890.

Ben Jonson's Works. As far as it has gone, the edition of various plays in the Yale Studies in English, is good.

J. J. Jusserand: *Histoire Littéraire du Peuple Anglais,* ii, 1904.

Lives of Shakespeare by J. Q. Adams, 1923, W. Raleigh, 1907, Sir Sidney Lee, 2d ed., 1915.

W. A. Neilson: *The Chief Elizabethan Dramatists excluding Shakespeare,* 1911.

G. T. Northup: *An Introduction to Spanish Literature,* 1923.

H. A. Rennert: *The Life of Lope de Vega,* 1904.

W. L. Renwick: *Edmund Spenser: An Essay in Renaissance Poetry,* 1925.

R. Schevill: *Cervantes,* 1919.

R. Schevill: *The Dramatic Art of Lope de Vega,* 1918.

Shakespeare's Plays, many editions, among the best are the Temple ed., the Arden ed., the ed. by W. A. Neilson, the Globe ed., and the Variorum by H. H. Furness.

G. G. Smith: *Ben Jonson,* 1919.

Edmund Spenser: *Faery Queen,* 1590-96; many editions.

J. A. Symonds: *Italian Literature,* 1888.

Torquato Tasso: *Gerusalemme Liberata,* many editions, best by Solerti, 1895. Several English translations; a good one by Sir J. K. James, 2 vols., 1865.

L. Tolstoy on Shakespeare, Eng tr. 1906. (Contains also an essay by E. Crosby on "Shakespeare's Attitude toward the Working Classes.")

Lope de Vega: *El nuevo mundo descubierto por Cristóbal Colon,* ed. E. Barry, 1901.

L. de Vega: *The King the Greatest Alcalde,* tr. by J. G. Underhill, *Poet Lore,* vol. 29, 1918.

A. W. Ward: *A History of English Dramatic Literature,*[2] 3 vols, 1899.

CHAPTER XIX. ART

GENERAL:

R. Bloomfield: *Renaissance Architecture in England* 1500-1800, 2 vols., 1897.

B. Bosanquet: *A History of Æsthetics,*[2] 1904.

B. Croce: *Der Begriff des Barocks und die Gegenreformation,* 1926.

Élie Faure: *History of Art.* Vol. 4. Modern. English translation, 1924.

W. Hauenstein: *Vom Geist des Barock,* 1924.

A. Jellinek und O. Frölich: *Internationale Bibliographie der Kunstwissenschaft,* 1902ff.

Klassiker der Kunst in Gesamtausgaben, Deutsche Verlags-Anstalt, Stuttgart und Leipzig. (Reproductions in separate volumes of the paintings and engravings of many of the masters).

J. Meier-Graefe: *Entwicklungsgeschichte der modernen Kunst,*[3] 3 vols., 1920.

A. Michel: *Histoire de l'art depuis les premiers temps chrétiens jusqu'à nos jours,* Tomes 5, 6, 1922.

S. Reinach: *Apollo,*[4] 1907. (French original; English translation).

W. Wiesbach: *Die Kunst des Barock in Italien, Frankreich, Deutschland, und Spanien,* 1924.

K. Woermann: *Geschichte der Kunst aller Zeiten und Völker* Band V, 1920.

1. ITALIAN DECADENCE

Max von Boehn: *Guido Reni,* 1910.

J. A. Crowe and G. B. Cavalcaselle: *History of Italian Painting,* 6 vols., 1903ff.

Salvator Rosa: *Poesie e lettere,* ed. G. A. Cesareo, 2 vols., 1892.

2. SPANISH ART

A de Beruete: *Velasquez*, 1906.

A. E. Calvert: *Murillo*, 1907.

Randall Davies: *Velasquez*, 1914.

C. Justi: *Diego Velasquez und sein Jahrhundert,*[2] 1903. (English translation of first edition, 1889).

C. Justi: *Murillo*, 1905.

P. Lafond: *Murillo* (1908?).

3. FLEMISH ART

A. Bertram: *Sir Peter Paul Rubens*, 1928.

L. Cust: *Anthony van Dyck*, 1900.

E. Dillon: *Rubens*, 1909.

M. Rooses: *Jacob Jordaens*, 1908.

M. Rooses: *Life of Rubens*, 2 vols., 1907.

M. Rooses: *L'Œuvre de Rubens*, 5 vols., 1886-92.

M. Rooses et C. Ruelens: *La Correspondance de Rubens,* 6 vols., 1887ff.

A. Rosenberg: *Rubens*, 1905.

4. DUTCH ART

W. Bode: *The Complete Work of Rembrandt*, 8 vols., 1897-1906.

J. Both: *Rembrandts Leben und Kun*st, 1908.

C. B. Brown: *Rembrandt*, 1907.

F. S. Degener: *Jan Steen, translated by C. J. Renier*, 1928.

J. C. Van Dyke: *Rembrandt and his School*, 1923. (Professor Van Dyke thinks that of the 800 or 1000 paintings attributed to Rembrandt, only 55 are genuine. Most experts believe that his destructive criticism has gone too far).

A. Fontainas: *Frans Hals* (1908?)

C. Hofstede de Groot: *A Catalogue Raisonné of the most eminent Dutch Painters of the 17th Century.* English transl. by E. G. Hawke, 7 vols., 1923.

E. Michel: *Paul Potter,* 1907.

C. Neumann: *Rembrandt,*[3] 1922.

Rembrandt: *Original Drawings reproduced in the Colors of the Originals,* ed. F. Lippminn and C. Hofstede de Groot, 4 series. The Hague, 1914-20.

Rembrandts Handzeichnungen, hg. von K. Freise, K. Lilienfeld, H. Wichman, vol. 1, 1921.

A. Rosenberg: *Adriaen und Isaak van Ostade,* 1900.

A. Rosenberg: *Terborch und Jan Steen,* 1877.

H. W. Singer: *Rembrandts Radierungen,*[2] 1910.

E. Verhaeren: *Rembrandt,* 1904.

5. FRENCH ART.

R. Bloomfield: *A History of French Architecture from the reign of Charles VIII to the death of Mazarin,* 2 vols., 1911.

R. Bonyer: *Claude Lorrain,* 1905.

P. Desjardins: *N. Poussin,* 1904.

W. Friedländer: *N. Poussin,* 1914.

INDEX

655

Rosweyde, H.
Acts of the Saints, 262
Lives of the Fathers, 262
Rousset, F., 142
Roy, H. de, 197
Royal Society, 83, 123, 130, 149,
152, 166f., 169, 174, 249
Philosophical Transactions, 166,
168, 174f.
and witchcraft, 451
Royal touch, 431
Roycroft, T., 281
Rubens, P. P., 584ff.
Rudolf, Emperor, 469
Ruisdael, J. van, 594f.
Rupert, Prince, 151
Rust, G., Bishop,
Discourse on Truth, 424

Sabbath-breaking, 502f.
Sagredo, G. F. di N., 69, 78, 85
Saint-Cyran, Abbé de, 370
Saint-Simon, C. de Rouvray, duke
of, 151
Saint-Sorlin, J. Desmarets de, 255
Salamanca, University of, 43, 329,
430
Sales, St. F. de,
life, 362
Sallo, D. de, 174
Sanchez, T., 181, 344, 437, 516
De Matrimonio, 367
Sandys, Sir E., 252
San Gallo, A. di, 573
Sarpi, P., 263f., 270, 365, 514
life and writings, 264ff.
History of Ecclesiastical Benefices,
265
Treatise on the Inquisition, 265
Right of Sanctuary, 265
Immunity of the Clergy, 265
History of the Council of Trent,
265ff.
Saumaise, C. de,
life and studies, 307
Saunders, N., 258
Savages, 119ff., 404
Scaliger, J. J., 107, 236, 306, 333,
346

Scaliger, J. J., life and work, 302ff.
De Emendatione Temporum, 289
f., 303
Thesaurus Temporum, 304
Scenery, appreciation of, 601f.
Schools, 315ff.
Science, 6ff., 606
astronomy, 17ff.
physics, 62ff.
mathematics, 87ff.
geography, 112ff.
biology, 122ff.
botany, 129ff.
medicine, 133, 138ff.
surgery, 141ff.
revolution, 144
fashionable, 151f.
defined, 154
inductive method, 157f.
journals, 172
Scioppius, C., 358
Scot, R.,
The Discovery of Witchcraft,
456
Scotland
and persecution, 475f.
Scotus, D., 337
Scribani, C.,
Politico-Christianus, 236
Selden, J., 385, 490
life and writings, 219ff., 228
On the Closure of the Seas, 219
Of the Law of Nature, 220
History of Tithes, 275
Titles of Nobility, 275f
*Privileges of the Baronage of Eng-
land*, 276
theological treatises, 288
and Bible, 294, 299
Sempere, H.,
Chivalry of the Fragrant Rose,
555
Seneca, 341
Serra, A.,
Treatise, 247
Servetus, M.
Errors concerning the Trinity,
132
circulation of the blood, 132f.
Severino, M. A., 132

Sévigné, Mme. de, 374, 468, 539, 542, 601
Sexual vice, 531ff.
Shakespeare, W., 42, 44, 138, 147, 150, 310, 515f., 526
life and plays, 560ff.
The Tempest, 562, 564
and Fletcher,
Cardenio, 558
Sheldon, Dr. G., 338
Shepard, T., 477
Sidney, Sir P., 43, 253
Sigismund III, 471
Simon, R., 280, 288
Histoire critique du Vieux Testament, 286f.
Critical History of the New Testament, 287
History of the Versions of the Bible, 287
History of the Principal Commentators, 287
Sixtus V, Pope, 282, 352, 430, 500, 508, 511, 513, 571
Skepticism, 398ff.
causes of growth, 401ff.
Deism, 408ff.
warfare of reason and religion, 414f.
Sleidan, J., 258
Religious and Political History, 263
Smith, H., 511
Snell, W., 66
Socinians, see Unitarians
Socinus, see Sozzini
Socrates, 156
Sorbonne, see Paris, University of
Sozzini, F., 392
life and writings, 394f.
Spain
decadence, 11
libraries, 352
and Inquisition, 463ff.
and theater, 565f.
Spee, F.
Criminal Procedure against Witches, 454
Spener, P. J., 397
Pia Desideria, 397

Spenser, E., 44, 150, 274, 359, 427, 519
Faery Queen, 425, 553ff.
life and writings, 553ff.
Spenser, J.,
Ritual Laws of the Hebrews, 288
Speroni, S., 255
Dialogue on Languages, 310
Spinola, A., 35
Spinoza, B., 201, 237f., 347
life and philosophy, 206
Theologico-Political Treatise, 206, 237, 239, 284ff., 486, 509
Ethics, 208
Political Treatise, 237
and Bible, 280, 284ff.
and skepticism, 405, 412.
and superstition, 455
Spontaneous generation, 138
Spratt, T., 151
Statistics, science of, 249
Steen, J., 593f.
Stevin, S., 44, 70, 91, 101, 104f., 236
life and discoveries, 67f.
L'Art Ponderaire, 68
The Decimal, 92f.
Appendice Algébraïque, 100
Stiefel, M., 94, 98, 106
Stigliani, T., 119
Stillingfleet, E., 401
Strada, F.,
Prolusiones Academicae, 64
Stubbs, H., 169
Stunica, D. à, 330
Commentary on Job, 43, 47
Sturm, C., 166
Sturm, J., 319
Suarez, F., 216, 242, 248
On Laws and God the Legislator, 242
Superstition, 425ff.
mythology, 425ff.
witch hunt, 434ff.
protest and skepticism, 450ff.
surgery, 141ff.
Sutton, T., 320
Swammerdam, J., 127f., 137
General History of Insects, 127
The Bible of Nature, 127

Sweden
and Protestantism, 13
Swift, J.,
Gulliver's Travels, 169
Sydenham, T., 140

Tacitus, 120, 343
Tagliacozzi, G., 142
Taquet, A., 55
Tartaglia, N., 72, 99f.
Tasman, A. J., 114
Tasso, T., 33, 427
Jerusalem Delivered, 118, 552f.
life and poems, 552f.
Tassoni, A., 255
Pensieri diversi, 41
Taylor, J., 543
*Discourse on the Liberty of
Prophesying,* 487
Holy Living, 503
Telescope, 34ff., 43, 45, 57, 61,
112
Telesio, B., 155, 544
Terborch, G., 595
Theater, 503, 558ff.
Theresa, St., 552
Thermometer, invention of, 84f.
Thou, J. A., de, 271f., 485
History of his own Time, 271
Tillotson, J., Archbishop, 366, 412,
475
Tilly, J. T., 82
Tintoretto, J. R., 574
Tirso de Molina, 568f.
Titian, 572
Tolerance
in Dutch Republic, 472
theory of, 481ff.
Torricelli, E., 345
life and theories, 74f., 79, 107f.
On the Motion of Falling Bodies,
74
Torture, 439f.
Tourneur, C., 563
The Atheist's Tragedy, 563
Trigonometry, 106
Tschirnhaus, E. W.,
Medicina mentis, 163
Tulp, Dr., 140

Turner, W.
New Herbal, 129
Tyndale, W., 292f., 299, 336
Tyrannicide, 241f.

Unitarians, 394f.
Universities, 326ff.
subjects taught, 326
Urban VIII, Pope, 48, 571, 574
Cum occasione, 371f.
Urbino, Duke of, 353
Usher, J.
*Annals of Old and New Testa-
ment,* 290f.
Usury, 510f.

Valla, L., 261, 547
Van Dieman, A., 115
Van Dyke, A., 589
Vanini, L., 198, 400, 418
Varchi, B., 71
Varchi, G., 71
Varenius, B., 117
Vatican Library, 354
Vega, G., de la, 245
Vega, L., de, 464
Plays, 566ff.
Velasquez, D. R. de, 580ff.
Venice, 264
Veronese, P., 574
Vermeer, J., 594
Vesalius, A., 144, 181, 195, 308
and culture, 5
De Fabrica Corporis Humanae,
18, 131
life and teaching, 131ff.
Vieta, F., 93, 103
life and work, 101, 106f.
Vincent de Paul, St., 362
Vinci, L. da, 71, 572
and anatomy, 131
Viret, P., 399
Instruction Chrétienne, 399
Virgil, 300
Vitellio, W., 65
Vives, J. L., 157, 350, 555
Vlacq, A., 97
Voet, G., 198